Cloud Computing and Virtualization Technologies in Libraries

Sangeeta N. Dhamdhere
Modern College of Arts, Science and Commerce, India

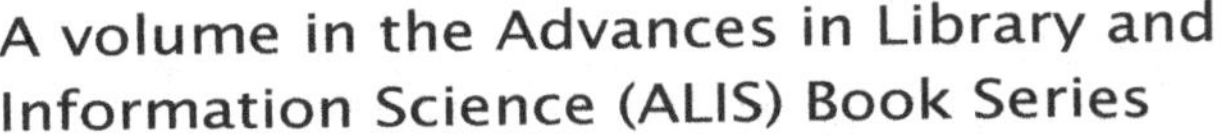

A volume in the Advances in Library and Information Science (ALIS) Book Series

Information Science REFERENCE
An Imprint of IGI Global

Managing Director: Lindsay Johnston
Production Manager: Jennifer Yoder
Publishing Systems Analyst: Adrienne Freeland
Development Editor: Monica Speca
Acquisitions Editor: Kayla Wolfe
Typesetter: Lisandro Gonzalez
Cover Design: Jason Mull

Published in the United States of America by
Information Science Reference (an imprint of IGI Global)
701 E. Chocolate Avenue
Hershey PA 17033
Tel: 717-533-8845
Fax: 717-533-8661
E-mail: cust@igi-global.com
Web site: http://www.igi-global.com

Library of Congress Cataloging-in-Publication Data

Cloud computing and virtualization technologies in libraries / Sangeeta N. Dhamdhere, editor.
pages cm
Includes bibliographical references and index.
ISBN 978-1-4666-4631-5 (hardcover) -- ISBN 978-1-4666-4632-2 (ebook) -- ISBN 978-1-4666-4633-9 (print & perpetual access) 1. Web services--Library applications. 2. Cloud computing. 3. Digital libraries. I. Dhamdhere, Sangeeta N., 1975- editor of compilation.
Z674.75.W67C586 2014
025.042--dc23

2013025035

This book is published in the IGI Global book series Advances in Library and Information Science (ALIS) (ISSN: 2326-4136; eISSN: 2326-4144)

British Cataloguing in Publication Data
A Cataloguing in Publication record for this book is available from the British Library.

All work contributed to this book is new, previously-unpublished material. The views expressed in this book are those of the authors, but not necessarily of the publisher.

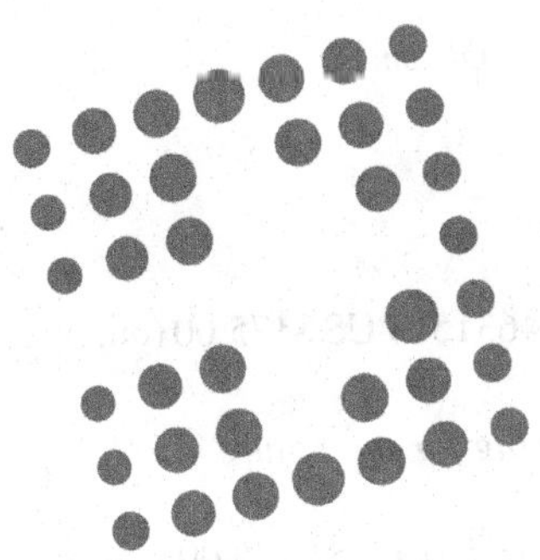

Advances in Library and Information Science (ALIS) Book Series

ISSN: 2326-4136
EISSN: 2326-4144

Mission

The **Advances in Library and Information Science (ALIS) Book Series** is comprised of high quality, research-oriented publications on the continuing developments and trends affecting the public, school, and academic fields, as well as specialized libraries and librarians globally. These discussions on professional and organizational considerations in library and information resource development and management assist in showcasing the latest methodologies and tools in the field.

The **ALIS Book Series** aims to expand the body of library science literature by covering a wide range of topics affecting the profession and field at large. The series also seeks to provide readers with an essential resource for uncovering the latest research in library and information science management, development, and technologies.

Coverage

- Academic libraries in the digital age
- Blogging in libraries
- Cataloging and classification
- Collection development
- Community outreach
- Digital literacy
- Ethical practices in libraries
- Green libraries
- Librarian education
- Mobile library services
- Remote access technologies
- University libraries in developing countries

IGI Global is currently accepting manuscripts for publication within this series. To submit a proposal for a volume in this series, please contact our Acquisition Editors at Acquisitions@igi-global.com or visit: http://www.igi-global.com/publish/.

The Advances in Library and Information Science (ALIS) Book Series (ISSN 2326-4136) is published by IGI Global, 701 E. Chocolate Avenue, Hershey, PA 17033-1240, USA, www.igi-global.com. This series is composed of titles available for purchase individually; each title is edited to be contextually exclusive from any other title within the series. For pricing and ordering information please visit http://www.igi-global.com/book-series/advances-library-information-science-alis/73002. Postmaster: Send all address changes to above address.

Titles in this Series

For a list of additional titles in this series, please visit: www.igi-global.com

Cloud Computing and Virtualization Technologies in Libraries
Sangeeta N. Dhamdhere (Modern College of Arts, Science and Commerce, India)
Information Science Publishing • copyright 2014 • 403pp • H/C (ISBN: 9781466646315) • US $175.00 (our price)

Revolutionizing the Development of Library and Information Professionals Planning for the Future
Samantha Schmehl Hines (Missoula College of the University of Montana, USA)
Information Science Reference • copyright 2014 • 312pp • H/C (ISBN: 9781466646759) • US $175.00 (our price)

Information Access and Library User Needs in Developing Countries
Mohammed Nasser AI-Suqri (Sultan Qaboos University, Oman) Linda L. Lillard (Clarion University, USA) and Naifa Eid AI-Saleem (Sultan Qaboos University, Oman)
Information Science Reference • copyright 2014 • 286pp • H/C (ISBN: 9781466643536) • US $175.00 (our price)

Collaborative Models for Librarian and Teacher Partnerships
Kathryn Kennedy (International Association for K-12 Online Learning, USA) and Lucy Santos Green (Georgia Southern University, USA)
Information Science Reference • copyright 2014 • 324pp • H/C (ISBN: 9781466643611) • US $175.00 (our price)

Collaboration in International and Comparative Librarianship
Susmita Chakraborty (North Bengal University, India) and Anup Kumar Das (Jawaharlal National University, India)
Information Science Reference • copyright 2014 • 346pp • H/C (ISBN: 9781466643659) • US $175.00 (our price)

Advancing Library Education Technological Innovation and Instructional Design
Ari Sigal (Catawba Valley Community College, USA)
Information Science Reference • copyright 2013 • 339pp • H/C (ISBN: 9781466636880) • US $175.00 (our price)

Library Reference Services and Information Literacy Models for Academic Institutions
Rosanne M. Cordell (Northern Illinois University, USA)
Information Science Reference • copyright 2013 • 355pp • H/C (ISBN: 9781466642416) • US $175.00 (our price)

Challenges of Academic Library Management in Developing Countries
S. Thanuskodi (Alagappa University, India)
Information Science Reference • copyright 2013 • 348pp • H/C (ISBN: 9781466640702) • US $175.00 (our price)

Robots in Academic Libraries Advancements in Library Automation
Edward Iglesias (Central Connecticut State University, USA)
Information Science Reference • copyright 2013 • 260pp • H/C (ISBN: 9781466639386) • US $175.00 (our price)

www.igi-global.com

701 E. Chocolate Ave., Hershey, PA 17033
Order online at www.igi-global.com or call 717-533-8845 x100
To place a standing order for titles released in this series, contact: cust@igi-global.com
Mon-Fri 8:00 am - 5:00 pm (est) or fax 24 hours a day 717-533-8661

Editorial Advisory Board

List of Reviewers

Table of Contents

Foreword xvii

Preface xix

Acknowledgment xxiv

Chapter 1
Digital Library and Its Requirements in the Global World 1
Surbhi Saini, Indira Gandhi National Open University (IGNOU), India

Chapter 2
Digital Information Management: Preserving Tomorrow's Memory 22
Pawan R. Agrawal, Silvassa Institute of Higher Learning, India

Chapter 3
Digital Preservation: Its Framework and Strategies in Cloud Computing Environment 36
Vijay Parashar, FET Library, Mody Institute of Technology & Science, India
Mohan Lal Vishwakarma, FET Library, Mody Institute of Technology & Science, India
Nisha Patle, FET Library, Mody Institute of Technology & Science, India

Chapter 4
Cloud Computing and Its Application to Information Centre 63
Nihal Alam, The Energy and Resources Institute (TERI), India
Ranjan Karmakar, The Energy and Resources Institute (TERI), India

Chapter 5
Application of Cloud Computing in Library Information Service Sector 77
Ajay Rawat, University of Petroleum & Energy Studies, India
Praveen Kapoor, University of Petroleum & Energy Studies, India
Rama Sushil, DIT University, India

Detailed Table of Contents

Foreword xvii

Preface xix

Acknowledgment xxiv

Chapter 1
Digital Library and Its Requirements in the Global World 1
Surbhi Saini, Indira Gandhi National Open University (IGNOU), India

This chapter introduces the basics of the digital library, including needs, benefits, and requirements, and briefly describes the digitization process. The role of library and information science professionals has now become a debatable one due to the advent of digital libraries and the Internet. The cloud computing and virtualization in digital culture is also discussed here. In this regard, the chapter covers cloud computing, including the characteristics, types, and how it works. The application of cloud computing in libraries is described with an example of the cloud in the academic library in Orissa. The advantages and disadvantages of cloud computing in libraries or in organizations are also covered here. The future prospects of the digital library using cloud computing technology is like an innovative application in libraries.

Chapter 2
Digital Information Management: Preserving Tomorrow's Memory 22
Pawan R. Agrawal, Silvassa Institute of Higher Learning, India

The most burning issue of today's electronic generation, where information generation is a task of seconds, is to save the information in a form that could successfully be read tomorrow. It is easily understandable that if one keeps a book in a drawer and open it after 10 years, one may hope to get it back and read it, possibly with some damage, but this is not the case for information stored in a Compact Disc (CD) or any other electronic device. This chapter projects at understanding digital preservation issues and identifying appropriate solutions to manage digital information. This chapter also aims to identify the projects undergoing throughout the world for digital preservation. This chapter overall discusses the speedy obsolescence, short-lived technologies, and other issues in digital preservation with the identified and possible strategies of digital preservation.

Digital preservation is the persistent archiving of digital assets for future access and reuse, irrespective of the underlying platform and software solutions. Existing preservation systems have a strong focus on grids, but the advent of cloud technologies offers an attractive option. The authors describe a middleware system that enables a flexible choice of cloud for ad-hoc computations that arise during the execution of a preservation workflow and also for archiving digital objects. The choice between different infrastructures remains open during the lifecycle of the archive, ensuring a smooth switch between different solutions to accommodate the changing requirements of the organization that needs its digital assets preserved. The authors also offer insights on the costs, running times, and organizational issues of cloud computing, proving that the cloud alternative is particularly attractive for smaller organizations without access to a grid or with limited IT infrastructure.

Information and communication technologies are developing very fast and providing us opportunities due to their benefits such as reduced cost, anytime, anywhere availability, as well as its elasticity and flexibility. Cloud computing is one of the newly emerged models for technology that provide us the facility of central remoting of servers to maintain data, software, and application through the use of the Internet. Nowadays it is widely applicable in many areas such as libraries, information centres, in-house, applications and digital library services. Our chapter will focus mainly on: Models of cloud computing, types of cloud suitable for information centres, application of cloud computing with examples, opportunity and risk in developing cloud services, and impact of cloud computing to information centres.

Cloud computing is a process that provides services on virtual machines. Through the Cloud the information can be stored permanently on the Cloud servers which can be accessed by the Internet. The main aim of Cloud computing is to bring scalability in the system, due to which CPU and memory will be fully utilized. It is up to a customer that one can increase or decrease the resources in the Cloud according to his need. Cloud computing provides a fascinating possibility for libraries that helps to increase data storage capacity, reliability, performance, and reduce technology cost. This chapter elaborates how libraries and information centers can enhance their resources infrastructure with minimum cost, make effective systems, and provide better services to the user community at minimum cost and time. The aim of this chapter is to explain how librarian, information and computer science professionals and knowledge workers apply Cloud computing in the libraries and information center management. Chapter begins with the Cloud computing introduction in the context of Libraries which is called Cloud libraries. How libraries are using Cloud services today and what can the Cloud computing solutions do for the libraries are presented in detail. The chapter describes the potential role of Cloud computing to serve library needs. At the end of the chapter some live examples, where Libraries are adopting Cloud Computing, like Dura Space, OCLC, Library Thing, Library Cloud and Seer Suite are discussed.

Cloud computing and Information Network both are emerging facets in the field of Information Science (IS). Cloud computing has potential to bring another wave of changes to organizations. Overall, planning and implementation of cloud computing will be beneficial in the terms of library level as well as institutional level to manage by cloud. In this chapter the authors present RECs/NITs resources to move on for managing cloud computing. Making the decision to use cloud-based services means balancing the elements of cost, risk, and benefit to decide whether those services advance the mission of the library as well as institute. RECs/NITs Libraries can take advantage of the cloud in numerous ways, such as data sharing including discovery tools, current status of research, and software as service which depends on the cloud, e-mail systems and social networking, and so forth. This chapter recommends a road for globalizing Regional Engineering Colleges/National Institutes Technology libraries.

Libraries all over the world suffer from common problems like flexibility associated with digital data, lower levels of efficiency, and costs involved in managing the entire IT infrastructure. Few options are available in collaborating with other libraries, which is the prime reason for subordinate levels of efficiency. For the past 20 years the use of Information Communication Technology (ICT) has fundamentally changed the practices and procedures of nearly all forms of endeavor within business and governance. Within education, ICT has begun to have a presence, but the cost of ICT is not affordable. The basic principle of cloud computing entails the reduction of in-house data centres and the delegation of a portion or all of the information technology infrastructure capability to a third party. Universities and colleges are the core of innovation through their advanced research and development. Subsequently, higher institutions may benefit greatly by harnessing the power of cloud computing. Cloud computing would help in bridging the gap between academic libraries and ICT. Sharing of data among the libraries will in principle reduce the overall cost and increase efficiency. Capital expenditure done on infrastructure will chiefly be converted into operational expenditure. It will also enhance the user's experience and will help in making the libraries a lot more scalable. In this chapter the authors discuss problems faced with academic libraries and development efforts to overcome that problem. Then they propose to improve current user service model with cloud computing.

Cloud computing is a new breed of service offered over the Internet, which has completely changed the way one can use the power of computers irrespective of geographic location. It has brought in new avenues for organizations and businesses to offer services using hardware or software or platform of third party sources, thus saving on cost and maintenance. It can transform the way systems are built and services delivered, providing libraries with an opportunity to extend their impact. Cloud computing has become a major topic of discussion and debate for any business or organization which relies on technology. Anyone connected to the Internet is probably using some type of cloud computing on a regular basis. Whether they are using Google's Gmail, organizing photos on Flickr, or searching the Web with Bing, they are engaged in cloud computing. In this chapter, an attempt has been made to give an overview of this technology, its connection with libraries, the models in which libraries can deploy this technology for providing services and augment the productivity of library staff and case studies.

The latest trend of Cloud Computing is progressing fast and using this technology it is possible to publish and store information on a virtual cloud based infrastructure. Virtualization technology has been adopted by many data centers in the industry. It shares resources on a single system efficiently and reduces infrastructure costs. Libraries are using various technologies along with Web tools at a time. Information sharing and an open access culture are developing fast in the education field. How libraries can make use of the application of cloud computing and virtualization technology for common data storage and managing multiple servers and provide cloud based information services to patrons will be discussed in detail in this chapter. This chapter also discusses in brief the applications of these technologies in libraries along with the university cloud library model and the role of cloud librarians.

World-wide electronic university libraries, with wide accessibility, are considered to be essential units in both academic and nonacademic information utilization. Within this context, the developed world wasted no time improving and expanding their libraries by applying the technology leverage offered by cloud computing. As institutions from developed countries expanded the use of cloud technology for library applications, it became clear that this technology was highly vulnerable to security threats. Nevertheless, this did not retard advanced nations from proceeding. Undaunted, they forged ahead and now are busy building appropriate cloud computing security infrastructures. Despite progress in this area, very little has been done to expand the university libraries in the sub-Saharan region using cloud computing technologies. Even less has been done in these developing countries to plan and develop the building of library computing security infrastructures. It was in view of this deficit that the University of Namibia's (UNAM) University Library electronic Identities Authentication (UL-eIDA) system was conceived to build a cloud computing security framework model suitable for the sub-Saharan region.

Whereas "Open Source" in software is still gaining momentum in many fields of applications, it is even more present in the "behind the curtains" scene of the Cloud. It is behind the scenes because Cloud tools are only operated by Cloud providers creating their infrastructure, not by end users. But as that infrastructure is going to be a crucial part of the IT environment of the future, like water and power supply have become for the wider living environments, it is good to note that this infrastructure is not limited to (commercial) proprietary technology and standards, but rather is subject to input from the major Open Source players. This chapter reviews the main technologies of this moment in Cloud software: CloudStack of Citrix and Apache, OpenStack of Suse and Openshift from RedHat. Also the CEPH-technology for distributed storage is added in this overview due to its obvious relevance for the Cloud. The brief review of these products confirms that FOSS indeed plays a major role in the Cloud, opening up that technology for open standards and "public" ownership of this soon-to-be an essential part of our IT environment.

Libraries invest millions of dollars in developing and maintaining library applications that are core to their libraries and help them to improve their competitive advantage through operational excellence of libraries. Continuous changes in the library environment forces the library to innovate and optimize their library process, resulting in continuous changes in the software applications that support the library processes. As a consequence, delivering applications rapidly that are defect free, scalable, and reliable becomes challenging. Testing becomes a critical and vital step in the process – not only in terms of coverage but also in terms of performance, security, and usability. Setting up test environments that closely mirror the production environment can be expensive – in terms of hardware, licenses, people to manage library infrastructure and its application. "Testing as a Service" – a new paradigm of Cloud-based "On Demand" testing service can help libraries to address this challenge. This chapter focuses on how libraries can optimize their IT budget through a strategic initiative in the form of "On Demand" testing. This chapter describes Requirements of Testbed Platform, Cloud Testing, and Benefits of testing using cloud environment for library Amazon Web Services – Public Cloud Services.

Cloud computing is a model to provide on-demand access of configurable computing services and resources to the network users without direct service provider interaction. Cloud computing is one of the new buzzwords in the business world. It is a generic term for computing solution where software and services are provided over the Internet. Also the cloud computing delivered and managed IT services in several different forms such as Platform, Infrastructure, and to publish Web services for the patrons. In this chapter we discuss technology, benefits, and initiatives and mainly compare about the Amazon Web Services (AWS) and Online Computer Library Centre (OCLC) cloud service players.

Cloud computing is an emerging computing model which has evolved as a result of the maturity of underlying prerequisite technologies. There are differences in perspective as to when a set of underlying technologies becomes a "cloud" model. In order to categorize cloud computing services, and to expect some level of consistent characteristics to be associated with the services, cloud adopters need a consistent frame of reference. The Cloud Computing Reference Architecture (CCRA) defines a standard reference architecture and consistent frame of reference for comparing cloud services from different service providers when selecting and deploying cloud services to support their mission requirements. Cloud computing offers information retrieval systems, particularly digital libraries and search engines, a wide variety of options for growth and reduction of maintenance needs and encourages efficient resource use. These features are particularly attractive for digital libraries, repositories, and search engines. The dynamic and elastic provisioning features of a cloud infrastructure allow rapid growth in collection size and support a larger user base, while reducing management issues. Hence, the objective of this chapter is to investigate and design reference architecture to Digital Library Systems using cloud computing with scalability in mind. The proposed reference architecture is called as CORADLS. This architecture accelerates the rate at which library users can get easy, efficient, faster and reliable services in the digital environment. Here, the end user does not have to worry about the resource or disk space in cloud computing.

Developing and maintaining Digital Libraries requires substantial investments that are not simply a matter of technological decisions but also organizational issues. While digital libraries hold plenty of promise both now and for the future, they have been slow in taking off. Some digital libraries have either been completely abandoned or they have been put on hold indefinitely. One of the reasons for this predicament is that developers of digital libraries have approached their implementation the same traditional way of building applications, which is also akin to how structures of physical information organizations are built. Digital Libraries with their universal functionality may be even more flexible and reusable, if designed in a service-oriented manner. Such design should allow decreasing the effort of the creation of new digital libraries and the maintenance and scaling of currently existing large installations. Service-oriented architecture offers a better approach to building digital libraries, including streamlining business components, employing reusable services and connecting existing applications to communicate efficiently. The SOA is still a fairly new concept in DL systems. This chapter investigates the applicability of SOA as a fundamental architecture within the system. Its objective is to design a Service-Oriented Architecture for Digital Library System (DLS) using Web Service technology. SORADLS includes different layers which provide primitive services to the library applications built on top of the DLS. DLS techniques of personalization, alert, and caching build SORADLS as services. This architecture provides a fast, safe, convenient, and efficient service to users connected through the Internet.

Cloud computing is leading the technology development of today's communication scenario. This is because of its cost-efficiency and flexibility. In Cloud computing vast amounts of data are stored in varied and distributed environments, and security to data is of prime concern. RSA or Elliptic Curve Cryptography (ECC) provides a secure means of message transmission among communicating hosts using Diffie Hellman Key Exchange algorithm or ElGamal algorithm. By having key lengths of 160 bits, the ECC algorithm provides sufficient strength against crypto analysis and its performance can be compared with standard algorithms like RSA with a bit length of 1024 bits. In the present work, the plain text is converted to cipher text using RSA or ECC algorithms. As the proposed model is intended to be used in Cloud environment, a probabilistic mathematical model is also used. While the data is being retrieved from the servers, a query is being used which uses the mathematical model to search for the data which is still in encryption form. Final decryption takes place only at user's site by using the private keys. Thus the security model provides the fundamental security services like Authentication, Security, and Confidentiality to the transmitted message and also provides sufficient strength against crypto analysis in Cloud environment.

Libraries are considered storehouses of knowledge in the form of books and other resources. Introduction of computers and information and communication technology paved the way for resources in electronic format. Hence, storage of library resources is categorized in two ways namely physical storage and electronic storage. The advantages of e-format are multiple users, increasing availability of free resource, sharing, storing, accessibility, retrieval, flexibility, compatibility, and so forth. As an evolutionary change in adapting to the electronic dissemination, electronic data can be stored virtually, externally, and retrieved in cloud computing. For cloud storage users, service providers and tools are considered as major components of the service architecture. Tool connects cloud storage server and thin client platform through the Internet. Green computing and green production technology are utilizing minimum resources and maximum production in an eco-friendly way. Data warehousing is collection of data, categorizing, filtering, eliminating replica data, format compatibility; security of data retrieval gives economic storage of files. Warehoused data with extract, transform, and load (ETL) tools are retrieved by data mining. This chapter discusses various architecture, service providers, models of service, certifications, billing models, security issues, solutions to security issues and eco-friendly economic storage.

On-demand computing power at modest cost, tied with faster Internet accessibility in the Cloud has offered the future of Cloud libraries. This chapter presents a snapshot of what is happening in the arena of Cloud libraries. It presents the features, its promises, components that drive a Cloud library, users and the services, infrastructure, information sources, and retrieval strategies in the Cloud. Further, it presents a Cloud strategic planning model for its realization in libraries. Whereas a lot of work has been done on the technical aspects and implications in health and medical services, there is lack of focus on the implication of Cloud computing in a library setting. This chapter is a self-conscious attempt in filling some of the gaps.

Digital libraries have arrived. New frontiers are being pioneered and technological superhighways being paved for a future researcher to tread on to go farther than humankind has ever gone before to create advanced knowledge-based communities. It is only possible to see how fast the horse will run its race once it has been tamed. Can the digital library be saddled with cloud computing and reined with e-books? The Industrial Revolution has brought disparity between poor and rich, widening the ozone layer gash. Advancements in nuclear technology have not necessarily resulted in worldwide peace. Identifying pitfalls and shortcomings in strategies and policies that govern developing technologies can help prevent issues and problems that can rear their heads at some later stage. This chapter continues to bring forth the issues concerning digital libraries and the challenges, current and ahead. Implications of such issues must be addressed constructively in time at several conceptual and factual levels in the context of a set of values that are ethically and scientifically acceptable by individuals from all walks of life worldwide.

Foreword

It is my privilege to pen the foreword to this important collection on the emerging vision of digital-age libraries "in the cloud" as viable, dynamic, and integrated enhancements to current centers for library and information resources, services, and facilities. The 19 chapters provide multifaceted, expert insight for information and knowledge management scholars, professionals, research staff, and students in higher education, especially within libraries, engineering, information technology, in computer, communication, and administrative sciences, in management and in all of primary, secondary, and higher education.

While physical, brick-and-mortar-based library resources, services and facilities persist in importance for teaching, learning, and research, the relative importance of virtual, cloud-based resources, services and facilities is increasing exponentially. We experienced a sea-change in the late and middle 1990's, when the World Wide Web opened new vistas with GUI's and hyperlinking. Whereas about 70% of current library resources, services, and facilities are physical and about 30% are virtual, cloud-based, and the relative importance of virtual, cloud-based libraries is growing exponentially. The capacity for physical libraries is slowing and has plateaued in most of the world, while the capacity for virtual, cloud-based libraries continues in its upward, dynamic, and accelerated growth. Within a decade, the relative percentages will likely be reversed, so that virtual, cloud-based library resources, services, and facilities will have grown to constitute 70% of the total capacity, and physical library resources, services, and facilities will remain generally static and will represent only about 30% of the total capacity.

It is in this likely scenario, that the current volume of expert essays demonstrates the value and validity of its strategic vision. The "library of the future" is virtual and cloud-based, and the 19 cogent essays in this volume guide the reader's vision into clear focus. These expert essays offer the proven effectiveness of case-study based data related to and extrapolated out into generic, adaptable frameworks and models. Many of the essays evidence theoretical and academic perspectives, where teaching, learning, research, and digital publishing are the coin-of-the-realm and innovative knowledge (applied and theoretical) is the value and product. Others stand firmly in the commercial environment, where bottom-line profit is the value and product. Some apply proprietary tools, products and networks; others demonstrate the advantages of open-source tools, products, and communities.

The contents of this volume should prove insightful, useful, and usable for an international audience, irrespective of high-technology capacity and infrastructure. Most of the issues are presented to allow for scalability – up to greater capacity, down to lesser technological infrastructures, and out to broad regional, national, and geographic environments. The target audience of this book is professionals, students, and researchers working in the fields of information and knowledge management in various disciplines, such as library, information, and communication sciences, administrative sciences and management, education, computer science, and information technology. Moreover, the book will provide insights and support executives concerned with cloud library management and development in different types of information and work communities and environments.

The esteemed editorial team, led by Sangeeta N. Dhamdhere, has attracted a substantive group of expert writers to present complex ideas in readable, inspiring, and ultimately practical terms. The authors represent broad professional perspectives and expertise from myriad fields: technology, knowledge creation, and management, education and pedagogy, business, communication media, and library and information science and administration. The authors represent a broad range of education, training, professional application and teaching over several continents and generations. This will certainly be an integral building block to the canon of digital-age libraries and will find a home in my consortium's collections, the Higher Education Library and Information Network / HELIN.

D. Russell Bailey
Providence College, USA

Donald Russell Bailey *is an international scholar in digital teaching, learning, and research and is currently Library Director at Providence College, Rhode Island, USA. Dr. Bailey has taught Western languages, literatures and cultures, comparative pedagogy and education (emphasizing East Asian educational opportunities) since 1973. Since 1994 he has served as a faculty administrator in higher education libraries in the US. He is best known for his work in The Commons (Information, Learning, Library, and Faculty Commons). His 2008 book, Transforming Library Service Through Information Commons: Case Studies for the Digital Age (with Barbara Tierney) has sold several thousand copies and continues to serve as a resource for libraries in the digital age. He is a frequent speaker internationally (US, Scotland, Czech Republic, Hong Kong, Hungary) and is currently pursuing the role of libraries in creating digital knowledge, especially digital humanities: drbailey@providence.edu, http://works.bepress.com/d_r_bailey/*

Preface

INTRODUCTION

Web technologies, e-publishing, and Open Access have reinforced libraries to reach beyond any physical, political or social barrier. Modern libraries are converting gradually to digital libraries. Cloud computing and server virtualization technology is a boon for libraries as it provides a common platform for all. Another major advantage is easy information storage and resource sharing being made possible on a single and efficient system that saves cost and time. Virtualization Technology is being adopted by many players in the industry. In the year 2012, when I was preparing for a research paper on cloud computing for an international conference, I searched for books and articles on this topic. I realized that very few books existed on this topic. This motivated me to develop a complete reference book based on the virtualization concept for libraries. I am thankful to IGI Global for accepting my book proposal. From then on it was challenge to assemble ideas from many experts from various parts of the world into one single book.

This book aims to provide relevant theoretical and practical information and the latest research findings in the area of virtualization of libraries. The chapters of this book are conceived by experts in this field and users of this technology. The authors have used their experience to present information which will be a useful asset to our target readers and professionals who are interested in improving their understanding in this area and who are inclined towards using this technology in their libraries to provide cloud-based information services to their patrons.

SPECIAL FEATURES

What makes this book unique is the unity in diversity. It is a collection of thoughts and ideas by not one but several authors from various walks of life. In an attempt to give a complete reference on Cloud Computing and Virtualization Technologies in Libraries, authors have been invited to present their contribution in form of chapters for this book. Hence it includes experts, researchers, IT educationists, IT professionals, Cloud professionals and LIS professionals, all forming an intelligent rainbow of knowledge. The International Review and Editorial team has put in a great effort to develop a quality product for the beginners and practitioners in the Cloud area.

This book focuses on the latest innovation of information technology and application of the Internet, which is 'Cloud Computing' and its application to virtualization of libraries. The reader, going through the chapters diligently, breezes through the entire concept of cloud computing and its application to the digital world of libraries. Starting its voyage with the definition and introduction of cloud computing, the book cruises along steadily through thicker clouds of knowledge. These clouds contain a variety of information viz. need of digital libraries, their architecture, application and implementation of cloud computing in digital libraries, issues and challenges faced in this process, green economic and secure libraries on cloud, digital preservation in cloud computing environment, different cloud libraries models, case studies, role and responsibilities of a future cloud librarian, open source in the cloud, various platforms available, their comparative studies, cloud library security, and finally recognizing the limitations and concerns associated with it. A person reading through the book not only familiarizes himself with the concept of cloud computing and virtualization of libraries, but also gets an insight on how digital libraries are valuable to the society.

STRUCTURE OF THE BOOK

Different chapters in the book are compiled in such a way that a person beginning to read with even the faintest idea of the digital library concept ends up acquiring a whole world of knowledge about the structure, benefits and challenges associated with it. The book is equipped with tremendous information. It also contains case studies, models and architecture of digital libraries and enriches the readers with valuable information, preparing them to face their respective professional fields with enthusiasm to implement the latest technology harnessed to benefit the inquisitive human mind. The book also gives food for thought to critics in this area, enabling them to think twice about the issues, concerns and limitations which need to be tackled with great care in order to optimize the benefits of cloud computing to virtualization of libraries in this frenzied world of innovations and technological advancements.

This reference book is a compilation of nineteen chapters, each one dedicated to different facet of cloud computing and virtualization technologies in libraries.

Chapter One introduces the Digital Library to the reader and gives information about its requirement in the global world. It explains the digitization process, recent trends and research activities, cloud computing, its types and methodology. It also describes the application of cloud computing in libraries with example of cloud in academic library in India, Library of Congress and OCLC. The chapter points out the change in the role of library and information professionals from a "book lending" person to a recognized "intermediary" between information and its users.

Chapter Two focuses on the need of digital information management and issues related to it. Digital preservation faces the problem of obsolescence and requires special concern. This chapter aims to identify the projects under process for digital preservation. It also describes the digital preservation techniques such as migration, emulation, Open Archival Information System, Metadata Harvesting and current trends of cloud computing in digital preservation and international efforts towards it with examples.

Chapter Three emphasizes that libraries and archives play a critical role in organizing, preserving, and providing access to the cultural and historical resources of society. It states that in a relatively stable world of printed, hand-written, and mechanically reproduced information, repositories have managed to preserve a rich array of scholarly communications, documentary evidence, and useful information for specialized scholars and for the general public. Finally it explains why the absence of a clear consensus about effective strategies and methods for digital preservation and the paucity of data on the resource implications of various proposed strategies serve as deterrents to concrete actions by institutions.

Chapter Four discusses how cloud computing, today's widely acclaimed phenomenon, creates a new business environment in libraries and has much to offer to the library world. It changes the way of thinking about library technology and shows great impact on librarianship since the technological environment is changing. As part of the evolution of technologies, libraries must be prepared for the new paradigm shift, and empower themselves to stay ahead in the game. This chapter focuses mainly on models of cloud computing, type of cloud suitable for information centers, opportunity and risk in developing cloud services and impact of cloud computing on information centers.

Chapter Five elaborates on how libraries and information centers can enhance their resources infrastructure with minimum cost, make effective systems and provide better services to the user community at minimum cost and time. Its aim is to explain how librarians, information professionals, computer science professionals & knowledge workers apply cloud computing technology in the libraries and information centre management. It explains the application of cloud computing in libraries and information centre. In the end it describes some real examples like Dura Space, OCLC, Library Thing, Chronopolis Project, Library Cloud and Seer Suite where Libraries are adopting Cloud Computing. It also discusses how resource scalability will have a direct impact on reducing the organizational capital and its operational cost and how integration of Libraries with Cloud computing will make the Library System greener.

Chapter Six presents a case study of application of cloud computing in NIT's in India with special reference to VNIT. Making the decision to use cloud-based services means balancing the elements of cost, risk, and benefit to decide whether those services help advance the mission of the library as well as institute. RECs/NITs Libraries can take advantage of the cloud in numerous ways, such as data sharing including discovery tools, current status of research, and software as service which depends on the cloud, email systems and social networking etc. The chapter recommends a road for globalizing Regional Engineering Colleges/National Institutes/Technology and Research Centers libraries in India.

Chapter Seven analyzes the current situation and existing problems of cloud computing in academic libraries. On this basis, with combination of cloud computing, SaaS, Web2.0, SOA and other technologies, this chapter proposes a CALIS-based cloud service strategy and the corresponding cloud library services platform (i.e., Nebula platform) model. The model is suitable for constructing a large-scale distributed network of public digital library services. The chapter further discusses problems faced by academic libraries and development efforts to overcome that problem. It also proposes to improve current user service model with cloud computing.

In Chapter Eight, an attempt has been made to give an overview of cloud computing technology and its advantages to the modern world. It also states its connection with libraries, the models in which libraries can deploy this technology for providing services and augment the productivity of library staff. It believes that with the introduction of cloud computing, libraries can certainly offer more effective, more professional and user-centric services.

Chapter Nine discusses in brief the applications of the cloud and server virtualization technologies in libraries along with information on common concepts, current examples of cloud libraries, open source platforms available, the proposed university cloud library model and cloud library access model. It emphasizes that technology is advancing at a phenomenal rate, but it needs to be harnessed in the most efficient way. It realizes that cloud computing, resulting in cloud libraries will provide a great leap forward in providing access to large quantity of information to users.

Chapter Ten looks towards expansion of University libraries in the sub-Saharan region using cloud computing technologies. It was in view of this deficit that the University of Namibia's (UNAM) University Library electronic Identities Authentication (UL-eIDA) system was conceived to build a cloud computing security framework model suitable for the sub-Saharan region. The UL-eIDA was intended to provide security in the cloud computing system. It employed security measures that utilized UL-eIDA card, firewalls, virtualization and VLAN configurations, DFUL-eIDA encryption mechanism and dynamic trust zone all worked in synergy to make the system forceful enough to combat security threats at any level.

Chapter Eleven looks into Open Source which has a strong position in the Cloud and for a good reason. The chapter discusses that commercial providers of the Cloud will have to adhere to the same standards, while hoping to add their strong 'warranty-based' service and reputation, an aspect in which Open Source still seems to lag a bit behind, at least in customer's perception. The chapter further illustrates that if libraries need more 'control' over their Cloud-environments, they can still go for the options – available in all FOSS-products that build their own Cloud. This is the only approach in which libraries would get in touch with the platforms themselves. Moreover it discusses advantages of open source for cloud, main contenders and distributed storage technology.

Chapter Twelve focuses on how library can optimize their IT budget through a strategic initiative in the form of 'On Demand' testing. The chapter describes requirements of Testbed Platform and Cloud Testing. It further states that the continuous changes in Library environment forces the Library to innovate and optimize their Library process, resulting in continuous changes in the software applications that support the Library processes. 'Testing as a Service' - a new paradigm of Cloud based 'On Demand' testing service can help Library to address this challenge in library. The Chapter describes the features of AMAZON EC2, S3, EBS and their limitations along with their security models.

Chapter Thirteen discusses the history, technology, benefits, and initiatives and mainly compares the Amazon Web Services (AWS) and Online Computer Library Centre (OCLC) cloud service players. It describes their services and Web, mobile and social applications.

The objective of Chapter Fourteen is to investigate and design reference architecture to Digital Library systems using cloud computing with scalability in mind. The proposed reference architecture is called as cloud oriented reference architecture of the digital library system, that is, CORADLS. This architecture accelerates the library users to get easy, efficient, faster and reliable services in the digital environment. Here the end user does not have to worry about the resource or disk space in cloud computing. This chapter describes the issue of scalability in the domain of Digital Library.

Chapter Fifteen designs a Service-Oriented Reference Architecture for Digital Library System (SORADLS) using Web Service technology. SOA has enormous benefits that digital libraries could use. The developers and information professionals must carefully and consciously learn, understand and apply the principles, requirements and techniques of SOA in order to see its full benefits. The proposed SORADLS explained with examples and different modules like personalization, Registration, Notification, Security, Caching and Storage with workflow of SORADLS in future research directions.

Chapter Sixteen discusses measures to provide security of data in a Cloud environment. ECC or RSA algorithms are discussed for security in a Cloud environment. ECC itself is a very secure algorithm for encryption. The advantage with this model is, it is not only free from linear and differential cryptanalysis but also free from chosen cipher text attacks. Thus the given model supports the important properties like authentication, security and confidentiality and resistance against chosen cipher text attacks at less computing resources when compared to algorithm like RSA.

Chapter Seventeen states how cloud storage users, service providers and tools are considered as major components of the service architecture. Green computing and green production technology are utilizing minimum resources and maximum production in an eco-friendly way. This chapter discusses various architecture, service providers, models of service, certifications, billing models, security issues, solutions to security issues and eco-friendly economic storage. The information in this chapter will help towards making data centre more economic, eco-friendly and secure to store ever growing data in a reliable environment acceptable by future generations and nature as a whole.

Chapter Eighteen presents a snapshot of what is happening in the arena of cloud libraries. It presents the features, its promises, components, users and the services, infrastructure, information sources and retrieval strategies in the Cloud. Further, it presents a Cloud strategic planning model for its realization in libraries. It points out to the lack of focus on the implication of cloud computing in a library setting. With the technological changes and a shift from library mission and services by being involved in traditional IT practices, there is an urgency to leverage library services on Cloud platform. This chapter is a self-conscious attempt in filling some of the gaps.

Chapter Nineteen addresses the limitations of digital libraries and concerns related to them. It brings forth issues concerning digital libraries and the challenges, current and ahead. Implications of such issues must be addressed constructively in time at several conceptual and factual levels in the context of a set of values that are ethically and scientifically acceptable by individuals from all walks of life worldwide. Therefore, identifying pitfalls and shortcomings in strategies and policies that govern developing technologies can help prevent issues and problems that can rear their heads at some later stage. Explosion of information should be harnessed in such a fashion that difference between the desired information and what is accessible could be minimized. This chapter gives a microscopic view of the issues related to various dimensions of digital libraries and cloud computing in a much systemized way and looks keenly at ways to tackle challenges lying ahead.

TARGET AUDIENCE

The target audience of this book will be professionals, students, and researchers working in the field of information and knowledge management in various disciplines, such as library, information and communication sciences, Cloud professionals, administrative sciences and management, education, computer science, and information technology. Moreover, the book will provide insight and support executives concerned with the cloud library management and development in different types of information and work communities and environments.

There is an emerging need for an easy-to-use resource guide to help LIS, Computer, IT and Cloud professionals to communicate, understand and implement the Cloud computing and Virtualization technology in their area. I am thankful to IGI Global for accepting my proposal on this topic and for giving me a chance to create a complete reference book on Cloud computing and virtualization technologies in libraries with the help of our contributors and editorial board members and reviewers who are experts in this area.

Sangeeta N. Dhamdhere
Modern College of Arts, Science and Commerce, India

Acknowledgment

I wish to acknowledge my sincere thanks to All Editorial Advisory Board Members, especially Dr. Paul Nieuwenhuysen, Professor, Vrije Universiteit, Brussels, Belgium, and Dr. Egbert De Smet, Professor, Antwerp Universiteit, Antwerp, Belgium for their constant support and guidance in editing and reviewing chapters and their proposals and spending their valuable time to make this book project a complete guide to cloud computing and virtualization technologies in libraries.

I also thank All Reviewers especially Dr. Shalini Lihitkar, HoD, LIS, Nagpur University, India; Mr. Siavash Mishiri, Director, Author and Consultant, EA, BPM, Cloud, Vistex Inc, Metanova, United Kingdom; Mr. Trevor A. Dawes, Circulation Service Director, Princeton University Library, New Jersey; and Mr. Deepak Mane, Cloud consultant/architect, TCS, India for reviewing the chapters contributed by experts from LIS, Cloud computing, Engineering profession, Software company, IT Lecturers from various part of world.

Many authors contributed their expertise and chapters for this project, and without their contribution I would not be able to present this comprehensive guide to cloud computing and virtualization technologies in libraries. I would like to express my many thanks to each chapter contributor. I am also thankful to D. Russell Bailey, Ph.D., Library Director of Providence College, Rhode Island, USA for spending time for going through the whole manuscript and express his views about this book as the foreword. I would also like to thank Mrs. Namita Gupta, IT Lecturer, International Maritime College Oman for reviewing the preface.

My sincere thanks to Hon. Dr. G. R. Ekbote, Chairman, Business Council, P.E. Society, Pune-05 and Prof. Shamkant Deshmukh, Secretary, P.E.Society, Pune-05 for extending their cooperation and motivation for all of the endeavors undertaken.

I want to express my gratitude to our Principal Dr. Sanjay Kharat, Modern College of Arts, Science and Commerce, Ganeshkhind, Pune, India who motivated and helped me to complete this project.

Most importantly, I cannot express enough thanks to my mother, father, and sister for their support and confidence in me to complete this book.

I thank IGI Global, USA publisher, and associate editors appointed for this project for publishing this book.

Lastly I thank all those who contributed directly or indirectly to complete this work.

Sangeeta N. Dhamdhere
Modern College of Arts, Science and Commerce, India

Chapter 1
Digital Library and Its Requirements in the Global World

Surbhi Saini
Indira Gandhi National Open University (IGNOU), India

ABSTRACT

This chapter introduces the basics of the digital library, including needs, benefits, and requirements, and briefly describes the digitization process. The role of library and information science professionals has now become a debatable one due to the advent of digital libraries and the Internet. The cloud computing and virtualization in digital culture is also discussed here. In this regard, the chapter covers cloud computing, including the characteristics, types, and how it works. The application of cloud computing in libraries is described with an example of the cloud in the academic library in Orissa. The advantages and disadvantages of cloud computing in libraries or in organizations are also covered here. The future prospects of the digital library using cloud computing technology is like an innovative application in libraries.

INTRODUCTION

Dr. S. R. Ranganathan was born for the development of the new subject of library science. But due to the impact of Information Technology, the subject has changed to Library and Information Science. He includes five laws designed to make the library as comfortable to the user as his or her home. The light of Ranganathan's five laws of library science is the motto *"Right information to the right user at the right time"* has the guru mantra of an information professional. The information world has expanded dramatically over the last few decades mainly due to the developments in information technology. These developments have resulted in new methods of communication. The speed of communication is moving at a high rate due to latest telecommunication and network system. The introduction of computers and application of optical technology for library and information activities have made for important achievements in information handling. But the resource sharing concept changed the realistic scenario and timely demand of information re-

DOI: 10.4018/978-1-4666-4631-5.ch001

sulted in distributed databases, and full text digital libraries came into existence. The digital library is the electronic library in which the access storage and dissemination of information is in the digitized form. The digital library is a logical extension of the networked environment and the development triggered thereof, and provides users with coherent access to a very rare, organized repository of information and knowledge. In a sense it is a global virtual library. The libraries networked thousand of electronic libraries/databases. The advent of digital libraries has made a noticeable impact on the role of library and information professionals as well as end users of information. In this chapter an attempt has been made to bring out certain points regarding challenges, which can be taken up as opportunities, posed by the digital library to library and information professionals. The digital libraries have several features in addition to computerization of traditional and routine work. These advancements have enabled information professionals to provide the quick and accurate digital information services to the users.

DIGITAL LIBRARY

The concept of digital library came in around 30 years ago. The digital library has different meanings in digital communities, such as electronic library, virtual library, library without wall, world library, Internet library, paperless library, and so forth. In all of the terms there is a little bit of difference, but here the concept of digital library will be pointed out. Digital library means a computerized network system where all the information are stored in electronic format, which can be accessed and transmitted through networks enabling retrieval of required information by a large number of users. Users can access their desired information using computer terminals at their work place.

Definition

In the information environment, a lot of authors give different views about the digital library. It is not possible to discuss all of them, but here are a few definitions which are very simple for understanding the digital library.

In *Online Dictionary of Library and Information Science (ODLIS)*, "digital library" has been defined as "A library in which a significant proportion of the resources are available in machine-Readable format, as opposed to print or microform."

Edward Fox has defined the digital library as "the new way of carrying out the functions of libraries encompassing new types of information resources, new approach to acquisition, new methods of storage and preservation, new approaches to classification and cataloguing, intensive use of electronic systems and networks and dramatic shifts in intellectual, organizational, and electronic process."

Need

The need only forces a man to invent something; that's why problems are often solved in the form of inventions. Today, the information explosion is the huge problem in front of librarians and librarians facing a problem to maintain their services, but digital technology may solve the problem and now libraries are in the position to provide an improved quality of library services.

In summary, the needs of the digital library are as follows:

- To minimize massive storage and space problem in libraries.
- To collect, store, organize, and access information in digital form.
- To encourage the economical and efficient delivery of information.

- To promote resource sharing.
- Accessible on the World Wide Web (WWW).
- To save library staff time by avoiding routine jobs.
- To fulfill the requirements of customers by providing better services.
- To have large digitized databases.
- Knowledge dissemination.
- Provide download and printing facilities.
- Provide easy and fast access to information irrespective of time and location.
- Provide access to rare books.

Advantages

The benefits of the digital library are as follows:

- Easier access to individual components within items (e.g., articles within journals).
- Better quality of library services provided to the user.
- Remote access to expensive and rare materials.
- Searching information is easy including full text.
- Ability to enhance digital images in terms of size, sharpness, color contrast, and noise reduction, and so forth.
- Integration of different media (e.g., images, sound video, etc.).
- The ability to satisfy requests for surrogates (e.g., photocopies, photographic prints, slides, etc.).
- Potential for presenting a critical mass of materials.

DIGITAL LIBRARY: REQUIREMENTS

Building a digital library is not an easy task. It requires a well-educated professional staff in the field of digital technology and information technology that also has a good knowledge of the library science field. The basic requirements of digital library are as follows:

- **Equipment:** Scanners, computers, and storage devices; audio and video capture equipment.
- **Software:** Scanning, optical character recognition, word-processing, spell-checking, image management, video and audio capture.
- **Human Resource:** Personnel and skills.
- **Funds (Cover):** Salaries, equipments, software, running costs, and so forth.

Digitization Process: Steps

The digitization process done in the steps which are explained below:

- **Scanning:** First it is important to scan the original books, paper, picture, maps, and photographs in images which are stored in a file. In this process, high resolution scanners, fax cards, electronic cameras, and other imaging devices may also be used to transfer normal paper based document into images.
- **Storage:** A server is the basic requirement with multiple CPUs with RAM in GB range. A few CD readers, writers, and so forth, are also used for storing each and every document in images.
- **Storage Engines:** Software is required for databases management, Web servers, content authoring and editing. A few multimedia PCs are required for running search engines successfully.

A digital image is composed of a grid of pixels arranged according to a set of rows and columns. Each pixel presents a very small portion of the images, and is allocated tonal values which are digitally represented in binary code (zeros and/or ones), so a digital image is actually a grid made up of zeros and ones. The binary digits for each pixel are called bits and are stored in a sequence.

RECENT TRENDS AND RESEARCH ACTIVITIES ON DIGITAL LIBRARY

Recent Trends on Digital Library

The library of traditional times and that of today in the changing digital era changes according to the need and requirement of the users. In the electronic era it is the effort of the library professionals that every user gets the information at his or her doorsteps. In the changing scenario of the libraries, the recent trends and research activities in digital libraries may try to make the path easy for the user, which means anybody can get the information at anytime, helping to dissolve the barrier boundaries among the users and information.

Architecture, Systems, Tools, and Technologies

This category refers to all technical, infrastructural, and algorithmic and system-related components of digital libraries (e.g., Shibboleth Project).

Digital Content and Collections

This category refers to individual digital objects and to collections of objects in repositories encompassing a variety of materials in different digital formats.

Metadata

Digital collections require well-structured metadata schemes to describe digital objects and content at various levels of granularity.

Interoperability

Interoperability is one of the most heavily discussed issues in digital library research. The requirement for interoperability derives from the fact that various digital libraries with different architectures, metadata formats, and underlying technologies wish to effectively interact–something they can do through applying a range of common protocols and standards.

Digital Right Management (DRM)

DRM technology is a key enabler for the distribution of digital content. It is an integrated secure digital content distribution technology.

Digital Archives, Preservation

In the digital era – to develop a digital archive in a different subject. The preservation and creation is real challenge in front of library professionals. It is very important to preserve the same. The Digital Creation Centre (DCC) was established to help solve the extensive challenges of digital preservation and digital creation and to lead research, development, advice, and support services for higher education institutions in the United Kingdom.

Digital Production and Digital Library Production Service (DLPS)

In a general way – to define “digital production” as the process by which creative ideas and assets (images, text, and interactive apps) are translated into an array of digital media–Web sites, banner ads, rich media applications, HTML e-mails, mobile and social media applications–so that the right messages are delivered via the right channel at the right time to the right users. These days, the DLPS service is provided by different libraries.

Deep Resource Sharing

The resource sharing among the libraries in a digital environment. The University of California has built nine campus libraries of distinction (and has launched the development of a tenth), comprising world-class collections that give a competitive edge to UC research and instruction. The UC libraries have also won an unparalleled reputation for innovation and service. Open Archives Initiative and Cross Ref (Cross Ref) all address different parts of the "data silo" problem.

Courseware Systems and the Library

The American universities and colleges develop the coursework system with technology, just to make the courses interesting and attract the students, or try to develop the interest among the students. The blackboard and the Web CT are commonly used now days.

Digital Portfolios

The digital portfolios are new tools for student assessment. Including this emphasis on the learning process and material results a student achieves throughout a course of study (e.g., Amsterdam University of Professional Education).

Collaborative Course Design

Today, teachers design a course material with the experts. The many learning environments build on a model for which origins can be traced back to early distance education. In this model, students are given a "box" containing all the materials for a source they need to master, a so-called, self-contained course (e.g., the DE site developed at Tilburg University to explain the complexities in decision making in Europe).

RESEARCH ACTIVITIES ON DIGITAL LIBRARIES

The Digital Libraries require research in several new key areas pointing to the development:

Proactive Systems

Proactive systems with functionality that facilitates collaboration, communication, and information creation.

Generic Digital Library Management Systems

Generic Digital Library Management Systems that provide basic system infrastructures that can be used to implement application specific digital libraries incorporating context-specific services.

Popular Examples

ILEJ (Internet Library of Early Journals)

ILEJ, the "Internet Library of Early Journals" was a joint project by the Universities of Birmingham, Leeds, Manchester, and Oxford, conducted under the auspices of the E-Lib (Electronic Libraries) Programme. It aimed to digitize substantial runs of 18th and 19th century journals, and make these images available on the Internet, together with their associated bibliographic data. The project finished in 1999, and no additional material will be added.

CAMiLEON Project (Creative Archiving at Michigan and Leeds: Emulating the Old on the New)

The CAMiLEON project is developing and evaluating a range of technical strategies for the long-term preservation of digital material. It has three main objectives: To explore the options for long-term retention of the original functionality and 'look and feel' of digital objects; to investigate technology emulation as a long-term strategy for long-term preservation and access to digital objects; and to consider where and how emulation fits into a suit of digital preservation strategies. The project began on October 1, 1999, and is a joint undertaking between the University of Michigan (USA) and the University of Leeds (UK) and is funded by JISC and NSF. The UK component of the project ended on December 31, 2002. The US component of the project ended on September 30, 2003.

NEDLIB: Towards a Networked European Deposit Library

NEDLIB stands for Networked European Deposit Library and is a project supported by the `Telematics for Libraries' programme of the EC. The aim of NEDLIB is to define the architecture for capturing, preserving, and accessing electronic publications, also in the distant future. The PANDORA (Preserving and Accessing Networked Documentary Resources of Australia) and (Preserving Access to Digital Information (PADI) are the part of same.

DELOS is a Network of Excellence

The DELOS Network of Excellence in Digital Libraries intends to advance the field in these new and exciting directions, with the aim of progressing to the development of the next-generation Digital Library system. To this end, DELOS coordinates a joint programme of activities of the major European teams working in digital library related areas. DELOS also aims at disseminating knowledge of digital library technologies to many diverse application domains, by providing access to technological know-how, services, test-beds, and the necessary expertise to facilitate their take-up. The research activities of DELOS have been organized in seven clusters: Digital Library Architecture, Information Access and Personalization, Audio/Visual and Non-traditional Objects, User Interfaces and Visualization, Knowledge Extraction and Semantic Interoperability, Preservation, and Evaluation.

Watermarking of Digital Audio

The Department of Information Technology Government of India has initiated a project titled Watermarking of Digital Audio and setting up of resource centre for DRM Systems" at C-DAC, Thiruvanthapuram. To start with, this resource centre shall develop robust watermarking algorithms for digital audio (e.g., PCM, MP3, etc.) and test and stimulate those watermarking techniques as a copyright protection mechanism of digital audio over the Internet. The project also involves adoption of various international standards to develop digital right management system for efficient and secured delivery of content (audio, video) over the Internet.

OeBF (Open E-Book Forum)

The OeBF is an international trade and standards organization. The goal is to produce industry-adopted specifications, which benefits publishers, technology companies, and consumers. It provides a forum for the discussion of issues and technologies related to e-books and for developing, publishing, and maintaining common specifications relating to electronic books and promoting the successful adoption of these specifications.

ODRL (Open Digital Rights Languages)

ODRL provides the semantics for a digital life management expression language and data dictionary pertaining to all forums digital contents.

OMA (Open Mobile Alliance)

OMA is an organization. OMA has tackled the issues of downloading and distribution of digital content through mobile phones with the standardization work of OMA downloads.

MPEG (Moving Picture Expert Groups)

MPEG is an ISO/IEC working group for standards development of coded representation of digital audio and video.

SDMI (Secure Digital Music Literature)

SDMI is a forum of worldwide record industry, consumer electronics, and information technology to develop specifications for most related digital right management solutions.

MAJOR DIGITAL LIBRARY INITIATIVES

- Cornell University Library (http://arxiv.org/archive/q-bio)
- Kurt Stüber's Online Library English version (http://www.biolib.de/)
- University of California, Berkeley (http://bscit.berkeley.edu/)
- Carbon Dioxide Information Analysis Center (http://cdiac.esd.ornl.gov/)
- The complete work of Charles Darwin online (http://darwin-online.org.uk/)
- BEN Bio sciednet (http://www.bioscied-net.org/portal/)
- California Digital Library (http://www.cdlib.org/)
- Rice University's Advanced Placement Digital Library (http://apdl.rice.edu/DesktopDefault.aspx?tabindex=3&tabid=33)
- HEC National Digital Library (DL) (http://www.digitallibrary.edu.pk/Index.php)
- Michigan Digitisation Project (http://www.lib.umich.edu/search/Website/biology)
- Utah Digital Newspapers (http://www.lib.utah.edu/digital/unews/)
- The Harvard University Herbaria (http://lib.harvard.edu/)
- Natural History Museum (http://www.nhm.ac.uk/research-curation/library/digital-library/index.html)
- Smithsonian Library's 'Digital Library' (http://www.sil.si.edu/DigitalLibrary.cfm)
- The digital library at Sapienza: universita di Roma and The efforts for open Access (http://bids.citicord.uniroma1.it/) and (http://bids.citicord.uniroma1.it/ricerca.aspx?testo=PADIS%20%E2%80%93%20PhD%20dissertations) text journals followed.
- British Library UK Web Archive (http://www.Webarchive.org.uk/ukw/)
- PANDORA, Australia's Web Archive (http://pandora.nla.gov.au/)
- The British Library's Digital Libraries Programme
- THOMAS - Library of Congress Digital Library
- California Digital Library (http://www.cdlib.org/)
- Gutenberg (http://promo.net/pg/)
- International Children's Digital Library (ICDL) (http://en.childrenslibrary.org/)
- The New Zealand Digital Library Project (http://nzdl.sadl.uleth.ca/cgi-bin/library.cgi)
- Digital Library of the Commons (http://dlc.dlib.indiana.edu/)
- Perseus Digital Library (http://www.perseus.tufts.edu/hopper/)
- The Sydney Electronic Text and Image Service (SETIS) (http://setis.library.usyd.edu.au/)
- The Berkeley Digital Library (http://sunsite.berkeley.edu/)
- Informedia Digital Video Library (http://www.informedia.cs.cmu.edu/)
- The Networked Digital Library of Theses and Dissertations (NDLTD)

- The Bradman Digital Library, Australia (http://www.slsa.sa.gov.au/bradman/)
- The University of Adelaide Digital Library (http://digital.library.adelaide.edu.au/)
- National Science Foundation Digital Library (http://nsdl.org/)
- The Cuneiform Digital Library Initiative (CDLI) (http://cdli.ucla.edu/)
- UQ e Space (http://espace.library.uq.edu.au/)
- Traditional Knowledge Digital Library (http://www.tkdl.res.in/tkdl/langdefault/common/home.asp?GL=Eng)
- Vidyanidhi (http://www.vidyanidhi.org.in/)
- The Digital Library of India (DLI) (http://dli.iiit.ac.in/)
- The Archives of Indian Labour (http://www.indialabourarchives.org/)

DIGITAL LIBRARY: CHALLENGES

The Librarians face a lot of challenges if they think about the digital library. The major challenges are as follows:

Infrastructure Constraints

The major hurdle is the weak computer infrastructure in libraries and also the lack of high capacity bandwidth for network and Internet access.

Lack of Professional Expertise

The lack of professional expertise in the present, changing environment, where the technological force forces us to adopt the changes, makes it only possible retraining existing staff members.

Absence of High Quality Contents

India has a stronghold of arts, folklore, spirituality, traditional knowledge, and so forth, that is unused and even may be lost after certain time because the rare books are difficult to use because of the bad condition of papers. As such, information is not disseminated. As the usage and reach of contents in digital form are far more wide-reaching than the printed text, and the process of digitization that may solve the problem best involves cost in terms of contents, systems, and expert manpower, care should be exercised on what sort of contents need to be digitized.

Support from the Authority/ Management

The prerequisites for the development and maintenance of state-of-the-art digital library systems and services are the proper funding, human resources, and IT skilled staff.

Lack of Policy

In India, the majority of libraries do not have laid down polices on ICT planning and strategies to meet the challenges posed by the technology push, the information overload, as well as the demand from the users.

Problem of Data Format

Digital library software usually accepts and processes all popular and standard digital formats such as HTML, word, RTF, PPT, or PDF. Most of the publishers put their materials in their own proprietary e-book reader formats, from which the text extraction becomes almost impossible. A majority of the scholarly content rests in journal literature and due to copyright issues it cannot easily find its way into the local repositories of the digital library.

Copyright/IPR Issues

In the new digital environment, issues of copyright, intellectual property, and fair use concerns are posing an unprecedented array of problems in front of libraries and librarians.

Lack of Proper Planning

In India's present situation of libraries, paper-based documents outnumber the electronic subscriptions and acquisitions. Some of the libraries need retro-conversion and digitization of library holdings too. Literature on related studies show that there is a severe lapse on the libraries with regard to proper planning of their information resources which are conducive for developing digital libraries. In the electronic resource, the multiplicity of complex formats and with different access terms and conditions is in the dissimilarity among the libraries. Nowadays, the information resources are scattered and distributed across a wide variety of publication types and a vast number of publishers. There is a dire need for proper planning and a meticulously framed content integration model, which is achieved and implemented through world standard digital library technology.

Digital Library Indexes

Current practices of providing indexes while creating a digital library is a matter of business, and lack of professionalism is well-noticed when a user gets wrong matches. The library and information professionals play a big role in the development of powerful indexes. If they are assigned a job of index preparation or even if they are consulted, the digital library will be fully utilized by users and also save the time of the research scholars or any other users of the library.

Copying Services

Today the digital libraries provide the required documents directly to the users on the screen, when they search digital libraries instead of providing photocopy services to the user which is done in the earlier days. Librarians are left out as nonentities in the digital environment when a user interacts with digital information through the Internet. Librarians participate and interact when they provide the bulletin board system, electronic conferences, and use net services. In the earlier days, library and information professionals actively participated, but today the scenario was changed to users directly sending and getting information through the Internet.

SERVICES

The objective of the digital library could be fulfilled by offering the following services:

Shared Cataloguing

It enables a librarian to use the catalogue information available in a major university library or a resource centre for cataloguing new publications added to the library. A document is catalogued only once at the time of entry into the network. Other libraries, which procure that document later, need not spend time in cataloguing it but can download the cataloguing information from the network.

Union Catalogue

A union catalogue of serials, books, and non-book materials held in different libraries of the country is created. This catalogue contains information not only about the available volume of a document in a library but also about the missing volume. Using the network, a user will be able to locate precisely the libraries where the sought document is available.

Online Cataloguing of Library/ Information Centre

The machine readable catalogue of the library or Information Centre can be made available through the internal Web.

The Document Supply/ Delivery Services

It will enable a library to request another library for a copy of a document to be transmitted via e-mail or fax. This service may be largely used for transmitting a few pages from documents say journal articles.

Inter-Library Loan Services

This service will enable a library to request another library through the network, for one or more books on inter-library loan basis for meeting the demands of its users. This may also include facility for reserving a book, if it is on loan in the lending library. The actual transmission of the book will be through postal mail or through courier services. Success of this service will depend on the cooperative spirit of the participating libraries. Libraries with richer collections will be major providers of these services. Success of this service will depend on the cooperative spirit of the participating libraries.

Referral Service

Requests for provision of information, which cannot be satisfied by a library, can be referred to another source from where the information can be had. In this service the users will be informed about the source to be approached to get the required information.

Selective Dissemination of Information

User requests are collected through e-mail. The descriptors are matched against latest available documents and the required users are contacted through e-mail.

Current Awareness Services

List of latest additions to the library, namely books, periodicals, patents, standards, audio-visual material, or any other can be put into the internal Web for user attention.

Bulletin Board

It is proposed to provide this facility to display/ view news, announcements, and so forth, with constant updating of information in an electronic bulletin board. The U.G.C. circulars can also be put on this board. Several bulletin boards can be made available in the networks for each specific category of user discipline.

E-Mail

E-mail is an important communication based service. It enables participants in the network to transfer/receive messages from any part of the world using data networks to which they are subscribing. E-mail provides facility through which other services like inter-library loan requests, location search in the union catalogue, document delivery, request transmission, referral service, and academic communication can be implemented.

ROLE OF LIBRARY PROFESSIONALS IN DIGITAL LIBRARY

Library professionals play a big role in the changing environment of digitization. The role of library professionals is as follows:

The librarians should learn new vocabularies to understand and use the technology fully; encourage interaction among the staff coming from the traditional library as well as a technology background; carefully match technologies and users, reach out and educate users and staff; be prepared to lose control over materials that have so long been the library's property; and connect and communicate with the local, national, and international professional events and work groups.

The librarians must retain the timeless service value of equity of access, personal service, and services tailored to the needs of individuals and at the same time explore new values such as integrating technologies, maintaining holistic computing environment, delivering core services through the network, making technology work for all, and collaborating across administrative lines.

The role of library professionals will change as the traditional tasks of cataloguing and classification are very likely to give way to more value-added services such as information searching, analysis, and dissemination.

The library professionals work more closely with the content of information resources and adopt skills from the knowledge management area.

The library profession should play a more active role in the buying and selling of electronic information contents and making this information available at the desk of the end user, through means such as the Internet.

The library professionals must become involved with the process of improving access to significant Internet content. The cataloguing of electronic resources is being adopted very effectively.

The search engines are largely dependent on the presence of suitable key words in the text of Web documents so as to be able to retrieve them. The World Wide Web Consortium (W3C) has developed the Resource Description Framework (RDF) into which metadata of different types can be entered. This creates a major opportunity for skilled practitioners to apply accurate and helpful descriptions to resources.

COMPETENCIES AND SKILLS OF A DIGITAL LIBRARIAN IN KNOWLEDGE MANAGEMENT

The following are the skills and competencies required for a digital librarian in the management of digital information systems and digital libraries:

Information Technology (IT) Skill

Not only the ability to use many packages, to search online databases and CD-ROMs, but the actual systems operation techniques.

Communication Skills

Financial planning, management, public relations, and marketing.

Human and Interpersonal Skills

Human behavior in terms of information seeking and social interaction and interpersonal relationships.

CLOUD COMPUTING AND VIRTUALIZATION IN THE DIGITAL LIBRARY

With the cloud computing in the digital library, services of libraries will have a new dimension in the near future. Now the services will become more user-centric, more professional, more effective, and so forth. In the future digital libraries will create more knowledge benefits to the users with the help of cloud computing.

Cloud Computing

In the geographical location, cloud computing refers to an innovative service offered over the Internet, which has completely changed the power of computer use. The different authors define cloud computing in the different ways as like in Wikipedia as "the delivery of computing as a service rather than a product, whereby shared resources, software, and information are provided to computers and other devices as a metered service over a network, typically the Internet" ("Cloud computing," 2011). Pettey and Forsling (2009) define cloud computing as "a style of computing in which massively scalable and elastic IT-enabled capabilities are delivered as a service to external customers using Internet technologies." Scale (2009) expresses the same thing in simple way as "simply the sharing and use of applications and resources of a network environment to get work done without concern about ownership and management of the network's resources and applications."

How is Cloud Computing Different from the Digital Library?

Cloud computing changes the way that traditionally installed things perform on the network, basically in the Internet cloud. Today the Internet cloud is the developed platform in which programmers write reusable, updated software components and soon not only this will be able to be embedded, coupled with other Web applications. In case of libraries, cloud computing is just a new breed of discussion. The most important and value proposition regarding cloud computing is that in outside libraries, it is more understandable. The example of cloud computing application is accessed through online databases and Union catalogs (Goldner, 2010).

Characteristics of Cloud Computing

Self-Healing or BackUp

In the cloud computing environment, the property of self-healing is the unique feature. In case of failure of the application or services, there is always a backup of the application ready to take over without disruption. In the same way, each copy updates itself.

MultiTenancy

Multitenancy means multiple tenants at the same instant of time. The system allows multiple users to share the infrastructure allotted to them without any of them being aware of the sharing. The servers on the available machine pool and then allotting the servers to multiple users is successfully done by virtualizing. But in any case the privacy of the users or the security of their data is not compromised.

Linearly Scalable

In the infrastructure the system is able to break down the workloads into pieces and service. Cloud computing services are linearly scalable. Generally, an exact idea of linear scalability can be obtained from the fact that if one server is able to process say 1000 transactions per second, then two servers can process 2000 transactions per second and soon.

Service-Oriented

Cloud computing systems are all service oriented means the systems are such that they are created out of other discrete services. The discrete services which are independent of each other are combined together to form this service. Clouding computing will allows reuse of the different services that are available and that are being created.

Service-Level Agreements (SLA) Driven

Businesses have agreements on the amount of services. Scalability and availability issues cause users to break these agreements. But cloud computing services are SLA driven so that when the system experiences peaks of load, it will automatically adjust itself so as to comply with the service-level agreements. The services will create additional instances of the applications on more servers so that the load can be easily managed.

Virtualized

The cloud computing environment is a fully virtualized environment. The applications in cloud computing are decoupled from the underlying hardware.

Flexible

Cloud computing can be used to serve a large variety of workload types - varying from small loads of a small consumer application to very heavy loads of a commercial application. In this manner the flexible character will take care of the entire environment (Gosavi, Shinde, & Dhakulkar, 2012).

Types of Cloud Computing

SaaS (Software as a Service)

In this applications or software is delivered as a service to the end user, who can access the program online using a Web browser or any other suitable users. SaaS services may be available on rental basis or on peruse basis. Example: Software package CRM or CAD/CAM, Salesforce, Hotmail, Google Apps, Skype, and many 2.0 applications etc. (Kroski, 2009).

PaaS (Platform as a Service)

In this application, a computing platform supplies tools and a development environment to help organizations to build, test, and deploy Web-based applications. It helps 'organizations not to make investment in the infrastructure required for building Web and mobile applications, but can rent the use of platforms. PaaS is based subscription model so users only pay for what they use. Example: Windows Azure, Google App Engine, and Force.com (Colayer, 2009).

IaaS (Infrastructure as a Service)

This type of cloud computing is also sometimes referred to as HaaS or Hardware as a Service and it involves both storage services and computing power. It this application delivers computer infrastructure as a platform virtualization environment as a service along with raw storage and networking. In the IaaS rather than purchasing servers, software, network equipment, clients instead buy those resources as a fully outsourced service. IaaS is priced on a pay-as-you-go model enabling clients to scale up or down the operations depending on their needs at any given time and pay only for what they use. In the simple way, hardware services such as processors, memory, networks etc on agreed basis for specific duration and price. Example: Amazon's Web services (Kroski, 2009).

On the other hand so many authors consider information, communication and monitoring as a service in cloud computing environment.

Communication as a Service (CaaS)

Allow for certain messaging tools via voice over IP (VOIP), Instant Messages (IM), and Video Conferencing.

Information as a Service (IaaS)

Allows customer to maintain owner and management of their application while off-loading infrastructure management to the Iaas provider.

Monitoring as a Service (MaaS)

Outsourcing of security service to a third party security team

Working of Cloud Computing

Gosavi, Shinde, and Dhakulkar (2012) discuss the working of cloud computing in the simple way as cloud computing system can be divided it into two sections: the front end and the back end. They connect to each other through a network (i.e., Internet). The front end is the side the computer user. The back end is the "cloud" section of the system. There are various computers, servers and data storage systems that create the "cloud" of computing services are available on the back end. A central server administers the system, monitoring traffic and users demands to ensure everything runs smoothly. Including this it follows a set of rules called protocols. Servers and remote computers do most of the work and store the data.

The provisioning service may deploy the requested stack or Web application as well.

- **User Interaction Interface:** This is how users of the cloud interface with the cloud to request services.
- **Services Catalogue:** This is the list of services that a user can request.
- **System Management:** This is the piece which manages the computer resources available.
- **Provisioning Tool:** This tool carves out the systems from the cloud to deliver on the requested service. It may also deploy the required images.
- **Monitoring and Metering:** This optional piece tracks the usage of the cloud so the resources used can be attributed to a certain user.
- **Servers:** The servers are managed by the system management tool. They can be either virtual or real (Reddy, 2012).

Teregowda, Urgaonkar, and Lee Giles (2010) state that the cloud computing changes the digital library culture and make the things for easer use in the retrieval of information. The infrastructure for Web based digital library search engines such as CiteSeerx face several challenges in the digital culture. The CiteSeerx indexes more than one and half million documents currently serving two million hits daily. The CiteSeerx provides autonomous citation indexing, full text indexing, and extensive document metadata from documents available from the Web across computer and information sciences and related fields. It utilizes terabytes of storage for storing the cached copies of crawled documents, database, index and information extracted from documents. Services supporting is in easily distributed with other machines. Reddy (2012) focuses that cloud computing offers price savings and the fact is that user only pay for the resources that he/she actually use. Mitchell (2010) states that "Libraries have been adopting cloud-based solutions for different services including electronic journal access management, statistics tracking, digital library hosting, and even integrated library system (ILS) hosting. This has allowed libraries to make strategic choices about the allocation of resources and to offer better service than would be possible if relying on in-house solutions" Sanchati and Kulkarni (2011) focus to improve current user service model in university library by using cloud computing. In the university library, services of libraries will have a new root in the near future. Cloud computing changes the screen of our country and provides library services that are more user-centric. Including in this cloud environment is a network environment and provides users high-quality service and security. The cloud computing techniques and methods applied to digital libraries can improve the utilization rate of resources.

APPLICATIONS OF CLOUD COMPUTING IN LIBRARIES

Bansode and Pujar (2012) discuss about the application of cloud computing in libraries. Similarly, focus on the advantage of the same. In the same manner as we now in the coin two side there in the same way if the things give us advantage than on the other hand give the disadvantages also, here Bansode and Pujar again try to catch a mind of user about the black side of cloud computing in libraries so that we will take care of this.

Automation

The software vendors and third party services offering hosting the service by (SaaS approach) on the cloud to save libraries from investing on hardware. The cost-benefit approach, the libraries will be free from undertaking maintenance such as software updates, backup, and so forth. For example vendors such as Ex-Libris, OSS Labs are offering this service on the cloud.

Digital Library Services

These days the updating of the software is important this kind work, vendors are now offering digital library services on the cloud using SaaS approach. For example vendors such as Duraspace, OSS Labs, and so forth, are offering this type service.

Office Applications

Now owing to cloud computing there are many applications which are made freely available on the Internet by companies like Google, Microsoft, and so forth. For example, Google Docs, a free office applications suite available on the Internet may be used in the libraries easily and free of cost.

Storage

The cloud computing provides new services, which offer space at no cost to store the files and documents. For example, Windows Sky Drive offers 25 GB to store files and share documents online. Amazon, Drop Box and many more initiatives offer storage space on the cloud to enable organizations and individuals to store and share their documents. In case of digital preservation, libraries are making use of services of CLOCKSS (http://www.clockss.org/clockss/Home) and Portico (http://www.portico.org/digital-preservation/) to get permanent access to the subscribed content irrespective of the publisher's existence.

Website Hosting

Website hosting is one of the earliest adoptions of cloud computing as many organizations including libraries preferred to host their Websites on third party service providers rather than hosting and maintaining their own servers. For example, Google Sites serves as a service for hosting Websites outside of the library's servers and allowing for multiple editors to access the site from varied locations.

Search Services

Libraries give various services such as Open URL providers, and federated and pre-indexed search engines on the cloud either by using commercial or open source solutions. For example, hosted Ex-Libris SFX Open-URL link resolver service offers libraries to linkup to the subscribed journal full-text articles.

Example: Cloud in the Academic Library in Orrisa, Library of Congress, and OCLC

Padhy and Mahapatra (2012) discusses about the application of the cloud computing in the academic library in Orissa. "While libraries can use cloud computing applications to create personalized portals for users, the Department of Library and Information Studies (LIS) at the university could use cloud computing as their back up methodology. This solution was proposed when confronted with the department to another building on campus. The method proposing is for the department is to create their own cloud server. This can be accomplished by the purchase of a Pogo plug device that connects to the network. It is a simple cloud server. With Pogo plug, faculty and staff will be able to access the cloud hard drives through a Web portal. Faculty should have a copy of the files on their desktop computer. It will need to be investigated if a free synchronization application like Toy Sync from Microsoft would be capable of automatically keeping folders synchronized without the need to do it manually. This solution has been proposed to the chair of the LIS Tech Committee." In the same way the Library of Congress has entered into a partnership with Dura cloud for a one year pilot program testing out cloud storage capabilities and OCLC has announced a new Web-scale, cooperative library management service.

ADVANTAGES AND DISADVANTAGES OF CLOUD COMPUTING

Advantages

The advantages of cloud computing is as follows:

- **Cost Saving:** Cloud computing technology is paid incrementally and saving costs for organizations. It offers price savings due to economies of scale and the fact that organizations such as libraries are only paying for the resources they actually use.
- **Easy on Installation and Maintenance:** Organizations will be free to concentrate on innovation and the IT staff may concentrate on other tasks. There is no need to procure any hardware to run the servers.
- **Increased Storage:** Cloud can hold more storage than a personal computer or the servers available in the libraries. It is possible to extend storage capacity as per the need.
- **Highly Automated:** Whenever new version release the cloud service provider take care of updating software so that the things easily manage. When the server is updated everyone using the service and also get access to the new version without updating anything on their end.
- **Flexibility:** Cloud computing offers much more flexibility, computing systems and saves time plus cost for organizations. It is possible for organizations like libraries to expand the services anytime, by requesting for an additional space on the servers.
- **Better Mobility:** The staff and the users of the library can connect to the library servers from any place or from wherever they feel comfortable.
- **Shared Resources:** A group of libraries can come together and can put their resources at one place, which in turn will enable them to provide access to more number of resources to their end users. Cloud computing allows people within and outside the organizations to have access to the resources.
- **Examples of Cloud Libraries:** OCLC, Library of Congress (LC), Exlibris, Polaris, Scribd, Discovery Service, Google Docs / Google Scholar, Worldcat and Encore.

Disadvantages

The disadvantages of cloud computing is as follows:

- **Data Security and Privacy:** The biggest concerns about cloud computing are security and privacy, when the organizations are dealing with sensitive data such as credit card information of customers. There is a risk of data loss owing to improper backup and systems failure.

- **Network Connectivity and Bandwidth:** The cloud computing is offered over the Internet. If the connection goes down due to any reason then the organizations suffer from loss of data connectivity till the time it is set. The service requires more bandwidth.
- **Dependence on Outside Agencies:** The cloud services being offered by third party services over the Internet, it is virtually difficult to have any control on the maintenance levels and the frequency. Migration to other service provider is also an issue, if the uniform standards are not followed by the host.
- **Limited Flexibility:** Flexibility may be limited in terms of special customization as services on the cloud will be common for all the customers.
- **Cost:** The cost could be higher, but may reduce depending on the usage of services. In the future may be organizations end up in paying higher charges.
- **Knowledge and Integration:** Deeper knowledge of cloud computing is essential as working of the service is totally dependent on the service provider. Integration is another issue as it will be difficult to integrate equipment used in data centers to host data with that of peripheral equipments in the organization such as printers, USB drives, and so forth.

CHALLENGES OF CLOUD COMPUTING

The IBM Academy of Technology Survey (2010) focuses the challenges which are generally faced by the professionals when they think about the application of cloud computing in there libraries or any work place ("Cloud computing insights from 110 implementation projects," 2010). The few challenges are given below:

- **Security:** Security is always an issue in public or shared environments. It is important that the cloud provider needs to make sure that data privacy and compliance is guaranteed. In the virtualized platform organizations need a way to organize, secure, manage and deploy images in a scalable manner.
- **Virtualization:** Virtualization is an important factor of cloud computing implementation. It is harder for clients to apply these technologies to other areas (network, applications, and desktop and clients). Automatic provisioning has been implemented in this client set, de-provisioning resources and reassigning those resources to other projects is always difficult.
- **Standardization:** Standardization is a major challenge for both processes and all technical layers. In cloud environment, the standardization of hardware and operating system/software stacks required.
- **Complexity and Integration:** Clients force that areas designed in such a way that reduce the complexity like providing additional pre-integrated offerings, improved functionality, flexibility, and decreased complexity for current offerings.

FUTURE PROSPECTS IN DIGITAL LIBRARY USING CLOUD COMPUTING TECHNOLOGY

In the drastic cut in budget, the cloud computing is the better option for the technology development in the library at the least cost. Reddy (2012) focus the future concept of cloud computing that offers price savings means only paying for the resources that actually use. Digital libraries may soon be building and managing their own data centers. Because of the security, privacy and reliability some companies to build their own private or hybrid clouds (A hybrid cloud is based in a privately-owned and operated data center). This hybrid model help digital libraries maintain more control over the applications and data stores that contain sensitive, private information about patrons. In addition, digital libraries can continually adjust the balance between the tight control of a private Information Technology infrastructure, and the flexibility and savings of cloud-hosted infrastructure. Digital libraries cooperate in the building and management of data centers, addition to this buy IT equipment, bandwidth and the services of IT professionals. Today, digital libraries express interest, a company like Google, Amazon, Microsoft or another cloud vendor might create a digital library Cloud similar to Google's Government Cloud or, a library vendor with deep IT resources (e.g., OCLC or Sirsi Dynix) might build digital library centric cloud services on top of cloud infrastructure leased from one of the more established players.

CONCLUSION

Cloud computing can bring about strategic, transformational, and even revolutionary benefits fundamental to digital libraries. Digital libraries offer new challenges to an emerging breed of digital librarians who should combine the principle and practice of information management with rapidly evolving technological developments to create new information products and services. The role of library and information professionals has changed dramatically from a "book lending" person to a recognized "intermediary" between information and its users. The issues of digital library, such as scientific, technological, methodological, economic technology are rapidly changing. The chapter is useful for the academic purpose in library and information science it covers all the areas of digital library and cloud computing. The librarian should aware about the digital library and tell this to the user so that users can access the document from anywhere at anytime. The digital library is like library in your hands whenever you feel suitable to search or whenever you want to visit the library, just start to search; that's why we call it a library without walls. This chapter is helpful for all the students and valuable for the academic purpose and research purpose. For organizations providing digital libraries with significant investment in traditional software and hardware infrastructure, migration to the cloud will bring out considerable technology transition; for less-constrained organizations or those with infrastructure nearing end-of-life, adaptation of cloud computing technology may be more immediate. The application of the cloud computing in libraries is helpful for the libraries as well as organizations. In the same way cloud computing reflects so many advantages but on the other side shows a lot of disadvantages. In the future cloud computing needs added research so that the problem will work out easily. The student understands about cloud computing when it is included in the syllabus, and updating the status of the syllabus will help the student to cope with the new technology. In case of digital culture, practical knowledge will lead the student to stand out in the challenging world.

REFERENCES

Aggregation, Integration, and Openness: Current Trends in Digital Libraries. (n.d.). Retrieved June 06, 2012, from http://www.kc.tsukuba.ac.jp/dlkc/eproceedings/papers/dlkc04pp105.pdf

An Overview of Digital Libraries: Issues and Trends. (n.d.). Retrieved July 22, 2012, from http://maltman.hmdc.harvard.edu/papers/DigitalLibraryOverview.pdf

Bansode, S. Y., & Pujar, S. M. (2012). Cloud computing and libraries. DESIDOC Journal of Library & Information Technology, 32(6). Retrieved January 04, 2013, from http://publications.drdo.gov.in/ojs/index.php/djlit/article/view/2848/1392

Cloud Computing Architecture in Digital Library. (n.d.). Retrieved February 04, 2013, from http://en.wikipedia.org/wiki/cloudcomputing

Cloud Computing Insights from110 Implementation Projects: IBM Academy of Technology Survey. (2010). Retrieved February 06, 2013, from https://www-304.ibm.com/easyaccess3/fileserve?contentid=215289

Colayer. (2009). What is Paas? Retrieved December 29, 2011, from http://ex.colayer.com/_cached/LINK_whatispaas/LINK_whatispaas.html

Collection Development in Digital Libraries. Trends and Problems. (n.d.). Retrieved December 07, 2012, from http://indjst.org/archive/vol.2.issue.11-12/dec09kavitha-29.pdf

Computing, C. (n.d.). Retrieved December 6, 2011, from http://en.wikipedia.org/wiki/Cloud_computing

D-Lib Magazine. (n.d.). Retrieved November 14, 2012, from http://www.dlib.org/dlib/july01/roes/07roes.html

Digital Library Research. Current Developments and Trends. (n.d.). Retrieved November 07, 2012, from http://eprints.rclis.org/bitstream/10760/4905/1/ASLRcolumn.pdg

Digital Library Technology Trends. (n.d.). Retrieved August 12, 2012, from http://daminfo.wgbh.org/digital_library_trends.pdf

Digital Object Identifier (DOI). An ISBN for the 21st Century. (n.d.). Retrieved June 15, 2011, from http://nopr.niscair.res.in/bitstream/123456789/4123/1/ALIS%20 50%283%29%20101-109.pdf

Digital Technology and Emerging Copy Right Scenario. (n.d.). Retrieved December 08, 2012, from http://nopr.niscair.res.in/bitstream/123456789/4905/1/JIPR%20 8%284%29%20276-301.pdf

Finding Topic Trends in Digital Libraries. (n.d.). Retrieved December 22, 2012, from http://Web.mit.edu/seyda/www/Papers/JCDL09_Topic-Trends.pdf

Fox, E. (2012). Digital library source book. Retrieved June 14, 2012, from http://vax.wcsu.edu/library.

Future Improvement of Cloud Computing in Digital Library. (n.d.). Retrieved February 16, 2013, from Cloud Computing in Libraries\Materials\What is Cloud Computing and how will it Affect Libraries Tech Soup for Libraries.html

Goldner, M. (2010).Winds of change: Libraries and cloud computing. Online Computer Library Center. Retrieved January 04, 2013, from http://www.oclc.org/multimedia/2011/files/IFLA-winds-of-change-paper.pdf

Gosavi, N., Shinde, S. S., & Dhakulkar, B. (2012). Use of cloud computing in library and information science field. International Journal of Digital Library Services, 1(3). Retrieved February 04, 2013, from http://www.ijodls.in/uploads/3/6/0/3/3603729/51-60.pdf

Gowda, M. P. (2008). Digital library. In A. K. Sahu (Ed.), *Information management in new millenium: opportunities and challenges for library professionals* (pp. 354–361). New Delhi, India: Ess Ess Publication.

Hybrid Cloud Computing. (n.d.). Retrieved January 26, 2013, from http://cloudcomputing.sys-con.com

Kaur, A. (2006). Role of libraries and library professionals in the digital environment. In P. V. Rao (Ed.), *Vistas of information management: Professor H.R. Chopra felicitation volume* (pp. 94–99). Chandigarh, India: Wisdom House Academic.

Kroski, E. (2009). Library cloud atlas: A guide to cloud computing and storage/stacking the tech. Library Journal. Retrieved February 15, 2011, from http://www.libraryjournal.com/article/CA6695772.html

Lal, M., & Hussain, A. (2010). Digital library: Challenges and opportunities. In R. K. Tiwari (Ed.), *Library Services in Electronic Environment* (pp. 339–343). Gurgaon, India: J.K. Business School.

Libraries, D. Technological Advances and Social Impacts. (n.d.). Retrieved June 22, 2011, from [REMOVED HYPERLINK FIELD]http://www.canis.uiuc.edu/news/Computerintro.pdf

Luvkush, & Chand, S. (2010). Digital trends in library and role of digital librarian. In R.K.Tiwari (Ed.), Library Services in Electronic Environment (pp. 67-77). Gurgaon, India: J.K. Business School.

Management, D. R. An Integrated Secure Digital Content Distribution Technology. (n.d.). Retrieved December 15, 2012, from http://nopr.niscair.res.in/bitstream/123456789/4878/1/JIPR%209%284%29%20313-331.pdf

Mitchell, E. (2010). Using cloud services for library IT infrastructure. Code4Lib Journal, 9, 3-22. Retrieved January 10, 2013, from http://journal.code4lib.org/articles/2510

ODLIS. Online Dictionary of Library and Information Science. (n.d.). Retrieved November 13, 2012, from http://www.dlib.org

Padhy, S. C., & Mahapatra, R. K. (2012). Cloud computing: Academic library in Orissa. VSRD Technical & Non-Technical Journal, 3(3). Retrieved January 15, 2013, from http://www.vsrdjournals.com/vsrd/Issue/2012_03_Mar/Web/5_Suresh_Chandra_Padhy_621_Research_Communication_Mar_2012.pdf

Pettey, C., & Forsling, C. (2009). Gartner highlights five attributes of cloud computing. Retrieved December 28, 2011, from http://www.gartner.com/it/page.jsp?id=1035013

Recent Trends in Statewide Academic Library Consortia. (n.d.). Retrieved June 22, 2011, from http://www.thefreelibrary.com/Recent+trends+in+statewide+academic+library+consortia-a019192264

Reddy, T. R. (2012). Digital era: Utilize of cloud computing technology in digital library. International Journal of Digital Library Services, 2, 92-106. Retrieved November 23, 2012, from http://www.ijodls.in/uploads/3/6/0/3/3603729/92-106.pdf

Rittenhouse, J. W., & Ransome, J. F. (2010). *Cloud computing implementation, management and security*. Boca Raton, FL: CRC Press / Taylor & Francis Group.

Saini, S. (2010). Digital library in new millennium: Opportunities and challenges for library professionals. In S. P. Singh (Ed.), *ICT impact on knowledge and information management* (pp. 204–209). New Delhi, India: Arihant Prakashan.

Saini, S., & Chand, S. (2011). Digital library: Challenges in the global world. In N. K. Swain, D. C. Ojha, & M. S. Rana (Eds.), *Paradigm shift in technological advancement in librarianship* (pp. 257–266). Jodhpur, India: Scientific.

Sanchati, R., & Kulkarni, G. (2011). Cloud computing in digital and university libraries. Global Journal of Computer Science and Technology, 11, 12. Retrieved January 07, 2013, from http://globaljournals.org/GJCST_Volume11/6-Cloud-Computing-in-Digital-and-University.pdf

Sangam, S. L., & Leena, V. (2000). Digital library services. In R. Vengan, H. R. Mohan, & K. S. Raghavan (Eds.), Information services in a networked environment in India (pp. 1.107-1.112). Ahmedabad, India: Inflibnet centre.

Scale, E. M. S. (2009). Cloud computing and collaboration. *Library Hi Tech News*, *26*(9), 10–13. doi:10.1108/07419050911010741.

Scholarly Digital Library Initiatives. World vs. India. (n.d.). Retrieved June 22, 2011, from http://publications.drdo.gov.in/ojs/index.php/djlit/article/viewFile/219/122

Teregowda, P., Urgaonkar, B., & Lee Giles, C. (2010). Cloud computing: A digital libraries perspective. IEEE Cloud 2010. Retrieved December 19, 2012, from http://clgiles.ist.psu.edu/pubs/ICCC2010-cloud.pdf

The Digital Library at Sapienza- University di Roma and the Effort for Open Access. (n.d.). Retrieved December 22, 2012, from http://eprints.rclis.org/bitstream/10760/8575/1/bids.pdf

Vengan, R. (2000). Digital library: A challenge to library and information professionals. In R. Vengan, H. R. Mohan, & K. S. Raghavan (Eds.), *Information services in a networked environment in India* (pp. 2.89–2.92). Ahmedabad, India: Inflibnet Centre.

KEY TERMS AND DEFINITIONS

Cloud Computing: Cloud computing is refer refers to an innovative service offered over the internetInternet. It completely changed the power of computers use.

Digital Culture: Digital environment is referred to as a Digital Culture.

Digital Library: Library in the digital culture is called as digital library.

Digitization: Digitalization is a process which is done in steps like scanning, storage, and storage engines.

Knowledge Management: Management of information in a systematic manner; and retrieved it inis able to be retrieved in a few seconds, give it to the user as knowledge.

Library Professional: People whothose are related to library work in theretheir profession.

Chapter 2
Digital Information Management:
Preserving Tomorrow's Memory

Pawan R. Agrawal
Silvassa Institute of Higher Learning, India

ABSTRACT

The most burning issue of today's electronic generation, where information generation is a task of seconds, is to save the information in a form that could successfully be read tomorrow. It is easily understandable that if one keeps a book in a drawer and open it after 10 years, one may hope to get it back and read it, possibly with some damage, but this is not the case for information stored in a Compact Disc (CD) or any other electronic device. This chapter projects at understanding digital preservation issues and identifying appropriate solutions to manage digital information. This chapter also aims to identify the projects undergoing throughout the world for digital preservation. This chapter overall discusses the speedy obsolescence, short-lived technologies, and other issues in digital preservation with the identified and possible strategies of digital preservation.

INTRODUCTION

The year is 2045, and my grandchildren (as yet unborn) are exploring the attic of my house (as yet unbought). They find a letter dated 1995 and a CD-ROM (compact disk). The letter claims that the disk contains a document that provides the key to obtaining my fortune (as yet unearned). My grandchildren are understandably excited, but they have never seen a CD before—except in old movies—and even if they can somehow find a suitable disk drive, how will they run the software necessary to interpret the information on the disk? How can they read my obsolete digital document? - Jeff Rothenberg, 1999

In recent few decades libraries are more recognized for their services of information dissemination in anticipation and on demand. This recognition has put libraries out of the reputation as a store house and custodian of documents. But it must not be forgotten that preservation is always necessary for a library and it is one of the major duties. Preservation is important not only for present but for the

DOI: 10.4018/978-1-4666-4631-5.ch002

future as well. A library collection may include books, journals, original manuscripts, audio sound recordings, videos, and digital collections.

'Preservation' or 'archiving' or to say 'permanent availability' of the documents is one of the processes which has been dramatically affected with the advent and highly acceptance of the digital world. When once the printed text was the only medium of information and was preserved successfully by the libraries at different location of the world. But, today preservation is not that much easy and carries a number of questions; first space of the preservation, as, it may always change with the links hyperlinks; assurance that the document will be preserved for long and will be available as and when required; and most importantly the preservation will take place keeping continuous track of the technological changes so that the document format does not become obsolete and could be read anytime.

Today, digital world has developed to an unavoidable extent and doing so it carries a number of advantages such as space, cost, and paper. At the same time this developments and advantages pose new challenges to all segments of the society including a layman, author, publisher, and library. A layman who was having a camera with negatives few years back now holds a digital camera similarly where one was keeping a diary to note phone no. and other important information, now s/he keeps mobiles, tablet and other technology to record those information. An author who uses to write his or her ideas on papers with pen or typewriter now uses a computer to store his/ideas. Publishers are turning their business from print to digital or developing new business model for electronic publishing. Moreover, the role of libraries is changed dramatically in the digital environment. They have to reshape and reconstruct their roles and policies as information disseminator and information preserver. Thus, all these segments of the society need new skills, tools and arrangements for the management and preservation of new digital information.

DIGITAL INFORMATION: WHAT AND WHY

Digital information is an invisible form of Information which requires some hardware and software to convert into visible information. An information is termed as digital information when, in order to secure the literature, we convert the printed text, images and other literature into machine readable format that can be stored onto a hard drive, DC, DVD or other optical and storage devices. Additionally, digital information can also be 'born digital' information where no other format of the same literature is available. National Library of Australia (2003) has defined digital information as

Digital materials include texts, databases, still and moving images, audio, graphics, software, and Web pages, among a wide and growing range of formats. They are frequently ephemeral, and require purposeful production, maintenance and management to be retained.

The digital information has following characteristics

1. **Dependency:** Digital information is always dependent. It requires some hardware and software to be read. Without these software and hardware digital information is useless as it cannot be read.
2. **Multipliable:** Digital information is multipliable. One can create a number of copies of information in digital format in very short time.
3. **Dynamic:** Digital information can be altered with user interaction. The user can not only alter the face of digital information but also the format of it using proper hardware and software.
4. **Economic:** Digital information is very economic in nature. Once it is produced it can be multiplied in as much copies as needed.

Additionally it does not require large floor to store it in the way printed information requires.

5. **Modular:** Digital information is can be broken in various components and reused in parts of as combination.
6. **Delicate:** Digital information is very delicate. It requires so much care of it from getting corrupted. Once it is corrupted, it is gone forever.

Some of these characteristics make digital information very important for the community. The use of digital information reduces utilization of paper which resulting saving trees and contributes towards green literature. Additionally being multipliable digital information does not require labour and fund to generate more copies of the single work. Rare manuscripts could also preserved by converting them into digital documents and thus rare documents also become accessible to the community. Digital documents require very less storage space and thus it does not require large floors for storage. Different type of digital information requires different amount of space for its storage but in general a compact disc of 700mb may store 260,000 text pages or 700 jpg image or video/audio of 80 minutes (Oracle Thinkquest, 2012).

With the development of information technology, the production of digital documents in increased dynamically, not only this but libraries and research centres which are having documents in print form are also going for a project for digitization of their printed documents. The School of Information Management at University of California done in 2003 at Berkeley put forward their observations related to digital information. Some of them are as following.

1. Print, film, magnetic, and optical storage media produced about 5 exabytes of new information in 2002. Ninety-two percent of the new information was stored on magnetic media, mostly in hard disks (1Exabytes = 1073741824 GB).
2. According to the Population Reference Bureau, the world population is 6.3 billion, thus almost 800 MB of recorded information is produced per person each year.
3. Amount of information produced in digital form doubles in every three year.
4. Information flow through radio, television, Internet, telephone contained almost 18 Exabyte, three and half times more than is recorded in storage media. (98% of this information sent and received through telephone calls and video and audio conferencing.) (Source: Lyman & Hal, 2003)

Hence, it is clear with the above presented informative statistics that most of the information in today's generation is produced in various digital forms such as text, audio, video, picture, multimedia, which are stored on storage devices and accessed through the computers. Digital information is a trend to 21st century which is most economic, compact and easily accessible from any corner of globe with the help of supporting devices. Information technology has really made the world very small through digital information and its real time sharing. The only need is to develop the strategies to preserve this information for future generation as might be the only source for them to see their past.

DIGITAL PRESERVATION: WHAT AND WHY

Gladney (2007) defines:

Digital preservation can be considered to be a special case of communication-asynchronous communication which the information sent is not delivered immediately, but is instead stored in a repository until somebody requests it. An information consumer will frequently want answers that resolve his uncertainties about the meaning or the history of information he receives. Digital preservation is a case of information storage in which he will not be able to question the information producers whose work he is reading.

Heslop, Devis, and Wilson (2002) consider digital preservation more important and threatening than preservation of print document. They consider digital materials preservation not as preservation of an object but as performance. This concept of digital preservation is very much similar to the concept of Gladney's concept of digital preservation.

Digital materials are always dependent on hardware and software tools that made digital material accessible to users. The access can be of a word processing document, a video, audio, Web page, an image or a database query. The access of all these materials is performed through coding, action and programs. The digital preservation requires the application of tools and technologies to require repetitive presentation of the same object.

Gladney (2007) provides a list of ten threats to digital information that have competency to damage, corrupt, or make it inaccessible. These threats are shown in Table 1.

However, some of these threats are rare to happen and some are frequent. First five threats are frequent threat that can take place any time while next five threats are rare and are possible only once in a while. Though the organizations working on digital preservation need to work on these threat too as the preservation is a long-term process.

Digital preservation or digital achieving, in modern term "permanent availability" of digital records, is required to ensure the availability

Table 1. Ten threats to digital information

Sr.	Threat	Description
1	Media and Hardware Failures	Failure causes include random bit errors and recording track blemishes, breakdown of embedded electronic components, burnout, and misplaced off-line HDDs, DVDs, and tapes.
2	Software Failures	All practical software has design and implementation bugs that might distort communicated data.
3	Communication Channel Errors	Failures include detected errors (IP packet error probability of ~10-7) and undetected errors (at a bit rate of ~10-10), and also network deliveries that do not complete within a specified time interval.
4	Network Service Failures	Accessibility to information might be lost from failures in name resolution, misplaced directories, and administrative lapses.
5	Component Obsolescence	Before media and hardware components fail they might become incompatible with other system components, possibly within a decade of being introduced. Software might fail because of *format obsolescence* which prevents information decoding and rendering within a decade.
6	Operator Errors	Operator actions in handling any system component might introduce irrecoverable errors, particularly at times of stress during execution of system recovery tasks.
7	Natural Disasters	Floods, fires, and earthquakes.
8	External Attacks	Deliberate information destruction or corruption by network attacks, terrorism, or war.
9	Internal Attacks	Misfeasance by employees and other insiders for fraud, revenge, or malicious amusement.
10	Economic and Organization Failures	A repository institution might become unable to afford the running costs of repositories, or might vanish entirely, perhaps through bankruptcy or mission change so that preserved information suddenly is of no value to the previous custodian.

(Source: Gladney, 2007)

or readability of the digital documents such as text, audio, video, images, or multimedia in the future. It is obligatory to save the unique results of research or unique creations of human mind in form of text, audio, video, images, and so forth, in digital format for the further generations. In print media library and archives used to store the printed document safely providing access of these documents to needy people. In electronic world the concern about the preservation is different. Digital preservation in electronic environment not only includes safety of resources in physical format but also its access, location, readability, compatibility with current and upcoming technology in other term 'safety from obsolescence' and remote access from any corner of world. National Library of Australia (2003) concerns about digital preservation on four levels and enumerates:

Digital preservation consists of the processes aimed at ensuring the continued accessibility of digital materials. To do this involves finding ways to re-present what was originally presented to users by a combination of software and hardware tools acting on data. To achieve this requires digital objects to be understood and managed at four levels: as physical phenomena; as logical encodings; as conceptual objects that have meaning to humans; and assets of essential elements that must be preserved in order to offer future users the essence of the object.

Here, Physical object is a carrier media such as DVD, or CD, Logical object consist a code in which file is written, Conceptual objects is a presentation to final user, and set of essential elements embody the features of the object for which the material is preserved. Thus, for the protecting intellectual creation of today's generation for the coming generations, or protecting cultural heritage in form of digital information for our ancestors, it is required to follow the digital preservation strategies and tools that can ensure long term preservation and easy access.

DIGITAL PRESERVATION: TECHNIQUES, STRETEGIES, AND STANDARDS

Digital preservation is process to select optimize and implement various tools and strategies for dealing preservation issues of digital objects. Graham (1994) favours three type of preservation in terms of digital objects. It includes Medium preservation, technology preservation and intellectual preservation.

Medium preservation is simply preservation of the storage devices in which digital objects are stowed, such as a magnetic tape, CD, DVD, Floppy, hard drives, and servers, and so forth.

The continuous research in information technology produces constant up-gradation and changes in the technological means which does not exclude the storage devices, computer hardware and software those are used in production, storage, display and dissemination of digital objects. Hence, it is required to preserve the technology also for the security of the digital object or to keep refreshing the digital objects with the technological changes.

The intellectual preservation is the preserve the originality of the digital object. It is a challenge for the people engaged in the digital preservation to preserve the document with its integrity, authenticity and, the form in which it was originally recorded.

The major problem with digital objects is that it is not viewable like a book or other printed documents and the technologies used in production, dissemination and storage is digital object are fragile. Thus, the preservation not only includes the preservation of digital objects using various techniques but also comprise periodic confirmation of such objects. The most promising techniques medium preservation and technology preservation are following.

Refreshing

The concept of refreshing, can be categorized as a technique of medium preservation, was initially identified as a preservation technique by Mallinson (1986) in his paper *Preserving machine-readable archival records for the millennia* presented during an International Symposium in 1985 and later published in *Archivaria.* In this paper the author insisted to move digital information to a more stable digital preservation medium to ensure long term preservation. This concept was later on recognized worldwide and today it is known as one of the preservation techniques. Conceptually, refreshing is an act to move the digital objects periodically to other storage medium to evade the deterioration or obsolescence of physical medium. This technique becomes more important because it is understood by the world that the any storage unit is not permanent and having an expiry date. Hence, it is required that before expiry of the storage device the information stored in the medium safely transferred into a new physical medium. Practically life of an optical disc is not more than 5 years if cared properly. Thus, it is required to refresh the physical medium to save and preserve the content of the storage device. However, the costing and labour charges are a consideration.

Two additional digital preservation techniques were proposed in Task Force (Garrett & Waters, 1996), that is, migration and emulation.

Migration

Migration is a digital and technology preservation technique that involves periodically migrating one file format to another which is more suitable in dynamic technological environment and to save the digital information from being obsolescent. For example - migrating WordStar file to Microsoft Word 3.0 to Microsoft Word 1997 to Microsoft Word 2010. Task force report on Archiving of Digital Information (Garrett & Waters, 1996) defines migration as:

Migration is the periodic transfer of digital materials from one hardware/software configuration to another or from one generation of computer technology to a subsequent generation. The purpose of migration is to preserve the integrity of digital objects and to retain the ability for clients to retrieve, display, and otherwise use them in the face of constantly changing technology.

In words of Besser (2001), "Migration seeks to limit the problem of files encoded in a wide variety of file formats that have existed over time by gradually bringing all former formats into a limited number of contemporary formats."

Migration helps to overcome the problem of hardware and software obsolescence. Though migration is used by computer users to make the document readable in heterogeneous environment as Microsoft Windows users produces their documents using Microsoft word software while Linux users use LaTEX for the same. Documents generated in one environment become unreadable in other environment. This situation developed a pragmatic technique, that is, to migrate the document in a third format which is readable in both environment (i.e., migrating such documents to pdf format or html format). This is a simple migrating technique used by all but this technique compels users to install new software to read the third format on their computers. A much better approach to this is to export the documents in ASCII format and import the same in any environment. Migrating to ASCII is simple but at the same time it just import the text contents and loses other settings such as text font, text colour, size, and so forth.

For such reasons, migration is not a single technique to migrate documents but several techniques of the same.

Emulation

Transferring old computer files into updated computers having more updated software and hardware poses threat of obsolescence of file format. Emulation is a technique used to resolve this issue. Emulation is an alternative approach to migration. This is similar to migration but it concentrates on the application software and hardware rather than the format of the information. This technique seems easy in comparison of migration because changing the file format every technological or hardware and software change is very difficult and laborious while incorporating some lines of coding that retain the ability of software to read earlier formats seems easy. For example MS Word was using .doc format before its 2003 version but the later versions, that is, MS Word 2007 and MS Word 2010 use .docx format. Though it is not possible without adding some add-in software to open docx format in MS Word 2003 software but at the same time MS office 2007 and MS Office 2010 has the ability to open .doc documents. In the same way now 64 bit programs are coming in light. These computers are designed in such a way that they can understand the maximum 32 bit software and can easily install on it and can read the information supported to these software.

Hence emulation does not stresses on changing the digital object itself but looks to recreate the environment in the computer in which the digital object used to be display. It helps to offer sustainable access to digital information in their authentic environment

Reinterpretation

Reinterpretation as a digital preservation technique was identified by Depocas, Ippolito, Jones, and Schaefer (2003) in their book. They defined reinterpretation as:

The most radical preservation strategy is to reinterpret the work each time it is re created. To reinterpret a Dan Flavin light installation would mean to ask what contemporary medium would have the metaphoric value of fluorescent light in the 1960s. Reinterpretation is a dangerous technique when not warranted by the artist, but it may be the only way to recreate performed, installed, or networked art designed to vary with context.

"Reinterpretation allows preservation professionals to make decisions about the characteristics of an object preservation or performance within some pre-defined boundaries. Currently, artist questionnaires are the primary means of developing a representation of a variable media art work with an eye towards reinterpretation" (Winget, 2005). This method was developed or posed for the preservation of digital media objects and virtually related to presentation, exposition, and performance of digital media objects. But the application of this method is rarely seen in other formats and even in art media this method is not appreciated by the artists.

In addition to the above techniques, the National Library of Australia (2003) has also pointed out some small but useful strategies for digital preservation.

- Working with producers (creators and distributors) to apply standards that will prolong the effective life of the available means of access and reduce the range of unknown problems that must be managed.
- Recognizing that it is not practical to try to preserve everything, selecting what material should be preserved.
- Placing the material in a safe place.
- Controlling material, using structured metadata and other documentation to facilitate access and to support all preservation process.
- Protecting the integrity and identity of data.

- Choosing appropriate means of providing access in the face of technological change.
- Managing preservation programs to achieve their goals in cost-effective, timely, holistic, proactive and accountable ways.

With the objectives of digital preservation several standards are developed time by time. Some of those prominent standards of digital preservation are as following.

Open Archival Information System (OAIS), developed in 2003, is most important and recognized standard of data preservation. It refers to an archive comprising an organization of people and systems that has the responsibility to preserve information and make it accessible to users. The reference model of OAIS is sketched in ISO 14721:2003 standard. The system is designated for the purpose of "long-term preservation" in respect of changing technology, media, data format, and user community. This standard has proposed a detailed reference model (Figure 1) for data preservation and access. The reference model involves three parts (i.e., Producer, Management, and Consumer).

Producer's role is played by the people or systems which provide the information to be preserve. Management role is played by those who finalize a complete OAIS policy as a unique component in a wider policy sphere while, consumers are those people or systems who interact with the OAIS services to browse and obtain the information of their interest.

Open Archive Initiative Protocol for Metadata Harvesting (OAI-PMH) is another standard for data preservation developed by Open Archive Initiative (OAI) in 2001. It is used to gather the metadata of the digital objects in an archive to build broader services using metadata from various archives. Primarily, it supports Dublin Core metadata description but may also support other metadata description. OAI-PMH uses Extensibl Mark-up Language (XML) with Hypertext Transfer Protocol (HTTP). The current version of OAI_PMH is 2.0 that was released in 2008.

DIGITAL INFORMATION: GUIDELINES

Digital information seen after the development of Internet in later part of 20th century and specially with the development of World Wide Web in 1991. Project Gutenberg was the major project to make documents accessible to people in digital format. Today a growing amount of information

Figure 1. Open Archival Information System (OAIS) reference model

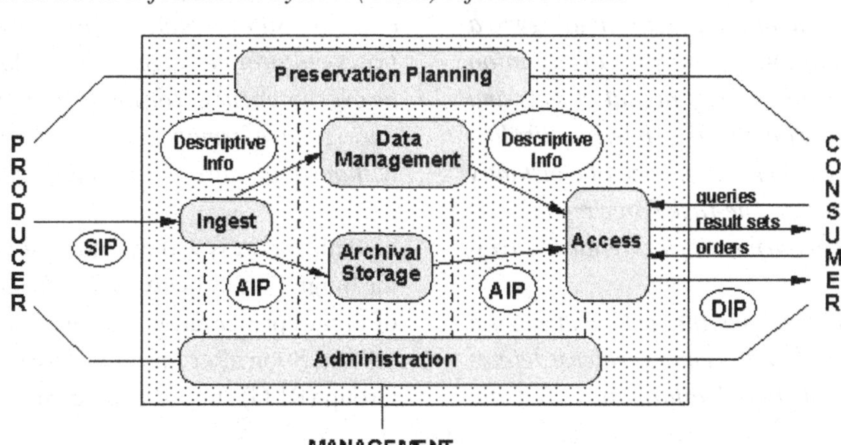

is created, stored, disseminated, and accessed in digital format. However, this change also drawn the attention of the various organization of the world concerning information preservation. The first attempt towards digital information preservation was made by U.S Commission on Preservation and Access and Research Libraries Group (RLG) in 1994 where they instituted Task Force on Archiving of Digital Information. The purpose of the Task Force was to "Frame the key problems that need to be resolved for technology refreshing to be considered an acceptable approach to ensuring continuing access to electronic digital records indefinitely into the future (Garrett & Waters, 1996).

The final report of the Task Force came in 1996 after an exhaustive research on issues of digital preservation. The summary of the report (Garrett & Waters, 1996) reads as following:

In taking up its charge, the Task Force on Archiving of Digital Information focused on materials already in digital form and recognized the need to protect against both media deterioration and technological obsolescence. It started from the premise that migration is a broader and richer concept than "refreshing" for identifying the range of options for digital preservation. Migration is a set of organized tasks designed to achieve the periodic transfer of digital materials from one hardware/software configuration to another, or from one generation of computer technology to a subsequent generation. The purpose of migration is to preserve the integrity of digital objects and to retain the ability for clients to retrieve, display, and otherwise use them in the face of constantly changing technology. The Task Force regards migration as an essential function of digital archives.

The Task Force envisions the development of a national system of digital archives, which it defines as repositories of digital information that are collectively responsible for the long-term accessibility of the nation's social, economic, cultural and intellectual heritage instantiated in digital form. Digital archives are distinct from digital libraries in the sense that digital libraries are repositories that collect and provide access to digital information, but may or may not provide for the long-term storage and access of that information. The Task Force has deliberately taken a functional approach in these critical definitions and in its general treatment of digital preservation so as to prejudge neither the question of institutional structure nor the specific content that actual digital archives will select to preserve.

The Task Force sees repositories of digital information as held together in a national archival system primarily through the operation of two essential mechanisms. First, repositories claiming to serve an archival function must be able to prove that they are who they say they are by meeting or exceeding the standards and criteria of an independently administered program for archival certification. Second, certified digital archives will have available to them a critical fail-safe mechanism. Such a mechanism, supported by organizational will, economic means and legal right, would enable a certified archival repository to exercise an aggressive rescue function to save culturally significant digital information. Without the operation of a formal certification program and a fail-safe mechanism, preservation of the nation's cultural heritage in digital form will likely be overly dependent on marketplace forces, which may value information for too short a period and without applying broader, public interest criteria.

This report is widely known for the favouring the 'migration' strongly over 'refreshing' a concept of digital preservation put forward by Mallinson (1986). Soon after this report Research Libraries Group (RLG) funded another study to know the status of digital archiving of its member institutions. Margaret Hedstrom and Sheon Montgomery (1999) summarized their study as under:

This report examined one component of an evolving infrastructure for long-term preservation of digital information: the responsibilities of archives, libraries, museums, and other repositories for preserving and providing access to valuable, digital resources. Although there is a gap between current models for digital preservation and the status of digital preservation in many institutions, most member institutions are seeking guidance on ways to close this gap. The members participating in this study look to RLG to make available concrete standards, guidelines, and training that will enable institutions at various stages in their digital preservation programs to work with confidence; that are flexible enough to evolve as technology and sources of information evolve; and that can be used to help ensure successful, quality services from third-party vendors. RLG is also seen as experienced in and committed to international coordination and to integration of archival, museum, and special collections into the mainstream of digital preservation activities. And members rightly expect that RLG will use consortial leverage on their behalf to identify and make real the standards and supporting services needed in a digital world.

Another major effort for digital preservation was done by the Library of Congress with the help of U.S. Government by passing a legislation to establish National Digital Information Infrastructure and Preservation Program (NDIIPP) in 2000. The goal of this plan was to seek solutions for collecting historical documents regardless of their formats, long-term preservation and storage, persistent and right based access for the public to the digital heritage of America (Library of Congress, 2002). This program included all major libraries and archives associated to digital preservation such as National Library of Medicine, Online Computer Library Centre (OCLC), Research Libraries Group (RLG), National Agricultural Library, National Institute of Standards and Technology, and so forth. In the final report of NDIIPP digital preservation architecture was designed for libraries towards digital preservation. This architecture consists of four layers namely interface, collection, gateway and repository that will work between digital object and the user of digital information. The detailed architecture can be referred from the NDIIPP report available at http://www.digitalpreservation.gov/documents/ndiipp_plan.pdf.

Another initiative in digital preservation took place in 2001 with the establishment of Digital Preservation Coalition (DPC). The major objective of DPC was to identify and develop tools to secure preservation of digital resources in United Kingdom (UK), and internationally to secure the global digital memory and knowledge base (Wikipedia, 2012). DPC is having organizations such as British Library, Cambridge University Library, Museums, Libraries and Archives Council, Joint Information Systems Committee, The National Archives, Oxford University Library Services and other academic and research organizations of United Kingdom in its member list. DPC has also sponsored am International Digital Preservation Award presented for initiatives undertaken in the field of digital preservation.

In field of Internet preservation, an initiative had been taken by International Internet Preservation Consortium (IIPC) established in 2003 with 12 member organizations. The objective of IIPC was to coordinate efforts to preserve Internet content for the future (International Internet Preservation Consortium, 2004). The major projects sponsored by IIPC are 'Web Curators Mailing List' (International Internet Preservation Consortium, 2004), development of organization tool, and several organisation of several conferences for digital preservation.

The Blue Ribbon Task Force on Sustainable Digital Preservation and Access (BRTF-SDPA) is another international initiative towards digital preservation collectively taken by National Science Foundation, Library of Congress and Joint Information System Committee, and so forth, in 2007. It published its report under the title 'Sustainable Economics for a Digital Planet: Ensuring Long Term Access to Digital Information.' The report provides general principles and actions to support long-term economic sustainability, context-specific recommendations tailored to specific scenarios analyzed in the report, and an agenda for priority actions and next steps, organized according to the type of decision maker best suited to carry that action forward (Blue Ribbon Task Force on Sustainable Digital Preservation and Access, 2010).

CLOUD COMPUTING: CURRENT TREND IN DIGITAL PRESERVATION

Cloud computing in simple term is computing with the software and hardware stays somewhere in the cloud. The term cloud is used here because of our unknowing about the location of software and hardware we use, but of course they exists somewhere in the world. Borko Furht (2010, p. 3) defines cloud computing as "as a new style of computing in which dynamically scalable and often virtualized resources are provided as a services over the Internet." The whole book is based on the various concepts of cloud computing, but, here the object to use this concept to understand the importance of cloud computing in terms of digital preservation.

We are very used to using various open access cloud computing services such as Wikis, blogs, e-mails, social networks, and so forth. Every one of us is surely having an e-mail ID or a Facebook ID where we store a huge amount of data such in form of emails in Inbox, Outbox and drafts, pictures, videos, comments, and shares in Facebook on daily basis. Now some questions arise here. First, do we know where these data reside? No, but we are sure it resides somewhere that is why we use the term clouds. Second, do we pay for these services used by us? No, but again we are sure it costs. Third and most important in our context, did we ever experience an automatic loss of an e-mail from our Inbox or Outbox? No in my case at least. I have never experienced an automatic loss of an e-mail from my Inbox or Outbox or drafts. I am using my e-mail address for last 10 years and it never happened in this duration. However, during this time technology changed rapidly, I had started with a Floppy disk then arrived a CD, then a DVD, then a USB, a memory card, an external hard drive, and so forth, and I surely experienced a data loss from these sources for one reason or another. Hence a short conclusion of the above discussion arrives that cloud computing is a great alternative for digital preservation although it may not be free or open access like emails and social networks.

Cloud computing has opened a new way to digital preservation with additional attractions like data access from any location of the world and cost effective storage. There are a number of known Web applications such as IBM Smart Cloud, Amazon Elastic Compute Cloud, and Microsoft Cloud Power, and so forth. Data preserved through cloud computing resides in the clouds and provides instant access from any location makes it easy to share and edit any document from any computer. Cloud computing servers reside at more than one location; hence it reduces the danger of having data at a single place and enables us to recover any lost data through the company. LOCKSS (Lots of Copies Keep Stuff Safe) is a project of digital preservation and is an ideal project that makes uses of cloud computing.

Cloud computing offers an option to the organizations for digital preservation without much worries. Institutions using cloud computing may not need to take care for the various technologies discussed earlier in this chapter for the purpose of digital preservation. They simply need to subscribe a service which provides digital preservation and become free of all worries. The cloud computing service provider will do all the work for preserving digital information.

To date, there is no example observed about the loss of data preserved through the use to cloud computing services and specifically paid services. The service providers use most of the digital preservation techniques discussed earlier to manage data stored in their servers. Additionally, being professional in their fields they are more efficient to use digital preservation techniques and could afford costly hardware and software. They store data not on a single server with a number of servers with additional mirrors that are helpful in easy recovery in case of loss of data from the primary server.

However, there are still some disadvantages, worries, and concerns that exist with digital preservation done through cloud computing also. First, technological obsolescence is a concern for digital preservation and cloud computing itself is a technology and may obsolete with the passage of time. A subscriber to the digital preservations service through cloud computing must take care of this issue while choosing it as digital preservation option. Second, the cloud computing services are managed by a third party, hence it is difficult to estimate the future cost for digital preservation. Generally, the preservation subscriptions are done on annual bases, three yearly bases, or five yearly bases. For the first phase, cost may be defined but after the expiry of this period of 1, 3, or 5 year(s), it is difficult to estimate the cost of subscription of cloud computing service or the raise in price for subscription. Cancellation of subscription is again a big deal to getting back all data without leaving a copy with the service provider and locating other service provider for digital preservation. Thus, cloud computing will also lead to an uncertainty toward future financial estimation for digital preservation.

Third threat is the hacking problem. As the cloud computing services works with the help of Web and Internet, there is possibility that the service of the cloud computing may get hacked. In that case the data preserved in the system may come under great threats such as information leak, loss of data, undesired changes in data, and so forth. Therefore, cloud computing may worrisome for the people who have information or data that they may not want to share. However, for the institutions such as libraries and data centre whose major objective is just to share information and they are not so concern about of leakage of information may not get worries about it.

There are several other threats those are exist while using cloud computing services such as change in preservation contract, difficult data access, unauthorized access to data, data goes offline for maintenance, and so forth.

Like every technology, cloud computing also comes with certain benefits and drawbacks. A user must understand both sides of the coin before making a decision about using cloud computing. However, if one see from one perspective and that is preservation then cloud computing is very successful to date. And there are many examples of digital preservation projects, some of them are discussed in this chapter, using cloud computing services.

INTERNATIONAL EFFORTS TOWARDS DIGITAL PRESERVATION

Digital preservation being an international concern draws attention of the world. A number of efforts, using above tools, strategies, and guidelines, took place during last few years some of major efforts towards digital preservation are CEDARS, Internet Archive, and so forth.

The Cedars (CURL Exemplars in Digital Archives) project was a UK digital preservation project initially funded by JISC through the Electronic Libraries Program (eLib). The project ran for four years from mid-1998 to the end of March 2002. The project was under the overall direction of the Consortium of University Research Libraries (CURL) and lead sites were the universities of Cambridge, Leeds and Oxford. The project aimed to promote awareness of the importance of digital preservation, to produce strategic frameworks for digital collection management policies and to promote methods appropriate for long-term preservation (UKOLN, 2002). Internet Archive is a non-profit organization established by Brewster Kahle in 1996 (Kahle, 2001). It offers permanent storage of and free public access to collections of digitized materials, including Web sites, music, moving images, and nearly 3 million public-domain books. The attractive part of this project is the way back machine which takes one back to the Web site content which is inaccessible now or to the Web sites which now does not exists on their URLs. It also archives all type of media uploaded on the Web such as images, pictures, text, and so forth, that may be called snapshot of the World Wide Web.

LOCKSS (Lots of Copies Keep Stuff Safe) is a project of Stanford University with the objective to collect, preserve and disseminate information published on the Web to their readers (Stanford University, 2008).

Some other major projects are Jstor, Open archives, NDIIPP, Digital Preservation Repository of University of California, and so forth.

CONCLUSION

Rapid technological invention has made our work easy but at the same time new inventions are bypassing one another so fast that they become obsolescent very soon. Digital preservation also facing this problem of obsolescence and requires special concern. A library spends a huge amount of money in purchasing digital books journals, and so forth, and to save it, one is required to use digital preservation techniques such as migration, emulation, and so forth. Digital information is like a time bomb which should be defused before it blasts and destroy everything. If we do not plan for the future with digital strategies and techniques, our dynasties will lose the past.

REFERENCES

Anderson, W. L. (2002). CODATA work in archiving scientific data. In B. Mahon, & E. Siegel (Eds.), *Digital preservation: The record of science* (pp. 63–67). Amsterdam: IOS Press.

Besser, H. (2001). Digital preservation of moving image material?. *The Moving Image, 1*(2).

Blue Ribbon Task Force on Sustainable Digital Preservation and Access. (2010). *Sustainable economics for a digital planet: Ensuring long-term access to digital information.* Retrieved July 3, 2012, from http://brtf.sdsc.edu/biblio/BRTF_Final_Report.pdf

Depocas, A., Ippolito, J., Jones, C., & Schaefer, C. A. (2003). *Permanence through change: The variable media approach.* New York: Guggenheim Museum Publications.

Garrett, J., & Waters, D. (1996). *Preserving digital information: Report of the task force on archiving of digital information.* Washington, DC: U.S. Commission on Preservation and Access and Research Libraries Group.

Gladney, H. M. (2007). *Preserving digital information.* Berlin: Springer.

Graham, P. G. (1994). *Intellectual preservation: Electronic preservation of the third kind.* Retrieved June 29, 2012, from http://www.clir.org/pubs/reports/graham/intpres.html

Heslop, H., Devis, S., & Wilson, A. (2002). *An approach to the preservation of digital record.* Retrieved July 2, 2012, from http://www.naa.gov.au/Images/An-approach-Green-Paper_tcm16-47161.pdf

International Internet Preservation Consortium. (2004). *Mission goal and charter*. Retrieved July 5, 2012, from http://netpreserve.org/about/mission.php

International Internet Preservation Consortium. (2004). *Web curators mailing list*. Retrieved July 5, 2012, from http://netpreserve.org/about/curator.php

Kahle, B. (2001). *The Internet archive*. Retrieved July 29, 2012, from http://archive.org/

Library of Congress. (2002). *Preserving our digital heritage: Plan for the national digital information infrastructure and preservation program.* Retrieved July 3, 2012, from http://www.digitalpreservation.gov/documents/ndiipp_plan.pdf

Lyman, P., & Hal, R. V. (2003). *How much information?* Retrieved June 17, 2012, from http://www2.sims.berkeley.edu/research/projects/how-much-info-2003/

Mallinson, J. C. (1986). Preserving machine-readable archival records for the millenia. *Archivaria, 22*, 147–152.

National Library of Australia. (2003). *Guidelines for the preservation of digital heritage*. Canberra, Australia: United Nations Educational, Scientific, and Cultural Organization.

Oracle Thinkquest. (2012). *What is CD ROM*. Retrieved June 14, 2012, from http://library.thinkquest.org/26171/whatiscdrom.html

Stanford University. (2008). *LOCKSS*. Retrieved July 29, 2012, from http://lockss.stanford.edu/

UKOLN. (2002). *CURL exemplars in digital archives (cedars).* Retrieved July 29, 2012, from http://www.ukoln.ac.uk/metadata/cedars/

Wikipedia. (2012). *Digital preservation coaliation.* Retrieved July 3, 2012, from http://en.wikipedia.org/wiki/Digital_Preservation_Coalition

Winget, M. (2005, June 7-11). *Digital preservation of new media art through exploration of established symbolic representation systems*. Paper presented at the ACM/IEEE Joint Conference on Digital Libraries' 2005 Doctoral Consortium. Denver, CO.

KEY TERMS AND DEFINITIONS

Digital Preservation: A process to preserve data in digital format.

Emulation: Imitating the functionalities of an obsolete system.

Migration: Transferring data from one format to a newer format.

OAIS: "An archive, consisting of an organization of people and systems that has accepted the responsibility to preserve information and make it available for a Designated Community" (OAIS 1.7.2).

Refreshing: Moving the data from one storage device to another.

Reinterpretation: A process of upgrading data but this term is used for software, music, and so forth. For example, when software is not able to work on upgraded hardware system, then the software needs to be reinterpreted according to new hardware.

Chapter 3
Digital Preservation:
Its Framework and Strategies in Cloud Computing Environment

Vijay Parashar
FET Library, Mody Institute of Technology & Science, India

Mohan Lal Vishwakarma
FET Library, Mody Institute of Technology & Science, India

Nisha Patle
FET Library, Mody Institute of Technology & Science, India

ABSTRACT

Digital preservation is the persistent archiving of digital assets for future access and reuse, irrespective of the underlying platform and software solutions. Existing preservation systems have a strong focus on grids, but the advent of cloud technologies offers an attractive option. The authors describe a middleware system that enables a flexible choice of cloud for ad-hoc computations that arise during the execution of a preservation workflow and also for archiving digital objects. The choice between different infrastructures remains open during the lifecycle of the archive, ensuring a smooth switch between different solutions to accommodate the changing requirements of the organization that needs its digital assets preserved. The authors also offer insights on the costs, running times, and organizational issues of cloud computing, proving that the cloud alternative is particularly attractive for smaller organizations without access to a grid or with limited IT infrastructure.

INTRODUCTION

Libraries and archives play a critical role in organizing, preserving, and providing access to the cultural and historical resources of society. In the relatively stable world of printed, hand-written, and mechanically reproduced information, repositories managed to preserve a rich array of scholarly communications, documentary evidence, and useful information for specialized scholars and for the general public. The introduction of digital technologies into the processes of production, distribution, and storage of information challenges the capacity of libraries, archives, museums, and other cultural institutions to carry out their responsibilities for preservation. This problem

DOI: 10.4018/978-1-4666-4631-5.ch003

has been the focus of numerous reports designed to raise awareness of digital preservation issues and to propose general strategies for addressing them. The general outline of digital preservation challenges is well established. Digital materials are especially vulnerable to loss and destruction because they are stored on fragile magnetic and optical media that deteriorate rapidly and that can fail suddenly from exposure to heat, humidity, airborne contaminants, or faulty reading and writing devices. Even if the media are preserved intact, digital materials become unreadable if the playback devices necessary to retrieve information from the media become obsolete or if the software that translates digital information from machine- to human- readable form is no longer available. Libraries, archives, and other repositories that traditionally have assumed responsibility for preserving information face technical, legal, and organizational Challenges in responding to the new demands of digital preservation. Repositories need access to technical resources – both information systems that support digital preservation and the technical expertise to use these technologies effectively. Institutions also face legal obstacles in fulfilling their mandates to preserve valuable information when copyright or licensing agreements prohibit duplication or local storage of digital information. Institutions can take action on their own, but there is a strong consensus that coordinated strategies and shared resources are essential to achieving broader solutions to digital preservation and enhancing the success of local efforts.

POSSIBILITY OF THE STUDY

The terms of reference for the study pointed out that the number of digital documents and resources to be managed and preserved is growing at a tremendous rate. Almost inevitably, the number of approaches being taken to the management and preservation of digital documents and resources is also growing rapidly. This raised four important questions that had to be addressed at the outset in order to build on the terms of reference and agree the scope and boundaries of the study.

PRESERVATION

The second question relates to what is actually meant by the term "preservation" in this context – why we need to preserve digital resources and what is involved in actually "preserving" digital resources.

Jeff Rothenberg(1995) provides one of the clearest accounts of some of the key challenges and tasks involved in preserving digital resources. The consultancy draws heavily upon his excellent article in this subsection. Digital preservation is broken down into three areas, each of which can then be further subdivided.

Preserving Bit Streams through Copying/Refreshing

Digital resources can be stored on any medium that can represent their binary digits. Rothenberg defines a "bit stream" as "an intended meaningful sequence of bits with no intervening spaces, punctuation or formatting". To preserve that bit stream the first requirement is to ensure that the bit stream is stored on a stable medium. If the digital medium deteriorates or becomes obsolete before we have read the digital information off the medium and copied it onto another medium then we have lost the data.

At a basic level, therefore, digital preservation involves the following tasks:

- Preserving the digital medium that holds the digital information by storing it in the correct environment and following agreed storage and handling procedures.
- Copying the digital information onto newer, fresher media before the old media de-

teriorates past the point where the digital information can be read or becomes so obsolete that we can no longer find a storage device to read it on.
- Preserving the integrity of the digital information during the copying process.

Preserving the integrity of the digital information at this level means preserving the bit configuration that uniquely defines the digital object. The Task Force on Archiving of Digital Information confirms that "there are various well-established techniques, such as checksums and digests, for tracking the bit-level equivalence of digital objects and ensuring that a preserved object is identical to the original". However, simply preserving the digital information on several copies of a stable, digital medium is not sufficient. We also need to be sure that the digital information can be retrieved and processed in future.

Retrieving a bit stream requires a hardware device such as a disk drive or a tape drive and special circuitry for reading the physical representation of the bits from the medium. Accessing the device from a given computer also requires a driver program.

So if we hold digital resources on a specific type of digital medium (CD-ROM; tape; diskette; punched card, etc.) we need a drive designed to accept that specific type of digital medium in order to read the data.

Today it is becoming difficult to find computer punch card reader suppliers so if you have not copied your old digital resources off punch cards and onto a newer media you will find it progressively more difficult to read them. The same problem could be experienced in future when CD-ROM drives or drives for specific formats of magnetic tape media become obsolete. This approach is referred to as copying or "refreshing."

In some cases, due to the way the digital resource has been recorded onto a specific type of digital medium, it can be difficult to retrieve the digital resource and write it onto a different medium. This is often the case with digital publications – digital resources that have been authored and published on a specific digital medium and are provided with proprietary access software to provide access to the data held in the publication.

The publisher may have set a limit to how much data could be copied or down loaded from the publication in one session. It may be impossible to copy the data using normal utilities without obtaining a key from the publisher. If the publisher cannot be contacted then it may prove impossible to copy or migrate data from the specific medium and hence no refreshing can take place. When the medium deteriorates or becomes obsolete the data will be lost.

A less extreme case would be where the data was authored and the access software was designed specifically for one type of digital medium. There would be a danger that if the data was copied to another type of medium – then all the links between the data and the access software used to retrieve the data would be lost and it might not be possible to use the access software at all. In such cases new access software would have to be written.

Such digital resources can be referred to as hardware-specific. Once the drives needed to read the media become obsolete and unusable it may prove impossible to access the digital publications in their original format using the original access software.

Ensuring We Can Interpret Data by Preserving Documentation

Rothenberg points out that—assuming you can physically read the bit stream—the next step is to be able to interpret it. This is not simple as a given bit stream (see Section 3 below) can represent almost anything from a sequence of integers to an array of dots in an image, and so forth.

Also, interpreting a bit stream depends on understanding its implicit structure which cannot be explicitly represented in the stream. A bit stream that represents a sequence of alphabetic characters may consist of fixed length chunks (bytes) each representing a code for a single character. To extract the bytes from the bit stream, thereby parsing the stream into its components, we must know the length of a byte.

One way to convey the length is to encode a key at the beginning of the bit stream but Rothenberg points out that this key must itself be represented by a byte of some length. A reader needs another key to understand the first one. The solution to this recursive problem is traditionally a "bootstrap" in the form of some human readable documentation which explains how to interpret the digital resource.

After the bit stream has been correctly parsed the next recursive problem involves interpreting the bytes. A byte can represent a number or an alphabetic character, according to a code. To interpret such bytes we need to know the coding scheme and the solution again is documentation that explains the byte encoding scheme. Hence, in addition to preserving the digital resource on a currently readable digital storage medium, we need to preserve documentation that allows us to interpret the digital resource.

Rothenberg goes on to point out that bit streams are usually stored as a collection or file of bits that contains logically related but physically separated elements. These elements are linked to each other by internal references consisting of pointers to other elements or of patterns to be matched.

Hence, in addition to simply reading the bit stream, there is a requirement to be able to interpret the information embedded in the bit stream. Most files contain information that is only meaningful to the software that created them. Word Processing files embed format instructions describing typography, layout and structure. Spreadsheet files embed formulas relating to their cells, and so forth. This embedded information and all aspects of the representation of a bit stream–including the byte length, character code and structure–comprise the encoding of a file. The files contain both instructions and data that can only be interpreted by the appropriate software.

Options For Ensuring We Can Interpret Data In Future

A word processing file does not represent a document in its own right. It merely describes a document that comes into existence when the file is interpreted by the program that produced it. In a very telling phrase, Rothenberg (1995) makes the point that "without this program or equivalent software, the document is a cryptic hostage of its own encoding."

To "preserve" a digital resource we need to ensure that we can decode the digital resource in future. There are two main approaches taken to solving this complex requirement. The conservative approach assumes that the only way to ensure that you will be able to fully decode the bit streams held in a file in future is to preserve the program used to create it. If you have documents held in "Microsoft Word version 6.0" format then you also need to preserve "Microsoft Word version 6.0". This approach is reviewed below as option one – preserving the original program. It leads to one of two preservation strategies: "technology preservation" or "emulation."

The optimistic approach is that the best way to ensure you will be able to fully decode the bit streams held in a file in future is to ensure that they are encoded in a format that is independent of the particular hardware and software used to create them. It is vital with this approach to also ensure that there is always software available to decode the current format. This approach is reviewed below as option two. It leads to one preservation strategy: "digital information migration."

Option One: Preserve the Innovative Program

Rothenberg is a strong advocate of this approach. He concedes that you do not always need to run the specific program that created a document in order to read that document. If it is simple document then similar software may be able to, at least partially, interpret the file. But Rothenberg feels it is naïve to expect that the encoding of any new digital document will remain readable by future software for very long.

His view is that IT creates new schemes that often abandon their predecessors instead of subsuming them. The latest version of the leading word processing package should be backward compatible with the previous one or two versions. However, in his view, it would be naïve to expect all future versions for the next ten years to be able to read all the files created on all the oldest versions of the package.

Where we are dealing with very sophisticated digital resources such as multimedia presentations, and so forth – there may be a total dependency between the digital resource and one version of one software package. Such a digital resource is therefore said to be "software- dependent."

Often–where some level of interchange is permitted between programs–it will involve some loss of data. Word Processing programs allow authors to save work as simple alphanumeric text using the American Standard Code for Information Interchange (ASCII) or other interchange formats such as Rich Text Format (RTF). However, Rothenberg points out those authors rarely save their work as pure text. They want to store format data and figures and footnotes. If this data is lost in the interchange then valuable content is lost. Rothenberg therefore argues that, if a scholar or researcher wants to view a complicated document as its author created it, he or she may have no choice but to run the application software that was used to create it. Hence in order to fully decode the bit streams held in a file and to view a digital resource such as a complicated document in its original format then we may also need to preserve the program used to create it.

If we archive the original program with the files it created then in future, when both are retrieved, there will also be a need to find and use the operating system software which the original program was designed to run on. Depending on how long the data and the original program are kept for then this can become a serious problem. The logical next step with this approach is, therefore, to plan to archive a copy of the operating system software with all the original application programs that run on it and all the files to be decoded by those application programs. Depending on how long the data and the application program and the operating system software are kept for, the final problem that occurs with this approach can then be finding the hardware on which to run the operating system software. There are only two solutions proposed to this problem.

The first is to preserve working replicas of all key computer hardware platforms. This is referred to as the "Technology Preservation" strategy. The second is to program future powerful computer systems to emulate older obsolete computer platforms and operating systems on demand. Your latest PC server could be programmed to emulate a specific VAX computer running a specific version of the VMS operating system, and so forth. This is referred to as the "Technology Emulation" strategy.

Both of these two potential digital preservation strategies are reviewed briefly below.

Option Two: Digital Information Relocation

This approach is the opposite of option one above. It assumes that the best way to ensure you will be able to fully decode the bit streams held in a file in future is to ensure that they are encoded in a format that is independent of the particular hardware and software used to create them. It is vital with this approach to also ensure that there is always software available to decode the current format.

Digital information migration could potentially be facilitated in the following ways:

- Through copying the digital information to an analogue medium.
- Through application programs that are "backward compatible".
- Through application programs that can "interoperate" with competing products.
- Through converting digital resources into a small number of "standard" formats that are hardware and software independent.

Digital information migration is the third digital preservation strategy covered by this study. It is reviewed in detail below.

Defining an Outline

The first question relates to the intended audience for this study. Who are the collection managers or caretakers and what are they trying to do? Are librarians, records managers, archivists and the managers of data centres all trying to do the same things with digital resources now – and in the future? If not then where do the similarities and the differences lie? What impact do these differences have on their preservation requirements?

In order to answer these questions the consultancy needed to identify an overall framework. An excellent framework has been developed and described by Daniel Greenstein. This is aimed at managers of collections of digitised scholarly and cultural information but is of even wider applicability. His objective in proposing the framework was to assist collection managers in identifying and addressing key issues and in developing their own data policies. The consultancy's objective in drawing on Greenstein's proposed framework in this study is to define and agree the context within which digital preservation is being addressed. Preservation is one of seven modules that together comprise Greenstein's proposed framework. The seven modules described by Greenstein are as shown in Table 1. Some of the key modules are further subdivided.

Table 1. Seven modules

	Module Name	Sub-Module Name	Sub-Sub-Module Name
1	Data Creation		
2	Data Selection & Evaluation		
3	Data Management	Data Structure	
		Data Documentation	
		Data Storage	
		Data Validation	Data Assessment
			Data Copying
			Media Refreshment
4	Resource Disclosure		
5	Data Use		
6	Data Preservation		
7	Rights Management		

- **Data Creation:** Decisions made when the digital resource was created – often outside the control of the collection manager but having a major impact on the options subsequently open to the collection manager.
- **Data Selection and Evaluation:** Decisions based on the digital resource's content, usability and relevance to the user base plus, on the ease with which the digital resource can be managed, catalogued, made accessible to users and preserved.
- **Data Management:** Broken down into four subsets.
- **Data Structure:** How a digital resource is formatted, compressed and encoded which determines whether the digital resource needs to be re-formatted, uncompressed and uuencoded or re- encoded.
- **Data Documentation:** The extent to which the digital resource's structure, content, provenance and history have been docu-

mented – which may determine whether the resource needs additional documentation.

- **Data Storage:** The computer hardware and media used to store the digital resource; whether the digital resource is stored online or offline and whether the storage is provided in-house or by a third party.
- **Data Validation:** Three procedures designed to ensure a digital resource's integrity.
- **Data Assessment:** Testing the digital resource's completeness; function and consistency.
- **Data Copying:** Making additional copies of the digital resource to guard against the loss or corruption of any one copy.
- **Media Refreshment:** Periodically copying one copy of a digital resource onto fresh media to protect against the corruption and content loss which may result from media deterioration.
- **Resource Disclosure:** Making information about a digital resource available to users e g via online catalogues.
- **Data Use:** How digital resources are to be delivered to end users and used by end users – will be influenced by how digital resources were created and managed and will influence how digital resources are managed.
- **Data Preservation:** Safe guarding the information content of any digital resource from the ravages of time, technological change and decaying magnetic media – different preservation strategies are appropriate for different data types and structures. Preservation requirements will impinge on how digital resources are structured, documented, stored and validated and possibly even on the conditions and methods by which digital resources can be accessed by end users.
- **Rights Management:** Intellectual property rights, data protection and confidentiality issues –need to develop both acquisition licenses and distribution licenses and implementation procedures.

Greenstein goes on to make the vital point that, in order to implement the framework in any one situation, the collection manager or caretaker needs to turn it into a data policy that suits their particular collection's needs. The needs of librarians and records managers and data centre managers will vary but they can all be described and differentiated within this framework.

Greenstein further makes the point that each collection manager needs a clear understanding of the collection's aims and its overall budget. In all cases cost will be a vital consideration. This is particularly true when it comes to the area of preservation. As we shall see below – some preservation strategies today require almost unlimited resources and hence are not practical for the majority of collection managers.

The last point that Greenstein makes which is vital to this study – is that all the key collection management issues and hence all the seven modules of the framework are closely interrelated. Decisions about whether to create or include a digital resource in a collection–and about its content and format–will impinge on how it can be managed and stored, on how or even whether it can be preserved and on how it can be delivered to end users. Equally, the uses intended for a particular resource or the method chosen to preserve it over time may impinge upon decisions taken when creating or including a digital resource into a collection.

The close inter-relations and dependencies between all aspects of digital collection management make it very difficult, in practice, to identify and isolate those actions that simply relate to preservation. There are some tasks that specifically relate to preservation but a successful preservation strategy depends upon good practice in almost all the other six areas identified in the framework.

For the same reason it has proved difficult to isolate just that subset of a data centre's budget which relates to preservation. Some costs specifically relate to preservation but one cannot infer that those are the only costs incurred when preserving digital resources. Given that a successful preservation strategy depends upon good practice in all the other six areas in the framework one also needs to allow for the costs incurred in each of those other six areas. This is the approach that has been adopted by the consultancy when drawing up the cost model.

THE DIGITAL PRESERVATION TACTICS

The third question relates to the range of potential digital preservation strategies that should be covered in the study and a definition and assessment of each one. The terms of reference for the study call upon the study to cover following three potential strategies for ensuring long term access to digital information.

- Technology preservation.
- Technology emulation.
- Digital information migration.

Above defined what we mean by digital preservation and placed these three strategies in the context of the two differing approaches that have been taken to digital preservation. It is rarely the case that a collection manager would want to adopt all three strategies for the preservation of one category of digital resources.

Normally the collection manager would select one or other strategy as being the most appropriate for each category of digital resource. However, it is quite possible that within one large collection there may be a requirement to adopt two or even three of the strategies for the long term preservation of a range of different categories of digital resources.

This explains the need for the first decision model. It aims to provide collection managers with guidance on the choice of the most appropriate long term preservation strategy for each of the different categories of digital resources.

The three strategies are described in more detail below. They are related back to the preservation requirements defined in section above. The consultancy refers to these definitions later in chapters four and five of the study.

Technology Preservation

This strategy involves the following tasks:

- Storing the bit streams on a stable digital medium.
- Preserving the digital medium while the bit streams are stored on it.
- Refreshing or copying the data to new media as required.
- Preserving the integrity of the digital information during the copying process.
- Preserving the original application program used to create or access the digital resource.
- Preserving the operating system software that the original application programs run on.
- Preserving the computer hardware platform that the operating system software was designed to run on.

The advocates of this strategy stress that to really replicate the behavior of a program and the look and feel of a document or publication then you needs to be running the original environment. While this is undoubtedly true in a purist sense it has to be balanced against the costs and the technical difficulties that would be faced by anyone trying to keep ageing computer hardware platforms running.

Already, in the brief history of computing, hundreds if not thousands of old proprietary computer hardware platforms have disappeared without trace. Examples of some of the more popular old platforms are still kept going by some computer enthusiasts as a hobby but they are fighting a losing battle trying to source old components. Today we are seeing the increasing dominance and ubiquity of a few computer platforms. In theory this should simplify the task of preserving these platforms in future. However, even here there are difficulties given the rapid obsolescence of computer components. It is unlikely that components for today's PCs could be sourced in ten years' time.

In general, this strategy cannot be regarded as viable for anything other than the short to medium term. The consultancy would see "technology preservation" being used as a relatively desperate measure in cases where valuable digital resources cannot be converted into hardware and/or software independent formats and migrated forward. This would usually be due to the complexity of the digital resource and the fact that it was created on a proprietary and obsolete application program. This strategy could be adopted where the only way to access a valuable digital resource was via an application that would only run on operating system software that would itself only run on an obsolete hardware platform. In this situation then collection managers would be best advised to seek out a specialist third party (if one could be found) with that hardware environment. They should then run the software and attempt to migrate the data off to at least a software-dependent format and ideally to a software independent format, which they can then migrate forward.

Any collection manager in charge of a large collection of digital resources who relied solely on this strategy would very soon end up with a museum of ageing and incompatible computer hardware.

Technology Simulation

This strategy has a lot in common with the technology preservation strategy described above. It involves the following tasks:

- Storing the bit streams on a stable digital medium.
- Preserving the digital medium while the bit streams are stored on it.
- Refreshing or copying the data to new media as required.
- Preserving the integrity of the digital information during the copying process.
- Preserving the original application program used to create or access the digital resource.

Where it differs from the previous strategy is in how it creates the operating system and hardware environment that the original application program was designed to run on. This strategy does not involve preserving ageing hardware and running the original operating system software on top of it. Rather, it involves software engineers performing the following tasks: designing and running emulator programs on current and future computer platforms and programming them to mimic the behavior of old hardware platforms and to emulate specific operating system software.

In other words you could configure your future PCs to look like a specific model of a VAX computer running a specific version of the VMS operating system, and so forth. Rothenberg advocates this approach but concedes that it will require extremely detailed specifications for the outdated hardware and operating system software.

Looking to the future, one can agree with Rothenberg that some applications and operating system software such as MS DOS (4.0) may remain ubiquitous so that all a collection manager would need to do would be to refer users to these programs. Also, when these ubiquitous proprietary programs become obsolete and hence less commercially valuable, then copyright restrictions tend to expire and they can stay available to future users.

In general, the consultancy would still see this as a short to medium term strategy or a specialist strategy where the need to maintain the look and feel of the original digital resource is of great importance to the collection's user base.

The consultancy would see technology emulation being primarily used in cases where digital resources cannot be converted into software independent formats and migrated forward. This would usually be due to the complexity of the digital resource and the fact that it was created on a proprietary and obsolete application program.

This strategy could be adopted where the only way to access a valuable digital resource was via an application that would only run on operating system software that would itself only run on an obsolete hardware platform. In this situation then collection managers would be best advised to seek out a specialist third party (if one could be found) able to emulate that hardware and operating system software environment. They should then run the software and attempt to migrate the data off to at least a software-dependent format and ideally to a software independent format so they can then migrate the data forwards. Any collection manager in charge of a large collection of digital resources who relied solely on this strategy currently would be taking a very significant risk. They would be depending on the technical ability of the software engineers to emulate a specific environment and sustain it and the commercial viability of anyone providing such a service.

Digital Information Relocation

This strategy assumes that the best way to ensure you will be able to fully decode the bit streams held in a file in future is to ensure that they are encoded in a format that is independent of the particular hardware and software used to create them. It is vital to ensure that there is always software available to decode the current format.

Another way of paraphrasing this strategy is to say that it is only worth preserving digital information if you can access it on current computer hardware and software platforms. As those platforms change so the collection managers must migrate their digital resources forwards to ensure the digital resources can also be accessed on the new platforms.

"There are a variety of migration strategies for transferring digital information from obsolete systems to current hardware and software systems so that the information remains accessible and usable. No single strategy applies to all formats of digital information and none of the current preservation methods is entirely satisfactory. Migration strategies and their associated costs vary in different application environments, for different formats of digital materials, and for preserving different degrees of computation, display, and retrieval capabilities."

Conversion Media

One basic migration strategy that the Task Force covers involves the transfer of digital resources from less stable to more stable media. They point out that the most prevalent version of this strategy involves printing digital information onto paper or recording it on microfilm. Paper and microfilm are more stable than most digital media and no special hardware or software is needed to retrieve information from them.

This strategy is, strictly speaking, outside the scope of this study. However, it is worth referring to briefly. It may be appropriate in those cases where collection managers are faced with having to preserve hardware and/or software – dependent digital resources for long periods of time with relatively low budgets.

The alternative strategies–technology preservation and technology emulation–are considered to be short to medium term strategies and are potentially extremely expensive. Hence, provided the digital resources are "document like"–they can be printed out onto paper or microfilm in a linear fashion–then printing or recording to microfilm should be considered. If nothing else it preserves a copy of the basic data while other migration strategies are explored.

Indisposed Compatibility

A second migration strategy relies on popular application software being "backward compatible." The latest versions of most popular word processing packages will be capable of decoding files created on earlier versions of the same package – particularly the previous two or three versions. If the leading application packages are "backward compatible" then migration simply involves testing the process and then loading files created on previous versions of the application program into the new version and saving them in the new file format.

While this strategy may work over the short term for simple digital resources created on some of the leading application packages it cannot be relied upon over the medium to long term or for more complex digital resources.

No one software supplier is in control of all the technical or commercial factors needed to guarantee the continued viability and support of their application software. They may go out of business and hence be unable to support their software. They may be forced to introduce a totally new software package and drop support for their old package. They may be forced to redesign the package to stay competitive with the result that the new version cannot read old files created on earlier versions.

Hence any digital information migration strategy which simply relied on "backward compatibility" of the leading application software packages would represent a short-term strategy that exposed the collection to many risks.

Interoperability

The third migration strategy relies on "interoperability" between rival popular application programs. You do not always need to run the specific program that created a digital resource in order to read that digital resource. Digital resources created on one application program can be exported in a common interchange format and then imported into a rival application program.

If such "interoperability" could be guaranteed between all the major competing application programs then "digital information migration" would be a much easier process. If your preferred CAD supplier ceased trading, you could export all your CAD designs in a common interchange format and then import them into your preferred new CAD application. You could export all your alphanumeric data from your old database engine and load them into your new preferred database engine. You could export all your text files from your old word processing application and load them into your preferred new word processing application. You could export all your raster image files from your old image processing application and load them into your new image processing application. The list of migration options would be endless.

If it is a simple digital resource then the fact is that, today, similar software may well be able to, at least partially, interpret the file. However, it is common where some level of interchange is permitted between programs, for the interchange to involve some loss of data. Word Processing programs allow authors to save work as simple alphanumeric text using the American Standard Code for Information Interchange (ASCII) or other interchange formats such as Rich Text Format (RTF). However, as Rothenberg (1995) points out, authors rarely save their work as pure text.

They want to store format data and figures and footnotes. If this data is lost in the interchange then valuable content is lost.

The more complex the digital resources then the more problems are involved in "interchange" and the more valuable data is likely to be lost in the process. How important the "loss of data" is will vary depending on the type of digital resource, the objectives of the collection manager and the needs of the users of the collection. Compared to all the data that is lost when digital resources are printed out to paper or microfilm, the data lost during such an "interchange" may be minor. On the other hand–when interchanging the data held in complex databases such as GIS databases and groupware databases–it could involve the loss of thousands of links that have taken years of effort to create and that represent the bulk of the value of the database.

While this strategy may prove useful over the short term–for migrating simple digital resources out of obsolete application packages and into preferred application packages–it cannot be relied upon over the medium to long term or for more complex digital resources.

No one software supplier is in control of all the technical or commercial factors needed to guarantee interoperability between their own and rival application packages. They may go out of business and hence be unable to support their software. They may be forced to introduce a totally new software package and drop support for their export and import options. They may be forced to redesign the package to stay competitive with the result that the new version cannot read old files created on rival packages. The interchange formats themselves may cease to be supported or may be replaced by newer, richer formats.

Hence any digital information migration strategy which simply relied on "interoperability" between the leading application software packages would represent a short-term strategy that exposed the collection to many risks.

Alteration to Usual Formats

A fourth and final migration strategy was again covered by the Task Force. They suggest that it is particularly appropriate for digital archives with large, complex, and diverse collections of digital materials. The proposed strategy is: to migrate digital objects from the great multiplicity of formats used to create digital materials to a smaller, more manageable number of standard formats that can still encodes the complexity of structure and form of the original. A digital archive might accept textual documents in several commonly available commercial word processing formats or require that documents conform to standards like SGML (ISO 8879). Databases might be stored in one of several common relational database management systems, while images would conform to a tagged image file format and standard compression algorithms (e.g., JFIF/JPEG).

This represents an enhanced version of the "interoperability" strategy. That strategy tends to rely on interchange formats that can be generated automatically from within the applications. Inevitably that tends to result in simple formats that involve the loss of significant data.

With this strategy the onus is placed on the collection manager to define the preferred formats and select the formats that are most appropriate for the digital resources they collect and the users they serve. The handling of text files or documents can provide us with one example of the difference between the "interoperability" and the "conversion to standard format" strategies. The interchange of basic text content has largely been solved today although the Task Force points out that there are still some issues that can affect interoperability:

"Text today is generally covered by a formal, international ASCII standard for representing character formats. Standard extensions exist for encoding diacritic characters in romance languages other than English and a new standard is slowly emerging to incorporate scripted languages under a new common encoding scheme (UNICODE). Alternative encoding methods, however, abound. IBM maintains its own EBCDIC character encoding scheme and Apple and Intel-based personal computers differ in the ways that they support extended ASCII character sets. For documents in which any of these character codes can adequately represent the contents, the differences in encoding schemes may matter little and digital archives can manage object integrity by mapping character sets from one to the other. However, for works involving multiple languages or complex equations and formula, where character mapping is imperfect or not possible, character set format takes on considerably more significance over the long-term as a matter of content integrity."

If we move beyond basic text content to cover text layout and structure coding then the differences between the two strategies become more apparent. So if we store documents in their native format then every time we interchange them we stand to lose valuable content. If, on the other hand the documents are marked up using agreed standards when they are created or when they are taken into digital collections then not only the basic text content but also the layout and structure of the documents can be preserved.

Selecting a Format

Decisions on which formats to convert digital resources into should be based on the structure of the digital resources themselves; on the objectives set by the collection manager and on the requirements of the users of that collection.

One important issue relates to whether the top priority is given to preserving the ability to process or edit the digital resource (auditability) or to preserving the format or visual presentation of the digital resource (format).

In most data centres one of the key objectives is to preserve the data and make it available in a format which allows it to be loaded into user application programs so it can be processed and new data derived from it. The data is the valuable resource and how that data is presented in the form of tables, graphs, and models, and so forth, is of secondary importance. In archives and records centres, on the other hand, the key objective may well be to preserve the format or visual presentation of the digital resource – to ensure its archival integrity.

In the latter case then one valid migration strategy for all electronic "document-like" records would be to convert them into a formatted page image format. Examples would include converting each electronic document into a series of PostScript page print files or to Adobe Acrobat PDF (Portable Document Format) files or to a series of page images stored in a raster graphics format. This strategy could be seen to be the digital equivalent of printing the digital resources out onto paper or microfilm. As with that strategy, this simple strategy would not cater for time-based data (audio and motion video) and is far from ideal for three dimensional graphics and relational database records.

A slight modification of this strategy for all electronic "document-like" records would be to hold them in their native file format but store with them "file viewer" software that enables users to view and print the documents as formatted page files but does not allow them to edit the documents. This latter strategy has some drawbacks as a "digital information migration" strategy. Firstly it would create a need to periodically migrate the "file viewer" software to ensure that the file viewer software could always operate in the current computer environment. In changing the preferred "file viewer" software the collection manager might find that the new "file viewer" cannot view some of the older files in the collection. In that case the collection manager has two choices. Firstly, he/she has to go back and migrate the old files in which case we are back to selecting the right format to convert them to.

Secondly, he/she has to resort to a "technology preservation" or "technology emulation" strategy and store the old "file viewer" software and the operating system software it runs on and preserve the required hardware environment for the operating system software.

Selecting the Most Applicable Extensive Duration Preservation Strategy

As described the terms of reference for this study called on the consultancy to "draw up a decision model for assessing the agreed categories of digital resources to determine the most appropriate method of long term preservation."

The consultancy has defined what is meant by digital preservation and has defined the three main strategies adopted for digital preservation. The three main strategies and key subsets of the third strategy are as listed in Table 2.

The consultancy also referenced Greenstein's framework which defines the context within which digital preservation is being addressed in this study. The framework defines seven modules, which must be addressed by any digital collection policy, of which preservation is one. The seven modules and key sub modules are as listed in Table 3.

The consultancy has defined 10 categories of digital resources and has reviewed the data types; applications; structures and management/distribution systems which can be employed to create, manage and distribute each category of digital resource. The diagram (Figure 1), shows seven key factors which need to be taken into account when deciding on the preferred preservation strategy for each category of digital resource.

Table 2. Three main strategies

	Preservation Strategy	Subset of Strategy
1	Technology Preservation	
2	Technology Emulation	
3	Digital Information Migration	Change Media
		Backward Compatibility
		Interoperability
		Conversion to standard formats

Table 3. Seven modules and key submodules

Module Number	Module Name	Sub-Module Name	Sub sub-Module Name
1	Data Creation		
2	Data selection and evaluation		
3	Data management	Data structure	
		Data documentation	
		Data storage	
		Data validation	Data assessment
			Data copying
			Media refreshment
4	Resource disclosure		
5	Data use		
6	Data preservation		
7	Rights management		

However, in section above, the consultancy has already reviewed the three preservation strategies and presented the third strategy–"digital information migration"–as being the preferred long-term strategy where it is technically and economically feasible. Migration was also the preferred long-term strategy of all the technical experts interviewed in the course of the study.

Given this level of consensus about the preferred preservation strategy, the consultancy proposes that, for each category of digital resource, the seven key factors should be reviewed and used in the following two ways:

Figure 1. 7 factors determining the appropriate preservation strategy for each category of digital resource

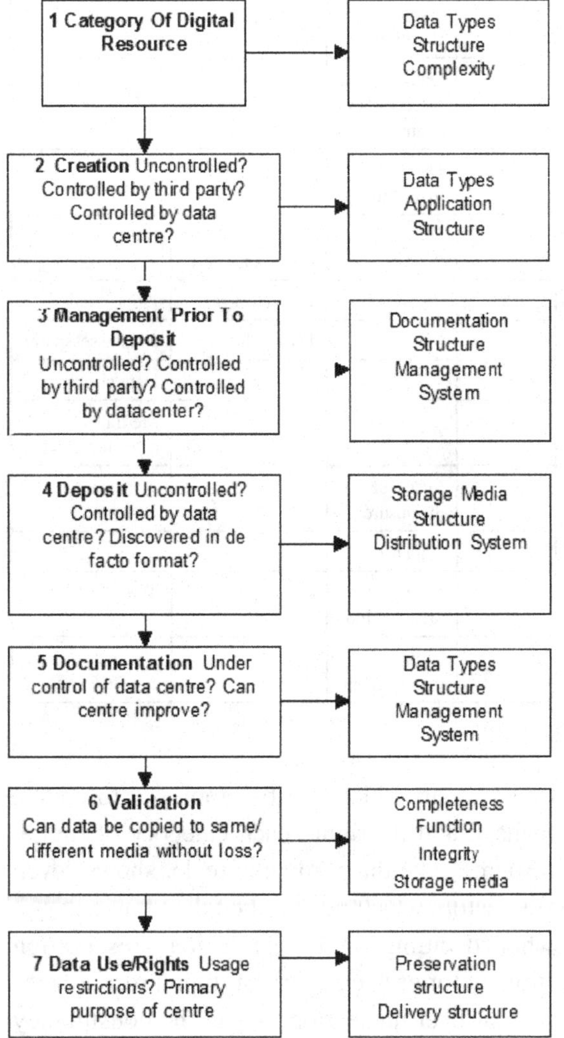

Firstly, to see whether any of them prevent the use of a "digital information migration" strategy. If one or more factors do appear to rule out the use of "digital information migration" for a specific category of digital resource then the other two strategies, "technology preservation" or "technology emulation," should be considered.

Secondly, if none of the seven factors appear to rule out "digital information migration" as the preferred strategy, the seven factors should be used to determine which subset of the strategy (change media; backward compatibility; interoperability or conversion to standard formats) is most appropriate for each category of digital resource. In some cases the review will indicate that there is a need to combine several of these subsets to form the perfect strategy for preserving a specific category of digital resource.

Classification of Digital Resource

The first key factor relates to the basic data types employed in each category and the structures applied to each category.

Data Categories

If the digital resource only contains one basic data type then this simplifies the management and preservation issues and helps to make "digital information migration" (migration) a more attractive and cost-effective option. The more data types contained within a digital resource then the more complex the management and preservation issues become and the less attractive some of the "migration" subsets become. If the digital resource only contains one basic data type and there are international or de facto standards for structuring and encoding that data type (ASCII for alphanumeric data) then this also makes the "interoperability" subset more attractive.

Data Constructions

If the digital resource is held in a standard processable form then this can simplify the management and preservation issues. It helps to make "migration" an attractive option. "Interoperability" and "conversion to standard formats" may both be considered as feasible subsets of the "migration" strategy in this case. If the digital resource can be said to be "document-like" (it can be printed out on paper as defined in above and can be exported in a standard formatted form then this can also simplify the management and preservation issues).

It helps to make "migration" an attractive option. "Change media" and "conversion to standard formats" can both be considered as feasible subsets of the "migration" strategy in this case.

If the digital resource is held in a proprietary processable form and, as indicated below, it was created on an obscure application program which is no longer supported, then this can make the management and preservation issues very much more complex. "Migration" may be resource intensive and very costly in this case. If a copy of the original application program still exists then the collection manager may have to resort to one of the other two digital preservation strategies, "technology preservation" or "technology emulation."

Digital Resource Creation

The second key factor relates to how the digital resource was created and covers several areas. The first relates to the application program used to create the digital resource.

Application Programs

If the digital resource was created using one de facto standard application program that is widely supported then this can simplify the management and preservation issues. It helps to make "migration" an attractive and cost effective option. "Backward compatibility" and "interoperability" may be considered as feasible subsets of the "migration" strategy. If the digital resource was created using an obscure application program which is no longer supported then this can make the management and preservation issues more complex.

Advices and Panels

The second relates to whether or not the digital resource was created in a controlled environment. The control could be imposed by the individual author or by the organisation he or she was working for or by the data centre or archive itself.

Historically, what controls there were would have been exercised by the authors themselves. If the author belonged to a profession then there may be standards followed for the production of formal interchange documents, and so forth. Organisations may impose controls by mandating the use of standard templates and house styles.

Finally, the data centre or the archive may actually be able to set the standards. One example where this is beginning to happen is in the Research Councils. The Research Councils sponsor research by individuals and institutions. The same Research Councils also fund their own data centres to archive the results of these research projects. Increasingly the data centres are able to define standards for documenting the data and standards for structuring the data. The Research Councils then make it a condition of any research grants that the research data should be presented in the data centre's standard formats at the end of the project.

The Public Record Office is the ultimate archive for government records. Increasingly, as government departments create more data sets and electronic records, the PRO will also become the ultimate government data centre. The PRO is in a position to advise government departments on how best to implement electronic records management systems and how they should structure their electronic records for deposit. They have already produced a draft set of guidelines. Clearly the more guidelines and controls are observed at the stage when digital resources are being created, the easier the task of managing and preserving those digital resources becomes and the more attractive the "migration" strategy becomes.

WHAT USAGE RESTRICTIONS/ REQUIREMENTS WERE IN OPERATION?

Depositors of digital resources may impose restrictions on the usage of their data. Some depositors might insist that users can only view or print their data – they should not be allowed to process or alter it in any way. A similar requirement might be that the digital resource must always be presented in the way intended by the author (e.g., certain aspects of the format cannot be altered).

Both these requirements would tend to lead the collection manager to a "migration" strategy built around the "change media" subset or the "convert to standard formats" subset. Digital resources may be converted to PostScript page files or Adobe PDF files or even to page images in TIFF.

There is one case where these requirements could lead the collection manager away from a "migration" strategy. This would be where the digital resource was created on a proprietary application program and held in a proprietary processable format. If the only way the digital resource could be interchanged involved the loss of formatting or presentation data (ASCII; RTF) then this may not prove acceptable. In that case the collection manager might have to adopt a "technology preservation" or "technology emulation" strategy to preserve the presentation or the "look and feel" of the original.

Alternatively, the users of a data centre that manages structured texts may indicate that they need to be able to access the texts in a processable form to edit and annotate them. In this case the collection manager would need to adopt a "migration" strategy built around the "convert to standard formats" strategy and select a standard processable format (e.g., SGML and an agreed DTD).

Applying the Model

Below the consultancy applies the decision model to the ten categories of digital resources defined for this study. Given the time and resources available for the study a very simplistic approach has been adopted. In reality there would be variations within each category.

The aim of the next ten brief sections is to show data managers how the decision model can be applied. It is not designed to provide definitive guidance. It has always been the view of the consultancy that the people best qualified to make the final decisions on preservation options are the people who understand the specific digital resources and data types to be preserved. If the model is useful then it should be taken up and applied by the data centre managers. Further work would then need to be done by specialists in each of the ten categories before any detailed guidance could be presented on how best to preserve each category of digital resource.

Data Sets

The bulk of data sets are taken to comprise a single data type – alphanumeric data. If the data has not already been "worked up" or validated then "working the data up" and "validating" the data can represent a very resource intensive task. If the data is not adequately documented then documenting the data can also represent a major task. The best approach to preserving data sets is to mandate depositors with documenting them fully and to mandate depositors with depositing them in a platform independent and ideally a software independent format.

The Data Archive at the University of Essex provide the following advice to depositors – "data held in a database management system should be written out as raw data files with identifiable delimiters, for example, comma delimited files, accompanied by data definition statements where appropriate."

The ideal preservation strategy for data sets is "Digital Information Migration" using the "Convert to standard formats" subset.

Structured Texts

The bulks of structured texts comprise one dominant data type, alphanumeric data, together with markup codes and, increasingly, tagged vector and raster graphics. Most data centres that specialise in the preservation of structured texts such as literary texts have adopted the "Digital Information Migration" strategy and specifically the "Convert to standard formats" subset.

Reference paper of Oxford Text Archive follows the Text Encoding Initiative (TEI) guidelines for using SGML to mark up literary works. There are various versions of TEI for different categories of literary work including plays, poems, and so forth. Oxford uses TEI Lite as a basic standard. Clearly there is a significant overhead involved in taking word-processed documents with proprietary markups and tagging them using TEI Lite. However, increasingly, regular depositors are following TEI Lite themselves.

For text only documents a well-equipped centre such as Oxford should not need to rely on any other preservation strategy. Problematic areas would be where a collection of texts were deposited that comprised text plus vector and raster graphics and the tags or links between the objects were held in a proprietary desktop publishing application or in a proprietary management system. If the desktop publishing application or the management system became obsolete then the centre would need to preserve the operating environment that they ran on until such time as they developed a migration strategy that allowed them to convert the digital resource into a format that could be migrated forwards.

Office Documents

Office documents cover almost all data types. The bulk would comprise alphanumeric data and raster and vector graphics. Increasingly there may be sound and moving video clips as well but these are covered separately below.

The Public Record Office draft guidelines are designed to address the long-term storage of electronic records created on office systems. They recommend the "Digital Information Migration" strategy and specifically the "Convert to standard formats" subset. The specific formats they recommend are PostScript; Adobe's PDF; TIFF; SGML and Comma Separated Variable ASCII for alphanumeric data.

Given their records management background the PRO favor "formatted forms" where the format and presentation of the document as well as its content is preserved. As a backup they would also endorse the "Change Media" subset where formatted page images of digital documents could be output to paper or microfilm. For modern digital office documents there should be no need to adopt any "Technology Preservation" or "Technology Emulation" strategies. A pragmatic short term solution for digital resources created on the leading de facto office applications would be to rely on the "Backward Compatibility" of the application. However, this should only be seen as a short-term solution and should always be backed up by converting the documents to a standard formatted form or changing the media.

Two main issues face data centre managers preserving images of paper documents.

The first issue–if the documents are not held in digital form at the time of deposit and hence have to be scanned and digitised–is what resolution should the images be scanned at and should they be captured and held as black and white; greyscale or colour images? The answer varies depending on the material to be captured. In addition, the cost of all the options also needs to be taken into account. High-resolution images take a long time to capture and create large file sizes. For standard office documents the "de facto" standard is 200-300dpi resolution, black and white or bitonal image capture.

The second issue relates to what file format the image data should be stored in, whether or not the image data should be compressed and, if so, what compression algorithm should be used. For standard office documents the "de facto" standard tends to be the CCITT Group IV facsimile compression algorithm and the compressed data is stored in TIFF. A problem area identified by the PRO is where–for a given collection of office documents–all the vital attribute data and context data plus the links between the documents were held in a proprietary office suite application or in a proprietary groupware database or document management system. If the office suite, groupware, or document management system became obsolete, then the centre would need to preserve the operating environment that they ran on until such time as they developed a migration strategy that allowed them to capture the links in a standard form. The effort involved in recreating the links on a preferred open management system would be prohibitive in most cases.

Design Data

Design data or product data can again cover almost all data types. The bulk would comprise vector graphics (CAD); raster graphics (old manual drawings) and alphanumeric data (text documents plus attribute data in databases). Design data can be held in two and three-dimensional formats. Data centers managing this category of digital resource recommend the "Digital Information Migration" strategy and tend to rely on a combination of the "Backward Compatibility," "Interoperability," and "Convert to Standard Formats" subsets. For interchange they tend to rely on the de facto "DXF" format or "IGES" for two and three dimensional vector graphics. Standard formatted forms include HPGL; Encapsulated PostScript, and TIFF.

Design data managers hold parts catalogues, technical manuals, standards and procedures in SGML and hold images of old drawings and reports, and so forth, in TIFF Group 4 format. As a backup many also endorse the "Change Media" subset where formatted page images of digital documents could be output to 35mm microfilm. For modern design data there should be no need to adopt any "Technology Preservation" or "Technology Emulation" strategies. A pragmatic short-term solution for digital resources created on leading CAD applications would be to rely on the "Backward Compatibility" of the application. However, this should be seen as a short-term solution and should be backed up by converting the documents to a standard formatted form or changing the media.

For older design data then "Convert to Standard Formats" is the preferred subset. "Technology Preservation" or "Technology Emulation" would be relied on only where valuable design data had been left on a proprietary platform which was now obsolete and where valuable data would be lost in translating the data to a standard format.

One problem area would be where–for a given product–all vital attribute and context data plus the links between the design data and documents were held in a proprietary Product Data Management system. Increasingly the trend would be to build the PDM system on top of a standard database engine and to hold all the design data and documents in standard formats.

If a proprietary PDM system was used and became obsolete, the centre would need to preserve the operating environment the PDM system ran on until they developed a migration strategy. The migration strategy would need to allow them to capture the links in a standard form and export the documents and design data in a standard form. The effort involved in recreating the links on a preferred open PDM system would be prohibitive in most cases.

Presentation Graphics

Presentation graphics can cover a range of data types. The bulk would comprise vector graphics (CAD); raster graphics; animation (moving graphics) and alphanumeric data. A judgment could be taken on how valuable the moving graphics were, for example, a PowerPoint presentation with build-up graphics could be archived as a series of static frames without much loss of value. Data centres managing this category of digital resource would be able to adopt the "Digital Information Migration" strategy and rely on a combination of the

"Backward Compatibility," "Convert to Standard Formats," and "Change Media" subsets. Standard formatted forms include PostScript, Adobe PDF, and TIFF.

As a backup, data centres could adopt the "Change Media" subset where formatted page images of digital documents could be output to microfilm or paper. For presentation graphics created on de facto standard packages there should be no need to adopt any "Technology Preservation" or "Technology Emulation" strategies. A pragmatic short term solution for digital resources created on the leading de facto presentation graphics applications would be to rely on the "Backward Compatibility" of the application. However, this should be seen as a short-term solution and should be backed up by converting the documents to a standard formatted form or changing the media.

For older presentation graphics then "Convert to Standard Formats" is the preferred subset. "Technology Preservation" or "Technology Emulation" would be relied on only where valuable presentations had been left on a proprietary platform which was now obsolete and where valuable data would be lost in translating the data to a standard format.

Visual Images

The bulk of visual images, self-evidently, will comprise one dominant data type: raster graphics data. Where large collections are held then attribute data relating to the images will be held as alphanumeric data and managed in a database. Most data centres that specialise in the preservation of visual images have adopted the "Digital Information Migration" strategy and specifically the "Convert to Standard Formats "subset. There are two main issues which face data centre managers preserving visual images.

The first issue–if the images are not held in digital form at the time of deposit and hence have to be scanned and digitised–is what resolution should the images be scanned at and should they be captured and held as black and white; greyscale or colour images. If the decision is colour then what coding scheme should be adopted? The answer varies depending on the range of material to be captured as images. In addition the cost of all the options also needs to be taken into account. High-resolution colour images take a very long time to capture and create very large file sizes.

The second issue relates to what file format the image data should be stored in and whether or not the image data should be compressed and, if so, what compression algorithm should be used. For visual images a well-equipped centre should not need to rely on any other preservation strategy.

Speech/Sound Recordings

It is important to distinguish between speech and all other sounds. Speech has a semantic content. Digital speech processing can be divided up into three areas:

- **Speech Coding:** The analogue to digital conversion of speech signals or waveforms; the compression of the digital signals and the reverse digital to analogue conversion for play back purposes. Standard digital telephony employs pulse code modulation and logarithmic coding and a sampling rate of 8 kHz and 8 bit code words is used to give a bit rate of 64 kbps. The bandwidth needed to transmit or record speech is smaller than that needed for other sounds e g music due to the narrower range of frequencies used when talking. Hence the number of bits needed to code 1 minute of speech is less than the number of bits needed to record 1 minute of music.
- **Speech Synthesis:** The translation by computers of a coded description of a message into speech (e.g., computers talking to people).

- **Speech Recognition and Speech Understanding:** The individual components of speech–the words–are recognised. This facilitates people talking to computers and dictating text or issuing commands, and so forth.

Non speech sounds do not generally have a complex semantic context. Non speech sound processing can therefore be divided up into two areas:

- **Sound Coding:** The analogue to digital conversion of sound signals, the compression and/or storage of the digital signal, and the reverse digital to analogue conversion for play back purposes.
- **Waveform Sound Can Be Uncompressed as on Audio Compact Discs or Compressed:** Any sound, including speech and music, can be recorded in this way. Compact Disc Digital Audio recording employs pulse code modulation and linear coding and a sampling rate of 44.1 kHz and 16 bit code words. The CD Audio standard supports stereophonic sound over two channels. Hence the aggregated bit rate for a stereophonic CD audio bitstream is 1.411 Mbps.
- **Music Can Also Be Described in a Symbolic Way:** We have used printed musical scores for centuries. For computer systems the Musical Instrument Digital Interface (MIDI) standard defines how to code all the elements of musical scores including notes, timing conditions and the instruments to play each note. MIDI is a much more compact coding technique than digitised samples.

The sound files which data centre managers need to preserve will generally contain sound data coded either as a digitised analog sound signal or as notes for a MIDI instrument. A MIDI file usually has a MID file extension. A WAVE or WAV file is the "de facto"standard for storing an analog signal in digital form under MS Windows. This is a very specialised area where individual studies need to be conducted by experts in the field of digital speech and sound recording and processing.

It appears that data centres managing this category of digital resource would be able to adopt the "Digital Information Migration" strategy and rely on a combination of the "Backward Compatibility," "Convert to Standard Formats" and Change Media subsets. For sound files created on de facto standard packages there should be no need to adopt any "Technology Preservation" or "Technology Emulation" strategies. A pragmatic short-term solution for digital resources created on the leading de facto applications would be to rely on the "Backward Compatibility" of the application. However, this should be seen as a short-term solution and should be backed up by converting the documents to a standard form.

Video Recordings

The bulk of digital video recordings, self-evidently, will comprise one dominant data type – motion video or moving image data. Increasingly digital video resources also contain interleaved audio data as well. Where large collections are held then attribute data relating to the moving images or interleaved audio and video data will be held as alphanumeric data and managed in a database. This is a very specialised area and is still a relatively new area where individual studies need to be conducted by experts in the field of digital video recording and processing.

Most data centres that specialise in the preservation of film and video recordings are still in the early stages when it comes to collecting and preserving digital video data. The bulk of holdings will still be in analogue film or videotape formats. Where practical, such centres have adopted the "Digital Information Migration" strategy and specifically the "Convert to Standard Formats" subset. The MPEG standards provide several standards for the compression of full motion video.

However, this is an area where early digital video material was inevitably created on proprietary applications and held in proprietary formats. Where the applications are now obsolete and unsupported then centres would have to turn to a "Technology Preservation" or "Technology Emulation" strategy to preserve the data until such time as they can work out an acceptable migration strategy.

Geographic/Mapping Databases

Geographic/mapping data can cover almost all data types. The bulk would comprise raster graphics (base mapping data) and vector graphics and alphanumeric data (attribute data – links, and so forth, in databases). Geographic data can be held in two and three-dimensional formats. This is a much specialised area where individual studies need to be conducted by experts in the field of GIS systems and mapping data.

Chris Perkins has already helpfully arranged cartographic software packages in increasing order of difficulty and functionality ranging from atlases and route planners right up to full Geographical Information Systems (GIS).

Data centres managing this category of digital resource recommend the "Digital Information Migration" strategy and rely on a combination of the "Backward Compatibility," "Interoperability," and "Convert to Standard Formats" subsets with "Change Media" as the backup option.

For modern mapping data there should be no need to adopt any "Technology Preservation" or "Technology Emulation" strategies. A pragmatic short-term solution for digital resources created on the leading de facto mapping applications and GIS systems would be to rely on the "Backward Compatibility" of the application. However, this should be seen as a short - term solution and should be backed up by converting the data to as standard a form as possible.

"Technology Preservation" or "Technology Emulation" would need to be relied on where valuable data had been left on a proprietary platform which was now obsolete and where valuable data would be lost in translating the data to a standard format.

The main problem area is where–for a given GIS database–all the vital attribute data and coordinates and all the links between the vector layers and the raster data are held in a proprietary GIS system which becomes obsolete. Here the centre would need to preserve the operating environment that the GIS system ran on until they developed a migration strategy. The migration strategy would need to allow them to capture the coordinates and the links in a standard form and export the documents and data in a standard form. The effort involved in recreating the links on a preferred GIS database would be very high in most cases.

Communicating Multimedia Publications

By definition multimedia publications comprise at least three data types. Most multimedia publications will comprise motion video and audio data interleaved; many will comprise animation and interleaved audio data and most will comprise some still images and graphics and alphanumeric data. Most of the early multimedia publications will have been produced on one of the CD formats and will have been authored and edited using proprietary multimedia editing and authoring packages. They will be accessed via proprietary access software.

This is again a very specialised area and is still a relatively new area where individual studies need to be conducted by experts in the field of interactive multimedia who appreciate the specific challenges and risks which a migration strategy pose to interactive multimedia publications. This is probably the most difficult category of digital resource to preserve today out of the ten categories covered by this report.

It is a fact that many valuable multimedia publications were created using proprietary editing, authoring and access software which is now no longer supported and which does not work on current hardware and software platforms. Given the fact, then data centre managers will have to adopt a "Technology Preservation" or "Technology Emulation" strategy to preserve the data until they can develop a practical migration strategy. It may prove impossible to migrate the data in future without the loss of considerable data.

Table 4 summarises the results gained in this first attempt to apply the model to the ten categories of digital resources defined for this study.

Table 4. Digital resources

	Digital Resource	Preservation Strategy	Subset of Strategy	Notes
1	Data Sets	Digital Information Migration	Convert To Standard Formats	
2	Structured Texts	Digital Information Migration	Convert To Standard Formats	
3	Office Documents	Digital Information Migration	Convert To Standard, Formats, Backward Compatibility, Change Media.	
4	Design Data	Digital Information, Migration	Backward, Compatibility, Interoperability, Convert To Standard Formats, Change Media.	Technology Preservation/ Emulation as short term strategy for product data on obsolete systems.
5	Presentation Graphics	Digital Information Migration	Backward Compatibility, Convert To Standard Formats, Change Media.	
6	Visual Images	Digital Information Migration	Backward Compatibility, Convert To Standard Formats, Change Media.	
7	Speech/Sound Recordings	Digital Information Migration	Backward Compatibility, Convert, To Standard Formats, Change Media.	A specialised area where additional work is needed by experts in the field.
8	Video Recordings	Digital Information Migration	Backward Compatibility, Convert To Standard Formats, Change Media.	A specialised area where additional work is needed by experts in the field, Technology preservation/emulation. needed in short term where data locked in proprietary systems
9	Geographic/ Mapping Databases	Digital Information Migration	Backward Compatibility; Interoperability; Convert To Standard Formats;	A specialised area where additional work is needed by experts in the field; Technology preservation/emulation needed in short term where data locked in proprietary systems
10	Interactive Multimedia Publications	Technology preservation/ emulation in short term for data in proprietary. systems until agreed migration strategies can be developed		A specialised area where additional work is needed by experts in the field.

HOW CLOUD PLATFORM OR SERVER VIRTUALIZATION WILL BE USEFUL FOR DIGITAL PRESERVATION

Digital preservation deals with the problem of retaining the meaning of digital information over time to ensure its accessibility. The process often involves a workflow which transforms the digital objects. The workflow defines document pipelines containing transformations and validation checkpoints, either to facilitate migration for persistent archival or to extract metadata. The transformations, nevertheless, are computationally expensive, and therefore digital preservation can be out of reach for an organization whose core operation is not in data conservation. The operations described the document workflow, however, do not frequently reoccur. This chapter combines an implementation-independent workflow designer with cloud computing to support small institution in their ad-hoc peak computing needs that stem from their efforts in digital preservation.

Digital preservation (DP) combines policies, strategies and actions to ensure that digital objects remain authentic and accessible to users and systems over a long period of time, regardless the challenges of component and management failures, natural disasters or attacks (Barateiro, Antunes, Borbinha, & Lisboa, 2009). This includes the preservation of materials resulting from digital reformatting, but particularly of information that is born-digital and has no analog counterpart. While DP has a vast literature exposing the wide array of associated issues, here we would like to focus on only three aspects: migration and transformation, scalability, and reusability.

The first aspect refers to the problem of keeping the content of legacy file formats accessible. This problem is most prominent with proprietary file formats for which documentation is not available. Once the vendor stops sup- port for the associated software products, these files face digital obsolescence. A common solution to the problem is migration in which older formats are transformed to a more persistent format.

Secondly, dynamic collections and environments for DP require technical scalability to face technology evolution. Existing static collections, for instance, a digitized historical archive, where no new items will be added, will have a fixed data size. Although it will not be necessary to add new components to increase the storage capacity, it may be necessary to replace components or transform the objects in the collection. These requirements ask for scalability. Achieving this of DP may require specific investments in an infrastructure for storing, maintaining, and managing data. Such costs can be prohibitive for organizations whose core business is not data conservation and that do not have a considerable budget for investments in information technology.

The third important aspect of DP that we would like focus on is to enable the reuse of digital content. Reuse of digital content covers its subsequent verification and its exploitation with a novel purpose, potentially by new consumers. Since consumers are unable to refer back to the creators, reuse of preserved digital objects depends on proper descriptions provided through the archive. In this sense, reuse of digital content asks for metadata on both the content and how it was transformed to its most recent form. This is where document process preservation helps, which provides an architecture-independent description of the intent behind a document process.

The above three points are not unrelated. Migration and transformation can be regarded as part of a larger problem described in the third point: we need to preserve not just the documents, but also how they were processed. The second point is, of course, crucial: Let it be migration or metadata extraction, these operations are computationally expensive. SHAMAN (Sustaining Heritage Access through

Multivalent Archiving) is an integrated project, cofunded by the European Commission under the seventh RTD Framework Programme. The aim of this project is to investigate the long-term preservation of large volumes of digital objects in a distributed environment, by developing a preservation framework that is verifiable, open and extensible. SHAMAN is focusing its research on: integrating data grid, digital library and persistent archive technologies; developing support for context representation and annotation, with deep linguistic analysis and corresponding semantics; and modeling of preservation processes. In this chapter, we describe a system developed in SHAMAN which combines a document process designer for digital preservation with scalable computational resources that are available for small organizations: cloud computing.

Figure 2. Architectural overview of Document processing in the cloud to support digital preservation

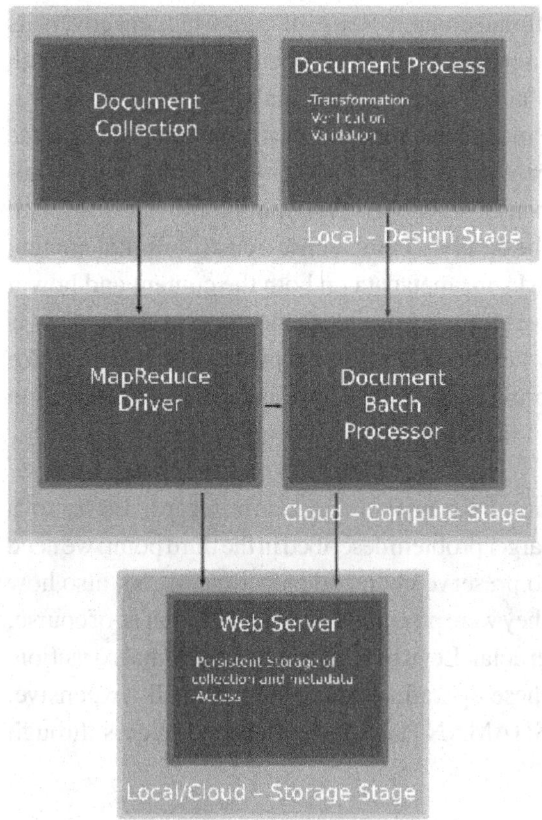

CONCLUSION

With a paradigm shift in the making toward a service-oriented architecture, digital preservation is one of the areas to benefit from this change. (See Figure 2.) Considerations suggest that especially small organizations should welcome the turn as an attractive upcoming solution to their related problems. To test the feasibility of this assumption, we tested the workflow designer in a cloud processing environment to show that the process is smoothly running. As first results by cloud computing suggest, even a single node m1 large instance has a performance close to that of a decent workstation which makes running Xeproc possible for everyone. Moreover, a single workstation may be more expensive to rent for a longer term than running the same calculations on a cluster, as shown in the average cost diagrams. By picking the cloud configuration with the lowest estimated average cost, bulky DP jobs can be done at an affordable price and with flexibility beyond that of fixed resources.

Therefore we believe that the architecture outlined in this paper advances the state-of-the-art in digital preservation for the following reasons:

- The procurement of an expensive server or a grid can be replaced by service-level agreements with the cloud provider.
- The flexibility is unprecedented in terms of scale and in terms document process design.
- Ad-hoc peak computations that are typical in document format migration are easily addressed.
- Persistent storage in the cloud is a viable alternative to local servers.

Archiving of Digital Information called for a deep infrastructure of institutions, services, technologies, and qualified personnel capable of supporting a distributed system of digital archives. This report examined one component of this infrastructure in detail: archives, libraries, museums, and other repositories that have been instrumental in preserving and providing access to scholarly communications, documentary heritage, and other cultural resources in traditional formats. It is clear that many of these institutions are beginning to add digital preservation to their array of preservation responsibilities, although most are taking only the first steps in this direction. Since 1995, the number of institutions that acquire digital materials and that convert traditional formats to digital form has more than doubled. Only one respondent does not anticipate taking responsibility for digital preservation within the next three years. There is a gap between current models for digital preservation and the status of digital preservation in many institutions. Institutions with large digital collections and more years of experience generally have policies in place that govern acquisition, storage, refreshing, and migration of digital materials. But the majority of institutions have not developed digital preservation policies or established methods to preserve digital information. Several factors help explain the slow pace of development of digital preservation programs. For many institutions, digital preservation is a new challenge and they are just beginning to confront the policy, technological and human resource implications of digital preservation. Institutions are seeking better methods and more affordable services to tackle the problems posed by technology obsolescence. Insufficient resources and inadequate planning for digital preservation also are considered major obstacles to digital preservation, and only a few institutions have experts in digital preservation on their staff or available through consultation arrangements. Finally, the absence of a clear consensus about effective strategies and methods for digital preservation and the paucity of data on the resource implications of various proposed strategies serve as deterrents to concrete actions by institutions.

REFERENCES

Barateiro, J., Antunes, G., Borbinha, J., & Lisboa, P. (2009). Addressing digital preservation: Proposals for new perspectives. [st *International Workshop on Innovation in Digital Preservation.* Austin, TX: Innovation in Digital Preservation.]. *Proceedings of InDP, 09*, 1.

Besser, H., Trant, J., & Robinson, P. (1993). *Introduction to imaging: Issues in constructing an image database.* Oxford, UK: Oxford University Computing Services.

Borbinha, J. (2010). SHAMAN: Sustaining heritage access through multivalent archiving. *ERCIM News, 80.*

Engel, F., Klas, C., Brocks, H., Kranstedt, G., Ja¨schke, G., & Hemmje, M. (2009, December). Towards supporting context-oriented information retrieval in a scientific-archive based information life cycle. In Proceedings of Cultural Heritage Online, Empowering Users: An Active Role for User Communities (pp. 135–140). Florence, Italy: Cultural Heritage Online.

Gennaro, R. D. (1996, September 23-26). JSTOR: The Andrew W. Mellon foundation's journal storage project. In A. H. Helal & J. W. Weiss (Eds.), *Proceedings of the 19th International Essen Symposium* (pp. 223-230). Essen, Germany: Universitatsbibliothek Essen.

Gennaro, R. D. (1997, August 31 - September 5). JSTOR: Building an Internet accessible digital archive of retrospective journals. In *Proceedings of the 63rd IFLA General Conference*. IFLA.

Innocenti, P., Ross, S., Maceciuvite, E., Wilson, T., Ludwig, J., & Pempe, W. (2009, October). Assessing digital preservation frameworks: The approach of the SHAMAN project. In *Proceedings of MEDES-09 1st International Conference on Management of Emergent Digital EcoSystems* (pp. 412-416). New York: ACM Press.

Jacquin, T., De'jean, H., & Chanod, J. P. (2010). Xeproc c: A model-based approach towards document process preservation in research and advanced technology for digital libraries. In M. Lalmas, J. Jose, A. Rauber, F. Sebastiani, & I. Frommholz (Eds.), *Proceedings of the 14th European Conference (ECDL 2010)* (LNCS), (vol. 6273, pp. 538-541). Berlin: Springer Berlin Heidelberg.

MacCarn, D., (1997, January - July). Towards a universal data format for the preservation of media. *SMPTE*, 477-479.

Matthews, G., Poulter, A., & Blagg, E. (1997). *Preservation of digital materials, policy and strategy issues for the UK: ISC/NPO studies on the preservation of electronic materials (report 41)*. London: BL Research & Innovation.

Mohlhenrich, J. (1993). *Preservation of electronic formats: Electronic formats for preservation*. Fort Atkinson, WI: Highsmith Press.

National Library of Australia. (1997). *Statement of principles: Preservation of and long term access to Australian digital objects*. Canberra, Australia: National Preservation Office.

Rothenberg, J. (1995). Ensuring the longevity of digital documents. *Scientific American, 272*(1), 42. doi:10.1038/scientificamerican0195-42.

Chapter 4
Cloud Computing and Its Application to Information Centre

Nihal Alam
The Energy and Resources Institute (TERI), India

Ranjan Karmakar
The Energy and Resources Institute (TERI), India

ABSTRACT

Information and communication technologies are developing very fast and providing us opportunities due to their benefits such as reduced cost, anytime, anywhere availability, as well as its elasticity and flexibility. Cloud computing is one of the newly emerged models for technology that provide us the facility of central remoting of servers to maintain data, software, and application through the use of the Internet. Nowadays it is widely applicable in many areas such as libraries, information centres, in-house, applications and digital library services. Our chapter will focus mainly on: Models of cloud computing, types of cloud suitable for information centres, application of cloud computing with examples, opportunity and risk in developing cloud services, and impact of cloud computing to information centres.

INTRODUCTION

Cloud computing is a new computing paradigm appeared in 2006, and the evolutionary offspring of parallel computing, distributed computing, utility computing, and grid computing, and the developmental outcome of network storage, virtualization, and load balance (Vaquero, Rodero-Merino, Caceres, & Lindner, 2009). The main idea of cloud computing is to build a virtualized computing resource pool by centralizing abundant computing resources connected with network and present the service of infrastructure, platform and software. This network that offers various computing resources is called "cloud" (Kamoun, 2009). As a supercomputing paradigm based on the Internet, cloud computing allows users to dynamically share a mass of hardware, software and data resource, and charges according to their actual usage. Therefore, computing power can be sold and purchased as merchandise easily by network in a low price, just like water, gas and electric power.

DOI: 10.4018/978-1-4666-4631-5.ch004

Cloud computing is an innovator thing similar to electric power changing from a single generator to a centralized electric power plant.

Cloud computing is a buzzword...The concept, quite simply, is that vast computing resources will reside somewhere out there in the ether (rather than in your computer room) and we'll connect to them and use them as needed. - Jonathan Weber (The Times Online)

BACKGROUND

In the networked environment of client-server technology new era was identified which is called as 'fourth Stage' in the evolution of library technology (Lavagnino, 1997), which defined the cloud computing as use of remote computing resources through the Internet. "At the foundation of cloud computing is the broader concept of converged infrastructure and shared services" (Wikipedia, n.d.).

More specifically, as National Institute of Standards and Technology (NIST) defines it, as "a model for enabling ubiquitous, convenient, on-demand network access to a shared pool of configurable computing resources" (Mell & Grance, 2011). By NIST's definition, the cloud is composed of three service or management models and four deployment models. The three service models include Software as a Service (SaaS), Platform as a Service (PaaS) and Infrastructure as a Service (IaaS). Private Cloud, Community Cloud, Public Cloud and Hybrid Cloud are the four common deployment models.

All these models share the same essential characteristics for end users:

- **On-Demand Self-Service:** Where end users can increase or decrease their service, such as mobile phone talk time or data storage size, as needed without requiring human intervention.
- **Broad Network Access (BNA):** This means that a user's can access the service through standard mechanisms like mobile phones and tablets in addition to desktop computers.
- **Resource Pooling:** It describes the nature of cloud computing – a cluster of hardware and software.
- **Rapid Elasticity:** Cloud-based services can be started at the minimum and easily adjusted in quantity as demanded by users at any time.
- **Measured Service (Mell & Grance, 2011):** Means system resources and performance are metered, similar to a traditional public utility, such as electricity.

The concept of cloud computing is in use for many years, but in recent years has it become a highlighted and come in picture. In the year 1990s, cloud computing was developed by major IT providers such as Sun, Microsoft, Google, and Amazon. Different products came into use for different levels of users. The most popular services for end users include web-based email systems (SaaS), e.g. AOL, Gmail, Hotmail, and Yahoo! Mail, and office applications such as Google Docs, Microsoft MS Office Online, Cloud-canvas.com, and Write.fm, etc. Developers can run their programs on the cloud (PaaS) like Google AppEngine, Windows Azure, and Force.com. Companies or organizations store or backup their large data on remote servers (IaaS), for example, Rackspace, Microsoft Azure, Animoto, Jungle Disk and Amazon's EC2 or S3 servers.

2011, the Primary Research Group (PRG) published a report of its recently conducted survey on library use of cloud computing (Primary Research Group, 2011). Participants included 70 libraries worldwide with the majority from the United States. The survey report reveals that 61.97 percent of libraries in the sample used free SaaS while 22.54 percent of libraries sampled used paid subscription SaaS; less than 3 percent of libraries surveyed used PaaS, and 4.23 percent used IaaS. Most libraries using PaaS or IaaS had annual budgets over $5,000,000. Smaller libraries usually used the servers of their parent organizations, while libraries with multi-million dollar budgets tended to use their own servers.

Few case studies also show the exploration and adoption of other models of cloud computing in libraries. For example, California State University libraries have migrated their key library systems to vendors' cloud-based servers (i.e. a public cloud) and to campus IT's internally virtualized environment (i.e. a private cloud) (Wang, 2012). The Burritt Library at Central Connecticut State University used Amazon's S3 to back up their high-resolution digital objects (Iglesias, 2011). Murray State University library experimented with Dropbox for library services (Bagley, 2011). University of Arizona Libraries have migrated their ILS, Digital Libraries website, Interlibrary Loan system and repository software to cloud-based services (Han, 2010). The Z. Smith Reynolds Library in Winston Salem, NC, started to use Amazon's EC2 for hosting its website, discovery services, and digital library services in 2009 (Mitchell, 2010b).

The service model represent server administration and maintenance responsibilities are moved from local personnel to the hosting vendor, while the management of the application remains in the traditional way, i.e. librarians are still able to access the backend of the system for local customizations as if they were managing the system locally.

Popular examples of the discovery tool include Ex Libris' Primo (Ex Libris Primo, n.d.), OCLC's WorldCat Local (OCLC, n.d.a), EBSCO's EBSCO Discovery Service (EBSCO, n.d.), and SerialsSolutions' Summon (SerialsSolutions, n.d.). Examples of the next generation library management services are Ex Libris' Alma (Ex Libris Alma, n.d.), Innovative Interfaces' Sierra (Sierra, n.d.), Kuali Foundation's Kuali OLE (Kuali, n.d.), and OCLC's WorldShare Management System (OCLC, n.d.b).

Although these solutions are cloud-based, their service model and data model are different. For example, WorldShare is a single shared instance and does not offer local installation option. The data model of WorldShare is OCLC's WorldCat, a world-wide union catalog, in which "the concept of importing or transferring bibliographic records into a local system no longer applies, because no local system needs to exist with this approach" (Breeding, 2012, p. 45). Similarly Alma can also be deployed as a local installation on either cloud-based or local infrastructure. Its data model is local but sharable with its community.

Shifting library core applications to cloud-based services will reduce or eliminate most or the entire local technical needs in managing server hardware and operating systems that underlie the applications also primary responsibility for managing system configurations remains about the same, it may be limited to processes such as customizing end user interfaces and branding. Application Programming Interfaces (APIs) are usually offered with the cloud-based applications for integrating with other systems or components of the local technical infrastructure. Because cloud computing services are provided via the Internet, the quality of the network connectivity and related aspects such as security and privacy are equally very important.

MAIN FOCUS OF THE CHAPTER

Adoption of many levels of cloud computing technology has moved into the focus and become an important topic of debate and discussion about the technologies. These technology drive new technology trend and the benefits of cloud computing, which increases number of libraries in shifting their key applications and services over the cloud.

Library Science history revealed that Librarians are "a product of the paradigm shift of the library" (Erlandson, 2010, p. 12). For easy conceptualizing the evolution of systems librarianship, the simple stage model defined by Lavagnino (Lavagnino, 1997) is borrowed.

The major role was born in the "second stage" when online catalog systems on mainframe and mini-computer technologies replaced the library's card catalogs.

Due to technologies advanced and microcomputers began to raise in libraries a 'third stage' and the ILS (Integrated Library System) was born, which give raise to systems departments. When server technologies replaced mainframes and minicomputers, and the Internet and World Wide web came into being which is called as 'fourth stage', where the roles and responsibilities and librarian expanded in depth, casing the evolution of expert librarianship or may called as System Librarian "is now a bona fide segment of the library profession" (Wilson, 1998, p. 21). It represents a blend of library science, computer operations, and management.

Wilson (Wilson, 1998, p. 37-42) defined, the skill sets required for a systems librarian that comprises library skills, managerial skills, and IT skills. Library skills include understanding of library mission and services, research process, data structures related to library materials, knowledge organization and classification, information retrieval and policy. IT skills include desktop and server operating systems administration, programming, database management, systems and network designs, as well as the Internet technologies. Also communication, ability in management is equally important for s sustainable system librarian.

Above quality are in part shared with other librarians and with computer specialists who may come from non-library backgrounds such as computer science, information science, or computer engineering.

CLOUD COMPUTING SYSTEM

Cloud computing involves a paradigm shift, both because the location of processing and data storage changes from the organization's computers to servers on the Internet (Kamoun, 2009; & Hayes, 2008), and because computational resources used have an elastic processing power and high availability, enabling one to talk about a new computational model (Voas & Zhang, 2009). As seen below, Figure 1 clearly depicts the relationship between cloud server to service directory through different modules.

Indeed, cloud computing is defined by the U.S. National Institute of Standards and Technology (NIST) as a "model for enabling ubiquitous, convenient, on-demand network access to a shared pool of configurable computing resources (e.g., networks, servers, storage, applications, and services) that can be rapidly provisioned and released with minimal management effort or service provider interaction" (Mell & Grance, 2011). EU (Jeffery, Neidecker, & Lutz, 2010) adopts a broader definition in its recent report and explains the cloud as an elastic execution environment of resources involving multiple stakeholders and providing a metered service at multiple granu-

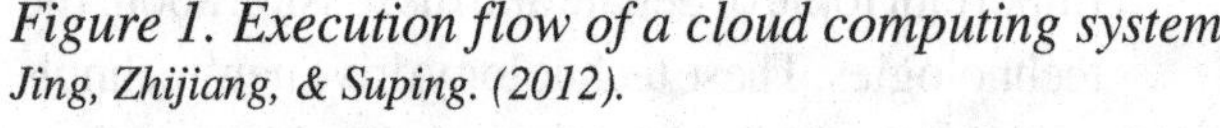

Figure 1. Execution flow of a cloud computing system
Jing, Zhijiang, & Suping. (2012).

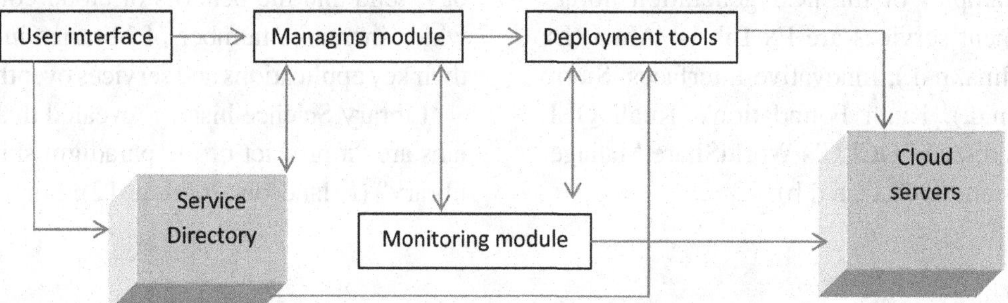

larities for a specified level of quality (of service). European Community for Software and Software Services (ECSS) describes cloud computing as the delivery of computational resources from a location other than your current one. Accordingly, it is a style of computing in which IT-related capabilities are provided "as a service" allowing users to access technology-enabled services from the Internet without knowledge of, expertise with, or control over the technology infrastructure that supports them. This cloud model is composed of five essential characteristics, three service models, and four deployment models. The five essential characteristics are (Mell & Grance, 2011):

1. **On-Demand Self-Service:** That is the unilateral provision of computing capabilities (e.g., server time, network storage) as needed, without requiring intervention of the service provider.
2. **Network Access:** Capabilities are accessed through standard mechanisms and by heterogeneous client platforms (e.g., mobile phones, tablets, laptops, and workstations).
3. **Resource Sharing:** Computing resources (e.g., storage, processing, memory, and network bandwidth) are pooled, by the provider, to serve multiple consumers using a multi-tenant model. The customer generally has no control or knowledge over the exact location of the provided resources but may be able to specify location at a higher level of abstraction (e.g., country, state, or datacenter).
4. **Elasticity:** Capabilities can be elastically provisioned and released, to scale depending on consumer's demand. The capabilities available typically appear to be unlimited, from the consumer's viewpoint.
5. **Measured Service:** Cloud systems automatically control and optimize resource use by leveraging a metering capability at a level of abstraction appropriate to the type of service (e.g., storage, processing, bandwidth, and active user accounts).

Service Models define the kinds of services provided by the service provider and are summarized in Table 1.

In every service model, the consumer does not manage or control the underlying cloud infrastructure including network, servers, operating systems, or storage, with the possible exception of user specific configuration settings for the provided applications, in the case of SaaS, or the provided application-hosting environment, in the case of PaaS. In the IaaS model, the consumer also does not manage or control the underlying cloud infrastructure but has control over the operating sys-

Table 1. Service models in cloud computing (Mell & Grance, 2011)

Service Model	Description	Resources Managed by the User	Examples
Software as a Service (SaaS)	The consumer uses the provider's applications running on a cloud infrastructure.	Possibly, user-specific application configuration settings.	Google Docs, Salesforce, SAP Business by Design are the examples for SaaS.
Platform as a Service (PaaS)	The consumer deploys to the cloud infrastructure applications created or acquired by him/her, libraries, services, and tools supported by the provider.	User has control over the deployed applications and, possibly, some configuration settings for the application-hosting environment.	Google App Engine, Windows Azure, Force.com can be the examples for PaaS.
Infrastructure as a Service (IaaS)	The consumer is able to deploy and run arbitrary software, which can include operating systems and applications, to the storage, networks, and other computing resources provided by the provider.	User has control over operating systems, storage, and deployed applications; and possibly limited control of select networking components (e.g., host firewalls).	Amazon, IBM, Microsoft's Azure are examples for IaaS.

tems, storage, and deployed applications. In what concerns to the possession and management of the cloud infrastructure, four deployment models can be considered (Cloud computing Issues and Impact & Borko, 2010):

1. **Private Cloud:** Cloud infrastructure is meant for exclusive use by a single organization.
2. **Public Cloud:** The cloud infrastructure is aimed at the general public, and exists on the premises of the cloud provider. It is owned, managed, and operated by a cloud service provider organization. For example, Google and Microsoft.
3. **Hybrid Cloud:** The cloud infrastructure is a combination of two or more distinct cloud infrastructures (private or public) that are bound together by standardized or proprietary technology that enables data and application portability (e.g., cloud bursting for load balancing between clouds).
4. **Community Cloud:** The cloud infrastructure is aimed at a specific community of consumers from organizations or groups with shared concerns. Its ownership, management and operation may be the responsibility of one or more of the organizations in the community, a third party, or some combination of them, and it may exist on or off premises.

ISSUES, CONTROVERSIES, PROBLEMS

Cloud computing offers many benefits as it allows to set up what is essentially a virtual platform and services to give you the flexibility of connecting to your business needs anywhere, any time. With respective to growing number of web-enabled devices used in today's information era (e.g. smart phones, tablets), access to your data is even easier. There are many benefits to moving library services to the cloud, but obviously the benefits come with risks—it's just a matter of knowing if the benefits outweigh the risks and vice versa. Table 2 gives you the complete picture of the cloud risk to libraries and its consequences which is evaluated by using five basic parameters (Cloud computing for business & Risks and Benefits of Cloud Computing).

SOLUTIONS AND RECOMMENDATIONS

The following solutions, suggestions and recommendations may be incorporated for a better application of cloud computing system with few examples:

IMPACT OF CLOUD COMPUTING TO INFORMATION CENTRES

The library community can apply the concept of cloud computing to amplify the power of cooperation and to build a more significant, unified presence on the Web, this approach of computing can help libraries in save their time and money while simplifying their services to end users.

The basic driving forces which constitute to virtualize the libraries and data centres to cloud computing are:

1. **Library Budget:** In an era of shrinking budgets especially for sector like library and documentation centres, it gets harder with each passing year to justify the purchase and maintenance of servers .Cloud computing offers price savings due to economies of scale and the fact that you're only paying for the resources you actually use. A report by the Brooking institution finds government agencies can save 20-25 of their IT costs and increase their business ability by migrating IT infrastructure to cloud (Cloud comput-

Table 2. Five basic parameters

Parameter	Risk	Benefits
1. Network	Cloud computing is totally dependent on the Internet connections and its major drawback of cloud computing is that you need Internet connection to access the cloud and this direct tie to the Internet means that system is prone to desecrates and service interruptions at any point of time.	Users are now more able to access data from servers irrespective of location, creating a more flexible and mobile work lifestyle for end user.
2. Developing Hybrid System / Standards	Many organization such as government and financial bodies have their own IT internal services and not like to put their data on cloud and following a legacy system due to unavailability of any standards that apply to all systems when it comes to connecting to new cloud systems	The low barrier of entry and the pay-per-use model offered by cloud computing makes it very versatile. Moving to cloud computing may reduce the cost of managing and maintaining your IT systems in library. Rather than purchasing expensive systems and equipment, Libraries can reduce operating costs in many ways like: • By including cost of system upgrades, new hardware and software in your contract • No longer need too much of IT expertized for running the server • Energy consumption costs may be reduced • There are fewer time delays
3. Reliability	Organizations usually outsource data and application services to a centralized provider. In cloud computing, we know that network dependency is a drawback due to outages. Centralized data can certainly add another risk to cloud computing: If the provider's service goes down, all clients are affected.	There is still more reliability in comparison to in-house systems because of the economies of scale. This may be: • The vendor is more able to give 24/7 technical support • Highly trained experienced staff to support the infrastructure at its best condition • Benefits will reach all their clients as compare this to each organization having a team of on-site IT people with varied skill set.
4. Data Security and protection	One can easily understand about the data protection and integrity if we can think of putting everything on cloud because there are always people out there who continuously improving their hacking skills.	There are security risks with cloud computing but small organization like Library/data centres which is smaller, new low-budget for implementing security systems and less know-how about security technology will have more security gain as compare to in house data storage system
5. Flexibility and Legal Licensing	Need to be aware of various legislative and regulatory requirements when storing personal data, if the data is being stored outside of Singapore (e.g. if your business uses an overseas service provider), you will also need to be aware of the legislation and regulation requirements in that geographic location.	Collaboration efficiency in a cloud environment gives more opportunity to share for value added services, communicate to outside of the traditional methods. Say for example working on a project/ services across different locations, you could use cloud computing to give employees, contractors and third parties access to the same files.

ing Issues and Impact, Winds of Change: Libraries and Cloud Computing & Cloud computing).

2. **Personal:** Getting tech guy is always problem in libraries; which is major concerns to set up IT infrastructure and services. It is cloud computing which decreases the pressure on information professionals to become hard-core IT professionals, if the services will be provided through cloud then this will reduces IT barriers to market entry.
3. **Sustainability of Cloud:** To set up a small data centres will required, a capacity planning, cooling management system, disaster plan and to get ready with the server crashes. These sets of problems can be resolved at one go; simply by adopting the cloud concepts. Also cloud computing yield a better infrastructure results in lower power network efficiency results in lower power consumption and smaller carbon footprints.
4. **Service Level Agreements (SLA):** Cloud computing provide cheap and pay-as-you-use computing resources are rapidly gaining momentum compare to alternative (SLA) between consumers and providers emerge as a key aspect. Due to the dynamic nature of the cloud, continuous monitoring on Quality of Service (QoS) attributes is necessary to enforce SLAs. In most of the case the SLA for cloud provider in term of up time of their server is remarkably satisfactory (Service Level Agreement in Cloud Computing).
5. **Cloud OPAC and Cloud Integrated Library system (ILS):** Over the past few years, numbers of ILS vendors have started offering cloud-hosted versions of their products. Even OCLC joined several other vendors last year when they began offering a cloud-based ILS tools that complement their existing cataloging tools (e.g. WorldCat and FirstSearch). Individuals and members of organizations were already choosing between desktop applications and cloud applications at large level when it comes to e-mail, RSS, file storage, word processing and other simple applications. (What is cloud computing and how will it affect libraries?)

APPLICATION OF CLOUD COMPUTING TO INFORMATION CENTRES

There is a vast implication of technological model to make the regular operational work of libraries more effective and less time consuming by using cloud computing concept.

1. **Ease access of Information to End Users:** Due to virtualization of data one can easily meet there information need irrespective of the distance ant time.
2. **Separation of Services:** There are numbers of services available under cloud one can use according to their need and requirement. Like account management to financial things such as licensing, fees, fines.
3. **Collaborate Closely with IT:** Finding solutions that help "go cloud" has considerably easier in recent years. For example, implementing cloud-based data storage used to involve custom solutions and an in-depth understanding of computing infrastructure. Services such as Dropbox (http://dropbox.com) and MobileMe (http://www.me.com) have made this process as simple as saving your data to a local folder on your hard drive.
4. Many Libraries using cloud tools as Google Chat, Skype, and Mailing Service for providing reference services.
5. Advertising the library new acquisitions and services using the Multimedia Resources of Cloud.

Table 3. Real world initiatives

1. 2011 OCLC delivered its Web-Scale Management Services, an ILS in the cloud.	6. The U.S. Library of Congress has entered into a partnership with Dura cloud for a one-year pilot program testing out cloud storage capabilities (see last month's interview with LC staffers for more), and OCLC has announced a new Webscale, cooperative library management service.
2. National Library of Australia's (NLA) Trove, has used the web to accomplish combining the collections of Australian libraries with other important Australian and international collections and information sources such a Wikipedia and to open much of this content so the public can tag it, edit it, collect it and review it.	7. HaithiTrust is a great example which shows us what cloud computing holds in store for the libraries. HaithiTrust is a repository for keeping huge amount of digitized data being shared among its members. It was founded in October 2008 and already has over sixty partners mostly including university libraries all around the world.
3. The Ohio LINK library consortium is using the Amazon's Web Services to host a handful of their Digital Resource Commons repository instances such as Kent State's Centennial Collection, and is testing server administration in the cloud, as well as the limits of Dspace repository software.	8. OAISTER is a service started by the University of Michigan and now managed by OCLC which seeks to harvest all the major digital repositories around the world.
4. The District of Columbia Public Library is using Amazon's EC2 service to host their website. They are also using Amazon's S3 service to back up their ILS, their upcoming digital repository uses Flickr, and Amazon EC2.	9. Europeana is gathering the digitized collections from European Galleries, Libraries, Archives and Museums.
5. At Western State College in Gunnison, Colorado, they are using Google's App Engine for their E-Library, and have also migrated two Microsoft Access databases that they used for serials circulations and government publication management.	10. OSS Labs, India has planned to move amazon's Elastic Cloud Computing platform due to Amazon's high durability of data, scalability, flexibility and the most important strong information security based on ISO 27000 Standards.

6. Acquisition Librarians managing diverse collections.
7. Electronic resource librarians managing burgeoning collections, and ever-changing list of vendors using the combined expertise and resources (Goldner, 2011).

EXAMPLES OF CLOUD COMPUTING IN LIBRARY AND INFORMATION CENTRES

In 2011 library vendors began to deliver Integrated Library Systems (ILS) and discovery tools as cloud solutions. Many vendors offer options to host the classic ILS as cloud solution, while some are developing a new generation of ILS especially for the cloud. It appears that most library systems will be delivered in the cloud in the future. For instance, Ex Libris will release Alma in early 2012. It is a cloud-based ILS with a discovery layer as its OPAC. Some of the real world initiatives of cloud solutions in libraries are listed out in the Table 3.

MAJOR CLOUD PROVIDERS FOR LIBRARIES AND INFORMATION CENTERS

- **Ex Libris:** Is a cloud service provider based in USA. Provides all the software and hardware cloud support and solutions for libraries and library consortia (Ex Libris: The Bridge to Knowledge).
- **Polaris Library System:** Is one of the cloud based library system available in the market. It offers acquisition and processing module (Polaris Library Systems).

- **DuraCloud:** Is the only service that makes it easy to move copies of your content into the cloud. Dura is the derivatives of DSpace digital library (Dura Cloud).

FUTURE RESEARCH DIRECTIONS

In the present era, the perceptions and proposed strategies in cloud computing environment (Liu, & Cai, 2013), the librarians make their livelihood simply by managing locally hosted library systems. This kind of situation is silently changing with the library systems moving onto the cloud: there will be less opportunity for systems librarians to perform routine systems administration work; instead, they will be acting more like coordinators of cloud-based library services, which involves dealing with campus IT and the vendors. As Iglesias (Iglesias, 2010, p. 74) states, "It is not that systems librarians are losing their role as technology specialists, but that they are increasingly becoming technology coordinators [. . .]"

Contrary to this, major changes will reduce the burden of handling constant and labor-intensive system upgrades, so librarians can use the time for other library functions. Opportunities exist in the areas of "providing tools to make it easier for the user to take existing knowledge and build new knowledge"; providing "contextual support" and "providing unique services that our users want, need and value" (Grant, 2012). Adding to this, developing new knowledge and skills and other emerging technologies will continue to be important for librarians. These technologies are closely related to library systems as cloud computing has broadened the network access from desktop workstations to mobile devices.

The rich features of cloud computing, that it is easy to use, flexible and with a lower upfront cost, can be both beneficial and challenging. By considering the advantage of these benefits, librarians may be able to explore new technology initiatives. However, at the same time, due to others' perception of these features, demands for quick responses to technological needs may be higher (Livingstone, 2011).

Librarians facing the new challenges in the cloud environment must update their IT professional skills "to accommodate emerging technologies and changing IT management and service delivery models" (EDUCAUSE, 2012). Of the skills noted earlier, all remain essential for systems librarians, except those that involve server operating system administration.

The traditional process of evaluating and purchasing systems will be changed to understanding and interpreting service level agreements (SLA) with campus IT or vendors. Having some understanding of pertinent legal terminology and institutional requirements is essential to systems librarians, because it will help them understand who holds accountability for the risks and costs associated with cloud implementation. When negotiating with the vendors for a contract term, it is wise not to commit to a contract for a long period of time in case that service is not the most suitable solution.

Unlike in a traditional environment where clients and servers are all located within the organization's network, cloud-based services are accessed via the Internet (except local private cloud) and may be provided by more than one provider. As a result, there are some special issues that systems librarians need to be aware of, for example, Internet connectivity, interoperability, data access, privacy, security, and sustainability, etc.

Besides this, librarians need to learn from the business world and take the advice from the experts of the field. For example, on cloud computing as a choice, Livingstone (Livingstone, 2011) pointed out, "[. . .] the Cloud system that was used for the successful prototype may NOT be the most appropriate choice for your full scale-up enterprise system." (p. 32); he saw the not-so-obvious impact of adding integration to other systems, that "integration effort could be much larger than the effort in implementing the Cloud system itself!" (p. 31); he also informed the community that "There are no universally accepted standards for the interchange of data and software programs between Cloud providers (and there may never be common standards), there is always likely to be a barrier in transferring from one Cloud environment to another system" (p. 87) Such advice on moving corporate enterprise systems to the cloud is also relevant and applicable to the library world.

Effective communication and broad collaboration will be even more important in the distributed cloud environment. Information professionals will need to communicate with library administrators about the importance of their involvement in decision-making, contribute by sharing their technical perspective, and educate non-technical staff of the new technology. They will also involve campus IT in all cloud discussions from day one for expert advice and input on issues related to parent institution's IT infrastructure, networking and security.

Based on the above viewpoints, there are certain strategies which came out based on the above discussion for Information Professionals/ Librarians

1. Stay abreast with latest cloud computing technology, the development of library related cloud services, and the new services provided by different database vendors.
2. Keep track of development of devices that can be used to connect with cloud-based services, e.g. smart phones and tablets.
3. Sharpen technical skills, such as standards related to technologies and library applications, mobile applications, and API services that can be used to enhance library services or for technological innovations.
4. Should know the issues related to cloud computing, e.g. the value and true cost, the risk, authentication, security, privacy, encryption, and SLA.
5. Improve the process of documenting and organizing, in order to provide tailored services to end users
6. Improve communication skills, which appear to be even more crucial in an environment that involves a variety of service providers.
7. Be conscious of your campus IT's strategic plan and its potential impact on library systems and services.
8. Get acquainted with technology needs that are required to reach the local library's strategic plan and goals.
9. Try to learn and explore from other colleagues and staff who may know more about a particular technology.

The above points drawn from the above discussion which is not an exhaustive but it draw some important and demanding aspect, which will be needed by information professionals.

CONCLUSION

Cloud computing, today's widely acclaimed phenomenon, creates a new business environment in libraries and had much to offer to the library world. It changes the way of thinking about library technology and shown great impact on librarianship since the technological environment is changing. Although there is not enough work has been done in Indian prospective to prove that such environmental changes will likely eliminate the need for systems librarians in the near future, library are facing a great challenge – how to embrace cloud computing. As part of the evolution of technologies adopted in the libraries, library must be prepared for the new paradigm shift, and empower themselves to stay ahead of the game, once again.

REFERENCES

Bagley, C. (2011). Parting the clouds: Use of dropbox by embedded librarians. In E. M. Corrado, & H. L. Moulaison (Eds.), *Getting started with cloud computing: A LITA guide* (pp. 159–164). New York: Neal-Schuman Publishers.

Borko, F. (2010). Cloud computing fundamentals. In F. Borko, & A. Escalante (Eds.), *Handbook of cloud computing* (pp. 3–19). New York: Springer Science Business Media, LLC.

Boss, G., Malladi, P., Quan, D., Legregni, L., & Hall, H. (2009). *Cloud computing*. Retrieved from http://www.ibm.com/developerswork/websphere /zones/hipods/ library.html

Breeding, M. (2012). *Cloud computing for libraries*. Chicago: American Library Association.

Cloud computing for business. (n.d.). Retrieved from http://www.business.qld.gov.au/business/running/technology-for-business/cloud-computing-business

Cloud computing issues and impact. (n.d.). Retrieved from http://www.ey.com/Publication/vwLUAssets/Cloud_computing_issues,_impacts_and_insights/$File/Cloud%20computing%20issues%20and%20impacts_14Apr11.pdf

Cloud computing. (n.d.). Retrieved from http://www.brookings.edu/research/topics/cloud-computing.

Dura cloud. (n.d.). Retrieved from http://duracloud.org/

EBSCO. (n.d.). Retrieved from www.ebscohost.com/discovery

ECSS. (n.d.). *White paper on software and service architectures, infrastructures and engineering – action paper on the area for the future EU competitiveness volume 2: Background information, version 1.3*. Retrieved from http://www.euecss.eu/contents/documentation/volume%20two_ECSS%20White%20Paper.pdf

EDUCAUSE. (2012). *Top-ten IT issues, 2012*. Retrieved from www.educause.edu/ero/article/topten-it-issues-2012

Erlandson, R. (2010). Digital culture: The shifting paradigm of systems librarians and systems departments. In E. Iglesias (Ed.), *An overview of the changing role of the systems librarian: Systemic shifts* (pp. 1–12). Cambridge, MA: Woodhead Publishing.

Ex Libris Alma. (n.d.). *The next-generation library services framework*. Retrieved from www.exlibrisgroup.com/category/AlmaOverview

Ex Libris Primo. (n.d.). *Empowering libraries to address user needs*. Retrieved from www.exlibrisgroup.com/category/PrimoOverview

Ex Libris: The bridge to knowledge. (n.d.). Retrieved from http://www.exlibris.co.il/

Goldner, M. (2011). Winds of change: Libraries and cloud computing. *Product and Technological Essence*, *5*(12), 1–13.

Grant, C. (2012). *Why and how librarians have to shape the new cloud computing platforms*. Retrieved from http://thoughts.care-affiliates.com/2012/06/why-and-how-librarians-have-toshape.html

Han, Y. (2010). On the clouds: A new way of computing. *Information Technology & Libraries*, *29*(2), 87–92.

Hayes, B. (2008). Cloud computing. *Communications of the ACM*, *7*(51), 9–11. doi:10.1145/1364782.1364786.

Iglesias, E. (2010). The status of the field. In E. Iglesias (Ed.), *An overview of the changing role of the systems librarian: Systemic shifts* (pp. 65–79). Cambridge, MA: Woodhead Publishing. doi:10.1533/9781780630410.

Iglesias, E. (2011). Using Windows home server and Amazon S3 to back up high-resolution digital objects to the cloud. In E. M. Corrado, & H. L. Moulaison (Eds.), *Getting started with cloud computing: A LITA guide* (pp. 143–151). New York: Neal-Schuman Publishers.

Jeffery, K., & Neidecker-Lutz, B. (2010). The future of cloud computing: Opportunities for European cloud computing beyond 2010. Retrieved from cordis.europa.eu/fp7/ict/ssai/docs/cloud-report-final.pdf

Jing, Y., Zhijiang, L., & Suping, Y. (2012). 2012 international workshop on information and electronics engineering (IWIEE): The community library anniance based on cloud computing. *Procedia Engineering, 29*, 2804–2808. doi:10.1016/j.proeng.2012.01.394.

Kamoun, F. (2009). Virtualizing the datacenter without compromising server performance. *Ubiquity, 2009*(9), 1-12. doi:10.1145/1595422.1595424

Kuali. (n.d.). *Kuali Open Library Environment*. Retrieved from http://kuali.org/ole

Lavagnino, M. B. (1997). Networking and the role of the academic systems librarian: An evolutionary perspective. *College & Research Libraries, 58*(3), 217–231.

Liu, W., & Cai, H. (2013). Embracing the shift to cloud computing: Knowledge and skills for systems librarians. *OCLC Systems & Services, 29*(1), 22–29. doi:10.1108/10650751311294528.

Livingstone, R. (2011). *Navigating through the cloud: A plain english guide to surviving the risks, costs and governance pitfalls of cloud computing*. Sydney, Australia: Rob Livingstone.

Mell, P., & Grance, T. (2011). *The NIST definition of cloud computing*. Retrieved from http://csrc.nist.gov/publications/nistpubs/800-145/SP800-145.pdf

Mitchell, E. T. (2010). Using cloud services for library IT infrastructure. *The Code4lib Journal, 9*. Retrieved from http://journal.code4lib.org/articles/2510

OCLC. (n.d.). *WorldCat local: overview*. Retrieved from www.oclc.org/worldcatlocal/overview/default.htm

OCLC. (n.d.). *WorldShare management services: Overview*. Retrieved from www.oclc.org/webscale/overview.htm

Peters, C. (2013). *What is cloud computing and how will it affect libraries?* Retrieved from http://www.techsoupforlibraries.org/

Polaris Library Systems. (n.d.). Retrieved from http: //www.gisinfosystems.com/

Primary Research Group. (2011). *Survey of library use of cloud computing*. New York: Primary Research Group.

Risks and Benefits of Cloud Computing (n.d.). Retrieved from http://blogs.sap.com/innovation/cloud-computing/risks-and-benefits-of-cloud-computing-020025

SerialsSolutions. (n.d.). *The summon service*. Retrieved from www.serialssolutions.com/en/services/summon/

Service level agreement in cloud computing. (n.d.). Retrieved from http://knoesis.wright.edu/library/download/OOPSLA_cloud_wsla_v3.pdf

Sierra. (n.d.). Retrieved from http://sierra.iii.com/

Vaquero, L. M., Rodero-Merino, L., Caceres, J., & Lindner, M. (2009). A break in the clouds: Towards a cloud definition. In S. I. G. C. O. M. M. Acm (Ed.), *Computer communication review 2009* (pp. 50–55). New York: ACM Press.

Voas, J., & Zhang, J. (2009). Cloud computing: New wine or just a new bottle. *IT Professional*, *11*(2), 15–17. doi:10.1109/MITP.2009.23.

Wang, J. (2012). From the ground to the cloud: A practice at California State University, East Bay. *CALA Occasional Paper Series, 10*, 1-8.

Wikipedia. (n.d.). *Cloud computing*. Retrieved from http://en.wikipedia.org/wiki/Cloud_computing

Wilson, T. C. (1998). *The systems librarian: Designing roles, defining skills*. Chicago: American Library Association.

Winds of change: Libraries and cloud computing. (n.d.). Retrieved from http://www.oclc.org/multimedia/2011/files/IFLA-winds-of-change-paper.pdf

ADDITIONAL READING SECTION

Abrishami, S., & Naghibzadeh, M. (2012). Deadline-constrained workflow scheduling in software as a service cloud. *Scientia Iranica D*, *19*(3), 680–689. doi:10.1016/j.scient.2011.11.047.

Miller, M. (2008). *Cloud computing: Web based applications that change the way you work and collaborate online*. New Delhi, India: Pearson Education, Inc..

Rhoton, J. (2010). *Cloud computing explained*. US and UK: Recursive Press.

Sun, A. (2013). Enabling collaborative decision-making in watershed management using cloud-computing services. *Environmental Modelling & Software*, *41*, 93–97. doi:10.1016/j.envsoft.2012.11.008.

Chapter 5
Application of Cloud Computing in Library Information Service Sector

Ajay Rawat
University of Petroleum & Energy Studies, India

Praveen Kapoor
University of Petroleum & Energy Studies, India

Rama Sushil
DIT University, India

ABSTRACT

Cloud computing is a process that provides services on virtual machines. Through the Cloud the information can be stored permanently on the Cloud servers which can be accessed by the Internet. The main aim of Cloud computing is to bring scalability in the system, due to which CPU and memory will be fully utilized. It is up to a customer that one can increase or decrease the resources in the Cloud according to his need. Cloud computing provides a fascinating possibility for libraries that helps to increase data storage capacity, reliability, performance, and reduce technology cost. This chapter elaborates how libraries and information centers can enhance their resources infrastructure with minimum cost, make effective systems, and provide better services to the user community at minimum cost and time. The aim of this chapter is to explain how librarian, information and computer science professionals and knowledge workers apply Cloud computing in the libraries and information center management. Chapter begins with the Cloud computing introduction in the context of Libraries which is called Cloud libraries. How libraries are using Cloud services today and what can the Cloud computing solutions do for the libraries are presented in detail. The chapter describes the potential role of Cloud computing to serve library needs. At the end of the chapter some live examples, where Libraries are adopting Cloud Computing, like Dura Space, OCLC, Library Thing, Library Cloud and Seer Suite are discussed.

DOI: 10.4018/978-1-4666-4631-5.ch005

INTRODUCTION

Today in the digital world where new technological trends flourish and fade on a daily basis, one new inclination promises more endurance. This trend is called Cloud computing. It will change the way of using computer and the Internet. Cloud computing is the third revolution in the IT after PC and Internet. With the advent of Cloud computing, unprecedented scenario has changed for computing and storing data. It has made tremendous impact on other commercial sectors and finding its place in the digital library domain. According to the definition given by NIST (National Institute of Standards and Technology), "Cloud computing is a model for enabling ubiquitous, convenient, on-demand network access to a shared pool of configurable computing resources (e.g., networks, servers, storage, applications, and services) that can be rapidly provisioned and released with minimal management effort or service provider interaction.

The main objective of Cloud computing is to bring scalability in the system, due to which CPU and memory could be utilized fully. It is up to a customer that he/she can increase or decrease the resources in the Cloud according to his/her need. Its feature of resource scalability will have a direct impact on curtailing the organizational capital and its operational cost. Cloud computing concept brings sharing of resources among customers and thereafter cost factor will come down. Customer only pays for the amount of used resources on subscription basis. Depending on the needs users can subscribe different types of Clouds Public Cloud, Private Cloud, Community Cloud and Hybrid Cloud. Public Cloud as the name depicts is public to the subscriber who can access the cloud space with an Internet connection. Private Cloud is usually setup for an organization which limits the access within the organization. Community Cloud is shared among the community (consist of two or more organizations) who is having similar requirements. Hybrid Cloud is an amalgamation of at least two different clouds, where the clouds included are mixture of public, private, or community. There are three different types of Cloud providers that one can subscribe: Software as a Service (SaaS), Platform as a Service (PaaS), and Infrastructure as a Service (IaaS).

Today in digital world, Cloud computing provides fascinating possibility for libraries that helps to increase data storage capacity, reliability, performance and reduce technology cost. As the growth of any library is completely dependent on the funds and its absence will deprive the library system in keeping pace with the improved forms of information. With incorporation of Cloud computing in our library system it helps to reduce the operation cost without worrying about any capital cost. Libraries with limited budget are not capable to purchase all book (eBooks) which make them difficult to keep pace with the ever growing information. Different libraries have their own data which may be present in other libraries also.

In this way they replicate the data. Cloud computing aspect of sharing resource can play a vital role here. As data in Cloud library is shared among different libraries so replication of data can be eliminated. Cloud library will help in scaling up or down of data capacity according to the requirement. The combined efforts of the libraries in Cloud computing will not only improve efficiency (due to sharing) but also make the system more scalable to save money. Incorporating Cloud into libraries will help in converting the principal investment on infrastructure into operation expenditure. Its objective is to pay on pro-rata basis for the cloud services for part of computer system used. With the implementation of Cloud computing model installation of server is not required in the libraries and the services are provided by the Cloud service provider on periodic subscription basis. Maintenance of all hardware and software taken care by the service provider, thus one can save the human resources and thereby saving money.

LIBRARIES AND CLOUD COMPUTING

Libraries and information center are in trouble to carry on pace with the growing call for improved and enhanced forms of information resources. Due to information explosion new publications are increasing very rapidly in all the form of information. Libraries are always budget constraints, even then libraries and information centers purchase lot of new publication in any form to keep track with the latest available literature. Obviously, with their limited budget it is not possible to procure all publications. Every library and information center tends to have certain information sources which may be available in some other library and information center also which leads to duplication of information sources.

However, if the libraries incorporate their information sources, there would be no more replication. This concept is called "Resource Sharing in Libraries and information center". Sharing resources between libraries and information centers may not be as simple as it may seem to be. Since long libraries and information centers are sharing their resources but this existing system is not very much effective due to many reasons. Now emerging technology i.e. Cloud computing can play vital role in resource sharing in libraries and information centers. Thereby our libraries and information centers will be more affluent in their collection and services.

All Library and information center have the outlook to improve their collection and services in relevance of today's society. Cloud computing is one possibility to move our libraries into the next generation libraries where libraries can maximize their resource with minimum cost with the help of resource sharing. Concept of cloud computing carry lot of benefits for libraries and confer them a different future. Due to cooperative effect of implementation of Cloud computing technology in libraries, libraries enjoy shared hardware and software, as a substitute for hosting hardware and software on behalf of individual libraries, as a result of all this operational cost of libraries comes down and library user can use enhanced resources also library workers workflow goes up with removal of all duplication of efforts to maintain catalogues, library resources etc. Cloud based library and information services could bring the power of library cooperation to core library management. Libraries will be freed to focus on innovation.

With the application of Cloud computing library and information centers can build up their own customized applications for library housekeeping activities and they can share these customized applications over the Internet as Web services for others to find and reuse. They can innovate collectively and increased visibility and accessibility of collections. Out of number of services provided by the Cloud, software as a service (SaaS) and data storage are the largest useful in library and information center. Traditionally, libraries and information centers need to purchase, installed, maintain and update hardware and software. software as a service (SaaS) provide send-off from all of these restrictions and reduce cost of managing library collection and services as all these services are available free of cost or on subscription payment basis.

Now library and information center are not responsible for maintenance of software and hardware as these activities are part of the service. Data storage like memory, components, devices, and media are also available in the Cloud services and also replace or work alongside traditional server storage. Like earlier, servers still necessitate cooling systems, regular maintenance, hardware, and backup systems but now libraries need not to worry about all these, outside vendors are looking after all these for Cloud data centers. Cloud data centers collect and store data in the server of data center and then the same is removed from an in-house server. Data are accessed through the Internet Web portal produced by the vendor, and libraries pay only for the services used by them on pro-rata basis.

Cloud computing is more useful in those libraries, where data or information resources are used and shared very rapidly with other libraries for research activities. When connected to the Cloud the digital libraries can become a large pool of data which can be a great help for patron institute of library and information centers connected to that Cloud. In the market, numbers of service providers like Google Docs, Facebook, Flickr, Amazon etc. are available where library and information centers can use the technology by paying a least amount. With the use of Cloud the library and information centers can spend fewer amounts on buying and maintaining the information documents etc. and other resources like hardware and networking infrastructure. Also the dependence on remote servers can be reduced.

Generally, concept of Cloud computing is applied in the university library system, where all the colleges that come under the university, can be connected directly to the library Cloud. All the information related to the library, can be uploaded to the Cloud and without worrying about the infrastructure, colleges can access this information and the chapter. The Cloud is cost efficient. Cloud solutions let a library and information center, to respond more promptly to service needs, by allowing a library and information center to scale its technology resources, employ a pay-on-demand resource model, and provide IT infrastructure on a subscription model that could be difficult to acquire and manage otherwise. Some of these services offload technical management responsibilities and even provide a level of data management for libraries. In Indian libraries Cloud computing concept is not much accepted due to the lack of service provider in this field. Those libraries which are willing to adopt Cloud computing are facing problems like non-availability of standard software, administrative procedures, budget constraints and connectivity problem etc.

IMPACT OF CLOUD COMPUTING ON LIBRARY AND INFORMATION CENTER

Libraries have the chance to perk up their services and significance in today's information era. Cloud computing is one way for this budge into the future. Concept of libraries changed drastically with the advent of computers, application of information technology and now emerging technology i.e. Cloud computing. It can bring several positive impacts on libraries and give them a different future.

Cost Savings

As libraries are always having budget constraints, Cloud environment pushup towards library cooperation with the help of technological advancement. It enables them to reduce the operational cost as well as capital cost. As with the use of this technology, customers need to pay only for the amount of resources, used on subscription basis.

Flexibility and Innovation

As Cloud environment encourage sharing of library resources and provide infrastructure on rented basis libraries are free for innovative work. Libraries don't have to decide between devoting their limited server resources to the OPAC's overflow traffic and some new innovations.

Broad, General IT Skills vs. Deep Specialized Skills

With the advent of cloud computing in IT, tremendous impact has been made on computer professionals. As cloud computing is new so lot of learning curve is there in professionals. Merely by knowing how to set up a network or configure a server will not help in setting up a cloud. Cloud computing need a complex project management and evaluation from competing vendors on the basis of variety of criteria. Cloud accountable is important when there is a large amount of online data stored on cloud. So cloud security will be major concern to the technologist to enforce contracts, write bindings which holds different vendors to some standards for reliability and security.

SCOPE OF CLOUD COMPUTING IN LIBRARIES AND INFORMATION CENTER

In today's state of affairs libraries and Information centers are take up advanced technology in their regular business and the concept of Cloud is one of them. Libraries and Information centers are willing to move towards implementation of Cloud technology to provide network based services so that all library housekeeping operations, digital libraries etc. are hosted on Cloud based network. In libraries there are two main areas where Cloud computing technology can be implemented.

- Automation of Housekeeping operations
- Digital Library

Implementation of Cloud computing in libraries and information centers day to day business needs a standard company. Company should have set of various software and hardware and experience in handling Cloud services in the Library housekeeping activities. It avoids duplication of various technical services like cataloguing, classification and indexing etc. In the market numbers of companies are providing cloud based services like Ex Libris, Dura Cloud, and Polaris Library System.

WHAT CAN CLOUD COMPUTING SOLUTIONS DO FOR LIBRARIES?

Are libraries finding the solution of the real problems in Cloud computing? The answer is yes. Libraries adopting cloud technology enhanced their resources through cooperation between different libraries and able to fabricate significant and cohesive presence on the Internet. This approach will facilitate libraries to save time and cost with the simplifying workflows. Following are the potential areas of step up of libraries.

- Libraries need not to invest much on hardware and software.
- Networking between different libraries are easy and cost saving.
- Libraries are able to store and maintain the same data thousand times.
- Libraries are able to strengthen the presence on the Web with the help of integration of data on a single server.
- Library cooperation is very easy and cheaper for libraries as all are using same technology.
- Library workers workflow goes up in the cloud environment as elimination of duplication of various jobs taken place and Information seekers are also work with more resources.
- Implementation of cloud technology in libraries reduces the carbon footprints, making libraries greener.

All these improvement are grouped into three basic areas: technology, data and community, offering general as well as many unique opportunities for libraries.

ANALYSIS OF CURRENT USER SERVICE MODEL IN UNIVERSITY LIBRARY

University libraries play an important role in academics and scientific research activities. Earlier libraries provide services based on their own resources. That was the only reason that they did not considered much demands of the users. But now in the cloud era libraries have changed completely and become modern. New digital libraries now have their improved view point and can consider the user requirement. Improved libraries will now focus more on user demands and their main objective will be to provide services to its users. Following, we present the current user service models in use.

WWW Service Model

World Wide Web is a client server model. It uses HTML language and HTTP (Hyper Text Transfer Protocol) for browsing the information on the browsers. It works on sending request and getting response mechanism. In WWW, client sends request to the server to access the data. Server in turn sends backs the result and the results are displayed on browser.

FTP Service Model

FTP stands for File Transfer Protocol. It is most widely used communication protocol for transferring files from server to client or peer nodes. It is a convenient protocol to use. It can be accessed through command mode or any FTP GUI software like cute FTP. It is having a Graphical User Interface. Integrating FTP service with libraries can help user to access library data/files. User can access id and password for security and help librarian to keep a record of the visitors.

BBS and E-Mail Service Model

BBS-Bulletin Board Service is a just like blank board service which is available on the Internet for the user, where user can write query. Librarian in return can respond to the query. User can consult librarian and can get quick answer without physically visiting to library.

IMPROVEMENT OF USER SERVICE MODEL IN ACADEMIC LIBRARIES

During the last few years there is a rapid development in the IT technologies which has increased the user and leads them in becoming more personalized. On the other hand with these rapid development libraries are promoting user centered services. For this they have to analyze the user requirement and fulfill the user demand. IT provides impetus to the library development. And also with the advent of cloud computing in libraries, it can conserve and utilize the resources and improve the user satisfaction.

Unified Search Service Model

Even though there are services like OPAC (Online Public Access Catalogue) and ILL (Inter-library loan) available, still library system is deprived on uniform platform to access and users feel still difficulty in accessing the shared resources. Integrating of cloud computing with libraries will help in resolving this problem and it will facilitate uniform distributed access interface. In addition it stimulates library resources so user can get platform for information retrieval.

Integrated Consulting Services Model

Every university library, now a days is providing a network of BBS or Email. For relentless improvement of user requirement digital libraries came into picture in ILS. Now further improvement in the ILS cloud computing CDRS (Cooperative Digital Reference Service) understand the sharing of services, resources and technology which will inculcate to a new system that will bring handiness to library users.

Real-Time Access Services Model

Today in the digital world, library users are paying more attention in digital and electronic form of journals and databases. It was a big challenge to the current library system. But with the advent of cloud computing, libraries can provide a sharing of library resources with collaboration of other university libraries. Cloud computing have great computational power, infinite capacity and sharing capability which will help to reduce the purchase of database (electronic journals and magazine) by different libraries. User can access the database with handheld devices, PCs and even with mobile phones, provided Internet connection should be present.

Knowledge Service Model

Knowledge plays a vital role in the development of any department and generating productivity. University libraries are main source of processing, storing and disseminating knowledge. With the emergence of cloud computing in libraries system, it helps in sharing the resource which saves resources and manpower in library consortium.

SERVICE PROVIDERS OF CLOUD COMPUTING FOR LIBRARIES

There are various Cloud service providers for LIS (Library information sector), some are discussed next.

Ex Libris

Ex Libris is a renowned Cloud technology service provider. Ex Libris basically based in USA and worked for automation solutions for academic and research libraries. Ex Libris worked for Cloud solution for libraries which include all the software and hardware support required to provide various library services to their users. For electronic, digital, and print materials, Ex Libris provides competent, comprehensible products that serve the need of library users and help them to move in to the future. It maintains remarkable patron base in more than 80 countries. Ex Libris built on assorted standard and contains various features like migration of data, customization, compatibility with Unicode; flexibility etc. and available for all libraries and consortia. Ex Libris developed the Alma next generation library management service which supports the all library housekeeping operations—selection, acquisition, metadata management, digitization, and fulfillment—for the full spectrum of library materials, regardless of format or location.

Polaris Library Systems

Polaris Library System is a product of a holding company called PLS Solutions, based in USA. It is a library automation solution available in the market used for automation of library housekeeping activities, integration of cataloging, circulation, acquisitions, serials control etc. Library can integrate various PC and printer with the help of Polaris ILS Client License at no extra cost. PLS accommodate various well know standards like

MARC 21 for bibliographic data, XML, Z39.50 for information retrieval, Unicode etc. Polaris is push libraries to work in a different way for collecting, storing, retrieval and dissemination of information and knowledge for the community members, also expanding their scope outside the physical library. Polaris Library System provides various solutions for different libraries like Polaris ILS, Polaris Inventory Manager, Polaris Course Reserves, Polaris Collection Agency Manager, Simply Reports etc.

Dura Cloud

Dura Cloud is a Cloud solution for digital library services. It is a managed service of Dura Space and is a not-for-profit organization providing services and technology for digitalization of content to be accessible for long term. Collaboration of the Dspace digital library software and Fedora Commons is known as Dura Space. D Space and Fedora Commons are two top open source solutions used by various libraries, research centers, and many other organizations involved in cultural heritage Fedora Commons offers solution for digital repository (Digital Library Solution) using standard software and hardware solution. Like other open source software's Dura Cloud also accommodate open source code and the code require to be installed on Computer System. Dura Cloud provides service for preservation of content simple and cost effective.

LIVE EXAMPLES: CLOUD COMPUTING IN LIBRARY AND INFORMATION SECTOR

OCLC

OCLC (Online Computer Library Center) is computer library service and research organization. It is public, membership and dedicated to the public purposes of furthering access to the world's information and reducing information costs. Taking a sneak peek into its history, OCLC began in 1967 as OHIO college library center to create a cooperative computerized network for OHIO libraries. Tracking towards the progress, the first library to implement online cataloging through OCLC was the ALDEN library on August 26, 1971. Thus it was the first occurrence of online cataloging by any library worldwide. Presently OCLC and all its associated member libraries cooperatively produce and maintain two services WORLDCAT: the OCLC online union catalogue and OPAC: the largest online public access catalogue in the world.

The big question arouses that why OCLC world share management services?

To confront this, there are three tier feature – Revolutionary, cost-effective and collaborative. It connects the content, technology of its member libraries to create first Web scale. The basic vision is to move services to "the Cloud" whereas libraries use the same shared hardware, services and data. OCLC includes unified acquisition, subscription and circulation and license management to the Cloud. Thus this generates cost benefits and efficiencies. The already operating OCLC services at Web scale integrate with the services. Scale is what matters in today's environment. Managing a computer network that create economies of scale and enabling more and more libraries to reduce costs and share resources have been built by OCLC and its members for more than 40 years.

OCLC-serve 72,035 libraries in 170 countries, serving the public purposes to further access the world's information with reduced library costs. The successful OCLC performance is justified with a tremendous number of 22 million transactions a day, with an average of 225 transactions per second. The WORLDCAT growth rises from 39 million records in 1998 to 34 million of records in 2011. Now, OCLC is generating Next-Generation services using 21st century Web technology. That will greatly amplify the power of library cooperation enabling users to participate in a network and community of libraries to reuse information and to give users a local, group and global research. Thus OCLC is proceeding strategically towards the direction of developing new Web scale services and also maintain and enhance existing services.

As discussed in OCLC parallel symposium -14 August, 2012, a truly next-generation library management system means meeting users at point of need and creating unified collection management and stream-lined workflows for staff. The future of Cloud based library automation means providing a technical platform which frees data and services for re-use and re-purpose by libraries and third party developers. Andrew Pace, OCLC executive director, Network library services summarized the challenges faced by libraries and OCLC's strategic and tactical plans to offer solutions for libraries that address the changing nature of their collections and the rising expectations of their users. OCLC PRESIDENT and CEO, JAY JORDAN emphasized on OCLC's long term strategy, building on promise of Cloud computing in order to achieve network effects. And thus it will allow every member to benefit from shared data and the participation of others.

For more than 30 years, OCLC has been conducting research for the library community. The researches outcomes are then known through various publications like journals, articles, presentations and reports. The presentations are basically organized into five categories: conference presentations, Dewey presentations, distinguished seminar series, guest presentations and research staff presentations. The research of OCLC taking OPAC to the Cloud was published in April 2009, announcing that they are going to offer a fully online Integrated Library System- ILS. Marshal breeding said- "while it's too early to predict the number of libraries that will shift from traditional ILS products to services offered through WORLD CAT, the dynamics of the library automation industry will inevitably change. OCLC now will compete with such companies as SIRSI Dynix, Ex Libris, innovative interfaces, Polaris, Serial solutions and a myriad of other companies that offer ILS products".

SeerSuite

Information retrieval applications or tools such as digital libraries and search engines are invaluable resources for finding the resources that are authoritative and relevant on the Web. The rate of growth of digital information which brings along processing, ingesting, indexing documents and then presenting such resources to the user in an effective and accessible manner has always been a challenge.

SeerSuite, an open source framework for digital libraries, enables users to build digital library search engines such as CiteSeerX. In addition SeerSuite enables users to crawl the Web in search of the most relevant documents, process these documents and access them through a Web based user interface. It includes a user portal CiteSeerX to support personalization and interaction. SeerSuite thus includes several components common to other information retrieval systems and Web applications. CiteSeer could be called a vertical research portal or a digital library. It uses a specialized function to find scholarly papers; it then extracts the text from PDF and PostScript files and creates a full-text index that can be further checked. CiteSeer enriches access to these materials by extracting author names, publication information etc.

However, rising demands from system use and the increasing size of CiteSeer's archive are causing query that are hidden to rise as well as significant weakening of system stability. It even suffers from design deficiencies. The most obvious problems are its lack of scalable storage and transaction-safe updates, which bring down the system's performance as well as its stability significantly.

With increasing popularity of Cloud computing and looking at the manner in which it is coming up providing simple solutions to data storage and redundancy problems. One of the most viable and economical solution would be considering taking the digital library on Cloud. The idea is to transfer such information retrieval systems on the Cloud in the most economical manner such that people are able to access the required apt information without paying for something which is not required or asked for and at the same time the digital portals store the required data without bearing the cost for obsolete or redundant information.

The aim is to extend the SeerSuite framework into the Cloud using CiteSeer. As a test bed to take advantage of a Cloud computing infrastructure both in house, for researchers and other users, who wish to expand features already available in SeerSuite. SeerSuite can also be hosted in "Infrastructure as a Service" platform (IAAS) with minimal refactoring. Such a hosting, however, is quite expensive with current Cloud offerings. The reason is large collection size and the volume of data transaction between the application and the user. The key question in this context is shifting to which one of the components or subset of CiteSeer to a Cloud would be the most cost-effective.

According to Lee Gills (College of Information Sciences and Technology, Pennsylvania State University), CiteSeerX, the successor to CiteSeer, has currently offered some unique aspects of search which is not present in other scientific search engines, such as table, figure, algorithm and author search. In addition, CiteSeerX continuously goes through the Web and author submissions. And now has nearly 1.5 million documents, close to 30 million citations, a million authors and comparable database tables. It has nearly 1 million unique users with millions of hit a day.

SeerSuite/CiteSeer is a modular by design, composed of services which can be hosted in the Cloud. Expense of hosting the whole of CiteSeer is prohibitive. Hence one of the recommended solutions is to host a component/service code. The goal here would be to identify optimal subset/components. Some of the identified cost components are Web services, crawler, repository, database, indexing and extraction. Develop and deploy a scalable Cloud based mechanism for crawling and processing documents from the Web and improving the metadata extracted. It makes available a Cloud infrastructure for repository and repository access. Expose metadata available in the Cloud through the index, repository and database by extending both the interfaces already available and add new interfaces, explore data access issues. Deploy my CiteSeerX in the Cloud, examining various privacy, confidentiality, integrity and security issues with user data. Develop an optimization model for evaluation of the various components and their processes for SeerSuite Cloud deployment.

LibraryCloud

LibraryCloud is platform as a service of Cloud computing. The idea of library as service of Cloud computing was originated by Digital Library. Digital library is a library in which the books, journals, white papers, research papers and many other collections are stored in the digital formats to secure them from being damaged and could be accessible via computers. The digital content can be easily stored on local networks or by wide networks of computer. Thus a digital library is a type of information retrieval system which can be retrieved at any point of time and from anywhere. These Digital Libraries have various benefits to explore, for example no physical boundary. This means that the work is accessible from anywhere and need not to go library physically. Another major advantage of these libraries is that they are accessible 24X7 for the reader hence round the clock availability.

It also supports multiple accesses, i.e. the same resources can be used by various institutions simultaneously. The "lending out" method is also deployed here, i.e. the material cannot be accessible after its lending time is expired. Information retrieval is another benefit, which says that whole pieces of the documentation and other collection are available to the user by any search term. Thus, digital library has very user friendly interface. Since the work is prone to degradation by repeated use, digitalization prevents it by proving access copies of the same. This is known as preservation and conservation. Last but not the least physical libraries have some limit to store the collections but the digital libraries can store much more and need very less physical space as compared to the physical library.

Seeing the above advantages, the idea of the researchers of Cloud computing, came up as service LibraryCloud. LibraryCloud is the metadata servers which gathers metadata from various institutions and thus are available through open APIs and other links. The target customers of such libraries are always scholars and researcher, because whenever there is need have searching; Google and Amazon are always the first choices to any users. But they are not aligned according to the need of public, or of scholars and re-searchers. The aim for LibraryCloud (as per the Web site of LibraryCloud) is to enable and encourage the collaborative developments of applications to provide huge collections of researches, Open Source software data available to all, especially for non- commercial use.

There are various silent features which LibraryCloud possess. One of them is the tool of browsing and discovery tools which not only helps researcher to find works but also give the guidance to search path. To support this they have three tools. First, ShelfLife this helps the researcher to understand the material. Second, StackView gives large collection brows able. Third, Library Dashboard provide data browser and visualize for large metadata. They also provide social networks around the library so as to provide best research work. Give semantic-related materials which have gone through testing. They also give recommendation for the engines to use for detailed researches. To deploy any idea the basic consideration is always the privacy.

Thus Library cloud is committed to supporting the privacy to its every user who is contributing to it. Talking about the security of the data, organization takes whole responsibility to secure data and check that it's sufficiently encrypted from others. Also, LibraryCloud, do all effort to eliminated access to data that can be re-identified. Also according to the Website of LibraryCloud, contributing organization has the responsibility to ensure that any information that is identifiable and permitted by license holder to be made public-ally available.

LibraryThing

'LibraryThing' was shaped by Tim Spalding, concept for Web developer and Web publisher based in Portland, Maine. "Library Thing" is one of the sites that offer services of social cataloguing where one can catalogue books of their interest. One can create catalogue (database) of books of one's interest: books own, books like to own, books one have read, books like to read or any combination of books. One can share this catalogue with others it is just like any social networking site like face book and twitter. One can use 'LibraryThing' to rate and reviews of the books read, read reviews written by others, get book recommendations based on a book read or review or from entire collection, and join groups, so that one can discuss books and read online. It authorizes people not only to contribute information and suggestion about books but also allows them to connect globally to share their interests. One can create free account to use LibraryThing to catalogue up to 200 books, which can be upgraded into a paid membership to catalogue more than 200 books. If one would like to unsubscribe LibraryThing account can send request for deletion of their account.

LibraryThing has no adverts, one can use it in different languages and it collects its data from wide range of library catalogues. Its interface is simple and easy to use. LibraryThing uses Amazon.com and Library of Congress, British Library and many other world libraries that provide open access to their collections with the Z39.50 protocol to collect data. It also collects data from users of all these libraries and amazon.com, who provide reviews, cataloguing information and adding tags. The protocol is used by a variety of desktop programs, notably bibliographic software like EndNote. LibraryThing appears to be the first mainstream Web use. There are various prominent enterprises that are providing solutions for libraries through partnerships between library automation vendors.

LibraryThing has online forums that allow one to communicate with other LibraryThing users about books, authors and other LibraryThing Websites. One can ask for help regarding use of LibraryThing. One can also do a keyword search for discussions on a certain book or author or topic using the search talk box. Like any other social networking sites groups can be created by the people in charge of LibraryThing, as well as list of user- created groups with the most members, most active groups and new groups. One can invite someone to checkout LibraryThing from their profile.

CONCLUSION

Integration of libraries can be done effectively by Cloud computing. Cloud computing will enable sharing of the electronic data that facilitates in reduction of duplicity. It will lead in curtailing the libraries budget. Its feature of resource scalability will have a direct impact on reducing the organizational capital and its operational cost. A lot of money can be saved through scalability. Integration of Libraries with Cloud computing will make Library system greener.

REFERENCES

Arora, D., Quraishi, S., & Quraishi, Z. (n.d.). *Application of cloud computing in university libraries*. Retrieved on 1st March 2013 from http://pioneerjournal.in/conferences/tech-knowledge/12th-national-conference/index.1.html

Goldner, M. (2011). Libraries and cloud computing. In *Proceedings of the 2011 SLA Annual Conference & INFO-EXP*. SLA.

Goldner, M. R. (2010). Winds of change: Libraries and cloud computing. *BIBLIOTHEK Forschung und Praxis*, *34*(3), 270–275. doi:10.1515/bfup.2010.042.

Khan, S., Khan, S., & Galibeen, S. (2011). Cloud computing an emerging technology: Changing ways of libraries collaboration. *Journal of Library and Information Science*, *1*(2), 151–159.

Kumar, D. K., M., Y.S.S.R., Ramakrishna, D., & Rohit, A. V. (2012). Application of cloud technology in digital library. *IJCSI International Journal of Computer Science Issues, 9*(3).

Pradeep, B. T., & Bhuvan, U. (n.d.). *CiteSeerx: A cloud perspective*. Retrieved on 1st March 2013 from http://static.usenix.org/event/hotcloud10/tech/full_papers/Teregowda.pdf

Sanchati, R., & Kulkarni, G. (2011). Cloud computing in digital and university libraries. *Global Journal of Computer Science and Technology, 11*(12).

Teregowda, P., Urgaonkar, B., & Giles, C. L. (2011). Cloud computing: A digital libraries perspective. In *Proceedings of the 2010 IEEE 3rd International Conference on Cloud Computing*, (pp. 115-122). IEEE.

Xiaona, F., & Lingyun, B. (2010). Application of cloud computing in university library user service model. In *Proceedings of the 3rd International Conference on Advanced Computer Theory and Engineering (ICACTE)*. ICACTE.

KEY TERMS AND DEFINITIONS

Cloud Computing: Cloud computing is the use of computing resources (hardware and software) that are delivered as a service over a network (typically the Internet).

Digital Library: A digital library is a library in which collections are stored in digital formats (as opposed to print, microform, or other media) and accessible via computers. The digital content may be stored locally, or accessed remotely via computer networks. A digital library is a type of information retrieval system.

FTP: File Transfer Protocol (FTP) is a standard network protocol used to transfer files from one host to another host over a TCP-based network, such as the Internet.

Library Thing: Library Thing is a portal that offers services of social cataloguing where one can catalogue books of their interest.

OCLC: Online Computer Library Center, Inc. (OCLC) is a nonprofit, membership, computer library service and research organization dedicated to the public purposes of furthering access to the world's information and reducing information costs.

Seer Suite: SeerSuite, is an open source framework for digital libraries, enables users to build digital library search engines such as CiteSeerX.

Chapter 6
Planning and Implementation of Cloud Computing in NIT's in India: Special Reference to VNIT

Ravikant M. Deshpande
Visvesvaraya National Institute of Technology, Nagpur, India

Bharati V Patle
Visvesvaraya National Institute of Technology, Nagpur, India

Ranjana D. Bhoskar
Visvesvaraya National Institute of Technology, Nagpur, India

ABSTRACT

Cloud computing and Information Network both are emerging facets in the field of Information Science (IS). Cloud computing has potential to bring another wave of changes to organizations. Overall, planning and implementation of cloud computing will be beneficial in the terms of library level as well as institutional level to manage by cloud. In this chapter the authors present RECs/NITs resources to move on for managing cloud computing. Making the decision to use cloud-based services means balancing the elements of cost, risk, and benefit to decide whether those services advance the mission of the library as well as institute. RECs/NITs Libraries can take advantage of the cloud in numerous ways, such as data sharing including discovery tools, current status of research, and software as service which depends on the cloud, e-mail systems and social networking, and so forth. This chapter recommends a road for globalizing Regional Engineering Colleges/National Institutes Technology libraries.

DOI: 10.4018/978-1-4666-4631-5.ch006

INTRODUCTION

We can't bind Sun rays,

We can't block the way of Water,

We can't bind knowledge in Libraries,

We can't stop the Technical Revolution,

Similarly, we can't stop progress in Cloud Computing.

Networking concept is extensively used in the libraries. They have developed robust frameworks for resource sharing and cooperative cataloging, leveraged publisher and aggregator platforms to deliver electronic collections, and created vibrant consortia and groups that share services across regions and countries. Cloud computing is a new paradigm in the delivery of e-resources on demand over the Internet. The technical foundation of cloud computing is based on Service Oriented Architecture (SOA) and virtualization of hardware and software, and Internet technologies. Cloud computing promises to change the way library computing is performed now, lift all technological barriers coming in the way of sharing distributed library resources and provide new tools to make access to global library resources easier and simpler and ensure that both libraries and all users can benefited from remote infrastructure and services.

The NITs (National Institute of Technology in India) have been in existence for 6 decades. They have very good developed hardware and software to manage their resources at institute level. But the resources that have been developed by them have little recognition on global level (Wikipedia, 2013). Hence the institute in general and libraries in particular has tremendous resources that can be put on the cloud thus allowing those resources to go global and sharable. The resources that are to be possibly shared have been further identified in this chapter. Moving on the cloud for the resources need careful consideration about data security, network access speed, skilled manpower, and legal issues to mention a few. There are lot of pros and cons to be considered before moving on to the cloud with well studied advantages and disadvantages.

LIBRARIES MOVING ON CLOUD

The fast growth of technology needs for shifting traditional libraries to modern libraries. Libraries all over the world suffer from common problems like flexibility associated with the digital data, lower level of efficiency, and huge cost involved in managing the entire IT infrastructure themselves. Few options are available when it comes to collaborating with other libraries as well which is the prime reason for subordinate levels of efficiency. Cloud computing would help in bridging the gap between digital libraries and IT. Sharing of data among the libraries will in principle reduce the overall cost and increase the efficiency. Capital expenditure done on infrastructure will chiefly be converted into operational expenditure. It will also enhance the users experience and will help in making the libraries a lot more scalable. (See Figure 1.)

CLOUD COMPUTING ESSENTIAL CHARACTERISTICS

On-Demand Self Service

A user can unilaterally provision computing capabilities, such as applications, server time, and network storage, as needed automatically without requiring human interaction with each service's provider (Chakraborty & Abhik, 2013). (See Figure 2.)

Figure 1. Shift from traditional library to modern library

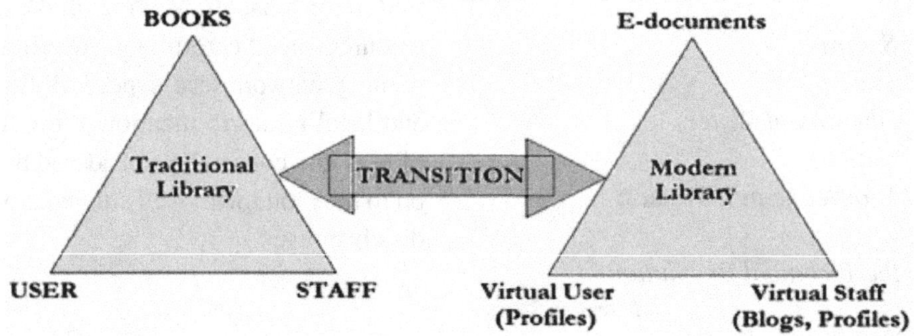

Broad Network Access

Capabilities are available over the network and accessed through standard mechanisms that promote use by heterogeneous thin or thick client platforms (e.g., mobile phone, laptops and PDAs).

Resource Pooling

The provider's computing resources are pooled to serve multiple users using a multitenant model, with different physical and virtual resources dynamically assigned and reassigned according to user demand. There is a sense of location independence in that the user generally has no control or knowledge over the exact location of the provided resources but may be able to specify location at a higher level of abstraction (e.g., country, state, or datacenter). Examples of resources include storage, processing, memory, network bandwidth, and virtual machines.

Rapid Elasticity

Capabilities can be rapidly and elastically provisioned, in some cases automatically, to quickly scale out and rapidly released to quickly scale

Figure 2. Essential characteristics of cloud computing

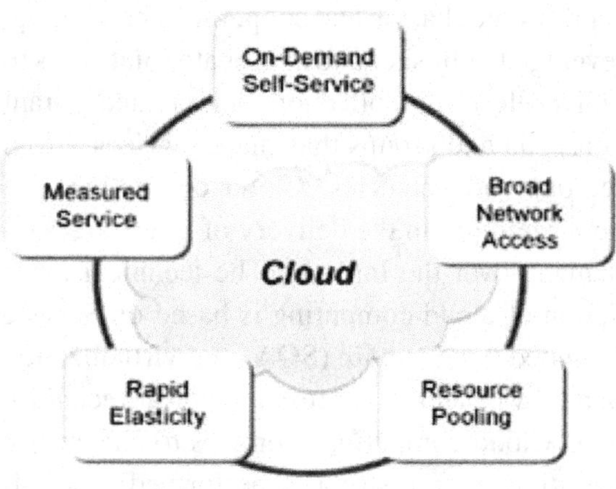

in. To the consumer, the capability available for provisioning often appear to be unlimited and can be purchased in any quantity at any time.

Measured Service

Cloud systems automatically control and optimize resource use by leveraging a metering capability at some level of abstraction appropriate to the type of service (e.g., storage, processing, bandwidth, and active user accounts). Resource usage can be monitored, controlled, and reported providing transparency for both the provider and consumer of the utilized service.

PLAN CLOUD LIBRARY SERVICES

Platform as a Service (PaaS)

Platform as a service is a type of service meant for cloud developers as a means to develop a platform to build up, install, and control SaaS applications. This platform usually includes databases; software glue with its infrastructure and services is Internet accessible by patrons. Cloud-computing platforms are emerging from a number of organizations like OCLC (WorldShare Platform), ExLibris (Alma), Serials Solution, Library Thing, Hathi Trust, SirisDynix, Summon, DuraCloud, Google App Engine. Microsoft Azure services, CloudFoundry, Amazon Web Service, and Enterprise KOHA have since demonstrated the usefulness of cloud computing in hosting libraries on to a common platform (Abidi & Abidi, 2012).

Software as a Service (SaaS)

Software as a service a software distribution form in which applications are hosted by services supplier and ended to clientele over the Internet (Abidi & Abidi, 2012). Clientele purchase the facility to access and utilize an application or service which is packed in the cloud. SaaS is usually available on demand and via the Internet and can thus be configured remotely. SaaS service providers offer special selections of software running on their infrastructure. SaaS is also known as software on demand. Thus, this service is highly cost-effective and location independent. The applications are accessible from various client devices through a thin client interface such as Web browser (e.g., Web-based e-mail).

Infrastructure as a Service (IaaS)

Cloud computing offers virtualized systems to access to computer hardware resources such as networks and storage. IaaS, Infrastructure as a service, defined by the variety of services to supply, i.e. servers, storage and network hardware. IaaS provides virtual machines and other related hardware and software systems through a service-based application programming interface (API). The capability provided to the consumer is to provision processing, storage, networks, and other fundamental computing resources where the consumer does not manage or control the underlying cloud infrastructure but has control over operating systems; storage, deployed applications, and possibly limited control of select networking components. Education ERP.net, Microsoft Flexiscale, Amazon S3, Cloudstatus, GoGrid, and Oracle Coherence are offering IaaS (Abidi & Abidi, 2012).

DEPLOYMENT MODELS OF CLOUD COMPUTING

Public Cloud

The public cloud is mainly is for public use, which can be accessed by everyone. It is mainly used by a large organization or institution. In this deployment the cloud infrastructure is accessible to the general public and shared in a "pay as you go" model of payment. The cloud resources are accessible via the Internet and the provider is responsible for ensuring the economies of scale and the management of the shared infrastructure. It is highly scalable and automated provisioning of commodity computer resource. The Google App Engine, Microsoft windows Azure, IBM Smart Cloud, and Amazon EC2 are example of public cloud. In this type of cloud, the organization does not access or use the public cloud which is accessible to the general public (Kumar, 2013; Singh & Surohi, 2013).

Private Cloud

Private cloud and internal cloud are terms used to describe offering that emulate cloud computing on private network. It is infrastructure to be operated within the organization, for the users who want to share specific information within the institution. In this model the cloud resources are not shared by unknown third parties. Clients' security and compliance requirements are not affected, though this offering does not bring the benefits associated with reduced capital expenditure in IT infrastructure investments. The general public does not have access to the private cloud neither does the organization use the public cloud.

Hybrid Cloud

Hybrid cloud is the combination of infrastructure of two or more clouds (i.e., public or private). One hybrid cloud servers its clientele with the collection of multiple public or private clouds as per their demand and requirement. A hybrid cloud exhibits the characteristics of both public and private clouds. It achieves maximum cost reduction through outsourcing which is a feature of public clouds, and maintains high degree of control over sensitive data, which is a feature of private cloud. An example for hybrid cloud would be library data stored in private cloud of each participating library and application running in the public cloud / community cloud

Community Cloud

A community cloud is applicable to serve a common function or purpose. In which cloud services are shared by several organizations and support a specific community that has shared and similar concerns. These services may be managed by the organizations or third party and may exist off site. It may be for one university or for several universities, but they share common concerns such as their mission, policies, online resources, union catalogues, security, regulatory compliance needs, and so on. This community cloud model

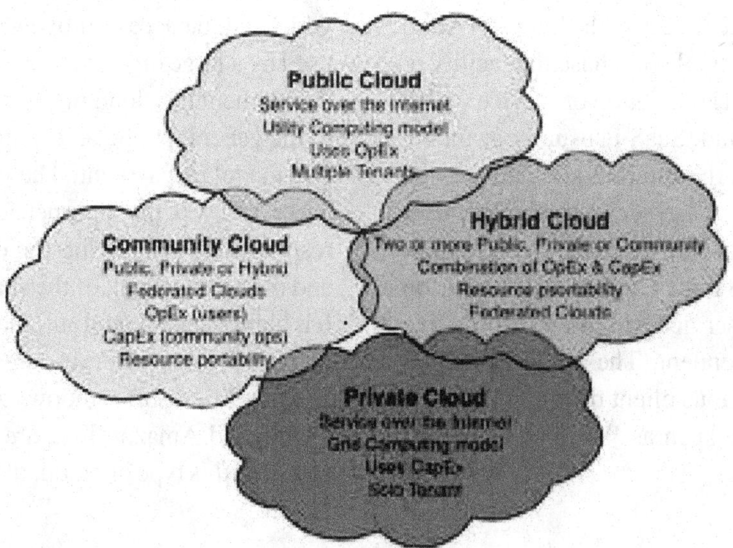

for library can be very suitable model and can be deployed at various levels (Institutional Consortia, National, and International) very similar to Government or G-Cloud. This type of cloud computing is provided by one or more agencies for use by all, or most libraries (Kumar, 2013).

ADVANTAGES/BENEFITS OF CLOUD COMPUTING

Web services will have a profound impact on library services which will be shared through cloud computing. Web-scale providers concentrate capacity in platforms whose benefits can be broadly shared. It is certainly an important trend for libraries to pay attention to, especially as libraries and resource centers struggle with dwindling budgets and staff. Like any other technology cloud computing does also have its advantages and disadvantages, which needs to be taken into consideration before implementing this new technology (Shagin, 2012).

Flexibility and Innovation

Many people love to use the cloud computing because of the great benefit of flexibility, and users can access stored data anywhere in the world, but the thing is you need a computer/laptop/smart phone/Android/Blackberry and other applicable devices with Internet connection. Staff and users can access the data and files outside the office and library at any time. Cloud computing provides flexibility in implementing changes and new technologies without high risk and cost. OPAC and the mobile Web application hosted in the cloud, the resources devoted to each will shrink and expand as traffic raises and drops. Further creating and configuring new virtual server instances is fast and easy in the cloud.

Cost Reduction and Increased Efficiency

One of the most significant features of cloud storage is cost effectiveness, as a library needs to pay only for the cloud space that its data actually requires and does not need to pay for storage overhead in advance. There is also no need or cost for file storage equipment, server setup and maintenance, staff time, power usage, and backup. A cloud provider can offer an infinite amount of resources to many users. Because of reduced cost and time, institutes can focus efforts elsewhere and be more efficient. Cloud computing offers price savings due to economies of scale and the fact that you are only paying for the resources you actually use. Like water and electricity, a computing cloud is a communally-shared resource that you lease on a metered basis, paying for as little as you need, when you need it.

Reliability

While Internet connectivity and the provider itself being subject to outages is a scary fact of the nature of cloud computing, there is still more reliability in comparison to in-house systems because of the economies of scale. The vendor is more able to give 24/7 technical support and highly trained experienced staff to support the infrastructure at its best condition, and the benefits will reach all their clients. Compare this to each organization having a team of on-site IT people with varied skill set.

Highly Secured Infrastructure

Cloud computing may affect libraries' IT infrastructure, the foundation of the library system. It is known that an IT unit within a library always takes on heavy duties and hold high responsibilities for an entire library. Usually, a library allocates a large amount of its budget to build up its infrastructure, such as computing abilities, networking equipment, and storage, however IT resources are not effectively used among the integrated library system (ILS) and various digital initiatives. Instead of relying on in-house IT infrastructure, some libraries have begun using cloud infrastructure for their IT services.

Security Gain

Yes, there are security risks with cloud computing. But as mentioned above, the traditional, in-house data storage system comes with risks as well. The gain here lies within smaller, newer libraries with low budgets for implementing security systems and less know-how about security technology. The cloud provider already provides the hardware and knowledge for the most current security measures. It is evident that implementing a new data system comes with serious risks to consider, but it is also clear that the benefits of cloud computing can be factors that help libraries grow especially well.

Fast Service (Always Up Time)

Cloud computing service providers are having cloud infrastructure, so the server is always in uptime. This results in your having no distractions in the resource centre. Depending upon libraries needs, they have to choose plans for fast access service.

More Storage Capacity

No need to worry about a lot of data and files to store, this provides more data to save the files in the server. Here depending upon the data and usage, you can choose the plan, available in different modes. Everything is online stored in the cloud and can be accessed at any time in the browser.

Simplicity of Integration

Cloud computing may play an important role in transforming the integrated library system (ILS) that provides core services for a library and is comprised of an online public access catalogue, a cataloguing module, a serials control module, and reporting module.

DISADVANTAGES OF CLOUD COMPUTING

Although many benefits are shown in cloud computing incorporation, libraries need to realize cloud applications are associated with some risks that may have a major impact on the libraries' information and services.

Network Dependency

Cloud computing is dependent on the Internet. The most basic drawback of cloud computing is that it needs Internet connection to access the cloud and this direct tie to the Internet means that this system is prone to outages and service interruptions at any time. This could occur in the middle of a task or transaction, meaning the action could be delayed or lost entirely if time sensitive.

Difficulty in Creating Hybrid Systems

This pertains especially to those Institutions that hold sensitive information. Organizations like government offices and financial institutions usually have their own IT services and will not take their data offsite despite the benefits of efficiency and performance. There really are no current industry standardized forms that apply to all systems when it comes to connecting to new cloud systems. With legacy systems, compatibility with a public cloud structure would need some IT magic and some hardware tweaks. And with a legacy system run organization, it's likely they will not part with these tried and true systems.

Centralization

Organizations usually outsource data and application services to a centralized provider. In cloud computing, we know that network dependency is a drawback due to outages. Centralized data can certainly add another risk to cloud computing: If the provider's service goes down, all clients are affected.

Data Integrity/Security

There is already a huge risk with data hosted in-house, so it's no secret that data offsite sits at even higher risk. With Data offsite, more avenues for attack and the fact that it will be travelling more makes it easier to be intercepted. With technology always improving, there are ways to make sure of better encryption. However with technology always improving, there are always people out there improving their hacking skills.

STATUS OF REC's/NIT's IN INDIA

India is a huge country with a population of more than 1 billion. In India, by tradition, education and learning are highly valued. In fact, India has one of the largest higher education systems in the world, with regard to the number of institutions. Education is a necessity. It is the most effective instrument with which the people can acquire the knowledge, skills, and capability to develop wisdom; it is developing nation. The seeds for some of India's higher education institutions were planted in the latter half of the 20th century. The National Institutes of Technology (NITs) are premier institutes of engineering and technology in India and are the new faces of the earlier Regional Engineering Colleges (RECs).

In the year 2002, the Govt. of India's Ministry of Human Resource Development, decided to upgrade all of the 17 existing Regional Engineering Colleges (RECs) as National Institutes of Technology (NITs), on the lines of the prestigious Indian Institutes of Technology (IITs). The NITs have the responsibility of providing high quality education in engineering and technology to produce competent technical manpower for the country. Libraries that are treasure houses of knowledge and information are one invaluable way to provide informal education since each library is a hub of all academic activities.

All the 30 NIT's (see Figure 4) now offer degree courses of Bachelor, Master, and Doctorate levels in various branches of Engineering and Technology. The entire nonrecurring expenditure and expenditure for postgraduate courses during the REC times were borne by the central government. On the other hand the entire recurring ex-

Figure 4. Locations of the 30 NITs

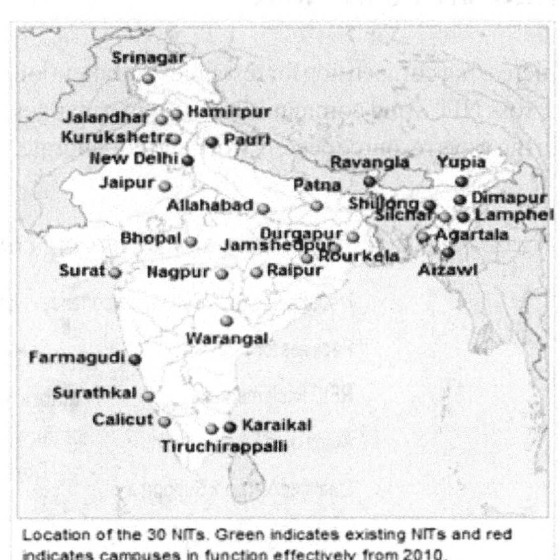

Location of the 30 NITs. Green indicates existing NITs and red indicates campuses in function effectively from 2010.

penditure on undergraduate courses was shared equally by the central and state government. NITs have a Central Library equipped with technical books, literature, fiction, scientific journals, and other electronic materials. Most have digitized their libraries. Some provide an intranet library facility. Every departmental library has high-speed connectivity. Electronic libraries allow students access to online journals and other periodicals through the AICTE-INDEST consortium, an initiative by the Ministry of Human Resource Development. Students also have access to IEEE documents and journals. While some have video conferencing facilities, others are upgrading under the World Bank funded TEQIP scheme.

All REC's / NIT's (see Figure 5) have various factors are responsible for moving on towards sharable e-resources as well as institution records for finding statistics easily and it should be provided access only to authorized, authenticated users and those users need to be able to trust that their data is secure in cloud computing.

CLOUD COMPUTING CHALLENGES SHAPING LIBRARY SERVICES REC's/NIT's IN INDIA

Increasing competition for resources and attention across NIT's and communities is driving changes in the ways resource centers work and collaborate. NIT's resource centers are investing in programs and technologies that can raise the visibility of and access to their resources. NIT's resource centres are coming together to face challenges for shaping library services (Anderson, 2011).

- Build capacity and impact through cooperation.
- The need for broader, diverse partnerships.
- Challenges of proving relevance.
- Finding new efficiencies as budget pressures intensify.
- Dynamics of serving an education system under reconstruction.
- Amplify the value they bring to the community they serve.
- Rethinking the library's role in the terms of greater collaboration and cooperation with other institutions.
- Redeveloping the library's online presence to better address user needs.
- The need for new types of analytics and metrics more closely tied to performance measures.
- Share innovative and efficient solutions to keep up with the rapid pace of change.
- Analyze data in new ways that link library value to student learning, educational value, and community impact.
- Demands to deliver resources electronically, ubiquitously, seamlessly.

Figure 5. NITs responsible factors for moving cloud computing

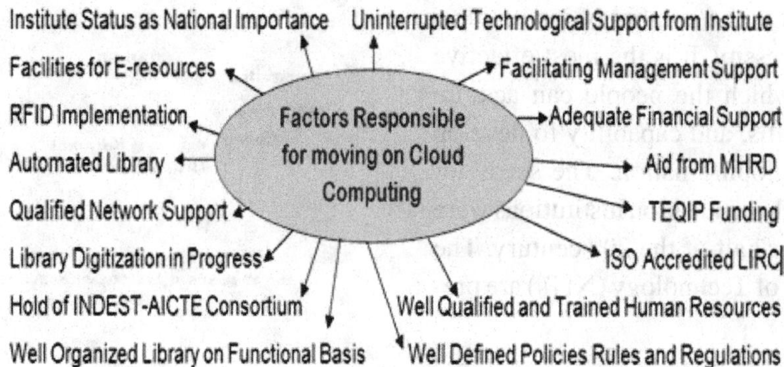

- Managing the transaction from print to electronic media.
- Keeping pace with the rate of technological change.
- Leverage their higher-value services.

THE STEPS TOWARD CLOUD COMPUTING FOR REC's/NIT's IN INDIA

Cloud adoption strategy helps in a world that is becoming more instrumented, interconnected, and intelligent. Cloud computing represents a smarter way to deliver services, use resources, control costs, and maintain a competitive advantage. Cloud computing can better satisfy their customers/patrons through improved visibility of IT resource use, better responsiveness, simplification, and cost-effective service delivery. Cloud computing can also increase the range of an organization's services, applications, and capabilities available to patrons/customers. Successful implementation requires an overall strategic vision combined with a pragmatic, evolutionary approach to deployment–one that all REC's/NIT's will develop through its many cloud engagements with customers around the world and within the nation. Tomorrow, VNIT will help NIT's, organizations around the world, and nations started on the journey toward cloud computing by following six strategic steps to cloud adoption.

Create the IT Strategy and Roadmap

For achieving goals of an organization it is very important to create a perfect roadmap and its IT strategy. Every organization has goals of rendering better services to public and for the same cloud service delivery, and the platform requirements and complexity associated with each. Goals can include:

- Centralization to reduce data centers and costs.
- Consolidation of servers and storage to reduce the carbon footprint.
- Virtualization to increase hardware utilization and standardize virtual images.
- Automation of service management processes application migration.
- Optimization of resources and dynamic provisioning of services.

Assess and Select Workloads for Cloud

REC's/NIT's have big collaboration of the huge country, so they have to first select workloads for the cloud, which is very beneficial for every person for upgrading their needs very easily. Workloads that are amenable to standardization, are self-contained applications or have a service-oriented architecture are more likely to be easily transported to a cloud environment. Identifying and prioritizing workloads which are assessed through the cloud delivery is the next step. Conversely, workloads that will be more difficult, risky, and costly to migrate to cloud computing are typically highly complex, require high amounts of data transfer, involve a high degree of customization, or are legacy systems that would require significant redesign to conform to cloud architecture.

Determine the Cloud Delivery Model

Once you have identified workloads, you can then establish which are more suited for delivery via a public cloud, private cloud, hybrid cloud, or community cloud. For public clouds, infrastructure and software-as-a-service workloads pose the least risk and offer the highest potential. These include audio, video, and Web conferencing, help desk and training infrastructure, desktop environments, and storage. For private clouds, data mining, text mining, analytics, security, and business continuity workloads offer higher potential and lower risk. In a community cloud, all type of the above environments are provided to the patron and library as well as an organizational point of view.

Determine the Value

It is very essential before implementing any new technology determine their value as per organizational aspect as well as their customer. Also determine increases in user productivity and resource utilization, avoidance of capital expense, and reduction of risk due to higher availability. Examine that cloud computing can bring, including time required for initial payback as well as projected payback. In determining, start by calculating the absolute saving that will be realized from all facets of IT operations related to the workload in question. For example hardware costs, software licenses and upgrades, system administration, system support, end user support, and provisioning.

Establish the Architecture

After selecting above steps, the final step prior to implementation will be to establish the architecture that will support your cloud initiatives, public, private, and community. It is very important to determine which type of cloud architecture is essential for an organization; for this we have to think over the following questions. Cloud architecture should address three domains: What are the services you will deliver or acquire? How will you create and deliver the services? How will users access the services? Underlying all three domains of the cloud platform is the architecture layer, which defines the dynamic infrastructure for cloud delivery and end user access.

Implement the IT Strategy, Roadmap, and Cloud Services

REC's/NIT's are very reputable; they have national importance acquiring organizations and innovative researchers; it is very essential to implement such a big innovative service to their researchers, students, staff, faculty, and every creative person who helps upgrade the national status and research activity. A key component of an IT strategy leading to the cloud is conditioning your infrastructure for cloud delivery. This may include virtualizing and automating existing systems, adding the service management capabilities requisite for cloud computing.

The cloud computing adoption framework can be a helpful tool in following these steps to implementation. The framework defines for cloud computing delivery model ad services, illustrates the key capabilities to consider in developing cloud computing strategies, and identifies key aspects required to successfully execute that strategy.

PLANNING AND IMPLEMENTATION OF CLOUD COMPUTING IN REC's/NIT's

Every new technology has advantages over the previous one, but necessarily lacks some of its predecessors attributes. Familiarity, which no doubt breeds contempt, breeds also comfort; that which is unfamiliar breeds distrust. Planning is a continuous process; it changes in the course of time and in the light of experience as we ourselves change. For fulfilling patron demands there is a necessity for improvement in the plan and implementation of new technologies. If the planning and implementation of innovative technologies in the library are introduced to understand and fulfill the needs of the 21st century digital native users on one face of the coin, then assessing and accounting for the success of these services is the other important face of the same coin

Cloud computing is a different form of IT infrastructure. Information software or other IT services are stored and accessed via third party servers connected to the Internet, rather than on individual computers or on private servers. This is not a new concept. Anyone who has a Web-based e-mail account such as 'Hotmail' or 'Gmail' is using a simple form of cloud computing. Amazon, Microsoft, Dell, IBM, Google, and Yahoo are just a few of the major IT companies who are developing or expanding their offerings to the commercial sector by giving businesses the opportunity to outsource various elements of their IT infrastructure with access achieved via the Internet (also known as "cloud-sourcing").

Cost savings and a reduced burden of running and maintaining IT infrastructure are the key features that make cloud-sourcing attractive. Removing storage and processing burdens on businesses can save huge amounts in capital cost (in terms of having to provide hard drives and servers to physically store and process data) and running costs (the housing and maintenance of on-site servers). There are also arguments that this can reduce a business's carbon footprint. To make Real-Time Library with Cloud-Scale Integration successful in today's global, 24×7 information environment and library/information center's operations need to be plugged into the Web. Library systems have to connect seamlessly to users and all the rich resources available online. In this Webcast, we need to learn about the technologies and operation models that enable real-time connections with users and resources, and find out the characteristics to look for when selecting a cloud integration platform.

Budgeting is a managerial device used for planning and facilitating resolutions about the distributing of resources. It is also one means of monitoring the results to ensure they conform to the plan. The budget expresses financially how the library will achieve its outcomes, and as such must be linked to the libraries priorities. Preparation of the budget should always be the role of the library advisory committee in consultation with other library staff. The first step in developing a library budget is to look at what the library hopes to accomplish in the next year. The availability of a current long-range plan will make this step much easier, because the plan should already document library users' need for resources and the library activities necessary to meet those needs.

The second step is to determine the total financial resources necessary for what the library wants to accomplish in the coming year. Often, increased funding is necessary because of increased costs, increased usage, and/or new services that will be offered. Additional resources for new services can also be made available by shifting resources from a lower priority to a higher priority services. Budgeting should not be seen as an isolated or incidental exercise. It must be inextricably tied to the notion of priorities and needs. The effective budget should be fair, appropriate, documented, and well-publicized. It is essential that forthcoming needs are clearly identified and cost effective.

REC's/ NIT's (see Figure 6) libraries are finding it difficult to keep pace with the ever growing need of enhanced and better forms of information. Ever year, thousands of books are bought by the NIT's resource Centers in order to keep track with the latest available literature on different subjects. Obviously, with their fixed budgets, not all books (or e-books) can be purchased. Every library tends to have certain data which may be present in some other libraries too, which leads to a lot of duplication of data. However, if the REC's/NIT's libraries integrate their data, there would be no more duplication since the libraries would be sharing the common data. The implementation of this technique, though, may not be as simple as it may seem to be. It is here that cloud computing can play its part. Cloud computing can help REC's libraries collaborate with each other in a facile manner. Every library has its own electronic data

Figure 6. Future of all NITs sharing through cloud

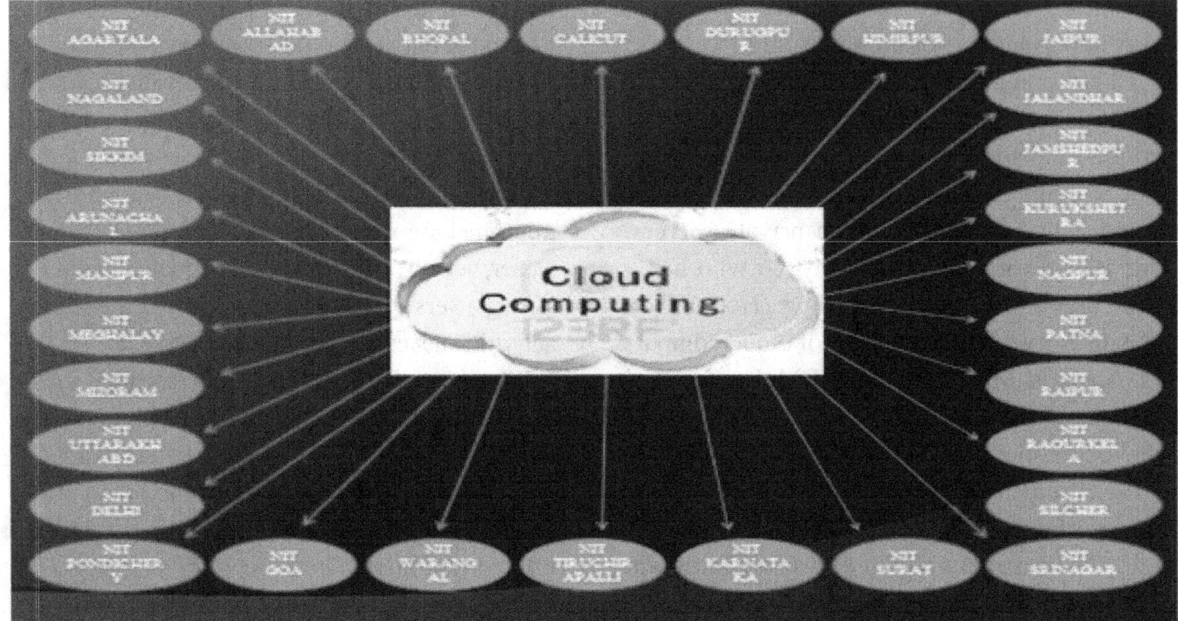

resources. If the all the electronic data resources are put together in a single place which may be accessed by a group of NIT's libraries, the whole electronic data base will become huge. This space which contains all the electronic data can be some cloud, say, a library cloud. This library cloud will contain the digitized data of different libraries and hence, will help libraries integrate their data. The need for maintaining and backing up the data will be no more the responsibility of the libraries since all the data will be stored in the cloud which shall be managed by some cloud provider.

It will also help the NIT's libraries in scaling up or down their data capacity whenever required. This scaling up or down is purely a function of need. Hence, the libraries would be consuming exactly the required space. Not a megabyte more! As a result, NIT's libraries will not have to predict their future needs and buy space and infrastructure beforehand. This coadjuvant effort of the NIT's libraries will not only increase the overall efficiency (since the data will be shared) but also open doors for innovation, make libraries a lot more scalable, and help save money as well. HathiTrust3 is a great example which shows us what cloud computing holds in store for the libraries. HaithiTrust is a repository for keeping a huge amount of digitized data shared among its members. It was founded in October 2008 and already has over 60 partners, including mainly university libraries all around the world.

SECURITY AND PRIVACY

There are numerous security issues for cloud computing as it encompasses many technologies including networks, databases, operating systems, virtualization, resource scheduling, transaction management, load balancing, concurrency control, and memory management. Therefore security issues for many of these systems and technologies are applicable to cloud computing. For example, the network that interconnects the systems in a cloud has to be secure. Furthermore, virtualization paradigm in cloud computing leads to several security concerns. Data security involves encrypting the data as well as ensuring that appropriate policies are enforce for data sharing. In addition, resource a location and memory management algorithms have to be secure. Security can be established using strong authentication, authorization and accounting procedure, establishing security of data at rest and in transit, locking down networks and hardening operating systems, middleware, and application software. It should be provide access only to authorized, authenticated users and those users need to be able to trust that their data is secure.

Cloud computing have wonderful security measure of encrypted and de-encrypted privacy in which there is arrangement of scrambled words which are not familiar to the machine language but it is familiar to human being these efforts are being made to identifying human being to a machine with security. There is interface of identifying correct human being to the machine so that machine will move on the information more securely if the person is identified. Somewhere scramble words are needed to be entering so that the correct human beings are too identified. Then only there is a foolproof security. For example in IRCTC debit card or credit card are being verified at IRCTC for visa verification.

Imagine RE • Design REC's/ NIT's in India Construct

As we know all type of revolution grabs everyone for achieving success. Creating and consuming a universe of content, challenges facing higher education, ability to leverage large information assets, type of research, spotting and predicting social and natural trades, analyzing user/consumer behavior, providing customized service prove worth the effort of reimaging, redesign, reconstruct REC's/NIT's in India towards cloud computing. Reengineering a Cloud computing platform in REC's/NIT's are needs to examine following major issues.

- Communicating Value.
- Data Curation.
- Digital Preservation.
- Higher Education.
- Information Technology.
- Mobile Environments (through mobile phones apps).
- Patron Driven e-book acquisition.
- Scholarly Communication.
- Staffing.
- User Behaviors and Expectations.
- Backups to the cloud can protect all kinds of organizational data.

PREAMBLE OF VNIT

Visvesvaraya National Institute of Technology, Nagpur is one of the thirty National Institutes of Technology in the country. Earlier, the Institute was known as Visvesvaraya Regional College of Engineering (VRCE). It was established in the year 1960 under the scheme sponsored by Govt. of India and Govt. of Maharashtra. In 2002, VRCE became VNIT with Deemed University status from UGC, and the Central Government took full financial and administrative responsibility. In August 2007, VNIT became the Institute of National Importance under the act of parliament.

The library was established in the 1960s when the state engineering college was in existence. The library has also received recognition as one of the best libraries in central India due to REC status. VNIT Library serves its users with the best services and to fulfill the requirements of the users as well as the organization. Since in this changing environment with the introduction of new technologies and the changing perception about the information and the information system, it is seen that the library needs to understand this change and work accordingly with the current situations and accept the current trends. As automation became a boon factor, LIRC VNIT changed itself from a traditional library to the new modern library with the introduction of different technologies available for library automation. From 1994 onwards LIRC VNIT is using LIBSYS software package for library activities. It made an infrastructure for LIBSYS software by using different networks like LAN and different points for user (OPAC) to consult the catalogue. After this it started with new technology (i.e., barcode technology in the year 2010) and now it has gone one step ahead with the implementation of Radio Frequency Identification (RFID). The status of VNIT is capable for the encroachment of cloud computing.

FACTORS RESPONSIBLE FOR MOVING ON CLOUD COMPUTING IN LIRC VNIT

Development needs up-gradation, and for perusing the next step, VNIT is ready to accept new technology. Above all, NIT's level factors are also seen in VNIT; therefore organization can be moving on cloud computing. These are the factors of LIRC VNIT that are responsible for cloud computing (Deshpande, Rahangdale, & Bhoskar, 2013).

- Institute Status as National Importance.
- Automated Library.
- Library Digitization in Progress.
- RFID Implementation.
- Hold of INDEST-AICTE Consortium.
- Facilities for E-resources.
- Well Organized Library on Functional Basis.
- Well Defined Policies Rules and Regulations.
- Qualified Network Support.
- Well Qualified and Trained Human Resources.
- Uninterrupted Technological Support from the Institute.
- Techno Savvy Chairman ET and LS.
- Facilitating Management Support.
- Adequate Financial Support.
- ISO Accredited LIRC.
- Aid from MHRD.
- TEQIP Funding.

RESOURCES AT INSTITUTE LEVEL THAT CAN BE MOVED TO CLOUD COMPUTING

National important acquired VNIT institute have robust framework for statistical, literary, cultural, educational resources so again for maintaining standard there is need of sharing these resources to every person. Therefore cloud computing architecture will open up new opportunities for more shared access and more use and creation of new information for the organization. A Cloud base information service for education and research institution will open up numerous opportunities for sharing data and information that are currently held within the servers of specific institute. VNIT can share following data through cloud computing.

- Faculty Profile.
- Student Profile (like a student grade report).
- Literary Events.
- Funding Criteria for Admission.
- Cultural Events.
- Technological Event Axis, Consortium, Yuddha, Love for Physics, Astronomy Club.
- Sharing of Virtual Class Room.
- Social Networking.
- National/International Conferences.

RESOURCES AT LIBRARY LEVEL THAT CAN BE MOVE TO CLOUD COMPUTING

Cloud computing represents one of the most important technology trends of our time. Every day we make use of computing and information resources through a Web browser powered by some distant and diffuse infrastructure. This model has become routine for personal use (e.g., e-mail, word processing, social networking, photo sharing, etc.). In more recent months and years, cloud computing has entered the library technology sphere. Cloud computing brings the opportunity for libraries to shift away from the need to own and operate their own servers to power their core automation applications and to instead shift to gaining similar functionality through Web-based services. In order to develop technology strategies in this context, it's essential for libraries to have a solid understanding of this new technology landscape, to move beyond a vague awareness of cloud computing (Breeding, 2012).

VNIT resource center have ready to encroach cloud computing for these knowledgeable resources which are beneficial for our patrons. Migration of libraries are responsible for researchers activity which are bust up our national level through moving library material on cloud computing. VNIT have valuable resource material:

- E-Books.
- E-Journals.
- NPTEL Lectures.
- Workshop Programmers.
- Institutional Repository (with the help of Greenstone).
- Assessment and peer review.
- Research Publications.
- National/International Conferences Papers.
- Thesis and Reports.
- Research Work.
- Digitization of rare books in PDF form (With the use of newly introduction of "RECAPTCHA" programme).

CONCLUSION

Big innovation requires big collaboration and Cloud computing will help the integration of REC's / NIT's libraries in a painless, easy manner. We can show the worth of libraries as community space. NIT's libraries will be able to share their electronic data resources which shall lead to reduction of duplicate data resulting in cutting down the overall budget of libraries. The dependency of libraries on external agencies for matters pertaining to IT is also expected to reduce considerably. Capital expenditure on hardware resources will be converted to operational expenditure. Scalability of cloud computing will also help in saving money. Libraries will also become greener by embracing the cloud. Server utilization, which will increase considerably, along with multitenancy, will help reduce carbon emissions annually. The more the NIT's libraries work together to aggregate and share data, utilize shared infrastructure and collaborate as a global community, the more value that can be delivered to the users of libraries.

REFERENCES

Abidi, F., & Abidi, H. J. (2012). Cloud libraries: A novel application of cloud computing. *International Journal of Cloud Computing and Services Science (IJ-CLOSER), 1*(3), 79-83.

Anderson, C. (2011). *Libraries Operating at Webscale*. Retrieved from http://www.oclc.org/content/dam/oclc/reports/worldshare-management-services/libraries-at-webscale.pdf

Breeding, M. (2012). *Cloud computing for libraries*. Chicago: ALA TechSource.

Chakraborty, A. K., & Abhik, C. (2013). Cloud computing for knowledge resource centre. In *Proceedings of 2nd International Conference on Academic Libraries* (pp. 68-75). New Delhi, India: Indo American Books Publication.

Deshpande, R. M., Rahangdale, B., & Bhoskar, R. (2013). Factors responsible for current status of libraries of national institute of technology in India. In *Proceedings of 2nd International Conference on Academic Libraries* (pp. 208-213). New Delhi, India: Indo American Books Publication.

Kumar, N. (2013). Cloud computing for academic library: A SWOT analysis. In *Proceedings of 2nd International Conference on Academic Libraries* (pp. 187-198). New Delhi, India: Indo American Books Publication.

Shagin, A. (2012). *Benefits of cloud computing*. Retrieved from http://blogs.sap.com/innovation/cloud-computing/risks-and-benefits-of-cloud-computing-020025

Singh, B., & Sirohi, K. (2013). Cloud computing use case for library. In *Proceedings of 2nd International Conference on Academic Libraries* (pp. 30-39). New Delhi, India: Indo American Books Publication.

Wikipedia. (2013). *National Institute of Technology*. Retrieved from http://en.wikipedia.org/wiki/National_Institutes_of_Technology

Chapter 7
A New Framework for Building Academic Library through Cloud Computing

Vijay Parashar
FET Library, Mody Institute of Technology & Science, India

Mohan Lal Vishwakarma
FET Library, Mody Institute of Technology & Science, India

Reema Parashar
FET Library, Mody Institute of Technology & Science, India

ABSTRACT

Libraries all over the world suffer from common problems like flexibility associated with digital data, lower levels of efficiency, and costs involved in managing the entire IT infrastructure. Few options are available in collaborating with other libraries, which is the prime reason for subordinate levels of efficiency. For the past 20 years the use of Information Communication Technology (ICT) has fundamentally changed the practices and procedures of nearly all forms of endeavor within business and governance. Within education, ICT has begun to have a presence, but the cost of ICT is not affordable. The basic principle of cloud computing entails the reduction of in-house data centres and the delegation of a portion or all of the information technology infrastructure capability to a third party. Universities and colleges are the core of innovation through their advanced research and development. Subsequently, higher institutions may benefit greatly by harnessing the power of cloud computing. Cloud computing would help in bridging the gap between academic libraries and ICT. Sharing of data among the libraries will in principle reduce the overall cost and increase efficiency. Capital expenditure done on infrastructure will chiefly be converted into operational expenditure. It will also enhance the user's experience and will help in making the libraries a lot more scalable. In this chapter the authors discuss problems faced with academic libraries and development efforts to overcome that problem. Then they propose to improve current user service model with cloud computing.

DOI: 10.4018/978-1-4666-4631-5.ch007

INTRODUCTION

Cloud computing is a technology that uses the Web (Internet) and central remote servers to maintain data, software, and application. Cloud computing allows users to use applications without installation in their local machine to access their personal and official files on any computer with Internet access. This technology allows users to access much more efficient computing by centralizing storage, memory and processing. This is not a new technology; it's associated with inception of the Web. In the libraries cloud computing is used to build a digital library and to automate housekeeping operations using third party services, software and hardware. Cloud computing refers to both applications delivered as a service over the Internet and the systems software in the data centers that provide services. In simple words the datacenters, hardware, and systems software is what we can call a cloud. A simple example of cloud computing is Yahoo mail, Gmail, and so forth. One does not need any software or server to store them. These services are free to all users till some limit, any extra storage capacity and advanced services are available at cost.

CLOUD COMPUTING

Various definitions and interpretations of 'Cloud 'and 'Cloud computing' exist and some of them are:

- "Internet based computing in which large group of remote servers are networked so as to allow sharing of data-processing tasks, centralized data storage a n d on l i n e access computer service or resources" (Dictionary.com, n.d.).
- "Cloud computing is a general term for anything that involves delivering hosted services over the Internet. These services are broadly divided into three categories: Infrastructure-as-a-Service (IaaS), Platform-as-a-Service (PaaS) and Software-as-a-Service (SaaS). The name cloud computing was inspired by the cloud symbol that's often used to represent the Internet in flowcharts and diagrams" (Search cloud computing, n.d.).
- "Cloud computing is a model for enabling ubiquitous, convenient, on-demand network access to a shared pool of configurable computing resources (e.g., networks, servers, storage, applications, and services) that can be rapidly provisioned and released with minimal management effort or service provider interaction. This cloud model is composed of five essential characteristics, three service models, and four deployment models" (Mell & Grance, 2009).

Cloud computing means cloud based networking environment. Cloud computing contains a set of a software and hardware resources that are available on the Internet and its services are managed by third-party. These services provide access to advanced software applications and highly configured servers. The service provider performs the role of consultant. Cloud computing is a Web based computing where shared resources, applications, and information are provided to the set of computers and other devices on demand using Web technology. Cloud computing is based on Internet; generally the Internet is commonly visualized as a cloud. Therefore, the process of cloud computing is being done through set of Web enabled applications loaded on the server with proper access rights. KPMG breaks this into essentially four different types of cloud computing: infrastructure, platform, applications, and services. To put this in more concrete terms, examples of each can be seen in Table 1.

Cloud computing can be understood as a way to use off-site computer processing power to replace content creation and servers that were traditionally hosted onsite. In layman's terms this

Table 1. Examples of Cloud Computing Types

Type	What It Is	Examples
Infrastructure	Buying space/time on external servers	Amazon A3 Bungee
Platform	An existing software platform to build your own applications on	Facebook
Applications	Software applications accessed with a Web browser	Google Docs Salesforce.com
Services	Ready to use services accessed with a Web browser	ADP

means "using Web services for our computing needs" (Kroski, 2009). Cloud computer allows content creation to be made "when data and software applications reside on and are drawn from the network rather than locally on any one workstation." By utilizing online applications, users can create and save their files online, share content (often for free), work collaboratively with others or create entire services that can all be accessed online without need of having the programs on their own computer.

These online services can reduce the need for expensive software, hardware, and even advanced technical knowledge from library staff since cloud computing services are often streamlined to be very user-friendly. As well, "the focus shifts away from which devices effectively store data and able to run applications to which devices can provide the easiest access to data and applications – which are stored at various places on the Internet" (Kroski, 2009).

SEGMENTS OF CLOUD COMPUTING

The Following are Different Segments of Cloud Computing

- **Application:** The application segment is the part of Internet technology which is proved already as the constructive and helpful model. When many individual applications are accessed through the central server of cloud, the library (institute) will demand sever a cost. On the other hand, the applications of on-demand are not similar in the price scheme and delivering process to the users. In short an application is the first segment without which a concept of cloud computing cannot be survived.
- **Storage:** The backbone of the main concept of cloud computing is called infrastructure or storage. All the vendors will permit the users to create their own cloud

Figure 1. Cloud Service Management Implementation Framework

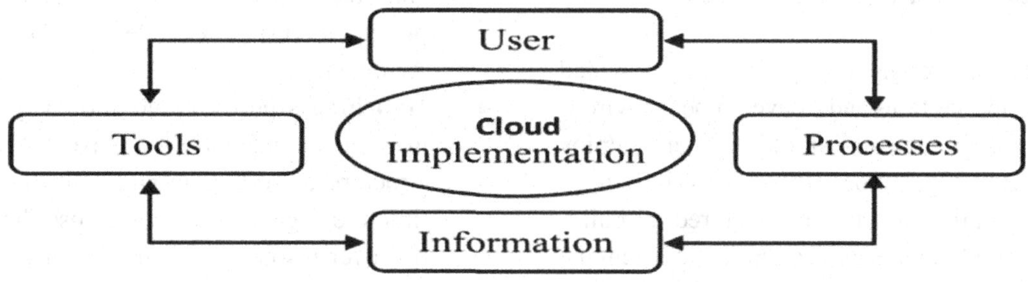

applications within the limited space. The popular S3 of Amazon is considered as a storage segment.

- **Connectivity:** Most important part of the cloud is connectivity. Without high speed Internet connectivity there will be no use of application and storage. Therefore, the high speed leased line Internet connectivity is necessary to connect with the cloud.

All above three segments are interrelated with each other and, out of three, if any one segment is missing then a concept of cloud will remain unfulfilled.

TYPES OF CLOUD

Software as a Service (SaaS)

Applications or software is delivered as a service to the customer who can access the program from any online device. Some of these Web-based applications are free such as Hotmail, Google Apps, Skype, and many 2.0 applications, while most business-oriented SaaS, such as Sales Force, is leased on a subscription basis. There is usually little customization or control available with these applications. However, subscribers benefit from low initial costs, have access to (usually 24/7) support services, and needn't worry about hosting, installing, upgrading, or maintaining the software.

Platform as a Service (PaaS)

With PaaS, a computing platform is provided which supplies tools and a development environment to help companies build, test, and deploy Web-based applications. Businesses don't need to invest in the infrastructure required for building Web and mobile applications but can rent the use of platforms such as Windows Azure, Google AppEngine, and Force.com. Applications which are built using these provider's services, however, are usually locked into that one platform.

Infrastructure as a Service (IaaS)

This type of cloud computing is also sometimes referred to as HaaS or Hardware as a Service and it involves both storage services and computing power. Amazon's Web Services, one of the major players in this area, offers two main products including the Elastic Compute Cloud (EC2), which provides computing resources, and Simple Storage Service (S3) for data storage.

Companies are using Amazon's Web Services to host or backup their Websites, for content delivery, to run high performance computing simulations, to host media collections, and much more. Most of these cloud services are available on a pay-per-usage basis, differing from the SaaS subscription model, enabling customers to scale up or down depending on their need at any given time and only pay for what they've used.

On the Basis of Usage

- **Private:** Private clouds are available only to the members of the organization. The cloud will facilitate user to store and disseminate their data on respective cloud (e.g., institutional cloud, ebay, etc.)
- **Public:** Any institute may use cloud service from third party which may available free or with cost can be considered as public cloud (e.g., Google apps, Windows Azure, etc.)
- **Hybrid:** As public cloud allow any organization to outsource their part of infrastructure to service provider, at the same time the organization would lose the control over resources and data management.

Figure 2. Cloud computing Models: Saas, Paas, Iaas

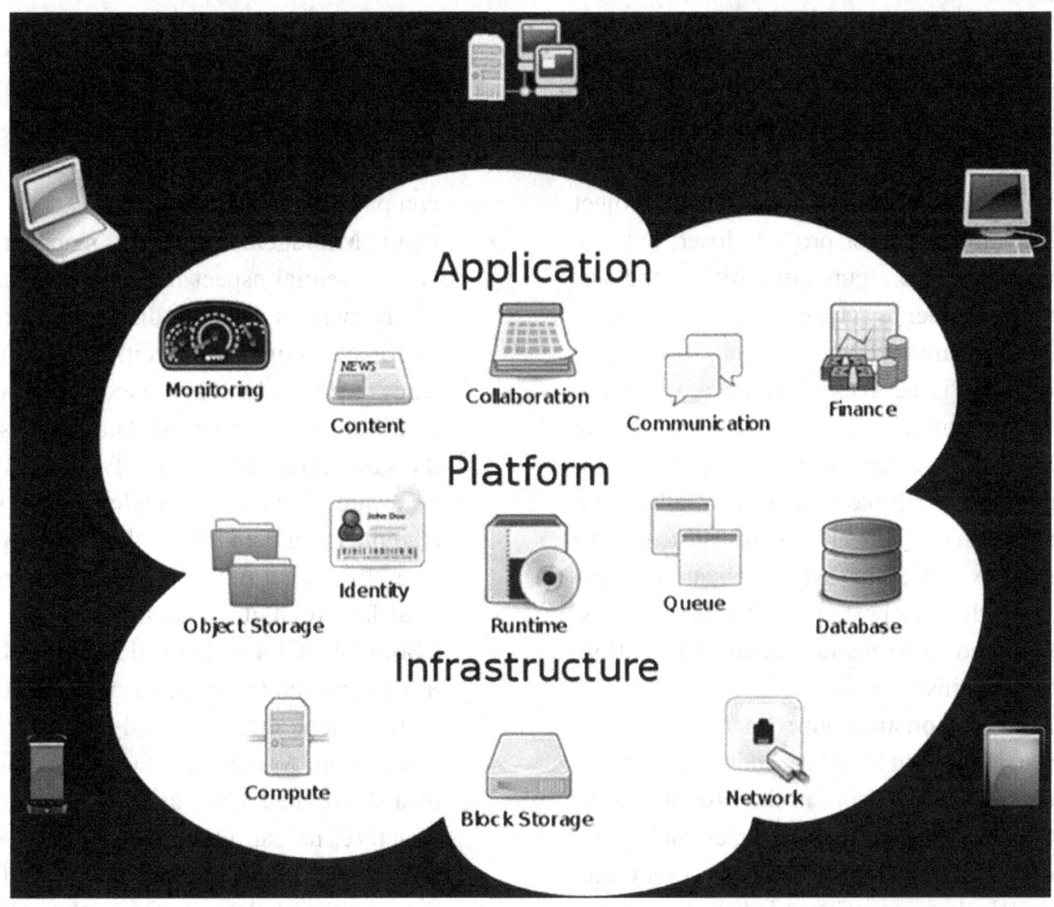

In this type of cloud a part of cloud will be given to public for use. (e.g., Google Apps, etc.)

- **Community:** Community clouds are specifically organized clouds and are limited for specific group (e.g., Institutional Gmail of GoogleApps, etc.)

On the Basis of Service

- **Infrastructure:** Infrastructure is provided by third party as service to the users to use them the way they want. (e.g., Amazon S3)
- **Platform:** Basically, platform is a set of computational resources using which one can use the infrastructure. In other words a set of computer application developed and hosted on the cloud to access and manage the data. (e.g., Google App Engine, Windows Azure [Platform])
- **Service:** Services are the set of applications developed by the service provider to use cloud infrastructure and platform. (e.g., Google Docs)

FEATURES OF CLOUD COMPUTING IN LIBRARIES

The following are different features of cloud computing:

- **Elasticity and Scalability:** Elasticity is one of the essential and core features of cloud systems. This is a very important feature of this service. Any modification and enhancement in the services is very easy and fast this makes service very scalable and resilient. One can easily add up required bandwidth, processing speed and data storage or number of licenses in very short time. One need not to plan any more for project costing, procurement, project implementation or project closer; but one need to place a purchase order to the service provider to get the service in due time.

- **Multi-Tenancy:** Multi tenancy is a highly essential issue in cloud systems, where the location of code and / or data is principally unknown and the same resource may be assigned to multiple users (potentially at the same time). This affects infrastructure resources as well as data / applications / services that are hosted on shared resources, but need to be made available in multiple isolated instances.
- **Energy Consumption:** Energy consumption is relevant to reduce additional costs of energy consumption. In the case of a traditional system one has to keep all the servers on as the data loaded on the server for round the clock access. Cloud is based on a network environment and therefore, principally allows reducing the energy consumption.
- **Reliability:** It's an amazing characteristic of cloud computing. Reliability is one needed characteristic of cloud computing which will increase when redundant Websites are accessed. Reliability is improved by having multiple sites for the same service, such that if one faces an outage, the other can take over the load.
- **Security:** Security is obviously essential in all systems dealing with potentially sensitive data and code. The cloud is managed and administered by a team of IT experts. Therefore, the data will be secure in terms of data loss and system crash.
- **Consumption-Based Billing:** The capability to build up cost according to the actual consumption of resources is a relevant feature of cloud systems. Pay per use strongly relates to quality of service support, where specific requirements to be met by the system and hence to be paid for can be specified. One of the great features of cloud is, if you don't use the resource then you pay nothing.
- **Data Management:** Data management is an essential aspect in sense of storage, where data is flexibly distributed across multiple resources. Implicitly, data consistency needs to be maintained over a wide distribution of replicated data sources. At the same time, the system always needs to be aware of the data location at the time of replicating data across the data centers. Therefore, data management is a tremendous feature of cloud environment.
- **Managing Cloud Activities:** One of the most considerable features of the cloud is management and monitoring of the cloud application. As cloud manager works within a distributed wide area network infrastructure; he can monitor it from all over the world. One of the biggest shifts from the traditional data center is that all the data stored, managed and administered in a cloud.
- **Self-Service Model:** One of the reason are behind popularity of cloud based environment is the self-service model. In some cases users have the ability to upload files, build programs, deploy, schedule, manage, and generate reports. This service is available to the users based on demand.

CLOUD COMPUTING IN THE CONTEXT OF LIBRARIES

Libraries are moving towards cloud and trying to provide network based services. Moving to cloud based services means that the library housekeeping operations, digital libraries etc. are hosted on a cloud based network. In the recent era many libraries are using Google Web technology knowingly or unknowingly to provide services. Earlier, if a person wanted to create document or spreadsheet he was using Microsoft's Office package, nowadays many libraries are processing documents, using Google Web technology (Google Docs) on day-to-day basis. Use of Google apps and other similar tools in the libraries shows a radical shift from traditional to advance technologies. Now libraries are providing a good number of services to their users to access various resources and computer applications from a single platform. This is an advantage of the cloud computing.

The concept of cloud computing is not much accepted in Indian libraries. The reason is the lack of good service provider in the field of library management, using advanced technology. Many libraries are thinking to adopt cloud computing but they are facing some problems in relation to standardize software, administrative procedures, budget constraints, connectivity problem etc. Nowadays, some foreign companies are providing cloud based services (e.g., Exlibris, Polaris Library Systems, Dura cloud, etc.).

AREAS OF LIBRARY WHERE CLOUD COMPUTING CAN BE APPLIED

In today's scenario libraries are adopting advanced technology in their day-to-day activity and the concept of cloud is one of them. In libraries there are main two areas which can be moved on the cloud.

1. Automation of housekeeping operations
2. Digital library

With a view to Indian libraries one need to examine all the criteria before choosing any cloud service. Because, when it is planned to use third party services one need to have thorough idea about the whole system. If one thinks that our all day-to-day activities can be moved then, first of all searching the standard company who has set of various software and hardware and experience in handling such services. There are many companies in the market which provide this kind of services.

How Libraries Impact through Cloud Computing?

Beyond the basic components like hosted email services that have a strong consumer base, cloud computing can be utilized to address needs which are specific to libraries? This can be broken down into the three types of cloud services, replacing a library's onsite technology environment with an online version, and then situations where a library can create its own cloud infrastructure. These areas offer "benefits to information professionals: outsourced infrastructure, greater flexibility, reduced barriers to innovation, and lower start up investments."

The three main types of cloud services are Software as a Service (SaaS), Platform as a Service (PaaS), and Infrastructure as a Service (IaaS) (Kroski, 2009). First, cloud computing offers the ability of libraries to use online software to handle a task like video chat through either Gmail video chat or through Skype. Both of these are free services though there is "little customization or control available with these applications" (Kroski, 2009). In other words, services you offer through a SaaS' interface will look like that of your competitors which will not distinguish you from them. On the other hand, since the services and application interfaces are often familiar with users, there would be a decrease in the learning curve for library staff and users.

Second, libraries can create applications in an online environment. These environments allow a library to "build, test, and deploy Web-based applications" (Kroski, 2009). PaaS gives the library the freedom to explore development options without having to purchase and maintains the required infrastructure. This way, if a particular program turns out to not be popular or a best fit for a library, they are not stuck with unwanted hardware and software which they could not recoup the costs from.

Third, a library no longer has to purchase their own servers to host their content. By using IaaS, a library can purchase server space and computing power. One of the major players in this arena is Amazon which offers the "Elastic Compute Cloud (EC2), which provides computing resources and Simple Storage Services (S3) for data storage" (Kroski, 2009). A library does not need to purchase a server which is underutilized but costs the same to purchase and maintain as if it were using all of its resources at all times. By using an IaaS, a library gains the benefit of only paying for the "resources you actually use" (Kroski, 2009).

Therefore the main benefit for moving to a cloud computing environment for a library is the ability to both try out new software without having to buy the hardware as well as being able to scale the computing power to meet the demand of users. A library's IT department can be more flexible in raising the amount of cloud computing they require by contacting their vendor instead of physically having to acquire new hardware to meet increased demands. This method will save the library money and staff resources.

Beyond Library Discovery Services

It is here that libraries can look to gain new efficiencies both internally and among the entire library community. When library software suppliers create the user personas that will use their software the focus is generally on external personas but there are also many internal personas that need to take advantage of new technologies and Web capabilities. One such example has been given with reference librarians now able to both better assist their patrons online but also to build a large network of librarians globally who can answer specific questions and be available 24/7. What other persons in the library can benefit from cloud solutions? Some examples are listed below:

- Acquisitions librarians managing increasingly diverse collections.
- Cataloging librarians seeking to describe an ever increasing body of information and information sources the library is managing.
- Serials librarians working to maintain control and access to collections across the Web.
- Electronic resource librarians managing burgeoning collections, and ever-changing lists of vendors.

The dramatic change in library collections often blurs the lines between traditional job roles in libraries. An acquisitions librarian probably also needs to manage licenses for electronic materials as well as manage purchasing for multiple formats, often for the same item. They need to access information from suppliers, reviewers, local constituency and other staff in a unified manner. This begs for an open system deployed where it can easily be accessed by external systems and pull in data and services in from those same systems. Cloud computing solutions can create the new workflows needed by librarians because it offers the opportunity for a cooperative platform for libraries to build on. There are four key principles of a cooperative platform:

- Openness, meaning that services and data are made available to support greater interoperability, not only within and between cloud services, but also with library-developed and third-party applications.
- Extensibility, meaning that the platform can easily accommodate the addition of new services and applications, developed either by the service provider or by members of the community.

- Data richness, meaning that a library can interact with and expose a wide variety of information about purchased, licensed, and digital content through this platform.
- Collaboration, meaning that libraries can harness the collective power of the community of libraries to innovate and share solutions.

And it is precisely this that the business world and social media have demonstrated can be done with cloud computing solutions. Through cooperative community building, libraries can have the same possibilities.

THE CLOUD IN THE ACADEMIC LIBRARY

While libraries can use cloud computing applications to create personalized portals for users, the Department of Library and Information Studies (LIS) at the University could use cloud computing as their back up methodology. This solution was proposed when confronted with the department to another building on campus.

The current proposal for back up within the LIS department is to have an external hard drive that is passed around to faculty members to back their data up on. However, this is a tedious process that also endangers the data due to the physical shuffling of the hard drive from place to place. The files that are to be backed up often exist on only the computers of faculty and staff or on flash drives. There is no centralized location of the files.

The method proposing for the department is to create their own cloud server. This can be accomplished by the purchase of a Pogoplug device that connects to the network. Pogoplug is an Internet enabled product that will allow the LIS department to connect their own external hard drives to it and then anyone with the access permissions will be able to access the data stored on the hard drives. In summary, it is a simple cloud server. With Pogoplug, faculty and staff will be able to access the cloud hard drives through a Web portal. Or they can also make their folder on Pogo plug appear as a folder on their desktop connected computer. In order to make this a backup solution, faculty should have a copy of the files also on their desktop computer. It will need to be investigated if a free synchronization application like ToySync from Microsoft would be capable of automatically keeping folders synchronized without the need to do it manually. This solution has been proposed to the chair of the LIS Tech Committee. The next likely step if the proposal goes through will be securing a Pogoplug and testing it on the network before full-scale implementation by all parties.

Libraries will want to consider what types of information or processes they want to trust to the cloud. The responsibility of libraries to preserve information at the Top Tech Trends panel, making the point that outsourcing its preservation in effect relinquishes that obligation.

Libraries will need to consider not only this type of ethical quandary, but also practical ones such as the privacy of sensitive information such as patron records, and concerns about records retention requirements. But it needn't be an all-or-nothing decision as libraries may choose to continue to host some of their own systems while using the cloud for less sensitive processes such as hosting library Websites, backing up media collections, or storing and accessing bibliographic data.

Libraries have already begun to adopt cloud services to alleviate their IT departments and increase efficiency. In addition to these libraries, the Library of Congress has entered into a partnership with Duracloud for a one-year pilot program testing out cloud storage capabilities (see last month's interview with LC staffers for more), and OCLC has announced a new Web-scale.

ANALYSIS OF CURRENT USER SERVICE MODEL IN ACADEMIC LIBRARY

University library, as a most important academic and scientific research base, charges for providing information services for its users. In the past, most libraries insisted that their service is based on their own library resources. So librarians scarcely considered users' demands. But today, modern libraries have changed this viewpoint. And librarians usually need to collect as more information as they can accord users' requirements? Then they will analyze the information and sort them out. Finally, they will provide them for users in some certain technical methods. However, services in modern libraries will increasingly focus on users' demanding in the future. And the ultimate goal of modern library is to offer appropriate, comprehensive and multi-level services for its users. Current user service models are mainly WWW service model, FTP service model, BBS and E-mail service model, and so forth, as follows:

- **WWW Service Model:** WWW (World Wide Web) is based on client-server model. It presents all kinds of information browsing systems with the bases of HTML language and HTTP protocol. The specific division is: WWW Servers are in charge of linking Web pages by hypertext links and WWW clients are responsible for displaying information and sending requests to servers. And the most significant feature of WWW service is its high degree of integration. In other words, it can connect all kinds of information and services seamlessly and provide user with vivid graphical user interface. In general, the WWW provides new means of searching and sharing information for people around the world. Meanwhile, it gradually becomes the best means of dynamic multimedia interactive for with people.
- **FTP Service Model:** FTP (File Transfer Protocol) is a widely used communication protocol. And it is comprised of various rules that support file transfer on the Internet. As such rules can permit online users for copy files from one host to another, it brings great convenience and benefits to users. Just as other Internet services, FTP are also based on client-server model. Meanwhile, it's easy to learn to use FTP service. First, you only need to start the FTP client program to connect with remote host, then you should issue file transfer command to remote host and after remote host; received the command, it will give response and implement the correct operation. Launching FTP service in university library network system is a good type that brings great convenience for users and library as well. By using FTP service in university library, users can make their own password, such as using their Email address, and this can let librarians obtain users visiting records easily. Furthermore, according to users' visiting records, librarians can offer corresponding services for them and improved users' satisfaction.

Internet and E-mail Service Model

BBS (Bulletin Board Service) is a kind of electronic information service system on the Internet. It is just like a public blank board on the Internet; all users can write their thoughts or release information on this board. And E-mail is just another kind of information service on the Internet. In a word, E-mail provides a very quick, simple and economical way of communication for the Internet users in the whole world. Through BBS system, library users can ask and consult librarians at any time. Usually they can get their response in a very short period of time. Meanwhile, librarians can communicate with more users at a time through BBS. What's more, university libraries can open lectures, release announcements and provide online help for users by BBS system. And through E-mail system, users can obtain their needed information and knowledge resources more quickly and economically as they don't need to visit libraries personally. In the new information environment, various IT technologies are updated timely. So current user service models are already out of date at some extent and they brought convenient services for users and their libraries. Facing the problems of shortage of funds, manpower and other material resources, current user service models cannot deal well with them effectively. What's worse, they may cause waste of resources and affect the quality of library services. BBSes were generally text-based, rather than GUI-based and early BBSes conversed using the simple ASCII character set. However, some home computer manufacturers extended the ASCII character set to take advantage of the advanced color and graphics capabilities of their systems.

STRUCTURAL DESIGN OF CLOUD AND IMPROVEMENT OF USER SERVICES IN ACADEMIC LIBRARIES

Architecture of cloud databases for libraries is a major view point of the selection of cloud services. One needs to keep some criteria for evaluation of databases, application, hardware configuration etc., which are available for the cloud.

With the rapid development of various IT technologies, users' information requirements are increasingly personalized. And now more and more libraries advocated user-centred services. So librarians should mine and study users' information requirements frequently. And only in this way, they can master the basic demands of their users. Furthermore, library can develop itself according to such information and improve users' satisfaction. University library, as we all know, is famous for its academic and teaching influences. And IT technology has been the driving force of library development. What's more, librarians can keep using new technology to develop library and optimize library service. With the expansion of Cloud Computing application, this paper proposes to apply cloud computing in libraries. By establishing a pubic cloud among many university libraries, it not only can conserve library resources but also can improve its user satisfaction.

Unified Search Service Model

Although there are OPAC (Online Public Access Catalogue) and ILL (Inter-library loan) services already, library users still cannot access the shared resources through uniform access platform. However, with the adoption of cloud computing in university library, the integrated library resources support distributed uniform access interface. At the same time, the uniform access platform can promote library resources, guide and answer users' questions by using high-quality navigation. As a result, users can grip more information retrieval methods and make better use of library resources.

Integrated Consulting Services Model

Today almost every university library can provide its users with network reference by BBS or Email. But with the constant improvement of users' demanding, integrated digital reference service came into being. And driven by Cloud Computing, CDRS (Cooperative digital reference service) can realize the sharing of technology, resources, experts and services of university libraries. Furthermore, it will develop Q&A smart joint service system, and this will bring great conveniences for library users.

Real-Time Access Services Model

In the era of digital libraries, library users paid more attention to electronic journals, electronic databases and so on. This is really a big challenge for university libraries. But by introducing cloud

Figure 3. Application of Cloud Computing in Academic Library

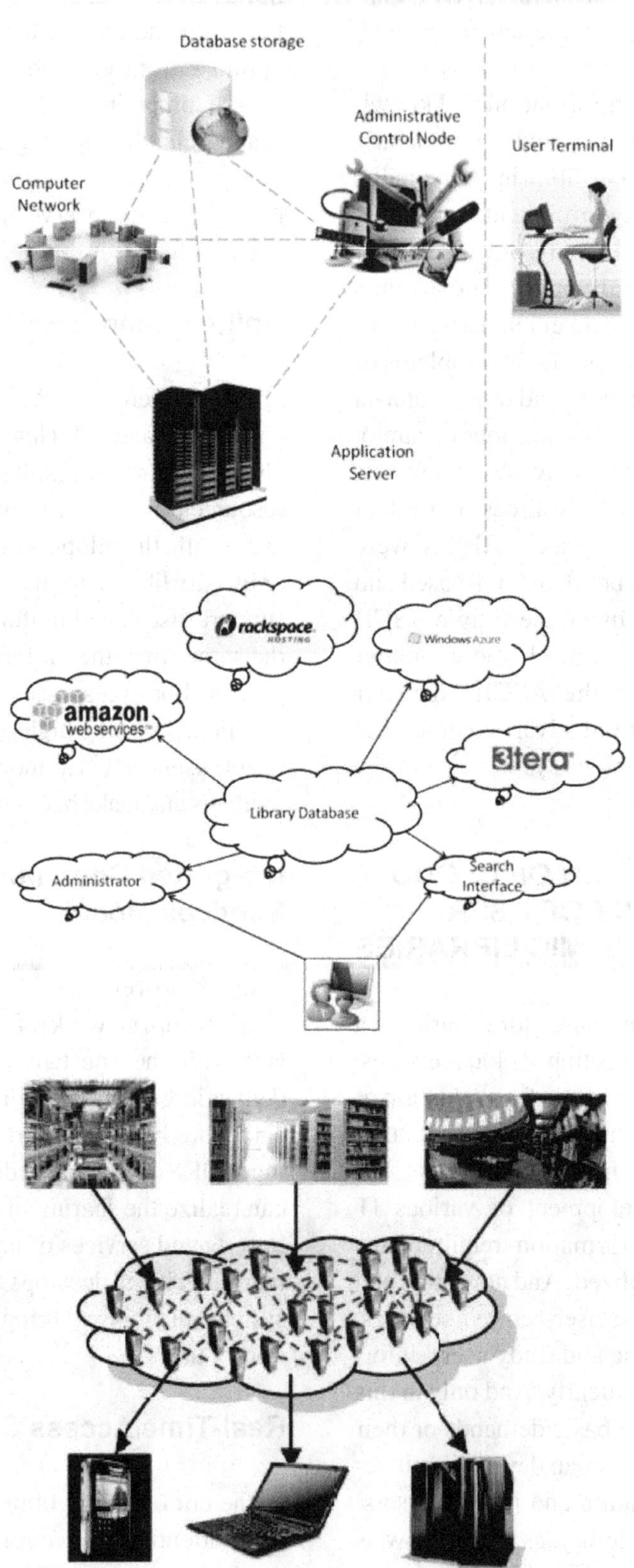

computing, university libraries can establish a shared public cloud jointly. As shared cloud can have infinite storage capacity and computing power theoretically, this can bring obvious benefits to libraries. On one hand, allied libraries no longer consider the hardware cost; on the other hand, it can help reduce the purchase of electronic database resources repeatedly among allied libraries. Meanwhile, users can visit the shared resources by any terminal equipment, such as PC, mobile phone or PDA, only if you can access to the Internet.

Knowledge Service Model

In the context of the knowledge economy, knowledge resource has become the main resource affecting productivity development. And university libraries are the main departments of storing, processing and spreading knowledge. So how to provide users with efficient transmission of information and knowledge services became urgent task for librarian's today. However, the emergence of cloud computing accelerated library's development. And the establishment of shared public cloud can save manpower and material resources greatly among university libraries. Therefore, with the aid of cloud computing, librarians won't have to maintain their own equipment's or deal with consultations personally. And librarians will have more time and energy to offer users with their needed knowledge-based services but not only information.

All-Oriented Service Model

Comparing with foreign university libraries, we can find that foreign libraries are intended to provide services for all the people. Besides the professors, teachers or students, all the people of that country can access to the library resources. In addition, they also permit users access to many libraries' resources by handling related certificate of that library. And fortunately, domestic libraries can also do this in the cloud environment. Anybody who can pass through the legal network identity authentication has the right to visit the joint resources of university libraries on the Internet. In other words, university libraries will offer services for the people with the help of cloud computing.

SERVICE PROVIDERS OF CLOUD COMPUTING IN LIBRARIES

- **Ex Libris:** Ex Libris is a well-known cloud service provider based in USA. They provide cloud solution in the field of libraries with all the software and hardware support needed to provide services to the users. Ex Libris is available for all type of libraries and also for consortia. Ex Libris is built on various standards and contains a number of features like compatibility with Unicode font, flexibility, migration of data, customization etc.
- **Polaris Library Systems:** Polaris is one of the cloud based library automation system available in the market. The company also provides standard acquisition and processing system. Also, with a Polaris ILS Client License, the library can integrate various PC and print management systems at no extra cost. The systems uses a number of well know standards like MARC 21 for bibliographic data, XML, Z39.50 for information retrieval, Unicode etc.
- **Dura Cloud:** Dura Cloud provides cloud solution for digital library services. Dura Cloud is a sister concern of Duraspace that is a collaboration of the Dspace digital library software and Fedora Commons. Fedora Commons is a framework for digital repository. It offers a complete solution for digital library with standard software and hardware solution. Dura Cloud also provides open source code and the code

needs to be installed on your machine. Where in case if you use Dura Cloud storage and software you have to subscribe Dura Cloud services with a nominal cost.

ADVANTAGES AND DISADVANTAGE

Like any other technology, cloud computing do also have its advantages and disadvantages, which needs to be taken into consideration before implementing this new technology.

Advantages

- Cost effective
- Flexible and innovative
- Round the clock access
- Simplified Cost and Consumption Model
- Enterprise Grade Services and Management
- Faster Provisioning of Systems and Applications
- Simplicity of Integration.
- Highly Secured Infrastructure.
- Compliant Facilities and Processes
- Flexible and resilient in disaster recovery.
- Reduces hardware and maintenance cost

Disadvantages

- Risk of data loss
- Failure in compliance
- Constant connectivity required
- Dependency
- Quality problems with cloud service provider
- Time and Budget Constraints
- Since all the development and deployment have been done by Cloud service provider, it is very difficult to get good grip on overall system.

SWOT ANALYSIS OF CLOUD COMPUTING WITH A VIEW OF LIBRARIES

SWOT analysis is a strategic planning method used to evaluate the Strengths, Weaknesses, Opportunities, and Threats involved in a project or in any venture. It involves specifying the objective of the project and identifying the internal and external factors that are favorable and unfavorable to achieve the objective. SWOT is a method to analyze a system as it displays good factors and bad factors for evaluation. Basically, SWOT analysis is used to evaluate market situation when a person wants to enter in the market. Nowadays Indian libraries can plan to move towards Cloud based environment, because most of the Indian libraries have budget constraints and therefore, before choosing cloud environment one needs to have some fare idea about the cloud and cloud computing services. Hence, SWOT analysis provides some evidences; we are trying to evaluate the cloud computing on SWOT principle.

- **Strengths:** India has a particularly strong IT industry that can be an important commercial factor for the western countries to consider in their future cloud related development. However, an Indian library does not have the economic strength to impact on the western countries. The main strength and hence advantage of India, however, consists in its consolidated and synergetic efforts to address new technological innovations, trends and governmental issues. As India has strong IT industry now, up-coming Indian companies are offering cloud services for Indian libraries at affordable prices. Moreover in India many institutes are not in condition to purchase high end server and costly software for their library; in this situation the cloud computing will provide great platform to host their data on cloud to serve their users.

- **Weakness:** However, India is not as fast as US and Europe in the development and considering the timelines of research to reach market-readiness as opposed to the fast movements in the market itself. The time is a critical resource with respect to positioning India in the global cloud development market. Implementation of cloud in the libraries is not a easy task as there are many administrative and financial matters involved. Adopting cloud services means we have to be depending on the service provider. Many Indian libraries do not have even Internet connection to connect with the cloud; in this case, it is very difficult to implement cloud based services.
- **Opportunities:** India is an emerging market for IT industry and Indian government is also providing help to Indian university libraries to get high speed Internet connection for research purpose, in view of libraries/institutions/ universities can consider cloud based library services to serve their users. Using cloud computing libraries can offer modern information services in user friendly format. With the use of these advanced technology library staff can also get an opportunity to learn new technological changes occurred in the field. As the cloud is a third party service if, any problem occurs, then the experts will provide the quick solution without interrupting library services.
- **Threats:** These opportunities are obviously counter weighted by some threats that particularly relate to the effort involved in the implementation. The threats namely connectivity problem, hidden cost for add-on services by service provider, compatibility, lock in period etc. The most important is migration of data from one service provider to other is a very difficult task.

CONCLUSION

This paper analyzes the current situation and existing problems of cloud computing in academic library. On this basis, on the combination of cloud computing, SaaS, Web2.0, SOA and other technologies, this paper proposes a CALIS-based cloud service strategy and the corresponding cloud library services platform (i.e. Nebula platform) model. The model is suitable for constructing large-scale distributed network of public digital library services. All library resources and service distributed on the Internet can be integrated as a whole, which forms a new type of adaptive control service system supporting interlibrary collaboration and service access, as well sharing resources from different libraries.

But in practice, cloud computing is facing large number of technical problems. IPv6 has improved the shortcomings of IPv4 and has solved the problem of security leakage. However, wireless networking around the city in anytime and anywhere will generate more information security problem than before. Cloud computing is associated with a range of severe and complex privacy issues. The main issues of cloud security are all related to data security which is the basic issue of cloud security. We need a measure to prevent our data from being obtained or damaged by some people who harbor vicious intentions. Therefore, it is necessary to encrypt data and make that the data obtained illegally cannot be deciphered.

Cloud computing technology is still relatively young in terms of maturity and adoption. The expectation is that it will undergo several changes in the future, in terms of resources, issues, risks, and ultimately best even though practices and standards. However it can potentially provide value for institutions of higher education. On-demand services can reverberate positively with the current university tight budgets across the nation and other parts of the world.

REFERENCES

Amrhein, D., de Andrade, A., Armstrong, J., Arasan, E., Bruklis, R., & Cameron, K. ... Zappert, F. (2009). *Cloud computing use cases: A white paper produced by the Cloud Computing Use Case Discussion Group*. Retrieved from http://www.cloudbook.net/cloud-computing-use-cases-group

CALIS-based cloud library service platform. (n.d.). Retrieved from http://www.lw20.com/2012021188925296.html

Carolan, J., & Gaede, S. (2009). *Introduction to cloud computing architecture: White paper*. Retrieved from http://webobjects.cdw.com/webobjects/media/pdf/Sun_CloudComputing.pdf

Dictionary.com. (n.d.). Retrieved from http://www.dictionary.reference.com

Dura Cloud. (n.d.). Retrieved from http://duracloud.org

Enterprise Features. (n.d.). Retrieved from http://enterprisefeatures.com/2011/03/8-key-advantages-that-cloud-computing-delivers-to-it

ExLibris: The bridge to knowledge. (n.d.). Retrieved from http://www.exlibris.co.il/

Golden, B. (2009). *The case against cloud computing, part four*. Retrieved from http://www.cio.com/article/480595/The_Case_Against_Cloud_Computing_Part_Four

Goldner, M. (2011). *Libraries and cloud computing*. Retrieved from http://www.sla.org/PDFs/2011ContribPaperGoldnerPace.pdf

Goldner, M. (2011). *Winds of change: Libraries and cloud computing*. Retrieved from http://www.oclc.org/multimedia/2011/files/IFLA-winds-of-change-paper.pdf

Google App Engine. (n.d.). Retrieved from http://code.google.com/appengine.

Hu, G. (2007). Research on information service model of university library in digital era (D). Tianjin Polytechnic University, 2007(12).

Huang, F. (2008). Research on the development of library information service models in the information culture environment (OJ). Xiangtan University, 2008(7).

Jacobson, A. (2010, June 26). Cloud computing for library services. Retrieved from http://libraralan.blogspot.com/2010/06/cloud-computing-for-library-services.html

Kroski, E. (2009, September 10). *Library cloud atlas: A guide to cloud computing and storage stacking the tech*. Retrieved from http://www.libraryjournal.com/article/CA6695772.html

Li, Y., Luan, X., & Li, S. (2009). Libraries Meeting Cloud computing Technology Era.*Academic Library and Information Tribune 2009, 1*(3).

Mell, P., & Grance, T. (2009). *The NIST definition of cloud computing*. Retrieved from http://www.nist.gov/itl/cloud/upload/cloud-def-v15.pdf

Mitchell, E. D. (2010, March 22). *Using cloud services for library IT infrastructure*. Retrieved from http://journal.code4lib.org/articles/2510

Padhy, S. C., & Mahapatra, R. K. (2012). Cloud computing: Academic library in Orissa. *VSRD-TNTJ*, *3*(3), 124–130.

Polaris Library Systems. (n.d.). Retrieved from http://www.gisinfosystems.com

Search cloud computing. (n.d.). Retrieved from http://searchcloudcomputing.techtarget.com/

Sultan, N. (2010). Cloud computing for education: A new dawn? *International Journal of Information Management*, *30*(2), 109–116. doi:10.1016/j.ijinfomgt.2009.09.004.

Terrence, W. (n.d.). *Features of cloud computing*. Retrieved from http://en.wikipedia.org/wiki/cloud-computing

Yang, M., & Yuan, X. (2009). *Digital Libraries under the Cloud Computing Environment (J)* (p. 9). Library Development.

Chapter 8
Libraries and Cloud Computing Models: A Changing Paradigm

Satish C. Sharma
Maharaja College of Management, India

Harshila Bagoria
Maharaja College of Management, India

ABSTRACT

Cloud computing is a new breed of service offered over the Internet, which has completely changed the way one can use the power of computers irrespective of geographic location. It has brought in new avenues for organizations and businesses to offer services using hardware or software or platform of third party sources, thus saving on cost and maintenance. It can transform the way systems are built and services delivered, providing libraries with an opportunity to extend their impact. Cloud computing has become a major topic of discussion and debate for any business or organization which relies on technology. Anyone connected to the Internet is probably using some type of cloud computing on a regular basis. Whether they are using Google's Gmail, organizing photos on Flickr, or searching the Web with Bing, they are engaged in cloud computing. In this chapter, an attempt has been made to give an overview of this technology, its connection with libraries, the models in which libraries can deploy this technology for providing services and augment the productivity of library staff and case studies.

INTRODUCTION ABOUT CLOUD COMPUTING

Cloud computing is a new technology which is an improvement of distributed computing, parallel computing, and grid computing. The basic principle of cloud computing is making tasks distributed among large number of computers but not in local computers or remote servers. This is a dynamic model, based on pay-per-use (subscription) or scalable system in which configuration of resources (hardware, platform/services) can be graded to suit the needs of the users for optimum utilization of resources. In simple words, it is a subscription-based or pay-per-use real time service over the Internet.

DOI: 10.4018/978-1-4666-4631-5.ch008

The vendors of this model also guarantee the utilization of these virtually interconnected resources by employing customized-service-level agreements (SLAs). According to Doerksen (2008), cloud computing is the user-friendly version of grid computing. However, Buyya, Yeo, and Venugopal (2008) have given much more elaborate definition which reads that cloud computing is a kind of "parallel and distributed system consisting of a collection of interconnected and virtualized computers that are dynamically provisioned and presented as one or more unified computing resources, based on SLA established through negotiation between the service provider and consumer."

Cloud computing takes the concept of virtualization even further by adding a couple of additional twists. In a cloud computing environment, the organization running an application neither typically own the physical hardware used for the applications nor usually know exactly from where the computation work of the applications is being processed. Cloud computing provides an organization with appreciably more flexibility and scalability to satisfy computing needs. Thus cloud computing means sharing and use of applications and resources of a network environment to get work done without concern about ownership and management of the network's resources and applications. This is a way to increase capacity or add capabilities without investing on new infrastructure, training new personnel, or licensing new software.

CHARACTERISTICS OF CLOUD COMPUTING

1. Self Healing
2. Multitenancy
3. Linearly Scalable
4. Service-oriented
5. SLA Driven
6. Virtualized
7. Flexible

CLOUD COMPUTING AND LIBRARIES

Libraries have been in transition since their inception as they are directly affected with environmental changes. There was a time, when biggest library used to be the one with largest collection and they were serving their users mainly with their own resources in an almost isolated manner. Then came an era of computers where libraries started getting connected with other collaborating libraries through networks and consortia for mutual advantage of sharing the resources at divided/shared cost with a shift of emphasis from acquisition to access. Emergence of electronic resources has an added impact on libraries which forced them to prepare to face different kinds of challenges from users to meet their multidimensional requirements.

Now, there is a new phase when libraries are adopting and utilizing the computing resources and services that are not even owned by it. Cloud computing and Web collaboration are emerging as two major concepts, supporting innovative developments in library automation. Cloud computing is emerging to help libraries to offer much improved services by strengthening the power of cooperation among libraries and showing their combined presence on Web. This will certainly help to enhance the efficiency of libraries by enabling them to access information through large global network of cooperating libraries and eliminating the IT related problems, thereby saving time, money and manpower. With these developments, heterogeneous resources are accessible to anyone, anywhere because of the application of domain independent software. Evidence of the library's active online or digital clients can be observed in the growing online social networks. In addition, forming of communities of interest among Web users indicate a growing movement toward Web collaboration which allows users without knowledge of the underlying Internet's infrastructure, to create content and have a contribution to what is being communicated and published daily. According to Farkas (2008), it can be useful for libraries as

Web provides opportunities for libraries to collect the tacit knowledge (through knowledge management) that 'resides in people's heads' (collected through interviews/ personal documents) and benefit from the library's 'community of users' supplying 'feedback and contributions.'

Using cloud computing can share the server in many application procedures, realizes the resource sharing, thus also reduced server's quantity, achieves the effect of reducing the cost. Therefore utilizing cloud computing in the digital library, gives our work, the life and the study inevitably obtaining a greater efficiency.

Libraries traditionally manage servers with huge volumes of data and face critical problems in their management due to lack of expertise and the cost involvement in acquisition and maintenance of required hardware and software. For example the university or research libraries hold the data of thousands of electronic journal downloads and thousands of digitally converted data of rare/ heritage documents. In any case there is a risk of data security and universal access. Therefore, the libraries can apply cloud computing to data integrity, upgrade and maintenance, intellectual property management, backups, disaster management, and failover functions. It facilitates reduced operational costs of IT resources; increases operational efficiency; extends distributed access through virtualized environment. By adopting this change, libraries can accrue increased reliability, declined costs due to economies of scale and other production factors. Many library staff members are already experienced users of cloud computing – without even knowing it. Some are using the cloud in the form of Google Docs. Staff users of Facebook take advantage of cloud, as do those who use photo sharing services such as Flickr. Through Web 2.0 applications, the information seekers are shifting much of personal computer usage to the cloud. For example, bookmarks are freed from the desktop by storing them on social bookmarking Websites such as Delicious, uploaded and shared videos on YouTube, used services such as slideshare to host presentations, some have designed applications for popular platforms such as Facebook.

ADVANTAGES OF CLOUD COMPUTING IN LIBRARIES:

From library perspective, cloud computing offers following advantages.

1. There is no need to own all infrastructure facilities as cloud computing takes care of it.
2. Provides large amounts of processing power comparable to supercomputer level.
3. It can be used as a personal workspace.
4. Since the service is not location specific, it provides opportunity for ubiquitous computing.
5. Virtualized technologies are a boon to green IT companies as virtual servers provide unlimited capacity, bandwidth, and increased security and disaster recovery solution.
6. Capital expenditure is minimized.
7. It is far more economic, as payment is based on utilization of service.
8. No need to copy all stuff from one PC to another when buying a new one. Moreover, one can create personalized repository of information that keeps growing as long as one wants.
9. A convenient tool to engage in the scholarship of teaching and learning.

CLOUD COMPUTING SERVICE MODELS IN LIBRARIES

Software-As-A-Service (SAAS)

This is a software delivery model which remotely provides access through Internet to business functions as a service. In SaaS, a provider licenses an application to customers for use as a service on demand. SaaS software vendors may host the application on their own Web servers or download the application for customers but it is disabled after use or after the demand contract expires. This type of cloud provides a wide range of applications (software) tools to end users. Any Web application is a cloud application in the sense that it resides in the cloud. Software as a Service provides network-based access to commercially available software. Google Docs (for word processing and spreadsheets), Netflix, Photoshop.com, Acrobat.com, Intuit QuickBooks Online, YouTube, SlideShare, Amazon, Facebook, Twitter, Flickr, and virtually every other Web 2.0 application is a cloud application in this sense. It offers several advantages like accessibility from any location, rapid scalability and bundled maintenance. Its applications in libraries are Open URL resolver, journal listing service, instructional guides, reserves statistics, and IM/chat service. Its major limitations are threat to data security and oppose open source movement. SaaS represents the potential for a lower-cost way for libraries to use software—using it on demand rather than buying a license for every computer, especially when most computers sit unused almost 70% of the time.

Types of SaaS

- **Business Utility SaaS:** Applications like Salesforce automation are used by businesses and individuals for managing and collecting data, streamlining collaborative processes and providing actionable analysis. Popular use cases are Customer Relationship Management (CRM), Human Resources and Accounting.
- **Social Networking SaaS:** Applications like Facebook are used by individuals for networking and sharing information, photos, videos, and so forth.

Platform-As-A-Service (PAAS) or Cloud Platform Services

It offers platform on which software developers can build new applications or extend existing ones saving the cost of underlying hardware and software. It provides an environment for software development, storage and hosting delivered as-a-service over the Internet. It facilitates the development and deployment of applications without the cost and complexity of buying, managing and configuring the underlying hardware, middleware and software layers. This platform typically includes a database, middleware and development tools, all are in the form of services through the Internet. Examples of PaaS are Google App Engine, Force.com, Microsoft Azure, WOLF, and so forth. Its applications in libraries are integrated library system, archives management software, initial Website applications, and so forth. The defining factor that makes PaaS unique is that it lets developers build and deploy Web applications on a hosted infrastructure. In other words, PaaS allows you to leverage the seemingly infinite compute resources of a cloud infrastructure.

Types of PaaS

Platform-as-a-Service (PaaS) solutions are created for different applications. Organizations need to carefully evaluate PaaS offerings and choose the platform which suits their needs:

- **Social Application Platforms:** Platforms such as Facebook provide APIs so that developers can write new application functionality and make it available to the platform's users.
- **Computing Platforms:** Platforms such as Amazon Web Services, Rackspace and others provide storage, processing and bandwidth as-a-service. As a developer you can upload a traditional software stack and run applications on their computing infrastructure.

- **Web Application Platforms:** Google Apps provides APIs and functionalities for developers to build Web applications that leverage its different services such as mapping, calendar and spreadsheets. More ideal for light weight Web applications!
- **Business Application Platforms:** Platforms such as WOLF provide a layer of abstraction from the underlying technical complexities and are specifically geared towards transactional business applications such as online databases and integration, workflow, and user interface services. Developers and business analysts can develop complex and robust business applications with a custom user interface – providing higher flexibility with lesser technical efforts and minimum maintenance.

The Main Ingredients of PaaS

Perhaps the best way to understand PaaS is to break it apart into its main components: platform and service, as seen in Figure 1. Now, consider the service being provided, which is referred to as a solution stack. A solution stack consists of the applications that will assist in the development process as well as the deployment of the application. These applications refer to the operating system, run time environments, source control repository, and any other required middleware. That said it is logical to assume that the two main ingredients of PaaS are the computing platform and the solution stack.

To illustrate these two "ingredients," let's look further into their definitions. A computing platform, in its simplest form, refers to a place where software can be launched consistently as long as the code meets the standards of that platform. Common examples of platforms include Windows™, Apple Mac OS X, and Linux® for operating systems; Google Android, Windows Mobile®, and Apple iOS for mobile computing; and Adobe® AIR™ or the Microsoft® .NET Framework for software frameworks.

Infrastructure-As-A-Service (IAAS)

This is another model of computing services and resources, also called utility computing. It delivers a computing infrastructure, typically a virtualization environment, as-a-service. Rather

Figure 1. A graphical interpretation of the relationship between classifications of cloud computing and the elements of PaaS

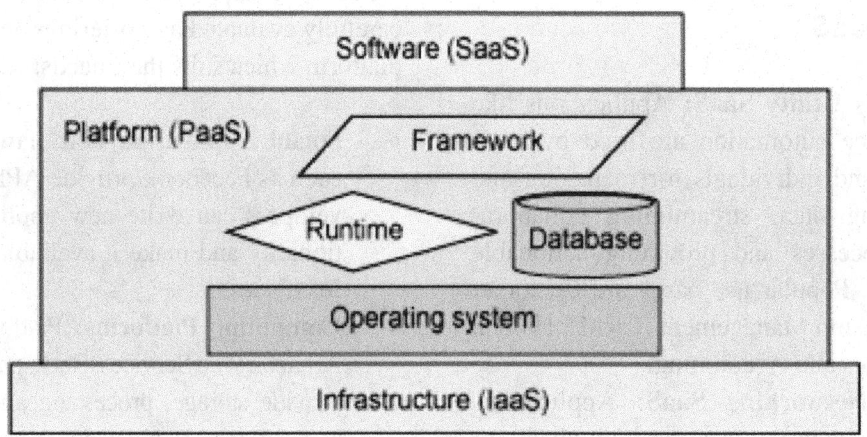

than purchasing and configuring servers, storage and network equipment, the client can utilize these resources as a fully outsourced service. The service is typically billed on a utility computing basis and the amount of resources consumed (and therefore the cost) will typically reflect the level of activity. For this service, users are charged according to usage. This type of cloud provides virtual hardware capacity to organizations on an elastic basis (flexible). Elasticity and scalability are the two terms associated with cloud computing that gives the ability to expand and reduce resources according to specific service requirement. Data Storage/hosting and archiving/preservation are important services among these. This system of packaging and storage requires minimum or no cost for hardware. Examples of IaaS are virtual servers leased by Amazon, Rackspace, GoGrid, and so forth.

Types of IaaS

There are different types of Cloud IaaS providers. IaaS providers may offer one or more of the following:

- Computing, Storage and Bandwidth
- Development and Test
- High Performance Computing
- Resource Sharing

Amazon was the pioneer in this, providing virtual machine instances, storage, and computation as innovative services. Amazon's Elastic Computer Cloud (EC2) is a major example of IaaS. Other examples include Rackspace's Mosso and Go Grid's Serve Path, and so forth. IaaS provides servers, software, data-center space and network equipment, available in a single bundle. Its applications in libraries are for hosting institutional repository discovery layer, ILS discovery layer.

Key Concepts of IaaS

- Cloudbursting
- Multitenant computing
- Resource pooling
- The hypervisor

The Value of IaaS

For businesses, the greatest value of IaaS is through a concept known as cloudbursting—the process of off-loading tasks to the cloud during times when the most compute resources are needed. The potential for capital savings through cloud bursting is significant, because businesses won't need to invest in additional servers that only run at 70% capacity two or three times in the year, the rest of the time sitting at 7-10% load.

However, for businesses to take advantage of IaaS in this capacity, IT departments must be able to build and implement the software that handles the ability to re-allocate processes to an IaaS cloud. There are four important considerations to building and implementing software that can manage such re-allocation processes:

- Developing for a specific vendor's proprietary IaaS could prove to be a costly mistake if the vendor were to go out of business.
- The complexity of well-written resource allocation software is significant and generally requires top-notch developer resources that do not come cheap. It will save organization's lot of time, frustration, and unanticipated expenses by budgeting more up front for the best resources.
- Sending data such as personal identities, financial information, and health care data put an organization's compliance at risk with U.S. Sarbanes-Oxley (SOX) Act,

Payment Card Industry (PCI), or Health Insurance Portability and Accountability Act (HIPAA) regulations.

- Understand the dangers of shipping off processes that are critical to the day-to-day operation of the business. A good idea is to start by drawing a table and placing processes that involve compliance-critical data in one column, business-critical tasks in the second column, and non-critical tasks in the third column. Then, plan on having the software only off-load the items in the third column for its first iteration.

In addition, organizations need to be careful of the current state of the cloud computing marketplace in terms of vendor lock-in. Virtual Machines (VMs) that can be moved to the cloud from data centers and between vendors' clouds can be an asset for businesses, but doing so requires that vendors support a standardized file format, which they have been reluctant to do.

The reality of the situation is that currently there is no specification placed in the open and under the authority of a standards body. In other words, there currently is no truly standardized format, which complicates things at best; because there is no guarantee that the format around which you build will be supported by anyone down the road. It is worth noting, however, that it is often possible to port a virtual appliance to another format, provided that the specification of the new format is open or that you have access to it. On a more promising note, major advances have been made recently in support of the Open Virtualization Format (OVF), which is a promising candidate to become a standard. Another promising candidate is the Virtual Machine Disk (VMDK) format. VMDK was originally a proprietary format for VMware, but now that the specification is open, it is supported by a number of third parties.

IaaS is easy to spot, because it is typically platform-independent. IaaS consists of a combination of hardware and software resources. IaaS software is low-level code that runs independent of an operating system—called a hypervisor—and is responsible for taking inventory of hardware resources and allocating said resources based on demand (see Figure 2). This process is referred to as resource pooling. Resource pooling by the hypervisor makes virtualization possible, and virtualization makes multi-tenant computing possible—a concept that refers to an infrastructure shared by several organizations with similar interests in regard to security requirements and compliance considerations.

With IaaS, you have the capability to provision processing, storage, networks, and other computing resources, where you can deploy and run arbitrary software such as operating systems and applications. Most use cases for cloud computing follow the same fundamental layering structure you are already used to: a software solution stack or platform is deployed on a network infrastructure, and applications are run on top of the platform. However, virtualization makes the cloud paradigm unique.

After understanding the three classifications of cloud computing, Table 1 shows cross-concept matrix for reference. A paradigm is a model to which the majority of users conform. As men-

Figure 2. The relationship among VMs, the hypervisor, and the computer

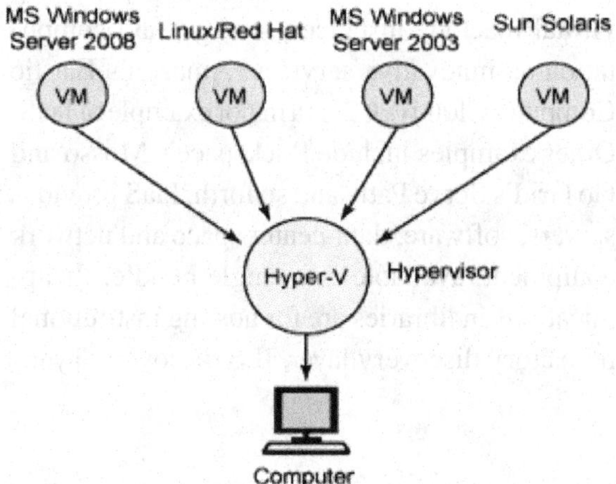

Table 1. Cross-concept matrix of the three classifications of cloud computing

	Paradigm Shift	Characteristics	Key Terms	Advantages	Disadvantages and risks	When not to use
IaaS	Infrastruc ture as an asset	Usually platform independent; infrastructure costs are shared and thus reduced; SLAs; pay by usage; self-scaling	Grid computing, utility computing, compute instance, hypervisor, cloud bursting, multi-tenant computing, resource pooling	Avoid capital expenditure on hardware and human resources; reduced ROI (Return on Investment) risk; low barriers to entry; streamlined and automated scaling	Business efficiency and productivity largely depends on the vendor's capabilities; potentially greater long-term cost; centralization requires new/different security measures	When capital budget is greater than operating budget
PaaS	License purchasin g	Consumes cloud infrastructure; caters to agile project management methods	Solution stack	Streamlined version deployment	Centralization requires new/different security measures	N/A
SaaS	Software as an asset (business and consumer)	SLAs; UI powered by thin-client applications; cloud components; communication via APIs; stateless; loosely coupled; modular; semantic interoperability	Thin client; client-server application	Avoid capital expenditure on software and development resources; reduced ROI risk; streamlined and iterative updates	Centralization of data requires new/different security measures	N/A

tioned a moment ago, IaaS marks the shift from the paradigm of infrastructure as an asset to that of Infrastructure as a Service. The other two classifications of cloud computing shown in Table 1 also mark a paradigm shift. For Platform as a Service (PaaS), the shift is from the paradigm of platform as an asset, where licenses are purchased in mass quantities. The same can be said for Software as a Service (SaaS), where the paradigm shift is from software being assets of the organization in the form of licenses to software being provided as a service.

CLOUD COMPUTING UNIVERSITY BASED MODELS

Cloud computing architects need to make some considerations about infrastructure models when moving from a standard enterprise application deployment model to one based on cloud computing. There are three basic service models to consider in a university based cloud computing, such as Public, Private, and Hybrid clouds.

Public Clouds

Public computing clouds are open to anyone who wants to sign up and use them. Public clouds are run by vendors, and applications from different customers are likely to be mixed together on the cloud's servers, storage systems, and networks. One of the benefits of public clouds is that they can be much larger than a company's private cloud and can offer the ability to scale up and down on demand, shifting infrastructure risks from the enterprise to the cloud provider.

IBM operates a cloud data center for its customers. Multiple customers share the same infrastructure, but each person's cloud is secure and separated as though behind its own firewall.

Private Clouds

The intention of designing the private cloud is basically an organization that needs more control over their data than they can get by using a vendor hosted service. Private clouds are built for the exclusive use of one organization, providing the utmost control over data, security, and quality of service. Private clouds typically sit behind the firewall of an organization (enterprise or university), and only people within that organization have permission to access the cloud and its resources.

Hybrid Clouds

Hybrid clouds combine both public and private cloud models. This model introduces the complexity of determining how to distribute applications across both a public and private cloud. If the data is small, or the application is stateless, a hybrid cloud can be much more successful than if large amounts of data must be transferred into a public cloud for a small amount of processing.

Virtual Computing Lab can work on Hybrid cloud model. It can provide services and infrastructure to the students and faculties of single university acting as a private cloud. It can also extend this services for inter university using public cloud. This requires more secure network.

IMPROVEMENT OF USER SERVICE MODEL IN LIBRARIES

With the rapid development of various IT technologics, users' information requirements are increasingly personalized. And now more and more libraries advocated user-centered services. So librarians should mine and study users' information requirements frequently. And only in this way, they can master the basic demands of their users. And furthermore, library can develop itself according to such information and improve users' satisfaction. University library is always famous for its academic and teaching influences. And IT technology has been the driving force of library development. What's more, librarians can keep using new technology to develop library and optimize library service. With the expansion of Cloud Computing application, this chapter proposed to apply Cloud Computing in libraries. By establishing a pubic cloud among many university libraries, it not only can conserve library resources

Figure 3. Application of Cloud Computing in Library

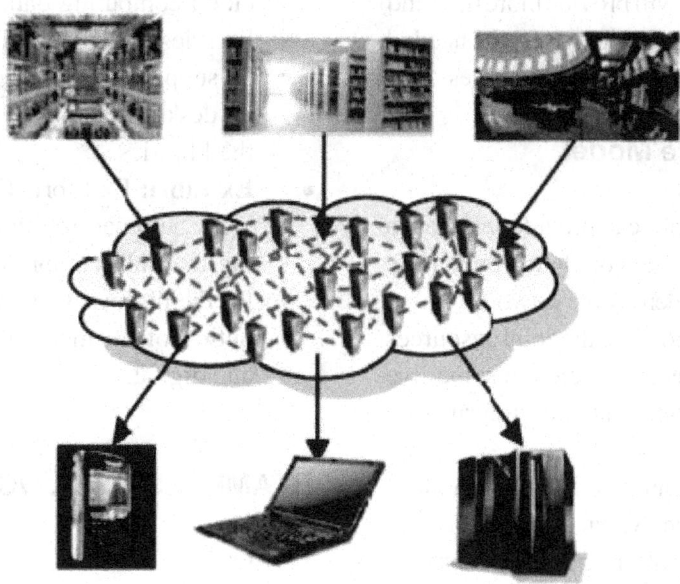

but also can improve its user satisfaction. And it can be illustrated in Figure 3. However, some more service models are as follows:

Unified Search Service Model

Although majority of libraries are using OPAC (Online Public Access Catalog) and ILL (Inter-Library Loan) services but a uniform access platform is not available to share the OPACs. However, with the adoption of cloud computing, the integrated library resources support distributed uniform access interface. At the same time, the uniform access platform can promote library resources, guide and answer users' questions by using high-quality navigation. As a result, users can grip more information retrieval methods and make better use of library resources.

Real-Time Access Services Model

Due to innumerable advantages of electronic resources, users prefer to access electronic journals and electronic databases. However, by introducing cloud computing, libraries can establish a shared public cloud jointly which can have infinite storage capacity and computing power bringing obvious benefits to libraries. It can help to reduce the substantial cost involved in hardware cost and purchase of electronic databases. Moreover, users can visit the shared resources by any terminal equipment, such as PC, mobile phone or PDA using Internet access.

Knowledge Service Model

In the context of knowledge economy, knowledge resources are directly affecting the productivity and national development. And libraries are the main departments of storing, processing and spreading knowledge. So the mode of dissemination of information and knowledge has become the most challenging task for librarians today. However, at this juncture, the emergence of cloud computing accelerated library's development. And the establishment of shared public cloud can help a great deal to save on manpower and resources. Moreover, with cloud computing, librarians won't have to maintain their own equipments or deal with users personally which will provide more time and energy to librarians to offer their users the needed information and knowledge-based services.

All-People Service Model

With this model, libraries can provide services to all the people with the help of cloud computing. Anyone who has legal identity the network authentication has the right to visit the joint resources of libraries on the Internet. There are some live examples of cloud computing for information management.

OCLC [Online Computer Library Catalog] Web Scale Management Services: It is from traditional ILS systems by offering member libraries one unified solution to help streamline routine tasks— like acquisitions and circulation. By moving these functions to the Web, libraries are able to share infrastructure costs and resources, as well as collaborate in ways that free them from the restrictions of local hardware and software. With Web scale management services, the libraries will be able to:

- Lower total cost of ownership for management services.
- Eliminate format-specific operations.
- Simplify critical (but routine) back-office operations.
- Reduce the support costs for disparate systems.
- Customize and extend library management services by using new applications and services available from an open, extensible platform.
- Make your data (and libraries' aggregated data) work harder for better decisions.
- Free staff time for high-priority services and local innovation.
- **LibLime:** Hosted in LibLime's distributed cloud computing data center, hundreds of libraries are able to alleviate their internal IT support needs. No software is installed on desktops and no servers are required in the libraries.
- **Ex Libri:** Ex Libris Group is a leading library automation solutions provider, offering the only comprehensive product suite for the discovery, management, and distribution of all materials—print, electronic, and digital.

EXAMPLES OF CLOUD LIBRARIES

1. OCLC
2. Library of Congress (LC)
3. Exlibris
4. Polaris
5. Scribd
6. Discovery Service
7. Google Docs / Google Scholar
8. Worldcat
9. Encore

CLOUD LIBRARY PLATFORMS

Many libraries are in the process of rethinking the effectiveness of the automation tools they're using to provide library services, both within and outside of their library buildings. Internally, the core component driving many of these services has been the integrated library system (ILS). The next generation of these systems is called "library services platforms," a term coined by the consultant Marshall Breeding.

The primary difference between the traditional ILS offerings and the new library services platform is that the ILS products were largely designed around the management of print collections. As libraries have moved increasingly to accommodate digital collections, they've found the ILS products unable to be reconfigured well enough to smoothly and efficiently handle the integration of all the workflows that are different, yet necessary, for both print and digital.

In addition, the older ILS do not take advantage of the latest offerings in computing technologies and architectures, particularly in the area of cloud computing. These all pitfalls of ILS were removed with the invention of new library services platforms.

The organizations developing and providing new library service platforms use a variety of descriptions: "Web scale management solutions," "uniform management systems," or just "services platform." The library platforms that have been announced yet include: WorldShare Management Services by OCLC, ALMA by Ex Libris, Sierra by Innovative Interfaces, Intota by Serials Solutions, Open Library Environment (OLE) by Kuali, and Open Skies by VTLS. In this section, these platforms are further elaborated in depth.

Sierra by Innovative Interfaces

Innovative Interfaces is one of the oldest, best known, most stable, successful and respected names in library automation. Sierra is the Innovative entry into the library services platform arena and represents a different approach than that taken by many of the other library services platform providers. Innovative approach is repackaging their previous product, Millenium, and modifying it to run on a new open source database (Postgres SQL), using a new open source indexing engine (Lucene), adding new open APIs, opening up some of the existing APIs, updating the interface, and adding new, functional modules. The totality of this package is called Sierra and it can be had as either software-as-a-service (SaaS) or a local install.

For libraries that decide to focus on meeting end user or member needs and defer reengineering back-end processes until later, Sierra will prove to be an entirely viable option. Libraries wanting to move to a hosted environment will be able to do so. (Innovative has long offered hosting for many of their products, including Millennium.) The product is available right now and offers a total range of library functionality, although workflows may not be as configurable as some competitors' offerings.

Innovative describes Sierra as an "open development" platform and is taking some very positive steps in this direction. Sierra clearly provides customers with access to more of the system APIs and Innovative is promising to deliver new APIs that will give access to additional data and services. (Librarians should request a detailed list of both the released and planned-for release APIs as part of their evaluation.) The Sierra literature talks about a developer community, coming soon, to be called the "Sierra Developers Connection." Sierra does offer some excellent reporting tools, a feature that has long been a plus for the Innovative Millennium product. These new tools include a new "Reporter" module that allows users to select fields and compose complex reports with relative ease (although some training is required). The data used to drive this module is copied nightly and includes the "core" ILS data. Another new tool is the "Decision Center," a tool for use by staff, typically the manager of collections. It appears to primarily use canned reports, but they can be run dynamically for instant use and analysis.

These reporting tools are offered primarily for use with data from the library or consortium using or sharing a Sierra implementation. Aggregation beyond this (such as would be required to compare your library to peer institutions across the country) involves additional steps to upload the data to Innovative's Data Center and to run the reports there.

Open Library Environment (OLE) by Kuali

This is the only open source software solution being offered among the new library services platforms. Backed by Kuali, development partners, and Mellon Foundation grant monies, a number of academic and research libraries have banded together to build, own, and govern this offering. The stated values of OLE membership include the ability to drive the product to meet the needs of member institutions, the ownership of the software as a long-term investment, and the ability to meet the enterprise needs of a research library that will also work for librarians in a consortial environment. The stated goal of the OLE project is to build a flexible, service oriented, enterprise library management system for academic and research libraries. As such, the product is a ground-up build of a new offering, but one that uses, where possible, some of the other Kuali open source software components. Currently the available functionality includes acquisitions, record loading, accounts receivable, and basic reports. Planned for future release are circulation, cataloging, inventory, financial processing, and ERM components. The product— designed to support the range and formats of scholarly information—interoperates and integrates with other systems while providing workflow configuration capabilities.

OLE is a SaaS offering, not a true cloud computing system and institutions using the product must select their own hosting service. Note this may change, however, as commercial partners sign on. Data sharing across system installations is done using the open linked data model.

OLE, like many of the new library services platforms, is at a very early development stage. Therefore, some features like interface design has not yet been addressed with any level of sophistication. OLE has hired an interface designer so this issue should be addressed in future releases. While OLE presentations are currently focusing on the open source benefits, rates of adoption and implementation will not likely increase until librarians can readily see how the product will solve today's problems and reduces expenses. At a high level, OLE, when compared to true cloud computing solutions, may not fully address issues such as data aggregation and analytics, multitenant architecture, and data center security/redundancy.

It is also not yet clear if OLE can acquire enough support among academic and research libraries to sustain itself over the long term. While the promise of OLE is strong, in comparison to competing library services platforms OLE remains focused on technical underpinnings and building support while other offerings are focused on showing functionality, well designed interfaces, and working examples of modifiable workflows. Nonetheless, over 70 libraries are current Kuali members and from the perspective of building a collaborative and community system, open and available to all, OLE has no peer among today's library service platform offerings.

Intota by Serials Solutions

Intota is a totally new product, written from the ground up, and is a true cloud computing solution. It is said to offer true multi-tenant software operations, shared data capabilities, and to fully support a powerful analytic and analysis engine. Plans also exist for multiple data centers, including international locations, within the next year. Intota is the latest entrant in the market for the revolutionary approach to a library services platform, so functionality is accordingly smaller at this point in time. The advantage of being the latest, though, is that what is being shown features some creative thinking and well thought-out integration of the workflows and processes that occur in the backrooms of all libraries. Intota's development is based on the premise that libraries are managing today's collection with yesterday's tools and that with the changing nature of the collection users want to be self-sufficient. Intota focuses on workflows, system maintenance, and assessment, the latter emphasis to aid libraries in showcasing their value. Overall, Intota is a total reconceptualization of library management systems providing functionality focused on selection, acquisitions, description (cataloging), fulfillment, a knowledgebase, and discovery.

It would also appear, based on Serials Solutions' selection of development partners, that Intota is a product designed to have broad appeal across all types and sizes of libraries. This carries some risks in the early stages of the product's life, so librarians, should carefully analyze their needs and understand when those needs will be addressed on the development timeline before committing to production use.

As for the openness of Intota, the company is promising a suite of documented, open APIs. Historically, Serials Solutions has been doing this with their other products for quite some time, so there is every reason to expect this trend will continue.

One of the real advantages of Intota is that it represents a total approach from end user discovery to the library's backroom. As a result, it offers tightly integrated processes, efficient and effective workflows, and data handling for both the print and digital environment. It will allow librarians to smash through the silos that existed in previous library automation systems.

Another important area where Intota is showing promise is analytics. At least in discussions, Serials Solutions is placing a major focus on assessment and analytics. Analytics are becoming more important because they allow the library to use data to understand the users in far greater detail and to predict, with higher accuracy, what types of services and content they'll need and when. This should be very appealing to librarians and will offer major steps forward in the profession in terms of being able to offer new, proactive services to users.

As for availability, while Serials Solutions is currently signing up and working with test partners for Intota, the product is not expected to be completed until late 2013, while many of the competing offerings are already largely complete and being installed.

At this point, the data center locations and security level certification(s) are unknown and thus customers need to closely analyze the security criteria discussed above during the procurement phase.

ALMA by Ex Libris

Alma is also an entirely new, true cloud computing product. The overall approach of Ex Libris is to provide libraries with comprehensive, unified resource management. In doing this, their intent is to avoid the duplication of effort and data required in maintaining separate ILS, ERM, institutional repository, discovery, and link resolution products. The goal is for library staff to be able to work in one environment.

Because Ex Libris traditionally addresses a narrower segment of the library marketplace (academic, research, national, and corporate libraries being their target market), one of the advantages they've had is that despite developing an entirely new product, they've also developed more depth of functionality than competing library services platforms. That functionality includes: selection (acquisitions and demand-driven acquisitions), print management (circulation, reserves, ILL), electronic management (licensing, usage tracking), digital asset management (repository functions), metadata management (cataloging, collaborative metadata management), and link resolution (Open URL). This product should move libraries from "just-in-case" to "just-in-time" collection development models. The product also features configurable workflows using a management tool that allows tasks to be assigned to staff. Due to the configurability of workflows, libraries can largely retain existing workflows and then reengineer them as time permits. Of course, it must also be noted that while much functionality exists at this point, there is some functionality still missing. This includes support for consortia capabilities, which will not be released until 2013. Also planned, but not yet released is support for EAD and MODS.

One of the new features offered as part of Alma is the "Community Catalog" used for the sharing/storage of metadata between libraries. Data in the Community Catalog uses the PDDL open data license. Among the data currently loaded are records from: CONSER, the Library of Congress, the British Library, and various journal metadata records. Ex Libris has laid the groundwork for a full implementation of cloud computing by placing data centers in the United States, the United Kingdom, and Australia. All of their data centers are independently SAS 70 certified. There is no planned capability to support local installations of Alma.

As a true cloud computing solution, Alma will be able to provide analytics based on shared data (provided customers agree) using Oracle's analytic tools. The result is that libraries should have comprehensive analytics across all their assets and users (and potentially across all libraries using the "Collaborative Business Intelligence" tools). As noted above, such analytics will allow libraries to better understand and anticipate usage patterns. Together, these capabilities should offer customers some powerful user-focused services in the future.

Ex Libris is another company that has long offered open APIs with their products. Plans for Alma include open APIs and support for SOA (Service Oriented Architecture). The company has long offered support for customers doing open source software extensions to their products via the EL Commons Website. The site includes both a Wiki and a code-sharing facility to encourage customers to share code, documentation, and presentations about code extensions they have developed. There are separate sections offered for each of their major products.

Because of the focus on depth of functionality rather than breadth of market, Alma appears to offer the richest level of functionality available in the new cloud computing library services platforms at this time.

WorldShare Management Services (WMS) by OCLC

WorldShare Management Services (WMS) is a fresh start, a totally new product that rethinks and recreates management software for libraries and offers a true cloud computing solution. Built by OCLC, it has the potential to benefit enormously from the "common good" and collaboration that OCLC represents. The philosophy underlying WMS is that libraries are more alike than different and that commonalities in management, workflows, and service are as similar as library collections, clients, and services. Yet, at the same time, OCLC understands WMS must support unique needs and must adhere to principles of vendor neutrality, wherever possible.

WMS is being designed for all types and sizes of libraries from those with millions of titles, circulations, and users to those with less than 100 users. The product uses all the data available in WorldCat®, the WorldCat knowledge base, the WorldShare™vendor information center, the WorldCat Registry™, and other centralized data repositories. This is a huge advantage for libraries.

However, as noted with other systems, one of the consequences of trying to appeal to that many types and sizes of libraries is that the functionality can be thin during the early stages of the product lifecycle. Librarians should carefully analyze their needs and understand when those needs will be addressed on the development timeline before committing to production use.

OCLC is offering solid and innovative methodology when it comes to installing the product. The community of early adopters works together during this process and the implementation process becomes a group experience. Libraries hold weekly meetings with their cohorts and discuss their plans, issues, and findings. OCLC has also developed training tutorials and recorded sessions that are available for library staff to use 24/7. Furthermore, live training sessions are available almost weekly at no additional charge to libraries.

Overall, this combination appears to be a very strong support system for implementing sites.

In the area of analytics, OCLC has announced plans to collect and use data to drive analytic-based services. Hadoop, an open source software framework from Apache, is being used and is extremely powerful. Hadoop has been the driving force behind many big data projects and the services that could result from its combination with OCLC's data could be quite impressive.

When it comes to openness, WMS seems to be promising on several different levels. OCLC wants their platform seen as one that enables libraries to build on top of it because they understand they can't do everything themselves. So, like many of the other platforms, they're saying WMS will offer a large number of open APIs for integrating with other applications. Unlike other platforms, though, OCLC's approach includes development of a common framework for services (F4S). This strategy is designed to allow OCLC to build consistent APIs, which are intended to translate into external developers being able to consistently develop new extensions. Furthermore, to do this they're using Open Social, a public specification defining a container and a set of common APIs for Web-based applications. This will allow library developers an open source method for creating apps, which they can then upload directly into the WMS interface, or use externally in other Open Social Containers. So in addition to APIs, OCLC has built the entire infrastructure for F4S and application processing, an App Gallery, and a management interface that allows users to modify the interface by adding their own apps. Of all the new platforms, this appears to be one of the most comprehensive approaches.

OCLC has two data centers in the U.S. and one each in Australia, Canada, and Europe. Within the next year, OCLC will be adding a second site in Europe. All of their data centers are certified to meet ISO 27001 and Lloyds Quality Assurance certifications.

Open Skies by VTLS

Open Skies is the very latest entrant into the library services platform. VTLS is taking an approach of repackaging their previous technology while combining it with other existing VTLS technologies and bundling in new capabilities. As with Innovative Interfaces and Sierra, this approach realizes many libraries are in no hurry to reengineer their backroom processes in light of the possible costs involved, but instead feel that they can get better support by initially focusing on end user-facing improvements. So VTLS has focused on adding support for multimedia, multi-format metadata, mobile devices, and greater interoperability with third-party systems through support for open APIs and SOA. They've added a unified Drupal™user interface on top of Chamo and other existing products. Through that interface, VTLS can offer data from their VITAL and Virtua systems to end users. Solr (a highly scalable, open source, search and index platform) is also employed in Open Skies. The specific steps involved are the merger of content from Virtua and Vital, the merger of Chamo and Visualizer into a new Chamo Discovery module, the creation of a common metadata management system for Virtual and Vital, and the development of enhanced displays of FRBR and RDA records.

Given this approach, there is no loss of existing functionality with this offering; rather, it is an approach that tries to integrate print and digital content; add streaming media support; allow events and activities to be supported; and provide basic preservation services for digital content, e-book collection management, and extensive support for mobile users.

Open Skies will be available either as a local installation or a SaaS offering. It does not meet the definition of a true cloud computing solution as defined above. Data centers can be provided by VTLS or self-hosted by the customer.

Openness is provided via basic support for linked data as well as open APIs that conform to Chamo structures (but this is not an open public specification).

Open Skies is scheduled to be released in early 2013 and should be demonstrable during ALA Midwinter in Seattle.

CLOUD COMPUTING IDEA DEVELOPED AT THE NORTH CAROLINA STATE UNIVERSITY (NCSU)

Virtual Computing Lab (VCL) is a cloud computing idea developed at the North Carolina State University (NCSU) through a collaboration of its College of Engineering and IBM Virtual Computing Initiative to address a growing set of computational needs and user requirements for the university. This system can deliver user required solutions for variety of service environments anytime and anyplace on demand/reservation.

Architectural Layers of Cloud Computing In VCL

Infrastructure as a Service (IaaS)

VCL delivers different infrastructure at one place. It provides a platform (internally no physical infrastructure) virtualization environment in the Universities. Using this, student need not to set up any specific physical infrastructure for their project assignment. VCL provides following services for infrastructure.

- Compute
  - Physical Machines
  - Virtual Machines
  - OS-level virtualization
- Network
- Storage

VCL manager provides appropriate virtualization (aggregation, dis-aggregation) of the available hardware resources before mapping the requested image onto that hardware. VCL services focus on controlling the resource at the platform level.

Platform as a Service (PaaS)

There are at least two perspectives on PaaS depending on the perspective of the producer or consumer of the services:

- The person producing (Here VCL) PaaS might produce a platform by integrating an OS, middleware, application software, and even a development environment that is then provided to a customer as a service.
- The person using (users in Universities) PaaS would see an encapsulated service that is presented to them through an interface. The customer interacts only with the platform through the interface, and the platform does what is necessary to manage and scale it to provide a given level of service. The Virtual appliances can be classified as instances of PaaS.

Using VCL, Students need not to physically install any specific services, solution stacks or databases on their machine. It provides the images to students where they can simply select these images and use them on a machine provided in a cloud.

- Services
- Solution Stacks
    - Java
    - PHP
    - .NET
- Storage
    - Databases
    - File Storage

Software as a Service (SaaS)

VCL allows any of the software as a service solutions, virtualization solutions, and terminal services solutions available today. VMWare, XEN, MS Virtual Server, Virtuoso, and Citrix are typical examples. VCL also as allows any of the access/service delivery options those are suitable from RDP or VNC desktop access, to X-Windows, to a Web service or similar. Figure 4 shows some of these VCL cloud services.

Benefits of Using VCL in Labs: A Cloud Solution

In universities, users are typically students and faculties. Cloud computing systems serving these users within a university environment must at least provide the following capabilities:

- Services and support to a wide range of users.
- A wide-range of course materials and academic support tools to instructors, teachers, professors, and other educators and university staff.
- Research level computational systems and services in support of the research mission of the university.

With these requirements, the major challenges of planning a cloud computing solution in a higher educational, research-oriented institute involves following factors:

Figure 4. VCL Cloud Services

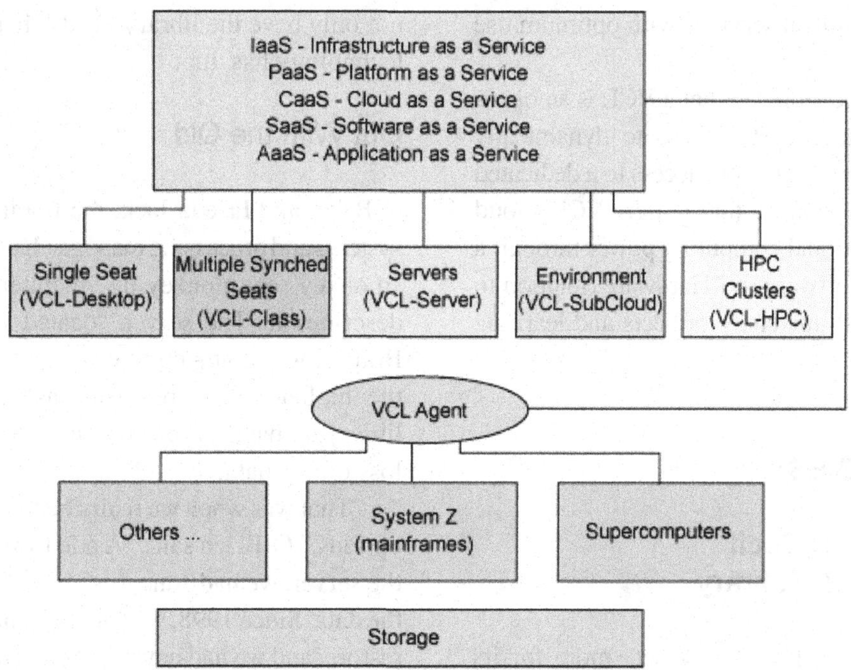

- Excellent resource utilization depending on different user demands
- Variety of diverse service environments
- Operating cloud infrastructure as an economically viable model

In universities the usage of resources will vary depending on the academic calendar. Demand for resources will be more during assignments and year-end time. The research projects and other research oriented activities are active throughout the year. So for a university based cloud computing system to be economically viable, it requires a proper scheduling mechanism to monitor demand and allocate the system resources. VCL provides good scheduling mechanism to identify the ebbs and flows of campus activities.

Here, by the observations and insights from the VCL environment at Universities, the important inference that can be identified in VCL is that, with the help of desktop and HPC utilization, VCL provides efficient utilization of the computational infrastructure in Universities labs. Also, using the VCL blades for both HPC and VCL desktops provides economical services with optimum use of resources.

This can be concluded that a VCL is an open-source Web based system used to dynamically provision and broker remote access to a dedicated computer environment for a user. VCL cloud provides exceptional computing power through a unique Open Software and Hardware Solution to run and host all university projects and learning programs.

CASE STUDIES:

Case Study 1: Cecil County Public Library

Cecil County Public Library gets more for its money with SirsiDynix ® Cloud.

If something were to happen now, we know that we could count on SirsiDynix to take care of it for us. That's something extra we got with Cloud that we didn't have before. - Lee O'Brien (Associate Director, Cecil County Public Library)

The breaking point was when the server room, by necessity, began doubling as office space for not four but five library staff. It was 2009, and the Cecil County Public Library had just reached more than one million in circulation for the first time. Excited but a tiny bit overwhelmed, the library directors began to rethink some of their processes.

A SirsiDynix customer since 1998, the Cecil County Public Library started out as "a turnkey library system," associate director Lee O'Brien said. Its operations were pretty basic, with just circulation, cataloguing and outreach functions. "It was a fairly simple installation originally," O'Brien said. "Then over the years the library just kept growing."

The Cecil County library system, consisting of headquarters at the Elkton Library and six other branch locations, now serves 56,000 patrons. And not only have the library needs changed, but the technology has, too.

Out With the Old

O'Brien and Frieda Jack, the library's technical systems and processing manager, had done enough "monkey see, monkey do" maintenance, as she describes it. The server, located at the Elkton Branch, was going on five years of use and, with the higher patron registrations and increased library demands, they couldn't afford to risk the loss of any data.

"That was when we really began to look at our options," O'Brien said. "Aside from maintaining the server, we had concerns about the security of the data. Since 1998, we had never had to do a full restore, and we had never lost data, but we always felt we were a hair's breath away from disaster."Just to keep the system operational required at least two hours of work each week, not counting the weekends, holidays or early hours when O'Brien and Jack would take care of required system updates. And in its current state, somebody physically had to touch the library server every day or they would rewrite data. (This would have been a serious headache had the library not upgraded to SirsiDynix® Cloud solution by the time the 56-inch snowstorms of early 2010 hit, putting the library out of connection with its physical server location for days.)

In With the New

Since upgrading to SirsiDynix Cloud, these former headaches, worries and after-hours experiments are no longer a concern for the library branch, which can now focus its saved time and resources on other library needs.

"For libraries in the situation we're in, with a very small IT staff, cloud computing really helps us be effective with our staffing," O'Brien said. "In addition to being responsible for running reports and system admin, our systems manager is also responsible for cataloguing, physical processing and statistical reports, so it's freed up time in her schedule to do other important things for the library."

And plus, O'Brien said, this isn't the '80s anymore. Technology threats are more complex now.

"We've always known that we should have redundant servers and that our data needs to be backed up and protected, but we just haven't had the resources or the expertise. Making that vulnerability goes away in this day and age is so important," O'Brien said. "If something were to happen now, we know that we could count on SirsiDynix to take care of it for us. That's something extra we got with Cloud that we didn't have before."

Case Study 2: New Jersey Institute of Technology (NJIT)

NJIT embraced the cloud in a strategy that evolved over several years, with their experiences informing a new organic strategy framed by the six viewpoints. These viewpoints are helping transform delivery of IT services at NJIT, offering a model for how these "views of the cloud" might do the same for other institutions.

Prerequisites for Cloud Success

The successful cloud examples at NJIT have three things in common:

1. **Authentication and Authorization for Cloud Services Should Be Done Locally:** Campus users need to benefit from using familiar log-in credentials to access cloud services, without sending user passwords directly to cloud providers. Most cloud providers support federated authentication methods like Shibboleth or SAML, which, in turn, work with the campus LDAP or Active Directory for seamless customer access, often through the campus portal's single sign-on features.
2. **Cloud Applications Should Be Branded with the Look and Feel of Campus Applications:** Most cloud providers allow some tailoring, ranging from appropriate placement of campus logos to adopting your color schemes and Website style sheets. Local branding disguises the true host of an application and provides a seamless transition as users click through from local to external cloud services and back again.
3. **Some Degree of Web Services Expertise will be Needed within the IT Support Staff:** The complexity of the cloud application will

drive the degree of extraction and sharing of data needed among local applications and those within a cloud. Integration with the campus can be as simple as building .csv extract files or it might range from designing XML imports to coding sophisticated APIs.

By focusing efforts and talents to meet these three prerequisites, NJIT has moved beyond the more limited perspective that views cloud computing as Web-enabled outsourcing. They have implemented multiple cloud-based services (see Figure 5) with the same financial and personnel resources that historically supported fewer solutions hosted on our site. The following sections explore specific examples of how NJIT has identified and embraced six cloud viewpoints.

View 1: Commoditized Services

In 2007 NJIT investigated replacing its Sun Java Messaging Server with a Webmail front end for student and alumni e-mail because its features paled in comparison to those available in consumer e-mail services (Gmail, Hotmail, AOL, and Yahoo), where most students were already forwarding their NJIT e-mail. Number of options were reviewed, some premises-based, others outsourcing to commercial providers, and even unified solutions consolidating all e-mail (student, alumni, faculty, staff) into a single service.

Outsourcing to established commercial service providers was quickly dismissed because of extremely high annual cost. Focus was then shifted to premises-based hosting models, with limited consideration given to new "no-fee" SaaS models from Google and Microsoft. Since both the companies were having similar basic feature sets, NJIT ultimately chose Google Apps for Education, finding that many of the value-add features and direction of Microsoft Live@edu were tightly coupled to other Microsoft offerings and only available to Windows users. Implementation of Google Apps for Education was relatively easy and handled by a systems administrator with working knowledge of mail routing, DNS, and directory services. Google mailboxes were predefined for existing NJIT students, who retained their @

Figure 5. Six Views of the Cloud

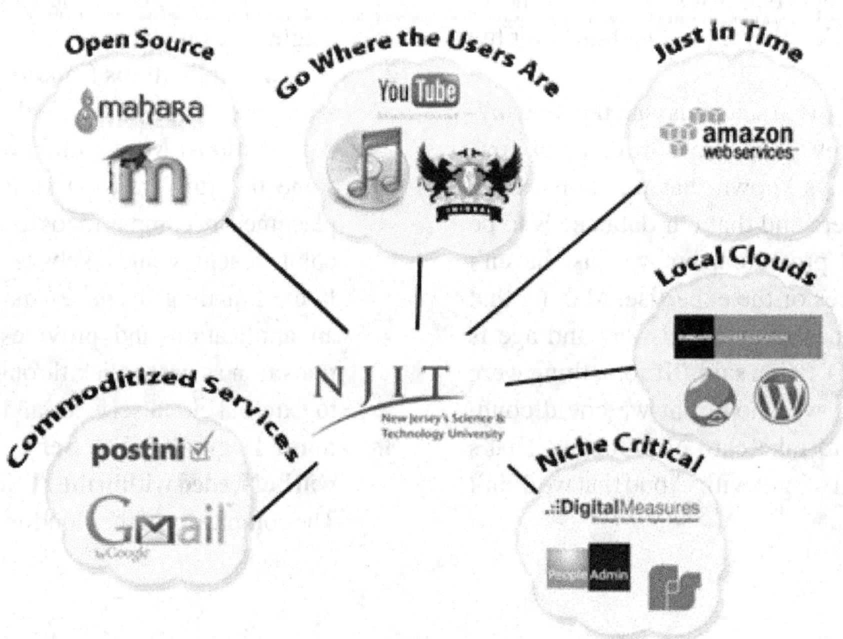

njit e-mail addresses. Successfully migrating to Google Apps was a significant accomplishment on a number of levels:

- First, the feedback from users was overwhelmingly positive — they immediately appreciated the increased functionality and service levels. The transition was not disruptive because of good communication plans. From the CIO's perspective, service levels increased and savings benefited the operational IT budget.
- Second, it demonstrated to systems administrators and technical staff that the cloud was a viable alternative. Security and privacy of data could be maintained with other than premises-based hosting. This was a major change for the technical staff.
- Finally, since these cloud services were branded with the NJIT look and feel and used the same authentication systems as other campus IT services, many users didn't know or care whether they were cloud-based or not. And that's the way it should be.

View 2: Open Source

Open-source software has come a long way and can meet mission-critical needs in a number of application areas. Open-source adoptions often follow the disruptive technology or disruptive innovation paths where they are introduced under the radar of more traditional and established applications.

In 2006 NJIT began exploring open-source and commercial alternatives as possible successors to current WebCT e-learning platform. In spring of 2008, with nearly 40 Moodle course sections, they selected MoodleRooms to host a supported version of Moodle. Several earlier "hiccups" with self-support of the downloadable version available from the Moodle community had proven time-consuming to our application support staff and disruptive to faculty and students.

In fall 2009, based on continued satisfaction with Moodle, a stable hosting partner, and predictable hosting fees, they chose Moodle as the successor e-learning platform to Blackboard's Campus Edition. The spring 2010 semester marked the end of Campus Edition use and the offering of 435 Moodle course sections. Moodle adoption had surpassed the highest level of WebCT adoption by 40 percent.

Based on positive experiences with cloud-sourcing Moodle as an e-learning platform, they launched Mahara in the spring of 2010 as an e-portfolio platform. Incremental growth again allows local adoption of the application to mature at its own pace. Because Mahara is integrated with Moodle installation, any student who wants to create a Mahara e-portfolio can do so without additional costs to the university.

In February 2010, NJIT joined the Open Courseware Consortium, a collaborative effort of more than 200 higher education institutions and organizations from around the world that make available free and open digital publication of high-quality educational materials organized as courses. From a financial perspective, the benefits of using open-source software with vendor support once again became an issue of cost avoidance.

View 3: Go Where the Users Are

Campus portals today are gateways to ERP and e-learning systems where students register for classes, pay bills, post class assignments, participate in threaded class discussions, and so forth. Institutions also need to truly understand which tools students are already embracing in their personal lives, how they actually use them, and their importance to students. Rising to this challenge, NJIT brought many direct and indirect benefits, as the following examples illustrate.

Schools on Facebook

Schools on Facebook is a Facebook application that allows students and student groups to build new NJIT connections and social networks within a separate, private, secure "NJIT-only" Facebook area. The application leverages a "place" where students already "hang out," know how to navigate, and feel comfortable. They can connect with campus organizations, find students in their classes, see other students from their hometown, create study groups — all things we saw students trying to do within the regular Facebook pages and groups we have had for several years.

iTunes U

A section of the iTunes Store, iTunes U allows institutions to provide both public and private means to distribute educational content. The private side would typically be used to distribute lectures meant for students registered in specific course sections. It has the infrastructure required for schools to manage access accordingly. NJIT currently has almost 1,500 individual files that support some 112 courses stored in the private portion of iTunes U. However, content can also be made available publically and searchable from within the iTunes store.

Aside from providing a no-fee digital asset repository with access control to individual classes, iTunes U provides the opportunity to showcase the scholarly work of faculty and students worldwide.

Figure 6. NJIT YouTube Channel

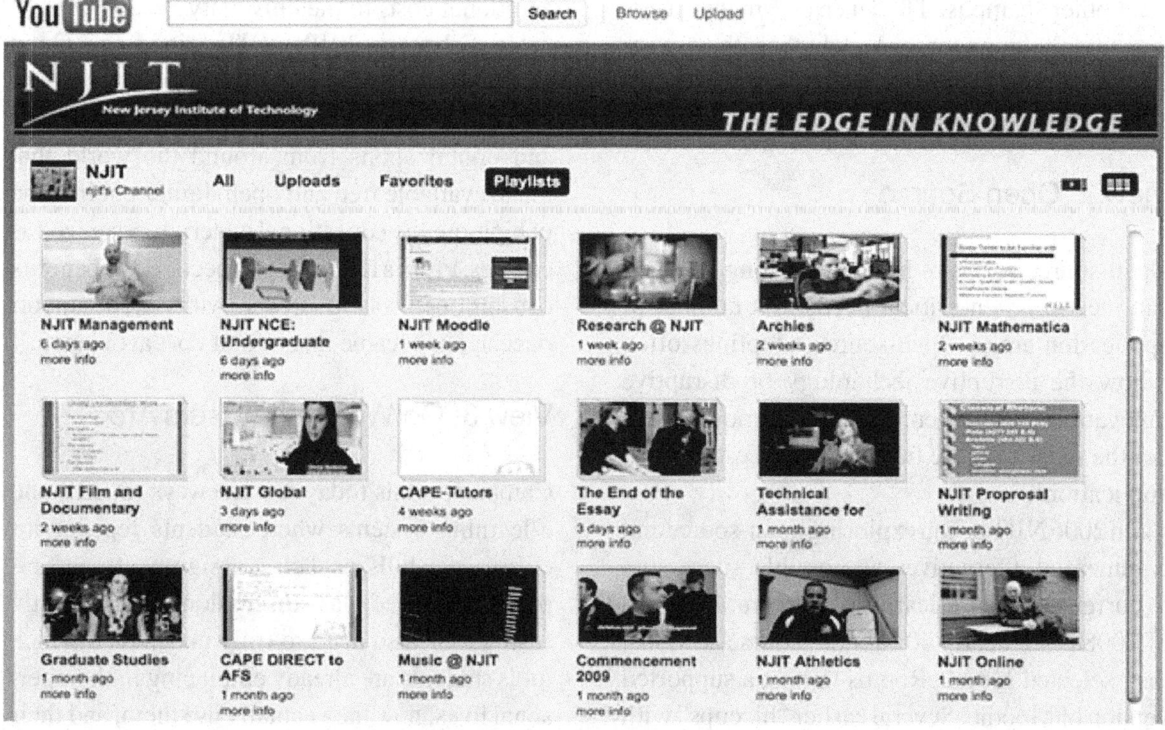

In a similar fashion, NJIT's YouTube (see Figure 6) and Flickr channels provide visibility and marketing not only for the scholarly activities of faculty and students but also as a venue to market and showcase the diverse activities of campus life and for the university to build and manage its brand. While some content is created explicitly for these sites, much of it was created for other purposes, which get more mileage by putting digital content in places where they will reach wider audiences of potential students, parents, alumni, students at other schools, and life-long learners.

View 4: Just-In-Time Computing

On-demand computing is a hallmark of the cloud-computing model. Amazon Web Services (AWS), for example, offers granular, by-the-hour pricing for virtual servers. The cloud-provided service is guaranteed at 99.95 percent reliability, which practically speaking might exceed what many campuses can guarantee for locally hosted services.

A recent example at NJIT involved a graduate course on distributed computing. The instructor divided two sections of his course (a face-to-face section and an online section) into 10 teams, each with 4-5 students. Each team received its own "cloud" with two Linux servers (an application server and a database server) for development of three-tier applications. Each team's servers have the same initial configuration of operating systems, database, and other tools preinstalled. Prior to the cloud model, such a real-world infrastructure of 20 separate servers could not have been provided to a single course.

Using this type of service gives students real-world experience with network security issues. As soon as a server is instantiated, that machine becomes a high-priority target for hackers. Upon getting to their virtual server, students need to immediately secure the operating system and properly manage the machine. In the context of a computer security class, this is a benefit because students get experience securing network resources.

The just-in-time cloud model opens a new world for educators by providing the infrastructure for realistic senior projects or capstone courses. The specialized needs for students doing theses and dissertations can be met easily without the significant overhead of setup and configuration. Researchers can test a concept and bring it beyond proof of concept without major investments in hardware and other infrastructure. Instructors and IT staff are discovering that capabilities once only imagined are now obtainable. These on-demand computing models also offer a significant resource for disaster recovery and business contingency planning.

View 5: Clouds Can Be Local, Too

Advances in virtualization technologies allow organizations to build their own "local" clouds. Managing virtual machines saves staff time, energy, and space. With virtualization, it is easy to provide redundancy for critical applications and plan for some degree of business contingency. Virtualizing a large number of disparate servers can lower an organization's total cost of ownership for server management.

At NJIT, IT staff designed a life-cycle replacement solution utilizing virtualization approaches with hardware for two local computational clouds and 30 percent spare capacity for growth:

- Cloud 1 runs Solaris Containers (Zones) for high transaction processing applications.
- Cloud 2 runs VMware to create virtual Windows and Linux machines.

Running a local virtualized environment also facilitates introducing new services for experimentation and innovation that might otherwise never have found a spare server.

View 6: Niche-Critical Applications

Campus IT managers always look for ways to meet the needs of their niche customers, who need to provide services to members of the campus community but don't have the clout to become an IT priority. Usage patterns of IT services for such niche customers often vary throughout the academic year. Cloud computing enables a new breed of software entrepreneurs to leverage the application service provider (ASP) business model and provide niche applications through a cloud. These entrepreneurs generally provide a single Web-based product or suite of similar products. Typically, all follow the "prerequisites for cloud success" discussed earlier that differentiate this approach from the traditional ASP, SaaS, or Web-enabled outsourcing models. NJIT has adopted a number of such niche applications with success. One of such niche application is Web-Based Self-Service for Real-Time Answers to Questions.

IntelliResponse provides a Web-based intelligent answer agent that allows customers to type common questions in an "Ask NJIT" branded text box and receive answers in real time. The system searches a database of commonly asked questions within a question domain and selects what it determines is the best answer. Management tools allow an administrator to review all questions submitted and further refine the accuracy of answers. Driving routine customer inquiries toward self-service mode and away from the more costly telephone and e-mail modes improves both customer satisfaction and staff productivity. NJIT has implemented several question domains, each administered by a separate university office. Those question domains currently cover separate topics in undergraduate admissions, graduate admissions, continuing professional education, library services, and the computing help desk.

CONCLUSION

With the unlimited growth of electronic resources and technological developments, libraries are facing the serious problem of budget constraints, which was never so acute earlier; moreover users' demands are multiplying and becoming more challenging. Under these circumstances, cloud computing which is a metered utility service like mobile or electricity, where users pay for real time use, is a great ray of hope.

It is a broad array of Web-based services, allowing users to obtain a wide range of technology-enabled services on a pay-as-you-go basis. As a result, it is becoming more popular day by day because of its important features such as: cost effectiveness, efficiency, user-friendliness, flexibility, data security, scalability, world wide connectivity, automatic adaptation, and so forth. So cloud computing is the broad concept of using the Internet to allow people to access technology-enabled payment based services that are greatly scalable and accessible from anywhere. The new trends in the automation spawned by recent Web development are making libraries to be more reliant on software and computing resources provided by outside companies in service delivery to users. Therefore, in this environment, libraries should constantly attempt to improve user service models by adopting new technologies. Although the use of cloud computing is still in its infancy, the effects of using it are quite obvious. With the introduction of cloud computing, libraries can certainly offer more effective, more professional and user-centric services. The cloud computing techniques and models applied to libraries, not only can improve the utilization rate of resources to address the imbalance in development between regions, but also can make more extensive use of cloud computing to our work life. The cloud environment is a highly developed network environment; it appears to the users as high-quality service and high security. And we all believe that libraries will create more knowledge benefits for our country with the help of cloud computing.

REFRENCES

Aggarwal, V. (2008). *Computing in the clouds.* New Delhi, India: Express Compute.

Buyya, R., Yeo, C. S., & Venugopal, S. (2008). Market oriented cloud computing vision, hype and reality for delivering IT services as computing utilities. In *Proceedings of 10th IEEE International Conference on High Performance Computing and Communications, Dalian.* (pp. 5-13). Melbourne, Australia: The University of Melbourne.

Cervone, H. F. (2010). Managing digital libraries: The view from 3000 feet. *OCLC Systems & Services, 26*(3), 162–165. doi:10.1108/10650751011073607.

Dhawan, N. (2011, July 23). Cloud computing can counter illiteracy. *The Times of India.* Retrieved from http://timesofindia.indiatimes.com/tech/careers/education/Cloud-computing-can-counter-illiteracy-Managing-Director-HP-India/articleshow/9335831.cms

Doerkson, T. (2008, August 5). *Cloud computing: The user-friendly version of grid computing.* Retrieved from http://jeremygeelan.ulitzer.com/node/593313

Farkas, M. (2008). Technology goes local: Collecting local knowledge with social software. *American Libraries, 39*(8), 50.

Goldner, M. (2010). *Winds of change: Libraries and cloud computing.* Dublin, OH: OCLC. doi:10.1515/bfup.2010.042.

Hamilton, D. (2008, June 4). Cloud computing seen as next wave for technology investors. *Financial Post.*

Sanchati, R., & Kulkarni, G. (2011). Cloud computing in digital and university libraries. *Global J. Comp. Sci. Technol., 11*(12), 37–42.

Sharif, A. M. (2010). It's written in the cloud: The hype and promise of cloud computing. *J. Enterprise Inf. Manag., 23*(2), 131–134. doi:10.1108/17410391011019732.

Shivakumar, B. L., Raju, T., & Revathy, H. (2010). Cloud computing: A dark lining in the dark clouds of crisis management of economic slowdown. *Asia Pacific Business Review, 6*(3), 99–105.

Thomas, P. Y. (2011). Cloud computing: A potential paradigm for practicing the scholarship of teaching and learning. *The Electronic Library, 29*(2), 214–224. doi:10.1108/02640471111125177.

Chapter 9
The University Cloud Library Model and the Role of the Cloud Librarian

Sangeeta N Dhamdhere
Modern College of Arts, Science and Commerce, India

Ramdas Lihitkar
Government College of Science, India

ABSTRACT

The latest trend of Cloud Computing is progressing fast and using this technology it is possible to publish and store information on a virtual cloud based infrastructure. Virtualization technology has been adopted by many data centers in the industry. It shares resources on a single system efficiently and reduces infrastructure costs. Libraries are using various technologies along with Web tools at a time. Information sharing and an open access culture are developing fast in the education field. How libraries can make use of the application of cloud computing and virtualization technology for common data storage and managing multiple servers and provide cloud based information services to patrons will be discussed in detail in this chapter. This chapter also discusses in brief the applications of these technologies in libraries along with the university cloud library model and the role of cloud librarians.

INTRODUCTION

The field of higher education has become one of the strongest adopters of virtualization as it allows the management of all resources like laboratories and libraries centrally and gives remote access to students through mobiles too. Today's librarians and IT experts are facing new challenges in managing electronic content archives. For giving quick and appropriate access to every piece of information libraries are adopting new technologies. What seemed a dream a few years back is becoming real nowadays. "Nowadays many university libraries are virtualizing servers

DOI: 10.4018/978-1-4666-4631-5.ch009

and desktops, collaborating with other campus organizations and saving money and staff time," states Karin Kelley, a virtualization analyst at the 451 Group (Roscoria, 2011). They are planning to build and maintain their own data centers for information sharing.

Cloud based services provide a means for libraries to free resources on information technologies and focus on libraries' core competences – to manage, organize, and disseminate information. "Cloud based services are also bringing cutting-edge services to libraries that have less information technology expertise," according to Qin Zhu, a member of the IEEE Library advisory council (2012). A very recent example is that in February 2012 the Library of Congress and OCLC announced a new beta cloud based service for Small Libraries (WSSL), with which libraries with fewer than 20,000 items in their collections may construct a low cost, simple, but dynamic Website. Features include basic patron and inventory management, with checkouts, returns, holds, and renewals, among other functions. Many libraries are now adapting 3M cloud libraries applications. Let's discuss more in detail on the application of cloud computing in libraries.

SERVER VIRTUALIZATION

Server virtualization is a method of running multiple independent virtual operating systems or applications on a single machine. According to Roscoria (2011), this technology is a way of achieving higher server density and now it is pretty much a no-brainer for everybody. Via net computing devices now many desktops are running simultaneously on one machine without CPUs in LAN. This technology is a huge boon from a consolidation perspective and the cost savings. Essentially instead of having one application per server you can now have multiple apps on one machine, which saves a huge amount on hardware resources. With this the use of library resources has increased and also the use of library software by library staff is increasing in developing countries.

The desktop virtualization model allows the use of virtual machines to let multiple network subscribers maintain individualized desktops on a single, centrally located computer or server. The central machine may be at a residence, business, or data center. Users may be geographically scattered, but all may be connected to the central machine by a local area network, wide area network, or via the public Internet. All publishers, suppliers, consortia are using this technology for giving access to their digital resources like e-books, e-journals, articles, scholarly materials.

CLOUD COMPUTING

Cloud Computing is the improvement of Distributed Computing, Parallel Computing, Grid Computing and Distributed Databases. The basic principle of Cloud Computing is making tasks distributed in large numbers of distributed computers but not in local computers or remote servers. "The idea of cloud computing has emerged for outsourcing of computing infrastructure, storage of client data and applications that are accessed via a remote server" (Hosch, 2009; Knorr & Gruman, 2008). Traditionally, companies sold product CD's and one had to buy a license to use them. Now companies like Tally, Frank Borland products provide subscription services on the Internet, without the need for the customer to set up anything and pay on a monthly or yearly basis or just for the usage. Cloud computing also provides a common computing platform where users can build their own applications for use by others through the Web.

Cloud Computing is Summarized as Follows

- **SAAS:** Software-As-A-Service
- **PAAS:** Platform-As-A-Service
- **IAAS:** Infrastructure-As-A-Service
- **DAAS:** Desktop-As-A-Service

INFORMATION COMMON

Information common and resources common usage and sharing is possible because of this emerging server virtualization and cloud technology. According to Wikipedia (n.d.), "An Information Commons is an information system like a physical library or online community that exists to produce, conserve, and preserve information for current and future generations. This concept refers to the shared knowledge-base and the processes that facilitate or hinder its use. It also refers to a physical space, usually in an academic library, where anyone and all can participate in the processes of information research, gathering and production.

Cloud computing and server virtualization technology enable the Internet to facilitate a decentralized production and distribution of information. It enables open source software and other commercial software to share software and hardware platform common to all users. Licensing in commons concept is also coming up. Creators have begun to use the licensing model to grant permissions for many uses in advance. The GNU General Public License (GPL), developed by Richard Stallman at MIT in the 1980s is an example of such license. "The GNU Free Documentation License is a form of copy-left intended for use on a manual, textbook or other document to assure everyone the effective freedom to copy and redistribute it, with or without modifications, either commercially or non-commercially" ("GNU operating system," 2013). The GPL allows works in the common to be secured in the common. Prices of scholarly journals dropped dramatically and publishing corporations restricted access to these journals through expensive licenses. Research libraries had no other choice but to cut many of their journal subscriptions. European and American academic communities began to find alternate ways to distribute and manage scholarly information.

The Scholarly Publishing and Academic Resource Coalition (SPARC) work to stimulate the emergence of new scholarly communication models that expand the dissemination of scholarly research and reduce financial pressures on libraries.

Cloud Libraries

Libraries can apply the concept of cloud computing to amplify the power of cooperation and to build a significant, unified presence on the Web to save money and time and to avoid duplication of work. Cloud computing can help libraries for resource, infrastructure, platform and software sharing. Different libraries under one educational trust can share and work on one platform so that consistency, uniformity, standards can be maintained. All libraries are already using the technology by the service providers like Google services, Facebook, Flickr, Slide Share, Social Book marking, file sharing, e-portfolio, Amazon, other Web tools and applications by paying a minimum amount. Because of digitization libraries have huge repositories of digital files both subscribed, institutional and purchased and the cloud is boon for storage and maintenance of such data. In developing countries some libraries have less technological infrastructure or platforms. With net computing solutions and cloud solutions they also can provide all the best services to their readers with a minimum investment. A few years ago each library had hardly one computer but now that scene has changed and you can see a couple of computers in every section. In digital libraries for net computing one can even arrange 50 workstations for readers' reference. Cloud libraries can be accessed and managed from anywhere, so there are no restrictions of place and device. One can access the libraries from one's mobile phone too from home, can send their queries to the librarian anytime and ask librarian's help. Librarians also can help readers from any place.

Because of Z39.50 libraries can import and export catalogue entries and can maintain standard catalogues according to Library of Congress or the National Library of that nation. It saves the time of member libraries. When data is maintained in the cloud, maintenance and backup of this data is done once and if a change is needed, once one library performs the change and all share it. Developing and Developed countries like India are spending on expensive technologies to assist their patrons in locating information owned by libraries or available online. There are very few softwares which are designed in standard formats and enable catalogue import/export facility and digital library solutions are very costly.

Many libraries cannot afford such softwares and go in for low cost local softwares which are designed just to keep records without following any library standards and so we see variations in catalogue entries. Already in many developed countries database vendors or integrated library system providers provide external servers to host library software and data. If universities provide such standard softwares or a uniform platform to all affiliated colleges through cloud it will be good for resource sharing, cooperative collection building, digitization, preservation, standardization of material and union catalogues.

3M™ Cloud Library

This application is an innovative way to browse, borrow and read popular fiction and non-e-books from local public library. Patrons can now enjoy an e-book collection with wireless browsing and

Figure 1. Example of 3M Cloud Library

borrowing, and Internet-free reading. Easy-to-use apps are available for most devices. They need valid library card to use this application. Patrons can use their personal accounts too to access e-books on their mobile devices like e-readers, PCs, Tablets, Kindle, Nook, iPad, iPhone, iPod Touch, Android-based tablets, Kindle fire, smart phones. More than 3,000 publishers have signed in with this application and provide access to more than 2 LACS titles through this common platform.

A recent example of use of this application is Kitchigami Regional Library System which launched the 3M Cloud Library eBooks service to all Kitchigami cardholders, providing downloadable eBooks for all ages.

DuraCloud

DuraCloud is a free open-source project and fee-based subscription service that is currently in use by a number of major institutions. It is a cloud based service developed and hosted by the Duraspace, a long-time NDIIPP partner and non-profit organization focusing on solutions for open access, institutional repositories, digital libraries, digital archives and data curation. The Library of Congress started working on a Pilot Program with DuraCloud to test perpetual access to digital content in 2009.

Private Clouds, Hybrid Clouds and Community Clouds

Private cloud is also called as internal cloud or corporate cloud that provides hosted services to a limited number of people behind a firewall. This kind of cloud can also be used in college libraries. A hybrid cloud is a composition of at least one private cloud and at least one public cloud. A hybrid cloud is primarily based in a privately owned and operated data center, but it can shift some of its traffic and data processing requests to public cloud vendors such as Amazon or Rackspace on an as-needed basis. This hybrid model would let libraries maintain more control over the applications and data stores that contain sensitive, private information about patrons. Moreover, libraries can continually adjust and fine-tune the balance between the tight control of a private IT infrastructure, and the flexibility and savings of cloud-hosted infrastructure. If reliability or security of one vendor becomes a concern, you're not committed to one company or one model of computing services.

Libraries presently cooperate with one another to buy IT equipment, bandwidth and the services of IT professionals, libraries may soon cooperate in the building and management of data centers. Alternately, if enough libraries express interest, a company such as Google, Amazon, Microsoft or another cloud vendor might create a Library Cloud similar to Google's Government Cloud. Or, a library vendor with deep IT resources (e.g., OCLC or SirsiDynix) might build library-centric cloud services on top of cloud infrastructure leased from one of the more established players.

Some Examples of Cloud Libraries are:

- Online Computer Library Catalog (OCLC)
- Library of Congress (LC)
- Exlibris
- Scribd
- Polaris
- Discovery services
- Google Docs
- World Cat
- Encore

Open Source Cloud Computing Platforms

Eucalyptus, OpenStack, Nimbus, Open Nebula, Open QRM, Zennos, Xen, EyeOS, Appscale, Google Drive, J-Cloud are examples of an open source multicloud library.

Paid Cloud Computing Platform and Servers

As commercial examples we can mention Amazon EC2, Appistry, AT&T, Enomaly, GCloud3, Zizmox, Google, Microsoft, RackSpace, Fanggle, DuraCloud, 3M Cloud Library Applications, etc.

With the rapid development and extensive use of ICT and Web technologies in libraries, users' information requirements are increasingly personalized. And now more and more libraries advocate user-centered services. And only in this way they can master the basic demands of their users. Furthermore, the library can develop itself according to such information and improve users' satisfaction. Farkas (2007) said about Web collaboration that it allows for libraries to be able to go to places where the patrons are and deliver relevant services where and when users need them.

Pasadena, Glendale, and a few other libraries in California tested a cloud library platform developed by 3M to lend out e-books recently in June 2012. They are using self-checkout machines too made by 3M. This cloud platform keeps everything in a synchronized way. Readers can download books within half a minute on iPhones, iPads, Nooks, Androids, or PC and Mac Computers. They can continue reading from one to another device.

As this technology has already entered in libraries, the future libraries are virtual libraries and cloud libraries. Slowly developing countries will also get solutions at reasonable costs.

THE UNIVERSITY CLOUD LIBRARY MODEL

Libraries are at the heart of any educational system. So university libraries are the heart of the university and fully depend on library resources. Traditional education is changing into distance education and e-learning. Universities are increasingly using digital media to accomplish their tasks and to offer user centered Web-based services. Being a most important academic and scientific research base, university libraries used to charge for providing information services for its users and member libraries. But today libraries have changed this viewpoint because of open access systems and use of digital media in research, preservation and dissemination of knowledge and delivery of education. In universities, readers are now accessing information from digital libraries and Internet. Comparing with university libraries, we can find that foreign libraries are intended to provide services for all the people. Besides the professors, teachers or students, all the people of that country can access to the library resources. In addition, they also permit users access to many libraries' resources by handling the related certificate of that library. And fortunately, domestic libraries can also do this in the cloud environment. Anybody who can pass through the legal network identity authentication has the right to visit the joint resources of university libraries on the Internet. In other words, university libraries will offer services for all the people with the help of Cloud Computing.

The role of libraries in managing e-resources and giving maximum information has increased. It has been observed that in developing countries affiliated colleges maintain their separate library and resources. As now many books and journals are available in electronic form libraries are purchasing/ subscribing to those resources or taking memberships of consortia. Universities are also investing a lot of funds for purchase and subscription of different resources. These resources are common to all colleges running same courses. If universities will give access to all these resources on their cloud for all affiliated colleges it will save time, money, and manpower. Universities and other funding agencies provide different grants for colleges for purchase of reading material. With the cloud technology member libraries will purchase new material to share rather than duplicate material. It will help to increase new resources for reference. Member libraries can give their resources to Inter-Library Loan.

Figure 2 shows a proposed model by the author for a Cloud University Library. Collections or materials in the university library for different courses can be stored on the cloud, for example, e-books, Journals, Databases, Question Papers, Question banks, theses dissertations, project reports, chapters from the books, conference proceedings, newspaper articles, manuscripts, presentations, guest lectures, images, working papers, Websites, edublogs, educational videos, CDs, DVDs, notices, circulars, newsletters, annual reports, and so forth. Also the university can keep the best library management solution on the cloud to access and use by member libraries or affiliated college libraries on the Cloud for uniformity, union catalogue and resource sharing purpose. The Library of Congress already initiated this Cloud-based activity for small libraries.

CLOUD LIBRARY ACCESS MODEL

Cloud computing solutions can create new workflows needed by librarians, because it offers the opportunity for a cooperative platform for libraries to build on. There are four key principles of a cooperative platform:

Figure 2. Proposed University Cloud Model by the author

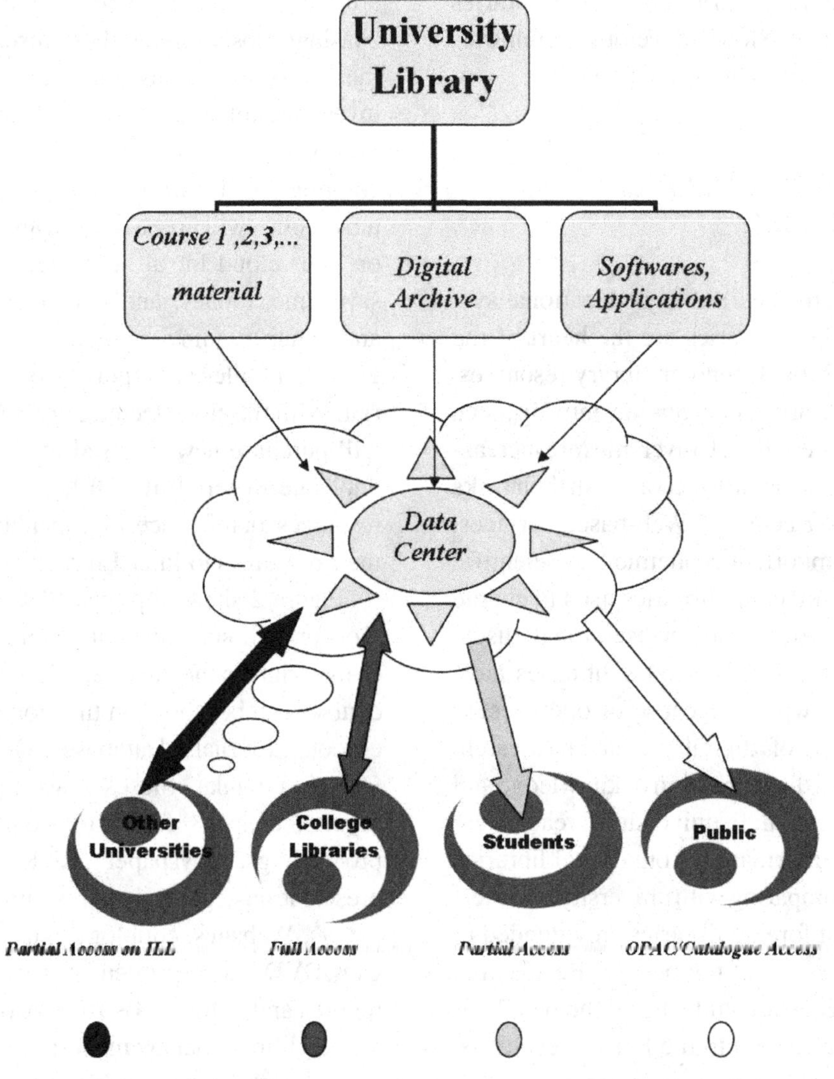

- **Openness:** Meaning that services and data are made available to support greater interoperability, not only within and between cloud services, but also with library-developed and third-party applications;
- **Extensibility:** Meaning that the platform can easily accommodate the addition of new services and applications, developed either by the service provider or by members of the community;
- **Data Richness:** Meaning that a library can interact with and expose a wide variety of information about purchased, licensed, and digital content through this platform; and
- **Collaboration:** Meaning that libraries can harness the collective power of the community of libraries to innovate and share solutions.

A Cloud University Library can be accessible with login password or IP address based. The OPAC can be available to all. Considering copyright issues, some resources will have limited access but the university can provide those on request through Inter-Library Loan. The future virtual library will be providing login and password details along with a tablet PC to the students at the time of admission itself. The university can design separate modules for different classes. All college librarians and university library staff can work together in the Cloud environment. They can contribute their best in providing Cloud-based services to all students and staff. Figure 3 shows the idea of a future college and university admission process. Students are provided a Cloud library kit with access code pin, validity, and tablet pc.

PROPOSED SUBSCRIPTION METHOD BY THE AUTHOR

The author suggests a second option for the university libraries with which they can provide Cloud-based services on subscription basis to its members and member libraries:

1. **OPEN ID:** A user can create his account for accessing information products available on the cloud. The library or individual can select the information or products they want

Figure 3. Future college and university admission process

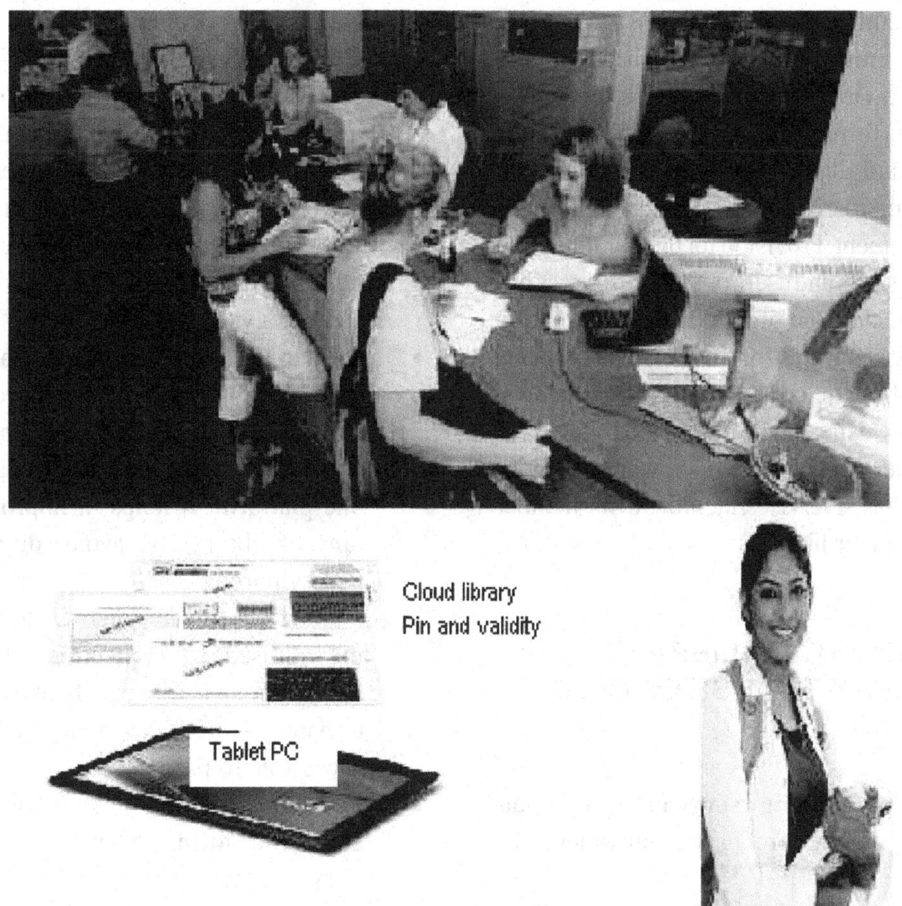

to subscribe or access. The centralized portal will have authentication and account summary. The portal will check his permission or member type, history and accordingly they will be providing the information.

2. **Payment/Billing:** For Inter-Library Loan to collect money for particular resource university should have payment service using which the library can credit/debit cards
3. **Tracking Usage/Subscription:** For tracking usage, users have to renew their membership every year. Temporary membership may be given on payment basis for a specific time. The Library Management System on the Cloud is protected by password and access is to member libraries only.
4. **Provisioning:** It is quite critical in the Cloud environment because at a time many users go through the resources stored in the Cloud and all member libraries use the same platform for LMS and Digital Resources management. Provision for the training to the library staffs and users of these resources has to be made from time to time. Information literacy programs for teachers and students should be organized frequently by the college libraries using the Cloud-based resources of universities. Figure 4 shows the flow of Cloud-based services/facilities to its member and member libraries.

ENHANCEMENT OF LIBRARY SERVICES BY THE USE OF CLOUD COMPUTING

- **E-Books Lending Service:** Cloud platform is now becoming popular to lend the e-books.
- **Union /Shared Catalogue/OPAC:** Network libraries can use same platform and give access to their collection on one platform. Through cloud computing creation of union catalogue become very easy.
- **Document Download Service:** One can download documents easily if permit access in the network.
- **Digital Preservation/Scanning Service:** Digitization and scanning work can be done centralized and so one can avoid duplication of such time consuming work. Libraries can preserve the collection is digital form in the form of archives.
- **Article Delivery Service:** Cloud computing can be used for article delivery service to the patrons by the libraries. Publishers are already using this technology for providing access to libraries.
- **Current Awareness Service:** To provide current awareness service to all patrons has become easy with cloud computing.
- **Document Sharing:** Document sharing has become easy with cloud computing.
- **Bulletin Board Service:** We can provide new services on bulletin board with this technology.
- **Information Common:** Information common like bibliographical data, content pages, cover pages, question papers, syllabus, and other reading material we can share on one platform. It helps in improving economy of library and avoids duplication of library purchase.
- **Collection Development:** Cloud computing is used for collection development. Duplications can be easily avoided and alternate resources can be located and made accessible to patrons.
- **File Sharing:** To share various files in electronic form become easy with the cloud computing.
- **Information Discovery:** Cloud provides a platform to store all information that one can access anytime from anywhere; so in-

Figure 4. Flow chart of Cloud-based services/facilities to university members and member libraries

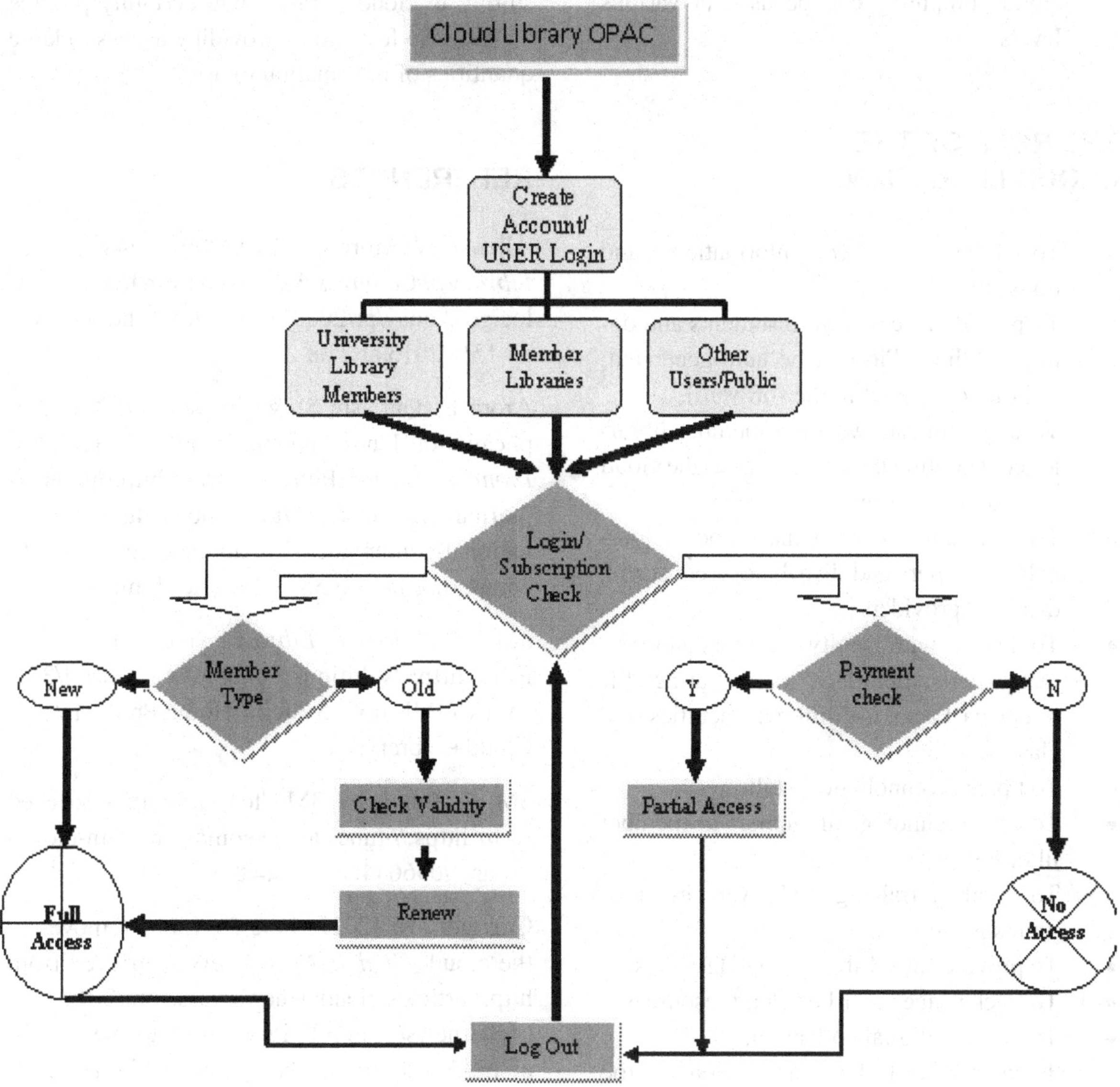

formation discovery and searching become easy and it is very useful for researchers.

- **E-Learning:** In the e-learning environment too, cloud computing is boon. Study material can be kept on the cloud for reference purpose and online examinations also can be conducted. Discussions, revisions can be done at a time from different places.
- **Information Literacy/Orientation:** Libraries can conduct information literacy and orientation courses on the cloud. They can keep the tutorials, videos, presentations and files on the cloud for user's orientation.
- **Social Interactions with the Users:** Can be possible because of cloud computing.

- **Online Demos:** For giving online demo, cloud computing can be used at various levels.

THE ROLE OF THE CLOUD LIBRARIAN

- To track member information and transactions.
- To provide Access Pin to students and define validity. (Pin can be auto-generated; Validity can be set in the software).
- To communicate with the member libraries contributing their resources to the cloud for resource sharing.
- To communicate with the e-books, journals publishers and distributors, consortia, database providers.
- To discuss with faculty members and subject experts, librarians for preparing different packages for different faculties and classes.
- To update technological skills.
- To give technological support to member libraries.
- To conduct training and awareness programs for readers.
- To provide Inter-Library Loan facilities.
- To track usage record of cloud resources.
- To develop digital collection.
- To keep record of physical resources too for providing referral service.

CONCLUSION

With the proliferation of scholarly resources, and the need to provide relevant information to users in a convenient manner, librarians have a great challenge before them. Technology is advancing at a phenomenal rate, but it needs to be harnessed in the most efficient way. Cloud computing, resulting in cloud libraries will certainly provide a great leap forward in providing access to large quantities of information to users.

REFERENCES

Allen, E., & Morris, C. M. (2009). *News from the Library of Congress*. Retrieved from http://www.loc.gov/today/pr/2009/09-140.html and accessed on 15/1/2013 at 2.08

Arora, D., Quraishi, S., & Quraishi, Z. (2011). Application of cloud computing in university libraries. *Pioneer Journal.* Retrieved from http://pioneerjournal.in/conferences/tech-knowledge/12th-national-conference/3654-application-of-cloud-computing-in-university-libraries.html

3M. ™ *Cloud Library*. (n.d.). Retrieved from http://solutions.3m.com/wps/portal/3M/en_US/3MLibrarySystems/Home/Products/Cloud+Library/

3M. *Company*. 3M Cloud Library. Retrieved from https://itunes.apple.com/us/app/3m-cloud-library/id466446054?mt=8

Corrigan, K. (2012, June 2). Library moves to the cloud. *Gledale News-Press*. Retrieved from http://articles.glendalenewspress.com/2012-06-03/news/tn-gnp-library-moves-to-the-cloud-20120601_1_library-moves-library-systems-library-patrons

Farkas, M. G. (2007). *Social software in libraries: Building collaboration, communication, and community online*. Medford, NJ: Information Today.

GNU operating system. (2013). Retrieved from http://www.gnu.org/licenses/licenses.html

Goldner, M. R. (2010). Winds of change: Libraries and cloud computing. *BFP*, *34*, 270–275.

Hickey, A. R. (2010). *20 Coolest cloud platform vendors*. Retrieved from http://www.crn.com/slishows/channel-programs/222400507/20-coolest-cloud-platform-vendors.htm

Hinkle, M. (2010). *Eleven open source cloud computing projects to watch*. Retrieved from http://socializedsoftware.com/2010/01/20/eleven-open-source-cloud-computing-projects-to-watch/

Hosch, W. L. (2009). *Google Inc*. Retrieved from http://search.eb.com/eb/article-9471099

How server virtualization works. (2010, May 17). Retrieved from http://searchservervirtualization.techtarget.com/video/How-server-virtualization-works

Hybrid cloud Definition. (n.d.). Retrieved from searchcloudcomputing.techtarget.com/definition/hybrid-cloud

Introducing clouds. (n.d.). Retrieved from http://code.google.com/p/jclouds/

Kitchigami Regional Library System Launches eBooks Service. (2012). Retrieved from http://www.northlandpress.com/AREAebookservice11612.html

Knorr, E., & Gruman, G. (2008). *What cloud computing really means*. Retrieved from http://www.infoworld.com/d/cloud-computing/what-cloud-computing-really-means-031

LeFurgy. B. (2012). *Top 10 digital preservation developments of 2011*. Retrieved from http://blogs.loc.gov/digitalpreservation/2012/01/top-10-digital-preservation-developments-of-2011/ and accessed on 15/1/2013

Mulvihill, A. (2012). *Ask a librarian*. Retrieved from http://www.highbeam.com/doc/1G1-256071262.html

Nandkishor, G., Sheetal, S., Shinde, S., & Bhagyashree, D. (2012). Use of cloud computing in library and information science field. *International Journal of Digital Library Services*, *2*(3), 51–60.

Next generation of archieving. (n.d.). Retrieved from downloads.sys-con-com/download/white-paper_autonomy_nextgen

Ou, G. (2006). *Introduction to server virtualization*. Retrieved from http://www.techrepublic.com/article/introduction-to-server-virtualization/607494

Peters, C. (2010). *What is cloud computing and how will it affect libraries?* Retrieved from http://www.techsoupforlibraries.org/blog/what-is-cloud-computing-and-how-will-it-affect-libraries

Pillai, A. S., & Swasthimathi, L. S. (2012). Study on open source cloud computing platforms. *International Journal of Multidisciplinary Management Studies*, *2*(7), 31–39.

Private cloud (internal cloud or corporate cloud) definition. (n.d.). Retrieved from searchcloudcomputing.techtarget.com/definition/private-cloud

Roscoria, T. (2011, August 1). *4 university libraries move down the virtualization path*. Retrieved from http://www.centerdigitaled.com/infrastructure/4-University-Libraries-Move-Down-the-Virtualization-Path.html

Sanchati, R., & Kulkarni, G. (2011) Cloud computing in digital and university libraries. *Global Journal of Computer Science and Technology*, *11*(12).

Scale, E. M. S. (2010). Assessing the impact of cloud computing and Web collaboration on the work of distance library services. *Journal of Library Administration*, *50*, 933–950. doi:10.1080/01930826.2010.488995.

Virtualization of the desktops. (n.d.). Retrieved from http://www.intelligroup.com/ppt/WhitepaperDesktopVirtualization.pdf

Wikipedia. (n.d.). *Information Common*. Retrieved from http://en.wikipedia.org/wiki/Information_Commons

Chapter 10
The University Library Electronic Identities Authentication System (UL-EIDA):
Enhanced by Segmented Virtual Machines and VLANs for Deployment in the Sub-Saharan Region

Jameson Mbale
Centre of Excellence in Telecommunications, University of Namibia, Namibia

ABSTRACT

World-wide electronic university libraries, with wide accessibility, are considered to be essential units in both academic and nonacademic information utilization. Within this context, the developed world wasted no time improving and expanding their libraries by applying the technology leverage offered by cloud computing. As institutions from developed countries expanded the use of cloud technology for library applications, it became clear that this technology was highly vulnerable to security threats. Nevertheless, this did not retard advanced nations from proceeding. Undaunted, they forged ahead and now are busy building appropriate cloud computing security infrastructures. Despite progress in this area, very little has been done to expand the university libraries in the sub-Saharan region using cloud computing technologies. Even less has been done in these developing countries to plan and develop the building of library computing security infrastructures. It was in view of this deficit that the University of Namibia's (UNAM) University Library electronic Identities Authentication (UL-eIDA) system was conceived to build a cloud computing security framework model suitable for the sub-Saharan region.

INTRODUCTION

The University Library electronic Identities Authentication (UL-eIDA) system was initiated as a cloud computing security framework model suitable for use in the sub-Saharan region. The system was built upon three operational layers: traditional, interface, and the cloud environment. In this work the terms "layers" and "environment" will be used interchangeably. These layers were then connected to the Cloud Provider which was subcontracted to acquire, provide and service the hardware and software.

DOI: 10.4018/978-1-4666-4631-5.ch010

The traditional layer consisted of: the University Library, UL-eIDA smart card authentication infrastructure, hardware firewall, server, and switch. The interface layer was composed of the VM/VLAN-Student, VM/VLAN-Staff, VM/VLAN-Community and generic firewalls. The cloud environment had the dynamic security zone (DSZ), and was divided into segmented VM/VLAN-Student, VM/VLAN-Staff, and VM/VLAN-Community networks.

The system was divided into three operational parts to support the conformity of data as it was processed in different environments. For instance, raw data could be processed in the traditional layer but not in cloud environment hence reformatting would be necessary. The data and equipment were virtualized to allow dynamic scaling of library applications. Boss, Malladi, Quan, Legregni, and Hall (2007) stated that by means of virtualization, the cloud is a pool of virtualized computer resources which allowed the dynamic scaling of applications abetted by the provisioning and de-provisioning of resources. In addition, the system was configured into three VLANs: VLAN-Student, VLAN-Staff, VLAN-Community networks. The VLANs provided a form of virtual isolation which constrained a group of users to limit their focus and efforts only to their networks. This provided security in the sense that it inhibited malicious intruders from crossing into other networks and domains to purposely destroy data.

The system uses the UL-eIDA, a smart card authentication infrastructure for strong authentication. With this technology, the user was authenticated once and got access to different networks without need for re-authentication. This is also known as "single sign on" technology, or merely SSO.

To further ensure that security was strong, the following measures were taken: first, the hardware firewall was installed and was used to filter data to-and-from the University library and interface layer. Second, a series of generic firewalls that filtered data to-and-from traditional and cloud environments. Third was the dynamic trust zone (DTZ) which was an assortment of security tools such as robust anti-virus software that screened and discarded all possible malicious malware.

The system employed the DFUL-eIDA Encryption infrastructure which was based upon the Delffi-Hellman algorithm (Forouzan, 2007). To conceal important information from intruders and hackers the DFUL-eIDA Encryption method applied mathematical principles where a symmetric key is used to both encrypt and decrypt messages. It was designed to work over an insecure public network. In a nutshell, a symmetric key might exist on the sender's system. Then certain information is then shared between the sender and receiver which allow the recipient to generate the same symmetric key allowing secure communications to proceed without having to ever exchange the symmetric or private key over the vulnerable network. This infrastructure is somewhat different than other more modern public key infrastructures which may use asymmetric keys whereby a private key is used to solely decrypt messages and a related public is only used to encrypt messages. The public key is transmitted or distributed between senders and receivers but the private key, which is used to decrypt messages and thus obtain information, is never exchanged between participants. In either method, intruders and hackers are completely deprived of private key access, which would be crucial for any breach of security.

The above security measures will be discussed in detail in later sections. However, the overview of security measures above should highlight how dynamic and robust the system is.

Statement of the Problem

Like any other universities world wide, libraries are key elements in providing both academic and non-academic information to a range of subscribers. Progressive nations have more recently taken steps to improve and expand their libraries by adopting the technologies of cloud computing. This was supported by Yuvaraj and Singh (2012) who pointed out that historically, libraries have been burdened by huge capital investments on IT infrastructure for various online as well as subscription based services. They further emphasized that with these large ICT investments, libraries were motivated to use subscription based cloud IT infrastructure as soon as it became available. As cloud computing became accessible, these institutions soon discovered that while ICT costs were reduced, this technology was highly vulnerable to security threats. As Kuyoro, Ibikunle, and Awodele (2011) explained, security issues in cloud computing had played a major role in slowing down its acceptance. In fact, security was ranked first as the primary challenge of cloud computing. Despite this issue, university libraries in the first-world forged ahead and are in the process of building university library cloud computing infrastructures.

Until recently, very little effort had been expended on expanding electronic university libraries in the less developed African regions, especially with regard to the utilization of cloud computing. So it made little sense to even consider the building of library security infrastructures. Kuyoro, Ibikunle, and Awodele (2011) even presented statistical evidence by stating that with regard to the development of cloud computing in Africa, the main concern for their stakeholders was the availability of high-speed access which registered 55% among survey respondents, followed by the issue of systems security which was estimated at a much lower 27%. Despite these concerns, UNAM's University Library electronic Identities Authentication (UL-eIDA) system was predicated upon a cloud computing security framework model. If it were successful, such a project might encourage many other developing African countries to follow this lead, and improve and develop their university libraries based upon the cloud computing business model.

Objectives of UL-eIDA

The UL-eIDA was developed in-line with the following objectives:

- Automate all the applications of the UL-eIDA system.
- Develop a dynamic and robust University library cloud computing security system for the sub-Saharan region.
- Empower the user for self service application as they use the cloud computing technology.
- Intensify and automate security mechanisms in all stages of the system.
- Use the UL-eIDA smart card infrastructure to authenticate users through-out all networks, and domains.
- Install firewalls in each operational environment to filter out unsafe data.
- Segment the network in order to manage security by constraining users to one virtual network at a time.
- Use the DFUL-eIDA key infrastructure to encrypt and decrypt the data in the UL-eIDA system.
- Reduce the running costs by out sourcing the IT/ICT University library services to the Cloud Providers.
- Virtualize the UL-eIDA data and equipment.
- Configure the servers and computers into VLANS.
- Employ temporary, symmetric session keys based upon the Diffie-Hellman cryptologic algorithm.
- Use the security tools in the dynamic security zone (DSZ) to screen all possible malicious malware.

RELATED WORK

As advanced nations moved aggressively into the cloud computing era, undeveloped nations in Africa usually lagged behind (International Telecommunication Union, 2012). Because of this, poorer countries found themselves in a situation where they were always trying to catch up and as a result, encountered incompatibility issues. But in this case, UNAM had no other choice but to join the advanced nations in addressing cloud security concerns. From a survey carried by Ayoub (2011) it was determined that more than 70% of professionals reported the need for new skills to properly secure cloud-based applications. Based upon their surprising findings they analyzed that on average, survey respondents in developing countries only had two or fewer years less of experience than their developed counterparts. They further stated that, on this basis developing countries were not that far behind and could be a target for security expansion in the future.

Ayoub (2011) also revealed that the role of the information security professional has been steadily changing during the past decade. They are now responsible for the security of many facets of an organization, including regulatory audit compliance, human resource awareness and training, legal compliance, data security, access control, and others. They categorically mentioned that as a result of the increased importance of such a position, information security professionals weathered the economic recession better than most other professionals in other industries.

Ayoub (2011) further emphasized that cloud computing was one of the most highly discussed topics in computing today. They discovered that organizations saw cloud computing as an enabler for more powerful, flexible and scalable computing. However, they highlighted numerous security concerns arising from the model of cloud computing, with no clear solution to issues such as audit compliance, data security, and access once the data left the host organization. They also indicated that information security professionals are a key part of the migration to the cloud but harbor serious concerns about cloud computing. They finally gave the following statistical list of security concerns of cloud computing in ranked order: first was the exposure of confidential or sensitive information with concern voiced by 85% of the respondents; second was sensitive data loss or leakage with 85%; third weak system or application access controls had 68%; fourth susceptibility to cyber attacks that made 67%; fifth was disruptions in the continuous operation of the data center (i.e., a disruption in the continuity of operations) which was 65%; sixth was inability to support compliance audits that was 55% and seventh was the inability to support forensic investigations which clocked in at 47%.

FORTINET (2011) is arguably, the leader of the worldwide unified threat management market and has a variety of products designed to extend traditional network security protection into the cloud. They stated that the only way to mitigate fears about moving to the cloud was to ensure that protection was in place at all points along the path of data, whether it be entering or exiting the corporate network, entering or exiting the cloud, and within the cloud itself. They discussed their Virtual Domains (VDOMs) as a method of dividing a FortiGate physical or virtual appliance into two or more virtual units that functioned independently. They further explained the VDOMs that could provide separate network security policies and completely separate configurations for routing and VPN services for each connected network or organization. They emphasized that such a native ability to split a single FortiGate device into multiple secure entities provided the enhanced levels of security and data segregation needed to build any cloud architecture.

They summarized the key advantages of FortiGate VDOMs in the following categories:

First was easier administration. The VDOMs provided separate security domains that allowed separate zones, user authentication, firewall policies, routing, and VPN configurations. VDOMs also provided an additional level of security because regular administrator accounts were specific to one VDOM and an administrator restricted to one VDOM could not modify information on other VDOMs. Any configuration changes and potential errors would apply only to that VDOM and limit any potential down time. Using that concept, you could further split settings so that the management domain was only accessible by a single administrator and did not share any settings with the other VDOMs.

Second was maintaining continuous path of security. When a packet entered a VDOM, it was confined to that specific VDOM and was subject to any firewall policies for connections between that VDOM and any other interface. When hosting separate clients or entities on single cloud architecture, the ability to guarantee that no data can pass from one connection to another was a critical requirement.

Third was savings in physical space and power. The FortiGate VDOM technology allowed the administrator to increase the number of protected domains without having to increase the amount of rack space and power consumed. This meant that, increasing VDOMs involved no additional hardware, no additional cabling, and very few changes to existing networking configurations. The administrator's ability to create virtual domains was limited only by the size of the VDOM license the client purchased and the physical resources of the client's FortiGate device.

FORTINET (2011) went on to identify new challenges around security once data was in the cloud. They identified the need to maintain control over data as it flowed from virtual machine to virtual machine. They mentioned that traditional hardware-based appliances had no control over the data once in the cloud, rather virtual security appliances were needed to inspect and protect the data in the virtualized environment. They emphasized that data entering and leaving the cloud should be subject to the same level of scrutiny as any other data entering or leaving the network.

FORTINET (2011) addressed additional challenges associated with securing data in the cloud. One major challenge was that the security architecture must also secure the multi-tenant nature of the traffic. It means the security architecture must have ability to enforce separate policies on traffic, depending on origin or destination. This requires that the security technologies in place must also have the ability to keep traffic entirely separate in order to avoid any risk of unauthorized access.

In VMWare (2010) the investigators explained that the first responsibility of the cloud provider was to provide a level of isolation between all of the different networks that were a part of the virtualization infrastructure. They further emphasized that the primary theme of the service provider's responsibility was offering a secured and isolated environment for each customer. They went on to say that each customer should only be able to access his or her own environment and no other customer's environment in any way. They argued that, no customer should have any visibility into the structure, systems, data or any other attributes of another customer's environment. They also stressed that companies should isolate customer data networks from each other and from any management networks. They explained that this could be accomplished in both a secured and scalable way using 802.1Q VLANs with firewalling established between the networks to ensure that no traffic was routed between networks.

In addition to the above discussion, VMWare (2010) identified that conventional infrastructure security controls designed for dedicated hardware do not always map well to the cloud environment. They explained that cloud architectures must have well-defined security policies and procedures in place. They emphasized that realizing full interoperability with existing dedicated security controls was unlikely and that there had to be some degree of compatibility between the newer security protections specifically designed for cloud environments and traditional security controls. They expanded the above discussion by stating that traditional environments segment physical servers with VLANs and that cloud environments should take the same approach and segment virtual machines by VLANs through Port Group configurations. They observed that since these were physical servers, traffic flows were visible to traditional network-based security protection devices, such as network-based intrusion prevention systems (IPSs). They said the concern in cloud environments was that IPS systems provided limited visibility to intervirtual machine traffic flows. They further illustrated that those were the flows between virtual machines on the same VLAN. Hence, by default, those traffic flows were not visible to traditional network-based security protection devices located in the datacenter network. They advised that administrators must make specific architectural and configurational decisions either to make the virtualization solution work with current security tools or to integrate security appliances into the virtualization architecture.

In FierceCIO (2009) the authors pointed out that cloud applications were inherently more vulnerable, though data in the cloud can be protected by implementing robust security mechanisms. They confirmed that the most successful developers had adopted a sort of "enlightened paranoia," building security into their products at the initial design stage. They assured that, by doing this, one would be able to deliver all of the advantages of cloud computing to customers with none of the headaches.

Peter (2009) pointed out that the cloud required the ability to apply global policies and tools that could migrate with, and control access to, the applications and data as they move from data center to cloud and as they travel to other points in the cloud. He indicated that the biggest areas of concern for both cloud vendors and customers alike were strong authentication, authorization, and encryption of data to and from the cloud. He also emphasized that users and administrators alike needed to be authenticated with strong or two-factor authentication to ensure that only authorized personnel were able to access data. In addition, the data itself needed to be segmented to ensure there was no leakage to other users or systems. He reported that most experts concurred that AAA services along with secure, encrypted tunnels to manage the user's cloud infrastructure should be at the top of the basic cloud services offered by vendors. He indicated that, since data could be housed at a distant location where you have less physical control, logical control become paramount, and enforcing strict access to raw data and protecting data in transit such as uploading new data, also become critical to the business as lost, leaked, or tampered data could have devastating consequences.

In Symantec (2011), those researchers advised that cloud applications required a change of mindset. They narrated that, to realize the benefits of a virtualized environment, it was necessary to accept that perimeters become logical rather than physical, dynamic rather than fixed. They reported that, whereas previously rights could be assigned to a physical machine and its location, the policies and privileges designated to a virtual machine must change when its workload does. They further cautioned that, a user's access to information and applications shouldn't just depend on who they were, but also where they were, what device they were using, and how they were using the information. They further stressed a rethink of policies because cloud computing required new tools and operating practices. They alleged that certification was a proven technique for establishing identity and trust and its role would become increasingly important as services move to the cloud. They also reported that certificates such as those provided by

VeriSign® Authentication Services, now part of Symantec, helped give companies and consumers the confidence to engage in communications and commerce online.

Zwattendorfer and Tauber (2012) and Clereq (2002) discussed the securing of cloud services using the single sign-on (SSO) model together with the mechanism of electronic identities (eIDs) and Secure Identity Across Borders Linked (STORK) framework. They explained SSO as a model that has an ability to authenticate just once in a distributed environment and gain access to several protected services. Thus, SSO established the capability to authenticate only once in a distributed network and to access several protected services and resources without reauthentication as opposed to frequent authentication processes that may annoy users and decrease usability. They emphasized that in case of username/password authentications, users just had to enter their credentials once at a service provider and they get automatically and seamlessly authenticated at other service providers. They supported their work by stating that security could be increased because authentication takes place at one single authentication authority only, which should be particularly protected. They maintained their argument that the main advantage of SSO was increased user comfort because a number of burdensome authentication processes could be omitted while still gaining access to several different protected services at the same time. Thus by using SSO, users normally just need to remember one strong password and the risk of reuse or of writing it down becomes lower.

Zwattendorfer and Tauber (2012), European Commission – MODINIS (2006) and European Commission – IDABC (2009) discussed the eIDs (eLECTRONIC IDENTITY AUTHENTICATION) as one mechanism which allowed for unique qualified identification and strong authentication. They stressed that the eID's identification and authentication mechanism fulfilled the higher security requirements. They further illustrated that eID solutions usually were user-centric and supported unique identification and strong authentication. They narrated that the eIDs have been rolled-out in many European Union Member States in recent years.

Alcalde-Morano et al. (2011), Leitold and Zwatterndorfer (2010) and Zwattendorfer and Tauber (2012) reported that the STORK framework, which had been designed and developed within the EU large scale pilot project STORK, constituted a secure and reliable eID interoperability framework supporting eID federation of various national eID solutions. They said the STORK project involved 18 European Union Member States. They narrated the STORK had started in 2008 and was finished by the end of 2011. They assured that by the help of this framework, citizens were able to securely authenticate at online services located in foreign European countries by actually using their own national eID, which had been issued by the citizens' home country. They cited an example that via the STORK framework Austrian citizens were able to authenticate at Spanish Governmental online services by using their Austrian eID.

UNAM's UNIVERSITY LIBRARY ELECTRONIC IDENTITY AUTHENTICATION (UL-eIDA) ARCHITECTURE

The University Library Electronic Identities Authentication (UL-eLDA) architecture is demonstrated in Figure 1. The architecture was divided into three (3) parts, and in this work was referred to as environments. These environments were the traditional, interface and cloud. The traditional environment was composed of the following components: library, University Library-electronic Identities Authentication (UL-eIDA) card, hardware firewall, server and switch. The interface environment had, the segmented virtual machines and generic firewalls. The cloud was composed of the different segmented clouds which included

Figure 1. The Segmented Library Cloud Computing System

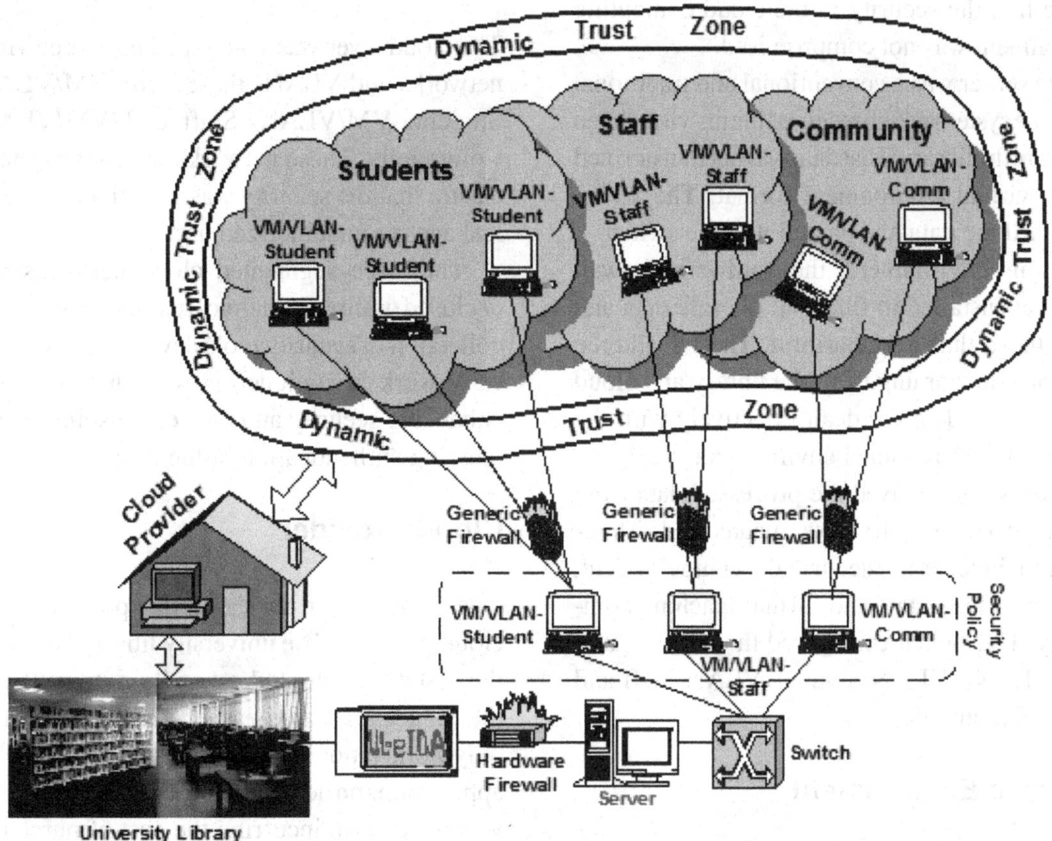

the student, staff and community. The other cloud components were segmented virtual machines and the dynamic trust zone. Outside these three environments, was an additional external component of the architecture called the cloud provider?

The Traditional Environment Components

The library is the main user of the UL-eIDA system. Its regular users were the students who comprised the great majority of subscribers, which in this case amounted to about 16,000 of them. These students accessed information on electronic periodicals, research articles, notes, etc. The next category of users was the community group who were library members from outside the University. The third faction was the members of staff. They also used the library to retrieve electronic periodicals, research articles, teaching materials, journals and conference resources. Having established the cloud system, the library has needed only workstation terminals to retrieve the work on demand. The library no longer maintains the hardware and software as these services were supplied by the cloud providers.

The University Library-electronic Identities Authentication (UL-eIDA) smart card was a core business component in this work. It is an electronic identity card which was programmed to authenticate only once in a distributed network and be able to access several protected services and resources from a segmented cloud computing environment without reauthentication. The UL-eIDA was programmed with a very strong authentication to ensure that the security in the cloud computing environment was not compromised.

The server was a conventional and traditional hardware system which received the un-virtualized data from the library. That data was not transformed to any virtual environment format. The server processed the data and passed it to the switch.

In this environment, the hardware firewall (HF) was installed to filter out the safe data and block those that were harmful. The HF filtered both the data coming from the library and cloud environment. The HF dealt effectively with the data from the traditional environment.

The switch received the processed data from the server. The system was segmented and virtualized into three parts: the virtual machine student, virtual machine staff and virtual machine community. The switch configured the network into three VLANs: VLAN-Student, VLAN-Staff and VLAN-Community.

Interface Environment

As discussed in the previous section, the system was virtualized and VLANs configured, to form VM/VLAN-Student, VM/VLAN-Staff and VM/VLAN-Community. These three components had the capacity to define security policies and procedures. In that way, the interface environment would manage to manipulate the virtualized data reformatting it and then passing it on to the cloud for further processing,

The generic firewalls filter the data that comes from either the traditional or the cloud environment. When the firewalls identify data which is benign, they pass it to the cloud component. If they identified data which was unsafe, they blocked it. Only data which was free from malicious threats reached the cloud passing through the dynamic trust zone for further screening and eradication of malware.

Cloud Environment/Layer

The cloud layer was segmented into three virtual networks and VLANs these were: VM/VLANs-Student, VM/VLANs-Staff and VM/VLANs-Community. These networks were segmented to ensure that the security was very tight to prevent leakages to unauthorized users.

The three segmented cloud networks were enclosed within a dynamic trust zone which was a collection of security tools developed to dynamically work in conjunction with the encryption, enhancing security and further consolidating the ongoing authentication of the data.

Cloud Provider

One of the major players in this project was the cloud provider. The university library contracted the cloud provider to host and run its systems in the cloud. As stated earlier, the library needed only workstations for the users to access the cloud applications on demand. Consequently, the library was freed from incurring the cost of purchasing and servicing the critical hardware and software. The most crucial technology was owned and hosted by the cloud provider. Therefore, it was a sole responsibility of that cloud provider to acquire, maintain and service all the equipment such as the servers, switches, routers and firewalls. In addition and in accordance with the user's requirements, the cloud provider was additionally contracted to develop and run application programs in the cloud. The cloud provider was also responsible for securing the whole system from any security threats. They had to procure all kinds of firewalls, antivirus software and pay for the licensing of these constituents. They frequently cleansed the systems with powerful anti-virus software to protect them from malware. They also protected the infrastructure from possibility of physical sabotage and other hazardous threats.

ENCRYPTION IN THE UL-eIDA

From the above discussed security measures employed, also an additional effective tool, encryption was used to strongly protect the data as it passed through different levels of UL-eIDA. As an EDUCAUSE Report (2010) stated that encrypting data in transit was important, as it had to satisfy the service provider's security procedures. This report further emphasized that cloud computing typically used server virtualization, and if the virtualization wasn't secure, data from one segment of a server could leak into another area. Hence, it was equally important to safeguard the virtualized servers used in the UL-eIDA system. To meet this requirement this work employed the encryption technology of Diffie-Hellman, which in this research was referred to as Diffie-Hellman-UL-eIDA (DFUL-eIDA). Forouzan (2007) discussed the Diffie-Hellman as an encryption tool which was designed for symmetric key sharing over an insecure communications channel, where two parties created a once-off symmetric session key to exchange data without having to worry about any future reuse of the key. It was further stressed that the sender and recipient neither have to meet to agree on the key nor for that matter to even know each other. In view of that, the UL-eIDA opted for the Diffie-Hellman, since such encryption technology better suited the system which has several levels of operation where remembering the key could be cumbersome. In that case the users on both sides of the communications channel had only to calculate the same symmetric key (K) for the session using the detailed Equation 1 and simplified Equation 2.

$$K = (c^x \bmod s)^y \bmod s = (c^y \bmod s)^x \bmod s = c^{xy} \bmod s \quad (1)$$

$$K = c^{xy} \bmod s \quad (2)$$

The UL eIDA used the DFUL eIDA, where the sender (S) and recipient (C) chose the two numbers s and c. While (K) stands for the calculated key. The advantage of this security tool was that these two numbers did not need be private as is the case with other methods. These chosen numbers, s represented the large prime number following the order of three hundred (300) decimal digits using one thousand and twenty four (1024) bits. The other digit c stood for the random number. This encryption method used many mathematical equations to derive the required symmetric keys. Some of the principal equations are given below:

$$R_1 = c^x \bmod p \quad (3)$$

$$R_2 = c^y \bmod p \quad (4)$$

$$K = (R_2)^x \bmod p \quad (5)$$

$$K = (R_1)^y \bmod p \quad (6)$$

Figure 2 illustrates the stages involving the DFUL-eIDA Encryption Mechanism as:

- **First Stage:** The sender chose a large random number x and calculated Equation 3.
- **Second Stage:** The recipient chose another large number y and calculated Equation 4.
- **Third Stage:** The sender sent R_1 to the receiver.
- **Fourth Stage:** The receiver sent R_2 to the sender.
- **Fifth Stage:** The sender calculated Equation 5.
- **Sixth Stage:** The receiver also calculated Equation 6.

From the third, it was realized that the sender did not send the value of x, but sent only R_1. Equally, in fourth stage the receiver sent R_2 to

Figure 2. The DFUL-eIDA Encryption Mechanism

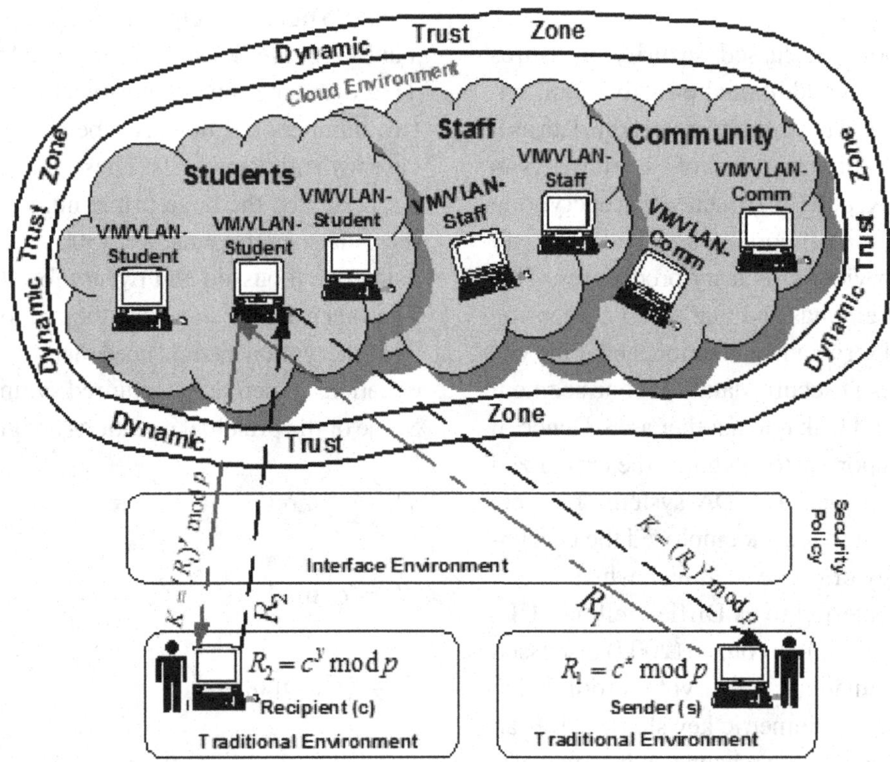

the sender. Also, the receiver in that did not send the value of y, but only sent R_2.

In view of the above, the sender calculated equation 7 and the receiver computed equation 8. In comparison with many encryption algorithms where the sender communicated the encryption key to the receiver, that risked the intruders to intercept the key, and thereafter maliciously accessed the data. However, in this work it was different, as both the sender and receiver did not know the key of the other. In fact, both the sender and receiver calculated and derived the same value without each one knowing the values of the other. In that way, it did not allow the intruders to intercept the data.

$$K = (R_1)^y \bmod p = (c^x \bmod p)^y \bmod p = c^{xy} \bmod p. \quad (7)$$

$$K = (R_2)^x \bmod p = (c^y \bmod p)^x \bmod p = c^{xy} \bmod p. \quad (8)$$

IMPLEMENTATION OF UNIVERSITY LIBRARY eLECTRONIC IDENTITY AUTHENTICATION (UL-eIDA)

The whole UL-eIDA architecture and its functional components were discussed in the previous section. The library was installed with workstations that were connected to the system administrator (SA) computers. These facilities only requested from the cloud system the application on demand at that particular moment. The users from the library ran the system to process the application requested. When the workstation was logged on, the user inserted the UL-eIDA card for authentication and sought authorization throughout. The UL-eIDA card was developed to run strong authentication, which was programmed to run in segmented cloud networks without re-authentication and compromising security. Then the authenticated data was passed through the tradition firewall to filter the data entering and exiting the traditional and cloud environment.

Then the safe data was then passed to the server where it was traditionally processed for the destined cloud environment. The traditionally processed data was forwarded to the switch. The switch virtualized and configured the VLANs into VLANs-Student, VLANs-Staff and VLANs-Community. These components transformed the traditional data to that of the cloud environment. Such a transformation massaged the data to fit the cloud environment. In addition, these components dealt with the security policies. These policies determined the suitable equipment, software, data, encryption and various technologies to be employed.

The policies also helped the configured VLANs to determine which segmented cloud environment the data was to be processed. Then this information was forwarded to the cloud environment through the generic firewalls, where data to-and-from traditional and cloud environment was filtered out and permitted the safe data to pass while blocking the unsafe information. After the data was filtered in the generic firewalls, it was forwarded to the cloud network. As the data entered the cloud network, it had passed through a host of security checks, within the Dynamic Trust Zone (DTZ). In the DTZ, the data was subjected to screening for all kinds of malware such as viruses, worms, logic bombs, Trojan horses, spyware, dishonest adware, most root-kits and other malicious programs. If any of the malware was detected by the DTZ, it was completely discarded or deleted. The DTZ was built in a style that it would only release data that was thoroughly cleansed. This purified data was then dispatched to their respective cloud networks: VM/VLAN-Student, VM/VLAN-Staff and VM/VLAN-Community for processing. In these networks, the data was processed and readied for application use. Also these three segmented cloud networks added additional security as it logically separated and isolated the VLANs thus making it extremely difficult for any intruder to maliciously and deliberately cross over into other networks.

DISCUSSION

The UL-eIDA was a highly dynamic and robust application and security designed cloud computing system. The system was designed with five levels of security checks and provided a thorough security screening. These five security levels were: the electronic identities (smartcards), hardware firewalls, generic firewalls, Dynamic Trust Zone, and encryption. The system was designed and divided into three operational layers and these were: traditional, interface, and cloud environments. In each of these clouds, it was assured that very close security checks were performed before the data was forwarded to the next component or environment. Therefore, the screening of the data before it left each environment ensured that no security was compromised.

It is worth pointing out that among the security components, the University Library Electronic Identities was, perhaps, the most critical module. The University Library Electronic Identities were designed to provide a very strong authentication that was capable of providing single sign on access throughout the entire system eliminating any re-authentication different cloud networks. If the user had to encounter multiple levels of authentication challenges, the whole process might possibly create boredom and frustration, with the whole system, and this could adversely impact the volume of usage.

Because of the security measures taken with the UL-eIDA system, the university library was able to reduce its security expenditures. Before UL-eIDA, the university library used to spend 55%

of the total allocated IT/ICT budget on combating security threats, by paying huge sums of money on securing and maintaining anti-virus licenses, firewalls, and resources, including CCTV cameras for spotting intruders on the premises.

From the allotted budget, shown in Figure 2, 40% of the budget was spent on acquiring and maintaining antivirus software, especially for license, in that particular academic year. About 10% of the cost was spent to acquire and service either the firewalls equipment or software. There was also a threat of unauthorized staff or intruders who might physically tamper with the equipment. At that time, the library bought CCTV cameras and positioned them on walls and locations around the building. The acquisition, installation, and maintenance of CCTV cameras cost 5% of the total allocated budget. From the total allocated budget only 45% was left for operation, physical maintenance and procurement of the rest of the hardware and software.

Since employing the UL-eIDA, the operational security costs incurred by the University Library plummeted as indicated in Figure 3. The total cost for the UL-eIDA was only 25%. The cost spent for anti-virus as compared to that of Old system, was 18%. For purchasing and servicing firewalls equipment and software cost 5% of the budget, whereas the internal and external intruders' expense was only 2%.

In comparison with the acquisition and running of the rest of the equipment and software during old system, the library was responsible for 100% of the costs. It had to purchase, maintain and service the entire IT/ICT infrastructure. This also compelled the library to employ a large IT/ICT workforce. Hence, it encountered significant costs for staff remuneration. Ever since the UL-EIDA system was implemented, the equipment and software running costs plunged significantly by as much as 68% as shown in Figure 3 and which was now borne by the cloud provider. Now the

Figure 3. Cost of Security Maintenance

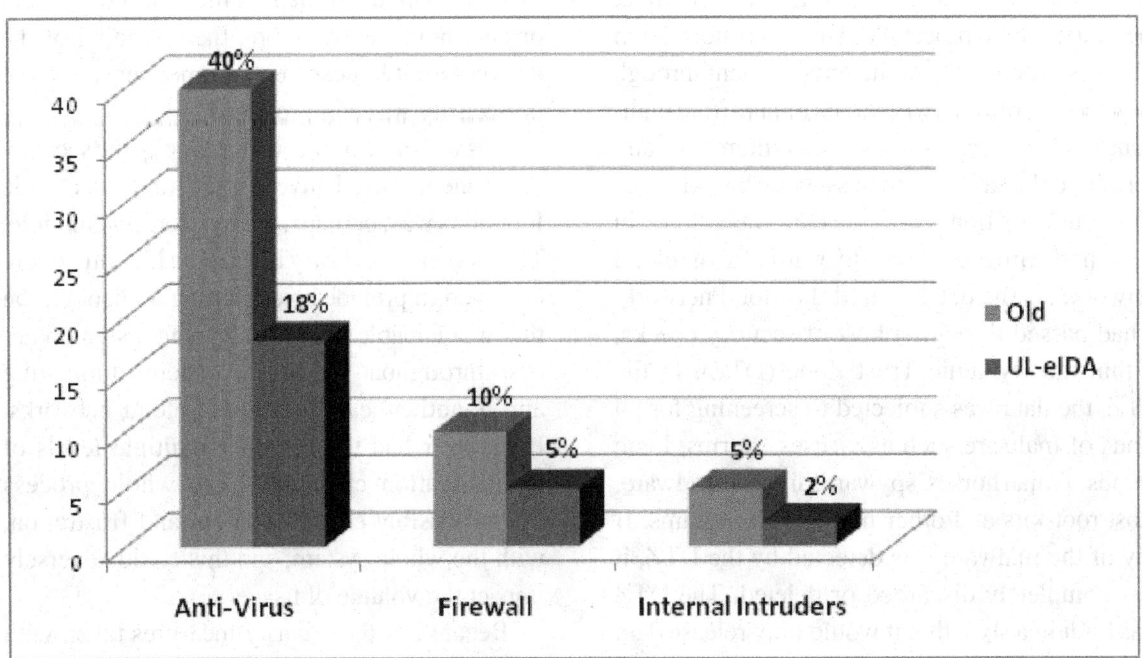

University Library's share was reduced to only 32% of the total capital budget for that particular academic year.

From Figure 4, the cloud provider was responsible for taking care of the majority of the acquisition and servicing of both IT/ICT equipment and software. They paid almost two thirds (2/3) of capital costs compared to the client who only paid one third (1/3) of the total budget. That meant the cloud provider purchased all major equipment and software required. Moreover, critical maintenance and services became their responsibility. Such a positive scenario unburdened the University Library from spending on large capital items such as equipment, software, and human resources. Within this arrangement, the users were only concerned with the services or applications they required at that particular moment and only paid for the services they processed on demand.

The technology of using virtual machines and configuring the VLANs together with segmenting the cloud networks into VM/VLAN-Student, VM/VLAN-Staff and VM/VLAN-Community, tremendously improved the security and performance of the entire system. The Network Administrator from the Cloud Provider configured the system into VLANs to separate the users into working groups of VM/VLAN-Student, VM/VLAN-Staff and VM/VLAN-Community in order to manage security and improve performance discussed above. That approach was also supported by Varadarajan (1997) who stated that VLANs allowed a network manager to logically segment a LAN into different broadcast domains. He further emphasized that VLAN's offered a number of advantages over physical networks such as: performance, formation of virtual workgroups, simplified administration, reduced cost and security. From his explanation, it justified the objectives of designing and implementing the UL-eIDA system, since it provided the technologies that enhanced security, performance and reduced operational costs.

The UL-eIDA used the DFUL-eIDA Encryption methods that applied mathematical principles where the key was never transmitted between the sender the receiver and where the same key was computed independently on both sides of the channel. The calculations involve modular arithmetic and the laws of algebra but which were based upon pieces of exchanged information that were not in themselves - sensitive. Because the DFUL-eIDA never transmits the session key this almost completely frustrates any intruder attempt to gain access to the secret number where they could open the data. In this method, the sender randomly chose a large prime number and calculated Equation 5. Similarly, the receiver chose the random number to calculate Equation 6. From these two calculations, the two were able to derive

Figure 4. Running Costs on IT/ICT Equipment, Software and Personnel

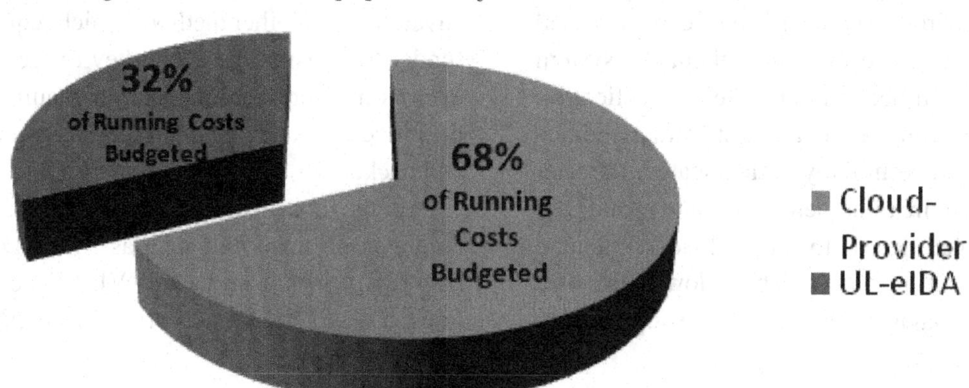

the same symmetric key without either of them knowing the value of x and y that they used in their computations respectively. Once the receiver finished computing the Equation 6, it was able to decrypt the data. No one else could gain access to the calculated value, thus thwarting any attempt at eavesdropping.

CONCLUSION

The UL-eIDA was intended to provide security in the cloud computing system. The UL-eIDA is a three layered system composed of: traditional, interface, and cloud environments. The entire system was connected to the cloud provider, who was contracted to run and maintain the hardware and software.

The data and equipment were virtualized. It is critical that the data in the UL-eIDA system was also virtualized so that it could be used in the cloud computing environment. As discussed in the earlier sections, the network was also configured and segmented into three networks as a way of separating the users into their independent operational environment in order to enhance security. This separation constrained any malicious users who might want to intrude into other networks to cause damage.

The UL-eIDA data and system security mechanism was robust, as the security measures were carefully built in from the design phase right up to the cloud computing environment. In the traditional environment, a UL-eIDA card was used to authenticate the user throughout the system without re-authentication. The authentication was made strong to safeguard it from malicious intruders. Once initially authenticated, the user does not require re-authentication and would gain unchallenged access to other cloud segmented networks and resources. This allowed the user to fluently navigate the networks as opposed to encountering several authentications that could irritate the user and diminish the amount of usage.

Before the data could be forwarded to the next operational environment, it had to be filtered by the firewalls. In the traditional environment, a hardware firewall was installed to filter out raw data between the Library and layers. The hardware firewall blocked unsafe data and passed safe data. What's more between the interface and cloud environment there were generic firewalls installed to filter data between these layers. Thus, the data from cloud or infrastructure environment was cleansed to prohibit possible security threats from complicating the next levels of operation.

The cloud was tightly surrounded by an arsenal of assorted security tools that included different anti-virus software. In this domain, data was subjected to a comprehensive scrubbing of all kinds of malware. All anti-virus products in this realm are subjected to constant updates to ensure that they keep up with new malware threats.

In this work, the DFUL-eIDA encryption mechanism was used. The sender encrypted the data after calculating symmetric key using the Equation 4 to come up with a session value for encryption. The receiver equally computed the same symmetric key using the Equation 5 to derive the session value which would enable the user to decrypt the data sent by the sender. One critical factor about this method is that both users need not know the value each one used and this makes it extremely difficult for intruders in the middle to intercept the encrypted files. This was a great advantage over other methods which required the sender to transmit the secret key to the receiver over an insecure communication channel and in the process risk having it intercepted by intruders and hackers.

All the above discussed security measures employed in this work such as: UL-eIDA card, firewalls, virtualization and VLAN configurations, DFUL-eIDA encryption mechanism and dynamic trust zone all worked in synergy to make the system forceful enough to combat security threats at any level. Thus the system left no stone unturned as security measures were in place at every level of data operation.

Besides the three operation environmental levels, the University Library subcontracted the Cloud Provider to run the system. The Cloud Provider purchased, installed, maintained and serviced all the critical hardware and software. All the running costs of the system were borne by them. It was their sole responsibility to run the system, especially ensuring that the data for the user was well secured, whether at traditional, interface or cloud environment levels. In view of that, it has relieved the University Library from incurring huge costs on purchasing, maintaining and servicing hardware and software. In conclusion, the transition to a cloud environment for the ULe-IDA appears to be a wise choice and one that will hopefully serve as a model for other developing African nations.

REFERENCES

Alcalde-Morano, J., Hernández-Ardieta, J. L., Johnston, A., Martinez, D., Zwattendorfer, B., & Stern, M. (2011). *Interface Specification*. Retrieved from https://www.eid-stork.eu/

Ayoub, R. (2011). The 2011 (ISC)2 global information security workforce study. Retrieved from https://www.isc2.org/uploadedFiles/Industry_Resources/FS_WP_ISC%20Study_020811_MLW_Web.pdf

Boss, G., Malladi, P., Quan, S., Legregni, L., & Hall, H. (2007). *Cloud computing. (Tech. Rep.)*. Armonk, NY: IBM.

Clercq, J. D. (2002). Single sing on architectures in infrastructure security. In G. Davida (Ed.), *Proceedings of InfraSec 2002* (pp. 40–58).

European Commission – IDABC. (2009). *eID Interoperability for PEGS: Update of Country Profiles*. Retrieved from http://ec.europa.eu/idabc/servlets/Doc2ba1.pdf?id=32521

European Commission – MODINIS. (2006). *The Status of Identity Management in European eGovernment initiatives*. Retrieved from http://ec.europa.eu/information_society/activities/ict_psp/documents/identity_management_eu_02_07.pdf

Fierce, C. I. O. (2009). Securing the cloud: Designing security for a new age. Retrieved from http://i.zdnet.com/whitepapers/eflorida_Securing_Cloud_Designing_Security_New_Age.pdf

Forouzan, B. A. (2007). *Data communications and networking* (4th ed.). New York: McGraw-Hill.

FORTINET. (2011). *Protecting the cloud: Fortinet technologies and services that address your cloud security challenges*. Retrieved from http://www.fortinet.com/sites/default/files/solutionbrief/Protecting%20the%20Cloud.pdf

International Telecommunication Union. (2012). *Cloud computing in Africa: Situation and perspective*. Retrieved from http://www.itu.int/ITU-D/treg/publications/Cloud_Computing_Afrique-e.pdf

Kuyoro, S. O., Ibikunle, F., & Awodele, O. (2011). Cloud computing security issues and challenges. [IJCN]. *International Journal of Computer Networks*, *3*(5).

Leitold, H., & Zwattendorfer, B. (2010). STORK: architecture, implementation and pilots. In *Proceedings of ISSE 2010 Securing Electronic Business Processes: Highlights of the Information Security Solutions Europe 2010 Conference*, (pp. 131-142).

Peter, S. (2009). *Securing the cloud: F5 white paper*. Retrieved from http://i.zdnet.com/whitepapers/eflorida_Securing_Cloud_Designing_Security_New_Age.pdf

Report, E. D. U. C. A. U. S. E. (2010). *Seven things you should know about cloud security*. Retrieved from net.educause.edu/ir/library/pdf/EST1008.pdf.

Symantec. (2011). The secure cloud: Best practices for cloud adoption. Retrieved from https://www4.symantec.com/mktginfo/whitepaper/TheSecureCloudBestPracticesforCloudAdoption_cta52644.pdf

Varadarajan, S. (1997). Virtual local area networks. Retrieved from http://www.cis.ohio-state.edu/

VMWare. (2009). *Securing the cloud: A view of cloud computing, security implications and best practices*. Retrieved from http://www.vmware.com/files/pdf/cloud/VMware-Savvis-Cloud-WP-en.pdf

Yuvaraj, M., & Singh, A. P. (2012). Cloud computing in conjunction with libraries: Descriptive literature review. *Asia Pacific Journal of Library and Information Science, 2*(2).

Zwattendorfer, B., & Tauber, A. (2012, December 10-12). Secure cross-cloud single sign-on (SSO) using eIDs. In *Proceedings of The 7th International Conference for Internet Technology and Secured Transactions* (pp. 150-155). London: ICITST.

Chapter 11
Open Source in the Cloud

Egbert de Smet
University of Antwerp, Belgium

ABSTRACT

Whereas "Open Source" in software is still gaining momentum in many fields of applications, it is even more present in the "behind the curtains" scene of the Cloud. It is behind the scenes because Cloud tools are only operated by Cloud providers creating their infrastructure, not by end users. But as that infrastructure is going to be a crucial part of the IT environment of the future, like water and power supply have become for the wider living environments, it is good to note that this infrastructure is not limited to (commercial) proprietary technology and standards, but rather is subject to input from the major Open Source players. This chapter reviews the main technologies of this moment in Cloud software: CloudStack of Citrix and Apache, OpenStack of Suse and Openshift from RedHat. Also the CEPH-technology for distributed storage is added in this overview due to its obvious relevance for the Cloud. The brief review of these products confirms that FOSS indeed plays a major role in the Cloud, opening up that technology for open standards and "public" ownership of this soon-to-be an essential part of our IT environment.

INTRODUCTION: THE CLOUD

For a recent seminar on "Cloud and Open Source" (Elewijt Centre, 2013), Figure 1 was used in the invitation and promotion publications:

The picture nicely shows the main application fields for Cloud: music, air-tickets, shopping, newspapers, e-mail, financial markets, business analysis, and so forth. No books or libraries, indeed. Maybe the feasibility, especially the financial one, is still not clear enough for libraries? Hopefully the chapters in this book shed some light on whether this is indeed the case and/or encourage libraries at least to consider their options.

The basics of Cloud, as should always be emphasized, are the three types of service (Infrastructure, Platform, and Software), as shown in Figure 2 below, also giving some examples:

Figure 3 (SUSE Cloud 1.0, 2013) presents nicely the respective degrees of coverage by either the provider or the customer for each of these four approaches, the green area representing the areas covered by the Cloud provider:

DOI: 10.4018/978-1-4666-4631-5.ch011

Figure 1. The Cloud scene

Figure 2. The three Cloud types of service

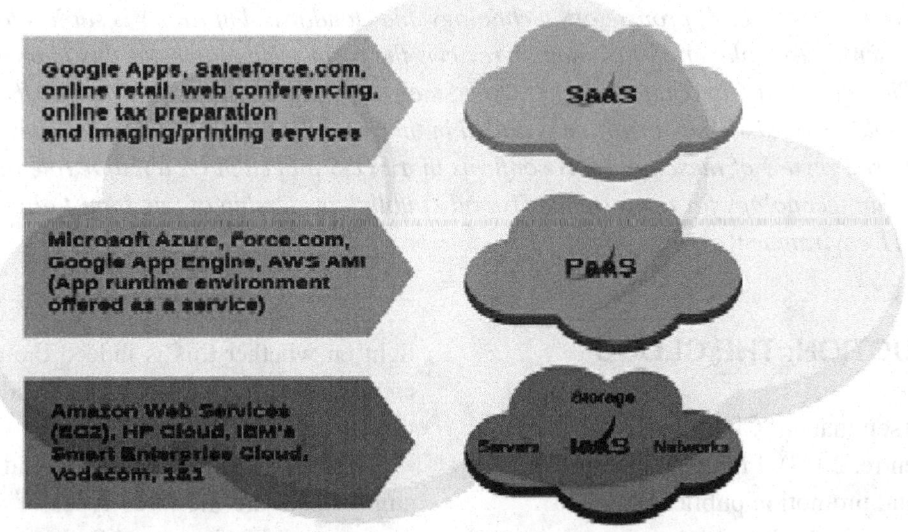

In any of these three types, the acclaimed advantages of Cloud are always: lower costs (in principle reduced upfront capital investment and reduced administration costs), more dynamic configuration, self-service provisioning and greater control and security (standard enterprise security inside a firewall).

The aim of this chapter however is to look at the role of Open Source in the Cloud. The answer to the abovementioned questions on financial viability for libraries might be different when Open Source solutions come into the picture. We will comment on the concepts of FOSS, its advantages for the Cloud and the main contenders and

Figure 3. The three Cloud services coverage

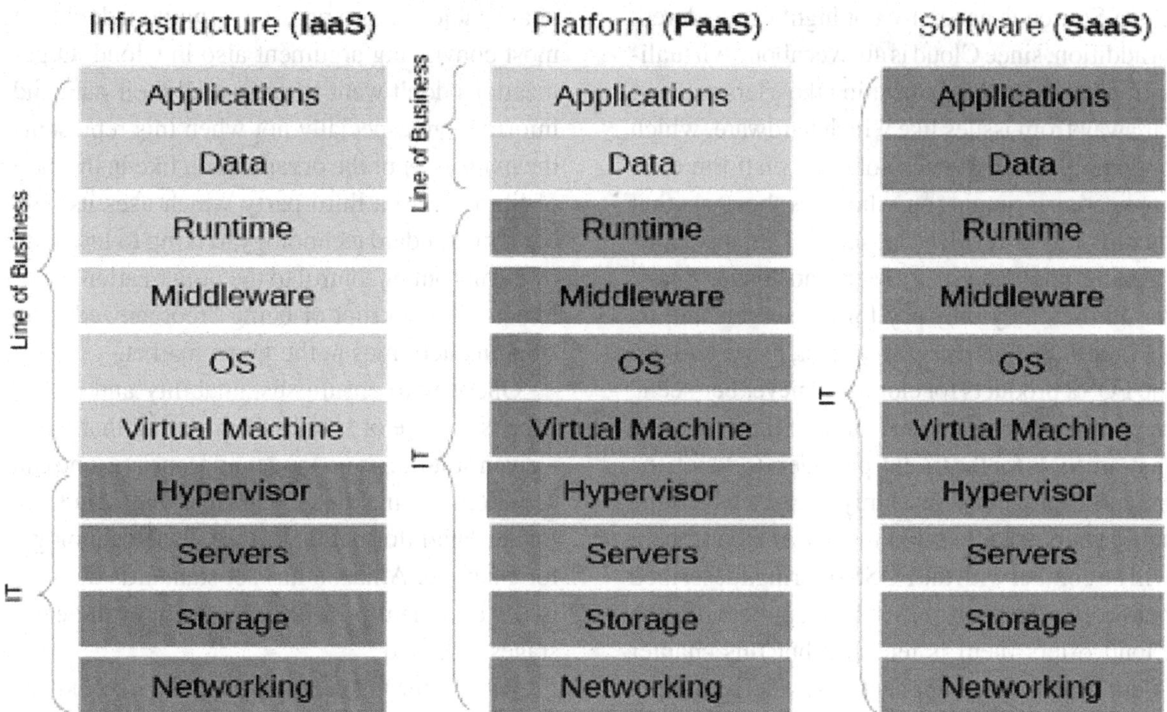

offerings in this area, before finally adding some conclusions on the relevance of Open Source for Cloud and libraries.

FOSS

Open Source software is gaining grounds in many fields, even in its "free" version (FOSS) which means that not only the source codes are available for scrutinization / improvements/study, but also the software itself is available for free, which means that the software is free in two meanings: free to use in all its aspects and non-paid. Well known examples of FOSS are Linux as an Operating System (with somehow popular versions like Ubuntu or strong contenders in the business market like Suse and RedHat), the Mozilla Firefox Web-browser, LibreOffice (a free replacement for Microsoft Office), Apache Web-server, Java/Ruby/Python programming, PHP Web-scripting and MySQL or PostgreSQL databases.

In the library and information field FOSS also is getting more attention: some of the best known tools for digital libraries and repositories (e.g., Greenstone and dSpace) are indeed FOSS, while even traditionally "commercial market" software like for library automation has some serious players in FOSS, with KOHA, PMB, Evergreen and (in the developing countries of the South) ABCD being the leaders, in many cases replacing commercial solutions. The "place to be" for this topic is the URL http://foss4lib.org, which lists 18 different softwares for library automation (FOSS4Lib, n.d.).

As a matter of fact, Open Source is also very strong in the Cloud technology, despite the fact that Cloud is characterized by spearheading complex technologies with high reliability and security requirements, two elements for which Open Source is generally not highly considered. In addition, since Cloud is all over about "virtualisation" of everything, meaning the users are kept far away from issues like which hardware, which operating system, which software platform their application is running on, who cares about whether there is FOSS involved? Users, or organisations offering applications to users, no longer "pay" for all that, they only pay for the service and its secured stable delivery. Moreover, as we will see the FOSS products for cloud will never be "seen" by even the paying organisations or their users, as they are tools for the Cloud-providers to which the organisations subscribe. Only in cases where the subscribers wish to build their own cloud, there will be contact with the FOSS offerings described below. For the users only which applications the Cloud offers them is relevant, but this chapter is not about which applications, whether or not FOSS, are running in the Cloud. In principle all applications (end-user software) can run and indeed run in the Cloud.

The purpose of the next sections of this chapter is to give a brief overview of the main players in the field from the Open Source scene with their main offerings. But let's first discuss some advantages of FOSS for the Cloud.

ADVANTAGES OF OPEN SOURCE FOR CLOUD

While the biggest companies in IT all have their own offering nowadays in Cloud-technology, one can still defend the position that all large scale cloud services are built on open source technology. The well-known argument defending OS as avoiding "vendor lock-in," meaning that in many commercial solutions the customer has to tie in with the solution-provider up to the degree of getting stuck when the provider stops providing for whatever reason (e.g., when their services become unavailable or too expensive) is without doubt the most convincing argument also in Cloud. Organizations don't want to entrust all their data and information, especially not when this represents the main asset of the organization like in the case of libraries, to a third party which uses its own but non-standard technology, risking to lose it all by events out of control to the organization itself, like going bankrupt or being "reorganized" and stopping activities in the given market.

One way to ensure sustainability and endurance is the use of standards, meaning that when a given solution is no longer appropriate, one can use another using the same formats and standards for the data/information. In the Cloud technology, for example, Amazon has set standards de facto by its dominant position especially in the early stages of Cloud.

What it means in reality is that Cloud-hosted data and information can be relatively easily transferred from one platform to another, resulting in the possibility to change providers without major efforts, time gaps or investments.

Since Cloud is mainly about "services;" we are not talking a "free" (as in non-paid) environment. Also in FOSS mostly services (e.g., expert advice, consultancy, tailor-made configurations and localizations) have to be paid and this for sure is not different in the Open Source world. One could even reason that since no profit can be made on the software side and the Cloud service is not a way to promote other products of their line, Open Source providers need to ensure their business model by realistic, or even higher prices.

Still, in view of the concept of Cloud itself, that is, in essence the network, storage and processing hard and software being abstracted from the customer, even to the extent that customers don't even need to know which software is running, the fact whether the software used is Open Source or not is irrelevant. More than anywhere else Open

Source can compete with commercial offerings strictly based on performance and features, not price or name and fame.

In the next part we look at such offerings and deal with the question on whether Open Source is indeed ready to take the challenge to compete with commercial offerings in the Cloud.

THE MAIN CONTENDERS: CLOUDSTACK, OPENSTACK, AND OPENSHIFT

Not surprisingly, some of the big names in Open Source are active in the Cloud market: Citrix and Apache with CloudStack, Suse with OpenStack and Redhat with Openshift. What these have in common is that they offer all the necessary Cloud technology to build concrete Cloud applications. In these sense end-customers, like, for example, libraries, don't "see" this technology except at the stage of setting up their Cloud application, often done by "brokers" and intermediary service providers?

In the same vein, the technology itself is to be situated at the less-visible underlying layers of the systems: this is about software which manages large clusters of storage (hard-disks and file-systems) and computing devices (CPU's, RAM) in order to keep them co-ordinated and monitored. The co-ordination involves not only constant monitoring (on failing devices, re-scaling according to needs...) but also automatic creation of redundancy and replication and - the only "visible layer" - the management software for configuring the many parameters of such systems: the "dashboard" and configuration panels.

All this is done regardless of whether the operating system and applications used on the "virtual machines" (the Cloud is all about virtualisation, both of hardware and software, infrastructure and services) are commercial or not. Running commercial systems on an Open Cloud platform is perfectly possible.

Based on our own checks on the promotion and documentation materials we claim that probably the most "mature" (not necessarily "best,"which we cannot evaluate) solution is the one offered by the consortium (with Citrix playing a leading role) around "CloudStack," while the most "pure" Open Source, community driven solution is the one of OpenStack (by Suse) with OpenShift (RedHat) combining a mix of the other two.

Let's briefly review each of these, describing their characteristics and development status.

CLOUDSTACK

CloudStack is the technology developed mainly by Citrix, in itself not an "Open Source" player however with large and appreciated input in several Open Source projects (comparable in this sense to, for example, IBM). The technology was handed over, together with its development control, to the Apache Software Foundation, one of the most widely acknowledged organisations for Open Source, so currently CloudStack is one of the impressively many Apache activities. They claim to "power the largest clouds in the world" for It-companies, telecom and broadcasting, more than 210 customers with together over 20.000 download per month, creating 1 billion USD in revenues. They further claim to have:

- 8x more paying customers deployments than VMWare.
- 15x more paying customers deployments than OpenStack.
- The only Cloud platform proven at large scale deployments (thousands of hosts).

They run both private and public clouds, but not the mixed type. However for public clouds two types are distinguished: hosted enterprise clouds and multi-tenant public clouds.

On top of the CloudStack technology a non-free Management Interface is offered under the name of CloudPortal, which is facilitating deployment of a concrete Cloud almost to the extent of being indispensable. With CloudPortal deployment is claimed to be a matter of a few hours, not days. However there is also an API, which allows customers to produce their own management software, an option still used by about half of the customers. This could be a viable solution for larger library consortia with the necessary manpower and skills to define and create their own interfaces.

The CloudStack and CloudPortal system is "aligned" along the Amazon Web Services standard (ensuring interoperability) and comprises the whole series of functions a customer might need:

All three types of Cloud services (Infrastructure, Platform and Storage) are supported. One strong asset to be mentioned is the tight quality control applied by Citrix using its own standards, ensuring no lower-reliability parts get through into the final system.

The functions of CloudPortal are the classic ones for Cloud:

- For the storage service: creating/scaling (up or down) volumes of storage and computing power, schedule snapshots and keeping their history.
- For the networking service: creating networks and filling them with VM's, IP assignment and load balancing.
- Setting rules for the previous task.
- Controlling traffic to VM's based on rules and firewalls.

The overall architecture picture nicely shows the multitude of Cloud actions to be taken in any system (the 3 arrows to the left are where external interfaces can "hook" into the system):

The "openness" of CloudStack is built on guaranteed operational compatibility to:

- When it comes to storage: any technology (local disks, iSCSI, FiberChannel, NFS, Swift).
- For computing services: any hypervisor (VMWare, XenServer, Oracle VM, KVM, Bare Metal).

Figure 4. Private and Public Clouds

Private Clouds

Public Clouds

On-premise Enterprise Cloud

- Dedicated resources
- Security & total control
- Internal network
- Managed by Enterprise or 3rd party

Hosted Enterprise Cloud

- Dedicated resources
- Security
- SLA bound
- 3rd party owned and operated

Multi-tenant Public Cloud

- Mix of shared and dedicated resources
- Elastic scaling
- Pay as you go
- Public internet, VPN access

Figure 5. Citrix CloudPortal

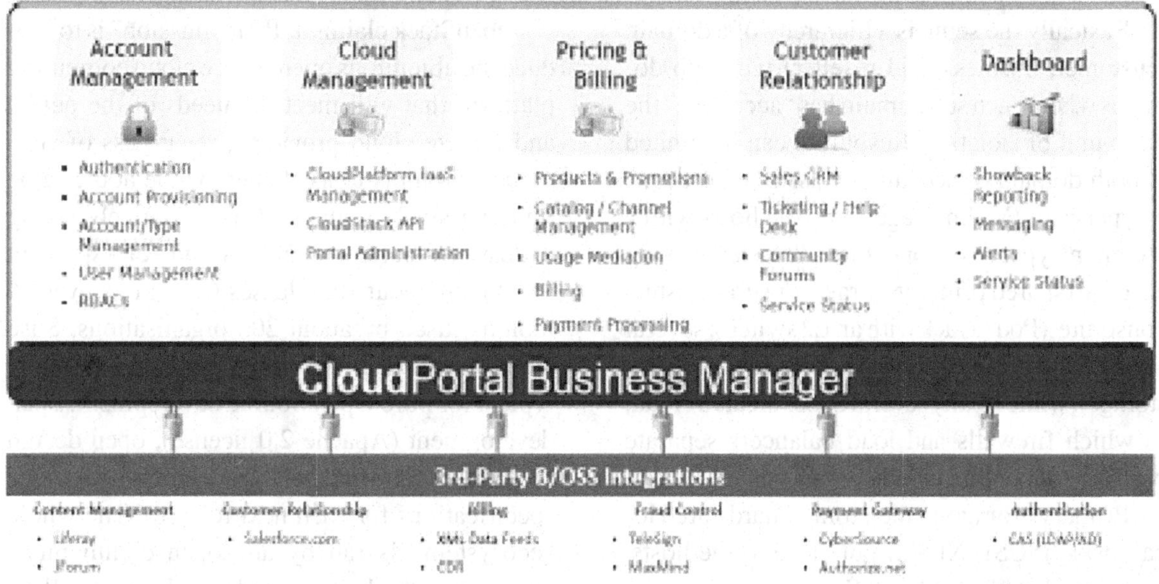

Figure 6. The Cloud internal architecture

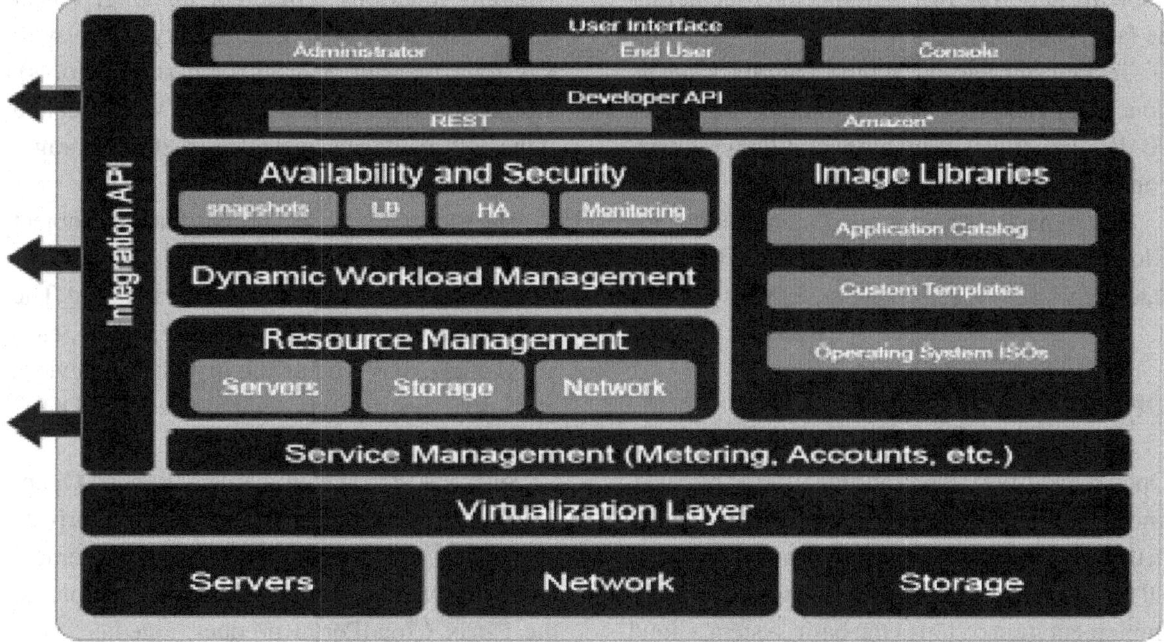

- For networking: network types, isolation, firewall protection, Load balancer and VPN.

Basically the setup is a hierarchy of a domain (customer, business, and reseller) with sub domains where each sub domain has "accounts," the basic unit of isolation. Resources can be limited at both domain or account levels. One host runs a hypervisor (VM manager) and the hosts with a common hypervisor constitute a "cluster" having access to shared primary storage. Several clusters constitute a Pod (a rack with an L2 switch), several Pods create a Zone (accessing shared secondary storage), while finally several zones create a cloud, in which firewalls and load balancers separate private from public clouds.

Primary storage is the storage hardware (local disks, iSCSI, NFS...) put close to the hosts, configured at cluster-level. Secondary storage is configured at zone-level to keep the snapshots, templates and ISO's, using NFS or the OpenStack implementation of Swift (another interoperability de facto standard).

Testing and learning about CloudStack can be done through accessing http://bit.ly/OHhO08. A 90-days free trial is available at http://www.citrix.com/products/cloudplatform/try.

The Apache development community for CloudStack can be found at http://www.cloudstack.org.

OPENSTACK

OpenStack is the Cloud solution offered by Suse, one of the main Linux providers with a strong hold in the larger enterprise market. As with CloudPortal for Citrix, they also offer their own OpenStack implementation on top of the basic system. Cloud Computing is defined as "On-demand access to a shared pool of computing resources or services that can be rapidly provisioned and released."

On-demand self-service, fast network-access and Internet, resource pooling, rapid elasticity and measure resource usage are the main characteristics (Mell & Grance, 2011).

OpenStack claims as their "mission" is to produce the ubiquitous open source cloud computing platform that will meet the needs of the public and private cloud providers, regardless of size, by being simple to implement while at the same time massively scalable. It is a relatively young endeavour, started by NASA and Rackspace in 2010 with about six releases (about one every 6 months) used by about 200 organisations, Suse being one of them. The project principles are really typical for pure Open Source development: open development (Apache 2.0 license), open design (with blueprints and half-year summits to define specifications for each next release). The whole "ecosystem" is ran by an "open community," meaning anybody interested, capable and willing to respect the philosophy can join.

Basically OpenStack exists of a series of standard functions (compute, imaging, object storage using Swift standard, identity control with Keystone, measurement and orchestration tools). The architecture, with on top the WWW-user and at the bottom the physical infrastructure (storage) is shown in the following figure:

The storage is based on two models: object storage and block storage. Amazon S3 and "Machine Image" standards are used for imaging. The main hypervisors1 (Xen, VMWare, KVM, etc.) are supported as well as the main block devices with one specific type emphasized: RADOS2 Block Devices (RBD).

Suse has its own implementation of OpenStack with Suse Cloud, offering public, private and mixed clouds, with an added management tool "Crowbar," more or less comparable to the Citrix CloudPortal product, together: Suse CloudPlatform.

The Crowbar add-on for cloud-creation is characterized by:

Figure 7. Suse OpenStack

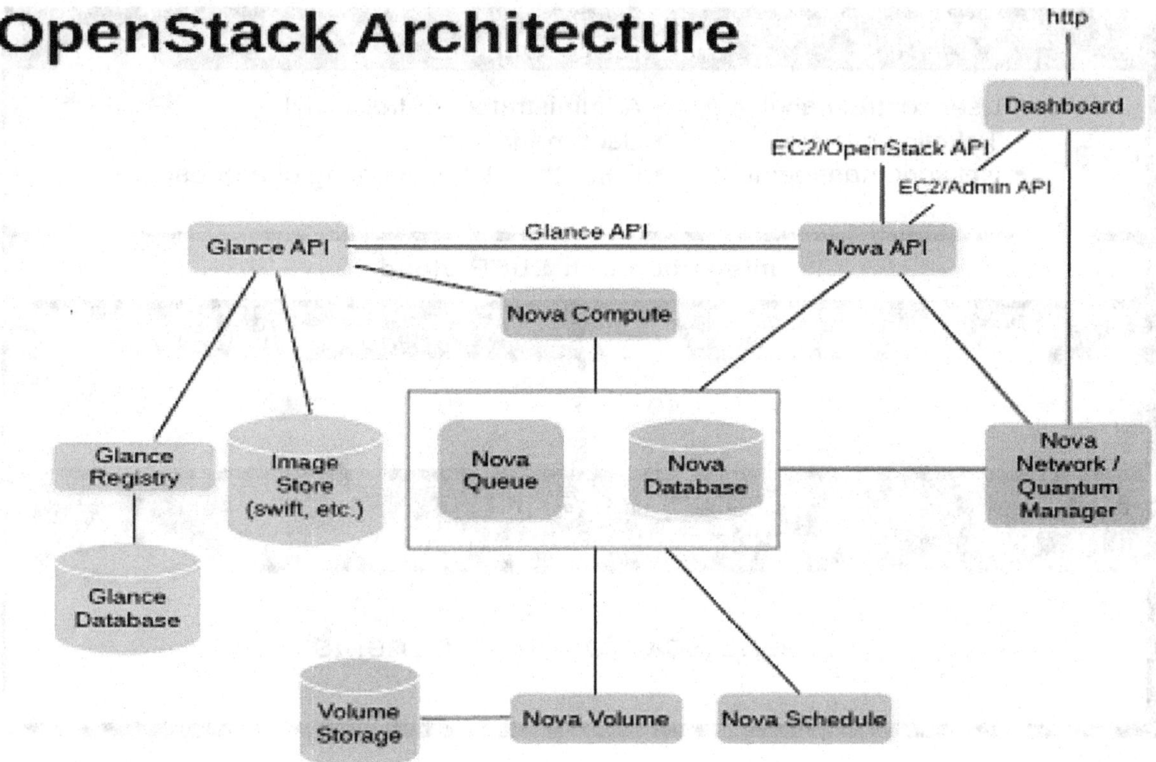

- Its mission as "A Zero Touch Cloud Installer".
- Delivering servers in boxes to full function cloud in less than two hours.
- Allowing also "bare metal" installations including BIOS and RAID configurations.
- Allowing users to choose how their system is to be configured (by "barclamps").
- Being not specific to OpenStack.

The "Chief" add-on is Suse's version of Cloud-Portal, which serves as an "Orchestration framework" to simplify installation and configuration.

OpenStack is especially proud of their wide and lively community (the "Linux of the Cloud") and the OpenStack foundation, guaranteeing long-term viability and benefits to the whole sector, not a single vendor.

Giving honour to who deserves it, Suse (of Suse Linux) is the main driving force behind OpenStack, integrating it into their larger Cloud offering as shown in the illustration under here:

Suse's administration server provides all functions (user dashboard, user instances views with easy-to-build instances (configurations of memory, storage, CPU, etc.).

Their documentation can be further explored at http://www.suse.com/documentation/suse_cloud10/ (SUSE Cloud 1.0., 2013).

OPENSHIFT

Next to Suse in the Linux enterprise-market stands, still quite long, RedHat. Also RedHat is developing its own Open Source Cloud platform: OpenShift.

Figure 8. Suse Cloud "ecologic system"

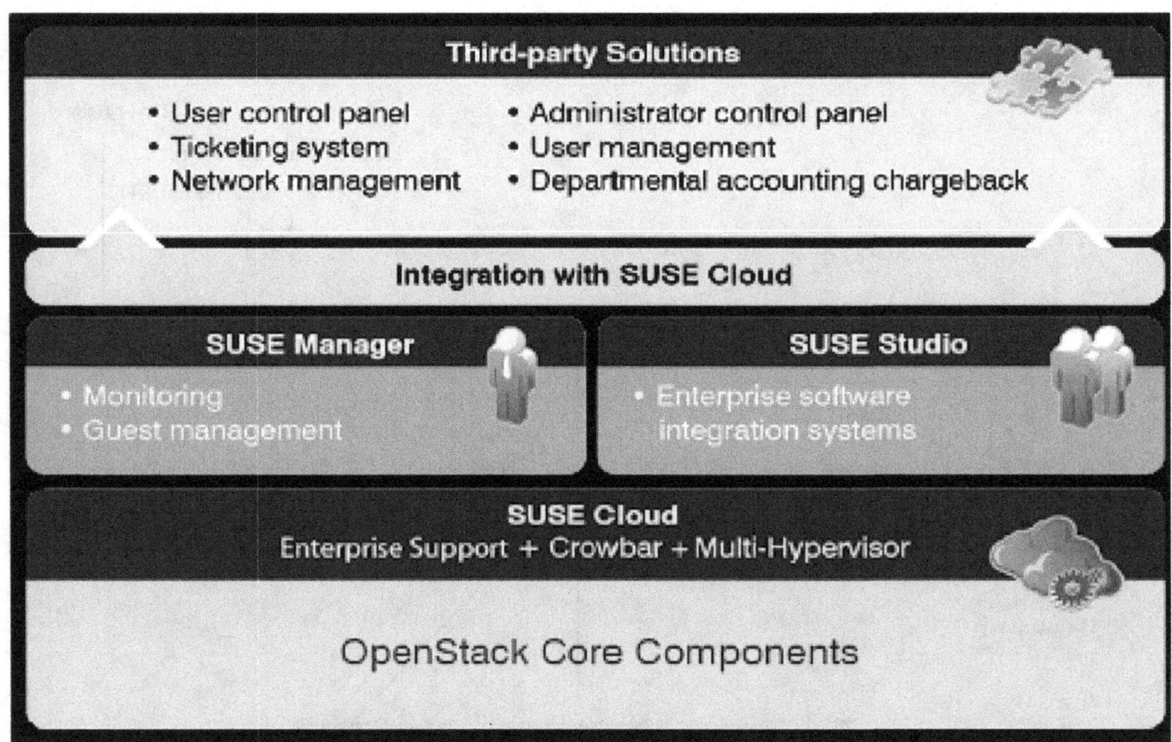

OpenShift is mainly a Platform-as-a-Service (PaaS) Cloud service. This means all levels of service (storage, hardware, virtualization, operating system and application platform) but NOT the application itself are "outsourced" to the Cloud.

A special feature of Redhat's OpenShift, making it really "open," is the concept of "cartridges," (i.e., plug-ins for tasks, produced by anyone capable and willing to do so sticking to the protocol for cartridges and offered on the "RedHat Marketplace"). RedHat itself has a full roadmap for J-Boss cartridges, showing they are serious about this possibility in OpenShift.

In OpenShift vocabulary a "broker" manages OpenShift "nodes." "Gears" represent secure containers in RHEL (e.g., the smallest coming with 512Mb RAM/1,5Gb HD).

However such "gears" are subject to automatic up- and down-scaling based on observed needs, meaning flexibility and scalability along with standards.

An OpenShift Source or Live-CD can be downloaded for testing. See http://openshift.redhat.com ("Cloud platform," 2013).

There are currently two versions under development:

- **OpenShift Online:** Only the application level remains for the customer, RH will run it for 18 months guaranteed (Public Cloud Service, only e-mail address to be provided), can actually be checked out (Techpreview status), a supported version comes out soon;
- **OpenShift Enterprise:** This version leaves more control for IT (Private Cloud Software), is for sale today since December 2012. Already a new version 1.1 was released on month later (January 1, 2013), the service is subscription based (no matter which version you want) and "feedback-driven."

DISTRIBUTED STORAGE TECHNOLOGY: CEPH

A special category of Open Source technology for Cloud focuses on storage. The main player here is CEPH. CEPH is a "distributed object store," running on commodity hardware, fully securing functionality by automated replicas and easy up- or down-scaling ("CEPH: The future of storage," 2013).

The automated replica method means that a (meta-data based) management software keeps track of where all objects (data/information/files) are stored. Using constant monitoring any failure is noted and automatically followed by creating a new replica on another storage unit.

Object storage devices are combined into a "cluster" serving objects to clients, intelligently peering to perform replication tasks. Monitors only maintain maps of clusters and provide consensus for "distributed decision making."

The RADOS Block Device (or RBD) is basically storage of virtual disks in RADOS, allowing decoupling of VMs and containers, live migration (quite important in critical systems !), with images striped across the cluster, with boot support in QEMU, KVM, and OpenStack Nova. Finally it has mount support in the Linux kernel. The combination with OpenStack of course means an enormous powerful platform, with Ceph adding live migration, snapshotting, copy-on-write cloning and a publicly available AMI ("CEPH: The future of storage," 2013).

Their CRUSH algorithm CRUSH is a pseudo-random placement algorithm, that ensures even distribution, is repeatable and deterministic, with a rule-based configuration and covering replica count, infrastructure topology and weighting.

The CEPH Metadata Server manages metadata for a POSIXcompliant shared filesystem, a directory hierarchy and its file metadata (owner, timestamps, mode, etc.). This way they claim to be capable to always find your data when your cluster is infinitely big and always changing.

CEPH uses the Open Source GPL2 license: each contributor owns his own code. Like the other Open Source providers they claim a "dynamic community" of developers ("CEPH: The future of storage," 2013).

A company building on CEPH services is, for example, InkTank ("Delivering the future of storage, 2013).

SUMMARY AND CONCLUSION

Let's summarize the hopefully not-too-much-advertisement-like descriptions of the main FOSS offerings for the Cloud, given above.

CloudStack, OpenStack and OpenShift are all three principally equivalent developments of a Cloud-platform, which Cloud providers can use to run their business. All three have big FOSS-players backing them, all three claim to adhere to de facto standards (Amazon, Swift, etc.) and being open to any "hypervisor" for virtualisation and standard storage technology. Since they are FOSS, all three–along with the narrower-aiming (storage only) CEPH project–claim to have dynamic and large developers communities.

It is simply too early in the Cloud history to evaluate whether there indeed would be performance and or reliability issues. Where CloudStack at this early moment seems to be a bit more "mature" (with many real-world but high-scale operational applications running), one could be attracted by the more FOSS-philosophy driven approach of CloudStack or OpenShift, but both these also can refer to running larger-scale implementations. It is simply *l'embarras du choix*: selecting one is the challenge. But it is a challenge preferable to not having any choice or not being allowed to choose.

So there is in fact only good news: Open Source has a strong position in the Cloud and for a good reason, discussed above – avoidance of vendor lock-in, which might be more of an issue than anywhere else in IT. This means that commercial providers of Cloud will have to adhere to the same standards, while hoping to add their strong "warranty-based" service and reputation, an aspect in which Open Source still seems to lag a bit behind, at least in customer's perception.

It is almost impossible to make any claim on the effect on pricing of the availability of FOSS in the Cloud. When looking for prices you will mostly get a response: "e-mail us" as the providers will want to assess your needs and financial capabilities before sticking out their neck. The only "figure" we found was an example of "50USD/user/month" subscription–it is all about subscribing to a service, not "purchase" of software, lowering significantly the financial impact of FOSS–which unfortunately does not say much about the real costs: If a user is a subscribing organisation (a "customer") this seems very low, if it would be an end-user it would be potentially a lot, certainly for libraries.

What is the meaning for libraries of all this? As explained above, libraries themselves will not directly "use" the Cloud platforms; they simply would continue using their applications, the main difference being that their infrastructure is totally abstracted into nodes/clusters/zones/domains (or whatever IT-slang the providers use) with auto-balancing traffic, auto-replicating and secured access-everywhere, that is, where there is Internet connectivity ("Cloud platform," 2013).

Libraries might feel that the old adagio of the "Personal Computer" (PC), that is, human beings owning and being in control of their own IT which has become an everyday tool to survive (economically, commercially, administratively or even socially/culturally), has been thrown upside-down in the Cloud, and therefore the Cloud deviates too much from their own mandate and philosophy. It will take a lot of positive experiences, for example, proving the economical superior model (running in the Cloud being cheaper indeed in a longer term when all costs are counted) of the Cloud. IT becomes a resource like the electricity power (or water) grids–libraries usually don't complain about not being in control of these essential resources–which ideally should be taken for granted (not still always the case, for example, in the South), allowing libraries to shift their focus more on what is the real essence: their services themselves and their quality (monitoring), not the underlying infrastructure offered by society.

If libraries need more control over their Cloud-environments, they can still go for the options–available in all FOSS-products described–to build their own Cloud. This is the only approach in which libraries would get in touch with the platforms themselves. Especially larger library consortia and networks could be capable of maintaining the needed human resources capacity for doing this, running their own Clouds. We tend to think that such perspective, especially in combination with the strong presence and claims of Open Source in the Cloud as described above, should encourage the library and information services field to embrace the Cloud fully.

REFERENCES

CEPH: The future of storage. (2013). Retrieved from http://www.ceph.com

Cloud platform. (2013). Retrieved from http://www.citrix.com/products/cloudplatform/try

Delivering the future of storage. (2013). Retrieved from http://www.inktank.com

Develop, host, and scale your apps in the cloud. (2013). Retrieved from http://openshift.redhat.com

Elewijt Centre. (2013, February 5). *Open source cloud day*. Retrieved from http://www.opensource-cloudday.be

FOSS4Lib. (n.d.). Retrieved from http://foss4lib.org/

Mell, P., & Grance, T. (2011). The NIST definition of cloud computing: Recommendations of the National Institute of Standards and Technology. Computer Security Division, Information Technology Laboratory, National Institute of Standards and Technology, Retrieved from http://csrc.nist.gov/publications/nistpubs/800-145/SP800-145.pdf

SUSE Cloud 1.0. (2013). Retrieved from http://www.suse.com/documentation/suse_cloud10/

ENDNOTES

1. A hypervisor is a 'supervisor' software to manage (create, maintain) virtual machines (VM's).
2. RADOS: reliable, autonomous, distributed object store.

Chapter 12
Testbed Platform:
Amazon Web Services for Library

Deepak Mane
Tata Research Design and Development Center, India

ABSTRACT

Libraries invest millions of dollars in developing and maintaining library applications that are core to their libraries and help them to improve their competitive advantage through operational excellence of libraries. Continuous changes in the library environment forces the library to innovate and optimize their library process, resulting in continuous changes in the software applications that support the library processes. As a consequence, delivering applications rapidly that are defect free, scalable, and reliable becomes challenging. Testing becomes a critical and vital step in the process – not only in terms of coverage but also in terms of performance, security, and usability. Setting up test environments that closely mirror the production environment can be expensive – in terms of hardware, licenses, people to manage library infrastructure and its application. "Testing as a Service" – a new paradigm of Cloud-based "On Demand" testing service can help libraries to address this challenge. This chapter focuses on how libraries can optimize their IT budget through a strategic initiative in the form of "On Demand" testing. This chapter describes Requirements of Testbed Platform, Cloud Testing, and Benefits of testing using cloud environment for library Amazon Web Services – Public Cloud Services.

INTRODUCTION

The recent sharp downturn in the economy is forcing libraries to reconsider their approach towards IT investments. In a world where companies are more focused towards improving efficiencies and return of capital employed, CIOs/CTOs need to reconsider how they can reduce their technology investments, or get higher return on the same or incremental investments. Testing is crucial to enhance user satisfaction and reduce support cost. However, testing requires libraries to invest in people, tools, and environments and can take up a significant percentage of the available budget.

DOI: 10.4018/978-1-4666-4631-5.ch012

But quality can never be compromised. New ways of development and testing on AWS are enabling libraries to ensure higher quality but with significantly lower investments.

REQUIREMENTS OF TEST LAB

Testing is a vital phase in any software development and maintenance initiative. Frequently changing requirements coupled with a reduced development life cycle has increased the pressure on testing teams to do more with less. A dedicated test lab is one of the solutions to handle this challenge. Traditionally, to support a test lab initiative, an organization would need to put the following infrastructure/resources in place:

- Target testing environment, similar to production environment of library.
- Multiple target software platform for compatibility testing of library.
- Skilled library professionals to design, develop, and execute test scripts; and analyze the results of the tests.
- A good test automation library software with multiple virtual user licenses.
- Sufficient bandwidth for simulating real life scenarios of library operations.

CHALLENGES FACED

Setting up a dedicated, in-house test lab of libraries comes with its own set of challenges. Some of the major challenges faced are:

- **Infrastructure:** Hardware and software resources, establishment of proper tools and processes, and other resources like bandwidth. This creates a strain on the overall budget.
- **Scalability:** To ensure that software works in a real life situation, it needs to be tested in a real life environment. It is not easy for an organization to create a scalable infrastructure that simulates the production environment.
- **Cost:** There is a major capital investment required to own a proper test lab. Since most of the cost is a fixed cost (hardware, software, and tool licenses) it also creates a challenge to allocate budgets for this kind of investment and justify the ROI.
- **Availability of Skilled Library Engineers:** Skilled test engineers, especially automation engineers, are not available easily and are very expensive.

CLOUD TESTING: NEW PARADIGM

Cloud Computing, one of the most highly publicized IT technology trends, is a new approach to deploy/test applications "over the Internet." Cloud Testing utilizes the same computing concept to extend current testing paradigms using shared, scalable, "on-demand" testing infrastructure that is allocated on a "pay as you go" basis. This model provides an unparalleled flexibility of ramping up and tearing down a testing environment in short notice. A new test harness can be launched in the cloud with all the necessary configuration work completed, including operating system, software, and so forth, in almost no time. Libraries need not procure any server, tools or licenses – they need to hook up, deploy the software, test, and start paying for just the resource usage. Same efficiency applies to shutting off a cloud environment – just cancel what you don't need. The Cloud Testing model's flexibility reduces much of the capital cost, risk and effort associated with establishing an appropriate testing environment for the enterprise. More importantly, libraries can focus on their core capabilities.

CLOUD

The term “cloud” is used as a metaphor for the Internet based on how the Internet is depicted in computer network diagrams. It is an abstraction for the complex computing infrastructure it conceals. Cloud computing is a style of computing in which virtualized and scalable computing resources are provided as a service over the Internet. Users need not have knowledge, expertise, or control over the computing infrastructure “in the cloud” that supports them.

Generally, cloud computing comprises applications delivered as a service over the Internet by the hardware and system software that support such applications in the data center. In essence, data center hardware and software is the cloud whilst services themselves are popularly known as Software as a Service (SaaS) (Armburst et al., 2009). From a hardware computing viewpoint, the cloud computing offers three new aspects hitherto unknown (Vogels, 2008).

1. “The illusion of infinite computing resources available on demand, thereby eliminating the need for Cloud Computing users to plan far ahead for provisioning.”
2. “The elimination of an up-front commitment by Cloud users, thereby allowing companies to start small and increase hardware resources only when there is an increase in their needs.”
3. “The ability to pay for use of computing resources on a short-term basis as needed (e.g., processors by the hour and storage by the day) and release them as needed, thereby rewarding conservation by letting machines and storage go when they are no longer useful.”

A BRIEF HISTORY

The evolution of cloud computing has been preceded by development of numerous computing models from CPU and storage as the foundation for computing technology through to utility computing. Each successive development of new model has been motivated by the need to achieve greater system efficiency through optimal system utilization (Elastra Corp, n.d.):

- **CPU and Storage (“Ad Initium”–At the Beginning):** This is the basis for all computing technology. The Moore’s law has successfully predicted increasing CPU power and memory capacity resulting in inexpensive computing technology. However, the data center composed from this technology suffers from superfluous capacity resulting in an inefficient system utilization model.
- **Virtualization (“Ex Uno Plures”–Out of One, Many):** This model solves the superfluous capacity problem by abstracting computing resources. It entails taking a server or disk unit and partitioning it into multiple logical units which can be accessed and consumed in an independent manner. Thus, it enables number of permutations for running a set of applications on the hardware, such that idle capacity is minimized.
- **Grid Consolidation (“E Pluribus Unum”–Out of Many, One):** This model consolidates capacity by combining multiple servers to satisfy a large-scale computing requirement. In essence, grid is the opposite of virtualization as it applies cumulative capacity of many servers to satisfy large-scale computing needs of an application.
- **Utility Computing (To Each According to his Needs):** This model leverages virtualization and grid consolidation to enable users to purchase only the capacity they need on an on-demand pricing model. This is analogous to electric utility where one pays only for the actual electricity used on an on-demand basis. Although utility computing makes computing resources more

efficiently available, software companies, enterprise IT organizations, and so forth, still face the challenge of how best to use the utility environment for applications in terms of deploying, scaling and managing their application infrastructure.

- **Cloud Computing:** This model promises a true on-demand computing to automate system deployment, scaling, monitoring and decouple application design and development from the deployment process along with pay-per-use pricing model. In essence, cloud computing is the sum of utility computing and applications offered as a service.

GENERAL ARCHITECTURE

The general architecture of the cloud, depicted in Figure 1, comprises four layers, namely: Bare Metal Hardware, Virtualization, Cloud Middleware and Application (services). The bare metal hardware layer is usually x86 commodity blade servers on which virtualization (VMWare ESX, Xen, KVM, etc.) enables virtual logical machine instances to be created. Each machine instance comprise a guest OS and an application along with its runtime environment. The virtualization capability is fundamental to the concept of cloud computing as it creates the perception of infinite computing resources on demand. The cloud middleware (Eucalyptus, Nimbus, etc.) enables the application layer to take advantage of the "elastic" nature of the computing resources based on its requirements.

TYPES OF CLOUD OFFERING

Today's cloud computing offerings can be distinguished based on the level of abstractions they export to the cloud users (or programmers) and the level of computing resource management

Figure 1. General Cloud Architecture

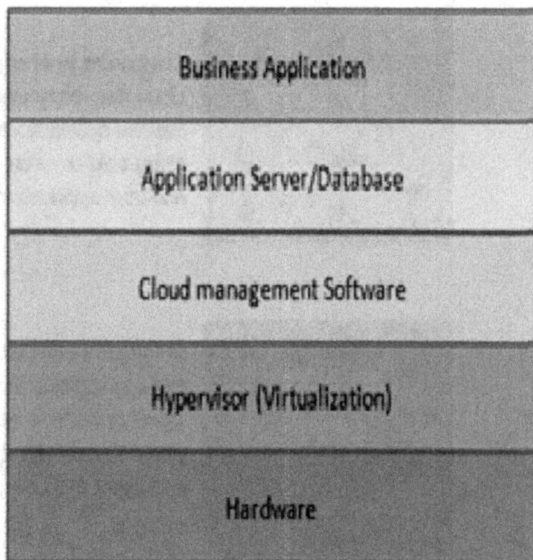

(flexibility) they offer as illustrated in Figure 2. Based on this characterization, cloud offerings can be broadly classified into three categories:

- **Infrastructure-as-a-Service (IaaS):** These cloud service providers offer computational resources such as servers, network, storage, and so forth, from a shared facility managed by the provider to cloud users on an on-demand basis. Examples of IaaS providers include Amazon Web Services and Flexiscale. Note that IaaS providers allow users to dynamically grow and shrink their resource allocations to match their demands; however, the responsibility of utilizing this elasticity effectively rests with the cloud user.
- **Platform-as-a-Service (PaaS):** The platform as a service providers export application-development platforms that broadly fall into two categories: (1) those that export application development platforms for certain domains or class of applications (e.g., the Google AppEngine and Force.com), and (2) those that export general-purpose application development platform (e.g., Microsoft's Azure). In either case, applications developed using these

Figure 2. Three levels of abstraction

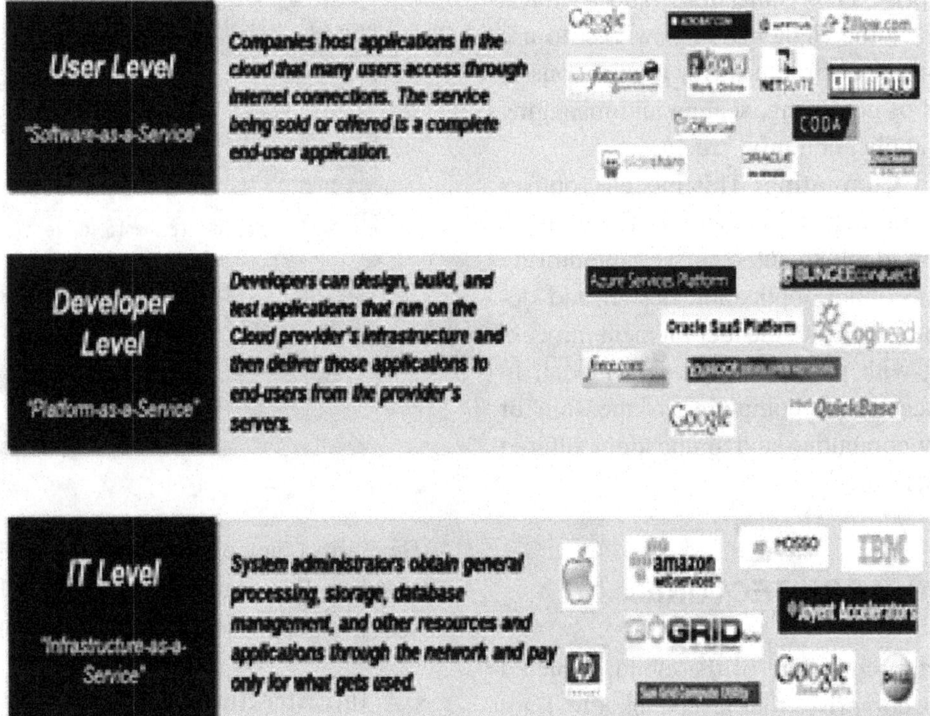

platforms are able to benefit from elasticity offered by Infrastructure-as-a-Service cloud providers. For instance, the Google AppEngine is directed at traditional Web applications; applications developed using the AppEngine API can scale automatically with increase in the number of resources as well as achieve high availability through replication. Force.com exports a platform for developing business application that solely interacts with the salesforce.com database. Microsoft's Azure platform, on the other hand, allows application to be developed using .NET libraries and compiled to common runtime language environment. The .NET libraries provide a degree of scalability and fail-over support, but require developers to declaratively specify application characteristics to take advantage of these features. Users do not get control of the operating system or runtime but are allowed choice of programming languages.

- **Software-as-a-Service (SaaS):** The Software-as-a-service cloud service providers offer specific application services, delivered over the Internet on some form of on-demand payment system. Examples include Salesforce.com and WebEx.

In addition, there are two variants of the cloud computing offerings that describe whether or not its services are available to global or select audience:

- **Public Cloud:** In this variant of the cloud, services are made available to global audience on a pay-per-use fashion with util-

ity computing being the service sold. Examples include Amazon Web Services, Google AppEngine, and so forth.
- **Private Cloud:** This variant refers to internal data center of a business or other organizations which is available to members of such entities only.

USING CLOUD FOR TEST ENVIRONMENT

As software applications become more critical for library changes, the software development process is becoming more agile, distributed and non cohesive. This, along with the emergence of a global delivery model, has resulted in smaller distributed teams operating independently for development, testing, and integration. To support this kind of development processes and the need for continuous testing, libraries spend a major part of their budgets in setting up test environments and automated tool licenses.

Cloud Computing reduces the cost by providing a test environment and easier provisioning. Scaling up and tearing down of a test environment is possible within a very short time, sometimes within minutes. This, along with "on demand" testing services by testing service providers, also helps libraries to reduce capex as well as opex

KEY BENEFITS OF TESTING IN CLOUD

All levels of testing can be carried out in cloud environments, and indeed, some types of testing benefit greatly from a test environment in the cloud. In an early pilot with a European Financial Services client, and in subsequent assignments with clients in the public and private sectors, we have identified a number of distinct differences and corresponding benefits to testing on the cloud.

- Flexibility
    - Different levels or grades of tests can be executed on separate environments at an organization's convenience.
    - Performance Testers no longer need to wait until the end of the testing phase to move to a production-like environment for their performance, load and stress tests. Instead a production-like environment can be brought into action at will.
- Simplicity
    - End-to-end Testing can be set-up in the cloud relatively simply, provided the necessary servers and images can be accessed to create an end-to-end environment;
    - The cloud also offers a new level of simplicity in terms of training or bug-fixing environments, which can be launched as quickly as the images and configuration can be put in place.
- Comprehensive and Indicative Testing
    - Even end-to-end tests for more generic business processes can be carried out in the cloud. All the necessary components can be published in the cloud to create the whole chain of systems. In this way, the whole business processes can also be tested;
    - In the cloud, a more realistic load can be generated than the virtual load generated by other tools. Cloud-enabled performance test tools generate the needed load and stress to test an application more accurately.
- Cost Reduction
    - There is a reduced need for expensive environments, which need to be used only when tests have to be executed;
    - Historically, internal testing and acceptance environments have been permanently available for testing projects within a company, creating a

permanent pressure on development budgets and infrastructure resources. Cloud environments however can be enabled and disabled at will, reducing the cost of environment management.

- Cleaner, Greener, Testing
  - It is intuitively true that the efficiencies cloud computing provides make it significantly greener than traditional, hosted models. That is true for testing, too. By sharing cloud resources for their test infrastructure, businesses will use IT resources on demand and eliminate waste. In addition, clients using cloud data centers can minimize energy use and deliver environmental savings in CO2 up to 55%.
- Geographic Transparency and Traceability
  - Test data is frequently sensitive and its location is therefore important, since data entering or exiting national borders can contravene national and international regulations, such as the EU Data Protection Directive. To address this, the Test Cloud solution is transparent about the geographic location where data and services are stored, and allows clients to keep data on their own servers, using a VPN connection.
- Driving Standardization
  - In one sense, creating test environments in the cloud is merely a temporary first step on a much longer journey. Cloud computing will give a huge impetus for the standardization of organizations infrastructure. That key shift will inevitably catalyze IT modernization and improve internal IT services maturity, impact upon application consolidation and portfolio rationalization, and change the way enterprises look at resourcing IT services internally

FORMS OF CLOUD-BASED TESTING

There are four different forms of cloud-based software testing. Each of them has different focuses and objectives.

- **Testing Application in a Cloud:** It assures the performance of a application in a cloud based on its non-functional service requirements.
- **Testing of a Cloud:** It validates the performance of a cloud from an external view based on the provided cloud specified capabilities and service features. Cloud and SaaS vendors as well as end users are interested in carrying on this type of performance testing.
- **Testing Inside a Cloud:** It checks the performance of a cloud from an internal view based on the internal infrastructures of a cloud and specified cloud capabilities. Only cloud vendors can perform this type of testing since they have accesses to internal infrastructures and connections between its internal SaaS(s) and automatic capabilities, security, management and monitor.
- **Requirements and Specifications:** This usually is performed by the cloud-based application system providers.

SUGGESTED APPROACH

To achieve maximum out of their cloud testing initiative, libraries need to have a cloud based test strategy before initiating the process. Libraries need to come out with a clear plan stating the testing goals, types of tests to be conducted, benchmarks, infrastructure requirements, and last but not the least, a gap analysis of required and available resources shown in Figure 3.

- **Define Test Strategy:** For a successful cloud based testing initiative, a test strategy should be defined. It should include the objective of this initiative (cost savings, scalability of the infrastructure, ROI), types of testing to be done on cloud (System testing, load testing, UAT), In source/outsource among other normal planning items like timeline, dependencies, and risks.
- **Identify Infrastructure Requirements:** Based on the test strategy, libraries need to identify resources required. These resources should include Hardware, Software requirements, Test Automation Tools and number of virtual users, Bandwidth, processing power, storage capacity, and so forth, libraries also should identify the usage requirements.
- **Identify Service Providers:** It is absolutely critical to identify a service provider with an established reputation to ensure quality and reliability of services. It is suggested that libraries identify service providers for providing end to end services starting from infrastructure, tool licenses, and provisioning. One important criterion to be evaluated is the time required for provisioning and tearing down the required infrastructure.
- **Test Execution:** Once a service provider is identified, libraries can start testing as per their plan. Organization should plan to optimize the usage of the infrastructure to minimize their cost.
- **Monitoring and Measurement:** It is important that the results of the cloud testing initiative are validated continuously on a scheduled or event-driven basis. This will enable libraries to intercept and resolve issues, find cloud usage patterns, and measure success against stated objective. This monitoring and measurement activities are key to demonstrate the ROI of cloud testing

Figure 3. Suggested Approach

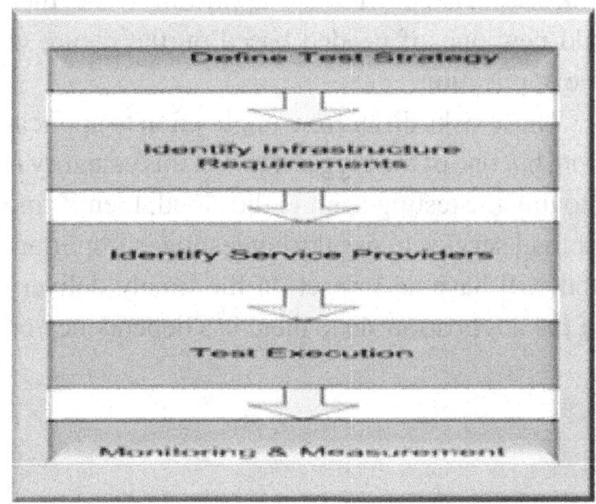

OPERATIONAL CHALLENGES OF TESTING IN CLOUD

Despite the bright upside, cloud-based testing has its limitations, too. Organizations must contend with a different set of challenges in their quest to reap cloud's benefits.

- **Lack of Standards:** Presently, there are no universal/standard solutions to integrate public cloud resources with user companies' internal data center resources. Public cloud providers have their own architecture, operating models and pricing mechanisms and offer very little interoperability. This poses a big challenge for companies when they need to switch vendors.
- **Security in the Public Cloud:** Security in the public cloud is still a major concern, and encryption techniques currently available today are considered insufficient.

Procedures are being developed to improve security and performance in the public cloud. For instance, service providers are developing virtual private clouds and client partitions. The main cause for concern is that the data may be stored in a remote location beyond an organization's legal and regulatory jurisdiction.

- **SLAs:** Terms and conditions of cloud service are sometimes hard to understand; misleading and biased toward the vendor.5 such areas include clauses governing data integrity, data preservation, data location and transfer, according to a study by The Center for Commercial Law Studies at Queen Mary, University of London 2010. Companies would do well to be diligent and proactive in sorting through these issues with their vendors.
- **Infrastructure:** Some cloud providers offer only limited types of configurations, technology, servers and storage, networking and bandwidth, making it difficult to create real-time test environments.
- **Usage:** Improper usage of cloud-based test environments can increase costs. Even though some vendors offer pay-as-you-go cloud based testing services, this approach can be expensive or out of sync with requirements, particularly if user estimates are too conservative or wildly overblown. Companies that apply pay-as-they-go approaches must first perfect their cost models or apply process-driven estimates rather than utilizing projections that are unsupported by data.
- **Planning:** Testing teams should rigorously plan their test environments, from utilization periods through disassembly. They should also be aware of the associated expenses, such as cost of encrypting data, before putting testing in a cloud environment, since these requirements will consume additional CPU and memory. It's important to monitor utilization of cloud resources to avoid over-usage and over-payment.
- **Performance:** As public clouds are shared by numerous users, there may be cases where a company might have to wait for the required bandwidth. There may also be cases where a service provider may suddenly announce disruption of service due to a maintenance window or network outage. Some of these issues can be resolved by working closely and proactively with the service provider.

RISKS AND MITIGATION FOR TESTING IN CLOUD ENVIRONMENT

There are potentially two types of risks: product risks and cloud computing risks.

Product Risks

When our application moves to cloud computing we have to identify if there are risks associated with the change from a traditionally-deployed application to a cloud-based service. The best way to approach this is to review the existing risks associated with the application and then add new ones if needed based on the nature of the application.

These risks differ from application to application, but one of the biggest risks in this category is moving the testing itself to the cloud. Identifying a cloud service to use during testing is important and will have an impact on the timely delivery of the application since there is a dependency on the setup and connectivity of this environment. Software testers have to incorporate these dependencies in their planning.

Cloud Computing Risks

There are risks that are inherited when we move to the cloud. Some of the advantages of moving to the cloud, like multi-tenancy (software application is designed to virtually partition its data and configuration, and each client organization works with a customized virtual application instance.) Or self healing (a process of self recovery during failure), can also involve risks. These are some areas that we need to consider when testing: self healing, multi-tenancy, type of cloud model utilized (SaaS, IaaS, PaaS), data governance, monitoring, data security. For each of these benefits we have to be able to identify the particular risks associated, and then plan to test for those so that they can be mitigated. Some examples are shown in Figure 4.

As software testers, we have to consider both product and cloud computing risks and try to mitigate them. For example if our application provides confidentiality, then we have to adequately test the security of the application to preserve confidentiality of the data. If we support multi-tenancy (i.e., then we also have to make sure that multiple tenants can run successfully without causing issues to one another. We will also have to do performance and load testing to make sure we can support the number of users we allow and also note the peak usage and breaking points

TESTING AS A SERVICE

Though having a cloud infrastructure solves most of the challenges related to test lab, libraries still find it difficult to find skilled testers who can prepare test strategies and perform test design and test automation. "On Demand" testing or "Testing as a Service" offered by leading testing service providers can help libraries in overcoming these challenges. In this model, the service providers take over the complete Cloud testing initiative. This helps to maximize the ROI as internal resources gets free and can be deployed for other core initiatives. This also helps to convert the fixed cost to variable cost. The flexible scale offered by the service providers also help to shorten the test cycle, resulting in a faster time to market.

AMAZON WEB SERVICES (AWS)

Amazon Cloud Computing Platform provides the following services in a quite cost effective manner.

- Simple Storage Solution (S3)
- Elastic Computing Cloud (EC-2)
- Simple DB
- Simple Queue Service (SQS)

AMAZON EC2

Amazon Elastic Block Store (EBS) offers persistent storage for Amazon EC2 instances. Amazon EBS defines an EBS volume that provides off-

Figure 4. Risks and Mitigation in Cloud computing

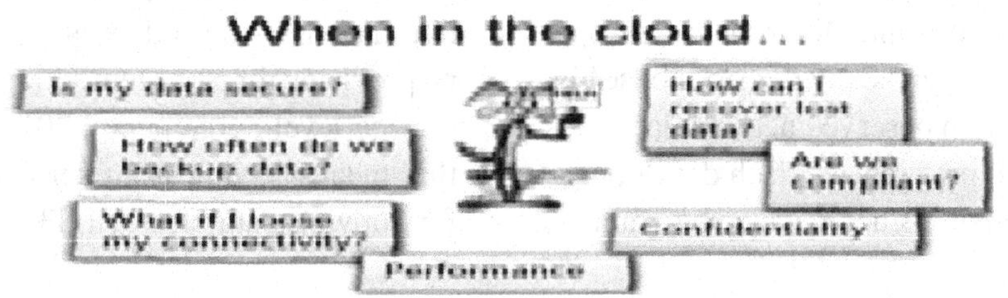

instance storage that persists independently from the life of an instance. Amazon EBS volumes are highly available and reliable which can be attached to a running Amazon EC2 instance and are standard block devices. EBS volumes offer greatly improved durability over local Amazon EC2 instance stores, as they are automatically replicated on the backend (in a single Availability Zone). For those wanting even more durability, EBS provides the ability to create point-in-time consistent snapshots of your volumes that are then stored in Amazon S3, and automatically replicated across multiple Availability Zones. These snapshots can be used as the starting point for new Amazon EBS volumes, and can protect data for long term durability. EBS is ideal for databases and file systems.

Features

Total boot time of an Amazon EC2 instance is related to the size of an Amazon AMI, Amazon EC2 (Linux) allows the user to boot an instance of a server in the range of few minutes ("Amazon simple storage service," n.d.). This guarantees a near instant availability of additional servers in cases where an application needs to scale up dynamically. This is typically the case when slash dotting occurs ("RightScale," n.d.). Once these servers are up and running, there is no CPU latency observed, since EC2 works on Oxen virtualization, which allows each virtual CPU time of its own, with no sharing.

Elastic Compute Cloud employs a pay-as-you-go model with no minimal fee from the user for the usage. The services are available in two regions, namely, the US and Europe. There are four unique availability zones in the US whilst there are two unique availability zones in Europe. This allows a developer the freedom to choose his/her region, based on observed network latencies and geographical preferences. Each developer is given full control of his/her instance by granting root access authority to the machine. This enables a user to deploy desired custom software on each instance with administrative rights and configure application level security settings as well. In order to run the same configuration on multiple servers, the same image is booted n times across n Amazon servers. Hence, minimizes system administration efforts. There are startup companies such Right Scale that have suite of system administration tools suitable for managing Amazon infrastructure.

EC2 is particularly cost-effective given its near instant launching of server instances and pay-per-use cost model for applications which experience unpredictable workload patterns. This type of demand pattern necessitates dynamic scaling of servers in order to satisfy Quos guarantees. Amazon EC2 provides wide range of machines, application runtime and development environment which allows a developer choice of required platforms and environment, such as REST, SOAP APIs, in several languages (Java, PHP, etc.) are provided in order to integrate this functionality within code as well (Hazelhurst, 2008).

As an added security feature, Amazon allows users to only present Web servers to the Internet. This is done by not having a public IP address associated with every EC2 instance running. For a multi-tier application, you can choose to have a public IP address on your Web server and have just an internal IP address on your database server. To access the database server, you would have to log into the Web server and then sash, telnet or RDP (Remote Desktop Protocol) from there to the database server.

Limitations

Once an EC2 instance is shut down, all data on that instance's hard disk is lost. Hence, there is no provision for persistent storage ("Amazon EC2 service level agreement," 2013). For user data, this means having a predefined backup policy for copying data between S3 and EC2. For system software, this backup is more difficult since changes may mean re-bundling and registering the new AMI which takes between 4 and 15 minutes depending on the size of the image and the power of the EC2 instance. This can be alleviated by taking a snapshot of EC2 instance every hour since cost of data transfer between EC2 and S3 is very cheap (i.e. 0.01 cent per 1 GB).

Amazon instances do not have static IP addresses. This means that every time an instance is shut down and started again, it acquires a different IP address. This is a huge drawback for applications that make use of mail servers. A mail server runs only with a static IP address. A reverse proxy approach in this case does not work because it is used as a measure to combat spam. One needs a different static IP address for different servers to be run; preferably in different class C networks, because search engines don't like dynamic IP addresses. Hence, the requirement for most developers today is a static IP for each running instance such that e-mail can be sent which can pass spam filters. Another issue with IP addresses is that DNS resolutions are not cached for an extended period of time and Amazon cannot guarantee the validity of an IP address at any given time. To overcome static IP address problem Amazon provide Elastic IP address service model which can be assigned as a static public IP to each EC2 instance.

EC2 provides only instance level support and no support in terms of dynamic scalability at the application level. This is a useful feature for most developers but is missing from EC2 today.

On the Operating system front, reserved instances available from EC2 currently support only variations of Linux. Also, no public Macintosh AMIs is available. While custom-made images can be created from scratch, for Linux, this customization is restricted to systems using the 2.6 kernel only. Lower compatibility versions of the Linux kernel are not supported. This would mean refactoring many legacy applications running on 2.4.x kernels.

Considering the pricing model, reserved instance charges are applicable only when instances are run in the same availability zone. EC2 also places a maximum threshold of 20 instances per account that can be run concurrently at any given time. To run more than 20, we are required to fill an additional form. Replication to local server incurs additional network cost. Amazon EC2 support, which is at the instance level only, is billed as an extra charge.

EC2 defines an Annual Uptime Percentage of at least 99.95% in their SLA. However, if the Annual Uptime Percentage for a customer drops below 99.95%, then the said customer is eligible to receive a service credit equal to 10% of their bill for the eligible credit period. Presently, Amazon does not offer SLA on I/O performance of EC2 instance. Furthermore, Amazon EC2 is based on X86 hardware therefore we cannot deploy X64 (Ultras ARC) application on Amazon EC2. Finally, if an application is running on 8 cores CPU then it is not possible to migrate or deploy such an application on an Amazon EC2 platform.

AMAZON S3

Amazon Simple Storage Service (S3) provides a simple Web services interface that can be used to store and retrieve any amount of data, at any time, from anywhere on the Web. It gives any developer access to the same highly scalable, reliable, fast, inexpensive data storage infrastructure that Amazon uses to run its own global network of Web sites ("Amazon S3 libraries," n.d.).

THE S3 STORAGE MODEL

S3 stores data as named "objects" that are grouped in named "buckets" ("Amazon S3 libraries," n.d.). Buckets must be explicitly created before they can be used; each user may create up to 100 buckets.

Bucket names are globally unique; an S3 user attempting to create a bucket named "food" will be told that the bucket name is already in use. S3 is designed to primarily store large objects and hence objects may contain any byte string between 1 and 5 Bytes. For each object, S3 maintains a name, modification time, an access control list, and up to 4 Kbytes of user-defined metadata. Each bucket has an access control list allowing read or read/write permission to be given to other specific AWS users or to the world.

Features

S3 provides persistent storage for EC2 instances, the one thing that EC2 instances lacks. Moreover, S3 is fast and scalable. It allows an unlimited number of objects to be stored in buckets. Additionally, in order to increase availability of data, Amazon allows sharing of an S3 bucket between multiple EC2 instances. Snapshots of user or application data can be stored on S3 and can be accessed from any availability zone.

In terms of throughput, S3 has maximum throughput (single threaded) of approximately 20 MB/s or 25 MB/s (multithreaded) for a small instance. This rises to 50 MB/s on the large and extra large instances. S3 is slow for file listing and search is by prefix only. Thus, S3 can be performance optimized by using multiple buckets. The write performance is optimized by writing keys in sorted order.

Amazon has public APIs for S3 in Java, PHP etc, to facilitate the use of storing and retrieving data from S3, from within the application (SlideShare, n.d.). S3 follows a similar pay model as that of EC2, with no upfront minimal fees to be paid to Amazon for usage of S3.

Limitations

S3 is subject to "eventual consistency" which means that there may be a delay in writes appearing in the system. In terms of performance S3 suffers from higher latency as well as higher variability in latency. S3 write latency can also be higher than read latency. S3 delivers dramatically faster throughput on large objects than small ones due to a high per-transaction overhead. It is designed to quickly fail requests that encounter problems; it is the client's responsibility to retry failed requests until they succeed. This is different than traditional Web servers, which implement a "best effort" policy for satisfying Web requests.

S3 supports PUT, GET, and DELETE primitives, but there is no way to copy or rename an object, move an object to a different bucket, or change an object's ownership. Although these primitives can be implemented by combining PUT, GET and DELETE operations, it can take days to move a few terabytes of data from one bucket to another using successive PUTs and GETs. Furthermore, moving data via this strategy can result in significant data transfer charges unless the GETs and PUTs are done from EC2.

S3 allows only 100 buckets per user account. If additional buckets are needed, we are required to fill out an application form that needs to be approved by Amazon. Maximum storage size of an object in a bucket is 5GB. S3 SLA describes a monthly uptime percentage of at least 99.9% during any monthly billing cycle ("Amazon EC2 libraries for Java, PHP, Perl, C#., " n.d.). For application critical data this may prove to be insufficient.

Fundamentally, S3 is not ideal for querying with respect to database and content distribution with respect to file system. When storing object data, developers can associate metadata with each object. Metadata entries are key-value associations that are stored with the object. Developers may create any metadata entries necessary to support the application. Amazon doesn't publish a maximum number of metadata entries that may be associated with an object ("Amazon elastic block storage," n.d.).

All types of business or services may not be comfortable with storing their data in the "cloud" especially those with extremely sensitive and confidential data e.g. financial ("Amazon elastic block storage," n.d.). Although, S3 promises 99.99% of uptime SLA, there were 2 major outages in February and July of 2008 which caused major disruption to services such as Twitter. Back in 2007 S3 had read/write speed issue ("Amazon elastic block storage," n.d.). Finally, Amazon does not provide de-duplication (version difference) at s3 level.

AMAZON EBS

Amazon Elastic Block Store (EBS) offers persistent storage for Amazon EC2 instances ("AWS public datasets," n.d.). Amazon EBS defines an EBS volume that provides off-instance storage that persists independently from the life of an instance. Amazon EBS volumes are highly available and reliable which can be attached to a running Amazon EC2 instance and are standard block devices. EBS volumes offer greatly improved durability over local Amazon EC2 instance stores, as they are automatically replicated on the backend (in a single Availability Zone). For those wanting even more durability, EBS provides the ability to create point-in-time consistent snapshots of your volumes that are then stored in Amazon S3, and automatically replicated across multiple Availability Zones. These snapshots can be used as the starting point for new Amazon EBS volumes, and can protect data for long term durability. EBS is ideal for databases and file systems.

Features

EBS provides unlimited size of block storage that can be formatted using a file system of your choice (ext3 for Linux and NTFS for Windows). No eventual consistency exists for EBS and it exhibits lower latency with less variation. It also has write-back caching policy for very low write latency. Unlike S3, it has a fast directory listing and searching.

EBS offers the same characteristic as "pay-as-you-go" model and no minimal fees, as the rest of the Web Services offered by Amazon. Snapshots of public datasets related to demographics, biology, and chemistry are available and new volumes can be pre-loaded with these datasets. Various databases currently available on AWS include Human Genome Data from ENSEMBL, Pub HEM Library from Indiana University and various census databases from the US Census Bureau.

Limitations

EBS volumes can only be attached to instances running in the same zone. Hence, in order to access data stored on a volume, say *vol1*, running in zone us-east-1c to an instance running in us-east-1b, we would require to create a snapshot of the volume *vol1* and load this snapshot into a newly created volume, say *vol2*, in zone us-east-1b. This incurs additional data transfer cost.

For a 20 GB volume, Amazon estimates an annual failure rate for EBS volumes to be from 1-in-200 to 1-in-1000. The failure rate increases as the size of the volume increases. Therefore you either need to keep an up-to-date snapshot on S3, or have a backup of the contents somewhere else such that it can be restored quickly to meet your needs in the event of a failure. EBS has a maximum throughput defined by the network. This is approximately 25 MB/s on a small instance and 50 MB/s on large instances and 100 MB/s on extra large instances.

The maximum number of volumes that can concurrently be used by an account is. Use of additional volumes requires an additional request form to be filled out. Amazon does not provide re-duplication at EBS Level. Amazon does not offer SLAs on EBS. Only one EC2 instance can be connected to an EBS volume i.e. sharing a single EBS volume amongst two or more EC2 instances is not feasible The Elastic Compute Cloud or EC2 is a Web service that provides resizable compute capacity in the cloud. Figure 5 shows how a user interacts with AWS:

Figure 5. Interaction of users with AWS

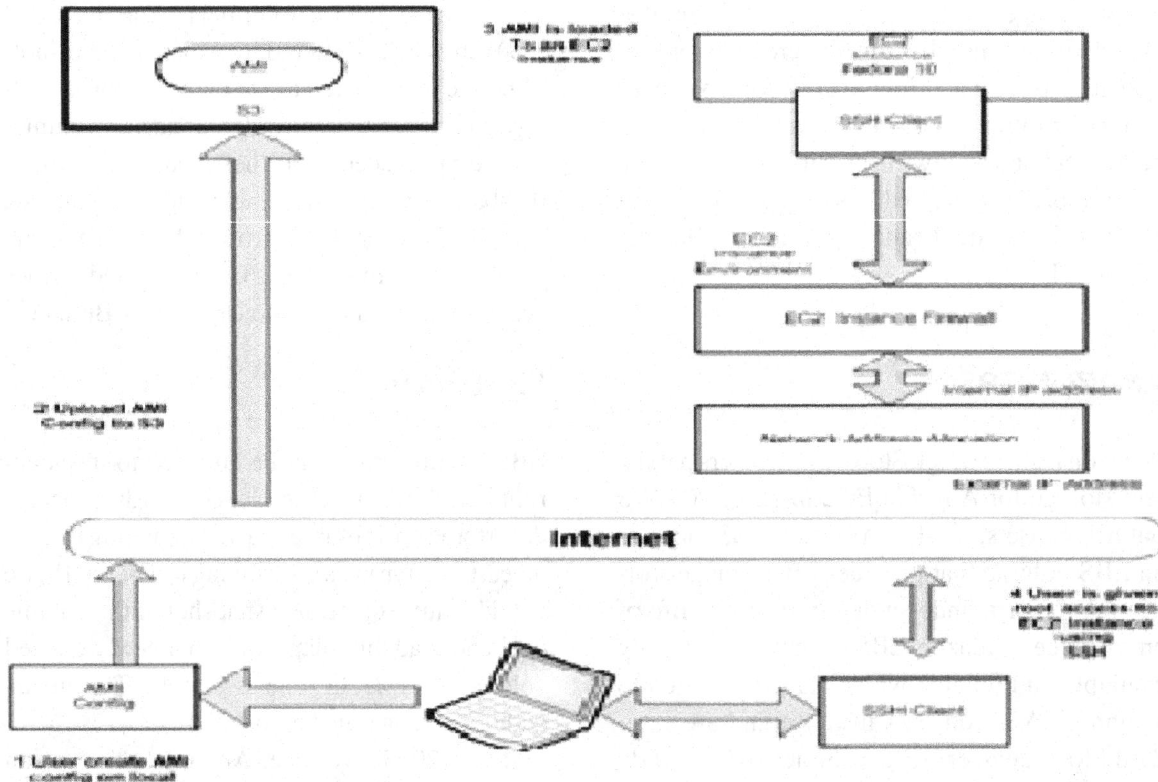

AWS SECURITY

Cloud Computing with Amazon entails storage of data, applications and its management within a controlled and secure premise. Hence, issues regarding end-to-end privacy and security become more complex. Amazon guarantees physical data security by housing data centers in nondescript buildings and employing military grade security.

Authentication

AWS supports two different schemes for identification and authorization. One uses a 40-character secret key and the HMAC algorithm to sign each request. The second scheme is based on X.509 certificates. Amazon creates each user's secret key and X.509 certificate and allows them to be downloaded from the dashboard. Access to the dashboard is granted to anyone with an Amazon username (an email address) and a password. AWS users may also upload their own X.509 certificates that they may have from other sources; these certificates are then trusted. Because all authentication credentials can be downloaded from the AWS Web dashboard, any individual with access to an account's password has full access to all of the resources pertaining to the account in question.

AMAZON EC2 SECURITY MODEL

For Amazon EC2, security is provided on several levels i.e. host OS, guest OS or Instance using firewalls and signed API calls ("Simple storage service APIs: Sample code and libraries," n.d.). Host OS security relies on cryptographically strong SSH keys that the user uses to log into the system.

On the other hand, guest OS security enables the user to grant root access to these machines. Use of privilege escalation, SSH key pairs or user generated key pairs is encouraged.

For network security, Amazon defines Security groups, which are akin to firewalls. Security groups in EC2 have a default "block-all-incoming-traffic" policy. A customer must manually open up ports for allowing inbound traffic to an instance. The traffic is configurable by protocol, port number, CIDR block or individual IP addresses. Similarly, outbound traffic can be controlled using pintables ("AWS toolikit for eclipse," n.d.). An instance can have multiple security groups, each with similar policies grouped together. As an additional layer of security, a firewall is configurable only by someone who possesses both the private key and the X.509 certificate, attached to each account. Given this setting of the firewall and the guest OS, it is possible to isolate two separate classes of administrators, the host administrator and the cloud administrator.

All calls to APIs must be signed with the account's X.509 certificate or the Secret Access Key. Amazon also recommends that the developer encrypt the API call using SSL, for added protection.

In order to safeguard the physical CPU (which runs instances) being compromised, Amazon uses a highly customized version of Oxen ("Amazon EC2 API tools," n.d.). This runs all the guest OS privileged instructions via the hypervisor, with elevated access to the actual machine underneath being impossible. Instance isolation on the same physical machine is achieved by placing the firewall (mentioned above) between the actual physical interface and the virtual interface of the instance. This ensures isolation similar to that offered by physically placing the machines apart. Physical RAM is protected using similar mechanisms.

To start or stop an instance, a user must possess the X.509 certificate and the private key. However, this can also be achieved via the AWS Management Console through a simple login and password. This creates vulnerability in the whole system. Moreover, AWS EC2 does not provide customer accessible audit log for forensic analysis in case of a breach.

MITIGATING ATTACKS

AWS provides standard provisions to circumvent attacks like Distributed Denial of Service (DDoS), man-in-the-middle attacks using mitigation techniques such as SYN cookies, limiting bandwidth, mutual authentication. IP spoofing is not possible and port scanning is ineffective, since all incoming ports are blocked by the security group default. The packet sniffer is rendered ineffective by the hypervisor, which does not deliver packets not addressed to it, even if the sniffer is placed in promiscuous mode. However, as with any new technology, there are bound to be exploits which are yet to be exposed. But they're more likely to be part of the management tools used to transfer and modify cloud data as well as remote tools used to access applications in the cloud than the clouds themselves.

AMAZON S3 SECURITY MODEL

Security for S3 poses a different problem. This is primarily due to the storage model employed by S3. The key challenges include being able to control access to the data in a bucket or an object. Hence, Amazon provides default bucket level and object level access controls mechanisms using an Access Control List (ACL) to prevent data from being read by anyone. Amazon S3 data is sent on end-to-end SSL encrypted links. This prevents data leakage or theft while in transit. Encrypted file systems are not provided by default, so the customer has to encrypt their data before storing it on S3 ("Simple storage service APIs: Sample code and libraries," n.d.). This might be because key escrow is difficult and taking responsibility for keys that essentially "lock" customer data is a daunting responsibility.

Since EBS is relatively new, it remains to be seen how the security policies around EBS are defined with respect to snapshots from EBS to S3 being encrypted and use of SSL for sending data between an EC2 instance and EBS volume.

TOOLS: AWS MANAGEMENT

AWS provides command line tools to control EC2 instances (Hazelhurst, 2008; "Amazon EC2 service level agreement," 2013). These are Java based tools for manipulating the Amazon Machine Image (AMI) and API tools for operations related to rebinding images, registering, and so forth. The Amazon EC2 AMI Tools are command-line utilities to help bundle an AMI, create an AMI from an existing machine or installed volume, and upload a bundled AMI to Amazon S3 ("Amazon EC2 service level agreement," 2013). The API tools serve as the client interface to the Amazon EC2 Web service and are used to register and launch instances, manipulate security groups, and so forth. ("Amazon EC2 AMI tools," n.d.).

Additionally, a free plug-in called AWS Toolkit for Eclipse allows developers to develop, deploy, and debug Java applications using Amazon Web Services ("AWs toolkit for eclipse," n.d.). The AWS Toolkit for Eclipse, based on the Eclipse Web Tools Platform, guides Java developers through common workflows and automates tool configuration, such as setting up remote debugger connections and managing Tomcat containers. The steps to configure Tomcat servers, run applications on Amazon EC2, and debug the software remotely are now done seamlessly through the Eclipse IDE.

Elastic Fox is a GUI extension for Mozilla Firefox 2.x that allows users to perform the same functions as those performed by the EC2 AMI and API tools ("ElasticFox extension for Mozilla Firefox, developer tools," n.d.). ElasticFox also integrates functions for performing actions related to EBS. S3Fox Organizer is a similar GUI-based tool related to S3, that allows one to upload objects to S3, create and destroy buckets as well as making file and folder management easy for S3 ("AWS management console," n.d.). S3Fox also enables access control to be defined to objects in various buckets.

AWS Management Console is another Web based tool that allows manipulations of all the Amazon services It allows users to start/stop EC2 instances, attach/detach EBS volumes, create snapshots, pre-load an EBS volume with a snapshot or a dataset, create security groups, bundle images, look for new AMIs, and a plethora of other such functions. A similar tool, called Cloud Studio is also used by enterprises to manage their AWS Cloud ("Cloud studio," n.d.).

Cloud42 is another GUI-based management as a service solution to Amazon Cloud Computing ("Cloud42," n.d.). Cloud42 allow management of EC2 resources and provides additional functionality to administrate EC2 AMIs and instances. Apart from the GUI Cloud42 offers a well-designed Web service interface which allows invocation of several functionalities from within other applications or even to orchestrate EC2 instances using BPEL processes. The tool features some enhanced functionalities like transferring files between your computing clouds or from an AWS S3 bucket. Furthermore, it is possible to remotely execute arbitrary commands on a running EC2 server instance only by using the GUI or the Web service interface. It also provides a notification mechanism that can be used to subscribe any kind of endpoint to event messages sent from EC2 instances according to the publish/subscribe pattern.

JungleDisk is another tool that provides reliable online backup and storage powered by Amazon S3 and Rackspace ("JungleDisk," n.d.).

SAMPLE TESTBED PLATFORM ON AWS

Let us consider the sample ANT pipeline shown earlier as an example to understand our solution. We created an AMI as a foundation for the executing the following activities on the various instances. A sample testbed platform can be seen in Figure 6 below.

- Source Code Analysis
- Unit / Integration Testing
- Acceptance Testing
- Load Testing

BENEFITS

Applying Amazon cloud computing facilities helped us accrue many benefits.

- **Reduction in Cost:** Capital Expenditure (owing to zero infrastructures)
- **Reduction in Cost:** Operational Expenditure (owing to a small "rent")
- **Reduction in Execution Time:** Rapid Feedback cycle

Figure 6. Sample testbed platform

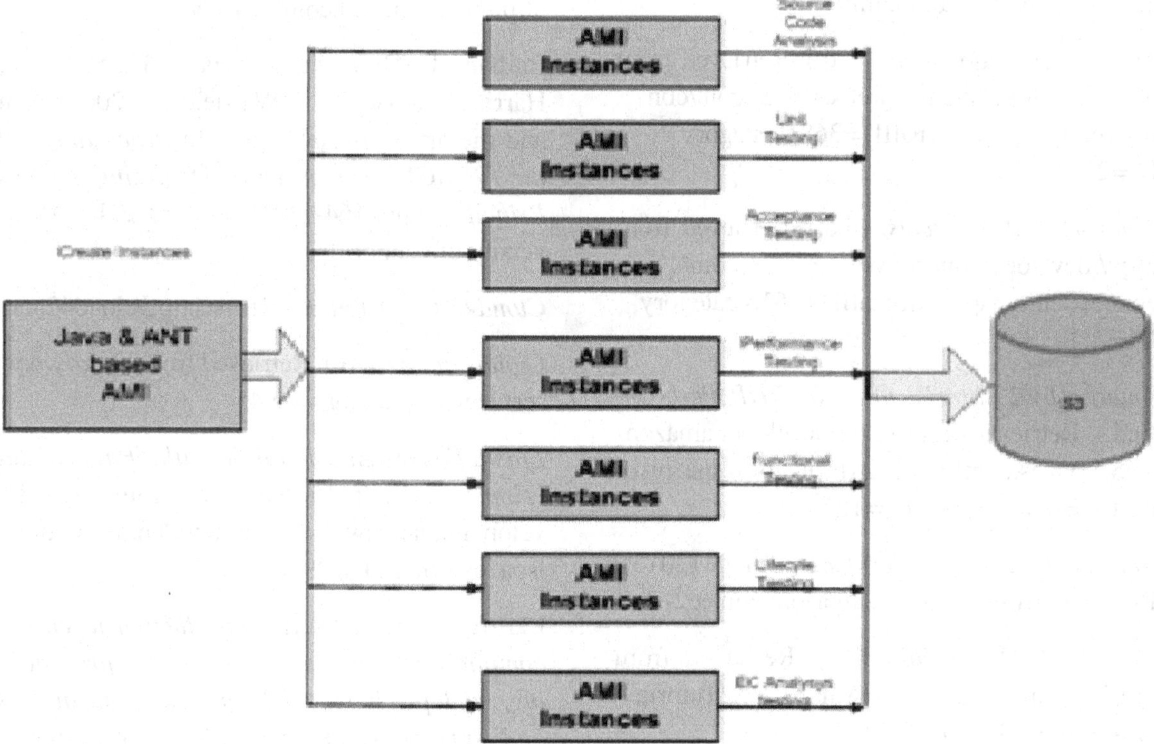

- **Quick Turn-Around:** Increase in Productivity
- **Reduction in Risk:** Increase in Quality

REFERENCES

S3Fox. (n.d.). Retrieved from http://www.s3fox.net/

Alestic. (n.d.). *Ubuntu on Amazon EC2*. Retrieved from http://alestic.com/

Amazon S3 libraries. (n.d.). Retrieved from http://developer.amazonwebservices.com/connect/kbcategory.jspa?resultOffset=0&categoryID=188

Amazon S3 service level agreement. (2013). Retrieved from http://aws.amazon.com/s3-sla/

Amazon autoscaling. (n.d.). Retrieved from http://aws.amazon.com/autoscaling/

Amazon EC2 AMI tools. (n.d.). Retrieved from http://developer.amazonwebservices.com/connect/entry.jspa?externalID=368&categoryID=251

Amazon EC2 API tools. (n.d.). Retrieved from http://developer.amazonWebservices.com/connect/entry.jspa?externalID=351&categoryID=251

Amazon EC2 libraries for Java, PHP, Perl, C#. (n.d.). Retrieved from http://developer.amazonwebservices.com/connect/kbcategory.jspa?resultOffset=45&categoryID=187

Amazon EC2 service level agreement. (2013). Retrieved from http://aws.amazon.com/ec2-sla/

Amazon EC2 tutorial. (n.d.). Retrieved from http://s3.amazonaws.com/AmazonEC2Tutorial/AmazonEC2Tutorial.html

Amazon elastic block storage (EBS). (n.d.). Retrieved from http://aws.amazon.com/ebs/

Amazon elastic compute cloud. (EC2). (n.d.). Retrieved from http://aws.amazon.com/ec2/

Amazon simple storage service (S3). (n.d.). Retrieved from http://aws.amazon.com/s3/

Armbrust, M., Fox, A., Griffith, R., Joseph, A., Katz, R., & Konwinski, A. ... Zaharia, M. (2009). *Above the clouds: A Berkeley view of cloud*. (Tech. Rep. No. UCB/EECS-2009-28). Berkeley, CA: University of California at Berkeley.

AWS management console. (n.d.). Retrieved from http://aws.amazon.com/console/

AWS public datasets. (n.d.). Retrieved from http://aws.amazon.com/publicdatasets/

AWS security white paper. (2008, September). Retrieved from http://s3.amazonaws.com/aws_blog/AWS_Security_Whitepaper_2008_09.pdf

AWS toolkit for eclipse. (n.d.). Retrieved from http://aws.amazon.com/eclipse/

Barham, P., Dragovic, B., Fraser, K., Hand, S., Harris, T., & Ho, A. ... Warfield, A. (2003). Xen and the art of virtualization. In *Proceedings of the 19th ACM Symposium on Operating Systems Principles* (pp. 164-177). Cambridge, UK: University of Cambridge.

Cloud42. (n.d.). Retrieved from http://cloud42.net/

Cloud studio. (n.d.). Retrieved from http://www.service-cloud.com/node/45

ElasticFox extension for Mozilla Firefox, developer tools. (n.d.). Retrieved from http://developer.amazonwebservices.com/connect/entry.jspa?externalID=609

Elastra Corp. (n.d.). *An introduction to elastic computing: A new software design, provisioning, and pricing model for online businesses and enterprises*. Retrieved from http://www.marketspaceadvisory.com/cloud/Envisioning-the-Cloud.pdf

Getting started with Amazon EC2. (n.d.). Retrieved from http://paulstamatiou.com/2008/04/05/how-to-getting-started-with-amazon-ec2

Google App Engine (GAE). (n.d.). Retrieved from http://code.google.com/appengine/

Hazelhurst, S. (2008). Scientific computing using virtual high-performance computing: A case study using the Amazon elastic computing cloud. In *Proceedings of the 2008 Annual Research Conference of the South African Institute of Computer Scientists and Information Technologists on IT Research in Developing Countries: Riding the Wave of Technology* (pp. 94-103). Wilderness, South Africa: University of Witswatersrand.

JungleDisk. (n.d.). Retrieved from http://jungledisk.com

Lakhe, P., Mane, D., & Nakrani, S. (2009). *Guidelines to create and run an Amazon Machine Image (AMI) on Amazon using Linux. (Tech Rep.)*. Pune, India: Tata Research Development and Design Centre.

Microsoft Azure. (n.d.). Retrieved from http://www.microsoft.com/azure/

RightScale. (n.d.). Retrieved from http://www.rightscale.com/

Simple storage service APIs: Sample code and libraries. (n.d.). http://developer.amazonwebservices.com/connect/kbcategory.jspa?categoryID=188

Slash dot effect. (n.d.). Retrieved from http://en.wikipedia.org/wiki/Slashdot_effect

SlideShare. (n.d.). *Intro to Amazon S3*. Retrieved from http://www.slideshare.net/parn09/intro-to-amazon-s3-presentation

Vogels, W. (2008, October). *A Head in the clouds: The power of infrastructure service*. Paper presented at the First Workshop on Cloud Computing and its Applications (CCA 2008). Chicago.

KEY TERMS AND DEFINITIONS

AMI: Eucalyptus Machine Image
AWS: Amazon Web Services
CIO: Chief Information Officer
CTO: Chief Technology Officer
EC2: Elastic Compute Cloud
OPEX: Operational Expenditure
ROI: Return on Investment
S3: Simple Storage Service
SLA: Service Level agreement

Chapter 13
Comparative Study of Amazon Web Services (AWS) and Online Computer Library Services (OCLC) Web Players

Ravikant M. Deshpande
Visvesvaraya National Institute of Technology, Nagpur

Suvarna H. Paunikar
Visvesvaraya National Institute of Technology, Nagpur

Nilima D. Likhar
Visvesvaraya National Institute of Technology, Nagpur

ABSTRACT

Cloud computing is a model to provide on-demand access of configurable computing services and resources to the network users without direct service provider interaction. Cloud computing is one of the new buzzwords in the business world. It is a generic term for computing solution where software and services are provided over the Internet. Also the cloud computing delivered and managed IT services in several different forms such as Platform, Infrastructure, and to publish Web services for the patrons. In this chapter we discuss technology, benefits, and initiatives and mainly compare about the Amazon Web Services (AWS) and Online Computer Library Centre (OCLC) cloud service players.

INTRODUCTION

Cloud Computing technology is a widely touted as the next revolution on the Internet in the delivery of scalable computing resources on demand. Cloud computing is a shift from product to service. Enterprises no longer buy and own computing resources as a product; instead they source them from the cloud as a service via Internet (Dhawan, 2013).

Cloud computing is the delivery of computing services over the Internet. Cloud services allow individuals and businesses to use software

DOI: 10.4018/978-1-4666-4631-5.ch013

and hardware that are managed by third parties at remote locations. Examples of cloud services include online file storage, social networking sites, Webmail, and online business applications. The cloud computing model allows access to information and computer resources from anywhere that a network connection is available. Cloud computing provides a shared pool of resources, including data storage space, networks, computer processing power, and specialized corporate and user applications (Office of the Privacy Commissioner of Canada, n.d.).

TYPES OF CLOUD PLAYERS

Google

Google technologies that use cloud computing (including Gmail, Google Calendar, Google Docs, Google App Engine, and Google Cloud Storage among others) provide familiar, easy-to-use products and services for business and personal/consumer settings. These services enable users to access their data from Internet-capable devices. This common cloud computing environment allows CPU, memory, and storage resources to be shared and utilized by many users while also offering security benefits. Google provides these cloud services in a manner drawn from its experience with operating its own business, as well as its core services like Google Search Security is a design component of each of Google's cloud computing elements, such as data storage, server assignment, compartmentalization, and processing (Google, 2012).

LibraryThing

LibraryThing is an online service to help people catalogue their books easily. The people can access a catalogue from anywhere even on their mobile phone. Because everyone catalogues together, LibraryThing also connects people with the same books, comes up with suggestions for what to read next, and so forth.

LibraryThing is a full-powered cataloguing application, searching the Library of Congress, all five national Amazon sites, and more than 690 world libraries. Users can edit their information, search and sort it, "tag" books with their own subjects, or use the Library of Congress and Dewey systems to organize their collection. LibraryThing uses Amazon and libraries that provide open access to their collections with the Z39.50 protocol. The protocol is used by a variety of desktop programs, notably bibliographic software like EndNote. LibraryThing appears to be the first mainstream Web use (LibraryThing, n.d.).

Reed Elsevier

Reed Elsevier is a world leading provider of professional information solutions. The company delivers improved outcomes to professional customers across industries, helping them make better decisions, get better results and be more productive (Reed Elsevier, 2013).

SeerSuite

SeerSuite is an application toolkit for search engines and digital libraries, that is, CiteSeerX. It includes automatic Metadata extraction, citation graph, full text indexing, ranking autonomous citation indexing, Web UI. It is a framework for scientific and academic digital libraries and search engines built by crawling scientific and academic documents from the Web with a focus on providing reliable, robust services (Source Forge, 2013).

CiteSeerX

CiteSeerX is an evolving scientific literature digital library and search engine that has focused primarily on the literature in computer and information science. CiteSeerX aims to improve the dissemination of scientific literature and to provide improvements in comprehensiveness, usability, efficiency, functionality, availability, cost, and timeliness in the access of scientific and scholarly knowledge (CiteSeerX, 2011).

TerraPod

Terrapod is a science vodcast (video podcast) and Website for youth ages 10-18. Its goal is to encourage kids to use filmmaking ("TerraPod," n.d.).

Atmos

It is object-based cloud storage platform to store, archive and access unstructured content at scale. Atmos provides the essential building blocks for enterprises and service providers to transform to private, hybrid, and public cloud storage ("Atmos," n.d.).

Chronopolis Project

Spanning academic institutions and disciplines, the Chronopolis digital preservation network provides services for the long term preservation and curation of America's digital holdings. Because of the ephemeral nature of digital information, it is critical to organize and preserve the digital assets that represent society's intellectual capital – the core seeds of knowledge that are the basis of future research and education ("Chronopolis," 2011).

Zoho

Zoho offers a suite of online Web applications geared towards increasing productivity and offering easy collaboration. Customers use Zoho Applications to run their business processes, manage their information and be more productive while at the office or on the go, without having to worry about expensive or outdated hardware or software ("Zoho," 2013).

Salesforce

Salesforce India's game changing technology and customer relationship Management cloud software addresses to all customer interface concerns, from sales and marketing and to, streamlining enterprise and saving invaluable time and resources ("SalesForce," n.d.).

SERVICE DELIVERY MODELS

The Service Models deployed as per the requirements are as follows:

Software as a Service (SaaS)

In the cloud, Consumers use a service and purchase the ability to access or that is hosted in the cloud. A best example of this is Salesforce.com, is where for the necessary interaction between the consumer and the service is hosted as part of the service in the cloud. In this area Microsoft is expanding its involvement and in Microsoft Office 2010, the cloud computing options for its Office Web Apps are available to Office volume licensing customers and Office Web App subscriptions through its cloud-based Online Services.

Platform as a Service (PaaS)

In this service model, consumers purchase access to the platforms, enabling them to deploy their own software and applications in the cloud. The operating systems and network access are not possibly managed by the consumer, and there might be constraints as to which applications can be deployed.

Infrastructure as a Service (IaaS)

Consumers manage and control the systems over the operating systems, applications, storage, and possibly limited control of select networking

Figure 1. Types of cloud players

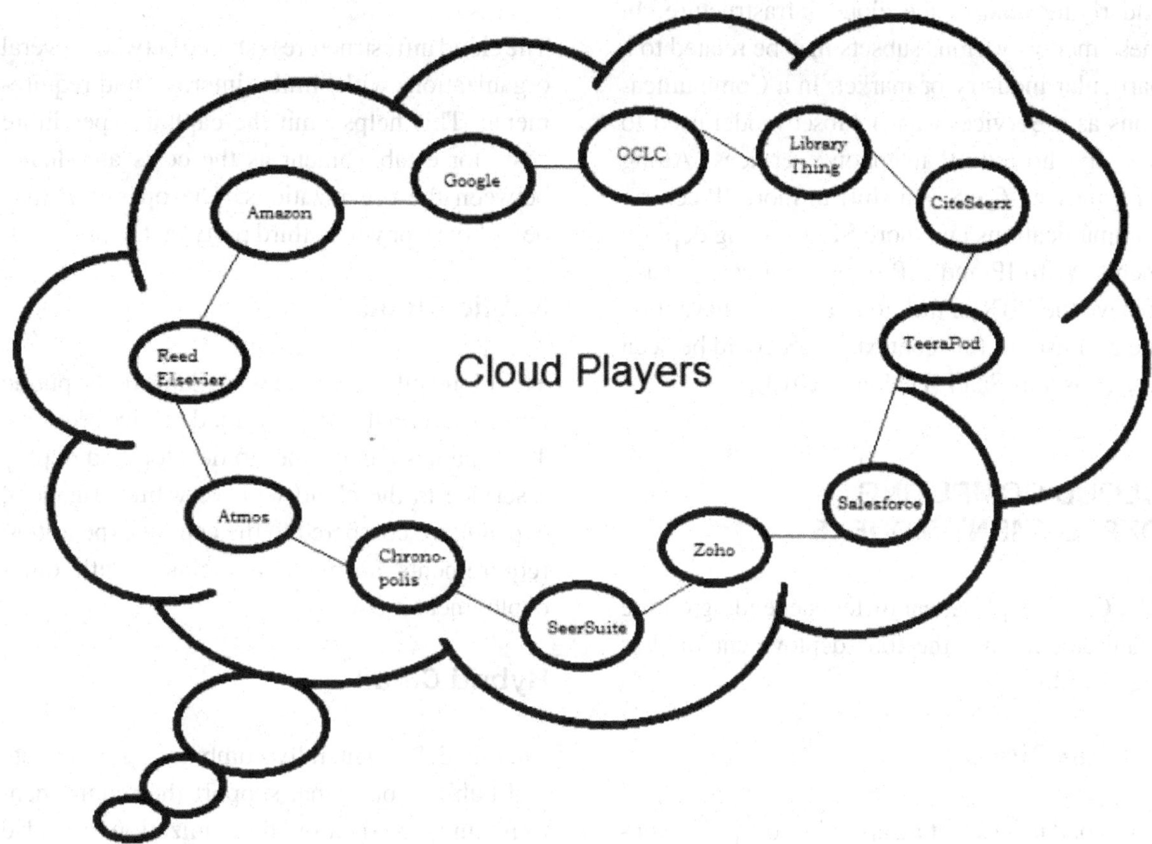

Figure 2. Cloud computing service model

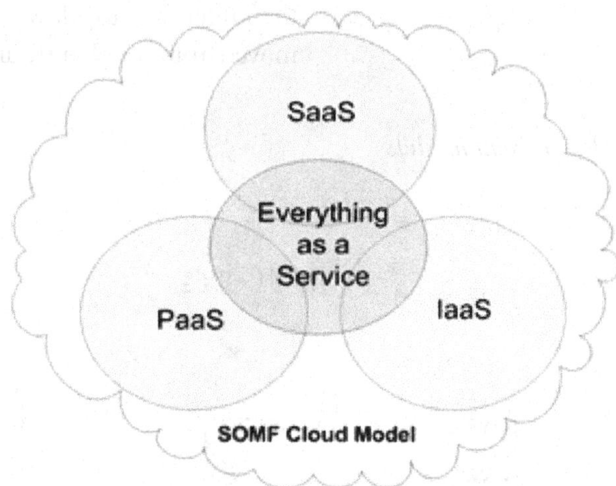

connectivity, (e.g., host firewalls), but docs not underlying control the cloud infrastructure. In these models various subsets may be related to a particular industry or market. In a Communications as a Service (CaaS) subset model used to describe hosted IP telephony services. Along with moving CaaS is a shift to more IP-centric communications and more SIP trunking deployments. With IP and SIP in place, it can be easy to have the PBX in the cloud as it is to have it on the premise. In this context, CaaS could be seen as a subset of SaaS (Dialogic, 2013).

CLOUD COMPUTING DEPLOYMENT MODELS

The Cloud deployment differs depending on the requirements and the four deployment models are as follows:

Private Cloud

The cloud infrastructure is deployed, and is maintained and operated by a single organization. The operation may be in-house or with a third party inside the premises.

Community Cloud

The cloud infrastructure is shared between several organizations with similar interests and requirements. This helps limit the capital expenditure costs for establishment as the costs are shared between the organizations. The operation may be in-house or with a third party on the premises.

Public Cloud

This cloud infrastructure is available to the public on a commercial basis by a cloud service provider. This enables a consumer to develop and deploy a service in the cloud with very little financial expenditure compared to the capital expenditure requirements normally associated with other deployment models.

Hybrid Cloud

This model is generally combination of private and public clouds that support the requirement to retain some data in an organization, and also the need to offer services in the cloud. The cloud infrastructure consists of a number of clouds of any type, but the clouds have the ability through their interfaces to allow data or applications to be moved from one cloud to another (Dialogic, 2013).

Figure 3. Cloud computing deployment models

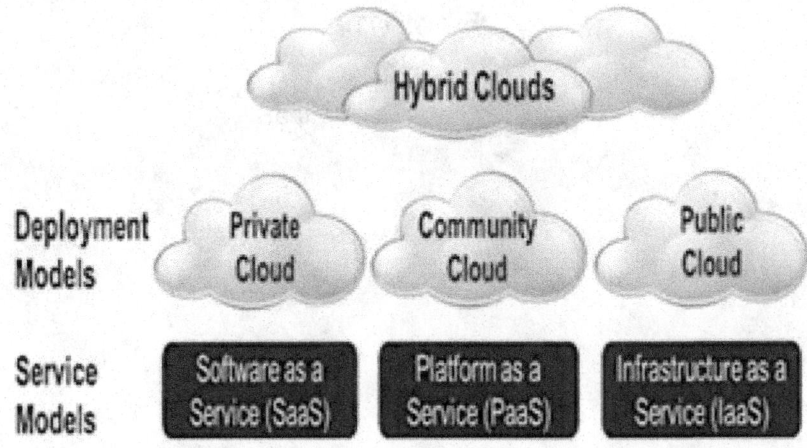

BENEFITS

The following are some of the possible benefits for those who offer cloud computing-based services and applications:

Cost Savings

Companies can reduce their capital expenditures and use operational expenditures for increasing their computing capabilities. This is a lower barrier to entry and also requires fewer in-house IT resources to provide system support.

Scalability/Flexibility

Companies can start with a small deployment and grow to a large deployment fairly rapidly, and then scale back if necessary. Also, the flexibility of cloud computing allows companies to use extra resources at peak times, enabling them to satisfy consumer demands.

Reliability

Services using multiple redundant sites can support business continuity and disaster recovery.

Maintenance

Cloud service providers do the system maintenance, and access is through APIs that do not require application installations onto PCs, thus further reducing maintenance requirements.

Mobile Accessible

Mobile workers have increased productivity due to systems accessible in an infrastructure available from anywhere (Dialogic, 2013).

HISTORY OF OCLC AND AWS

The original name of the OCLC was the Ohio College Library Centre. OCLC exist in 1967 through the collaboration of Ohio university presidents, vice presidents, in July 5, 1967 the group work for to sign the articles of incorporation for the nonprofit organization. The group met with Frederick G. Kilgour, a former Yale University medical school librarian, to design the shared cataloguing system. Kilgour wanted to merge the latest information storage and retrieval system of the time, the computer, with the oldest, the library. His vision of an active rather than passive system, where the library would go to the people was a revolutionary idea for 1967. The plan was to provide electronic catalogue through computer network and database in order to streamline to increase library management efficiency. The goal of this network and database was to bring libraries together to cooperatively keep track of the world's information in order to best serve researchers and scholars (Wikipedia, 2013b).

In 2006, Amazon Web Services Officially launched, provide online services for other Web sites or client-side applications. The AWS offer uses their applications to other developers. Amazon Web Services offerings are accessed over HTTP, using REST and SOAP protocols. In 2004, an engineer at Amazon presented a paper on how the company could make a profit on the infrastructure required to run the Amazon.com store. In November 2004 the first AWS service launched for public usage was Simple Queue Service. In June 2007, Amazon claimed that more than 330,000 developers had signed up to use Amazon Web Services (Wikipedia, 2013a).

INTRODUCTION OF CLOUD PLAYERS

Online Computer Library Centre

In 1967 OCLC is a worldwide library cooperative, owned, governed and sustained by members. The public purpose is a statement of commitment to each other – that the people will work together to improve access to the information held in libraries around the globe, and the best ways to reduce costs for libraries through cooperation. The public purpose is to establish, maintain and operate a computerized library network and to promote the evolution of library use, librarianship, and to provide processes and products for the benefit of library customers and libraries, including such objectives as increasing availability of library resources to people, library patrons and reducing the rising rate of library per-unit costs, all for the fundamental public purpose of furthering assisting to access and use of the ever-expanding body of worldwide scientific, literary and educational knowledge and information (OCLC, 2013a).

Amazon Web Services

In the cloud from Websites Amazon Web Services offers a complete set of infrastructure and application services that enable to run virtually everything and mobile applications to large data projects and enterprise applications. Today, hundreds of thousands of patrons of all classes take advantage of these services in nearly every industry, including public sector, education, financial services, insurance, Internet, real estate, retail, healthcare and media (Amazon Web Services, 2013).

SERVICES OF ONLINE COMPUTER LIBRARY CENTRE (OCLC)

OCLC WorldShare Management Services include cataloguing, acquisitions, license management and circulation that are a unified, Web-based environment and extends delivery tool for library users and a powerful discovery. The OCLC WorldShare Management Services modify libraries to share infrastructure costs and resources, as well as cooperate in ways that free from the restrictions of local hardware and software.

WorldShare Management Services

- **Shared Data:** The collective data connects WorldCat, publisher data, vendor records, local holdings records, knowledge base, authority records and more.
- **Entirely Web-Based:** To reallocate resources to more important projects and tasks. When no longer have to purchase hardware and software, or manage updates.
- **Radically-Improved Workflows:** Logical integration of ordering, receiving and cataloguing saves time.
- **Intuitive and Streamlined Staff Interfaces:** Common interface manages all physical and licensed and digital materials.
- **Increased Visibility on the Web:** OCLC partnerships direct users from the open Web straight to library.
- **Single Search Access:** Google-like searching with WorldCat Local the discovery interface for WorldShare Management Services delivers content from library and the world's library collections.

- **Applications from OCLC WorldShare Platform:** Sharing and use of new applications, Creation, enhances staff and patron experience (OCLC, 2013b).
- **Amlib:** The next generation of library and knowledge management.
    - It provides a single, integrated solution for all libraries include public, school, college, tertiary institutions, corporate or special.
    - To access a range of resources for everyday reference in one easy search provided through federated searching.
    - Supports the addition of electronic images, pictures and documents to catalogue records.

Amlib solution is based on:

- Excellence in customer support.
- State-of-the-art library software that is robust, proven and easy to use.
- Experience in helping libraries migrate to Amlib in a timely, professional manner (OCLC, 2013c).

1. CBS Metadata Management Solution

CBS comprise of components for online cataloguing, batch import and export of bibliographic and authority records, inter library loan and management information. In the systems Clients can choose to implement individual components in accordance with their requirements, to create a completely adapt solution.

In 1978 the shared cataloguing system known as GGC is first implementation of CBS. More than 200 libraries and documentation centres use the GGC every day to catalogue their collections. Thirty years later and the software are in use around the world. In recent years, OCLC has used CBS software as the foundation for a national resource sharing service in the UK, known as Unity. In 2008, new updating functionality was introduced, which enables CBS catalogues to update behind the scenes in real-time in WorldCat. Regional cataloguing activity can now be consistently integrated with global exposure on the Web of the world's library collections.

CBS can be used purely as a back-office utility or can be made publicly accessible and searchable through international standardised interfaces, like Z39.50, SRU or by using its own powerful search engine interface. In addition, it fully integrates with other discovery tools.CBS can be implemented either onsite as a hosted and maintained by OCLC or local installation (OCLC, 2013d).

Benefits

- The major library consortia used tried and tested software in all over the world for over thirty years.
- A partnership approach to developing catalogues and services based on CBS software.
- CBS offers complete flexibility in the choices a consortium has to make. Catalogues using CBS can be configured to handle multiple metadata types and formats and an install of the software can be hosted by OCLC or either onsite at a partner institution.
- Whatever the objectives of union catalogue activity might be to help shared cataloguing, interlibrary loan or end user resource discovery. CBS has a suite of constituent available for the job.
- Regional cataloguing activity can be synchronous with global exposure of library collections, through up to the minute updating on WorldCat (OCLC, 2013e).

Features

- **Batch Import**: It is used for batch loading bibliographic and authority records with efficient record conversion and matching/ merging facilities.
- **Batch Export**: It used for record conversion and sorting with ability to apply style sheets for layout.
- **Synchronisation**: It is use for online update function (SRU protocol). The client can synchronise with WorldCat and the target is used for loading updates in the CBS database from local or regional catalogues.
- **Management Information**: Providing online statistics about the system, usage and database characteristics. The data can be configured using Business Objects for presentation purposes.
- **Z39.50 and SRU Update**: It functions allowing local cataloguing clients to integrate local cataloguing processes with shared union cataloguing processes.
- **Interlibrary Loan Functionality**: To creation and maintenance of ILL requests with automatic holding analyses based on the detailed library holdings information maintained in the CBS union catalogue (OCLC, 2013e).

2. OLIB

From nearly two decades OLIB has served a wide range of health, education, government and other special libraries with software that satisfied their library management needs. OLIB has proven its worth in over three-hundred libraries around the world, furnish unique combination of library efficiency, ease-of-use and superior multi-media capabilities. It leads the way for libraries whose vision is to extend the reach of their service.

OLIB achieved another milestone in its evolution, with the launch of OLIB Web in 2008. OLIB Web provides a comprehensive range of staff management functionality required by libraries, but in a Web environment. There is no client software to be installed on library PCs, staff just click on the browser in any location, at any time.

OLIB Web can be run with a system distribute at the library site or it can be used in conjunction with OCLC's secure hosted environment in the UK to provide library with a fully hosted solution. This development has increased the range of OLIB service models now available, and is proving priceless to those wishing to sustain their bid for a functionally rich system at a cost within reach of most small to medium-sized libraries (OCLC, 2013f).

Benefits

- The Web View OPAC empowers users to help themselves by providing access to usefully packaged data, for example, reading lists and by furnishing self-service functions. It also reduces staff time spent on routine circulation queries. It capable the library to extend services beyond traditional catalogue searching to offer enquiry and purchase request facilities.
- Customisation via the Layout Manager tool provides the flexibility to broaden the scope of the catalogue to deliver information on any media type, with options to create user-defined catalogue screens for media as diverse as WWW sites and key contacts. In addition it able authorised library staff to 'customise' the system to meet local requirements in terms of ter-

minology, workflow and general working practices whilst maintaining a supportable environment.

- Compliance with wide range of library and IT standards and initiatives including MARC21, Z39.50, SIP, ISO ILL and OAI. It ensures interoperability with third-party systems and data sources, enabling bibliographic and user data import, cross-searching of third-party catalogues and integration with self-issue devices.
- Significant experience of data conversion from legacy systems ensures smooth and efficient data migration from current library management systems to OLIB. Also provide options to improve quality of data by removing inconsistencies and inaccuracies as part of the process, saving valuable staff time in manual data tidying whilst improving data recall (OCLC, 2013g).

Features

- Full range of library housekeeping modules.
- Choice of Web or Windows-based system.
- Hosted solution or local implementation.
- Sophisticated range of user services available in the Web View OPAC.
- Customisable input screens offering flexibility. [23]

3. SISIS-SunRise

The library management and service tasks SISIS-SunRise assists in both for in-house and cross-business processes. This opens up significant potential for optimizing business processes. The concept of standardized interfaces and using standard protocols (SIP2, Z39.50, RFID, etc.) simplifies the integration of any additional modules, new devices or services into the SISIS-SunRise application. Individual requirements can also be put into practice quickly and economically.

These open up a significant potential for optimizing business processes. For example, use a supplier's online order server to determine what media want to order, which people then order by e-mail or in XML format. The acquisition process is initiated and followed up in the SISIS-SunRise system, and the order is documented in the cataloguing and circulation system. Electronically available data, for example, delivery notes for issue entries, is processed electronically and directly transferred to the journals index ("SISIS-SunRise," 2013).

SISIS-SunRise completely provides all the requirements of a modern library system. Equipped with cutting-edge technology, flexible and user-friendly, it strengthens as a service provider and ables to continuously expand range of services. This applies to all work processes in library, from acquisitions and cataloguing (including external data processing) to circulation. From user searches in local and worldwide data holdings data can be made available on the Internet and in external systems. The system's high degree of flexibility means use it in academic and public libraries of any size, as well as in specialized libraries ("SISIS SunRise at a glance," 2013).

Benefits

- A modern, powerful library and information system.
- Standardized interfaces and protocols guarantee internal and external flexibility.
- Standards (Z39.50, SIP2) and the newest technology ensure connectivity.
- User-friendly and ergonomic user interface.
- Efficient and cost-effective ("SISIS SunRise at a glance," 2013).

Features

- Covers all the work processes of a library (acquisitions, journal and e-media management, catalogue, circulation, user searches, administration, statistics, etc.)
- A large number of additional service options can be integrated (book safeguarding, self-service, SDI service, automatic payment and posting processes, SMS and e-mail service, etc.)
- A cross-processes administration tool for all functional areas.
- Available modules include Acquisition, Cataloguing, Circulation, WebOPAC.
- Available add-on products include IDM Connector.
- Available add-on products unique to Sunrise include EC-Pay, ELLI, FIBU Interface, Sunrise e-Mail, Sunrise SMS ("SISIS SunRise at a glance," 2013).

4. Electronic Collection Management

One of the significant implementation of OCLC provides libraries with the tools to manage and maximize the use of their electronic collections. For adding the e-books, e-resources and digital items already indexed in WorldCat, OCLC is working with libraries and partners to build a comprehensive knowledge base of the e-collections licensed by all member libraries. The WorldCat knowledge base supports a complete set of applications to streamline and automate electronic collection management and put electronic materials in the hands of users wherever they start their search.

OCLC WorldShare License Manager makes together the two key features of electronic resource management – knowledge about licenses that govern their purchase and use, and linking technology that connects users to needed content in a single place. WorldShare License Manager helps library staff more effectively manage license agreements, rights, access and resolution to full text from the same interface, take out the need to devise work arounds to connect different systems. A globally maintained vendor information centre provides license templates for global management of public and shared licensing terms by staff at all participating libraries.

EZproxy is authentication and access software in the world's leading access and authentication solution. More than 2,500 institutions in over 60 countries have purchased EZproxy software. EZproxy helps provide users with remote access to Web-based licensed content offered by libraries, and is easy to set up and maintain. EZproxy is now also available as a hosted solution, giving libraries the option to outsource the set-up and ongoing management of their proxy configuration.

WorldCat Local included OpenURL resolution functionality, A–Z lists for e-journals and e-books, and a citation finder at no additional charge. This enables OCLC public interfaces to integrate instant link resolution with "View now" links in search results, from which users can link to the full-text resources they need.

Taking a service-oriented approach, several solutions utilize services from the WorldShare Platform to simplify and streamline the processes that accompany the management, discovery and delivery of electronic articles and e-books ("Electronic collection management," 2013).

DIGITAL COLLECTION MANAGEMENT

OCLC offers a digital background with a wide range of solutions to support the digital life cycle, including managing, sharing and preserving primary source materials. Whether they have digital collections of photos, audio/video files, documents, newspapers, maps or any combination of materials, OCLC can provided the expertise and services users need.

1. The Web Based Share Digital Collections

contentdm Digital Collection Management Software can provide everything in digital collections available to online researchers, anywhere. Whatever the format local history archives, newspapers, books, maps, slide libraries or audio/video—contentdm can handle the storage, management and delivery of collections to users across the Web.

2. Maximize Web Visibility of Digital Collections via WorldCat

With the help of efforts in building digital collections, the unique treasures are showcased on the Web. Priority given to resources for creating these collections, broadening visibility and access are of foremost importance. The WorldCat Digital Collection Gateway provides a self-service tool for uploading the metadata of unique digital content to WorldCat the premier database of library materials. Once metadata is in WorldCat, collections are more visible and discoverable by users who search WorldCat.org, as well as Google, Yahoo! and other popular Websites. The Gateway is compatible with all OAI-compliant repositories, such as contentdm, and is available at no pay ("Digital collection management," 2013).

3. Resource Sharing

OCLC WorldShare Interlibrary Loan is time saving new service that will replace WorldCat Resource Sharing, as part of libraries OCLC Resource Sharing subscriptions provides interlibrary lending tools. The new service centralizes workflows now managed in multiple systems, will provide new functionality to speed fulfilment of interlibrary loan requests, and will save time for library staff and library users. A phased in rollout is in progress, leading toward general availability in mid 2013.

WorldCat represents a broad range of subjects and languages. Also, the addition of new functionality and services, such as the WorldCat knowledge base and WorldShare License Manager, brings new features that speed digital delivery and enhance article sharing among libraries. These new features streamline staff article processing procedures and enhance customer service, making it possible to fill requests for electronic materials within hours.

4. WorldCat Resource Sharing

WorldCat Resource Sharing provides time-saving, efficient inter-library lending tools that simplify library workflows and connect information seekers to materials in 10,000 libraries in 40 countries. From 1979 the system has been continually updated and automated reducing staff time and effort and providing members with a high fill rate. Soon, the new WorldShare Interlibrary Loan service will go beyond traditional interlibrary loan to provide a truly integrated delivery solution for libraries. The service will integrate discovery and delivery of electronic, digital and print materials within a single interface. It will also support evolving workflow changes in libraries, such as the option to purchase needed items rather than borrow them ("Resource sharing," 2013).

SERVICES OF AWS

Compute and Networking

Amazon Elastic Compute Cloud (Amazon Ec2)

In the cloud computing Amazon Elastic Compute Cloud (Amazon EC2) is a Web based service that provides resizable compute capacity. It is designed to make Web-scale computing easier for developers. Amazon EC2's simple Web service interface allows acquiring and configuring capacity with minimal friction. It provides with complete control of computing resources and run on Amazon's proven computing environment. Amazon EC2 reduces the time required to obtain and boot new server instances to minutes, allowing to quickly scaling capacity, both up and down, as computing requirements change. Amazon EC2 changes the economics of computing by allowing paying only for capacity that actually use. Amazon EC2 provides developers the tools to build failure resilient applications and isolate themselves from common failure scenarios.

Amazon Ec2 Functionality

Amazon EC2 presents a true virtual computing environment, allowing using Web service interfaces to launch instances with a variety of operating systems, load them with custom application environment, manage network's access permissions, and run image using as many or few systems ("Amazon elastic compute cloud," 2013).

Amazon Route 53

Amazon Route 53 is a highly available and scalable Domain Name System (DNS) Web service. It is designed to give developers and businesses an extremely reliable and cost effective way to route end users to Internet applications by translating human readable names like www.example.com into the numeric IP addresses like *192.0.2.1* that computers use to connect to each other. Route 53 effectively connects user requests to infrastructure running in Amazon Web Services (AWS)–such as an Amazon Elastic Compute Cloud (Amazon EC2) instance, an Amazon Elastic Load Balancer, or an Amazon Simple Storage Service (Amazon S3) bucket – and can also be used to route users to infrastructure outside of AWS.

Amazon Route 53 Functionality

Amazon Route 53 has a simple Web-services interface that gets started in minutes. DNS records are organized into "hosted zones" that configure with Route 53's API. To use Route 53, simply:

- Subscribe to the service by clicking on the sign-up button on this page.
- Create a hosted zone that can store DNS records for domain. Upon creating the hosted zone, receive four Route 53 name servers across four different Top-Level Domains (TLDs) to help ensure a high level of availability.
- Hosted zone will be initially populated with a basic set of DNS records, including four virtual name servers that will answer queries for domain. If can add, delete or change records in this set using the AWS Management Console or by calling the *Change Resource Record Set* API. A list of supported DNS records is available.
- Inform the registrar with the registered domain name to update the name servers for domain to the ones associated with hosted zone ("Amazon route 53," 2013).

Storage and CDN

Amazon Simple Storage Service (Amazon S3)

Amazon S3 is storage for the Internet. It is designed to make Web-scale computing easier for developers. Amazon S3 provides a simple Web services interface that can be used to store and retrieve large amount of data, at any time, from anywhere on the Web. It gives any developer access to the same highly scalable, reliable, secure, fast, inexpensive infrastructure that Amazon uses to run its own global network of Web sites. The service goal is to maximize benefits of scale and to pass those benefits on to developers ("Amazon simple storage service," 2013).

Amazon Elastic Block Store (Ebs)

Amazon Elastic Block Store (EBS) provides block level storage volumes for use with Amazon EC2 instances. Amazon EBS volumes are network-attached, and persist independently from the life of an instance. Amazon EBS provides highly available, highly reliable, predictable storage volumes that can be attached to a running Amazon EC2 instance and exposed as a device within the instance. Amazon EBS is particularly suited for applications that require a database, file system, or access to raw block level storage ("Amazon elastic block store," 2013).

Aws Import/Export

AWS Import/Export accelerates moving large amounts of data into and out of AWS using portable storage devices for transport. AWS transfers data directly onto and off of storage devices using Amazon's high-speed internal network and bypassing the Internet. For significant data sets, AWS Import/Export is often faster than Internet transfer and more cost effective than upgrading your connectivity.

AWS Import/Export supports importing and exporting data into and out of Amazon S3 buckets in the US East (N. Virginia), US West (Oregon), US West (Northern California), EU (Ireland), and Asia Pacific (Singapore) Regions. The service also supports importing data into Amazon EBS snapshots in the US East (N. Virginia), US West (Oregon), and US West (Northern California) Regions. In addition, AWS Import/Export supports importing data into Amazon Glacier in the US East (N. Virginia), US West (Oregon), US West (Northern California), and EU (Ireland). To start using this service, click on the "Sign Up for AWS Import/Export" button ("AWS import/export," 2013).

Amazon CloudFront

Amazon CloudFront is a Web service for content delivery. It integrates with other Amazon Web Services to give developers and processes an easy way to distribute content to end users with low latency, high data transfer speeds, and no commitments.

Amazon CloudFront can be used to deliver entire Website, including dynamic, static and streaming content using a global network of edge locations. Requests for content are automatically routed to the nearest edge location, so content is delivered with the best possible performance. Amazon CloudFront is optimized to work with other Amazon Web Services, like Amazon Simple Storage Service (Amazon S3), Amazon Elastic Compute Cloud (Amazon EC2) Amazon Elastic Load Balancing, and Amazon Route 53. Amazon CloudFront also works seamlessly with any non-AWS origin server, which stores the original, definitive versions of files. Like other Amazon Web Services, there are no contracts or monthly commitments for using Amazon CloudFront – pay only for as much or as little content as actually deliver through the service ("Amazon CloudFront," 2013).

Databases

Amazon Relational Database Service (Amazon Rds)

Amazon Relational Database Service (Amazon RDS) is a Web service that makes it easy to set up, operate, and scale a relational database in the cloud. It provides cost-efficient and resizable capacity while managing time-consuming database administration tasks, freeing up to focus on applications and business. Amazon RDS gives access to the capabilities of a familiar MySQL, Oracle or Microsoft SQL Server database engine. This means that the code, applications, and tools already use today with existing databases can be used with Amazon RDS. Amazon RDS automatically patches the database software and backs up database, storing the backups for a user-defined retention period and enabling point-in-time recovery. Benefit from the flexibility of being able to scale the computer resources or storage capacity associated with Database Instance (DB Instance) via a single API call ("Amazon relational database service," 2013).

Amazon Redshift

Amazon Redshift is a fast, fully managed, petabyte-scale data warehouse service that makes it simple and cost-effective to efficiently analyze all data using existing business intelligence tools. It is optimized for datasets ranging from a few hundred gigabytes to a petabyte or more and costs less than $1,000 per terabyte per year, a tenth the cost of most traditional data warehousing solutions.

Features and Benefits

Amazon Redshift delivers fast query and I/O performance for virtually any size dataset by using columnar storage technology and parallelizing and distributing queries across multiple nodes. We've made Amazon Redshift easy to use by automating most of the common administrative tasks associated with provisioning, configuring, monitoring, and backing up, and securing a data warehouse.

Powerful security functionality is built-in. Amazon Redshift supports Amazon VPC out of the box and can encrypt all data and backups with just a few clicks. Once provisioned cluster can connect to it and start loading data and running queries using the same SQL-based tools use today ("Amazon Redshift," 2013).

Deployment and Management

Aws Management Console

Manage AWS, Wherever Are Access and manage Amazon Web Services through a simple and intuitive Web-based user interface. Or use the companion mobile app for Android to quickly view resources on-the-go. Making AWS Simpler to Access and Use the AWS Management Console provides a simple Web interface for Amazon Web Services. Log in using AWS account name and password. If enabled AWS Multi-Factor Authentication, it will be prompted for device's authentication code ("AWS management console," 2013).

Aws Identity and Access Management (Iam)

AWS Identity and Access Management (IAM) enable to securely control access to AWS services and resources for users. Using IAM can create and manage AWS users and groups and use permissions to allow and deny their permissions to AWS resources.

First time users should visit the IAM Best Practices section of IAM user guide. To get started using IAM, sign in to the AWS Management Console.

IAM also enables identity federation between corporate directory and AWS services. This lets use existing corporate identities to grant secure access to AWS resources, such as Amazon S3 buckets, without creating new AWS identities for those users ("AWS identity and access management," 2013).

Aws Cloud Formation

AWS Cloud Formation gives developers and systems administrators an easy way to create and manage a collection of related AWS resources, provisioning and updating them in an orderly and predictable fashion.

The use AWS Cloud Formation's sample templates or create own templates to describe the AWS resources, and any associated dependencies or runtime parameters, required to run application. don't need to figure out the order in which AWS services need to be provisioned or the subtleties of how to make those dependencies work. Cloud Formation takes care of this for. Once deployed, can modify and update the AWS resources in a controlled and predictable way allowing to version control AWS infrastructure in the same way as version control software. Can deploy and update a template and its associated collection of resources (called a stack) via the AWS Management Console, Cloud Formation command line tools or APIs. Cloud Formation is available at no additional charge, and pay only for the AWS resources needed to run applications ("AWS CloudFormation," 2013).

WEB, MOBILE, AND SOCIAL APPLICATIONS ON AWS

Web, Mobile, and Social included the collection of tools and technologies required to power Internet applications. AWS provides on-demand access to scalable Web and application servers, storage, databases, content delivery, cache, search and other application services that make it easier to build and run applications that deliver a great customer experience ("AWS applications," 2013).

Table 1 and Table 2 compare OCLC and AWS cloud players and services.

As per above table the comparative analysis shows that cloud based services is made based on some important parameters and competitive features which are decisive in the choice for the users.

CONCLUSION

OCLC's Digital Archive goes pretty far down the path of a preservation-worthy archive of digital files. Amazon's S3 is an inexpensive, network-oriented file hosting service, and as such it doesn't have many of the features built into that we seen in a preservation archive service (OCLC). Beyond raw file service, one would need to add layers of software and human activities to perform the functions that Digital Archive provides now. Looking at OCLC's Digital Archive and Amazon S3 is almost an apples-to-oranges comparison,

Table 1. Comparison of OCLC and AWS Cloud Players

Online Computer Library Services	Amazon Library Services
Definition–OCLC is a nonprofit, membership, computer library service and research organization dedicated to the public purposes of furthering access to the world's information and reducing information costs (Wikipedia, 2013b).	Definition–Amazon Web Services is a collection of remote computing services (also called Web services) that together make up a cloud computing platform, offered over the Internet by Amazon.com (Wikipedia, 2013a).
Benefits	**Benefits**
• Comprehensive, expedited access to partners' collections. • Access to restricted, non circulating, and special collections materials that partners would not normally lend. • Costs of interlibrary loan and document supply held to minimum through agreements to supply one another at fixed below-market prices. • On-site access for one's constituency: partners give each other's visiting faculty and scholars the same degree of access to collections and services that they provide for their own communities. • Collegiality, trust, mentoring, sharing expertise and going the extra mile. [43]	• No Upfront Investment–Replace upfront infrastructure investment with low monthly costs. • Low Ongoing Cost–Reduce your overall IT costs. • Flexible Capacity–Eliminate guessing on your infrastructure capacity needs. • Speed & Agility–Develop and deploy applications faster. • Apps not Ops–Focus on projects that differentiate your business, not the infrastructure: Cloud computing lets you shift resources away from data centre investments and operations and move them to innovative new projects. • Global Reach–Take your apps global in minutes: Whether you are a large global company or small start-up, you may have potential customers around the world (Amazon Web Services, 2013).

Table 2. Comparison between OCLC & AWS Services

Types of Services	OCLC	AWS
System Management	✓	✓
Physical Security	✓	✓
Data Security	✓	✓
Data Backups	✓	×
Disasters Recovery	✓	Unclear
Virus Checking	✓	×
Content Delivery	✓	✓
Metadata Management Solution	✓	×
Resource Sharing	✓	×
Networking	✓	✓
Digital Archive	✓	×
Online Databases	✓	✓
Terminology Services	✓	×
Cataloguing	✓	×
Web Traffic (Repository Service)	✓	✓
Special Collection	✓	×
Electronic Data Exchange	✓	×
Simple Storage Service	×	✓
Software Service	✓	✓
Mobile Application Service	×	✓

both in price and in functionality. Comparing functionality first, S3 is missing critical components of a preservation storage system namely, rigorous access control and a content backup/restore facility. Comparing costs, though, S3 is dramatically cheaper and OCLC is high costing. But the functionality playing field in OCLC is more featured and huge amount of major service in the OCLC. So the OCLC is better than AWS.

REFERENCES

Amazon CloudFront. (2013). Retrieved from http://aws.amazon.com/cloudfront/

Amazon elastic block store. (2013). Retrieved from http://aws.amazon.com/ebs/

Amazon elastic compute cloud. (2013). Retrieved from http://aws.amazon.com/ec2/

Amazon redshift. (2013). Retrieved from http://aws.amazon.com/redshift/

Amazon relational database service. (2013). Retrieved from http://aws.amazon.com/rds/

Amazon route 53. (2013). Retrieved from http://aws.amazon.com/route53/

Amazon simple storage service. (2013). Retrieved from http://aws.amazon.com/s3/

Amazon Web Services. (2013). *What is cloud computing?* Retrieved from http://aws.amazon.com/what-is-aws/

Atmos. (n.d.). Retrieved from http://india.emc.com/storage/atmos/atmos.htm#!

AWS applications. (2013). Retrieved from http://aws.amazon.com/web-mobile-social/

AWS CloudFormation. (2013). Retrieved from http://aws.amazon.com/cloudformation/

AWS identity and access management. (2013). Retrieved from http://aws.amazon.com/iam/

AWS import/export. (2013). Retrieved from http://aws.amazon.com/importexport/

AWS Management Console. (2013). Retrieved from http://aws.amazon.com/console/

Benefits of SHARES participation. (2013). Retrieved from http://www.oclc.org/research/activities/shares/benefits.html

Chronopolis. (2011). Retrieved from http://chronopolis.sdsc.edu/

CiteSeerX. (2011). *About CiteSeerX*. Retrieved from http://csxstatic.ist.psu.edu/about

Dhawan, S. M. (2013). Library Transformation to the Cloud Environment: Issues and Strategies. In S. M. Dawan, S. Mujumdar, & S. Deshmukh (Eds.), *Library Services through Cloud Computing Moving Libraries to the Web* (pp. 76–81). Delhi, India: Indo American Books.

Dialogic. (2013). *Dialogic making innovation thrive*. Retrieved from http://www.dialogic.com/~/media/products/docs/whitepapers/12023-cloud-computing-wp.pdf

Digital collection management. (2013). Retrieved from http://www.oclc.org/en-europe/services/digital-collection.html

Electronic collection management. (2013). Retrieved from http://www.oclc.org/en-europe/services/electronic-collection.html

Google. (2012). *Google's approach to IT security: A Google white paper*. Retrieved from https://cloud.google.com/files/Google-CommonSecurity-WhitePaper-v1.4.pdf

LibraryThing. (n.d.). Retrieved from http://www.librarything.com/about

OCLC. (2013a). *Public purpose*. Retrieved from http://www.oclc.org/about/purpose.en.html

OCLC. (2013b). *OCLC WorldShare™ management services*. Retrieved from http://www.oclc.org/en-europe/worldshare-management-services.html

OCLC. (2013c). *Amlib*. Retrieved from http://www.oclc.org/en-europe/amlib.html

OCLC. (2013d). *Cbs*. Retrieved from http://www.oclc.org/en-europe/cbs.html

OCLC. (2013e). *Cbs at a glance*. Retrieved March 07, 2013, from http://www.oclc.org/en-europe/cbs/about.html

OCLC. (2013f). OLIB. Retrieved from http://www.oclc.org/en-europe/olib.html

OCLC. (2013g). Olib at a glance. Retrieved from http://www.oclc.org/en-europe/olib/about.html

Office of the Privacy Commissioner of Canada. (n.d.). *Fact sheet: Introduction to cloud computing*. Retrieved from http://www.priv.gc.ca/resource/fs-fi/02_05_d_51_cc_e.pdf

Reed Elsevier. (2013). *About us*. Retrieved from http://www.reedelsevier.com/aboutus/Pages/Home.aspx

Resource sharing. (2013). Retrieved from http://www.oclc.org/en-europe/services/resource-sharing.html

SalesForce. (n.d.). Retrieved from http://www.salesforce.com/in/

SISIS-SunRise. (2013). Retrieved from http://www.oclc.org/en-europe/sunrise.html

SISIS-SunRise at a glance. (2013). Retrieved from http://www.oclc.org/en-europe/sunrise/about.html

Source Forge. (2013). *SeerSuite*. Retrieved from http://sourceforge.net/projects/citeseerx/?source=navbar

TerraPod. (n.d.). Retrieved from www.terrapodcast.com/

Wikipedia. (2013a) *Amazon web services*. Retrieved from http://en.wikipedia.org/wiki/Amazon_Web_Services

Wikipedia. (2013b). *OCLC*. Retrieved from http://en.wikipedia.org/wiki/OCLC

Zoho. (2013). Retrieved from http://www.zoho.com/company.html

Chapter 14
A Cloud-Oriented Reference Architecture to Digital Library Systems

K. Palanivel
Computer Centre, Pondicherry University, India

S. Kuppuswami
Kongu College of Engineering, India

ABSTRACT

Cloud computing is an emerging computing model which has evolved as a result of the maturity of underlying prerequisite technologies. There are differences in perspective as to when a set of underlying technologies becomes a "cloud" model. In order to categorize cloud computing services, and to expect some level of consistent characteristics to be associated with the services, cloud adopters need a consistent frame of reference. The Cloud Computing Reference Architecture (CCRA) defines a standard reference architecture and consistent frame of reference for comparing cloud services from different service providers when selecting and deploying cloud services to support their mission requirements. Cloud computing offers information retrieval systems, particularly digital libraries and search engines, a wide variety of options for growth and reduction of maintenance needs and encourages efficient resource use. These features are particularly attractive for digital libraries, repositories, and search engines. The dynamic and elastic provisioning features of a cloud infrastructure allow rapid growth in collection size and support a larger user base, while reducing management issues. Hence, the objective of this chapter is to investigate and design reference architecture to Digital Library Systems using cloud computing with scalability in mind. The proposed reference architecture is called as CORADLS. This architecture accelerates the rate at which library users can get easy, efficient, faster and reliable services in the digital environment. Here, the end user does not have to worry about the resource or disk space in cloud computing.

DOI: 10.4018/978-1-4666-4631-5.ch014

INTRODUCTION

Digital library provides a convenient, along with the increasing knowledge level, the requirement of digital library and growing. But because of uneven economic development in different regions causes the digital library's resources to be relatively short, to university digital library as an example. Various colleges and universities while are raising the respective teaching level unceasingly, have established a digital library to purchase its own database resources, but because of the teaching focus and economic conditions, library resources between university's has the differences, meanwhile looked from the whole that the Digital library has certain flaw. Data resources between various universities are relatively independent, building redundant projects possibility was high, has created the manpower, the financial resource and the resources waste, or some colleges and universities to use only part of database resources, inadequate use of resources, and cannot play resources maximum utilization. Digital library representative one kind of new infrastructure and the environment, through the cloud computing, it may use resources more effective, and can solve the defects of digital library.

Digital Library Automation solutions provide timely, efficient and effective enterprise library management services, complete with easy-to-use library and knowledge management functionality (Teregowda, Urgaonkar, & Lee Giles, 2010). These transformative library services remove information access barriers, such as proprietary information silos, to seamlessly make information access equitable. The end result is open access throughout the organization to information services and resources such as: electronic journals, lab notes, databases or other knowledge assets. The Digital Library Software (DLS) solutions transform:

- Delivery of core library services: making them more efficient and accessible.
- User satisfaction: due to improved information access and knowledge management.
- Library operations: making them more streamlined and less costly.
- The library's ability to provide for future growth and changing information demands.

With the rapid development of various IT technologies, Library users' information requirements are increasingly personalized. And now more and more libraries advocated user-centered services. Library can develop itself according to such information and improve users' satisfaction. University library, as we all know, is famous for its academic and teaching influences. And IT technology has been the driving force of library development. The Library Administrator can keep using new technology to develop library and optimize library service. With the expansion of Cloud Computing application, this paper proposed to apply Cloud Computing in libraries (Goldner, 2010).

Digital library provides a convenient, along with the increasing knowledge level, the requirement of digital library and growing. Digital library representative one kind of new infrastructure and the environment, through the cloud computing, it may use resources more effective, and can solve the defects of digital library. Based on cloud computing in the cost calculation, performance, team cooperation and the advantages of the geographic location, because simultaneously the different application procedure has used the different mutually independent platform, each application procedure completes on own server. Using cloud computing can share the server in many application procedures, realizes the resource sharing, thus also reduced server's quantity, achieves the effect of reducing the cost, therefore utilizes cloud computing in the Digital library. Every cloud computation's server may be the computation server, saves the server or the wide band resources and so on.

The objective of this chapter is to investigate and design a scalable reference architecture for DLS using Cloud Computing. The CORADLS able to define the operating library model from a business, organizational, managerial, risk, compliance and technology perspective. In doing so, all library stakeholders will have a clear appreciation of the implications for their business. CORADLS effectively reduce complexity and speed up the development of new products, product lines and portfolio. It provide a guideline for inter-operability and standards. It Model the functions and services of implementation systems. The proposed reference architecture is called CORADLS and this architecture is explained in main focus of this article section

This chapter is organized as follows: The background information needed to write this chapter is discussed in Background section. Also discussed necessary architecture and models that required to write this chapter. The proposed architecture is presented in the main focus of this article and discussed the direction of the future research. Finally this chapter is ended with conclusion.

BACKGROUND

This section provides the necessary background on commonly used technology in Cloud environment. This chapter gives a brief overview of the Digital Library, Cloud Computing and Reference Architecture.

Digital Library

Digital Library is currently used to refer to systems that are heterogeneous in scope and yield very different functionality (Shrawankar & Dhage, 2011). Digital Library range from digital object and metadata repositories, reference-linking systems, archives, and content administration systems to complex systems that integrate advanced digital library services. Digital Library functionality is supposed to be, and integrating solutions from each separate field into systems to support such functionality, sometimes the solutions being induced by novel requirements of Digital Libraries.

Despite the great variety and diversity of existing digital libraries, in reality only a limited range of concepts are defined by all systems as core functionalities. These concepts are identifiable in nearly every Digital Library currently in use. The concepts provide a foundation for Digital Libraries and they are content, user, functionality, quality, policy and architecture.

- **Digital Content:** The digital content concept encompasses the data and information that the Digital Library handles and makes available to its users. Digital content is used to aggregate all forms of information objects that a Digital Library collects, manages and delivers.
- **Library User:** The library user concept covers the various actors entitled to interact with Digital Libraries. The different users of DL are Teacher, Student and Administrator.
- **Functionality:** DLs bare minimum of functions would include new information object registration, search and browse. The Digital Library ensure that the functions reflect the particular needs of the Digital Library's community of users and/or the specific requirements relating to the digital content it contains.
- **Policy:** The policy represents the set or sets of conditions, rules, terms and regulations governing interaction between the Digital Library and users, whether virtual or real. Examples of policies include acceptable

user behavior, digital rights management, privacy and confidentiality, charges to users, and collection delivery (OASIS, 2013).

Digital Library System (DLS) is a software system that is based on a defined (possibly distributed) architecture and provides all functionality required by a particular DL. Library users interact with a Digital Library through the corresponding DLSs. Reference model, reference architecture and concrete architecture are the elements constituting the DLU framework more specifically.

Digital Library Management System

The Digital Library Management System (DLMS) functionality includes Digital Library Portal (DLP), Catalog, Library Administration, System/database configuration and Integration. The DLP provides the users a branded knowledge portal with access to custom links, RSS feeds, blogs, and wikis, along with an OPAC that provides access to your resources in text, audio and video formats. The Digital Library Portal uniquely provides thesaurus, review & rating, document submission, security classification, inquiry reference management and advance booking.

- **Catalog:** This highly flexible and functional repository can manage a wide variety of physical and electronic materials, with sophisticated cross referencing, poly hierarchical thesaurus and full-text electronic document indexing. Catalog functions provides custom data templates, unique search navigation, circulation& self-circulation, auto cataloguing and copy/bulk copy management.
- **Library Administration:** Includes acquisitions, reporting and enhanced inquiry reference management. Acquisitions manages suppliers and acquisition of all types of materials including books, electronic materials and serials. Reporting runs or schedules any report, from any location, in PDF, XLX, RTF and TXT formats. Enhanced inquiry reference management includes incoming email capture, status tracking and automatic administrator alerts and user-responses.
- **System/Database Configuration:** The Digital Library System Administrator (DLSA) can easily design and maintain the database by creating fields, content types and record templates, or we can do it for you.
- **Integration:** It streamlines processes and share information integrating the library management system with other aspects of the organization. Using this facility, we can create a single sign on (SSO), automatically reflecting changes in a user's record.

The library community can apply the concept of cloud computing to amplify the power of cooperation and to build a significant, unified presence on the Web. This approach to computing can help libraries save time and money while simplifying workflows.

Cloud Computing

The Digital Library has brought new opportunities for the advancement of digital library. Cloud computing can take the library facility at the most convenient state to its stakeholders than other technical approaches. Many people are getting more used to with the e-copies of books, journals, newspaper and other resources than paperback format. Cloud computing can provide the optimum library services to the people by centralizing the resources and disk spaces of any digital library. Cloud computing can provide an uninterrupted service to its stakeholders. The implementation of cloud computing in digital library can provide many scopes for people from different professions.

Librarians, Computer experts, and people from other professions have different scopes while cloud computing has integrated as part of any digital library.

The three typical kinds of cloud computing services are processing clouds, storage clouds and application clouds (Behrendt et al, 2011). Processing Clouds that provide scalable and mostly affordable computing resources that run enterprise programs, which is also sometimes known as Infrastructure as a service (IaaS), Storage Clouds that offer an alternative to local file systems also known as a Platform as a Service (PaaS), and Application Clouds also called Software as a Service (SaaS), that allow a thin client to interact with services that are completely hosted on an external infrastructure.

- **Software as a Service (SaaS):** Applications or software is delivered as a service to the customer who can access the program from any online device. The customers benefit from low initial costs, have access to (usually 24/7) support services.
- **Platform as a Service (PaaS):** With PaaS, a computing platform is provided which supplies tools and a development environment to help companies build, test, and deploy Web-based applications. Applications which are built using these provider's services, however, are usually locked into that one platform.
- **Infrastructure as a Service (IaaS):** It involves both storage services and computing power. IaaS provides computing resources, and Storage Service for data storage. Most institutions are using IaaS to host or backup their websites, for content delivery, to run high performance computing simulations, to host media collections, and much more.

While libraries can use cloud computing applications to create personalized portals for users, the Library could use cloud computing as their back up methodology. Libraries have already begun to adopt cloud services to alleviate their IT departments and increase efficiency. Mentioned below are some of the advantages of this technology:

- **Cost Efficient:** Cloud computing is probably the most cost efficient method to use, maintain and upgrade.
- **Unlimited Storage:** Storing information in the cloud gives you almost unlimited storage capacity. Hence, you no more need to worry about running out of storage space or increasing your current storage space availability.
- **Backup and Recovery:** Since all the data is stored in the cloud, backing it up and restoring the same is relatively much easier than storing the same on a physical device.
- **Automatic Software Integration:** In the cloud, software integration is usually something that occurs automatically. This does not need to take additional efforts to customize and integrate DL applications as per user's preferences.
- **Easy Access to Information:** Once register in the cloud, it can access the information from anywhere, where there is an Internet connection. This convenient feature lets the users move beyond time zone and geographic location issues.
- **Quick Deployment:** Lastly and most importantly, cloud computing gives you the advantage of quick deployment. Once you opt for this method of functioning, your entire system can be fully functional in a matter of a few minutes. Of course, the amount of time taken here will depend on the exact kind of technology that you need for your business.

The benefits of cloud based services are enormous.

- First of all, cloud based networks offer highly scalable data solutions to your business needs.
- With increased agility in business processes, your revenues increase while infrastructure costs are reduced.
- Moreover, globalizing your network infrastructure makes your business processes location independent.
- With streamlined processes, increased accessibility and improved flexibility, resources are leveraged to optimal levels.

Cloud System Architecture

In cloud computing, scalable and elastic IT-enabled capabilities [7] are delivered as a service to customers using the network. The most important capabilities are a self-service portal; a pool of shared resources; and release of resources; and ubiquitous access. Cloud System provides the above capabilities using the three-layer architecture shown in Figure 1. Within this architecture, the delivery layer provides application service delivery; the demand layer contains the self-service portals and is where services are actually consumed by end users or subscribers; and The supply layer provides all the infrastructure services for Cloud system; this is where the physical and virtual assets reside

The Cloud system is based on the converged infrastructure. Employing a shared services model, with pools of compute, storage, and network resources, the Converged Infrastructure is an ideal foundation for cloud computing. Cloud system provides a complete management environment to help ensure the cloud service meets the needs of the end user. Cloud system offer added features as governance, application readiness, service monitoring, and enhanced security.

Cloud Computing Reference Architecture (CCRA)

The reference architecture is an architectural design pattern indicating an abstract solution that implements the concepts and relationships identified in the reference model (Reed, Jr., 2004). There may be more than one reference architecture that addresses how to design digital library systems built on the reference model. The Reference Architecture based approach has been proven to be useful in several customer engagements. According to Rational Unified Process (RUP), "a Reference Architecture, is in essence, a predefined architectural pattern, or set of patterns, possibly partially or completely instantiated, designed, and proven for use in particular business and technical contexts, together with supporting artifacts to enable their use. Often, these artifacts are harvested from previous projects".

The Cloud Computing Reference Architecture (CCRA) is intended to be used as a blueprint/guide for architecting cloud implementations, driven by functional and non-functional requirements of the respective cloud implementation. The CCRA defines the basic building blocks - architectural elements and their relationships which make up the cloud. The CCRA also defines the basic principles which are fundamental for delivering & managing cloud services. The CCRA is more than just a collection of technologies and products. They consist of several architectural models and are much like a city plan. The CCRA defines how your cloud platform should be constructed so that it can satisfy not you're your current demands and but also be extensible to support the future needs of a diverse user population. So this blueprint should be responsive to changing business and technology requirements and adaptable to emerging technologies. By delivering best practices in a standardized, methodical way, an RA ensures consistency and quality across development and delivery projects.

Figure 1. Architecture of Cloud System

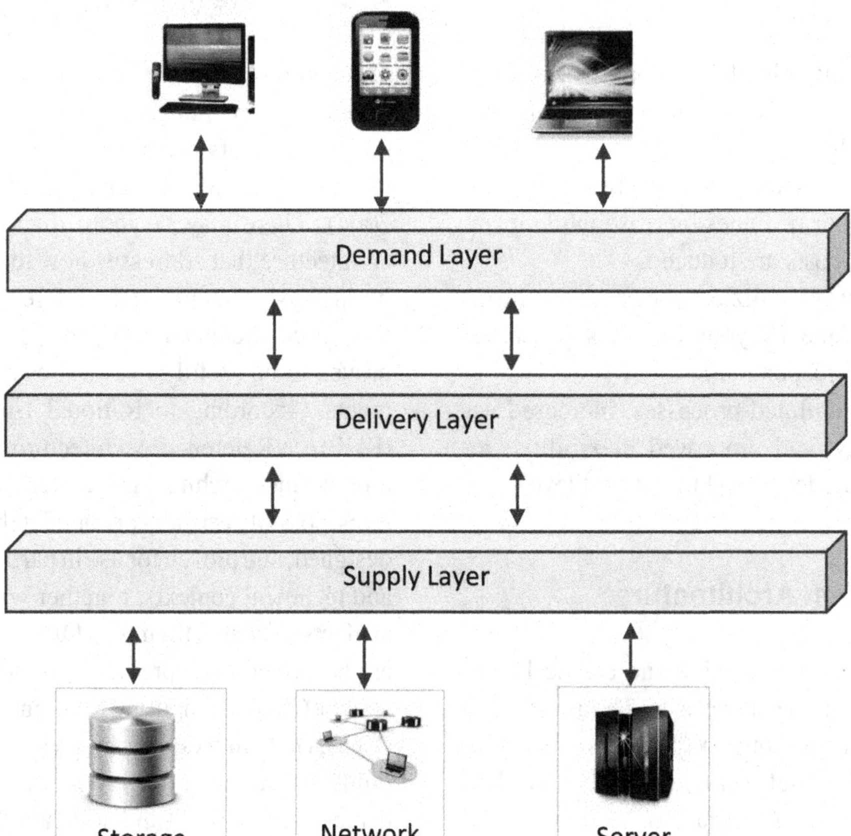

Literature Review & Related Works

This section presents the literature review on various cloud computing models available. Various models of cloud computing are Unified search service, integrating consulting service, Real-time access service, Knowledge service and All-oriented service and they are discussed below (Sanchati & Kulkarni, 2011).

- **Unified Search Service Model:** With the adoption of Cloud Computing in Digital Library, the integrated library resources support distributed uniform access interface. The uniform access platform can promote library resources, guide and answer users' questions by using high-quality navigation. As a result, users can grip more information retrieval methods and make better use of library resources
- **Integrated Consulting Services Model:** The integrated digital reference service can realize the sharing of technology, resources, experts and services of Digital Libraries. This will bring great conveniences for library users.
- **Real-time Access Services Model:** By introducing Cloud Computing, Digital Libraries can establish a shared public cloud. As shared cloud can have infinite storage capacity and computing power theoretically. It can bring obvious benefits to libraries.
- **Knowledge Service Model:** Digital Libraries are of storing, processing and spreading knowledge. The establishment

of shared public cloud can save manpower and material resources greatly among university libraries.

- **All-oriented Service Model:** Digital Libraries provide services for all the people like the professors, teachers or students can access to the library resources. They permit users access to many libraries' resources by handling related certificate of that library.

Review on DL Architectures

There are number of research regarding Cloud Computing architectures on Digital Library systems. A broad collection of reference architectures and reference models were considered. The existing architecture/models systems are revisited and analyzed in terms of the above quality attributes. These reference architecture / model identifies the main components of the reference architecture and indicates inter-relationships between the components. For brevity's sake only those relevant architectures/models are described and compared below.

Suresh Chandra Padhy and RK Mahapatra [1] proposed to improve current user service model with Cloud Computing. This paper explores the application of cloud computing in academic library in Orissa.

Pradeep Teregowda discuss constraints and choices faced by information retrieval systems like CiteSeerx by exploring in detail aspects of placing CiteSeerx into current cloud infrastructure offerings (Teregowda, Urgaonkar, & Lee Giles, 2010). We also implement an ad-hoc virtualized storage system for experimenting with adoption of cloud infrastructure services. Our results show that a cloud implementation of CiteSeerx may be a feasible alternative for its continued operation and growth.

Matt Goldner (2010) defines cloud computing and shows how it is different from other types of computing. It also discusses how cloud computing solutions could be beneficial to libraries in three basic areas: technology, data and community.

Lee Badger (2011) introduced a conceptual model, the NIST Cloud Computing Reference Architecture and Taxonomy. It presented USG target business use cases and technical use cases in the cloud. It discussed security challenges in the context of cloud computing adoption, high-priority security requirements, and current and future risk mitigation measures requirements. It also presented a subset of the analysis that drove the rationale for the requirements.

G. Athanasopoulos (2010) represents the first release of the Digital Library Reference Model produced by the DL.org project. It has been produced by using the DELOS Digital Library Reference Model released by the DELOS Network of Excellence as firm starting point. This release maintains, consolidates and enhances the previous one by applying a number of revisions and extensions.

Reference Architectures for SOA based Enterprise applications have been presented in the paper (Reed, Jr., 2004). Best practices have been discussed. The use of SOA would reduce the time-to-integrate any new application.

HP CloudSystem (2011) provides these capabilities using the three-layer architecture, which enables IT as a service. Within this architecture, the supply layer provides all the infrastructure services for CloudSystem; this is where the physical and virtual assets reside. The delivery layer provides application service delivery. The demand layer contains the self-service portals and is where services are actually consumed by end users or subscribers.

In cloud computing, scalable and elastic IT-enabled capabilities are delivered as a service to customers using the Internet. The most important capabilities are a self-service portal; a pool of shared resources; automated provisioning, flexing, and release of those resources; a facility to meter and charge for usage; and ubiquitous access.

MAIN FOCUS OF THE CHAPTER

This section of the chapter describes the proposed reference architecture called a CORADLS. This includes the identification of Digital Library services, proposed model / architecture and evaluating the proposed architecture.

Motivation Example

Cloud computing can take the library facility at the most convenient state to its stakeholders than other technical approaches. Many people are getting more used to with the e-copies of books, journals, newspaper and other resources than paperback format. Cloud computing can provide the optimum library services to the people by centralizing the resources and disk spaces of any digital library. The motivation behind to propose Reference Architecture to Digital Library is shown in Figure 2.

Figure 2. Motivation of Example of Digital Library

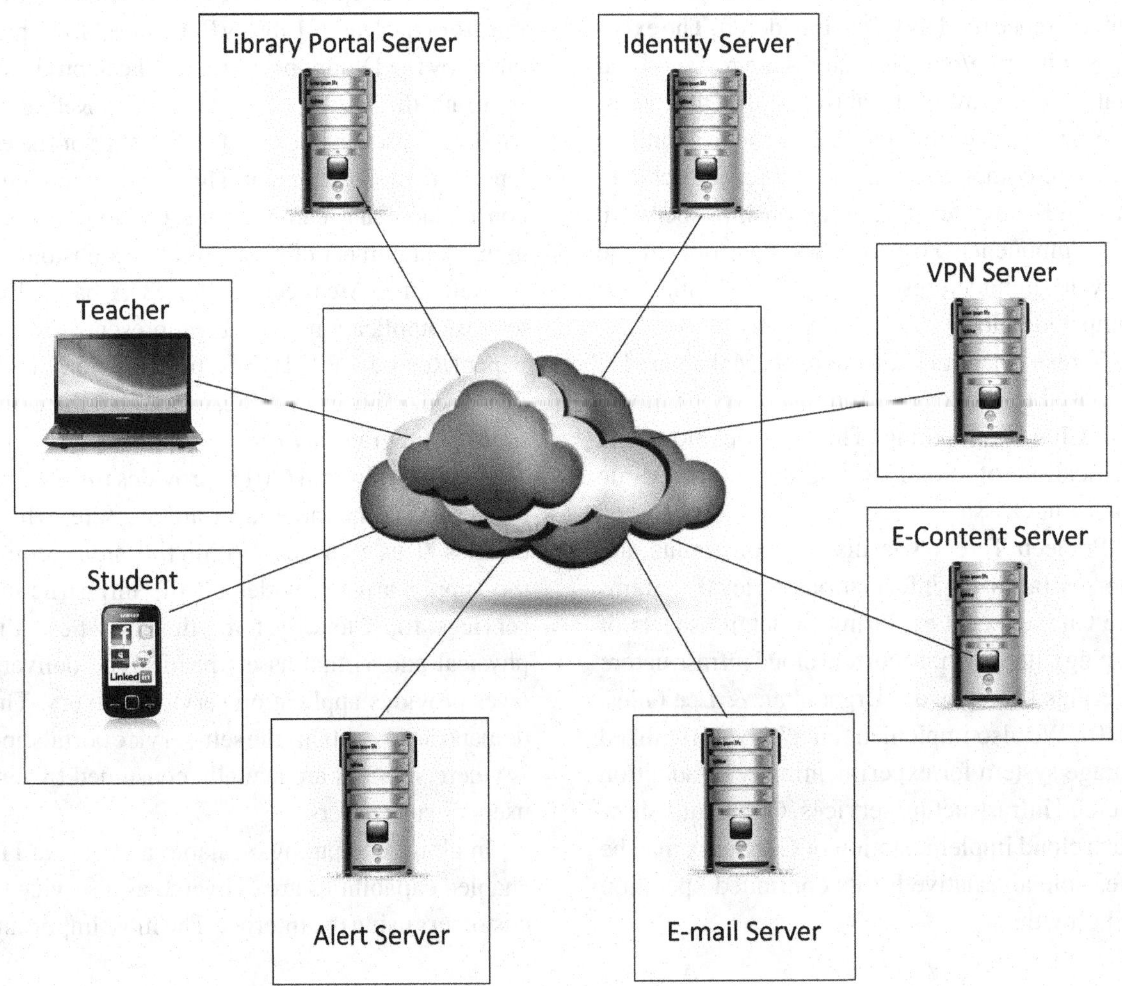

The Library users are connected to the Digital Library Portal Server (DLPS) via internet. The Authentication Service is the entry point of Identity Server. A user must pass an authentication process before accessing the Identity Server console and its corresponding management functions. A user attempting to access a service or application protected by Identity Server must also authenticate before access is allowed. The Authentication Service invokes authentication modules to collect and validate the necessary credentials. Identity Server also provides APIs that allow applications to participate in a single sign-on functionality enabling a user to authenticate only once yet access multiple resources.

A VPN Server comes handy in establishing connection between two or more computers in order to access the systems remotely over a public network. The basic function of a VPN server is to make way for a secure network between participating computers. This helps the users connected to the network to communicate with each other without being affected by any third party intruder. The Notification Server listens for notification requests from E-content Server and processes the request to send a message through e-mail, pager, or SMS service. The Notification Server processes and handles notification events, leaving E-content Server resources free to handle file transfers. The Notification Manager lets you configure the logging and account information necessary for the notification Server to communicate with it.

Challenges and Issues

The challenges and issues occurs in Figure 1 are performance and scalability. Scalability without the right infrastructure can degrade efficiency when service delivery policies can't be applied intelligently across Digital Library applications. This can result in poor performance for users and, ultimately, undesirable downtime. Some of the challenges in designing DL applications are as follows:

- **Ensure Availability:** The higher density of virtual machines increases the potential for a failed application to affect the availability DL applications. With flexible, intelligent scalability technology, we can automatically handle application failure without affecting other applications.
- **Scale Seamlessly:** Seamless, transparent scaling of applications in the cloud requires collaboration across application delivery and provisioning systems.
- **Improve Performance:** The library users expect content to load in the blink of an eye. This expectation is difficult to meet with the complexity of systems and variability in location, user devices, and application profiles.
- **Maximize Resources:** Caching consume significant resources, leading to decreased capacity and poor performance. Commoditization of server sizing intensifies this effects, requiring DL applications to scale out faster and incur higher costs.

So it needs solutions to

1. Offload this services to a shared application delivery tier, improving performance and capacity.
2. Ensure the elasticity of DL applications we expect from the cloud computing initiatives.
3. Employ a variety of offload, acceleration, and optimization technologies that help you achieve this seemingly impossible goal.
4. Enable the multi-tenant architectures required to protect DL applications from noisy or failing neighbors.

Designing a consistent operational architecture, it can rely on repeatable and intelligent scalability policies. By integrating with leading virtualization and cloud computing architecture, they help automatically maintain optimal performance and availability.

Statement of the Problem

The Architecture concept refers to the Digital Library System entity and represents a mapping of the functionality and content offered by a Digital Library on to hardware and software components. There are two primary reasons for having architecture as a core concept: (i) Digital Libraries are often assumed to be among the most complex and advanced forms of information systems; and (ii) interoperability across Digital Libraries is recognized as a substantial research challenge.

A clear reference architectural for the Digital Library System offers ammunition in addressing both of these issues effectively. Challenges adding to the DL concerns of IT include:

- The need to maintain compliance with stringent privacy and security regulations.
- The need to provide users with access to DL applications and organizational computing resources.
- The growing need to support user owned devices in the network environment.

As Cloud Computing has become more and more popular, various Cloud Computing architectures have been defined for Digital Library Applications. However, to effectively achieve the potential of cloud computing, there is need for the definition of system architecture of the Digital Library systems involved in the delivery of cloud computing, so that it can be used as a reference for the architects (Liu, Zhang, Hu, & He, 2012). There is no reference architecture available to design Digital Library Systems with scalability. Hence, the problem statement is to have one reference architecture for DLS supporting DLs constructed by federating local resources and multiple organizations, and another one for personal DLs or for specialized applications.

Solution to the Problem

The Solution to the problem is to investigate and design a scalable reference architecture for DLS using Cloud Computing. The proposed reference architecture is called CORADLS. CORADLS is layered architecture and it consists of demand layer, supply layer and delivery layers. This architecture provides several benefits. Because it includes a SaaS approach for data along with PaaS option and even an IaaS offering, the data can be stored based on the security, consistency, and other properties desired. Because the access is provided through a single interface (but a scalable one), there is ultimate flexibility in the type of storage access, from auto-detection of the data and where it is to be stored or the security of the data, and perhaps even in-transit transform into a desired shape or format.

The architecture is designed to support maximum scalability and high service levels through virtualization and an optimized management environment. It enables new levels of scalability while providing a very cost-effective modular solution. This enables institutions to start with a cost-effective small pilot and then grow and expand over time to support an enterprise-scale online learning environment. Some of the critical design factors are flexible infrastructure, building services, scalability of users and contents, and caching the data (Subramanyam, 2012). Here, we take the design considerations based on functionality.

1. **User Performance:** The Library users can interact with multiple channels such as mobile, Laptop, or online. Some of the content that must be retrieved when a user approaches the DL server are how frequently the user comes back and what are the interests of the user.

2. **Security:** Library transactions are always critical and should be secured so security as service will enable security requirements including multi-factor authentication.
3. **Scaling of Library User Systems:** The Library administrator should enhance the number of systems available for users.
4. **Common Infrastructure:** Identify the common functionalities and provide them with a common infrastructure for better coordination and implementation.
5. **Collaboration Services:** Design Library applications for collaboration services like sharing the information on common utilities, information, attractive provisions offers, etc.
6. **Load Balancing:** Handle load balancing using Infrastructure as a Service.

Requirements

The main objective of cloud computing is to use a specific software through calculation and the data stored in a desired computer distribution which causes the enterprise to reduce cost and improve performance. Digital library represents one kind of new infrastructure and the environment; through cloud computing technology since it uses resources more effectively and can solve the constraints in digital library. Cloud providers should provide mechanisms to support data portability & system portability, service interoperability, security and privacy (NIST, 2013).

- **Portability:** For portability, customers or library users are interested to know whether they can move their data or applications across multiple cloud environments at low cost and minimal disruption. From an interoperability perspective, users are concerned about the capability to communicate between or among multiple clouds. This can be data portability and system portability.
- **Interoperability:** Service interoperability is the ability of cloud consumers to use their data and services across multiple cloud providers with a unified management interface.
- **Security:** Security in cloud computing architecture concerns is not solely under the purview of the Cloud Providers, but also Cloud Consumers and other relevant actors. Cloud-based systems still need to address security requirements such as authentication, authorization, availability, confidentiality, identity management, integrity, audit, security monitoring, incident response, and security policy management.
- **Privacy:** Cloud providers should protect the assured, proper, and consistent collection, processing, communication, use and disposition of personal information in the cloud (NIST, 2013).

DL Services Identified

The services identified during design of CORA-DLS are registration, DL portal service, Alert/Notification service, Library service, Monitoring service, Remote Connection service, etc. The services can be specified as a set of messages of a XML. The Services Layers implement the necessary functionality to transform the request from a service consumer application to a suitable format, communicating with the application/product implementing the functionality and returning the result. A brief description of the services is as follows

- **Registration Service:** It enables an application to register as a participant. The Registration service provides methods for collecting the information required to build the User personal details. The tasks have to be covered by registration are registration process, sending e-mails to the registered users, conform registration and enable/disable of users account.

- **DL Portal Service:** CORADLS provides role-based portals and interfaces. They enhance the user experience for designing, building, and consuming private and public cloud services. Among the interfaces CORADLS provides consumers of services, service designers, service assurance, and IT administration.
- **Alert/Notification Services:** Library users receive an e-mail or SMS alerts or notifications whenever adding/updating content to the DL Server. The chief function of the notification service is to notify the library users with the latest information they are interested in automatically without any users' information retrieval and request (Zheng, Chen, & Bai, 2003). The users only need to do is to register the kind of their subject. The information types to be notified are subject information, subject navigations, the digital magazines/journals, book records in the OPAC and the library news/notification, new services provided by library.
- **Personalization Services:** The personalization services in a Digital Library environment would help the users to find information resources available in a digitally chaotic world (Zheng, Wu, & Zhuang, 2004). The reasons of developing a digital library include increasing access to information serving and users' needs and bringing organization to the unstructured universe of electronically available information.
- **Digital Reference Services:** Digital Reference Services include either finding the required information on behalf of users, or assisting users in finding information themselves. Instruction in the use of library resources and services, and user guidance in which users are guided in selecting the most appropriate information sources and services. Web based reference services are also now being provided by academic libraries in the virtual reference environment (Pomerantz, 2003).
- **Library Service:** The Digital Library has Discovery service, Indexing service, Metadata service and Repository service. The Discovery services are capable of searching quickly and seamlessly across a vast range of local and remote content and providing relevancy-ranked results to the library users (Vaughan, 2011).
- **The Indexing Service:** Provides the generic functionality of an inverted file, mapping elementary tokens to documents/entities (Sinha & Sanyal, 2011).
- **The Metadata Service:** Associates metadata records to all the objects managed by Digital Library and organized as repository (Mazurek, Stroinski, Werla, & Weglarz, 2006). In the context of Digital Libraries, the Metadata Service becomes equivalent to the service providing the corresponding interface.
- **The Repository Service:** Provides the functionality of a content repository which contains all the content that is available in the storage server (Sinha & Sanyal, 2011). It provides an effective solution to concerns such as copyright management or mirroring.
- **Security or Identity Service:** Security service offers authentication, authentication, access control and confidentiality (IBM Developer Network, 2003). The authentication handles the authentication requests sent to the DL portal. It is passed log-on credentials for a user and returns an authentication certificate. Authorization

follows authentication and that is, once a user or system has be authenticated. The confidentiality is the security service for ensuring non-disclosure of sensitive information traveling through networks.

- **Remote Connection Service:** This service offers establishing connection to the DL Server from a remote place. It accepts the requests from the authorized Library users and allow them to access the contents available in the DL server.
- **Monitoring Service:** Monitoring Service can be implemented as support to predict, track and remediate site problems in a timely and efficient manner. This secure service will interpret events and activate the proper response mechanism with user defined notification rules, including e-mail or SMS. The user friendly DL web portal gives Library users easy access to up-to-date contents such as e-books, e-journals, e-theses, etc. and dynamically generated reports.

The above identified services are registered in the services registry. The registry manager can either start/restart or stop the services.

Cloud Computing DL Model

The cloud computing model allows access to information and computer resources from anywhere that a network connection is available. Cloud computing provides a shared pool of resources, including data storage space, networks, computer processing power, and specialized corporate and user applications. The design uses layered web application architecture (Palanivel & Kuppuswami, 2011). Figure 3 shows the proposed Cloud Computing Model for Digital Library (Hewlett-Packard, 2011). It consists of Subscriber Tier, Service Tier, Application Tier and Storage Tier (Reddy, 2012).

- **Subscriber Tier:** All the Library users or subscribers are exists in the Subscriber Tier. Various users of the Library are stu-

Figure 3. Cloud Computing Model for Digital Library

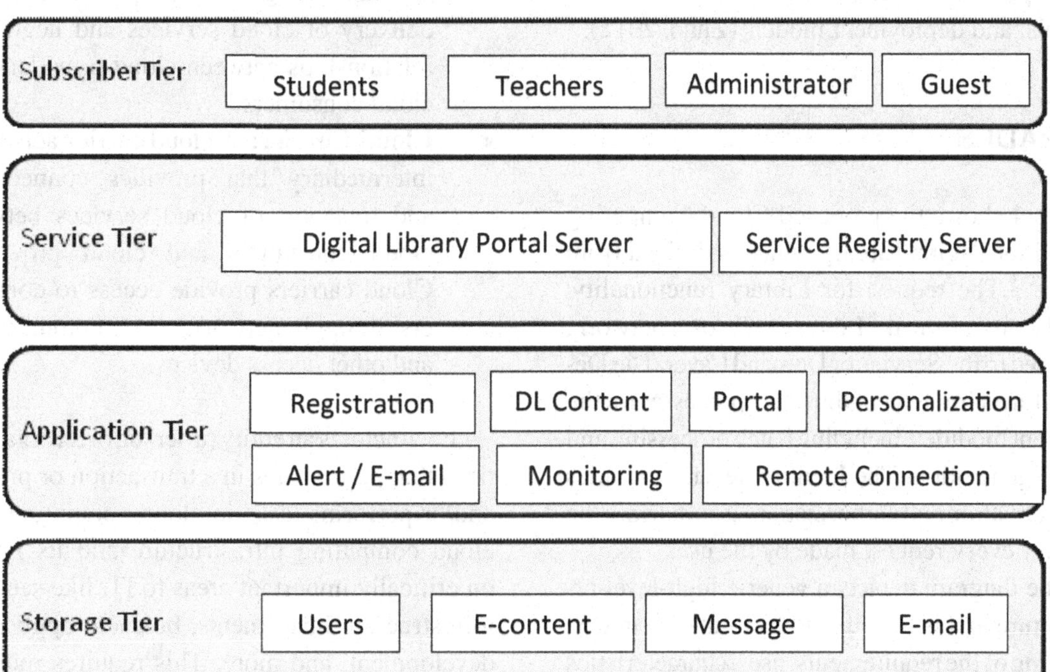

dents, teachers, guests and administrator. The Library users connects to the DLPS via Desktop, Laptop, etc.

- **Service (Demand) Tier:** The Digital Library portal service and Service registry are exists in this tier. All the services discovered in the above section should be registered in the Service Registry. The registered Library users demand the necessary content to the DL Applications.
- **Application (Delivery) Tier:** Various applications related to the DL are placed in this layer. These applications perform registration, user identity, search or query, send alerts/ notifications, monitoring, remote connection management, etc.
- **Storage (Supply) Tier:** All the data or content are available in Storage tier. They supply necessary data/ information to the registered users or subscribers. The data are available in the form of databases like user database, e-content database, e-mail database, message database, etc.

This cloud model promotes availability and is composed of essential characteristics, service models, and deployment models (Zhao, 2012).

CORADLS

Figure 4 shows the proposed Cloud Computing Model for Digital Library which is derived from Figure 3.The request for Library functionality, which comes from the Library users over network, is passed to the Service or Demand Layer. The Demand Layer implements business processes for the different modules, including batch processing and report generation. The Identity Service includes authentication and authorization. It authorizes the user for every request made by the user.

The diagram depicts a generic high-level architecture and is intended to facilitate the understanding of the requirements, uses, characteristics and standards of cloud computing (Behrendt et al., 2011). The cloud computing reference architecture defines the actors: cloud consumer, cloud provider, cloud carrier, and cloud broker. They are described below:

- **Cloud Consumer:** The cloud consumer (example Student, Teacher, Guests) is the principal stakeholder for the cloud computing service. A cloud consumer browses the service catalog from a cloud provider, requests the appropriate service, sets up service contracts with the cloud provider, and uses the service.
- **Cloud Provider:** A cloud provider (Digital Library Applications, SMS, Notification, E-mail, Monitoring, etc.) is the entity responsible for making a service available to interested parties. A Cloud Provider acquires and manages the computing infrastructure, runs the cloud software, and makes arrangement to deliver the cloud services to the Library users through network access.
- **Cloud Broker:** A cloud broker is an entity that manages the use, performance and delivery of cloud services and negotiates relationships between cloud providers and cloud consumers.
- **Cloud Carrier:** A cloud carrier acts as an intermediary that provides connectivity and transport of cloud services between cloud consumers and cloud providers. Cloud carriers provide access to consumers through network, telecommunication and other access devices.

Each actor is an entity (a person or an organization) that participates in a transaction or process and/or performs tasks in cloud computing. The cloud computing infrastructure and its impact on critically important areas to IT, like security, infrastructure investments, business application development, and more. This requires multiple

Figure 4. Reference Architecture CORADLS

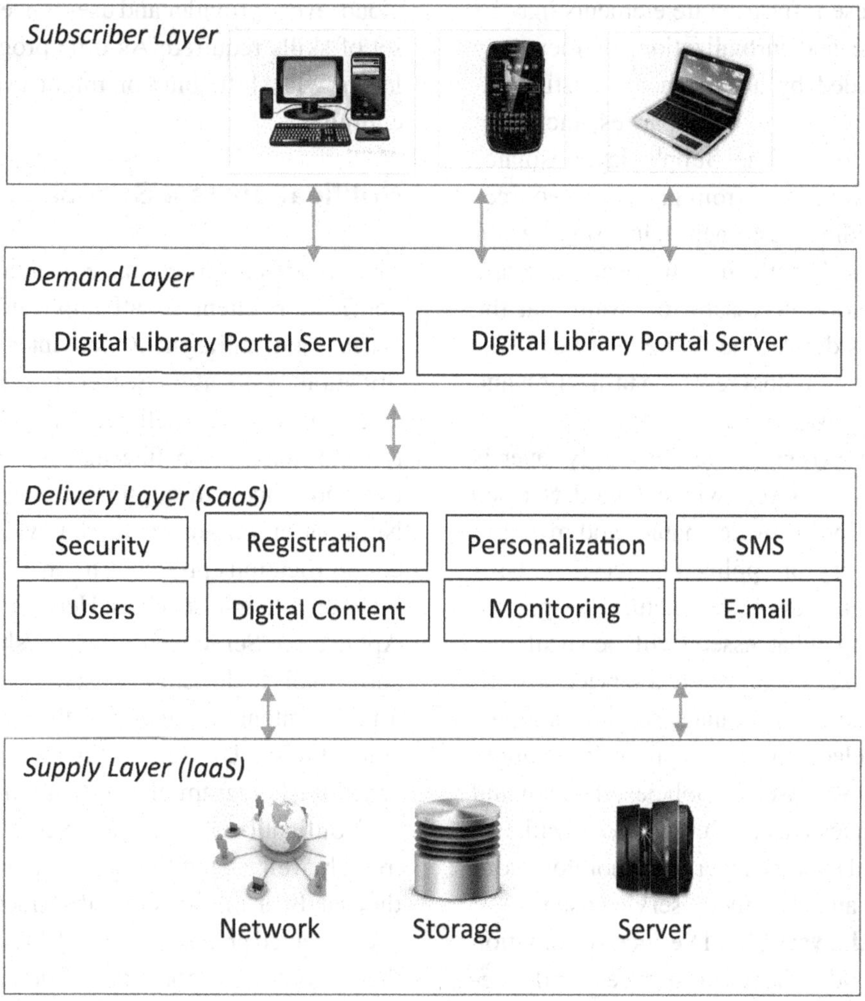

skills for using applications on the cloud computing environment. These layers have made it easier for the users to define the roles and responsibilities and the skills demanded by the users at each level. The above four key layers of a cloud computing environment will help understand the functionality and the technical skills required, in order to understand the system as well as perform tasks more efficiently.

Layered Architecture

CORADLS consists of various layers like supply layer, delivery layer and demand layer and their functions are explained below:

- **Consumer Layer:** The consumer are students, teachers, guests designer and administrator. The consumer layer is more strictly and carefully separated from the services and service provider to allow pooling and substitution of cloud services or providers. This end layer is more about the data consumers. As these data consumers use a different kinds of protocols and APIs, Enterprise Search Layer and Data Manipulation Layer appropriately exposes the services for them to be consumed.
- **Supply Layer:** The supply layer provides for service delivery of infrastructure elements such as compute, network, storage,

and other resources both physical and virtual. These infrastructure elements may be hardware and virtualization, or they may be provided by a customer's existing infrastructure or by third parties, including public clouds. The Supply layer isolates the Delivery layer from physical resources by providing customer-facing service abstractions. It performs all governance and orchestration necessary to ensure that the resources deliver the desired service. This layer also monitors resource utilization and generates usage data records.

- **Delivery layer:** Above the supply layer is the delivery layer, where Cloud Service Automation software enables and manages the delivery of application services. User interfaces allow infrastructure design, for specifying what assets will be available, and service design, where a service designer can add to and manage service catalogs. It also selects the most appropriate Supply layer to use, based on policies, the Demand layer requested, and Supply layer availability. The Delivery layer also monitors consumers' and customers' service usage.
- **Demand layer:** Cloud Service Automation also provides the portal services for the demand layer, where consumers or business users can request services. The Demand layer exposes services and products to the consumer through a user portal. It maintains a catalog of all internal (provided by the Delivery layer) and external (aggregated) services available to end users. The Demand layer authenticates end users to determine their authority to create or modify services, generates service billing and settlement information, and provides visual feedback on customers' Quality of Experience and Service Level Agreement compliance.

As more functionality moves to the internet cloud, every provider and user is needs to develop set of skills required. As time progresses, these layers will shift, blur or might even disappear entirely.

Notification as a Service

This Notification Service provides a single notification client to all applications, support synchronous and asynchronous interface to the Notification Application Server (Pomerantz, 2003). The Notification Application provide capability to send notification like instant /short messaging, and e-mails through multiple channels. The Notification minimizes the knowledge of different notifications produces in order to facilitate a loose coupling of services. Here, the Notification Application Server sends instant/short messages and e-mails to the Library users whenever adding a new contents or updating the existing digital content to the DL Server. Figure 5 illustrates the functioned diagram of Notification system.

Notification Application Server perform extremely well even if the application must support thousands or millions of subscribers because of a set-oriented processing model. In all applications that send notifications, the basic requirement is to evaluate subscriptions at the right times, either when an event related to the subscription is available, or according to a schedule.

Managing IT notification and problem resolution continues to be increasingly challenging and critical for enterprises of all sizes, academic institutions, government entities and other large organizations throughout the world. Notification as a service allows enterprises to take maximum advantage of the growing trends toward Software as a Service (SaaS) and to leverage on-going improvements in IT notification technologies, while minimizing operating costs and avoiding future forklift upgrades.

Figure 5. Structure of Notification Service

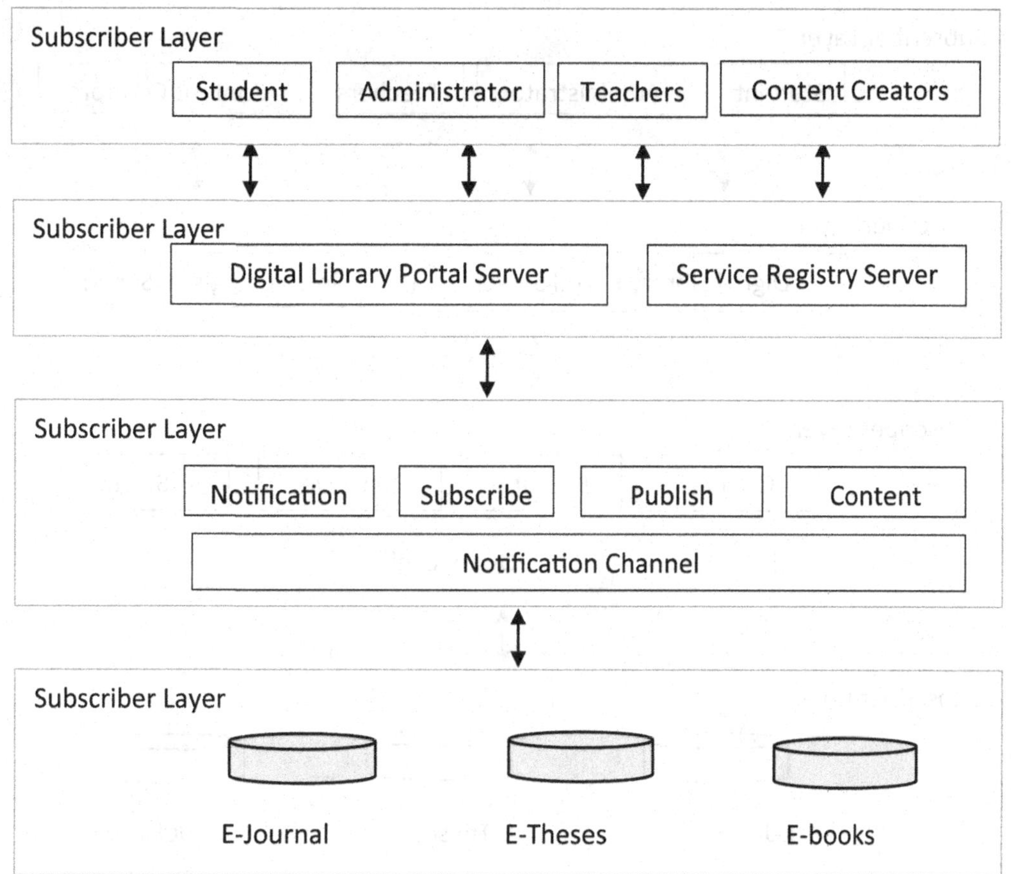

Query as a Service

Query as a Web Service is a Library application that allows the users to quickly create queries and publish them as web services. It has a client component that creates queries from universes, and a server-side web service that allows developers to create web services from specific Business Objects queries.

DLPS need to present data in a tabular format to the Library users. Figure 6 illustrates the how DLPS server delivers the data to Library users in a tabular format. The functionality provided by the search component are dynamic query generation based on Library user input, sort order, joins, etc (Vaughan, 2011). In order to make the changes in the architecture as transparent as possible to the user, CORADLS provides a list of the services references if such functionality is activated. There are multiple ways to invoke the query service according to users' preferences. One straightforward way to access the service is by an embedded URL. For example, the Library users want to search a digital content/ object related to Computer Science, then they have to type 'Computer Science'. By activating the link on the query interface, it can obtain the extra services exposed by other providers.

The advantages of the storing the results in XML format while avoiding the disadvantages of increased data volumes and reduced query performance caused by the enrichment process.

Figure 6. Structure of Query Service

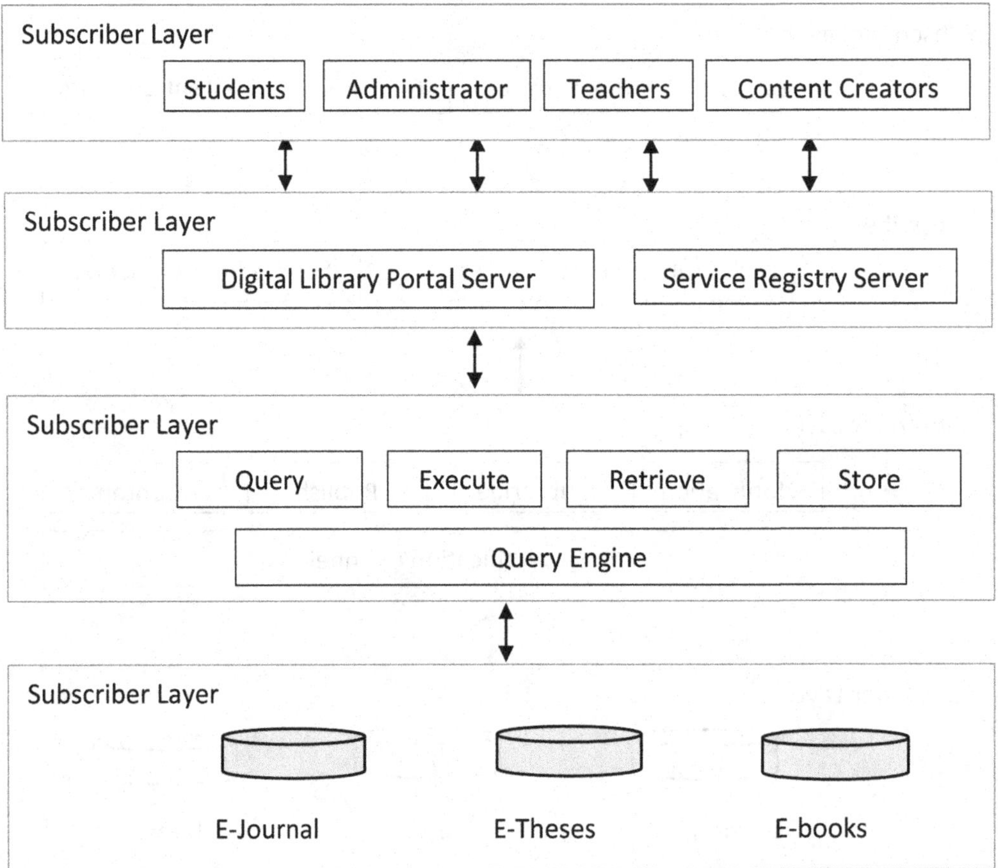

Security as a Service

Security-as-a-Service solutions for the cloud protect Digital Library Web Applications against the most common threats and attacks. Security-as-a-Service solutions for the cloud provides solutions to secure the application and infrastructure stack. It delivers both critical Web protection and cost effective management. Security-as-a-Service solutions for the DL includes Information, Data, User Account, Access Rights, Intrusion & Detection, Firewalls, Virtual Private Network, RFID, etc. Security component offers authentication, authentication, access control and confidentiality [18, 30]. Figure 7 shows that how the security module works in CORADLS.

The authentication handles the authentication requests sent to the DLPS. It is passed log-on credentials for a user and returns an authentication certificate. Authorization follows authentication and that is, once a user or system has be authenticated. Authorization means making a decision about whether an authenticated or even an authenticated identity is allowed to access a resource.

The confidentiality ensures non-disclosure of sensitive information traveling through untrusted communication networks. Information at rest includes security, user, and application information. It is commonly rely on ton cryptographic techniques such as encryption.

Single sign-on (SSO) is mechanism can permit library user to access all resources without the

Figure 7. Structure of Security Service

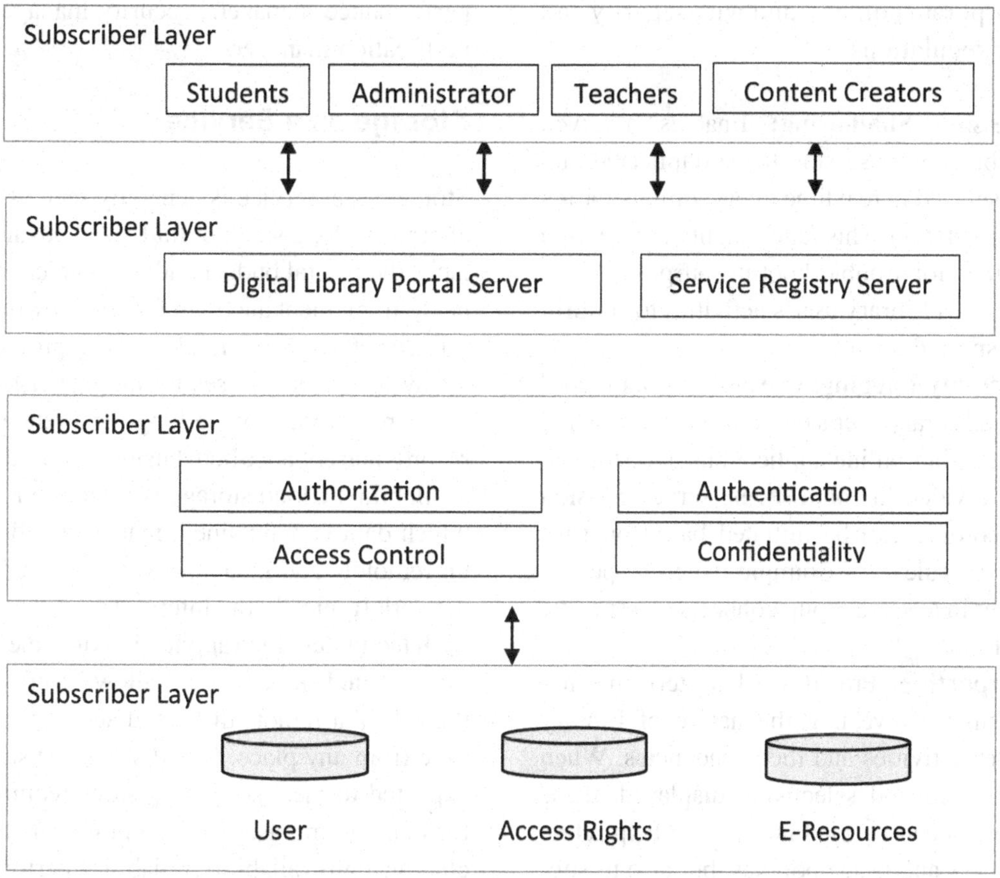

need to enter multiple passwords. Single sign-on reduces human error, a major component of systems failure and is therefore highly desirable but difficult to implement.

Preservation must also ensure that information resources remain intact; unauthorized tampering with the content of electronic resources could have grave implications for its continued value. Security technologists will aid in preservation by preventing corruption or destruction of information resources and ensuring their authenticity.

The security services enhance both security and performance. This increase website performance, no installation of firewall, anti-virus software, remote access, etc.

Monitoring as a Service

Application monitoring tools pursues with all or at least a part of DL application. A monitoring tool that is itself delivered as a service so that it can log onto one central web based dashboard which is hosted by the vendor of the monitoring service and see what is going on with all of DL applications matter where they are located. Monitoring as a Service is referred as MaaS. The extensive monitoring, tracking and auditing capabilities of DLAs help administrators identify and react to misuse due to malicious intentions, undetected compromises, policy gaps, errors or oversights. They also provide extensive support for compliance with corporate policies, and with security and privacy regulations.

- **Session Shadowing:** Enables a given Library user session to be duplicated and displayed in real time on an administrator's workstation. This functionality can be used either for troubleshooting purposes or to watch a Library user's activities to confirm suspected misuse.
- **Activity Logging:** Creates a visual record of a Library user's on-screen activity while accessing online applications and stores it as a video file on a secure server. Session recording can be initiated based on triggered rules, for example, when a specific user in a watch group connects to a specific DLA.
- **Reporting:** Provides a long-term mechanism for revealing the nature of Library user activities and their tendencies. When gathered and selectively displayed, these details can be used not only to help refine access and usage policies, but also to support forensic analysis.

Monitoring-as-a-Service is an outsourced service to provide security mainly to platforms that are run on the Internet for conducting business. Maas became highly popular in the last decade. Safe monitoring involves protecting DLs from cyber threats, in which a team prepared is crucial to maintain the confidentiality, integrity and access to IT assets. However, time and resources constrain the limits of security operations and their effectiveness for the vast majority of companies. With this, it is vital to continue vigilance on security infrastructure and information.

This service monitor and manage the quality of service of the architecture, including its performance, security, and manageability. This service also includes building blocks such as performance managers, security managers, and notification managers.

Storage as a Service

Storage as a Service is generally seen as a good alternative for a small or mid-sized business that lacks the capital budget and/or technical personnel to implement and maintain their own storage infrastructure. SaaS is also being promoted as a way for all businesses to mitigate risks in disaster recovery, provide long-term retention for records and enhance both business continuity and availability. Cloud storage is a service model in which data is maintained, managed and backed up remotely and made available to users over a network (typically the Internet).

It facilitates cloud applications to scale beyond their limited servers. SaaS allows users to store their data at remote disks and access them anytime from any place. Cloud storage systems are expected to meet several rigorous requirements for maintaining users' data and information, including high availability, reliability, performance, replication and data consistency; but because of the conflicting nature of these requirements, no one system implements all of them together.

The types of storage layers for Infrastructure-as-a-Service (IaaS) include capabilities such as web or virtual machines (VMs), storage for online file sharing, backup or archiving, database, search and development tools. These capabilities enable cloud providers themselves or third parties to create customized solutions by combining the various cloud functionalities or layers with services provided. SaaS cloud storage solutions include file, document, music, photo and video sharing and backup/restore along with archiving capabilities. Other cloud storage options include database, cloud drives and other applications exploiting back-end cloud storage. Cloud storage solutions also extend to products and solutions used for deploying public, private and hybrid clouds.

Workflow of CORADLS

The Digital Library Portal Server (DLPS) provides single window access to the user. User interface is based on the keywords related to meta-data.

- The Library users login into the DLPS. The security checks the user whether authorized user or not. The authorized user can submit query to the central server.
- The DLPS translates the query and passes the query to the Storage Server.
- The Searching service checked with indexing services. Searching service do the ranking on the outcome of the indexing service. Application servers execute query provided by the central server and return results.
- The Searching services passes the response to the DLPS.
- The DLPS reformulates the ranked response according to the format expected by primary servers.
- The DLPS server returned results to user after translation, summarization, filtering etc. of the content as required or the link to the content.

This system works with meta-data information of the digital content present in the distributed digital repositories. Whenever any new content is added to any digital repository of the primary service, a set of metadata information moves to central server and as per the policy, central server updates the index files accordingly. The advantages of the CORADLS are availability, scalability, performance and maximize resources and they were given below:

- **Availability:** Improve capacity and performance of applications by offloading services, simplifies provisioning of application delivery services and increase virtual machine density for maximum efficiency
- **Scalability:** Increase operational efficiency by transparently scaling applications and ensure availability by proactively monitoring application health and capacity.
- **Performance:** Improve response time by offloading resource-heavy processing to the network, enhance performance by integrating feedback from application services into provisioning decisions and speed delivery times by applying the appropriate device-, location-, and application-specific policies that can optimize content to reduce bandwidth and transfer times.
- **Maximize Resources:** Ensure availability with seamless application-layer failover, enable a multi-tenant service delivery strategy to ensure fault isolation and self-service capabilities and integrate on- and off-premises cloud resources to ensure the highest levels of availability.

Evaluating CORADLS

In order to assess the success of Cloud Computing in DL, it is assessed the following central areas.

- The quality of the Library service has been very positive. Many libraries have become comfortable using SaaS-style services for other solutions and are increasingly reliant on Internet connectivity. So moving the Digital Library application infrastructure outside the campus network proved to be a non-issue. Both SaaS and PaaS solutions are difficult to implement in libraries.

- The DLAs often require specialized software or configurations which are either localized or simply application specific.
- By using an infrastructure level service, it is able to bring DLAs online without having to find a service that supported the correct s versions of the underlying technology.
- The impact of cost comparisons on cloud computing indicate that minimal cost savings may not be a sufficient inducement to change.
- Efforts to concentrate on investigations and aim at the development of a common platform that could span over different cloud implementations.

FUTURE RESEARCH DIRECTIONS

Service-oriented and cloud computing combined will indeed begin to challenge the way in which we think about enterprise computing. However, the potential for sharing could not only remove historical barriers but also encourage organizations to think more collaboratively. This research work is still at an initial stage and is carried out in the context of the first author's doctoral research. The research scope is to explore and propose a framework for improving the cross-platform development and deployment of cloud applications.

- There is a wide range of available platform offerings that a cloud developer can choose from today.
- Each platform may have unique characteristics and use certain technologies, tools, APIs etc. Moreover the provided services may vary significantly across platforms.
- A realistic approach would be to focus on a certain set of platform offerings, services, technologies whose scope is to support all type applications.
- Many of the activities loosely grouped together under cloud computing have already been happening and centralised computing activity is not a new phenomena.
- There are concerns that the mainstream adoption of cloud computing could cause many problems for distributed users.

CONCLUSION

Libraries have the opportunity to improve their services and relevance in today's information society. Cloud computing can bring several benefits for libraries and give them a different future. Cloud computing which is applied in digital libraries, analyzes current situation and existing problems of the cloud computing in digital library All library resources and service distributed on the Internet can be integrated as a whole, which forms a new type of adaptive control service system supporting interlibrary collaboration and service access, as well sharing resources from different libraries.

This chapter described the issue of scalability in the domain of Digital Library. It also described the proposed reference architecture for Digital Library systems. The main issues of cloud security are all related to architecture are scalability and security which is the basic issue of cloud computing. Cloud computing technology is still relatively young in terms of maturity and adoption. However, there are some issues like caching, routing, etc., to be resolved to build a highly scalable reference architectures in Digital Library systems.

REFERENCES

Athanasopoulos, G., Candela, L., Castelli, D., Innocenti, P., Ioannidis, Y., & Katifori, A. ... Ross, S. (2010). *Coordination action on digital library interoperability, best practices and modelling foundations: The Digital Library Reference Model*. Retrieved from http://www.dlorg.eu/uploads/DL%20Reference%20Models/The%20Digital%20Library%20Reference%20Model_v1.0.pdf

Avancini, H., Candela, L., Manzi, A., & Simi, M. (2006). *A powerful and scalable digital library information service*. Retrieved from http://www.ercim.eu/publication/Ercim_News/enw66/ avancini.html

Badger, L., Bohn, R., Chu, S., Hogan, M., Liu, F., & Kaufmann, V. ... Leaf, D. (2011). *US government cloud computing technology roadmap volume II release 1.0 (draft): NIST cloud computing program information technology laboratory*. Retrieved from http://www.nist.gov/itl/cloud/upload/SP_500_293_volumeII.pdf

Behrendt, M., Glasner, B., Kopp, P., Dieckmann, R., Breiter, G., & Pappe, S. ... Arsanjani, A. (2011). *Introduction and architecture overview: IBM cloud computing reference architecture 2.0*. Retrieved from http://www.teamswift-solutions.com/CCRA.IBMSubmission.02282011.pdf

Council, C. I. O. (2012). *Creating effective cloud computing contracts for the federal government: Best practices for acquiring IT as a service, in coordination with the Federal Cloud Compliance Committee*. Retrieved from https://cio.gov/wp-content/uploads/downloads/2012/09/cloudbestpractices.pdf

Goldner, M. (2010). *Winds of change: Libraries and cloud computing*. Retrieved from http://www.oclc.org/content/dam/oclc/events/2011/files/IFLA-winds-of-change-paper.pdf

Han, L., & Wang, L. (2011). Research on digital library platform based on cloud computing. *Advances in Computer Science, Environment, Ecoinformatics, and Education Communications, 214*, 176–180. doi:10.1007/978-3-642-23321-0_27.

Hewlett-Packard. (2011). *A white paper: Understanding the HP cloud system reference architecture reference architecture*. Retrieved from www.hp.com/go/cloudsystem

IBM Developer Network. (2003). *Web services security*. Retrieved from http://www.ibm.com/developerworks/webservices/library/ws-security.html

Liu, J., Zhang, L. J., Hu, B., & He, K. (2012, June). *CCRA: Cloud computing reference architecture. Paper presented at the 9th International Conference on Service Computing (SCC 2012)*. Honolulu, HA.

Mazurek, C., Stroinski, M., Werla, M., & Węglarz, J. (2006). *Metadata harvesting in regional digital libraries in PIONIER network, 23*(4), 241-253.

NIST. (2013). *Copy data objects out of a cloud*. Retrieved from http://collaborate.nist.gov/twiki-cloud-computing/bin/view/CloudComputing/UseCaseCopyFromCloud

OASIS. (2013). *OASIS privacy management reference model technical committee*. Retrieved from http://www.oasis-open.org/committees/pmrm/charter.php

Padhy, S. C., & Mahapatra, R. K. (2012). Cloud computing: Academic library in Orissa. *VSRD Technical Non-Technical Journal, 3*(3), 124–130.

Palanivel, K., & Kuppuswami, S. (2011). Service-oriented reference architecture for personalized e-learning systems (SORAPES). *International Journal of Computers and Applications*, *24*(5), 35–44. doi:10.5120/2956-3907.

Palanivel, K., & Nagalingam, U. (2011, November). Service-oriented reference model to security for digital library (SORMSDL). In B. R. Babu & P. N. Rao (Eds.). Information Security in the Digital Era: Society for Electronic Transactions and Security, 230-243.

Pomerantz, J. (2003). Integrating digital reference service into the digital library environment. *The Digital Research Agenda, 23*(47).

Reddy, T. R. (2012). Digital era: Utilize Of cloud computing technology in digital library. *International Journal of Digital Library Services*, 2(2), 92–106.

Reed, P. R., Jr. (2004). *Reference architecture: The best of best practices*. Retrieved from http://www.ibm.com/developerworks/rational/library/2774.html

Sanchati, R., & Kulkarni, G. (2011, July). Cloud computing in digital and university libraries. *Global Journal of Computer Science and Technology, 11*(12).

Shrawankar, M. G., & Dhage, S. (2011). Enhancements in libraries using cloud computing. In *Proceedings of the 2nd National Conference on Information and Communication Technology NCICT(5)*. New York: Foundation of Computer Science.

Sinha, R., & Sanyal, R. (2011). *Creating aggregative digital repository in distributed environment using service oriented architecture: New dimensions in special libraries services.* Paper presented at ICoASL 2011. Tokyo, Japan.

Subramanyam, G. V. B. (2012). *Cloud-based reference architecture: Design factors of financial supply chain systems*. Retrieved from http://cloudcomputing.sys-con.com/node/2112881

Teregowda, P., Urgaonkar, B., & Lee Giles, C. (2010). Cloud computing: A digital libraries perspective. Paper presented at IEEE Cloud 2010, Computer Science and Engineering. Pennsylvania State University, University Park, PA.

Vaughan, J. (2011). *Web scale discovery services*. Chicago: ALA TechSource Publications.

Zhang, Y., Wu, J., & Zhuang, Y. (2004). The personalized services in CADAL digital library. The College of Computer Science, ZheJiang University. Hangzhou, China.

Zhao, Y. (2012). *Enterprise and solution architecture forum, 2012*. Retrieved from www.Architechllc.com.

Zheng, Q., Chen, Z., & Bai, X. (2003). *Research on the application of notification service for service-oriented digital library*. China: Shanghai Jiao Tong University Library.

Zheng, X., & Fang, Y. (2010). *An AIS-based cloud security model*. Paper presented at the International Conference on Intelligent Control and Information Processing (ICICIP). Dalian, China.

Chapter 15
Service-Oriented Reference Architecture for Digital Library Systems

K. Palanivel
Computer Centre, Pondicherry University, India

S. Kuppuswami
Kongu College of Engineering, India

ABSTRACT

Developing and maintaining Digital Libraries requires substantial investments that are not simply a matter of technological decisions but also organizational issues. While digital libraries hold plenty of promise both now and for the future, they have been slow in taking off. Some digital libraries have either been completely abandoned or they have been put on hold indefinitely. One of the reasons for this predicament is that developers of digital libraries have approached their implementation the same traditional way of building applications, which is also akin to how structures of physical information organizations are built. Digital Libraries with their universal functionality may be even more flexible and reusable, if designed in a service-oriented manner. Such design should allow decreasing the effort of the creation of new digital libraries and the maintenance and scaling of currently existing large installations. Service-oriented architecture offers a better approach to building digital libraries, including streamlining business components, employing reusable services and connecting existing applications to communicate efficiently. The SOA is still a fairly new concept in DL systems. This chapter investigates the applicability of SOA as a fundamental architecture within the system. Its objective is to design a Service-Oriented Architecture for Digital Library System (DLS) using Web Service technology. SORADLS includes different layers which provide primitive services to the library applications built on top of the DLS. DLS techniques of personalization, alert, and caching build SORADLS as services. This architecture provides a fast, safe, convenient, and efficient service to users connected through the Internet.

DOI: 10.4018/978-1-4666-4631-5.ch015

INTRODUCTION

The library services are always followed by library works. Information and communication technology (ICT) have brought changes in the concept of traditional library work as well as service. The recent trend and change in the information related field especially in collection, storing, processing and dissemination of information have resulted in to the evolution of digital libraries. Now most of the reference books like encyclopedias, dictionaries, directories, hand books, and so forth, are published in electronic form. At present, most of the digital libraries have been highlighted mainly on providing access to diverse digital information resources. A digital library is an information retrieval system in which collections are stored in digital formats and easily accessed by networked computers (Bergeron, 2004). Advantages of digital libraries include limitless storage, no physical boundary, multiple accesses, instantaneity of retrieval, round-the-clock availability, indestructible, preservation and conservation, and so forth.

The Digital Library is completely dealing with the digital data in the form of text, graphs, images of photo copies, sounds, and so forth. Digital Library and its storage systems need various technologies, including scanning, OCR, digital storage techniques, data compression, indexing and search algorithms, display devices and the Internet. The digital searching becomes so easy, inexpensive, fast and ubiquitous that users will not tolerate, or will not access, traditional materials, special techniques for non-textual materials, such as music, images, videotape, and so forth. For the Digital Library, the core data required for it must be in the Digital format. So if the collected data of any format should be converted into digital form. Converting text, images, and objects to digital form requires much more than digital photography or even high-resolution scanning and requires some process, like:

- Initial input, either scanning or keyboarding.
- Conversion to one of a set of standard digitals.
- Optical character recognition (OCR) to capture text characters for searching.
- Creation and input of metadata and cataloging information.

The provision of personalized reference and information services is considered as one of the important characteristics of the library and information profession (Baman, 2004).

Digital Library System

Digital Library System (DLS) stores content digitally and is accessible by computers. DLS retrieves comprehensive yet accurate information and virus-free, delivering it instantly at the click of the mouse across the intranet. This efficient and interactive software platform, boasts the most up-to-date information on every subject that is quickly retrievable by keying in some elementary fields in the search options. This eliminates the innumerable hours spent crawling search engines which more often than not spews out contradicting and unreliable information while restricting unnecessary Internet access, which is difficult to control/monitor.

The key principles of DLS architecture are open architecture, modularization, federation and distribution. The Open Architecture partitioned into set of well-defined services and these services accessible via well-defined protocol. The Modularization promotes interoperability and scalable to different clientele (research library, informal Web). Federation enables aggregations into logical collections. The Distribution distributes the content (collections) and services in the network environment. It also distributes the administration and management of DLS.

Digital Library Services

Digital library is simply an online system providing access to a wide variety of digital content and services. Digital content can include virtually any kind of electronic material, such as various kinds of electronic media (images, video, etc.), licensed databases of journals, articles, and abstracts, and descriptions of physical collections. Digital Library services are also varied, but typically serve the same roles that traditional collection development and access services have in physical libraries: selection, specialization, and administration.

In a digital library, collection selection means acquiring, describing, storing, and delivering electronic resources. Metadata is used to describe the intellectual and technical attributes of the resource's objects. Storage is not only distributed across an institution but around the world through subscription or collaboration with remote partners. Many digital objects can be delivered directly over the Web, while some may require special viewing applications.

Digital Libraries with their universal functionality may be even more flexible and reusable, if designed in a service-oriented manner. Such design should allow decreasing the effort of the creation of new digital libraries and the effort of maintenance and scaling of currently existing large installations. Standardized interfaces to such services should also allow to reuse them in other systems and to use services from other systems as components of digital libraries.

Service-Oriented Computing

Service-Oriented Computing (SOC) is a relatively new paradigm of computing where tasks are subdivided and performed by independent and possibly remote components that interact using well-defined communications protocols. In particular, the Service-Oriented Architecture (SOA) refers to a framework built around XML and XML messaging. It is often argued that SOA can be adopted by an organization to increase reuse, modularity and extensibility of code, while promoting a greater level of interoperability among unrelated network entities.

Service-Oriented Architecture (SOA) allows many applications or components of systems to be loosely joined and yet perform different functions efficiently. SOA was used, as this is arguably ideal for loosely-coupled systems that need to interconnect with other systems. In order to produce digital library infrastructures of a high quality, an effective discovery phase of the constituent components and careful monitoring of the infrastructure are mandatory. Service-Oriented Architecture would require that you implement a general purpose service that renders in different formats (Osei-Poku, 2009). This removes the need to keep building multiple copies of services that would be needed by many applications. In the future if the digital library decides to render content in a completely new format, the same general purpose service could be called to do the rendering. In designing a user experience layer, it is necessary to connect interface elements to back-end services.

Reference Architecture/ Model for DLS

The building of a Digital Library requires a cooperative and distributed development model that, as far as possible, promotes the sharing and reuse of current Digital Library products. In order to support this model, an abstract solution to the problem of implementing a Digital Library–in other words, reference architecture–is fundamental.

In the area of Digital Library (DL), a pragmatic approach has required in developing systems via specialized methodologies, usually by adapting techniques borrowed from other disciplines. This approach has produced a plethora of heterogeneous entities and systems–commonly classified as 'Digital Library Systems'–and has resulted in a lack of agreement on what should constitute the fundamental aspects of DL technology. This makes the interoperability, reuse, sharing, and cooperative development of DLs extremely difficult. Moreover, the role played by DLs undergoes continuous evolution, making current systems inadequate for future applications. Modern DLs are conceived as systems to support the whole process of dealing with human knowledge production, maintenance, and communication.

To overcome the above limitations and lay the foundations upon which to build future DL systems, it is aimed at producing a Digital Library Reference Model. A reference model is an abstract framework for describing and understanding the significant relationships between entities in an environment. It consists of a minimal set of unifying concepts and relationships within a problem domain and is usually independent of specific standards, technology, implementations or other concrete details. Its goal is to enable the development and integration of systems by using consistent standards or specifications supporting that environment.

The main outcome of this chapter is to design a Reference Architecture to Digital Library Systems, which provides an abstract solution to the problem of organizing and implementing DL systems. This reference architecture is based on a loosely coupled component-oriented approach. Such an approach is fundamental for the purposes of the reference architecture, since it allows for: (i) easy tailoring of the DL through component selection and replacement; (ii) reuse of the components in different contexts; (iii) distributed installation (since each component can be independently implemented); and (iv) easy support for heterogeneity issues by using or providing an appropriate component dealing with the particular issue.

The chapter is structured as follows. Background describes the theoretical background of this chapter such as Digital Libraries, Web Services, Web Service Notifications, Publish-Subscribe and Personalized DLs. Literature review was done in section 3. Various architectures using Web Services and SOA were identified and studied. Section 4 describes the architecture of SORADLS. The description includes the requirements and architecture. Finally, section 5 concludes the paper and provides recommendations for future works.

BACKGROUND

This section introduces the background information required to depict this chapter. It includes digital library and Web service technology. Also, a literature review was done in this section.

Digital Library

Digital Library conjures up an image of a sprawling universe of information available through the Internet and accessible via home or office workstations, fulfilling the promise to provide information at any time, to any place, and for any user. A digital library must have a number of characteristics such as coherence, searchability, preservation, service and opportunities, in addition to being a collection of digitized materials. Digital libraries should have a coherent, organizing principle, sorting materials by topic or by type of material, for instance (Gupta & Ansari, 2006). The ability to find and use materials on the Internet is a major challenge for most users. Information on the Internet is, in many cases, ephemeral and presents considerable challenges for archiving.

Few digital libraries have built services into their offerings of collections. Digital libraries can build in services where users can ask questions, use frames to provide guidance and instruction, and can develop FAQs (frequently asked questions) files to assist users. Digital libraries offer new opportunities to enhance the value of collections to users. Digital libraries are offering a wealth of information to a large community of users and will become an increasingly valuable part of the Internet as they are developed in a coherent and imaginative way.

Web Service Technology

A Web Service is a software system designed to support interoperable machine-to-machine interaction over a network (Ort, 2005). Web Services expose only their interfaces to the public. Such an interface can be completely described using a Web Service Description Language (WSDL) document that characterizes the Web Service interface in terms of operations that the Web Service provides, messages that are exchanged to do so and data types that are used to construct those messages. An important characteristic of Web Services is that implementation details of the systems are hidden behind the interface.

The use Web services also bring about the important benefit of collaboration. Many digital libraries need to collaborate with other digital libraries, physical libraries, publishers, retailers, and so forth. The use of service-oriented architecture and specifically the use of Web services could increase the level of collaborations and cooperation and also remove all bottlenecks that impede cooperation. In addition to that, it could make the digital library agile enough to meet increasing demands on it.

- **SOAP:** It is an application-level protocol based on XML used for data exchange and remote procedure call in distributed applications, usually for accessing Web Services (Gudgin et al., 2007). Due to its XML-based design, SOAP is platform and programming language independent. SOAP messages are transmitted embedded into or on top of other application-level protocols such as HTTP, SMTP, or JMS.
- **WSDL:** The Web Service Description Language (WSDL) provides the possibility to completely describe a Web Service interface through the use of an XML document that conforms to an XML Schema as defined by the WSDL specification of the W3C. WSDL provides machine-processable information on how to interact with a given Web Service to a Web Service consumer application. Since the Web Service is fully described by the WSDL document, it is possible to generate client code for interaction with a given Web Service by using the definitions given in the WSDL document (Chinnici, Moreau, Ryman, & Weerawarana, 2007).
- **UDDI:** The Universal Description Discovery and Integration (UDDI) specification defines a Web Service registry that allows possible Web Service consumers to dynamically discover Web Services that provide a certain service. While WSDL describes the Web Service interface, UDDI allows the discovery of the Web Service interface by clients. The UDDI registry is actually a Web Service itself and makes use of WSDL to describe its interface. The main purpose of the UDDI registry is to allow client applications to dynamically discover Web Services that provide a required service. The use of UDDI allows the client applications to discover a replacement for failed Web Services (Clement, Hately, von Riegen, & Rogers, 2008).

Web Service Notifications (WSN) is to allow Web Services to notify other interested entities of events that have occurred inside the Web Service (Vinoski, 2004). In the basic form of publish-subscribe interaction, a Web Service publishes a topic of events to which other interested entities may subscribe. Occurrence of an event inside the publishing Web Service then triggers the Notification of subscribed entities. Additional to this basic form, Web Service Notifications may also involve an intermediary Web Service, called a Notification broker that may introduce additional features and enhanced scalability to the Web Service Notification architecture.

WS-Security is a good choice for interoperability with external partner but might have a negative effect on performance when used internally (IBM, 2002). The security services view therefore needs to provide specifications of the available security services, the use of related standards as well as proprietary standards or technologies both for internal use as well as for external use. Additionally the specific use of open standards needs to be documented, as they usually provide a large degree of flexibility.

Service-Oriented Architecture

Service-Oriented Architecture is an architectural style which utilizes methods and technologies that provides for enterprises to dynamically connect and communicate software applications between different business partners and platforms by offering generic and reliable services that can be used as application building blocks (Ort, 2005). In this way it is possible to develop richer and more advanced applications and information systems. Although SOA is not a new concept, especially after the invention of Web Services, the new developments in this area bring about a new way of constructing software application architectures, a new approach to rebuild available software infrastructures and possibility of communicating with other enterprises according to the available services.

SOA contains the following entities in its conceptual model, described as follows:

- **Service Consumer:** It is the entity in SOA that looks for a service to execute a required function. The consumer can be an application, another service, or some other type of software module that needs the service. The location of the service is discovered either by looking up the registry, or if it is known, the consumer may directly interact with the service provider.
- **Service Provider:** It is the network addressable entity that accepts and executes requests from consumers. It provides the definite service description and the implementation of the service. The service provider can be a component, or other type of software system that fulfills the service consumer's requirements.
- **Service Registry:** It is a directory which can be accessible through network and contains available services. Its main function is to store and publish service descriptions from providers and deliver these descriptions to interested service consumers.

Publish-Subscribe

Publish/subscribe is a well-known communication pattern for event-driven, asynchronous communication (Meiler & Schmeing, 2009). The pattern is particularly well suited in situations where information is produced at irregular intervals. By using publish/subscribe instead, the consumers subscribe to information from the applications instead, and receive a notification each time new information is available. This means that the consumers receive the information the moment it is available (instead of having to wait for the next polling), and the network traffic is reduced. Thus, the asynchronous nature of the publish/subscribe paradigm makes it a very important mode of communication in distributed systems.

Personalized Digital Libraries

Personalization is defined as the ways in which information and services can be tailored to match the unique and specific needs of an individual or a community (Callan et al., 2003). Personalization is about building customer loyalty by creating a meaningful one-to-one relationship; by understanding the needs of each individual and helping satisfy a goal that efficiently and knowledgeably addresses each individual's need in a given context. The key element of a personalized environment is the user model. A user model is a data structure that represents user interests, goals and behaviors. The more information a user model has, the better the content and presentation will be tailored for each individual user. A user model is created through a user modeling process in which unobservable information about a user is inferred from observable information from that user; for example, using the interactions with the system.

DLs are more than simple Web pages that give access to information. They also comprise, among others, a structure for the organization of the information, metadata regarding the semantic of the information and knowledge about who uses them and for what purposes. This implies that, if usually designing a good Web page is problematic, the process of designing a good digital library is even more complex due to the syntactic and semantic organization/architecture that is needed (Palanivel, Amouda, & Kuppuswami, 2009). In general, the services provided by DL through their interaction elements (interface) can be classified as follows:

- Mechanisms for the personalization of content. These mechanisms make it possible for each user to create a personal DL that contains only the information that is interesting and relevant to that user.
- Mechanisms to help in the process of navigation. These services present each user with an environment that better suit the way in which that user interacts with the DL.
- Information filtering (IF) and information retrieval (IR) mechanisms. These services provide ways to find and filter the vast amount of information that a user accesses and receives.

Review and Related Works

Several research papers have been published on DSs recently using Web services and SOA are reviewed and the research papers that are related to this work are discussed below:

Baman (2004) highlighted present scenario of digital library services in India. It outlines the initiatives taken by the UGC, India, the INFLIBNET Centre, DELNET, IITs, RECs, National Research Organizations/ Institutions of India in the digitization of libraries and information centers in order to provide digital library services. Further it suggests that in a developing country like India where resources are limited, funds are inadequate the library and information professionals should develop their skill and proficiency to meet the challenges of technological developments and changes emerging out of digital library services.

Kodali, Farkas, and Wijesekera (2004) proposed the concept of *generalized subject* that encompasses all access permissions of a given user, regardless of the multiple permissions in different access control models. Finally, we develop methods to generate secure views for each generalized subject and retrieve them using a secure multimedia server.

Zheng, Chen, and Bai (2003) researched the architectures, main technique points and methods of these four notification service modules under the framework of Web service and information grid. In this paper, the notification services in the individualized Portal System of Shanghai Jiaotong University Library are introduced.

Gupta and Ansari (2006) discussed the concept of Interoperability in the digital library environment. It also covered infrastructure requirement for digital library research, research issues and priorities-Interoperability, objects and repositories, collection management and organization, user interfaces.

Han and Wang (2011) Consisted of four lays: infrastructure layer, data layer, management layer, and service layer. The structure and function of each layer are described in great detail. The new digital library platform can be used to solve the problem of library resource storing and sharing effectively, and provide fast, safe, convenient and efficient services to users.

Buchanan and Hinze (2005) discussed the lessons learned from building such a distributed alerting service. We present our prototype implementation as a proof-of-concept for an alerting service for open DL software.

Sherikar, Jange, and Jadhav (2006) attempted to notify the significance of Digital reference Services in the Internet world and suggests the criteria Planning and implementing Digital Reference Services in an academic and research world. Further, the Web-based reference services, which could be used by the libraries are compiled and concludes with challenges of system of Digital Reference Services.

Osei-Poku (2009) looked at some of the major benefits of service-oriented architecture and how digital libraries can tap into these benefits by adopting and implementing the requirements of service-oriented architecture. The essay concludes that digital libraries are better-off adopting service-oriented approach than maintaining the status quo.

In a survey of these architectural paradigms and their exploitation in current DLSs is reported. This study aimed at identifying the similarities among these paradigms as well as their distinguishing peculiarities in fulfilling the various requirements arising in the Digital Library arena. The major outcome of this study consists in the recognition of the complementary nature of these architectures and of the needs to combine them in order to fruitfully exploit the available resources in different contexts.

PROPOSED ARCHITECTURE: SORADLS

This section describes digital library systems using the reference architecture in different application contexts. The proposed reference architecture is called SORADLS and this architecture is designed using Web Services and SOA. The Reference Architecture can have multiple instances once implemented in a concrete scenario.

Motivation Example

The motivation behind to design scalable SORADLS is presented in figure 1. The users are connected to the Digital Library Web Portal Server (DLWPS). The Digital Library Application Server (DLAS) includes various applications like authentication, library contents, OPAC and alert systems. The library users logs in once and gains access to all digital contents. The users submit the query and the DSWPS retrieves the content and displays to the user. To improve the data access rate it maintains a caching server. The library users are connected to the Library portal server and availed various services offered by the portal in distributed environment.

Here the main challenge is as the number of users and e-resources grows instead of having a manageable size of e-learning users/resources.

Figure 1. Motivation example for SORADLS

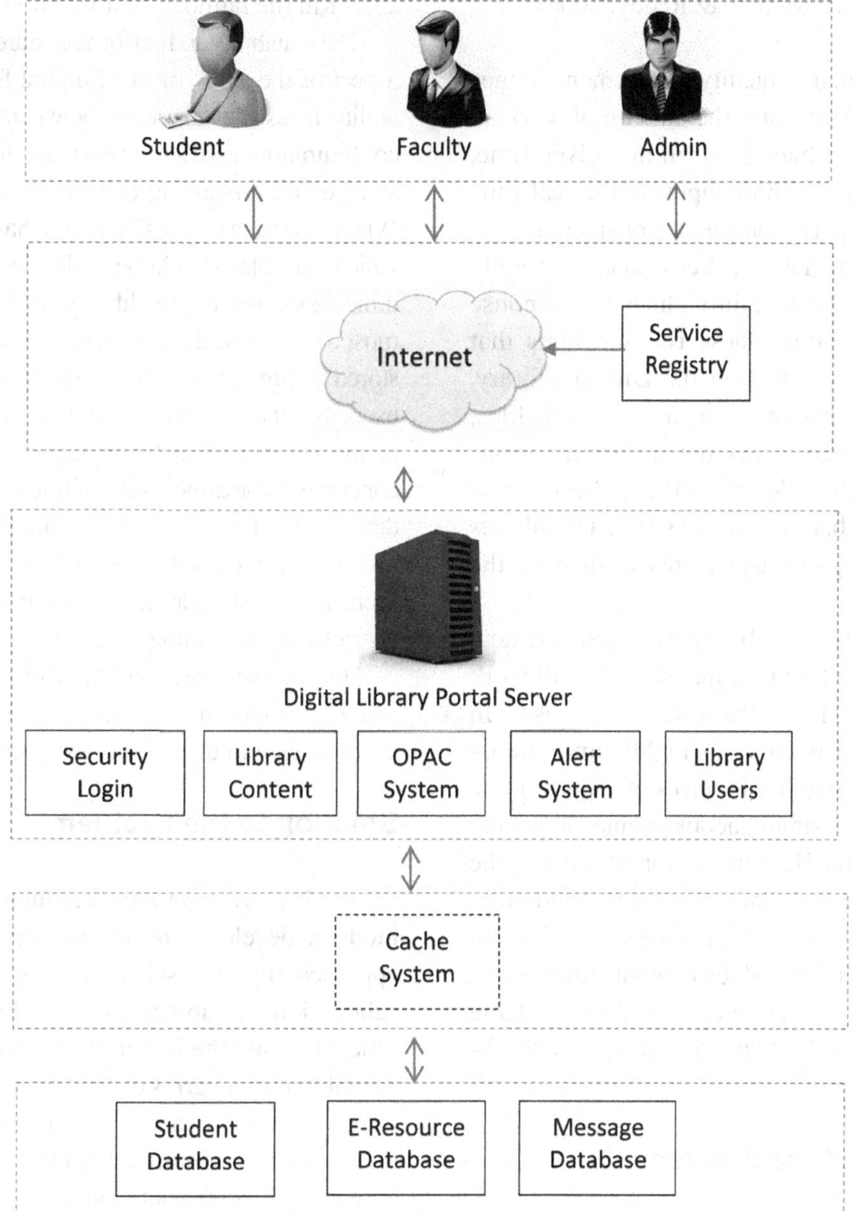

Some more challenges are provides a flexible DLS in distributed environment, provide support interoperability between hardware/software, delivers appropriate performance using scalable architecture, needs to be adaptable e-learning architecture and needs to be a seamless integration of individual components in DLS.

Challenges in Digital Library Systems

Quality of Service in a Digital Library can be highlighted in terms of both functional and non-functional requirements. The Performance and the Scalability are the critical non-functional requirements / quality attributes of the Digital Library (Pratha, Mattam, Ambati, & Reddy, 2006).

- A Performance quality requirement defines a metric that states the amount of work an application must perform in a given time, also called as throughput. In the real-time systems performance is considered very critical in DLS's. Performance usually manifests itself in throughput and response time measures. These two measures that have major effect on the Digital Library. When streaming the audio/video files, client system slows down due to various reasons like file size, disk space, congestion, and bandwidth and so on. This affects the throughput and response time of the system.
- Scalability can be represented as how well a solution to some problem will work when the size of the problem increases. In the digital library it is highlighting the issue of scalability in terms of request load, data size, simultaneous connections and bandwidth. Here the major concern is the simultaneous connections and bandwidth that need to be established in a Digital Library. In general the content delivery can take place by providing the downloadable file. This will reduce the flexibility for library users.

Statement of the Problem

Digital Libraries (DL) are concerned with the creation and management of information resources, the movement of information across global networks and the effective use of this information by a wide range of users. One of the services offered by a DL is to retrieve "relevant" digital objects and return them to the user. To provide their services over a long time, digital libraries have to be scalable to support for future growth in different dimensions, for example in the number of users and/or in the number of stored documents.

The scalability and performance are the important aspect of the assessment of digital libraries. Scalability faces the mismatch between the hardware configurations and the current needs for information storage and processing and the growing of users. When assessing a digital library, it has to be defined which variables should be scaled, that is, in which dimensions the digital library should grow. The most common scaling variables are the number of stored documents and/or the number of supported users, but the number of different document types or the number of different services may also be concerned. The dimensions of scaling belong to the definable factors of scalability and they are settled once because scalability requires the built-in ability to change, which is, due to efficiency reasons, usually restricted to the scaling dimensions.

Hence, the statement of the problem is to provide a solution for better scalability and better performance to digital library systems.

Solution to the Problem

Digital Libraries are focusing more attention on modular development around services. A SOA approach supports scalability and the addition, subtraction, or substitution of technologies over time. Defining the functional components of the digital library in terms of services allows changes to be made in isolated or semi-isolated parts of the code with little impact on the other software components. It is easier to integrate new capabilities and improved technologies into the system if designers follow SOA principles while developing the system. Once defined and developed, services can be reused or modified, supporting flexibility and a modular architecture.

The solution to the above problem is to design a scalable architecture to DLS, that is, Service-Oriented Reference Architecture for Digital Library Systems (SORADLS). SORADLS is a layered architecture and using SOA and Web Services. SORADLS provides the developer a flexible architecture. SORADLS addressed the challenges are to build a distributed system for alerting in digital libraries integrated with the DL software and collections. SORADLS support distributed as well as local collections that are federated and creates fluent user access to documents independent of access paradigm (seeking or alerting), that is, alerting equivalent of searching and browsing.

In the context of SORADLS reliability refers to the ability of the architecture instances to provide around the clock service with minimal downtime, scalability to the ability to support increasing number of user requests and documents in the collection, and robustness to the ability of the instance to continue providing services while some of the underlying services are unavailable or resource constrained.

SORADLS is focused on the development of a new platform for storing digital contents. It has been designed to overcome traditional library limitations that characterize the process of building Service-Oriented Digital Library. The features of SORMSDL are as follows:

- Allow content creators/providers to easily share their archives through the Web interface or with application.
- Allow the archivist and administrator to define the way data should be rendered to the end users.
- Allow the archivists to provide for each archive of digital contents a specific visualization template and a set of search forms.

User interfaces to SOA-based systems need to submit requests (typically in XML over the Web) and parse and reformat or transform responses (typically also in XML) in order to generate portions of the Web interface. This communication is easily accomplished using Ajax.

Digital Library Services

In a broad sense a digital library is simply an on-line system providing access to a wide variety of content and services. Content can include virtually any kind of electronic material, such as various kinds of electronic media (images, video, etc.) licensed databases of journals, articles and abstracts, and descriptions of physical collections. Digital Library services are also varied, but typically serve the same roles that traditional collection development and access services have in physical libraries: selection, specialization and administration.

In a digital library, collection selection means acquiring, describing, storing and delivering electronic resources. Metadata is used to describe the intellectual and technical attributes of the resource's objects. Storage is not only distributed across an institution but around the world through subscription or collaboration with remote partners. Many digital objects can be delivered directly over the Web, while some may require special viewing applications.

Specialization motivates the creation of a variety of access services for searching, browsing and discovering resources. Digital objects need to be organized and indexed for different purposes. Obvious structures for organizing and indexing digital objects include collection catalogs, finding aids and databases -- but virtual collections can also be built from multiple resources. For example, an instructor may want to combine references to objects in the library catalog, electronic journals and electronic reserves in an on-line course page. Mechanisms to find and access these objects must work in different on-line contexts. In addition, patrons should be able to perform their own specialization by accessing digital library content and services through personalized portals.

Administration is handled by core services that usually interact with other digital library services rather than directly with patrons. These services must often be recreated for each new environment and digital library system. How they are developed and maintained is critical to the long-term success of a digital library project, especially when technical resources are limited. For example, a naming service can provide a technology- and location-independent mechanism for identifying and retrieving digital objects; without it, access services must be modified when resources move or are ported to a new platform.

Access control presents a growing challenge as digital libraries include an increasing variety of electronic resources from different sources. Different mechanisms (e.g., proxy, login names/passwords, certificates or other vouchers) are required to grant access depending on who and where the patron is and what resource is being accessed. Without a core service, each special access service must handle the task of choosing and performing the specific login or else pass the responsibility on to the patron.

Managing large amounts of digital information requires a robust server and a storage system that is reliable and has strong performance. While small digital collections do not need to worry as much about the details of storage, large digital libraries are likely to see significantly high levels of activity from users who will expect to access resources quickly and reliably. Decisions about the storage hardware, server allocations, databases, and distribution approaches, along with bandwidth considerations, are key in establishing the digital library as a resource that teachers, students, researchers, and the general public regard as reliable. If a user cannot access content easily, if a video can be viewed only after it has been downloaded, if music does not play at an even speed, or if content becomes corrupted or lost over time, for example, the community will not view the digital library as a credible source of information.

Storage decisions for large digital libraries have the most impact when the content is centrally located rather than distributed among systems that have differing architectures for managing the content. Repositories that are content aggregators increasingly have looked to clustered storage solutions to provide reliable and robust performance. Disc speed, failover capabilities, and automatic error correction functionality found in clustered storage solutions help ensure high availability of the content and a performance that is adequate to meet user needs.

Services Identified in DLS

The services identified in SORADLS are personalized, information, digital reference, notification, Web scale discovery, indexing, and so forth, are presented below. All the identified services are registered in the UDDI registry.

- **Registration Services:** The registration service registers or unregisters the library users. The service also updates the existing registration information.
- **Notification Services:** The chief function of the notification service moduleof the portal project of service-oriented digital library is to notify the users with the latest information they are interested in automatically without any users' information retrieval and request. The users only need to do is to register the kind of their subject (Buchanan and Hinze, 2005).
- **Personalization Services:** The personalization services in a digital library environment would help the library users to find information resources available in a digitally chaotic world. However there is a demand for end-user instruction on the use of digital libraries and the digital library professionals who are subject specialists should help users to formulate disciplinary search strategies and provide assistance in developing new digital information resources (Zhang, Wu, & Zhuang, 2004).

- **Digital Reference Services:** Digital Reference Services include either finding the required information on behalf of users, or assisting users in finding information themselves. Web based reference services are also provided by academic libraries (Pomerantz, 2003). These libraries use customer relationship management (CRM) software packages for providing Web-based reference services in the virtual reference environment.
- **Indexing Service:** The Indexing service provides the generic functionality of an inverted file, mapping elementary tokens (e.g., word, date, etc.) to documents/entities (Sinha & Sanyal, 2011). In the context of API, two instances of this service are used to independently index documents and their citations. It is interesting to see that, as we extend API to deal with additional semantic objects – e.g. acknowledgements – we can take advantage of the service granularity to add a new index service for those objects without affecting existing indexes.
- **Metadata Service:** The Metadata service associates metadata records to all the objects managed by DL. Hence we can organize this service as repository (Mazurek, Stroinski, Werla, & Weglarz, 2006). In the context of CiteSeer and Digital Libraries, the Metadata Service becomes equivalent to the service providing the corresponding interface.
- **Repository Service:** The Repository service provides the functionality of a document repository which contains all the documents that are available from the API (Sinha & Sanyal, 2011). One important feature of this Service is that it is aware of file duplicates. It evolves towards a federation of such repositories, the service nature of the electronic repository will permit many such services to join in the federation, hence providing an effective solution to concerns such as copyright management or mirroring.

Services described above should allow composing a digital library, giving the core functionality required in such systems. The above description is focused on functional requirements of digital library services. The above identified services are registered in the services registry. The registry manager can either start/restart or stop the services.

Layered Architecture of DLS

The design uses layered Web application architecture (Palanivel & Kuppuswami, 2011). Figure 2 shows that the architecture of SORADLS. It consists of DL User Interface layer, DL Application layer, DL Resource, Caching layer and Storage layer and they are presented below:

The User Interface Layer (UIL) handles the interaction between users and the DLWPS. It consists of an HTML based browser user interface and displays information to the user and interpreted commands from the user into actions upon the DL components. The user interface provides the mechanism by which people interact with the computer's functionality. Typically a user's understanding of a computer application is governed by the behavior of the user interface. In a Web application, the interface is hosted within a user's Web browser. The user clicks on information and fills out forms. Because of the architecture of the Web, search is exclusively user-driven. A user requests a piece of information (by clicking on a link) and the server responds. The important ramification of this is that new pages are always requested by the user – the server does not spontaneously push new information to the client. Designing an effective application requires designing a user interface that is appropriate for the users and which helps them complete their tasks

Figure 2. Reference Architecture of SORADLS

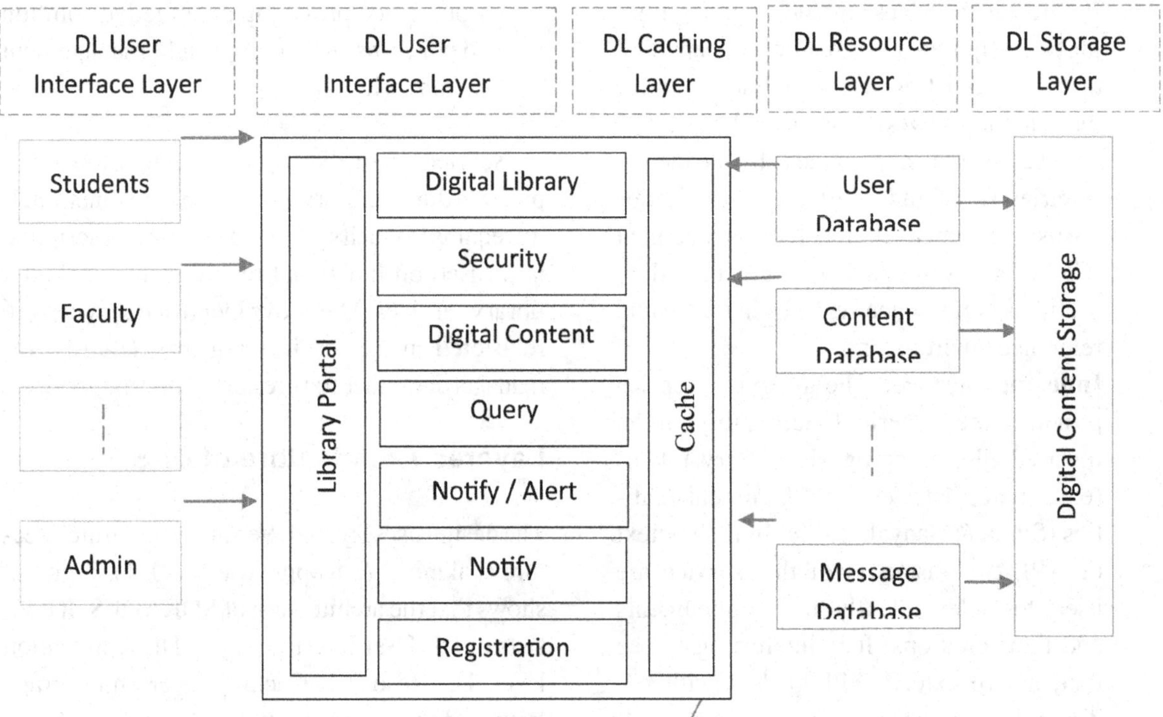

quickly and efficiently. Understanding user needs and testing possible interface designs with users is essential.

The DL Application layer serves as supporting components of the library services. It accepts requests from the User Interface Layer and need to be able to respond to those requests. The DL application layer provides uniform interfaces to distributed components of the digital library. It helps tie together the storage, delivery, searching, and browsing of electronic resources. By wrapping the digital libraries core services inside an application layer, existing and new resources can be more easily integrated into the digital library. This scalability is achieved through a middleware architecture that "brokers" communication between components.

Frequently accessed data is cached by DL Caching layer for efficient access. Its functions are very similar to a caching layer in a digital library for static users. An additional built in functionality is that data which is frequently accessed by many users is communicated to the broadcast module. The cache is also used to store answers to imprecise queries waiting to be transmitted to users/hosts. Caching is used by DLS's to reduce the response time for users. The role of caching is even more important when data is accessed by users. SORADLS supports caching to have a continuous data display during the voluntary disconnection periods. If the period of disconnection is known, then the amount of data that can be displayed in that time period is computed and is "prefetched" and stored in the cache.

The responsibility of DL Resource Layer (Database Layer) is storing persistent data. The communication should be where a component sends SQL requests to data sources and data sources sends responses back to components. The DL Resources Layer integrates heterogeneous collections distributed repositories and connects the resources related in space and time into a multidimensional mesh structure storage system. The Resource layer provides users with a uniform organic whole that is seamlessly linked to its heterogeneous parts. Service methods incorporated in the Resources layer are the abstracts database, full-text databases, citation databases, resource navigation databases, online public access catalogue, the special expert system, integrated periodicals and the integrated agricultural research basic data, among others.

The storage layer is responsible for physical storage of metadata and content. This can easily be modified, and will shortly be extended to cover multiple file systems to enable larger volumes of content to be stored. The Storage Layer describes the network of nodes and links. The run-time layer describes mechanisms supporting the user interaction with the hypermedia. The within-component layer covers the content and structures within hypermedia nodes. Between these three layers there are two interface mechanisms: the anchoring mechanism which acts as an interface between storage layer and within-component layer, and the presentation specification mechanism which acts as an interface between storage and run-time layers.

The caching layer can simply try to keep copies of query results but usually several queries are triggered in sequence, for example, because more than one attribute of a component is needed by client applications to do their work. Frequently accessed data is cached by this layer for efficient access. Its functions are very similar to a caching layer in a digital library for static users. An additional built-in functionality is that data which is frequently accessed by many users is communicated to the broadcast module. The cache is also used to store answers to imprecise queries waiting to be transmitted to users/hosts.

The DLSs are complex systems whose implementation and management beneficiate by their decomposition into smaller and more manageable parts. The Reference Architecture applies the decomposition technique and proposes a loosely coupled component oriented approach (Estefan, Laskey, McCabe, & Thornton, 2008). This approach is fundamental for the purposes of the reference architecture since it allows for

1. Easy design of the DLS through component selection and replacement.
2. Reuse of the components in different contexts.
3. Distributed installation and maintenance since each component can be independently implemented and deployed.
4. Easy supporting of heterogeneity issues by using or providing an appropriate component dealing with the particular problem.

Various modules of the proposed architecture are registration, security, caching, notification, and so forth are presented below.

Personalization Module

The users interact with portal through DLWPS, that is, personalized index page, reader page, setting page. The individual reads the content of book through Reader page, at the same time the logging module of portal records all book pages read by him/her. Reader page also provides functionality to make it easy for user to bookmark the book pages of interest and add current book to his personal collection. Moreover, one can set the personalized rules through setting page, which are regarded as one's preference. The monitoring module is applied on the logs recorded by logging module to discover the frequent sequential access pattern and then do the recommendation.

Registration Module

Registration provides an easy-to-use Web interface for potential users of an application to "register" themselves and request sign-in credentials. Administrators receive requests and decide whether to grant them or not. When a user is registered, a Library credential is created on his behalf and used whenever he uses the Library application.

Figure 3 shows that the function of Registration Service. Registration combines certification authority with a back-end database and a Library Web portal to automate user registration requests. The registration interface solicits basic data from user, including a desired ID/password combination. Requests are forwarded by email to an administrator and the data from the requests are stored in a database. The administrator uses administrative functions in the Web portal to process requests. Users receive email notification when their accounts are ready for use. When an account is created, the portal generates a credential for that account automatically. This library credential is issued by the application administrator, so it is most likely only "valid" for use with the specific application and no others.

When a user logs into the Library portal, the application obtains a certificate from the security service using the user's ID/password, and the application can then use this security to authenticate to any other service that recognizes credentials issued by the application administrator.

Notification Module

The function of the notification service module of the DL Web portal of service-oriented digital library is to notify the users with the latest information they are interested in automatically without any users' information retrieval and request. The users' only need to do is to register the kind of their subject.

Considering the actual application of DL Web portal system, the content types to be notified including: the subject information, subject navigations and pertinent Internet resources; the latest digital magazines users customized; the individual information; subject references; book records in the Internet Public Access Catalog System; public information; the library news/notification; new services provided by the library.

As interactive information seeking may be achieved by more than one method, for example, searching and browsing, alerting users of changes in content can be achieved in many ways. Bringing new content to the attention of readers is a common task in a physical library. To match this need, the accession shelf or acquisition section is used to highlight new material that the library

Figure 3. Structure of Registration Module

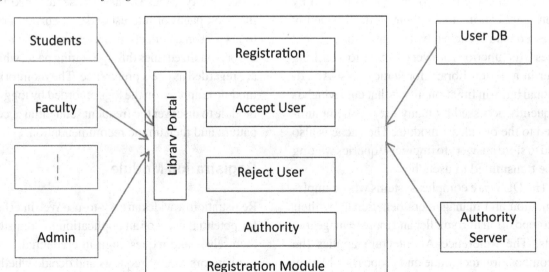

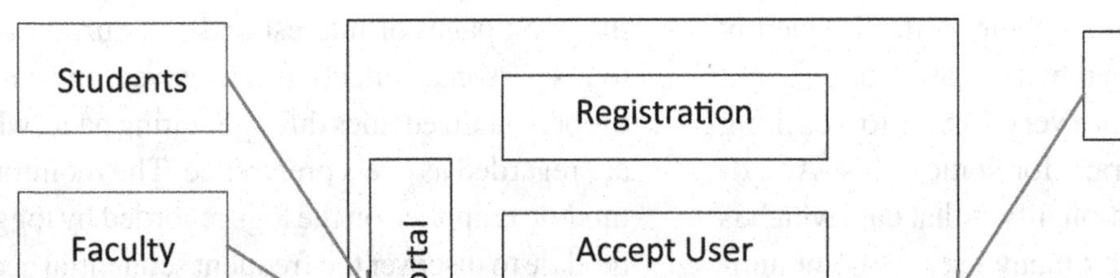

has obtained. An alerting service could provide an analog of this – a part of the classification hierarchy that lists recently added documents. A well personalized notification provides a similar service to the personal recommendations given by a librarian.

The alerting means such as selective dissemination of information or information filtering, or event notification system. An event occurs when a change occurs in a digital library. This results in an event message being sent that carries the information about the event. Often, alerts are generated during the library's building cycle (i.e., when a number of new documents are added and indexed in the library). The alerting service stores and indexes the profiles in a profile repository. Changes in the library are either automatically reported to the alerting service. The alerting has the process of profile creation, observation, filtering and notification. Figure 4 shows the Notification Service.

Security Module

Security module offers authentication, authentication, access control and confidentiality (Vaughan, 2011; IBM, 2007). The authentication handles the authentication requests sent to the DL portal. It is passed log-on credentials for a user and returns an authentication certificate. Authorization follows authentication and that is, once a user or system has be authenticated. Authorization means making a decision about whether an authenticated or even an authenticated identity is allowed to access a resource. The confidentiality is the security service for ensuring non-disclosure of sensitive information traveling through untrustworthy communication networks or at rest, such as in data stores, volatile memory, and so on.

Figure 5 shows the security module of SORADLS. SORADLS allows administrators to define access permissions on per user-based manner. That is, there is a direct relation between the subjects (users) and the objects (contents) determined by the access privilege, like given by an access control lists. The policies provide controlled information flow between the protection objects and subjects. To provide information confidentiality, data is permitted to flow only from a dominated security label to a dominating security label. A user plays within the organization determines his/her access privileges. Privileges are assigned to roles, and

Figure 4. Structure of Notification Module

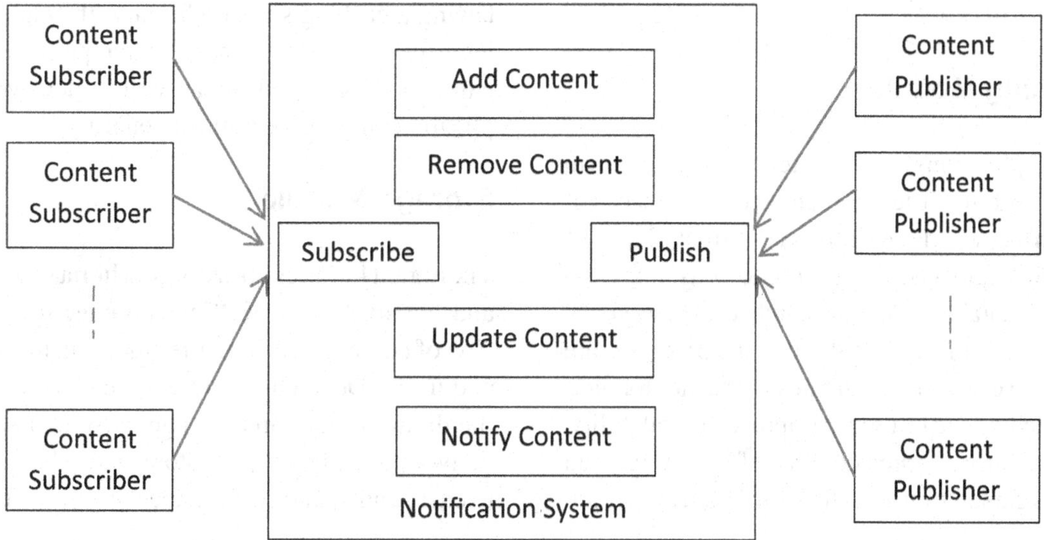

Figure 5. Structure of Security Module

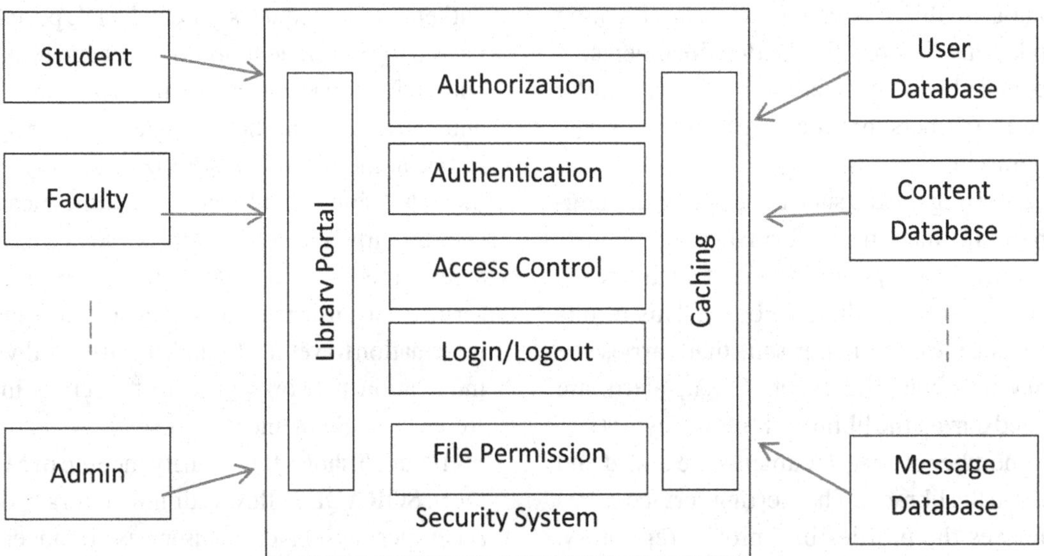

users are assigned to roles. A user is allowed to activate any assigned roles and the corresponding privileges within a session.

Security Service protect Digital Library Web Applications against the most common threats and attacks (Palanivel & Nagalingam, 2011). It delivers both critical Web protection and cost effective management. Security service for the DL includes access to Information, Data, User Account, Access Rights, Intrusion and Detection, Firewalls, Virtual Private Network, RFID, and so forth.

Caching Module

DL Applications can be often made to perform better and run faster by caching critical pieces of data in memory. Frequently accessed data, layers of HTML fragments, results of time-consuming/expensive database queries, search results, sessions, results of complex calculations and processes are usually very good candidates for cache storage.

Caching can be used to improve the scalability, performance and predictability of SORADLS and serves the same purpose for distributed library applications. By caching, the state of the content is transparently stored in a cache local to the client. Subsequent calls to the same content are solved by retrieving the value from the local cache rather than from the actual content. Main problems in caching are the efficient implementation of a caching mechanism and the issue of maintaining a local state that is synchronized with the actual state of the remote object. The structure of caching module is shown in the Figure 6.

DL application architectures benefit from having a caching solution because they are read intensive and usually have better performance gains using cache whereas write intensive applications may not get much benefit.

Storage Module

The digital libraries utilize digital library services and thus are capable of efficient storage and provision of content, fulfilling the requirements of the end-users. Depending on the type of content in the digital library and the approach adopted for delivering it, higher speed storage may be needed to ensure adequate performance (e.g., for stream-

Figure 6. Structure of Caching Module

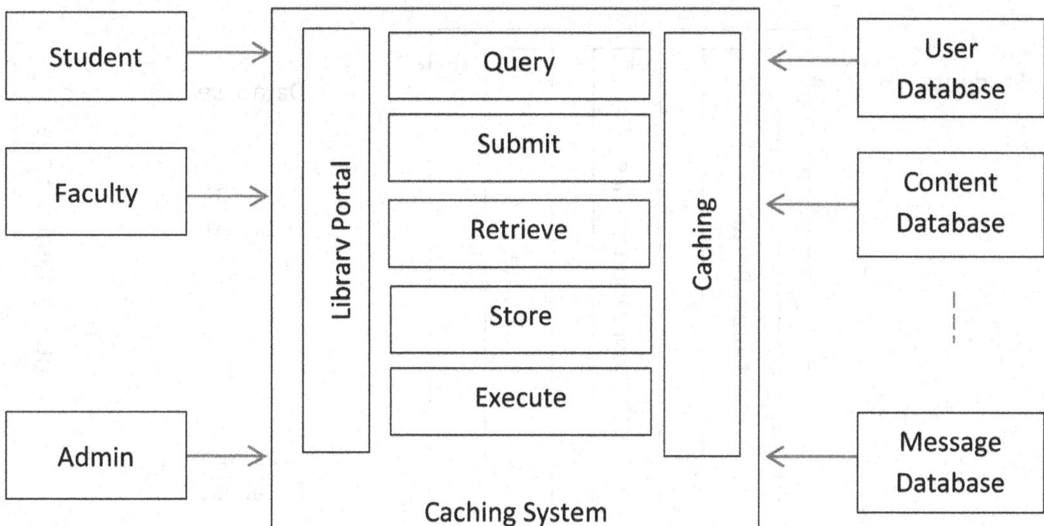

ing music); text-only content may not require a speed as high, but will still require failover and automatic error correction. One of the main challenges in designing an archival repository is how to configure the repository to achieve some target "preservation guarantee" while minimizing the cost and effort involved in running the repository.

The database contains objects and is focused on transactions and version tracking of objects central to digital libraries implementations. Objects stored in the main database include document metadata, author, citation, keywords, tags, and hub (URL). The tables in the main database are linked together by the document they appear in and are identified by the document object ID. The databases store metadata and relationships in the form of tables providing transaction support, where transactions include adding, updating or deleting objects. The database design partitions the data storage across three main databases. This allows for growth in any one component to be handled by further partitioning the database horizontally. The basic premise behind storage services architecture is thinking about infrastructure as a granular set of reusable services that can be invoked as needed by the appropriate DL application. This approach allows organizations to optimize on cost, performance, recovery, and other metrics that are fundamental to DL processes. The structure of storage is shown in Figure 7.

Storage scalability provides a trivial basis for scaling DLS storage where the metadata and/or data collections reside in databases. In addition, specific techniques may be employed to achieve scalability at higher levels.

Workflow of SORADLS

The system is focused to create security model using Web service. In our system, main role or service is of central server. Library Portal server provides single window access to the user. User interface is based on the keywords related to meta-data.

- User login into the library portal. The security checks the user whether authorized or not. The authorized user sends a query in any language to the central server.
- The Portal server translates the query to the requested languages. Portal server passes query to the searching service.

Figure 7. Structure of Storage Module

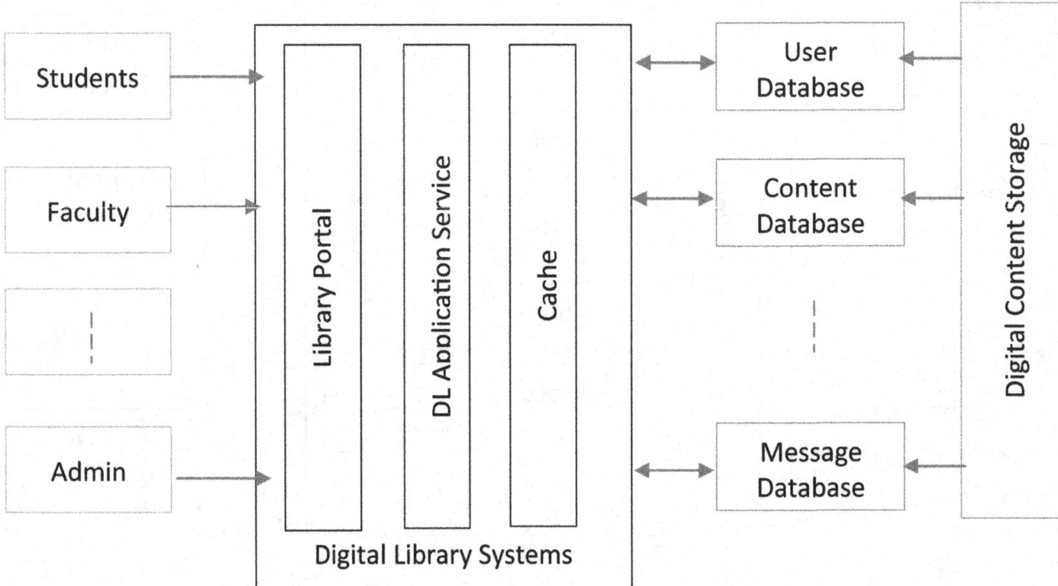

- Searching service checked with indexing services. Searching service do the ranking on the outcome of the indexing service. Searching services passes the response to the central server.
- The Portal server reformulates the ranked response according to the format expected by primary servers.
- Application servers execute query provided by the central server and return results.
- The Portal server returned results to user after translation, summarization, filtering and so forth, of the content as required or the link to the content.

This system works with meta-data information of the digital content present in the distributed digital repositories in their respective language. Whenever any new content is added to any digital repository of the primary service, a set of metadata information moves to central server and as per the policy, central server updates the index files accordingly.

FUTURE RESEARCH DIRECTIONS

Current research challenges include the following:

- As e-resources and datasets become very large, the standard algorithms for handling data change and new algorithms are actively being sought.
- The system interoperability is still difficult at best. It needs which are significantly more simple standards and protocols.
- Integrating DLS tools into Operating Systems can result in more widespread use and adoption.
- New services can provide annotation and linking capabilities and these should be provided in DLSs.
- Finally, any distributed or large DLS needs to monitor its metadata for duplicates and quality issues. Services to make such assessments are gradually being improved but still considered to be a difficult problem.

- Developing self-sustainable and expandable DL systems, offering high-quality information and services.
- Establishment of an Initiative for an Integrated Digital Library, which leads to the development of comprehensive Digital Library Universities and research institutions.

CONCLUSION

This chapter addressed the performance and scalability issues that are unique to Digital Library Systems. This chapter also analyzed the technology that best fits the Digital Library and proposed Reference Architecture solution. In sum, the scalability should be kept in mind during the planning and development phases for a digital library. Scalability is critical to support long-term growth of the system. Building a modular system, SOA, will enable flexibility, code reusability, and stronger system sustainability. DLS are common and interoperability is a key consideration for any system. Most systems are therefore not run in isolation, but as one part of a larger networked information system, where scalability adds a new dimension to the architecture.

This chapter discussed the application of service-oriented architecture in digital library. It is quite clear that SOA has enormous benefits that digital libraries could use. The developers and information professionals must carefully and consciously learn, understand and apply the principles, requirements and techniques of SOA in order to see its full benefits. While the current methods of building applications worked very well for a lot of systems, they may not work very well for digital libraries. The complexity and the expectations for digital libraries are so high that, there is the need to find a better and equally higher approach to creating a platform that will serve digital libraries better.

The Service-Oriented Digital Library (SODL) has changed the service mode from inactive service to active service. Users much more welcome notification service because of its server model, real time, and the tightness between the contents and subject. The SODL has changed the service mode from inactive service to active service. The service depth, service contents, service quality are most concerned by users. Users much more welcome notification service because of its server model, real time, and the tightness between the contents and subject. Along with the further research of digital library technology, the efficiency and quality of notification service are enhanced effectively.

REFERENCES

Avancini, H., Candela, L., Manzi, A., & Simi, M. (2006). A powerful and scalable digital library information service. *ERCIM News*, *66*, 24–25.

Baman, P. (2004). Emergence of digital library services in India. In *Proceedings of the 2nd International Convention on Automation of Libraries in Education and Research Institutions* (CALIBER 2004). New Delhi, India.

Bergeron, B. (2004). Creating a digital library. *MedGenMed : Medscape General Medicine*, *6*(1), 52. PMID:15208563.

Buchanan, G., & Hinze, A. (2005). A generic alerting service for digital libraries. In *Proceedings of the 5th ACM/IEEE-CS Joint Conference on Digital Libraries (JCDL '05)*, pp. 7–11.

Callan, J., Smeaton, A., Beaulieu, M., Borlund, P., Brusilovsky, P., & Chalmers, M. … Toms, E. (2003). Personalization and recommender systems in digital libraries. (Tech. Rep.) Dublin, Ireland: Joint NSF-EU DELOS Working Group.

Chinnici, R., Moreau, J. J., Ryman, A., & Weerawarana, S. (Eds.). (2007). *Web services description language (WSDL) version 2.0 part 1: Core language*. Retrieved from http://www.w3.org/TR/2007/REC-wsdl20-20070626/

Clement, L., Hately, A., von Riegen, C., & Rogers, T. (Eds.). (2008). *UDDI version 3.0.2: UDDI spec technical committee draft*. Retrieved from http://uddi.org/pubs/uddi_v3.htm

Estefan, J., Laskey, K., McCabe, F., & Thornton, D. (Eds.). (2008). *OASIS reference architecture for service oriented architecture version 1.0: Public review draft 1*. Retrieved from http://docs.oasis-open.org/soa-rm/soa-ra/v1.0/soa-ra-pr-01.pdf

Gudgin, M., Hadley, M., Mendelsohn, N., Moreau, J. J., Nielsen, H. F., Karmarkar, A., & Lafon, Y. (Eds.). (2007). *SOAP version 1.2. part 1: Messaging framework (2nd ed.)*. Retrieved from http://www.w3.org/TR/2007/REC-soap12-part1-20070427/

Gupta, V., & Ansari, M. A. (2006). *Interoperability as a bench mark in digital libraries*. Retrieved from http://ir.inflibnet.ac.in/bitstream/handle/1944/1259/275-280.pdf?sequence=1

Han, L., & Wang, L. (2011). Research on digital library platform based on cloud computing. *Communications in Computer and Information Science*, *214*, 176–180. doi:10.1007/978-3-642-23321-0_27.

IBM. (2002). *IBM developer network*: *Web services security*. Retrieved from http://www.ibm.com/developerworks/websphere/library/techarticles/0605_chung/0605_chung.html

IBM. (2007). *Understanding SOA security design and implementation*: *IBM Redbook*. Retrieved from http://www.redbooks.ibm.com/abstracts/sg247310.html

Kodali, N., Farkas, C., & Wijesekera, D. (2004). An authorization model for multimedia digital libraries. *International Journal on Digital Libraries*, *4*(3), 139–155. doi:10.1007/s00799-004-0080-1.

Kruk, S. R., Decker, S., & Zieborak, L. (2005, August 22-26). JeromeDL - adding semantic web technologies to digital libraries. In Proceedings of 16th International Conference, DEXA 2005, Copenhagen, Denmark (pp. 716-725). Berlin: Springer.

Mazurek, C., Stroinski, M., Werla, M., & Weglarz, J. (2006). Metadata harvesting in regional digital libraries in PIONIER network, 61-704. Poznan, Poland: Poznan Supercomputing and Networking Centre.

Meiler, P., & Schmeing, M. (2009). *Secure service oriented architectures (SOA) supporting NEC (Tech Rep.)*. Brussels, Belgium: North Atlantic Treaty Organization.

Ort, E. (2005). *Service-oriented architecture and Web services: Concepts, technologies, and tools*. Retrieved from http://www.oracle.com/technetwork/articles/javase/wstools-141839.html

Osei-Poku, W. (2009). *Service oriented architecture*. Retrieved from http://works.bepress.com/raspino/4

Palanivel, K., Amouda, V., Kuppuswami, S. (2009). A personalized e-learning using web services and semantic web. *International Journal of Computer Engineering and Information Technology Winter ed.*, *21*(5), 27-37.

Palanivel, K., & Kuppuswami, S. (2011). Service-oriented reference architecture for personalized e-learning systems (SORAPES). *International Journal of Computers and Applications*, *24*(5), 35–44. doi:10.5120/2956-3907.

Palanivel, K., & Nagalingam, U. (2011). Service-oriented reference model to security for digital library (SORMSDL). In B. R. Babu, & P. N. Rao (Eds.), *Information security in the digital era* (pp. 230–243).

Pomerantz, J. (2003). Integrating digital reference service into the digital library environment. In R. D. Lankes, S. Nicholson, & A. Goodrum (Eds.), *The Digital Reference Research Agenda* (pp. 23–47). Chicago: Association of College and Research Libraries.

Pratha, L., Mattam, M., Ambati, V., & Reddy, R. (2006, November 17). *Multimedia digital library: Performance and scalability issues.* Paper presented at the 2nd International Conference on Universal Digital Library. Hyderabad, India.

Sherikar, A., Jange, S., & Jadhav, S. (2006). *Digital reference services in the Web based information world.* Paper presented at the Convention on Automation of Libraries in Education and Research Institutions (CALIBER 2006). Gulbarga, India.

Sinha, R., & Sanyal, R. (2011). *Creating aggregative digital repository in distributed environment using service oriented architecture: New dimensions in special libraries services.* Paper presented at the International Conference of Asia Special Libraries (ICoASL 2011). Tokyo, Japan.Thurlow, I., Duke, A., & Davies, J. (2006). *Applying semantic web technology in a digital library.* Paper presented at European Semantic Web Conference (ESWC 2006). Budva, Montenegro.

Vaughan, J. (2011). *Web scale discovery services.* Chicago: ALA Techsource Publications.

Vinoski, S. (2004). Web services notifications. *IEEE Internet Computing, 892*, 86–90. doi:10.1109/MIC.2004.1273491.

Zhang, Y., Wu, J., & Zhuang, Y. (2004). *The personalized services in CADAL digital library.* Retrieved from http://www.ulib.org/conference/2006/23.pdf

Zheng, Q., Chen, Z., & Bai, X. (2003). *Research on the application of notification service for service-oriented digital library.* Retrieved from http://www.ulib.org/conference/2006/27.pdf

Chapter 16
A Randomized Cloud Library Security Environment

A. V. N. Krishna
PujyaShri Madhavanji College of Engineering & Technology, India

ABSTRACT

Cloud computing is leading the technology development of today's communication scenario. This is because of its cost-efficiency and flexibility. In Cloud computing vast amounts of data are stored in varied and distributed environments, and security to data is of prime concern. RSA or Elliptic Curve Cryptography (ECC) provides a secure means of message transmission among communicating hosts using Diffie Hellman Key Exchange algorithm or ElGamal algorithm. By having key lengths of 160 bits, the ECC algorithm provides sufficient strength against crypto analysis and its performance can be compared with standard algorithms like RSA with a bit length of 1024 bits. In the present work, the plain text is converted to cipher text using RSA or ECC algorithms. As the proposed model is intended to be used in Cloud environment, a probabilistic mathematical model is also used. While the data is being retrieved from the servers, a query is being used which uses the mathematical model to search for the data which is still in encryption form. Final decryption takes place only at user's site by using the private keys. Thus the security model provides the fundamental security services like Authentication, Security, and Confidentiality to the transmitted message and also provides sufficient strength against crypto analysis in Cloud environment.

INTRODUCTION

Cloud computing is the use of computing resources (hardware and software) that are delivered as a service over a network (typically the Internet). The name comes from the use of a cloud-shaped symbol as an abstraction for the complex infrastructure it contains in system diagrams (see Figure 1). Cloud computing entrusts remote services with user's data, software, and computation.

Today many of the largest software companies operate almost entirely in the cloud, the top five software companies by sales revenue all have major cloud offerings, and the market as a whole

DOI: 10.4018/978-1-4666-4631-5.ch016

Figure 1. Cloud computing environment

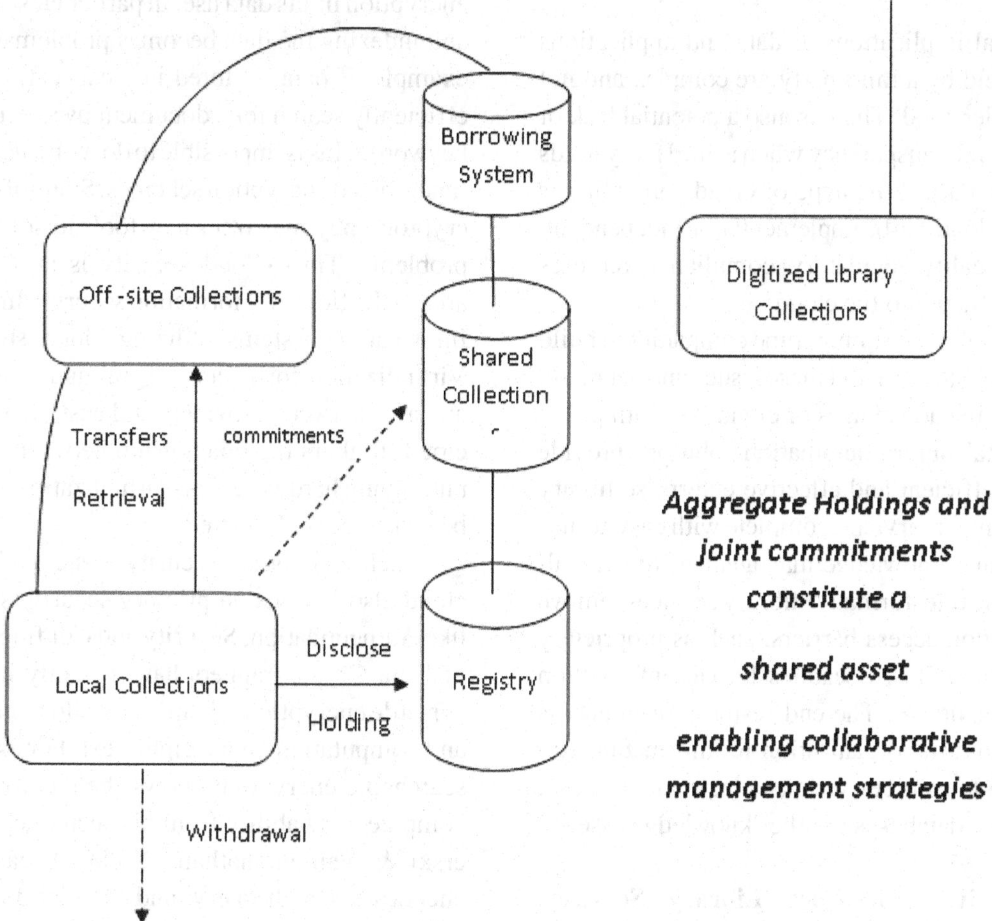

is predicted to grow at a very fast pace. Yet, despite the trumpeted business and technical advantages of cloud computing, many potential cloud users have yet to join the cloud, and those major corporations that are cloud users are for the most part putting only their less sensitive data in the cloud.

Mell and Grance (2012) define the "security" concerns that are preventing companies from taking advantage of the cloud as:

- Traditional Security
- Availability
- Third-Party Data Control

Traditional Security

These concerns involve computer and network intrusions or attacks that will be made possible or at least easier by moving to the cloud. Cloud providers respond to these concerns by arguing that their security measures and processes are more mature and tested than those of the average company.

Availability

These concerns center on critical applications and data being available. Well-publicized incidents of cloud outages include G mail, Amazon.

Third-Party Data Control

The legal implications of data and applications being held by a third party are complex and not well understood. There is also a potential lack of control and transparency when a third party holds the data. Part of the hype of cloud computing is that the cloud can be implementation independent, but in reality regulatory compliance requires transparency into the cloud.

All this is prompting some companies to build private clouds to avoid these issues and yet retain some of the advantages of cloud computing.

Digital library automation solutions provide timely, efficient and effective enterprise library management services, complete with easy-to-use library and knowledge management functionality. These transformative library services remove information access barriers, such as proprietary information silos, to seamlessly make information access equitable. The end result is open access throughout the organization to information services and resources such as: electronic journals, lab notes, databases or other knowledge assets.

- **Delivery of Core Library Services:** Making them more efficient and accessible.
- **User Satisfaction:** Due to improved information access and knowledge management.
- **Library Operations:** Making them more streamlined and less costly.
- The library's ability to provide for future growth and changing information demands.

Privacy-Enhanced Business Intelligence

The report ("Privacy in Cloud," 2009) finds that for some information and for some business users, sharing may be illegal, may be limited in some ways, or may affect the status or protections of the information shared. A different approach to retaining control of data is to require the encryption of all cloud data. The problem is that encryption limits data use. In particular searching and indexing the data becomes problematic. For example, if data is stored in clear-text, one can efficiently search for a document by specifying a keyword. This is impossible to do with traditional, randomized encryption schemes. State-of-the-art cryptography may offer new tools to solve these problems. Thus Cloud security is an evolving area in the field of information security. In library Information systems utilizing cloud structure, Virtualization forms an integral and intermediate layer between providers and customers of the cloud. It alters the relationship between OS and underlying hardware. This virtualization needs to be protected and secured.

Much like other security systems Library cloud also focuses on primary security services like Authentication, Security and Confidentiality of Data Cryptographers have recently invented versatile encryption schemes that allow operation and computation on the ciphertext. For example, searchable encryption allows the data owner to compute a capability from his secret key (Brakerski & Vaikuntanathan, 2011). A capability encodes a search query, and the cloud can use this capability to decide which documents match the search query, without learning any additional information. Other cryptographic primitives such as homomorphic encryption and Private Information Retrieval perform computations on encrypted data without decrypting.

Historically, encryption schemes were the first central area of interest in cryptography (Stallings, 2006). They deal with providing means to enable private communication over an insecure channel. A sender wishes to transmit information to a receiver over an insecure channel that is a channel which may be tapped by an adversary. Thus, the information to be communicated, which we call the plaintext, must be transformed (encrypted) to a cipher text, a form not legible by anybody other than the intended receiver. The latter must be given some way to decrypt the cipher text, i.e.

retrieve the original message, while this must not be possible for an adversary. This is where keys come into play; the receiver is considered to have a key at his disposal, enabling him to recover the actual message, a fact that distinguishes him from any adversary. An encryption scheme consists of three algorithms: The encryption algorithm transforms plaintexts into cipher texts while the decryption algorithm converts cipher texts back into plaintexts. A third algorithm, called the key generator, creates pairs of keys: an encryption key, input to the encryption algorithm, and a related decryption key needed to decrypt.

Any symmetric encryption scheme uses a private key for secure data transfer. In their work on "A simple algorithm for random number generation, the authors presented a simple algorithm which generates random numbers (Krishna & Vinaya, 2009). Krishna, Vinaya, and Pandit (2007) presented a probabilistic algorithm which generates multiple cipher texts for one plain text which is relatively free from chosen cipher text attack. Most of the products and standards use public-key cryptography for encryption and digital signatures. As these cryptographic techniques mature, they may open up new possibilities for cloud computing security use RSA today. Recently, Elliptic Curve Cryptography has begun to challenge RSA (Stallings, 2006). The principal attraction of ECC compared to RSA, is that it appears to offer better security for a smaller key size, thereby reducing processing overhead. Figure 2 shows the rates of challenges for cloud computing (Mell & Grance, 2010).

SECURITY MODEL

In Cryptography, encryption is the process of encoding messages (or information) in such a way that eavesdroppers or hackers cannot read it, but that authorized parties can. In an encryption scheme, the message or information (referred to as plain text) is encrypted using an encryption algorithm, turning it into an unreadable cipher text. This is usually done with the use of an encryption key, which specifies how the message is to be encoded. Any adversary that can see the cipher

Figure 2. Rate of challenges to cloud on demand

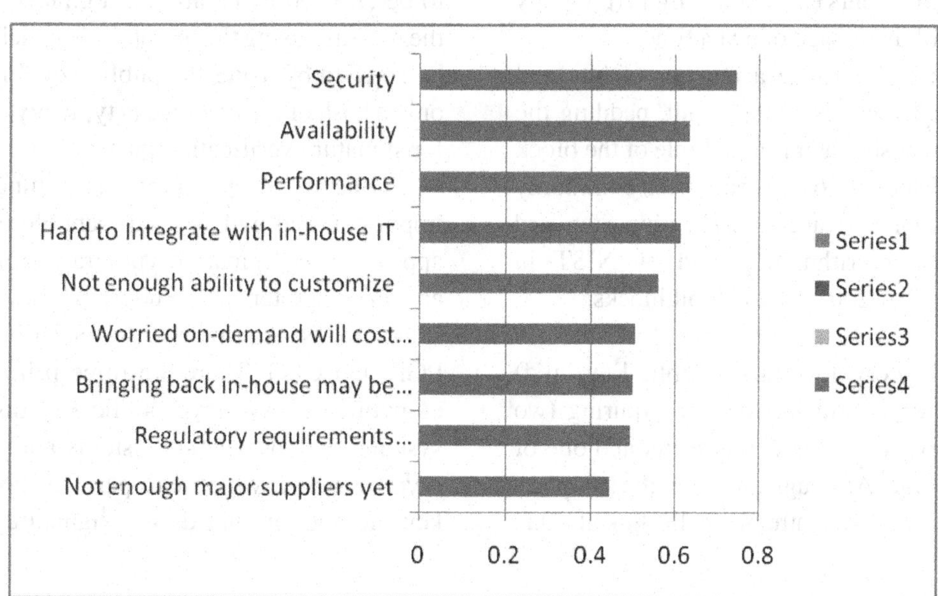

text should not be able to determine anything about the original message. An authorized party, however, is able to decode the cipher text using a decryption algorithm that usually requires a secret decryption key that adversaries do not have access to. For technical reasons, an encryption scheme usually needs a key-generation algorithm, to randomly produce keys. There are two basic types of encryption schemes Symmetric Key and Public key Encryption.

Symmetric-key algorithms ("Symmetric Key," n.d) are a class of algorithms for cryptography that use the same cryptographic keys for both encryption of plain text and decryption of cipher text. The keys may be identical or there may be a simple transformation to go between the two keys. The keys, in practice, represent a shared secret between two or more parties that can be used to maintain a private information link. This requirement that both parties have access to the secret key is one of the main drawbacks of symmetric key encryption, in comparison to Public key Encryption.

Symmetric-key encryption can use either stream cipher or block cipher.

- Stream ciphers encrypt the digits (typically bits) of a message one at a time.
- Block ciphers take a number of bits and encrypt them as a single unit, padding the plaintext so that it is a multiple of the block size. Blocks of 64 bits have been commonly used. The Advanced Encryption Standard (AES) algorithm approved by NIST in December 2001 uses 128-bit blocks.

Public-key cryptography ("Public Key," n.d) refers to a cryptographic system requiring two separate keys, one of which is secret and one of which is public. Although different, the two parts of the key pair are mathematically linked. One key locks or encrypts the plain text, and the other unlocks or decrypts the cipher text. Neither key can perform both functions by itself. The public key may be published without compromising security, while the private key must not be revealed to anyone not authorized to read the messages.

Public-key cryptography uses asymmetric key algorithms (such as RSA), and can also be referred to by the more generic term "asymmetric key cryptography." The algorithms used for public key cryptography are based on mathematical relationships (the most notable ones being the integer factorization and discrete logarithm problems) that presumably have no efficient solution. Although it is computationally easy for the intended recipient to generate the public and private keys, to decrypt the message using the private key, and easy for the sender to encrypt the message using the public key, it is extremely difficult (or effectively impossible) for anyone to derive the private key, based only on their knowledge of the public key. This is why, unlike symmetric encryption algorithms; a public key algorithm does not require a secure initial exchange of one (or more) secure keys between the sender and receiver. The use of these algorithms also allows the authenticity of a message to be checked by creating a digital signature of the message using the private key, which can then be verified by using the public key. In practice, only a hash of the message is typically encrypted for signature verification purposes.

Public-key cryptography is a fundamental, important, and widely used technology. It is an approach used by many cryptographic algorithms and cryptosystems. It underpins such Internet standards as Transport Layer Security (TLS),] PGP, and GPG. There are three primary kinds of public key systems: public key distribution systems, digital signature systems, and public key cryptosystems, which can perform both public key distribution and digital signature services.

Diffie-Hellman Key exchange is the most widely used public key distribution system, while the Digital Signature Algorithm is the most widely used digital signature system.

The distinguishing technique used in public-key cryptography is the use of asymmetric key algorithms, where the key used to encrypt a message is not the same as the key used to decrypt it. Each user has a pair of cryptographic keys – a public encryption key and a private decryption key. The publicly available encrypting-key is widely distributed, while the private decrypting-key is known only to its proprietor, the recipient. Messages are encrypted with the recipient's public key, and can be decrypted only with the corresponding private key. The keys are related mathematically, but the parameters are chosen so that determining the private key from the public key is either impossible or prohibitively expensive. The discovery of algorithms that could produce public/private key pairs revolutionized the practice of cryptography, beginning in the mid-1970s.

In contrast, symmetric key algorithms variations of which have been used for thousands of years–use a single secret key, which must be shared and kept private by both the sender and the receiver, for both encryption and decryption. To use a symmetric encryption scheme, the sender and receiver must securely share a key in advance.

Because symmetric key algorithms are nearly always much less computationally intensive than asymmetric ones, it is common to exchange a key using a key exchange algorithm, then transmit data using that key and a symmetric key algorithm. PGP and the SSL /TLS family of schemes use this procedures, and are thus called hybrid crypto systems.

Description

The two main uses for public-key cryptography are:

- **Public-Key Encryption:** A message encrypted with a recipient's public key cannot be decrypted by anyone except a possessor of the matching private key – it is presumed that this will be the owner of that key and the person associated with the public key used. This is used to attempt to ensure confidentiality.
- **Digital Signatures:** A message signed with a sender's private key can be verified by anyone who has access to the sender's public key, thereby proving that the sender had access to the private key and, therefore, is likely to be the person associated with the public key used. This also ensures that the message has not been tampered with. An analogy to public-key encryption is that of a locked mail box with a mail slot. The mail slot is exposed and accessible to the public – its location (the street address) is, in essence, the public key. Anyone knowing the street address can go to the door and drop a written message through the slot. However, only the person who possesses the key can open the mailbox and read the message.

An analogy for digital signatures is the sealing of an envelope with a personal wax seal. The message can be opened by anyone, but the presence of the unique seal authenticates the sender.

A central problem with the use of public-key cryptography is confidence (ideally, proof) that a particular public key is correct, and belongs to the person or entity claimed (i.e., is "authentic"), and has not been tampered with, or replaced by, a malicious third party (a "man-in-the-middle"). The usual approach to this problem is to use a Public Key Infrastructure (PKI), in which one or more third parties – known as certificate authorities–certify ownership of key pairs. PGP, in addition to being a certificate authority structure, has used a scheme generally called the "Web of thrust", which decentralizes such authentication of public keys by a central mechanism, and substitutes individual endorsements of the link between user and public key. To date, no fully satisfactory solution to this "public key authentication problem" has been found

When using symmetric algorithms, both parties share the same key for en- and decryption. To provide privacy, this key needs to be kept secret. Once somebody else gets to know the key, it is not safe any more. Symmetric algorithms have the advantage of not consuming too much computing power. A few well-known examples are: DES, Triple-DES (3DES), IDEA, CAST5, BLOWFISH, and TWOFISH.

Asymmetric algorithms use pairs of keys. One is used for encryption and the other one for decryption. The decryption key is typically kept secretly, therefore called "private key" or "secret key," while the encryption key is spread to all who might want to send encrypted messages, therefore called "public key." Everybody having the public key is able to send encrypted messages to the owner of the secret key. The secret key can't be reconstructed from the public key. The idea of asymmetric algorithms was first published 1976 by Diffie and Hellmann.

Asymmetric algorithms seem to be ideally suited for real-world use: As the secret key does not have to be shared, the risk of getting known is much smaller. Every user only needs to keep one secret key in secrecy and a collection of public keys that only need to be protected against being changed. With symmetric keys, every pair of users would need to have an own shared secret key. Well-known asymmetric algorithms are RSA, DSA, and ELGAMAL.

However, asymmetric algorithms are much slower than symmetric ones. Therefore, in many applications, a combination of both is being used. The asymmetric keys are used for authentication and after this have been successfully done; one or more symmetric keys are generated and exchanged using the asymmetric encryption. This way the advantages of both algorithms can be used. Typical examples of this procedure are the RSA/IDEA combination of PGP2 or the DSA/BLOWFISH used by GnuPG.

The work is broadly divided into three modules.

- Plain text to be converted to cipher text using RSA or ECC algorithm.
- Probabilistic Model being used to generate Basin values.
- Output of RSA or ECC is scalar multiplied with the value of basins generated from mathematical model to be stored in cloud server.

The RSA Algorithm

The RSA algorithm involves three steps:

1. Key Generation
2. Encryption
3. Decryption ("Public Key," 2000)

Key Generation

RSA involves a public key and a Private Key. The public key can be known to everyone and is used for encrypting messages. Messages encrypted with the public key can only be decrypted using the private key. The keys for the RSA algorithm are generated the following way:

1. Choose two distinct prime numbers p and q.
    a. For security purposes, the integer's p and q should be chosen at random, and should be of similar bit-length.

2. Compute n = pq.
    a. n is used as the modulus for both the public and private keys. Its length, usually expressed in bits, is the key length.
3. Compute ?(n) = (p?–?1)(q?–?1), where ? is Euler's totient function.
4. Choose an integer e such that 1 < e < ?(n) and greatest common divisor gcd(e, ?(n)) = 1; i.e., e and ?(n) are co prime.
    a. e is released as the public key exponent.
    b. e having a short bit length and small Hamming weight results in more efficient encryption – most commonly 216 + 1 = 65,537.
5. Determine d as d ??e?1 (mod ?(n)), i.e., d is the multiplicative inverse of e (modulo ?(n)).
    a. This is more clearly stated as solve for d given de ? 1 (mod ?(n))
    b. This is often computed using the extended Euclidian algorithm.
    c. d is kept as the private key exponent.

By construction, d?e ? 1 (mod ?(n)). The public key consists of the modulus n and the public (or encryption) exponent e. The private key consists of the modulus n and the private (or decryption) exponent d, which must be kept secret. p, q, and ?(n) must also be kept secret because they can be used to calculate d.

Encryption

Alice transmits her public key (n, e) to Bob and keeps the private key secret. Bob then wishes to send message M to Alice.

He first turns M into an integer m, such that 0 ??m < n by using an agreed-upon reversible protocol known as a padding scheme. He then computes the cipher text c corresponding to:

c=me (mod n)

This can be done quickly using the method of exponentiation by squaring. Bob then transmits c to Alice.

Decryption

Alice can recover m from c by using her private key exponent d via computing:

m=cd (mod n)

Given m, she can recover the original message M by reversing the padding scheme.

Elliptic Curve Cryptography

Elliptic Curve Cryptography (Cilardo, Coppolino, Mazzocca, & Romano, 2006) makes use of elliptic curves in which the variables and coefficients are all restricted to elements of a finite field. In ECC we normally start with an affine point called Pm(x,y). These points maybe the Base point (G) itself or some other point closer to the Base point. Base point implies it has the smallest x, y co-ordinates, which satisfy the EC. A character in a message is first transformed into an affine point of the elliptic curve by using it as a multiplier of Pm. That is, if the ASCII value of a character is A, then we determine P0 m=A (Pm). This is one step towards introducing sophistication and complexity in the encryption process. The newly evaluated P0 m is a point on the EC, determined by applying the addition and doubling strategy of ECC technique. Then as per ECC algorithm, P0 m is added with kPB, where k is randomly chosen secret integer and PB is the public key of user B, to yield (P0 m+ kPB). This now constitutes the second part of the encrypted version of the message. The other part, namely, kG, which is the product of the secret integer and the Base point, constitutes the first part. Thus the encrypted message is now made up of two sets of coordinates, namely, (kG, P0 m+ kPB). In this paper we have assigned kG=(x1,y1) and (Pm+kPB)=(x2,y2).

An example of indirect data-mining that might be performed by a cloud provider is to note transactional and relationship information. For example, availability also needs to be considered in the context of an adversary whose goals are simply to sabotage activities. Increasingly, such adversaries are becoming realistic as political conflict is taken onto the Web, and as the recent cyber attacks on Lithuania confirm. An example of indirect data-mining that might be performed by a cloud provider is to note transactional and relationship information. For example, the sharing of information by two companies may signal a merger is under consideration.

Homomorphic encryption (Craig, 2010) schemes that allow simple computations on encrypted data have been known for a long time. For example, the encryption systems (Goldwasser & Micali, 1982) support either adding or multiplying encrypted ciphertexts, but not both operations at the same time. In a breakthrough work, (Stehlé & Steinfeld, 2010) constructed a fully homomorphic encryption scheme (FHE) capable of evaluating an arbitrary number of additions and multiplications (and thus, compute any function) on encrypted data.

Broadly this work deals with the importance of security aspects in Cloud computing in the present day scenario. The very important feature with Cloud is security to data stored and security to data transmitted. To maintain security to data the best technique that can be employed is encryption. Encryption to data supports the very important features like security, confidentiality to data and authentication of users.

The organization of our work is as follows. The work started with discussing the features of RSA and Elliptic Curve Cryptography. In the following sections the concepts of probabilistic model are discussed.

We review here only some of the most important facts about elliptic curve cryptography. Let p > 2 be a prime number and let q = pm, for some m in N. Let Fq(also written as GF(q)) be a finite field of q elements. If q is prime, we can think of Fq as the set of integers modulo q (Zq).

Let a1; a2; a3; a4; a6 in Fq.

We say that the elliptic curve over Fq is the set of solutions (x; y) in Fq for the Weierstrass equation

E: y2 + a1xy + a3y = x3 + a2x2 + a4x + a6

in background together with a special point O, called the point at infinity. After a change of variables, equation above can be simplified to the

Following forms (known as simplified Weierstrass form for curves of characteristic p):

E: y2 + xy = x3 + ax2 + b if p = 2

y2 = x3 + ax2 + bx + c if p = 3

y2 = x3 + ax + b if p > 3

When p = 2 we need b = 0, when p = 3 we need a2 (b2 /4ac) b3 = 0 and when p > 3 we need 4a3 + 27b2 = 0 to ensure that E has no multiple roots, so it is possible to draw a tangent line in any point of the curve. It is well known that the points of an elliptic curve define a group law, with O as the identity element. We now define some useful concepts in elliptic curves:

Point multiplication (scalar point multiplication): let s be an integer and P an elliptic curve point. We define [s] P as the sum of P with itself s times. There are well defined formulae for adding two points P and Q of an elliptic curve (R = P + Q) or for computing the scalar point doubling. We remark that [s]P can be efficiently computed (i.e., computed in polynomial time) using double-and-(add or subtract) algorithm and curve order (#E): is the number of points of a given curve E.

The Weiestrass equation defining an elliptic curve over GF (p), for q > 3, is as follows: y2 = x3 + ax + b, where x, y are elements of GF (p), and a, b is integer modulo p, satisfying 4a3 + 27b2 = 0 mod p.

Here p is known as modular prime integer. An elliptic curve E over GF (p) consist of the solutions (x, y) defined by Equations 1 and 2, along with an additional element called O, which is the point of EC at infinity. The set of points (x, y) are said to be affine coordinate point representation. The basic Elliptic curve operations are point addition and point doubling. Elliptic curve cryptographic primitives [13] require scalar point multiplication. Say, given a point P(x, y) on an EC, one needs to compute kP, where k is a positive integer. This is achieved by a series of doubling and addition of P. Say, given k = 20, entails the following sequence of operations P, 2P, 3P, 6P, 12P, 24P, 48P, 96P, 192P, 193P, 386P.

Let us start with P (xP, yP). To determine 2P, P is doubled. This should be an affine point on EC. Use the following equation, which is a tangent to the curve at point P.

S = [(3x2P + a)/2yP] mod p

Then 2P has affine coordinate's xR, yR given by:

xR = (S2 ? 2xP) mod p

yR = [S(xP ? xR) ? yP] mod p

Now to determine 3P, we use addition of points P and 2P, treating 2P = Q. Here P has coordinates (xP, yP) and Q = 2P has coordinates (xQ, yQ).

Then: xR = (S2 ? xP ? xQ) mod p

yR = (S(xP ? xR) ? yP] mod p

Therefore we apply doubling and addition depending on a sequence of operations determined for k. Every point xR, yR evaluated by doubling or addition is an affine point (points on the Elliptic Curve).

Implementation Details of ECC: Once the defining EC is known we can select a base point called G. G has [x, y] coordinates which satisfy the equation y2 = x3 +ax+b (Ramasamy, Prabakar, Devi, & Suguna, 2009). The base point has the smallest x, y values which satisfy the EC.The ECC method requires that we select a random integer k(k < p), which needs to be kept secret. Then kG is evaluated, by a series of additions and doublings, as discussed above. For purpose of this discussion we shall call the source as host A, and the destination as host B. We select the private key of the host B, called nB. k and nB can be generated by random number generators to give credibility. That would be digressing away from the main discussion. Hence we make suitable assumptions for these two parameters. The public key of B is evaluated by PB = nBG. [3] Suppose A wants to encrypt and transmit a character to B, he does the following. Assume that host A wants to transmit the character 'm'. Then the ASCII value of the character 'm' is used to modify Pm as follows: P0m= mPm. Pm we said is an affine point. This is selected different from the Base point G, so as to preserve their individual identities. P0m is a point on the EC. The coordinates of the P0m should fit into the EC. This transformation is done for two purposes. First the single valued ASCII is transformed into a x,y co-ordinate of the EC. Second it is completely camouflaged from the would-be hacker. This is actually intended to introduce some level of complexity even before the message is encrypted according to ECC. As the next step of ECC, we need to evaluate kPB, here PB is a public key of user B. Determining this product involves a series of doubling and additions, depending on the value of k. For a quick convergence of the result, we should plan for optimal number of doubles and additions. The encrypted message is derived by adding P0m with kPB, that is, P0m+kPB. This yields a set of x2, y2 coordinates. Then kG is included as the first element of the encrypted version. kG is another set of x1, y1 coordinates. Hence the entire encrypted version for purposes of storing or transmission consists of two sets of coordinates as follows: Cm = (kG, P0m + kPB), where kG =(x1, y1), (P0 m + kPB) = (x2, y2).

Probabilistic Model

With probabilistic encryption algorithms, a crypto analyst can no longer encrypt random plain texts looking for correct cipher text (Krishna, Vinaya, & Pandit, 2007). Since multiple cipher texts will be developed for one plain text, even if he decrypts the message to plain text, he does not know how far he had guessed the message correctly. To illustrate, assume a crypto analyst has a certain cipher text ci. Even if he guesses the message correctly, when he encrypts the message the result will be completely different cj. He cannot compare ci and cj and so cannot know that he has guessed the message correctly. Under this scheme, different cipher texts will be formed for one plain text. Also the cipher text will always be larger than plain text. This develops the concept of multiple cipher texts for one plain text. This concept makes crypto analysis difficult to apply on plain text and cipher text pairs.

In the ECC algorithm, a random value is used in encryption process. The cipher text is generated as C1 and C2 where C1 gives (Pm+k*G*Pb) and C2 gives k* G where Pm refers to plain text, G is a global parameter; Pb is the public key of receiver and kis the random value. The cipher text is generated as C1 and C2 to provide for decryption process. This makes for more data overhead and more computing overhead during the encryption and decryption process. In the present work, a probabilistic model is used at both sender and receiver which generate the random value which is used in C1. Since a probabilistic model is used, this work does not need the generation of C2 which reduces data and computation overhead.

Probabilistic features are incorporated in the output of ECC model to make it free from chosen cipher text attack.

It involves following steps:

1. Algorithm for generating sequence.
2. Generating Basins with unequal values based on equality of values.
3. Mapping the basin value in the output of ECC.

Algorithm for Generating the Sequence:

1. Consider the sequence for 0 to n values where n is a positive integer.
2. Convert each element of the sequence into ternary form of a given digit number.
3. Represent the values of step 2 in a matrix form of (n+1) * (digit number).
4. Subtract 1 from each element of the matrix specified in step 3.
5. Consider a random matrix key of size (digit number*digit number).
6. Multiply the output of step 4 with the output of step 5.
7. Convert all positive values of matrix to 1, negative values to -1 and zero by 0.
8. Add 1 to each element of output of step 7.
9. Convert ternary values of step 8 into decimal form. A sequence is generated.

Algorithm for Generating Basins from Sequence Generated:

1. Consider the sequence of values starting from 0 to n where n be an integer.
2. Read the sequence generated from algorithm 1.
3. Read the starting element of step 1 and store the first element of step 1 and the corresponding first element of step 2 in a separate basin.

4.1 Compare the element of step 3 with the elements of step 2. If there is a match, store the corresponding elements of step 1 in the basin specified in step 3. Neglect already visited elements.

4.2 Repeat step 4.1 with the remaining elements of the basin of step 3 and store them in the same basin. This will form one basin.

5. Go to next element of step 1 which is not visited earlier.

In cloud computing, querying is processed on the encrypted data. Without decrypting the data, the query needs to be processed and output is transmitted to users in encrypted form only. In the present work, a new mathematical model is used which uses a nonce value and a dynamic time stamp to generate a distributed sequence. This sequence is used as key to generate indexed encrypted values of stored data in the server of the Cloud environment. When a query is to be processed, this mathematical model is used to decrypt the index values of stored encrypted data. Thus known the index values to encrypted message, data is identified and used for transmission to intended users.

IMPLEMENTATION DETAILS:

Example of RSA Encryption and Decryption:

Choose two distinct prime numbers, such as:

p=61 and q=53.

1. Compute n = pq giving

n=61*53=3233.

2. Compute the totient of the product as ?(n) = (p???1)(q???1) giving

3. Choose any number 1 < e < 3120 that is coprime to 3120. Choosing a prime number for e leaves us only to check that e is not a divisor of 3120.

e=17.

4. Compute d, the modular multiplicative inverse of e (mod ?(n)) yielding d=2753.

The public key is (n = 3233, e = 17). For a padded plain text message m, the encryption function is m17 (mod 3233).

The private key is (n = 3233, d = 2753). For an encrypted cipher text c, the decryption function is c2753 (mod 3233).

For instance, in order to encrypt m = 65, we calculate:

c=6517=2790 (mod 3233).

To decrypt c = 2790, we calculate:

M=27902753=65 (mod 3233).

Example for ECC Algorithm

The Elliptic Curve is y2 mod 13 = (x3 ? 5x + 25) mod 13. The base point G is selected as (4, 11). Base point implies that it has the smallest x, y co-ordinates which satisfy the EC. Pm is another affine point, which is picked out of a series of affine points evaluated for the given EC. We could have retained G itself for Pm. However for the purpose of individual identity, we choose Pm to be different from G. Let Pm= (6, 4). The choice of Pm is itself an exercise involving meticulous application of the ECC process on the given EC, the secret integer k, and the private key nB of the recipient B. In the present work we use the basin say, b (2) to consider the values.

Example with Probabilistic Features

Random Value to be Generated from Probabilistic Model

Step 1: Consider a ternary vector at 81 values (i.e., from 0 to 80).
Step 2: Representing them in matrix form (see Table 1.)
Step 3: r = r – 1 (see Table 2)
Step 4: Consider a 4 X 4 matrix (see Table 3)
Step 5: A X r= (see Table 4)
Step 6: r = Sign (A*r) (see Table 5)
Step 7: R = r+1 (see Table 6)
Step 8: Converting output of step 7 to integer form as: (see Table 7)
Step 9: Model for generating Basins:

1. n [81]= 0 1 2 3 4 5…80
2. r [81] = output of step 8.
3. Read n[0]=0. Store the values of n[0],r[0] in a basin.

4.1and4.2 Step4.1 is repeated with other elements of basin

Table 1.

0	0	0	0
0	0	0	1
0	0	0	2
0	0	1	0
0	0	1	1
0	0	1	2
.	.	.	.
.	.	.	.
.	.	.	.
2	2	1	2
2	2	2	0
2	2	2	1
2	2	2	2

Table 2.

−1	−1	−1	−1
−1	−1	−1	0
−1	−1	−1	1
−1	−1	0	−1
.	.	.	.
.	.	.	.
.	.	.	.
.	.	.	.
.	.	.	.
1	1	0	1
1	1	1	−1
1	1	1	0
1	1	1	1

Table 3.

A =

1	5	−6	1
2	1	3	2
3	−2	−3	3
4	2	4	4

Table 4.

−1	−8	−1	−14
0	−6	2	−10
1	−4	5	−6
−7	−5	−4	−10
.	.	.	.
.	.	.	.
.	.	.	.
.	.	.	.
7	5	4	10
−1	4	−5	6
0	6	−2	10
1	8	1	14

Table 5.

$$\begin{vmatrix} -1 & -1 & -1 & -1 \\ 0 & -1 & 1 & -1 \\ 1 & -1 & 1 & -1 \\ -1 & -1 & -1 & -1 \\ . & . & . & . \\ . & . & . & . \\ . & . & . & . \\ . & . & . & . \\ 1 & 1 & 1 & 1 \\ -1 & 1 & -1 & 1 \\ 0 & 1 & -1 & 1 \\ 1 & 1 & 1 & 1 \end{vmatrix}$$

Table 6.

$$\begin{vmatrix} 0 & 0 & 0 & 0 \\ 1 & 0 & 2 & 0 \\ 2 & 0 & 2 & 0 \\ 0 & 0 & 0 & 0 \\ . & . & . & . \\ . & . & . & . \\ . & . & . & . \\ . & . & . & . \\ 2 & 2 & 2 & 2 \\ 0 & 2 & 0 & 2 \\ 0 & 2 & 0 & 2 \\ 2 & 2 & 2 & 2 \end{vmatrix}$$

b (0) = (0, 3, 4, 6, 12, 13, 15, 30, 39, 5, 31, 57, 10, 36)

The basins formed with corresponding elements:

b (1) = (9, 54, 7, 24, 33, 18, 19, 21, 22, 45, 48, 1, 27, 16, 42)

b (2) = (20, 60, 8, 17, 25, 26, 34, 43, 51, 54, 69, 78, 2, 11, 28, 29, 37, 46, 54, 55, 63, 72, 32, 35, 58, 59, 61, 62, 71, 9, 18, 19, 21, 22, 45, 48, 38, 64, 47, 56, 73, 7, 24, 33, 16, 42, 53, 79, 1, 27)

b (3) = (23, 74, 44, 70, 49, 75)

b (4) = (40, 14, 66)

b (5) = (80, 41, 50, 65, 67, 68, 76, 77)

Step 10: Mapping the basin values to the output of ECC:

The values of any basin may be considered as 'k' of the encryption and decryption process of ECC. This is again encrypted by the output of mathematical model to generate final encrypted data to be stored in the Cloud server. Consider a case where basin b(2) is considered for identifying the value used in encryption process. Hence we shall assume that k = 20, and nB = 16. Plaintext is "m", which is made equivalent to 22. Therefore,

PB = nBG = 16(4, 11) = (8, 3)

P0m = 22(4, 11) = (6, 4)

kPB = 20(8,3) = (4,2)

P0m + kPB = (2, 10) + (4,= (4, 2) 2)

Encrypted version of the message 'm' is (11, 1);

CRYPTO ANALYSIS

Encryption and decryption of data is done at two levels.

Encryption:

Level 1: Encryption of data is done using RSA or ECC algorithm.

Table 7.¬

R = r(4,1) + 3 * r(3,1) + 9 * r(2,1) + 27 * r(1,1).

0	33	60	0	0	6	0	9
20	54	57	60	0	0	40	0
19	20	54	54	60	54	54	74
9	20	20	33	60	60	0	6
26	9	20	26	57	60	61	0
40	80	19	20	23	54	6	71
54	74	80	20	20	47	60	60
71	6	26	26	20	26	26	60
61	80	40	80	80	20	23	26
61	71	80	74	80	80	20	47
80							

Level 2: The model also uses probabilistic model to generate random values used in encryption process.

Level 3: Decryption of data is done at server level using Basin values of Mathematical model.

Level 4: Decryption of data of level 1 is done at user's site using their private keys.

1. It uses probabilistic features to generate cipher text which makes it relatively free from chosen cipher text attacks. If a simulation game, Game 2 to be generated, then each plain text character must be mapped by 3-450 combinations of cipher text which gives sufficient strength against crypto analysis. The complexity of the model is increased by O (Number of basins formed (number of values of each basin)).
2. Thus the complexity of the proposed model (see Table 8) is exponential in nature.

To use RSA or Diffie-Hellman to protect 128-bit AES keys one should use 3072-bit parameters: three times the size in use throughout the Internet today. The equivalent key size for elliptic curves is only 256 bits. One can see that as symmetric key sizes increase the required key sizes for RSA and Diffie-Hellman increase at a much faster rate than the required key sizes for elliptic curve cryptosystems. Hence, elliptic curve systems offer more security per bit increase in key size than either RSA or Diffie-Hellman public key systems.

Table 8. NIST recommended key sizes

Symmetric Key Size (bits)	RSA and Diffie-Hellman Key Size (bits)	Elliptic Curve Key Size (bits)
80	1024	160
112	2048	224
128	3072	256
192	7680	384
256	15360	521

CONCLUSION

This work discusses the measures to provide security to data in a Cloud environment. ECC or RSA algorithms are discussed for security in a Cloud environment. ECC itself is a very secure algorithm for encryption. A plaintext character 'S' is taken for implementing the algorithm proposed in this paper. Each character in the message is represented by its ASCII value. Each of these ASCII value is transformed into an affine point on the EC, by using a starting point called Pm. This Pm may be selected to be different from the Base point G. The purpose of this transformation is twofold. Firstly a single digit ASCII integer of the character is converted into a set of coordinates to fit the EC. Secondly the transformation introduces non-linearity in the character thereby completely camouflaging its identity. This transformed character of the message is encrypted by the ECC technique. However, in ECC the cipher text is represented as C1 and C2 to accommodate random values which give strength against crypto analysis. This work also discusses a probabilistic model which generates random values which are used in encryption of data. So this system generates cipher text as C1 only which provides for lesser data and computing overhead on the transmitting medium. This model generates multiple cipher texts for one plain text. Any one cipher text can be used for secured data transfer. The advantage with this model is, it is not only free from linear and differential cryptanalysis but also free from chosen cipher text attacks. Thus the given model supports the important properties like authentication, security and confidentiality and resistance against Chosen cipher text attacks at less computing resources when compared to algorithm like RSA. It provides sufficient security for the same key length at reduced computing and data over head in a Cloud environment.

REFERENCES

Cilardo, A., Coppolino, L., Mazzocca, N., & Romano, L. (2006). Elliptic curve cryptography engineering. *Proceedings of the IEEE, 94*(2), 395–406. doi:10.1109/JPROC.2005.862438.

Cloud Computing Security. (2009). *FTC questions cloud computing security.* Retrieved from http://news.cnet.

Craig, G. (2009). Fully homomorphic encryption using ideal lattices In M. Mitzenmacher (Ed.). In *Proceedings of STOC '09 the 41st Annual ACM Symposium on Theory of Computing* (pp. 169-174). New York: ACM.

Craig, G. (2010, August 15-19). Toward basing fully homomorphic encryption on worst-case hardness. In T. Rabin (Ed.), *CRYPTO: Proceedings of the 30th Annual Cryptology Conference (2010).* Santa Barbara, CA (LNCS 6223, pp 116-137).

Diffie, W. (1988). The first ten years of Public Key cryptography. [). New York: IEEE.]. *Proceedings of the IEEE, 76*, 560–577. doi:10.1109/5.4442.

Goldwasser, S., & Micali, S. (1982). Probabilistic encryption and how to play mental poker keeping secret all partial information. In *Proceedings of STOC '82 the 14st Annual ACM Symposium on Theory of Computing* (pp. 365-377). New York: ACM.

Krishna, A. V. N., Vinaya, A. B., & Pandit, S. N. N. (2007). A generalized scheme for data encryption technique using a randomized matrix key. *Journal of Discrete Mathematical Sciences and Cryptography, 10*(1), 73–81. doi:10.1080/09720529.2007.10698109.

Mell, P., & Grance, T. (2010). *Effectively and securely using the cloud computing paradigm.* Retrieved from http://www.csrc.nist.gov/groups/SNS/cloud-computing/cloud-computing-v26.ppt

Privacy in Cloud. (2009). *Risks to privacy and confidentiality from cloud computing.* Retrieved from http://www.worldprivacyforum.org/pdf/WPF_Cloud_privacy_Report.pdf/

Public Key cryptography. (2000). *Standard Specifications for Public Key Cryptography.* Retrieved from http://www.Stanadard Specifications for Public Key cryptography, IEEE Standard

Public Key. (n.d). Public key algorithm. *Retrieved from* http:// wikipedia.org/wiki/Public-key_cryptography

Ramasamy, R. R., Prabakar, M. A., Devi, M. I., & Suguna, M. (2009). Knapsack based ECC encryption and decryption. *International Journal of Network Security*, *9*(3), 218–226.

Stallings, W. (2006). *Cryptography and Network Security* (4th ed.). Upper Saddle River, NJ: Prentice Hall.

Stehlé, D., & Steinfeld, R. (2010, December 5-9). Faster fully homomorphic encryption. In M. Abe (Ed.), *ASIACRYPT: Proceedings of the 16th International Conference on the Theory and Application of Cryptology and Information Security (2010).* Singapore (LCNS 6477, pp 377-394).

Symmetric key. (n.d). *Symmetric key algorithm.* Retrieved from http://wikipedia.org/wiki/Symmetric-key algorithm/

ADDITIONAL READING SECTION

Aydos, M., Yanik, T., & Kog, C. K. (2001). High-speed implementation of an ECC-based wireless authentication protocol on an ARM microprocessor. *IEEE Proceedings of Communication, 148*(5), 273-279.

Boneh, D., Goh, E. J., & Nissim, K. (2005, February 10-12). Evaluating 2-DNF formulas on ciphertexts. In *Proceedings of the 2nd Theory of Cryptography Conference, (TCC 2005).* Cambridge, MA (LNCS 3378, pp. 325-341).

Brakerski, Z., & Vaikuntanathan, V. (2011). Fully homomorphic encryption from ring-LWE and security for key dependent messages. In *Proceedings of the 31st Annual Cryptology Conference.* Santa Barbara, CA (LCNS 6841, pp. 505-524).

Chen, G., Bai, G., & Chen, H. (2007). A high-performance elliptic curve cryptographic processor for general curves Over GF(p) based on a systolic arithmetic unit. *IEEE Transactions on Circuits and Wystems. II, Express Briefs*, *54*(5), 412–416. doi:10.1109/TCSII.2006.889459.

Cheng, R. C. C., Baptiste, N. G., Luk, W., & Cheung, P. Y. K. (2005). Customizable elliptic curve cryptosystems. *IEEE Transactions on VLSI Systems*, *13*(9), 1048–1059. doi:10.1109/TVLSI.2005.857179.

Krishna, A. V. N. (2005). A simple algorithm for random number generation. *Journal of Scientific and Industrial Research*, *64*, 794–796.

Krishna, A. V. N. (2011). A new nonlinear model based encryption scheme with time stamp and acknowledgement support. *International Journal of Network Security*, *13*(3), 202–207.

Krishna, A. V. N., & Pandit, S. N. N. (2004). A new algorithm in network security for data transmission. *Acharya Nagarjuna International Journal of Mathematics and Information Technology*, *1*(2), 97–108.

Krishna, A. V. N., & Vinaya, B. A. (2006). Web and network communication security algorithm. *Journal on Software Engineering*, *1*(1), 12–14.

Krishna, A. V. N., & Vinaya, B. A. (2009). Training of a new probabilistic encryption scheme using an optimal matrix key. *Georgian Electronic & Scientific Journal*, *2*(19), 24–34.

Krishna, A. V. N., & Vinaya, B. A. (2010a). A new model based encryption scheme with time stamp and acknowledgement support. *International Journal of Network Security*, *11*(3), 172–176.

Krishna, A. V. N., & Vinaya, B. A. (2010b). A new nonlinear, time stamped and feedback model based encryption mechanism with acknowledgement support. *IJANA, 21-24.*

Lauter, K. (2006). The advantages of elliptic cryptography for wireless security. *IEEE Wireless Communications*, *11*(1), 62–67. doi:10.1109/MWC.2004.1269719.

Lee, J., Kim, H., Lee, Y., Hong, S. M., & Yoon, H. (2007). Parallelized scalar multiplication on elliptic curves defined over optimal extension field. *International Journal of Network Security*, *4*(1), 99–106.

Moon, S. (2006). A binary redundant scalar point multiplication in secure elliptic curve cryptosystems. *International Journal of Network Security*, *3*(2), 132–137.

Paillier, P. (1999, May 2-6). Public-key cryptosystems based on composite degree residuosity classes. In *Proceedings of the International Conference on the Theory and Application of Cryptographic Techniques*. Prague, Czech Republic (LNCS 1592, pp. 223-238).

Raines, A., & Potoczny, H. B. (2006). Cryptanalysis of an elliptic curve cryptosystem for wireless sensor networks. *International Journal of Security and Networks*, *2*(3/4), 260–271.

Shi, Z. H., & Yan, H. (2008). Software implementation of elliptic curve cryptography. *International Journal of Network Security*, *7*(2), 157–166.

Smart, N. P., & Vercauteren, F. (2010. May 26-28). Fully homomorphic encryption with relatively small key and ciphertext sizes. In *Proceedings of the 13th International Conference on Practice and Theory in Public Key Cryptography*. Paris (LNCS 6056, pp. 420-443).

Sweeny, L. (1997). Weaving technology and policy together. *The Journal of Law, Medicine & Ethics*, *25*, 2–3.

Wang, H., Sheng, B., & Li, Q. (2006). Elliptic curve cryptography-based access control in sensor net-works. *International Journal of Security and Networks*, *1*(3/4), 127–137. doi:10.1504/IJSN.2006.011772.

Yongliang, L., Gao, W., Yao, H., & Yu, X. (2007). Elliptic curve cryptography based wireless authentication protocol. *International Journal of Network Security*, *4*(1), 99–106.

KEY WORDS AND DEFINITIONS

Asymmetric Encryption: Public-key cryptography refers to a cryptographic system requiring two separate keys, one of which is secret and one of which is public. Although different, the two parts of the key pair are mathematically linked. One key locks or encrypts the plaintext, and the other unlocks or decrypts the cipher text. Neither key can perform both functions by itself. The public key may be published without compromising security, while the private key must not be revealed to anyone not authorized to read the messages.

Cloud Computing: Is the concept of using someone else's computer equipment instead of your own. It allows a person or a business to forget about technical details like whether a hard drive is big enough and puts that concern on another party. Sometimes those third parties charge for the use of the equipment or computer programs, which they are making available for you to use. Other times, the service is available as a public service.

Cloud Computing Security: (Sometimes referred to simply as "cloud security") Is an evolving sub-domain of information security. It refers to a broad set of policies, technologies, and controls deployed to protect data, applications, and the associated infrastructure of cloud computing. Cloud security is not to be confused with security software offerings that are "cloud-based."

Homomorphic Encryption: Is a fully homomorphic encryption scheme (FHE) capable of evaluating an arbitrary number of additions and multiplications that is compute any function on encrypted data.

Probabilistic Encryption: Is an encryption process which generates multiple cipher texts for one plain text. This encryption is free from chosen cipher text attacks.

Symmetric Encryption: A class of algorithms for cryptography that use the same cryptographic keys for both encryption of plain text and decryption of cipher text. The keys may be identical or there may be a simple transformation to go between the two keys. The keys, in practice, represent a shared secret between two or more parties that can be used to maintain a private information link.

ENDNOTES

1. ECC Algorithm: Elliptic Curve Cryptography Algorithm.
2. Mod: Modular Function.
3. RSA Algorithm: Rivest-Shamir-Adleman Algorithm.

Chapter 17
Green Economic and Secure Libraries on Cloud

Kalpana T.M.
Shri AMM Murugappa Chettiar Research Centre, India

S. Gopalakrishnan
National Institute of Fashion Technology, India

ABSTRACT

Libraries are considered storehouses of knowledge in the form of books and other resources. Introduction of computers and information and communication technology paved the way for resources in electronic format. Hence, storage of library resources is categorized in two ways namely physical storage and electronic storage. The advantages of e-format are multiple users, increasing availability of free resource, sharing, storing, accessibility, retrieval, flexibility, compatibility, and so forth. As an evolutionary change in adapting to the electronic dissemination, electronic data can be stored virtually, externally, and retrieved in cloud computing. For cloud storage users, service providers and tools are considered as major components of the service architecture. Tool connects cloud storage server and thin client platform through the Internet. Green computing and green production technology are utilizing minimum resources and maximum production in an eco-friendly way. Data warehousing is collection of data, categorizing, filtering, eliminating replica data, format compatibility; security of data retrieval gives economic storage of files. Warehoused data with extract, transform, and load (ETL) tools are retrieved by data mining. This chapter discusses various architecture, service providers, models of service, certifications, billing models, security issues, solutions to security issues and eco-friendly economic storage.

INTRODUCTION

Cloud computing (CC) is storing of metadata externally. In this digital environment large, mixed and multiformat resources are available, which need to be stored in library and this forces evolutionary change to library in collection development, storage, and retrieval and dissemination process. Users differ from local to global users, from techno savvy to amateur and child to senior citizens. As the users requirement and approach are different, dissemination process and methodology should

DOI: 10.4018/978-1-4666-4631-5.ch017

differ and service should be tailor made. Storage becomes a bigger problem in personal or desk top computers. To share and secure data, file servers are installed and every time servers are upgraded at higher costs, infrastructure facilities like air conditioning bigger sophisticated rooms, special server experts to install and configure, and so forth, are required. This needs heavy investment in the form of infrastructures, servers, software and hardware consultants in server installation, sophisticated rooms, air conditioning for maintaining the room temperature, power backup for servers, and so forth. In almost all situations, all these investment procedures, engage a lot of time before and after investment. To avoid this, cloud computing comes to rescue, which is cost-effective and data are stored externally. Thus, it is very simple to pay minimum rent and store data retrieved from anywhere globally when ever needed. No need for wired connections.

In this modern world resource centres are dumped with large volumes of e-resources from open source and subscribed access, user details and transactions, backup files, and so forth. Whenever, the servers are overloaded, it slows down the processing speed of the systems not only to that particular computer but the entire network in few topologies. Data are taken back up in traditional external storage devices like CDs, DVDs, external hard drives, and so forth, for individual users and smaller organizations, but in a medium and bigger organization data generated cannot be taken back up in CDs or DVDs, because in due course the process or technology may become outdated. Therefore, refreshing of these stored data is made mandatory due to technological evolution and transforms it to new technologies to retrieve the data. Failure of retrieval can become possible and data will be lost forever, for example, floppy discs, magnetic tapes, drums, and so forth, which have become obsolete now. Retrieval of 100% data stored in obsolete technologies is not possible without professional intervention. So such information should be retrieved, restored, converted and disseminated into today's technologies. So this cloud computing having many latest required advantages can be taken for consideration. Every new invention and discovery has its own advantages and disadvantages. This chapter discusses features, technologies requirements, rates and investment-required pros and cons of storing externally in cloud environment in general and with special reference to the library and resource centre.

CLOUD COMPUTING MEANING AND SCOPE

Cloud computing is storing metadata in different electronic formats remotely and accessing from any point of globe via Internet through satellite. This is a service to the heterogeneous community that may be private individual to corporate. All the software, references, end users databases, and so forth, can be stored and hence all these remotely stored applications can be accessed using simple thin client computers like laptops, iPads, mobile devices (Furht & Escalante, 2010).

COLLECTION DEVELOPMENT WITH CLOUD COMPUTING

With the increasing contents and information explosion, availability of resources for free, stimulates the intention to all the users to collect more and more data, data availability with relevancy is enormous and collecting and storing of required data for future retrieval made inevitable. Such collected information, should be well stored without data loss. External storage devices like CDs and hard drives are used, but on long run, and when technology becomes obsolete or data is corrupted and the source becomes irretrievable. Data will not perish as this technology as estimated will have long run, making data collection and storage live for long. Moreover collected information with reference to libraries almost published earlier and confidentiality to some extent is not a hindrance.

SCOPE AND SUITABILITY OF CLOUD COMPUTING IN LIBRARY ENVIRONMENT

Cloud computing in library environment will help in resource sharing with confidentiality, authenticity with reference to intellectual property concepts other than few manuscripts, working notes, and so forth. Storage is a gigantic problem especially because of size of resources available in different formats from videos, audio files, images, and so forth, which comparatively occupies more space for storage. Resources available in science faculty doubles every 2 years and social sciences every 3 years and this leads to information explosion and one cannot gain access and store all available information for his own research. So with the help of library professionals, researchers access to relevant information under selective dissemination of information service to relevant extent.

Gained or so collected information should be stored for future references. When a university or Indian Institute of Technology's (IIT's) and Indian Institute of Management's (IIM's) are considered, where 100's of departments, lakhs of users gain access to millions of resources making storing and retrieving a problem. Figure 1 shows the future of cloud computing worldwide and the storage trend followed in present scenario (Miller, 2011).

NEED FOR CLOUD COMPUTING

In the above mentioned situation for storage many big storage servers should be installed at heavy investment in manpower in specialized integration, hardware requirements, hi-tech air-conditioning to maintain temperature, battery backups, and infrastructure facilities. But cloud computing for

Figure 1. The future of cloud computing

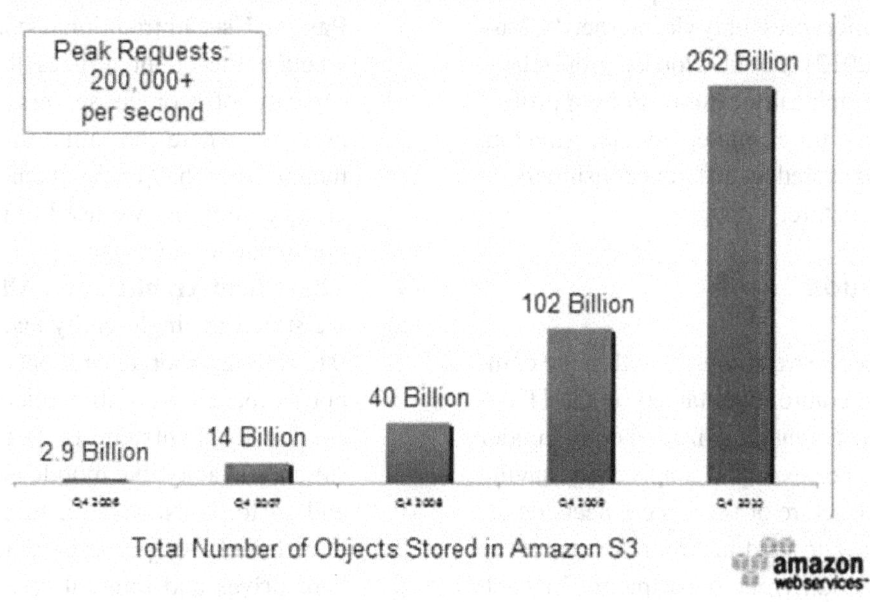

non-confidential resources can be considered as the best option. In the present, cloud computing considered as an alternative solution for storage but security issues has been considered as a major hitch that has put immense pressure on service providers. Moreover, in competitive atmosphere, cloud computing service providers have brought out excellent measure to keep data in a tamper proof environment.

ARCHITECTURE OF CLOUD COMPUTING

Cloud computing architecture is the integration of software and hardware components. There are many types of architecture depending on the requirement of the users and service provider's signature features. Few to mention are

Public Clouds

Public cloud applications, storage, and other resources are made available to the general public by a service provider. These services are free or offered on a pay-per-use model. Generally, public cloud service providers like Amazon AWS, Microsoft and Google own and operate the infrastructure and offer access only via Internet ("Cloud computing," 2012). Public clouds: proprietary, different geographical location run by a professional company, for example, Google, Amazon, Microsoft, and shared by different consumers on shared infrastructure.

Private Clouds

Privately owned servers, mostly within the campus, with total control maintained by the IT department of the parent organization comes under private cloud. For example, a university having its own infrastructure of servers connects its affiliated colleges, located far from the university geographically, different departments in each college, department libraries, many libraries of the particular university like medical library, engineering library, arts library, and so forth, are networked with Internet access.

Virtual Private Clouds

Virtual private clouds allow service providers to offer unique services to private cloud users.

- **Inter-Cloud:** Very similar to Internet. Data stored in others clouds and when ever needed only access is gained. This is gaining moment as it is very cost effective.

ADVANTAGES

- **Fast Deployment:** All the software connected to that cloud will be installed once and authentication for running software is instructed with IP address mapping. This software service system helps the client operations to work faster. From one software installation any number of same programs can be run. All the files downloaded are stored in same cloud (as allotted) so duplication of files can be avoided.
- **Pay for Use:** In traditional storage servers, whether the client utilizes the maximum capacity of storage servers, installed in premises where the initial investment and maintenance has to be taken care. But in cloud computing we need to pay rent proportionate to the usage.
- **Thin Client Architecture:** All the software are stored in single entity and so recovery rate is faster, moreover client systems need not be loaded with all applications for accessing so clients can be thin having low storage capacity like mobile phones, iPads, and so forth. Nowadays, thin clients also have broad storage assisted with external hard drives and internal micro SD cards,

but with an additional investment. These storage devices can be used as supplements but cannot compensate the need for cloud computing.

- **Lower Costs:** Costs on maintenance and management of servers is very less when compared to traditional individual storage, as the individually maintained servers should be upgraded whenever the data storage is increased. Such provisioning needs lot of infrastructure investment like power backup, clean air conditioned rooms, server maintenance experts, and so forth, if the servers are to be upgraded for increasing storage needs further secured clean environment should be allocated. Comparatively, security and load audit should be done continuously for tamper proof system. Such services can be delivered by experienced server professionals which makes it even more costly. Such continuous and periodic check will help in mapping rare combinations of data which are required for further policy or strategy designing.
- **Scalability:** Each and every time up gradation too needs heavy investment in case of traditional storage but in cloud computing flexibility in upgrading, widening the storage or shrinkage also is possible instantly. Pay for use business model is widely used strategy for pricing by the service providers, so instant reduction and widening helps to maintain bills within the budgets.
- **Rapid Provisioning:** Provisioning of extra storage needs hours together for scaling up due to infrastructure and hardware integration, but in cloud provisioning is done instantly as the entire infrastructure facilities are already installed and only provisioning is done on request.
- **Faster Elasticity:** Elasticity in including more files or clients, extending geographical locations, shifting of premises, and so forth, all of these situations will not affect the end user. Flexibility and elasticity is the main advantage of this computing.
- **Low cost Disaster Recovery:** Cost of recovery of data in case of natural calamities and accidents like fire, flood, and so forth, is very high in case of private server storage and percentage of recovery rate cannot be determined but comparatively possibility of disaster is very less and moreover recovery rate is higher and so data safety is ensured. Among cloud storage service providers, especially geographically far apart, back up of data centers are stored with mutual consent. Hence when any calamity occurs and the data centre is at risk of data loss, the entire stored backup can be retrieved and this mechanism helps in 100% data recovery. This cannot be ensured with individual storage servers.
- **Hypervisor Protection Against Intrusions:** All initiatives in protecting documents from intrusions are possible for scaling service providers and so to some extent data or user authenticity are promised. If the information security is broken or breached with the cloud, the service provider will be in a critical position to compensate for the losses, has to face a legal suit, and so forth. Therefore, information security is at maximum at the service provider's cost.
- **Real Time Analysis of System Tampering:** All the operations are saved on data access and therefore system tampering can be easily ruled out and this avoids lost or alteration of data at any levels and thus giving best possible in maintaining confidentiality. Data retrieving and accessing pattern

and mapping are done round the clock, to check the intrusion under regualr security audit with more professional touch and hence system tampering cannot be possible. Moreover, if such tampering of information occurs, further intrusions can be easily and immediately identified that helps to prevent further loss.

- **On Demand Security Services:** In earlier days, security of information was taken as a different service, but nowadays in package schemes it is also covered as one of the bundle packages like provisioning, and so forth. Security issues can be handled in a better professional and authentication way. Intrusions, tampering can be easily ruled out by user behavior, content, location authentications and can be well secured by multilevel certifications.

REQUIREMENTS

- **Internet:** for transferring data to virtual hosts.
- **Public Network:** Telecommunication service providers like Aircel, Airtel, BSNL, and so forth.
- **Virtualization Hosts:** virtual space allotted for individual for storing.
- **Management Node:** the node where files that are to be taken to cloud are kept and floated to virtual space.
- **Private Network:** for collection or sharing to all the users within the organization.

DISADVANTAGES

Any modern management system are analyzed with advantages, disadvantages, suitability, flexibility adaptability, legal provisions, cost benefit analysis, skilled manpower, technical support, after service, and so forth. Few disadvantages with reference to cloud computing in all the above discussed features are

- **Recurring Cost:** Rent paid to the service provider is a recurring cost, and no capital or infrastructure can be shown out of the rent or advance paid, where as in traditional individual server all the investments are in the form of infrastructure development.
- **Connectivity:** If the connectivity between the server and the client fails due to any reason like poor power supply, any technical fault in Internet connectivity, and so forth, information cannot be retrieved instantly till the error is rectified in both ends. Though it is possible in individual server system also, rectification depends on the size, maintenance, service provider, and so forth.

DIFFERENT PRICING STRATEGIES

Charging of different service provided vary from service providers on services, their infrastructure facilities, efficiency, special offerings, business model, sales sophistication, and so forth (Garter Hype, 2009). For storage pricing bandwidth was first used as a standard metric, which declined due to the availability of broad band width at reduced costs. Operational costs like electricity consumption was also considered for pricing, but it was considered meaningless in just calculating a service through electricity consumption that may vary due to power fluctuations, but actual service would have been rendered. Finally infrastructure utility model became the best business model for pricing strategy. For storage, SAAS CPU usage, racks installed, virtual machines created and contacted, and so forth, were taken into consideration for pricing. Few other models worth mentioning are number of incidents, contacts, service calls, per user model, data usage model, mail box, transactions, and so forth ("Pricing cloud services," 2009).

CLOUD COMPUTING TOOLS

1. Abiquo can manage thousands of virtual machines without control of physical infrastructure.
2. Bitnami based on Amazon cloud starting from basic to enhanced services.
3. Mor.ph it is an operational management platform for managing many sophisticated services focused on business applications.
4. Scalr tamper proof, fault tolerant database monitoring tool to ensure security and regular backups for easy retrieval of lost data.
5. CloudStack.
6. CrowdDirector.
7. RightScale.
8. rPath.
9. Symplified.
10. Kaavo.
11. Cloudera.
12. Monitis.

("15 recommended cloud computing tools," 2009).

STATISTICAL ANALYSIS AND PREDICTIONS ON CLOUD COMPUTING

The Info graphic below shows there will be around constant increase of 25% of spending

1. Marketing research team IDC predicts not only the amount of spending will increase and also the users.
2. Around 33,000 cloud service providers are available globally.
3. Mobile devices utility is directly proportional to the cloud service utility.
4. There will be around 10 billion mobile application users. This implies the use of mobile and smart devices which are thin clients; therefore, information and data are necessarily stored in clouds (Miller, n.d.).
5. Market size of Cloud computing will be about $150 Billion by 2013.
6. Amazon EC2 expects to earn around $750 million.

60% of workload like software updation, data backup, and so forth, will be shouldered by the cloud service providers (Ingthorsson, 2011).

TOP 10 SERVICE PROVIDERS

1. Amazon Web Services
2. Rack Space
3. Century Link
4. Salesforce
5. Verizon
6. Joyent
7. Citrix
8. Blue Lock
9. Microsoft
10. VM ware

OPEN SOURCE RESOURCES FOR CLOUD COMPUTING

Software can be classified in different models on features; one such model is based on monetary aspect. Software available free of cost downloadable from the Internet is free software and under this if the source code is available it is free open source software, else it is free software. If it is available on payment it is commercial model where the source code is blocked normally and again it is further classified in to two namely outright purchase and yearly subscription model.

During the recent economic recession many open source software came into existence at par in excellence with commercial software in functionality, security and many more features, almost in all fields, including cloud computing. Following are few such open source cloud computing components.

1. Eucalyptus system is one such software very similar to AmazonEC2 with original architecture with latest updates.
2. Redhat cloud is a linux based player supported by many presentations by senior professionals in cloud environment available in open source mode.
3. Traffic server is used-in-house at yahoo to manage its own traffic. Traffic server can manage, authentication, load and stress balancing, allocation, partitioning, routing, and so forth, exceptionally.
   Cloudera is a deployment software that specializes in cluster based, query reporting, automated auditing and virtualization.
4. Enomaly is Elastic Company Platform is a perfect cloud management software with exceptional performance in provisioning.
5. Joyent specializes in fast deployment of cloud infrastructure extraordinary perfection in functionality with private and public cloud infrastructure
6. Similar open source cloud software are Zoho, Globus Nimbus, Reservoir, Open Nebula are few worth mentioning (Rupley, 2009).

SECURITY ISSUES

Security of the data stored in cloud computing can be hacked and retrieved by various hacking techniques like creating similar Websites, loggers, password tracking software. Especially data become more confidential in financial sector like banking services, insurance, online trading, health database, and so forth. When these are retrieved by unauthorized persons by breaking passwords, then user's accounts can be used to transfer funds without any authentication. Therefore, the financial sector maintains their servers with utmost safety to avoid security breach. When core banking and integration of all banking services were taken up, server nodules were created for increasing the processing speed ("Top five cloud computing security issues," 2009; Dawei Sun, 2011).

SOLUTIONS TO SECURITY ISSUES

Security issues and breach of confidentiality can be overcome to a maximum extent by implementing multilevel security check, login certification by content check, location mapping, multi window password lock, cryptographic storage, biometric authentication, password with special characters, alpha numeric with capital letters, two way user id passwords, and so forth. Beyond all these security checks intrusions are very difficult but possible and so most confidential data and governmental issues are not recommended under cloud storage.

SECURITY ISSUES WITH SPECIAL REFERENCE TO LIBRARY

Data in library are almost published earlier except few confidential data like access passwords, and so forth. Only books can be lent with this by unauthorized persons, where costly and reference books normally will not be lending in the libraries and kept for reference and reading only inside the library premises. Thus security breach does not affect in storing in library environment as it is in financial sector, if selected files are locally stored for confidential issues. Solutions to overcome security breach can be attained by few of the following implementations. For each level of hacking there are different ways to protect the data from being hacked by scrupulous persons. Even further hacking can be addressed with multilevel check points (Zissis & Lekkas, 2012; Sood, 2012).

1. **User Control Management:** User access details can be collected and a separate database namely usage control container from where access control, statistics mapping, authentication, and so forth, can be implemented in different contexts namely
2. **Passwords:** For every window there will be a password check, where passwords should be different and strong. Password strength can be exercised maximum with mixed characters like alphanumeric, special characters and capital letters, while avoiding date of birth, nick names, spouse and children names, and so forth. Periodic change in passwords recommended, where earlier used passwords are not accepted, because this tends the user to have passwords generated in a cyclic pattern and does not serve the purpose of changing it periodically. Tracking of such passwords are made easier to hackers.
3. **Image Based Authentication:** Biometric and image authentication has also gained momentum nowadays because of its encrypted storage, replication or duplication is comparatively complicated when compared to other alphanumeric authentication. With new edition of gadgets where authentications are possible using image processing techniques, this adds to security on gadget handling. Similar mechanisms can be tried ("Image processing and cloud computing_architecture overview," n.d.).
4. **Geographical or Location Mapping:** If the user tries to access, from unusual locations or multiple times from different locations at a time (due to usage by unauthenticated persons), can clearly be identified as misuse of password or breach of security. Such an account should be immediately blocked and after getting proper justifications from the user, account can be activated. Nowadays mobility of the user has increased and these criteria alone cannot be considered.
5. **Multiple Certifications:** In accessing safety lockers, the bank official and the user has to login with the key password simultaneously into the correct slot. If this authentication fails, then one cannot open the locker. Such principle is often used in most confidential login. Similar mechanisms can be used for external or guest users. With special reference to library context, multiple password authentications can be used where the library staff and the user can jointly login to access the cloud storage.
6. **Encryption:** Cryptographic separation of data is just by converting using cryptographic algorithms and so confidential data can be encrypted on production on storage and on retrieval is done after encryption by authenticated person through proper certification channels. This setup can be used in storing research, raw data in cloud computing for publishing.
7. **Authorization:** Authorization to content, time, IP address, and so forth, is few fields where authentication can be scaled and drafted. For example for research scholars access to scholarly Websites is more than enough, other social networking and entertainment political Websites can be blocked. Such restrictions can be implemented to authorization in accessing required information to their administrative capacity and other files can be blocked for access to all except for the top level management. To avoid risk of breach of security in top level management no person can be given full administrative rights to access all the documents including staff of cloud computing storage service providers. As in the case of banking sector, Teller can access only to the credit transactions. Card management systems can access only card transactions and only the user can have more control to online transactions, in authenticated Websites. Loggers are software

which is used to collect individual's user's username and password through duplicate Websites of banks and other financial related Websites that resembles the genuine Website.

Statistics can be used as a tool to detect, evaluate and plan for the future breach and intact security systems. Periodic statistical assessment of usage can help in following:

1. Policy framing in future and current use.
2. Need and budgeting for storage.
3. Trend identification of research.
4. Storage requirements.
5. Duplicate downloads.
6. Best practices compared to other cloud users.
7. Breach of security.
   a. In access to files, software, and so forth.
   b. Retrieval of information and downloading, and so forth.
   c. View and listing.
8. **Behavior Assessment:** User who behaves unusually for example, try to access from different geographical location without prior intimation, different IP address, content search and download is very different namely science student goes for cultural or entertainment Websites, and so forth, can be well assessed in user evaluation thus giving maximum confidentiality and limited authenticity. However, regular user impede with all options in search and procedure to access, but comparatively new intruder cannot have the idea of already searched and stored resources and goes for quick searches and this behavioral change recorded can easily be chased and sought for intrusions. In library environment usage mapping can be clearly ruled out by the subject and its relevancy. Though interdisciplinary researches are considered, access and usage trends can be easily sorted out if clear watch is done on regular basis. So if there is any discrepancy the user account is intimated or locked and after justifications and users' consent the account accessibility can be revived.
9. **File Distribution Management System:** File distribution management system is very similar in concept with database management system but functionality differs. Implementing these management systems can enhance the security in distribution of information. There are few commercially available packages like Seculore, that helps the user to customize each and every file with time, geographical location, user identity, times of usage, print, copy, redistribute, and so forth, and this can be altered whenever needed by authenticated persons.
10. **File Compression as Security Tool:** Files when compressed with password will have dual benefit. Compressed data occupies less space for storage and retrieval of information is possible with authenticity. This gives enhanced security and economic storage. Much commercially available and free open source software with all secure features is available. Data should be secured and compressed at the user end, then can be stored in cloud. Integrated file distribution management system with data compression is also available in models commercially available software like AirZip, and so forth.
11. **Security Certification:** Organization such as Cloud Security Alliance has come out with security and load, stress testing management and if the service provider meets the standards under different rating patterns and provides certification for security. Proper guidelines and requirements are stated by the certification providers and this gives maximum preparatory modes and means to security. Such certifications will enhance the standard of the company practicing cloud storage and meaningful impact among the customers especially in financial and bank-

ing sector. With reference to library such certifications can endeavor for improving the status of library and best practices to international standards.

12. **Standards for Information and or Data Security:** Information security is the major concern that prevents many organizations from shifting to cloud environment. Therefore to make the cloud computing more reliable in security, functionality, recovery, foolproof standards are coded. Any cloud service provider that has certifications like ISO 27001 has a more secure infrastructure resulting in compact and tamperproof information. In the United States, the more confidential data are related to finance and health insurance. Such information is stored in cloud with utmost security measures, and being a government agency certify with regular standards recommended to store most confidential data related to one's personal finance and health.
13. **Virtualization:** Virtualization of storage may affect users in connectivity, when compared to traditional library resources and if the network connectivity is interrupted, it affects accessibility to the resources. Moreover virtualization is the concept of multiple accesses to one resource at a time. Hence load and stress testing are done to all storages whether it is inter or intra connected. Operating response and retrieval time is tested with multiple virtual users.
14. **Time-Based Solutions:** Time based login access: according to the shift timings, or class hour timings students or users access can be monitored or even restricted. This resembles the principle as in parental control options in modern television sets. Time between password and login name should be very minimum. Ideal window and data feeding time between passwords, and so forth, can also be restricted. Flexibility in time management should be locally permitted as the need for change may be required often. Total access time can also be restricted and auto logout options will enhance the time management and control. Periodic change of passwords should be made mandatory, as in the case of many Internet banking applications, as this ensures password tracking loggers to avoid breach of security password over a period of time.

TYPES OF SERVICES

There are many types of public cloud computing:

- **Infrastructure as a SERVICe (IaaS):** Large number of servers with high density in storage are installed at a most sophisticated environment, access to the users are given through Internet connectivity in the form of authenticated user name and password.
    - **Platform as a Service (PaaS):** Storage of information in a remote centre and accessibility is given through a customized platform only through which stored data can be accessed.
    - **Examples are Content:** SpringCM, Xythos OnDemand, GoogleBase Force.com, Google App Engine, Bungee Labs Connect, Etelos, Intiuit Quickbase, LongJump, Apprenda SaasGrid, Oracle Saas Platform, MS Azure
    - **Data:** Amazon S3, Box.net, Google Base, Amazon SimpleDB, Trackvia, Microsoft SSDS.
- **Software as a Service (SaaS):** Software that helps to access the information stored in cloud environment. Google Docs are now even upgraded as Google drive where the individual can store retrieve using Gmail account. Accessibility and avail-

ability of space and information makes this SAAS service more popular as most of them are provided free of cost initially. On continuous usage, it may be charged. Compared to traditional electronic storage it need not be carried all along as it is stored in cloud. Few examples for SaaS are Salesforce, Google Docs, Facebook, LinkedIn, and Doodle

- **Network as a Service (NaaS):** Networking of authenticated systems in different geographical locations makes cloud more adaptable under a wider security umbrella. Therefore networking itself has emerged out as a separate service in recent years and implements utmost security systems.
- **Storage as a Service (STaaS):** Storage in service providers wide range of infrastructure facilities especially for offsite back up and retrieval services. This service si efficiently used in disaster and recovery management among cloud service providers. For example cloud storage service provider A is located in America and service provider B located in Eastern country stores data in vice versa model with regular backups of their clients' information. This enables to retrieve data even at a higher risk of natural calamity. For security purposes backup or information stored in others' servers are encrypted and compressed for economic storage.
- **Security as a Service (SecaaS):** Service through compact and infallible security with proper certifications gives security as a service, a need for the more confidential data storage like governmental, military and revenue information. Breach of such information may lead to total threat in national security in the focus of financial, social, cultural and communal harmony.
- **Data as a Service (DaaS):** DAAS is the form of collection and distribution of information service. This type of service has not gained momentum. The reasons can be as follows:
    - Request sent to service provider should respond.
    - Instant retrieval is comparatively not possible.
    - Authenticity of information cannot be ensured.
    - Relevancy cannot be guaranteed as the service provider cannot put on requestor's shoes.
- **Desktop as a Service (DaaS - see above):** DaaS is similar to SaaS and the user desktop applications are stored in cloud and can be accessed through connectivity. Such service providers take the utmost responsibility in updating, loading and maintaining the software. Concept reminds from the Virtual Desktop Interface (VDI) (Wikipedia)
- **Database as a Service (DBaaS):** Data base provider stores data in cloud and gives access to the distributable content in the form of authentication through a cloud service provider. So cloud service provider takes the authentic responsibility for database distribution and rights authentication.
- **Test Environment as a Service (TEaaS):** Testing of cloud computing software, storage management systems, certifications, and so forth, comes under this service. Before launching of applications authentication and certification are gaining importance among software user and for such service standardized methods and models are to be practiced. (Wikipedia)
- **Backend as a Service (BaaS):** Back end of an application will be having database

software. Storing of information in the form of data alone can be categorized under backend as a service.

- **Integrated Development Environment as a Service (IDEaaS)**
- **Integration Platform as a Service (IPaaS):** See Cloud-based integration (Cloud Computing, 2012).
    - **Integration:** Boomi, Mule OnDemand, OpSource Connect (OSB), Amazon SQS, Microsoft BizTalk Services.
    - **Orchestration:** ProcessMaker, Appian Anywhere, Skemma, Intensil.
    - **Billing, Contract Management:** OpSource/LeCayla, Aria, eVapt, Amazon DevPay, Zuora.
    - **Security:** OpenID, OAuth, Ping Identity.
    - **Cloud Deployment:** rPath, CohesiveFT, VMWare, Xen, Parallels, Bea Weblogic Server VE, 3Tera AppLogic, Elastra Cloud Server.

SUPPORTING SERVICES REQUIRED TO ENHANCE CLOUD COMPUTING

- **Unit and Total Load Testing:** A calculation automated tool used to show the users service and transaction rate, time consumption at a time for sharing against usage by multiple users.
- **Access Control:** Methods of access, modes of login, time limitations, usage limitations, and so forth.
- **Billing:** Pay per use, renting, and so forth, are few different models of billing according to the requirement of the individual users.
- **Security:** Different levels of security and check gates, including timely access multiple level entries, passwords security, strength of password generation, dynamic password, encryption on storage at source, encryption on storage at servers, and so forth.
- **Configuration Management:** Allotment of memory, at different usage slots like peak hours, lean hours, and so forth.

DATA WAREHOUSING

Data warehousing is collection of data, categorizing, filtering, eliminating duplicate data, format compatibility, security of data retrieval, and so forth. Data are clipped through tools will have very compressed form of table and so size of such files will be comparatively less, making storage of files very easy. Further compression of data will help in storing bulky data in to smaller files. Data warehousing can be further explained with the following example. In an academic institution administrative office will have students' personal details, accounts and finance department will have fees details added with admission details, Admission details will have personal details incorporated. Faculty particular student belong to will have academic profile with personal details and finally library will have information seeking behavior, book circulation, fine and fees, and so forth, with personal details. Therefore, personal details of the candidate with all added information from each department will be clipped to one that can relate to each department's need, and answer query with personal details from one database. Few examples of ware housing tools are Prism warehouse manager, Platinum info refiner, info pump, QDB, Vality, and so forth.

DATA MINING

Data that are warehoused with Extract Transform and Load (ETL) tools are then retrieved by data mining. Benefits of mining are that the data available will be user friendly and simplified query. This facilitates decision making more apt, time saving and economic. Web mining is a similar concept of data mining but to cluster the search queries that can result in more relevant answers.

Latest versions of data mining are provided with semi automatic analyzer. It helps to map different or heterogeneous data structures and points out the changes in regular pattern. Auto mapping and reporting tool helps to reduce pressure in handling large database. Moreover, it can be effectively used in mapping the information seeking behavior, usage pattern; change in utility of services, and so forth, and its reports can be used for security audit purposes. Therefore, data mining and warehousing not only helps in economic storage, but also in effective reporting, security audit and policy or decision making. Few examples for Data mining tools are Clementine, IBM's Intelligent Miner, SGI's MineSet, and SAS's Enterprise Miner.

NEED FOR ECONOMICS IN STORING

Most of the cloud computing service providers work with pay for use charging system. So, the files to be stored should be small in size and be extracted when required. Naturally, if usage size is comparatively small, this draws smaller bills for storage space utility. Compactness can be ensured by compression, but retrieval will be complicated. So meaning compression can be done with data warehousing tools as it eliminates all duplicate data, sort and append.

GREEN COMPUTING

Green computing is acquisition, processing, storage and retrieval including hardware and software components in maximum efficiency with minimum energy, carbon foot print, emission of heat in production, usage, recyclability, biodegradability, safe disposability, reduced use of heavy or hazardous or precious metals, and so forth. Green computing in common language is information communication technology sustainability or green IT. Green computing can be practiced in any level of production contributing to the green environment to the extent possible. Many companies like HP, Dell, and CISCO, and so forth, have now incorporated green computing concepts.

NEED FOR GREEN TECHNOLOGIES

Physical or Web libraries, both will utilize energy. But when accounted for, do all libraries have taken enough steps to sustain nature friendly environment in libraries especially in the energy and environment. Traditional library with physical print books or the digital libraries with computer emit radiations and accumulate dust. Nowadays, more importance is given in getting sustainability evaluation and certification especially in newly constructed buildings. In few countries, it has been made mandatory for newly constructed buildings to get sustainability rating to showcase the environment friendly techniques used in raw materials and energy efficiency. When a new technology is gaining momentum, adaptability will increase. Such drastic increase if not analyzed properly, its impact on environment will be very drastic resulting in irreparable damages. For example, if the energy consumption in cloud computing servers is intense than the local servers including data transaction then adapting cloud may not be advisable on global view. So any technology that has high adaptability should be tested for energy efficiency, nature friendly aspects and if not available more research and alterations can be brought like introducing solar energy as mandatory for cloud computing servers, where it becomes sustained energy efficiency with more adaptability. Technologies like green computing, green roofing, and so forth, will have major impact on nature in diminishing usage of fossil fuels, carbon sequestration, emission of green house gases, sustainable energy for temperature control, and so forth.

GREEN COMPUTING AND DATA WAREHOUSING

Compression of data meaningfully, makes the space consumption and file size comparatively smaller. Hence, requirement of storage space is minimized, which in turn reduces the resources like materials used, energy in production and energy in storage and retrieval is minimized, thus contributing to green tomorrow. Few tools like DATAllegro, Kickfire have the capability to process exponentially more transactions with a smaller hardware footprint. Meanwhile, extreme data compression is currently advertised by special DBMS like ParAccel, Vertica, which also results in a smaller hardware footprint.

ENERGY CONSUMPTION AND CARBON FOOT PRINT

Energy consumption by the cloud computing environment will increase as it works 24/7, when compared to small business enterprises that maintains individual servers because they are not kept running when not in use. But, when such medium and small enterprises move to the cloud, then automatically the system is kept live round the clock. Though, carbon foot print is diminished when clustering, integration of small servers that are maintained individually by enterprises, it is compensated with more energy consumption on continuous running.

Power supply fluctuated according to the request is a more complex model to implement, but will have some impact on saving power consumption. All the users of particular cloud service provider are classified into small area groups according to their functionality and grouped together. For example, many companies from one geographical area are grouped together and working hours of such group will differ from another group from a different location and this again will differ in intensity of request and function. These hours are considered as peak hours and lean hours are kept idle with minimum power for operating is allocated.

Calculation of individual power consumption, grouping according to the user timing, type, and so forth, measuring the need and allocating should be done with more professionalism to get a fruitful energy saving and economic service (Kuribayashi, 2012).

ENERGY SUSTAINABILITY FROM RENEWABLE ENERGY SOURCES AND GREEN TECHNOLOGIES

Another way to save environment from hazardous carbon emission from ICT industry (which are drastically increasing fuel consumption) is to move to environment friendly renewable source of energy like solar, tide, wind, and so forth, for generating power. In countries like India gifted with rich solar power as a source of renewable energy round the year (if utilized properly) power shut downs, heavy investment on fossil fuel research, source searching, refining, and so forth, can be avoided. At average calculations, investments on erecting solar power panels can be recovered within 6 to 8 years but production continues till the life of installed power panels that are estimated from 25 to 60 years depending on the quality and maintenance. This means saving more than 10% to 20% of the total budget every year and this saved fund can be utilized for improvement on regular basis. During hot seasons regular production is supplemented with extra power generated that can even be supplied to others commercially paving way for earning additional revenue (Kalpana & Gopalakrishnan, 2012a). According to the featured article published in Down to Earth a magazine on Science and Environment states that the spiritual centre caters to the feeding needs with a capacity to serve 50,000 people for a single meal solely from the energy generated by solar panels installed in the roof top of the University. Excess energy generated are stored and utilized for later needs after sunset for the next 16 hours. (Paliwal, 2013). When such a great conservation and zero emission solar energy is generated to cater a substitution of around 200 liters of diesel and 1.5 tons of carbon emission for cooking 50 kgs of rice in 12 minutes it is possible to save fossil energy. Almost all cloud computing service providers runs 24/7 with many servers integrated, will consume lots of fossil energy. If it is made mandatory by the government to implement renewable energy as source to fulfill their energy requirement including temperature maintenance, power backup, and so forth, increase in fossil energy requirement at least can be avoided.

GREEN ROOFING

Green roofing is the new technique introduced in Boston National Library eliminating the cost of cooling systems and gives an enhanced look, a natural temperature control, greening the environment and producing more oxygen. Roofs are covered with a thin layer of specially designed structure that can lodge plants with small root structures like Korean grass. Such erections can be used effectively in rain water harvesting, recycling of effluents and other waste water. Moreover it helps to maintain temperature inside the building in a more eco friendly way.

Indoor Plantations

Planting of small plants, shrubs helps to maintain green fresh air circulation and removes toxic substances from air in a natural way by absorbing odour and emissions from building materials. This strategy is implemented in almost all organizations as this compliments to the interior decoration giving a lush green lively environment. Few more advantages are

- Ecologically maintains temperature.
- Utilizes flood water naturally.
- Reduces CO_2 emissions from fossil fuel production and consumption.
- Reuses waste materials.
- Salvages and decompose the organic wastes.
- Generates renewable pollution free green energy.
- Supplies oxygen to environment and saves ozone depletion.
- Absorbs sound and so reduces noise pollution.
- Absorbs pollutants and dust particles like cigar smoke, and so forth, and reduces air pollution levels and gives clean air for breathing.
- Produces oxygen and helps in air circulation in rooms populated with electronic devices that run continuously emitting lots of heat.
- Absorbs pollutants mainly from raw materials used in construction and interior infrastructures emits gases with odours, especially when it is new.

INDOOR PLANTS AND ITS EFFECTS ON HUMANS

Data centre is not just the store house of information, but also of dust and pollution. Indoor planting is keeping gardens inside the rooms for giving lush green color to room, fresh air, and pollution-free environment. Natural environment can give long lasting comforts among humans. Materials used in construction and indoor fittings and fixture will emit chemical substances like Benzene, Formaldehyde, and so forth. NASA has conducted research on indoor plants and their capacity to absorb air pollution from cigar smoke and they proved to be best natural pollution control method.

Table 1. Indoor plants that can remove harmful chemical pollutants

Chemicals	Pollutant Sources	Pollutant Removing Plant Varieties
Benzene	Inks, oils, paints, plastics, rubber, dyes, detergents, gasoline, pharmaceutical, tobacco smoke, synthetic fibers	English Ivy, Dracaena marginata, Janet Craig,Warneckei, Chrysanthemum, Gerbera Daisy, Peace lily
Formaldehyde	Foam insulation, plywood, pressed-wood products, grocery bags, waxed paper, fire retardants, adhesive binders in floor coverings, cigarette smoke, natural gas	Azalea, Philodendron, Spider plant, Golden Pothos, Bamboo palm, Corn plant, Chrysanthemum, Mother-in-law's tongue
Trichloroethylene	Primarily used in the metal degreasing and dry cleaning industries; also in printing inks, paints, lacquers, varnishes, adhesives	Gerbera Daisy, Chrysanthemum, Peace lily, Warneckei, Dracaena marginata

(Kalpana & Gopalakrishnan, 2013). Table shows some examples of indoor plants that can remove harmful pollutants.

All the above mentioned building materials are used in datacenters so that they emit toxic substances that may affect even the sophisticated infrastructure. Hence traditional technologies that can give a major impact on the environment should also be considered for better, safe and eco friendly infrastructure (Flickety, n.d.).

CONCLUSION

Hence, any new technological evolution should affect libraries, because the resource centre analyzes the need and serves the right information to right person at the right time. Mainly information sharing, storing, retrieving, dissemination through latest technologies in information and communication should be upgraded instantly to beat the race of efficiency in service. Today's users are well-informed and mostly techno-savvy. Therefore library professionals should also update themselves to serve users more confidently and economically, resulting in maximum benefits at minimum availability. This technological intervention will surely help in storing information in a more cost effective and authenticated access. Collection development need not depend on storage capacity hereafter as large is possible with minimum rents and improve collection to maximum in digital environment. (Kalpana & Gopalakrishnan, 2012a; Kalpana & Gopalakrishnan, 2012b). Users nowadays prefer digital libraries than traditional print libraries due to major advantages like easy storage, retrieval, sharing, availability, and so forth. Therefore, libraries should also progress towards evolutionary changes towards digital environment, as expected by users. Green energy, pollution free environment, and so forth, are popular and existing concepts, but when all suitable technologies integrate together they complement each other, giving a drastic change overall. Finally data centre should be economic, eco-friendly and secure to store ever growing data in a reliable environment acceptable by future generations and nature as a whole.

REFERENCES

Cloud computing. (2012). Retrieved from http://en.wikipedia.org/wiki/Cloud_computing#Public_cloud

Dawei Sun, G. C. (2011). *Surveying and analysing security: Privacy and trust issues in cloud computing environments. Advances in Control Engineering and Information Sciences* (pp. 2852–2856). Beijing, China: Elsevier.

Dorey, P. G., & Leite, A. (2011). *Commentary: cloud computing – a security problem or solution?* London: Elsevier. doi:10.1016/j.istr.2011.08.004.

Flickety, K. E. (n.d.). *How to purify air using indoor plants*. Retrieved from http://www.wikihow.com/Purify-the-Air-Using-Plants

Furht, B., & Escalante, A. (2010). *Handbook of cloud computing* (1st ed.). New York: Springer. doi:10.1007/978-1-4419-6524-0.

Gartner Hype. (2009). *Pricing and positioning cloud computing services*. Ingram Micro Partner Smart Services Division.

Image processing and Cloud computing _ architecture Overview. (n.d.). Retrieved from http://computer-vision-talks.com/2011/04/image-processing-cloud-computing-architecture-overview/

Ingthorsson, O. (2011, November 30). *5 Cloud computing statistics you may find surprising*. Retrieved from http://cloudcomputingtopics.com/2011/11/5-cloud-computing-statistics-you-may-find-surprising/

Jianhua Che, Y. D. (2011). Study on the security models and strategies of cloud computing. *International Conference on Power Electronics and Engineering Application* (pp. 586-593). Beijing, China: Elsevier.

Kalpana, T. M., & Gopalakrishnan, S. (2012a). Collection development and cloud computing. *International Conference on Collection Development in Digital Environment* (pp. 99-104). Chennai, India: University of Madras.

Kalpana, T. M., & Gopalakrishnan, S. (2012b). Increased collection with ecofriendly strategies. *International conference on collection Development in Digital Era* (pp. 421-424). Chennai, India: Univeristy of Madras.

Kalpana, T. M., & Gopalakrishnan, S. (2013). Self sustainability in academic libraries in digital era. In Thanuskodi (Ed.), Challenges in Academic Libraries in Digital Era. Hershey, PA: IGI Global.

Kuribayashi, S. I. (2012). Reducing total power consumption method in cloud computing environment. *International Journal of Computer Networks and Communications*, *4*(2), 69–84. doi:10.5121/ijcnc.2012.4205.

Miller, M. (n.d.). *Cloud computing info graphics*. Retrieved from http://pinterest.com/markmillerit-pro/cloud-computing-infographics/

Miller, R. (2011, January 30). Amazon S3 cloud stores 262 billion objects. Retrieved from http://www.datacenterknowledge.com/archives/2011/01/30/amazon-s3-cloud-stores-262-billion-objects/

Netmetix. (n.d.). *Top 10 cloud computing statistics*. Retrieved from http://netmetix.wordpress.com/2011/11/09/top-10-cloud-computing-statistics/

Paliwal, A. (2013, March 15). *Bon appetit with sun: Down to earth*. Retrieved from http://www.downtoearth.org.in/content/bon-appetit-sun

Pricing cloud services: Cost structures. (2009, February 23). Retrieved from http://gettogreen.blogspot.in/2009/02/cloud-computing-cost-structure-and.html

15. *recommended cloud computing management tools*. (2011, March 25). Retrieved from http://www.cloudtweaks.com/2011/03/15-recommended-cloud-computing-management-tools-for-your-business/

Rupley, S. (2009, November 26). *11 Top open source resources for cloud computing*. Retrieved from http://gigaom.com/2009/11/06/10-top-open-source-resources-for-cloud-computing/

Sood, S. K. (2012). A combined approach to ensure data security in cloud computing. *Journal of Network and Computer Applications*, *35*, 1831–1838. doi:10.1016/j.jnca.2012.07.007.

Top five cloud computing security issues. (2009, April 29). Retrieved from file:///F:/presentations/cloud%20computing%20security%20issues/Top-five-cloud-computing-security-issues.htm

U.S. Department of Health and Human Services. (n.d.). *The security rule*. Retrieved from http://www.hhs.gov/ocr/privacy/hipaa/administrative/securityrule/

Wikipedia. (n.d.). *Desktop as a service*. Retrieved from http://en.wikipedia.org/wiki/Desktop_as_a_service

Zissis, D., & Lekkas, D. (2012). Addressing cloud computing security issues. *Future Generation Computer Systems*, 583–592. doi:10.1016/j.future.2010.12.006.

Chapter 18
Cloud Libraries:
Issues and Challenges

Mayank Yuvaraj
Banaras Hindu University, India

ABSTRACT

On-demand computing power at modest cost, tied with faster Internet accessibility in the Cloud has offered the future of Cloud libraries. This chapter presents a snapshot of what is happening in the arena of Cloud libraries. It presents the features, its promises, components that drive a Cloud library, users and the services, infrastructure, information sources, and retrieval strategies in the Cloud. Further, it presents a Cloud strategic planning model for its realization in libraries. Whereas a lot of work has been done on the technical aspects and implications in health and medical services, there is lack of focus on the implication of Cloud computing in a library setting. This chapter is a self-conscious attempt in filling some of the gaps.

INTRODUCTION

Greek mythology tells of critters plucked from the earth`s surface and treasured as a celestial body in the sky. Analogous developments have erupted in the computing world where data, software, hard disk and platforms have been swept from desktop PCs and server rooms and installed in the compute Cloud. "The Cloud phenomenon is very real because of its position to drive technology, deliver usability and force standardization" (James, 2010).

In general, Cloud computing has stripped the computing power from CPU and brought a shift in the geography of computation leading to delivery of computing power on the Web (online CPU). "The Cloud is the content bazaar of the Web" that is "massive" and "ignoring or prohibiting the Web is to prohibit electricity" (James, 2010). The "Cloud" element of Cloud Computing can be seen as an acronym that stands for C- Computing resources, L- that is Location independent, O- accessed via Online means, U- used as an Utility and D- On Demand availability. Cloud Computing

DOI: 10.4018/978-1-4666-4631-5.ch018

has severely infested the structure and functions of library`s trinity: books to e-books, users to virtual users, staff to virtual staffs. Under the ascendancy of technological developments library services have underwent phenomenal changes taking the shape of Cloud libraries. This chapter is written with an aim to present the various shades of Cloud computing enabled Cloud libraries their needs, features components, major players, infrastructure as well as strategies of realization. Cloud library in general is a fundamental transformation of the entire brick- and- mortar library which offers an auspicious opportunity to introduce Web-based dynamic library services. A Cloud library is a trinity of users, Cloud (Internet) and staff which are interconnected through computing. In a Cloud library the library services are consumed and delivered over the Internet.

CLOUD COMPUTING AND LIBRARIES: ISSUES

There is an intellectual contestation of varied interpretations regarding the implication of Cloud computing in libraries. Sadeh (2007) feels that "The widespread adoption of Web search engines and other Internet tools and services and the emergence of players such as Google Scholar and Windows Live Academic in the scholarly information-retrieval arena have reduced users' dependence on library support to fulfil their information needs." The Web has also expanded the scope of services provided by librarians. Vaquero, Rodero-Merino, Caceres, and Lindner (2009) opine that Cloud computing and Web collaboration is two major concepts that underlie new and innovative developments in library automation. Cloud services allow for more optimal resource utilization, easier access, and more effective cost reduction.

The growing Internet usage among library users plus the time users spend on the Internet has made it imperative for the libraries to offer their services online. Today`s information consumers have more alternative and attractive ways of finding information than the traditional libraries. The "change in users` perceptions and their preference for Internet tools and services such as Web search engines, e-mail, blogs, and RSS feeds" needs to be studied and redesign the library services (Sadeh, 2007).

Yang (2012) asserts that "The Cloud-based new generation of ILS allows many libraries to share useful data. For instance, sharing of full-text journal titles from electronic databases, many libraries subscribe to the same database." Historically, libraries have turned to huge capital investment on IT infrastructure for various online as well as subscription based services. With these success libraries are motivated for using subscription based IT infrastructure in the Cloud. "In the field of library automation there are several commercial suppliers already offering various adaption's of their products which make the use of the cloud possible to a lesser or greater extent" (Romero, 2012). According to Tomer and Alman (2011) Cloud computing is important in the context of LIS for two reasons "First, the embrace of Cloud computing by many organizations, including OCLC, OhioLink, SirsiDynix, and the Library of Congress suggest that this mode of computing will have a significant impact on the configuration, the economics, and perhaps the personal requirements of library computing in years to come."

Moreover, libraries are in a unique position to experiment with Cloudcomputing given their service oriented mission and need to find appropriate solutions using limited resources. Fox (2009) observes that the goals of the organization have an impact on their use of Cloud solutions. Sachdeva, Rana, Kapoor, and Shahid (2011) argue that "There are many reasons for why Cloud-computing is being in common. Technologically we use Cloudcomputing because we can and it`s convenient. Economically, it is cost effective and pocket friendly, and finally it makes interactivity easier to achieve with the target audiences" (p.161).

Fox (2009) further argues that libraries may be governed by the policies and regulations that dictate how they can use Cloud-based solutions. On the other hand, Yang (2012) opines that "As Resource Description and Access, our new cataloguing rule, will replace AACR2 and be implemented in the future; the new Cloud-based ILS will provide a unified approach to bibliographic data" (p,7). Cloud computing is also going to change the practise of traditional reprographic services offered in the libraries. Khater (2010) argues that "With the development of cloud computing and the digitization of human knowledge, translation has begun to see major breakthroughs by moving from rule to statistical based translation algorithms. Any individual, application or device is now enabled to translate content in endless languages, facilitating communication and breaking a major barrier – language." There is a tremendous amount of enthusiasm around Cloud-based solutions and services (filtering, sorting, categorization and analytics to help users manage the vast repositories of both structured and unstructured information) as well as the cost-savings and flexibility that they can provide (Rhoton, 2009).

TRANSITION TO CLOUD LIBRARIES

The changes in the libraries were largely the product of inertia of libraries and the evolution of information technology that led to revolutions from which libraries could not prevent themselves. Modern libraries to a large extent are built on technology. Post 1950 information technology became an integral part of the library operations. The changes in the libraries ran side by side along with technology. The path breaking change however to library services came with the use of Internet services (networking). This paved the way for services being accessed and delivered via the Web. This concept matured into Cloud services. By hosting the data stored in a database in the Cloud these services are offered.

The development of technology that brought significant effect over the libraries has been presented in Figure 1.

"Richard West and Peter Lyman have suggested a three-phase procession of the effects of information technology on organizations: modernization (doing what you are already doing though more efficiently); innovation (experimenting with new capabilities that the technology makes possible) and transformation (fundamentally altering the nature of the organization through these capabilities)" (Lynch, 2000). In order to flesh out the genesis of Cloud libraries there is a need to gauze the development of Cloud libraries on these three lines.

Modernization of Libraries

No value is much more satisfying than a commitment of library and information professionals to satisfy people with their quest of information. In order to come true to their mission libraries even took the aid of technology from time to time. Initially libraries were reluctant to go along with the erosion of winds of Information Technology but the changes in information seeking behaviour of the library users precipitated its need. Implication of Information Technology in libraries led to automation of library operations, rise of

Figure 1. Development of technology

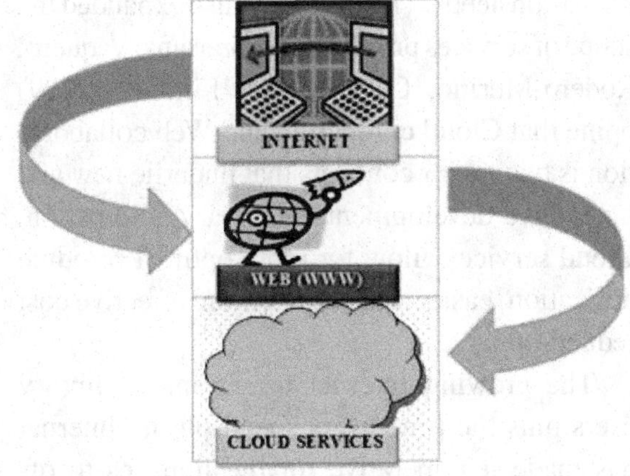

electronic resources and databases followed by digital libraries. Almost all of these services were based in Cloud which unfamiliarly librarians as well as library users are using. "Users who have had the experience of using Web 2.0 services like Wikipedia, Blogger, and Flickr etc have already experienced Cloud computing, maybe unknowingly" (Abidi & Abidi, 2012). "Furthermore, cloud computing remarkably boosts the learning ability of the students With this technology, learning approaches and strategies unheard of before, or, at the very least, thought to be undoable, are now being used on a large scale" (Cenon, 2012). The quick development of Cloud libraries have been brought by the emerging computing technologies that are offering reasonably priced metered usage of computing infrastructures and massive storage capacity.

Innovation in Libraries

Libraries are constantly in search of solutions as well as viable means to reach out to users expectations. With the dawn of Internet era library users were gripped with Google fever due to which users preferred to seek information from the luxury of their home and offices rather than coming to libraries. Henceforth, libraries rejuvenated and retooled themselves with globally networked institutional repositories, digital libraries and databases to meet the user needs. Pervasiveness of Information Technology brought out by the device-independent nature of Cloud computing provides the perfect platform for Cloud libraries. "Provided that it has an Internet connection and a Web browser, it really does not matter if the computer is a traditional desktop or laptop PC, or even a net book, tablet, smart phone, e-book reader, surface computer, ambient device or any of the other new computing appliances" (Barnatt, 2010).

However, with the provision of proxy based access to electronic resources there was misuse of library resources. Most of the libraries used user ids and passwords as their access control to Cloud resources which was shared and sometimes forgotten. Libraries used digitized handwriting, voice prints, finger prints and access token networks as an alternative to passwords.

Transformation of Libraries

Modern libraries are largely driven by the technologies. Choudhary et al. (2008) argue that "Prior to the Internet library networking was limited to cross-linking services between libraries. Post Internet, library networking has taken on a much more fundamental service role, as it is becoming the library service itself, as physical services becomes virtualized." It was the result of conjunction of libraries with the information technology only that led to library automation, digital preservation and digital libraries. Further, with the coming of Cloud computing technology libraries has lot to offer its users which unconsciously are moving from ground to Cloud. Commenting on the future of Cloud computing in libraries Carl Grant at ALA annual conference in Anaheim opined that "These new Cloud-computing platforms are the technological foundations of that great age of librarianship. They're going to let us define new and better librarianship based services that will truly give us the capability to differentiate ourselves from other information end-user services" ("Thoughts from Carl Grant," 2012).

To understand the nature and characteristics of Cloud computing driven Cloud library there is a need to demarcate the boundary between traditional brick-and-mortar libraries with that of a Cloud library. A comparative take on both of them has been presented in Table 1.

NEED OF CLOUD LIBRARIES

Goldner (2010) has put forth various issues which justify the inevitability of Cloud libraries has been mentioned below:

Table 1. Brick-and-mortar vs. cloud library

S.No	Brick-and-Mortar Library	Cloud Library
1.	They are available in-house.	They are available virtually.
2.	Network connectivity is desirable to access the resources of this library.	Network connectivity is essential to access the resources of this library.
3.	They are available to a local population to a specific group of users.	They are available for a larger population irrespective of geographical location.
4.	They are dependent on software and hardware.	They are independent of software dependency but are hardware dependent.
5.	They involves large extent of physical maintenance like dusting, fumigation, binding, chemical treatment etc.	They do not require any physical maintenance.
6.	They contain print as well as digital documents.	They contain only digital documents.
7.	In this library, librarian has to focus on library services as well as computer based services like (library automation and digital library).	In this library, librarian has to only focus on services not on any aspects of IT.
8.	There is no such loss of data.	There is a greater risk of data loss so data has to kept as back up.
9.	There is always growth of library documents and requires expansion of library building.	It does not involve physical storage or library building but needs database storage capacity.
10.	For availing the services user has to come to library.	It brings the information to the user which can be accessed by any device having Web browser via Internet.
11.	In this library the library staff interacts face to face with the library user.	It involves virtual interaction with the library user through social networks and blogs.
12.	The services of this library can be accessed by the devices available in the library only.	There services can be accessed by any device that has a Web browser and has a network connection.

- Most library computer systems are built on pre-Web technology.
- Systems distributed across the Net using pre-Web technology are harder and more costly to integrate.
- Libraries store and maintain much of the same data hundreds and thousands of times.
- With library data scatter across distributed systems the library's Web presence is weakened.
- With libraries running independent systems collaboration between libraries is made difficult and expensive.
- Information seekers work in common Web environments and distributed systems make it difficult to get the library into their workflow.
- Many systems are only used to 10% of their capacity. Combining systems into a cloud environment reduces the carbon footprints, making libraries greener.

FEATURES OF CLOUD LIBRARIES

The feature of Cloud computing enabled Cloud libraries is enlisted below:

- It contains a variety of information resources stored and accessed in Cloud ranging from text to graphics and audio-video.
- These resources do not require installing any software for its readability or view ability, except the broadband connectivity and Web browser.

- The Cloud library users and services are distributed in the world.
- It links the resources of many libraries.
- They are the painless IT solutions where user has to hardly bother to install or update the application or software that is being delivered.
- The Cloud library services are offered on Pay-per-use basis.
- The Cloud libraries are independent of time, space, and language and technology barrier.
- It enables an effective and efficient interaction among the different users and library professionals through blogs and social networking.
- It offers more advanced and dedicated applications for the libraries.
- It creates a digital world in the cloud where data, computing capabilities (Virtual CPU) and servers are stored and protected.
- It offers platform to design innovative applications for the library users.

PROMISES OF CLOUD LIBRARIES

Before switching to any new technology one should look for the promises that it can offer to its clients. A Cloud library offers following promises:

- Transaction Processing of resources and services.
- Availability of computing services as a commodity.
- Scalable Web-services.
- Scalable Web-servers.
- Integrated applications.
- Open accessibility.
- Cuts operational and capital costs.
- Interoperability and user choice.
- Economic value.
- Facilities to develop niche critical applications.
- Availability of Cloud library resources all the time.
- Frees valuable library personnel to focus on delivering services than maintaining hardware and software.
- Greener IT practises where combined operations can result in more efficient power consumption.
- Conduit for innovation without the need for internal IT.
- Lower operating costs.
- It is reliable and easy to use that does not require any maintenance and paperwork.

CLOUD LIBRARY COMPONENTS

Cloud computing environment has brought abrupt shift from local data centre, which had single data entry and exit point, to a global network having large data centres and thousands of data entry exit nodes. It is essential to understand the fundamental components that run a Cloud library. A Cloud library essentially comprises of three components: clients, data centre, distributed servers. Each element has a designated function that plays a specific role in delivering a functional Cloud based library services to the end user.

Client

They are the devices through which users interact with Cloud libraries to seek information on the Cloud. They are of three types:

1. **Thick Clients:** They are the regular computers that use Web browsers to access the information in the Cloud. Users can even store their information on their hard disks or memory.
2. **Thin Clients:** They do not have internal hard drives but rather let the servers do all the work to seek information from the Cloud.

3. **Mobile Clients:** It includes mobile devices like PDA, smart phones, Windows mobile phones or iPhones to seek information from the Cloud.

Data Centres

It comprises of collection of servers which houses the applications or resources of library to which a library user subscribes. There are two types of data centres: private or enterprise data centres and public or Internet data centres. A Private data centre is owned by the organization and provides the Web-hosting, applications and storage functions needed to maintain full operations. On the other hand, in Public data centres are managed and located in share or jointly by the public. Through Public data centres applications and data are typically accessed through the Internet. They vary with each other in terms of bandwidth type, use of layers in the traffic control, extent of server virtualization and the number of servers.

Distributed Server

All the servers need not be housed in the same location. The existence of servers depends on the size, speed of physical server and the applications that are supposed to run on a virtual server. However, users get the feel that all the servers are working next to each other.

CATEGORIES OF CLOUD LIBRARIES

Although Cloud phenomena is front and centre of people consciousness yet the concept of Cloud library is yet to be implied. There are no any fixed principles or built guidelines for the preconditions of a Cloud library. However, to imply Cloud computing in libraries constructive research method can be used, which is based on the theme of construction of new knowledge drawing ideas from existing knowledge used in new ways, with possibly adding a few missing links. Employing the constructive research method I used the current state of the art on Cloud computing to produce a conceptual schema of Cloud libraries. There can be four categories of Cloud libraries:

- **Open Cloud Library Model:** In an open Cloud library model the Cloud computing implementation to libraries is shared by the general public with wide array of library services. These libraries are owned and managed by an enterprise that offers freely Cloud services on pay-per-use.
- **Closed Cloud Library Model:** In a closed Cloud library model Cloud computing implementation to libraries restricts access to internal users such as a particular library patrons and staff. These services stay within a firewall.
- **Centrally funded Integrated Cloud Library Model:** In this model, Cloud computing implementation to libraries will depend on the parent body, usually a government agency like UGC, CSIR, IIM, and IIT for its design and maintenance. Libraries have almost same funding agencies as well as share a common user group who requires more the less similar services. Under these favourable cases an integrated Cloud library has the utmost potency to reach out to its readers in the Cloud for example IIT`s NPTEL programme. They can develop global search mechanism.
- **Publisher`s Cloud Library Model:** The electronic age has offered end user salvation with a new, diversified and multi-sensory environment, where users can communicate freely and express themselves more fully, in an electronic realm through electronic resources channels. These channels are e-books, e-journals, e-magazines, e-thesis, e-prints which are owned and controlled by a publisher or third party.

Libraries can provide access to these resources through digitized handwriting, voice prints, finger prints and access token networks as access control.

CLOUD LIBRARY USERS

Cloud library users can be divided into three groups based on different levels of their involvement with the Cloud library infrastructure

On the Basis of Use of Cloud Library

- **Active Cloud Library User:** An individual who uses the Internet at least once in a month to access the library resources and services available in Cloud.
- **Claimed Cloud Library User:** An individual who has used the library resources and services available in Cloud at any point in time in past.
- **Learned Cloud Library User:** An individual who possess technical know-how to access and use library resources stored in the Cloud.
- **Potential Cloud Library User:** Those individual which are the members of a Cloud library but have never accessed the library resources or services available in Cloud.

On the Basis of Accessibility to Cloud Library

- **Prominent Users:** These users possess necessary infrastructure and tools to access the library resources and services available in Cloud.
- **Laggards:** These users do not possess necessary infrastructure and tools to access the library resources and services available in Cloud.

On the Basis of Design of Cloud Library

- **Front-End Users:** They are the ones who access the Cloud resources and services through their devices.
- **Back-End Users:** They are the programmers and developers who create programmers or applications according to the user requirements.

CLOUD LIBRARY SERVICES

The various ranges of services that can be offered via the Cloud computing enabled libraries are enlisted below:

- Cloud-based access to library collections through the OPAC.
- Delivery of services as well as documents as an utility.
- Just-in-time during need on demand library services.
- Cloud based recommender system to make user friendly retrieval strategy, for example Biblio commons.
- Cloud based discovery layers to make the special collections of the library accessible to users which are not catalogued.
- Cloud based software of citation management enables users to share content, form communities and recommend a resource.
- Cloud based efficient management and organization of scholarly communications.
- Cloud based library apps enrich user to access the library data.
- Cloud based Stack Map, shelf-mapping software enable users in mapping the physical location of a book.
- Appealing feature of Cloud libraries services includes global accessibility to vast

library resources and the inherent resilience to failures.

- Cloud library services are metered that integrates telemetry as a part of service offerings.
- CAS and SDI services through emails, RSS feeds or Web feeds, Social networking Websites and blogs.
- Cloud based self-service for real time queries.
- Global Cooperation in maintaining bibliographic and authority records.
- Global collaboration on decision on collection development, preservation and digitization.
- Collaborative management of Cloud resources.

CLOUD LIBRARY INFRASTRUCTURES

Many scholars have called the concept as hype and questioned the verity of Cloud libraries. Nonetheless as personal computing, brought decentralization to the computing world that enabled users to run software of own choices. Correspondingly, Cloud computing provides users with infrastructure to run Web based software and applications of their desires. Under such circumstances libraries should not derail from the Cloud revolution. With the total empowerment of end users in Cloud, libraries should gasp fresh air and capitalize their agenda for Cloud libraries. The schema of creating a Cloud library infrastructure has been presented in Figure 2.

Since, a Cloud library generally runs through Web-based applications or programmes it is indispensable to understand how a library can move in the Cloud. For creating a Cloud library any library be it Public or Academic or Special has to depend to computing resources available in the Cloud. These computing resources are owned and provided by Cloud intermediaries.

Cloud Storage Providers

A Cloud storage provider offers an organization and users with an infrastructure to store and save their data on online hard drives. The data in these

Figure 2. Cloud Library typical infrastructure

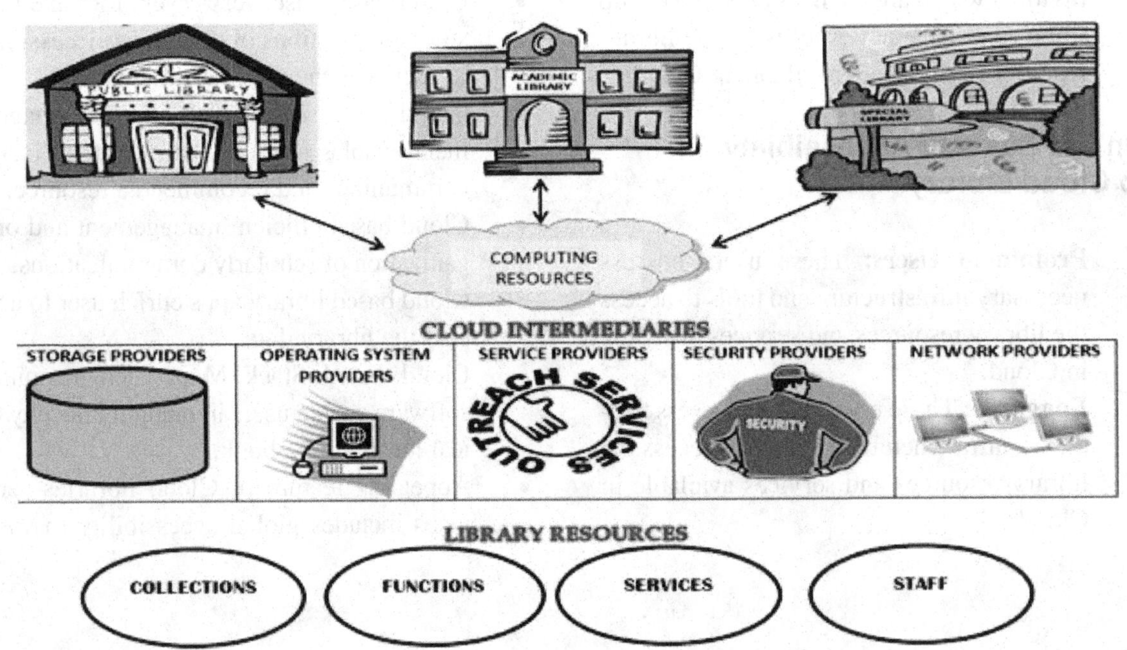

hard drives are stored in faraway data centres. The stored data can be accessed from anywhere provided the network connectivity. Some of the Cloud storage providers are:

- **Sitefinity Documentation:** It offers unshared space away from the database to stock images, videos, documents and other files. It stores the metadata in its database where as the actual file is in the file system or Cloud storage.
- **ZipCloud:** They offer security to data storage with simplicity and safety. It uses bank level encryption that shields files and folders and ensures privacy.

For selecting a Cloud storage provider librarians should take care of various things:

1. While selecting the Cloud storage provider librarians should not run after the provider offering services at a cheap rate. Librarian should comparatively analyse the features like, storage spaces, data uploading downloading speeds and the reliability offered out of the cost. He should ascertain that there is the facility of money back guarantee in case of dissatisfaction.
2. Cloud computing is independent of location and can be accessed on any media having network connectivity. Under such circumstances the library data stored in the Cloud should be compatible with PC, Mobile devices, tablets, android apps, iPad and iPhone apps.
3. Then, features like backups (automated or scheduled), file and folder sharing facilities as well as data restoration should be looked for.
4. Lastly, the Cloud storage infrastructure should be easy to use and supplemented by phone, e-mail, chatting supports and video tutorials.

Cloud Operating Systems Providers

Cloud Operating system provider enables the end user connected to the Internet to run various bits of software and desired applications. Any user at any time can run the software through the Internet from Cloud server. It removes the obligation of software updates and hardware along with operating system`s dependency. Cloud operating systems providers have deprived the computer system with operating systems by putting them in Cloud. Cloud operating systems have eradicated the technical Web of configuration and knowhow, ensuring painless IT operations. Some of the Cloud operating system providers are:

- **Zimdesk:** It is virtual CPU on the Web. It constitutes desktop, operating system and favourite applications which are all available online. Zimdesk is available as both a subscription Web-based service and enterprise version for business, government and education. To access the services of Zimdesk one needs to sign up through quick registration.
- **Kohive:** An online collaborative workspace that mimics a computer desktop by design. It is based on the notion that most people work from varied geographical locations that needs to be supplemented by services like social networking, file sharing and e-mail.

For selecting a Cloud operating system provider librarians should take into account various aspects:

1. Firstly, librarians should comparatively evaluate the price of the operating systems in terms of subscription (either on use basis or any subscription plan), Inbound and Outbound bandwidth prices, plan costs per hour and its details and the additional IP costs.

2. Then the features in terms of paid basis and offered freely should be weighed. Auto scaling, load balancing, monitoring, root accessibility along with file and Web hosting services should be given principal importance.
3. Also, compatibility of operating system, processor speed and the programming languages (Java, PHP, Ruby and others) support should not be ignored and carefully evaluated.
4. Lastly the support services offered by the provider needs to be examined.

Cloud Services Providers

Cloud services provider offers user with services via Cloud computing networks: private (private Cloud), public (public Cloud) and hybrid (Public + Private) networks. It offers some components of Cloud computing- Infrastructure as a Service (IaaS), Software as a Service (SaaS) and Platform as a Service (PaaS) to other individuals or organizations. Some of the Cloud operating system providers are:

- **StratoGen:** It offers one stop solution of necessary infrastructure to leverage the Cloud for your organization. It allows end user to cost effectively scale out hosted infrastructure from a single VMware workstation to multi-site environments. It provides the facility to run multiple virtual machines along with the actual machines.
- **Amazon Elastic Compute Cloud (Amazon EC2):** It is a Web service that provides end user with resizable computing capacity in the Cloud. It provides complete control over computing resources and offers the user a flair to work in an environment verified by Amazon.

For selecting a Cloud service provider librarians should take care of various things:

1. Firstly, price comparison of the various Cloud service providers should be done by the librarians.
2. Then, the storage space and features made available by the service provider like emails, contacts, calendars, documents editing, music and videos playing support as well as slideshows creation and presentation facilities should be checked.
3. Also, librarians should ascertain that the services are accessible by all the Web enabled devices and supports all configurations.
4. Lastly, end user service support system is a prerequisite of any Cloud based service infrastructure.

Cloud Security Providers

Library works involves large data due to which security perceptions are still the biggest obstacle to wider Cloud adoption in the libraries. Cloud security provider attempts to keep the Cloud infrastructure secure, safe and protected. The Cloud security providers at their level best try to protect the assets of an organization in the Cloud from various threats. Some of the Cloud security providers are:

- **Firehost Secure Cloud Hosting:** It provides secure, powerful and flexible hosting for application of various sizes. It offers a powerful and secured portal with no any setup fees and contracts.
- **Cloudmark:** It is a Cloud based e-mail security solution. It can be deployed quickly and easily that does not require any setup costs and management resources.

For selecting a Cloud security provider librarians should take care of various things:

1. Firstly, librarians should check out the range of scalability and control offered by the Cloud security provider.

2. Preferences should be given to processing speed, disk space allocations, availability of SSD storage and the bandwidth.
3. Then, librarians should check out the level of security provided. Cloud security should include unlimited firewall zones, Web application protection, network isolation, secured access to Virtual Private Network (VPN).
4. Also, it should be ensured that it offers the features of data backups and third party application support.

Cloud Network Providers

The true potential of a Cloud library can be realized only with universal, high-speed network connectivity. Attempts have been undertaken in this regard and airlines have started satellite based Wi-Fi flights. Downtown areas are being wired with hotspots.

Cloud network providers are still evolving. The Cloud is a popular public access Wi-Fi provider that has over thousands of hotspots. It provides simpler, faster and the most reliable broadband connectivity for the people wherever they go. Through The Cloud anyone can be entertained at any place, work anywhere in the Cloud, chat on Skype and face time at any moment. It provides accessibility to computing resources in Cloud with Wi-Fi connectivity.

CLOUD LIBRARIES AND RANGANATHAN`S FIVE LAWS

There has been shift of library users towards cloud. Users have developed a tendency to remain connected to the Web through cloud services like Web mails (Gmail, Yahoo mail, Sify mail), online storage systems (Skydrive, Idrive, Box.net). There has been sharp increase in the usage of Web-based office tools (Google Docs and Zoho) in the recent times. Further, to keep themselves abreast of recent developments users are using Web-based RSS readers (Bloglines, Google Reader). All these activities are performed in cloud which can be used through a Web browser with Internet connectivity. Cloud has evolved as a global entertainment (YouTube, Flickr, Hulu) as well as Social network (Orkut, Facebook, hi5) also. Various platforms in the cloud are offering Web based useful applications: Pando (sharing large files), Adobe Photoshop Express (online photo editors), Jump Cut (edit videos online). Above all, cloud is being used as open source development network to share the source codes (Drupal).

With the orientation of library users towards cloud, libraries need to reengineer themselves in the cloud ecosystem. Since, time immemorial Ranganathan`s five laws has been the soul of library professional practises. These laws can be adapted well in Cloud and justify the shift from brick-and-mortar libraries to cloud libraries. They are the foundation for any Cloud based library services.

First Law: Books Are For Use

It stresses that the centrality of existence of the libraries lies in providing unrestrained and unfettered accessibility to the documents. Libraries are the nodal centre for serving people with information. As such, the virtualization trend brought out by Cloud computing demands for a cloud based library that can be accessed from the luxury of home at any time. A library can host its database in the cloud backed by a search engine through which users can search the documents through a Web OPAC and gain access to the documents. Moreover, library staffs should maintain virtual profiles (blogs, social networks) to interact with its users and redesign the library services.

Second Law: Every Reader, His or Her Book

It argues that library user have manifold information need and there is always a chunk of knowledge to satisfy that. It attempts to eradicate the monopoly of people over the recorded knowledge. It demands to nurture open avenues of available knowledge. Through cloud libraries can develop integrated search mechanism and global tagging to discover resources. Also, it is the obligation of the library authorities, states, library staffs as well as the readers to realize such dream. Moreover, with the freedom to generate information in the cloud it is the responsibility of the librarians to judge its genuineness.

Third Law: Every Book, its Reader

This law stresses on user literacy to promote documents which are unknown to users to check the wastage of library resources. With the 2.0 universe in the picture there is a need to redesign and redevelop library services. The future demands for collaborative, customized, seamless services which can be realized by a Cloud library. Employing Cloud based tools like blogs, folksonomies, podcasts, social media, RSS feeds and multi format references (IM, MMS, and SMS) librarians can reach to the users.

Fourth Law: Save the Time of the User/Staff

With the continuous expansion of print and electronic resources library users feel drowning in the sea of information. New channels and tributaries of information generation and dissemination have made the water perilous and polluted in the Cloud. The law henceforth stresses for organized and handy library tool to navigate the resources in the Cloud. It also demands for usage of reference 2.0 services in the libraries.

Fifth Law: Library is a Growing Organism

In the analogue world spaciousness was an elemental issue which has been significantly inescapable phenomena in the Cloud also. With the future of Cloud libraries it demands for higher database size and platforms to adept in the Cloud. From time to time the changes in libraries have further emphasized for developing skills and staffs too.

In a nutshell, it can be ascribed the five laws of library science necessitates the Cloud library services and resources with the change in trend brought by Cloud computing strategies. With the change in library user behaviour the existence of libraries at stake can re-vigour through Cloud based library solutions and services.

PLAYERS OF CLOUD LIBRARIES

There are four categories of players that play important role in the Cloud library paradigm, as shown in Figure 3.

Cloud Infrastructure Consumers

Any library and individual who prefers to use Cloud computing infrastructure are the consumers. Library purchases the Cloud infrastructure and hosts its databases on any Cloud service provider`s server. Users can access this infrastructure through any Web-browser enabled device which will be metered.

Figure 3. Players in cloud library environment

Cloud Infrastructure Providers

A Cloud infrastructure provider owns and controls Cloud computing systems to deliver services (Software, Platform or Infrastructure) to libraries. Currently there is plenty of big and small players in the Cloud dominated by Google, Amazon and Microsoft. However, there is ample space for outsiders also. Cloud market offers opportunity to collaborate and partner among the service providers.

Cloud Infrastructure Integrators

The role of Cloud infrastructure integrators is to collaborate with big infrastructure holding Cloud provider to bring their services to customers. They especially benefit a larger section of smaller, lesser experienced entrants to Cloud markets that have not achieved expertise in Cloud.

Cloud Infrastructure Regulators

Lillard, Garrision, Schiller, and Steele (2010) state that "Cloud computing comes with its own set of standards, terminology and best practises that can be difficult to manage within the traditional information security context."Although Cloud computing industry does not have any committed regulatory body yet it is being governed by the Internet regulations. However, as the Cloud computing operations face problems like data security, ownership, location, privacy and intellectual property there is an utmost need of a regulatory body.

INFORMATION SOURCES IN CLOUD

Web has been a nodal point of revolution from information generation to its access and usage to retrieval which is usually stored in Cloud. In the Cloud environment there is need for the librarians to master the art of information searching and literacy in order to stand true to their mission and services. T. Scott Plutchak the Director, Lister Hill Library of the Health Sciences, University of Alabama, Birmingham says: "While the great age of libraries is coming to an end, the great age of librarians is just beginning." With the scattering of information in the Cloud there is an utmost need to authenticate information in order to provide right information and overcome information pollution. In attempting to deal with the Cloud computing technology in libraries there is a need to understand study and manage information stored in Cloud media, a media form so potent and different from previous media technologies. Some of the information sources in Cloud are:

- **Conference Proceedings Databases:** Conference proceedings in academic fields are the amassment of academic papers that are published relating to an academic conference. They are published to inform a wider audience of the papers presented at the conference. They are pivotal tool for the cutting-edge developments in a field. Further conferences being a standard tool for information sharing entire scientific community does not attend it for which the publication of conference proceedings are an exemplary solutions. Publication of conference proceedings in the Cloud ensures wider readability and coverage.
- **Courseware/Tutorials/Slides/Manuals:** They are Power point slides of course contents or other topics aimed at exploiting and bringing interest of the people through visuals. There are plenty of sources in the Cloud that provides access to presentations or tutorials that can be accessed as well as downloaded online.
- **E-Journals:** They are the scholarly carriers of intellectual productivity via electronic means. They are published on the Web based platforms. They are of two types: open source (freely available) and

closed source (available on some charge or on subscription basis). In the Cloud environment various electronic journal publishers and distributors have come with time that provides accessibility to libraries on subscription or Pay-per-use basis.

- **Patent Databases:** Patents are the exclusive rights granted to an inventor regarding his or her monopoly over the product. It is very handy tool as the inventors can scan through the patent databases or indexes trying to get his or her works patented.
- **Science News Magazines:** They are the publications bearing intellectual activity designed to decipher information about the natural world and to understand the life`s mysteries. As scientific fields are evolving every day, one always wants oneself to keep abreast of recent developments that one can get through the online science magazines.
- **Blogs:** This is a personalized electronic journal published on the Web comprising of posts displayed in chronologically reverse order. It is the work of a single individual. It is a good tool to interact with the library users virtually and disseminate information in the Cloud. However, the authenticity of information on these channels needs to be checked, as it can provide wrong and misleading information.
- **Thesis and Dissertations:** Thesis or dissertations are the documents submitted for presenting an author`s research work and findings. There are online archives of thesis and dissertations hosed by the institutions in the Cloud.
- **Institutional Resources:** These are the resources of an organization or institution hosted on the Web. It is very instrumental in delivery an institution`s scholarly works to the user globally.
- **Abstracting and Indexing Databases:** They contain index as well as abstracts of the articles held at one place in the Cloud. Users can access these databases through their concerned libraries.
- **Library Catalogues:** Catalogue is a tool representing the documents in libraries. These holdings can be searched by author, title, subject or keywords. Online catalogues are an exemplary tool for resource sharing in the Cloud. It can be used to scan through the catalogues of other libraries also.
- **E-Books:** An e-book is an electronic representation of a book usually a parallel publication of a print copy, but occasionally "born digital". Also, referred as paperless book, e-book is read on any Web-browser enabled devices having broadband connectivity which is an integral part of Cloud libraries.

CLOUD LIBRARY STRATEGIC PLANNING

When any organization take initiative to move its services from ground to Cloud it needs strategic planning and decision taking. For implying Cloud computing in libraries there is a need to examine Cloud library model`s benefits and risks, its potentiality in achieving the objectives and to spot approaches for its realization. For planning a Cloud library, I propose Cloud Library Strategic Planning (CLSP) model as shown in Figure 4.

Models are mental or pictorial representation of an event or phenomenon which is employed to study such phenomenon that cannot be seen or felt. This model was developed with a need to figure out the steps in planning a Cloud library. CLSP model includes four stages:

Step I: Determining Objectives

The first step is to analyse the status of library and with a clearly defined vision establish pre-

Figure 4. Cloud library strategic planning (CLSP) model

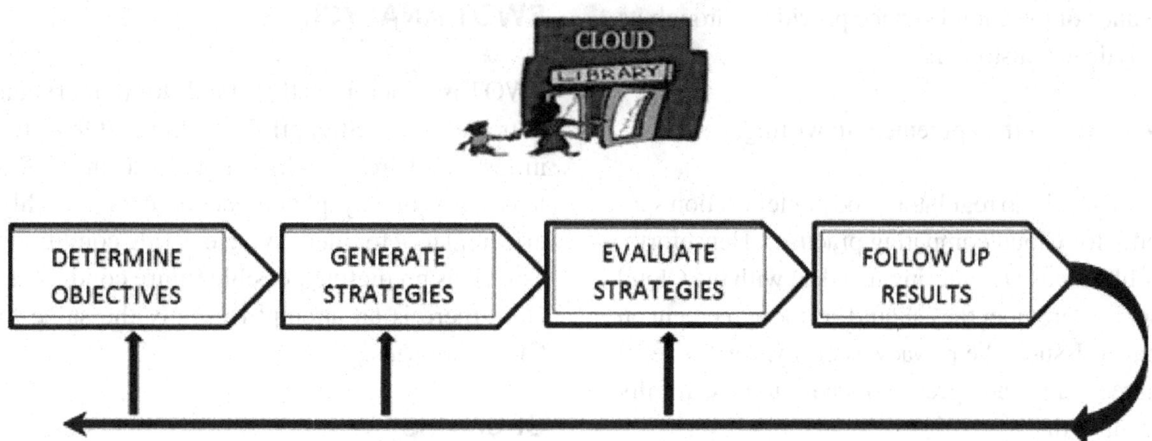

cise and measurable objectives of Cloud library, which should take care of user requirements. With inadequate time and resources librarians must make decisions as to what can and cannot be accomplished. Librarians should ensure that the identified objective and its scope serves the library users needs at its utmost efficiency and effect.

Step II: Generate Strategies

Following establishing objectives librarians develop specific actions on the way to accomplish the objectives. At first there is need to evaluate the prospects and impediments in the adoption of Cloud computing to libraries. It can be evaluated through the comprehensive guides of NIST and ENISA. Moreover, the viability of Cloud library proposal can be gauged through SWOT analysis.

Step III: Evaluate Strategies

After determining the course of actions, there needs to be important decision making in various instances in the Cloud computing-based adoption of services in libraries. Primarily, there are six avenues which involve strategic decision taking in carving out a Cloud library niche.

- To settle issues on selection of Cloud based services.

Cloud computing involves three stacks of service layers SaaS (Software as a Service), PaaS (Platform as a Service) and IaaS (Infrastructure as a Service). Strategic decision has to be taken regarding the selection of services and dealing with the Cloud service provider.

- To settle issues on deployment models of Cloud based services.

There are four models for deploying Cloud services Public, Private, Hybrid and Community. It also involves calculated decisions suited to a particular library and the infrastructure that it wants to host.

- To select Cloud provider.

Selecting a Cloud provider is elemental to Cloud computing implication to libraries. Before negotiating a deal with the Cloud service provider librarians should look for service models on offer, pricing schemes, billing mechanism, data loss and recovery supports, privacy and security policies.

One can also judge the genuineness and performance of the Cloud service providers through its privileged customers.

- To get the agreement in writing.

There is no regulatory body or legislation specific for Cloud computing practises. Henceforth, if librarians are entering in a deal with the Cloud service provider they should get the agreement on paper. Issues like privacy, security, service level agreements and agreements have to be carefully dealt with.

- Facilities of data export and import.

Librarians should ensure that the Cloud service provider provides the facilities of data export and import. Library may sometime wish to change its Cloud service provider or the provider may close its services. Henceforth, it is inevitable to ensure that data migration facilities are provided.

- Start a Pilot implementation.

The Cloud computing implication should start with a pilot implementation not substantially but partially to frame future considerations of adopting the same.

Step IV: Follow-Up Results

Lastly, the Cloud computing infrastructure in libraries has to be deployed according to chalked out plan and the progress should be followed up by evaluation and validation. Results are evaluated in terms of the determined objectives. In case of dissatisfaction and failure in achieving the expected outcomes libraries should diagnose the solutions and reframe the objectives to ensure the objectives achievement.

CLOUD LIBRARIES: SWOT ANALYSIS

SWOT is an acronym that stands for four crucial nuts and bolts (Strengths, Weakness, Opportunities and Threats) which is used to judge the feasibility of any phenomenon. It is a highly effectual tool for identifying existing conditions as well as predicting possible future conditions. Here there is an attempt to imply the same to Cloud libraries.

Strengths

- Shared library resources and computing resources delivered via Web.
- Cost savings on maintaining and delivering services.
- No hardware and software maintenance in the libraries.
- Focus on library goals and services.
- Subscription based services checks the waste of resources.
- Data and services mobility.
- Ubiquitous availability of the libraries.
- Contiguous digital library environment in the Cloud.
- Absolutely no significant effort is required.

Weakness

- Reliance on the network connectivity.
- Unclear cloud regulations and legislations.
- Huge dependency over Cloud resources for computing works.
- Opaque data location in the Cloud and privacy restrictions.
- Trust over storing data in the database of Cloud library service provider.
- Lack of planning co-ordination.

Opportunities

- Interoperability of the library services in the Cloud.
- Agility and the flexibility of Cloud library services.
- Growth in Cloud services.
- Dependence of the users over the Web.
- Preference of library users to electronic information over the print media.
- Use of wireless technologies.

Threats

- Abuse and Nefarious Use of Cloud Libraries.
- Insecure Interfaces and APIs.
- Malicious Insiders.
- Shared Technology Issues.
- Data Loss or Leakage.
- Account or Service Hijacking in the Cloud.

CLOUD LIBRARIES INITIATIVES

Cloud Computing has been recognised as a legitimate areas of research and application. Its implications is scattered across a wide range of disciplines. Some of the notable initiatives exclusively in the libraries have been enlisted below:

I. OCLC`s Web Scale

OCLC`s Web scale is an exemplary Cloud computing solution for the libraries. OCLC for a long time has been offering libraries with global accessibility to its readymade database of catalogues stored in the cloud. They have started World Share management services that are aimed to move library routine activities like acquisitions, circulation, subscription and license management to the Web powered by a cloud database. It is supposed to save time, money and resources and streamline the library operations.

II. Ex-Libris Cloud

It is a leading provider of library automation solutions of print, electronic and digital documents that caters to the library`s needs of resource description, management and distribution. Some of the products of Ex-libris offered in cloud are:

- **Primo Discovery and Delivery:** It is a one stop solution for the libraries to provide its resources in the cloud that can be accessed by the users remotely.
- **Integrated Library System (Aleph and Voyager):** It is an integrated library solution providing variety of different library modules offered in the Cloud. It is Web-based and can be used by any institutions and consortia.
- **SFX Scholarly Linking:** It is an Open URL link resolver that can be hosted locally or managed by Ex Libris. It contains menu driven links to full text or other scholarly services for users and librarians separately backed by a powerful knowledge base. It also contains tools for user statistics, managing collections and report analysis.
- **Metalib Meta Searching:** It enables users to search multiple, diverse remote resources at a same time.
- **Verde E-Resource Management:** It is a single point tool for the libraries to manage electronic products and collections.
- **Digital Asset Management Tools (Digitool and Rosetta):** It is an important tool to create, manage and provide access to databases of digital collections.
- **Alma:** It is next generation library management service designed to consolidate, optimize and extend the range of library services in the cloud. It offers unified resource management, collaborative metadata management, intelligent collection development and Cloud based services to reduce the investment of libraries on own-

ership of Cloud infrastructure and provide accessibility to shared services and data.

III.OSS Labs

OSS Labs are exploiting Amazon`s elastic cloud computing platform to provide Koha (open source Integrated library system) and Dspace (open access scholarly or published repository software) hosting and maintenance services to the subscribing libraries. It has offered painless IT solutions for the librarians who are independent of obligations to update and maintain it and are focusing on library missions. In the near future it is expected that OSS labs in India will be providing cloud based solutions to the library users also.

IV. Duraspace`s DuraCloud

It is an open source platform that offers on-demand storage and services in the Cloud to the library users and staff. It claims to be the only service through which one can move copies of their content into the Cloud. A user can view, manage, stream and transform the stored data from anywhere at any time.

V. Shared Academic Knowledge Base plus or KB+

It is a part of JISC`s (Joint Information System Committee, UK) digital library infrastructure which offers services over the Cloud with libraries or users accessing it through their desktop PC or devices having Web browser across the Internet. It includes database covering all subscribed resources from a UK higher education perspective. The database covers publication information, holdings, subscription management, organizations, licences, usage statistics and financial data in an online catalogue across all UK academic libraries. Cloud based services do not attempt to develop a new electronic resource management system. It focuses on creating a global database and developing a community of library practises. It aims to simplify the challenge of collating accurate, quality and timely data across UK universities. It keeps a check on inconsistency of delivery of data to the libraries.

VI. 3M Library Systems

The 3M Cloud library offers a user friendly flexible e-book lending system. Users can browse, read and issue the titles of their interest. Through the latest mobile technology it offers users with the facilities to explore and borrow e-books from anywhere at any time. Users can make their personal accounts to access these services. They are also provided with bookmarking facilities.

ROLE OF CLOUD LIBRARIANS

Cloud librarians are a new genus of librarians having lineage from Cybrarians (Librarians engaged in Cyber space). They are a group of highly skilled and competent librarians who can work in a Cloud landscape and nurture the Cloud libraries. The role of these librarians has been mentioned below:

1. A cloud library involves librarians to deal with Cloud resource and players and select the best bargain. A librarian should look for the best solution at least cost with quality service ensuring optimal satisfaction.
2. A cloud librarian should maintain his virtual profile by creating his or her blog or social network profile to interact with the user. The same platform can be used for providing reference services and educating the users on cloud resources or how to use the Cloud infrastructure.
3. A Cloud librarian should use his or her strategic planning and decision making ability at different stages of developing a Cloud library.

4. A Cloud librarian should have command over managing each and every aspect of Cloud library services irrespective of his place of work in a library section.
5. A Cloud librarian should have troubleshooting abilities.
6. A Cloud librarian should be well equipped and should have sound knowledge of the devices used in the Cloud.

CHALLENGES OF CLOUD LIBRARIES

Although Cloud computing is a low cost solution for organizations like libraries, it suffers from a number of challenges.

- Cloud libraries demands for globally integrated Cloud infrastructure which is difficult for multilingual information resources.
- There is high uncertainty of storing the information on hard disks in the Cloud, unlike the certainty of information engraved on the stones.
- Unavailability of library intermediaries in Cloud environment affects the information competency of the users.
- Cloud libraries largely depend on high speed network connectivity. Availability of the same is doubtful in the present scenario. Given an initiative to improve the same can only make the realization come true.
- Limited transparency offered by the cloud service provider to the Cloud libraries may be barrier for its adoption.
- There is always a concern over putting the proprietary data into the hands of Cloud service provider.
- Most of the Cloud service providers offer a single pattern of *Terms* and *Conditions* for every user who will not negotiate with individual users or the libraries.
- Uncertainty and doubt surrounding the ownership of data in the cloud.
- Data retention or permanence in the cloud

FUTURESCOPE

Any technology is always very easy, people are hard to adopt because the processes are harder. The future of Cloud libraries is very Cloudy but seeing the trend denial of Cloud computing will strip users from the brick-and-mortar libraries. Although it appears harmless to the unconscious library users and staff but these clouds carry substantial storm to the practise of librarianship. As discussed earlier there has been drastic change in user behaviour; users prefer information in the Cloud at their home. Some of the central issues for Cloud libraries that need to be worked out in the future are:

- Frame "Canon of Cloud Libraries" that should be the guiding principle for the alliance of libraries with Cloud computing.
- Addressing the problem of Cloud library legislations.
- Addressing the expenses and justifying the issues over Cloud library budget.
- Defining the scope and boundaries of the library services in the Cloud.
- Resolving the data trust, privacy, migration and backups.
- Identifying competencies for new breed of Cloud librarians.

CONCLUSION

In a nutshell, the Cloud library paradigm is all about virtualized Web based services, providing painless and economic computing to users and librarians. "Clouds" of computing power comprising inexpensive applications is being offered on Internet through the Cloud provider. It is still evolving and in a state of flux. New players are constantly joining the Cloud race and everyone is using some form of Cloud unconsciously. With the technological changes and shift from library mission and services by being involved in traditional IT practises there is an urgency to leverage library services on Cloud platform. Cloud has an essence of future and by 2020 everything is supposed be in the Cloud. So we have to nurture a library structure in Cloud landscape following the trend.

REFERENCES

Abidi, F. & Abidi, H. J. (2012). Cloud libraries: A novel application for cloud computing. *International Journal of Cloud Computing and Services Science (IJ-CLOSER), 1*(3), 79-83.

Barnatt, C. (2010). *A brief guide to cloud computing*. London: Constable & Robinson.

Cenon. (2012). *How universities implement cloud computing*. Retrieved from www.cloud.tweaks.com/2012/02/how-universities-implement-cloud-computing/

Fox, R. (2009). Library in the clouds. *OCLC Systems & Services, 25*(3), 156–161. doi:10.1108/10650750910982539.

Goldner, M. (2010). Winds of change: Libraries and cloud computing. Retrieved from www.oclc.org/multimedia/2011/.../IFLA-winds-of-change-paper.pdf

James, R. (2010). Records management in the cloud? Records management is the cloud? *Business Information Review, 27*(3), 179–189. doi:10.1177/0266382110377060.

Khater, R. (2010). Cloud computing and the monolithic narrative. Retrieved from http://www.arabmediasociety.com/?article=764

Lillard, T. V., Garrison, C. P., Schiller, C. A., & Steele, J. (2010). *Digital forensics for network, Internet and cloud computing: A forensic evidence guide for moving targets and data*. New York: Elsevier.

Lynch, C. A. (2000). From automation to transformation: Forty years of libraries and information technology in higher education. *EDUCAUSE Review, 35*(1), 60–68.

Rhoton, J. (2009). *Cloud computing explained: Implementation handbook for enterprises*. Retrieved from http://www.amazon.com/Cloud-Computing-Explained-Implementation-ebook/dp/B003LO1H2W

Romero, N. L. (2012). Cloud computing in library automation: Benefits and drawbacks. *The Bottom Line: Managing Library Finances, 25*(3), 110–114.

Sachdeva, M., Rana, P., Kapoor, R., & Shahid, M. (2011). Cloud computing: Pay as you go technology In *Proceedings of the 5th National Conference on Computing for National Development*. (pp. 161-166). New Delhi, India: BVICAM.

Sadeh, T. (2007). Time for a change: New approaches for a new generation of library users. *New Library World, 108*(7/8), 307–316. doi:10.1108/03074800710763608.

Thoughts from Carl Grant. (2012, June 28). *Why and how librarians have to shape the new cloud computing platforms*. Retrieved from http://thoughts.care-affiliates.com/2012/06/why-and-how-libraries-have-to-shape.html

Tomer, C., & Alman, S. W. (2011). Cloudcomputing for LIS education. In E. M. Corrado, & H. L. Moulasion (Eds.), *Getting started with Cloud computing* (pp. 59–68). New York: Neal Schuman.

Vaquero, L., Rodero-Merino, L., Caceres, J., & Lindner, M. (2009). A break in the clouds: Towards a cloud definition. *ACM SIGCOMM Computer Communication Review*, *39*(1), 50–55. doi:10.1145/1496091.1496100.

Yang, S. Q. (2012). Move into the cloud, shall we? *Library Hi Tech News*, (1): 4–7. doi:10.1108/07419051211223417.

ADDITIONAL READING SECTION

Askhoj, J., Sugimoto, S., & Nagamori, M. (2011). Preserving records in the cloud. *Records Management Journal*, *21*(3), 175–187. doi:10.1108/09565691111186858.

Barnhill, D. S. (2010). Cloud computing and stored communications: Another look at Quon v. Arch Wireless. *Berkeley Technology Law Journal*, *25*(1), 625–638.

Blokdijk, G., & Menken, I. (2009). *Cloud computing - The complete cornerstone guide to the cloud computing best practices: Concepts, terms, and techniques for successfully planning, implementing and managing enterprise IT cloud computing technology*. Retrieved from http://www.ebooksx.com/Cloud-Computing-The-CompleteCornerstone-Guide-to-Cloud-Computing-Best-Practices-Concepts-Terms-andTechniques_312071.html

Buyya, R., Yeo, C. S., Venugopa, S., Broberg, J., & Brandic, I. (2009). Cloud computing and emerging it platforms: Vision, hype, and reality for delivering computing as the 5th utility. *Future Generation Computer Systems*, *25*, 599–616. doi:10.1016/j.future.2008.12.001.

Convery, N., & Ferguson-Boucher, K. (2011). Storing information in the cloud – A research project. *Journal of the Society of Archivists*, *32*(2), 221–239. doi:10.1080/00379816.2011.619693.

Grossman, R. L., Gu, Y. H., Sabala, M., & Zhang, W. Z. (2009). Compute and storage clouds using wide area high performance networks. *Future Generation Computer Systems*, *25*, 179–183. doi:10.1016/j.future.2008.07.009.

Joshua, A., & Ogwueleka, F. N. (2013). Cloud Computing with related enabling technologies. *International Journal of Cloud Computing and Services Science.*, *2*(1), 40–49.

Leavitt, N. (2009). Is cloud computing really made for prime time? *Computer*, *42*(1), 15–20. doi:10.1109/MC.2009.20.

Lin, G., Fu, D., Zhu, J., & Dasmalchi, G. (2009). Cloud computing: IT as a service. *IT Professional*, *11*(2), 10–13. doi:10.1109/MITP.2009.22.

Rittinghouse, J. W., & Ransome, J. F. (2010). *Cloud computing implementation, management, and security*. London: CRC Press.

Sultan, N. (2010). Cloud computing for education: A new dawn*? International Journal of Information Management*, *30*, 109–116. doi:10.1016/j.ijinfomgt.2009.09.004.

Thomas, P. Y. (2011). Cloud computing: A potential paradigm for practicing the scholarship of teaching and learning. *The Electronic Library*, *29*(2), 214–224. doi:10.1108/02640471111125177.

Voas, J., & Zhang, J. (2009). Cloud computing: New wine or a just a new bottle. *IT Professional*, *11*(2), 15–17. doi:10.1109/MITP.2009.23.

Wolf, R. (2010). Cloud computing. *North Carolina Libraries*, *68*(2), 30–31.

KEY TERMS AND DEFINITIONS

Cloud Centre: A large service provider that rents its infrastructure to other organization or an enterprise.

Cloud Client: Computing devices used to access Cloud resources.

Cloud Librarians: They are well-trained and competent professionals involved in Cloud Computing practises to serve the library users with information.

Cloud Library: It is a library which runs from the resources and services stored in the Cloud. Cloud library is an attempt to serve the library users by offering information in Cloud accessible Web-browser enabled devices.

Cloud Sourcing: Cloud sourcing involves the usage of Cloud service to do a work.

Cloud: It is an abstraction of the infrastructure that runs the Internet. The Cloud symbol is borrowed from IT textbook`s illustrations which represents the demarcation point of the responsibility of the user and service provider on the Web.

Cloudware: They are the applications or software that aid in building, deploying and running Cloud based solutions.

Chapter 19
Cloud Libraries–Limitations and Concerns

Namita Gupta
International Maritime College Oman, Sultanate of Oman

Syed Asim Raza Rizvi
International Maritime College Oman, Sultanate of Oman

ABSTRACT

Digital libraries have arrived. New frontiers are being pioneered and technological superhighways being paved for a future researcher to tread on to go farther than humankind has ever gone before to create advanced knowledge-based communities. It is only possible to see how fast the horse will run its race once it has been tamed. Can the digital library be saddled with cloud computing and reined with e-books? The Industrial Revolution has brought disparity between poor and rich, widening the ozone layer gash. Advancements in nuclear technology have not necessarily resulted in worldwide peace. Identifying pitfalls and shortcomings in strategies and policies that govern developing technologies can help prevent issues and problems that can rear their heads at some later stage. This chapter continues to bring forth the issues concerning digital libraries and the challenges, current and ahead. Implications of such issues must be addressed constructively in time at several conceptual and factual levels in the context of a set of values that are ethically and scientifically acceptable by individuals from all walks of life worldwide.

INTRODUCTION

The advancement in the information technology with every passing day brings the nations, organizations and individuals closer. Business models are transforming, means and methods of waging wars are revolutionizing, data is being mined into useful information to disseminate knowledge, corporations' yearly budgets are burgeoning at faster than many wealthy countries' social security expenses. New crimes are emerging at a faster pace than the laws and regulations that are developed to restrain them. Health risks are reaching almost epidemic levels whether they are related to physical, psychological and emotional or social issues.

What defines advancement when it comes to technology? The running cars and the humming engines are signs of prosperity or that of dying healthy environment is a concern that most of the well educated individuals who are pro green computing often wonder about. Advancement in computer science specifically, and information

DOI: 10.4018/978-1-4666-4631-5.ch019

technology in general has its pros and cons. At what stage are we standing on one of the two sides is yet to be realized.

Cloud computing is pervasive like its carrier-the Internet. It is a multilayered foundation upon which the phenomenon of virtual libraries has begun to spawn incessantly creating in its wake new patterns of economies and stake holders. This is a phenomenon which could be vastly appreciated on account of its advantages. Highly secure and guarded edifices that conventional knowledge based data centers are, would they be accessible to the masses once the local public libraries would be rendered obsolete? Would local libraries have to assume a different role for survival? It is still debatable.

Digital Libraries are being implemented in every major university and educational institution in the modern world. They are evolving and gaining strength in terms of popularity. Not only the privileged few but also the laymen across the world could reap benefits from this relatively cheaper and possibly more convenient form of education. However, if we ask the similar question: What is the opportunity cost and how it can be evaluated?

This knowledge age is at the doorsteps of the modern world. The need to record, store, and disseminate timely information has ushered in a new era of electronic books, digital libraries and cloud computing. The asynchronous and synchronous hybrid educational models' commercial and social success depends upon vital elements like storage, preservation, dissemination of data, information or knowledge. Digital library is the route toward that success, but not without a price. It is fraught with well known though widely neglected issues like escalating physical and psychological health concerns, no regard for copyrights, democratization of knowledge for the haves and complete disregard for the unprivileged ones.

Copy right issues, controversies surrounding e-books in libraries, digital divide within a country, matters of confidentiality, technical issues about uniformity in user interfaces and interoperability issues between distributed Digital Libraries, dependability of storage issues on the cloud, matters of differences in taxonomy of intellectual property in the form of different media and their accessibility by the end users, Issues in implementation of cloud computing for Digital Libraries, overdependence on Internet technology applications such as online courseware, drop boxes, and e-libraries are meaningless unless compatibility with human needs and nature in the form of ergonomics is thoroughly tested and proven. With e-mails being continuously monitored, faces being scanned and credit cards being stolen, how can human needs such as to be free and not contained, to be able to trust and not be paranoid, to be progressive and not suppressed, to be protected and not exploited, to be able to socialize and shake hands over a cup of coffee or tea with likeminded people without being observed through digital cameras, be satisfied?

Concepts such as e-learning having been reinforced by cloud computing and e-libraries with all their bells and whistles to impress the untrained eyes are not yet ready, just like a fabric waiting to be tailored into a modest smart dress for the society. They are not flawless. It is a well known fact that mostly, outcomes are results of intentions. Do we need to peek into the room of a fifteen year old lad who has five hundred friends all over the world, has read a vast number of comic books online, but has not seen the kid who is just about his age and has moved recently in his neighborhood.

Does it matter if all the books in the world are monopolistically controlled by one corporation? Should corporations like Google be allowed to manipulate world's best writers and publishers? Should every aspect of academia be guided by the stock market or should there be checks and balances? What will be the nature of relationship between the publishers and the writers? Will there be many writers and not as many readers? Excess in life causes issues of different kinds so who will control the supply and demand and on what basis? One needs to ponder over such queries.

Here we need to ask of ourselves one critically important question. Where are we headed? Are e-libraries going to create smart people with almost no social skills? E-libraries are paving way for e-learning. Is e-learning efficiently customizable according to the students' individual needs? A teacher usually inspires students in the class, although sometimes through negative sentiments just like in Einstein's case. Who would be held accountable for the resounding success of a student in academics and equal failure in personal life? Are educational giants gradually taking over the world's business sweeping away any competition from the smaller fish? How far reaching are affects on the minds of the students out on excursion with their teachers to the local botanical garden or a zoo? Does it stand the test of similar significance in students' lives when it comes to e-learning? Electronic reading habits have more adverse effect on health as compared with traditional ones, what does scientific research have to say about it? Will digital divide cause even greater gap between the rich and the poor? Not everything is visible with open eyes sometimes. Complexities of online learning software can in itself be the first hurdle in the students' academic career. Moreover, students with better funding could be at an advantage when compared with under-privileged individuals when it comes to latest gadgets. Will infrastructure of cloud computing, e-libraries and e-learning in the developed nations have any impact on socioeconomic agendas of underdeveloped nations? These questions must be answered unambiguously to satisfy inquisitive minds.

LIBRARY ISSUES

Publishers vs. Libraries

The increased demand for e-books has triggered a war between publishers and libraries regarding who owns the e-books, how can they be lent, what should they cost? (Vinjamuri, 2012). These questions pose a series of intractable challenges for both publishers and libraries. By changing the model for pricing an e-book, both parties could find a clear and equitable resolution to the current impasse. Publishing is also changing dramatically as it is trying to cope with the uproar in e-books and the rise in power of Amazon, a river of low priced indie titles and the diminishing bookstores.

The republication of materials on the Web by libraries may require permission from rights holders, and there is a conflict of interest between libraries and the publishers who may wish to create online versions of their acquired content for commercial purposes. In 2010, it was estimated that 23% of books in existence were created before 1923 and thus out of copyright. Of those printed after this date, only 5% were still in print as of 2010. Thus, approximately 72% of books were not available to the public (Vemulapalli, Halappanavar, & Mukkamala, 2002).

Sharing of Resources between Universities: Interoperability Issues

With more and more courses being introduced in university curriculums, demand for Digital Libraries is ever growing, and hence they tend to buy their own database resources. But there is no uniformity in different universities when it comes to using various platforms. This is again because of the fact that there are too many options available in the market. All this puts a ceiling on the comfort of sharing of resources between universities which can substantially help bring down the economic factor. A Digital Library is a place which can store information in various forms. It generally has a well researched architecture and user interface which allows users to retrieve information and interact using searching and browsing at different levels. But even in the presence of all these amenities, Digital Libraries are not being utilized to the utmost. When it comes to global sharing of resources, it is not as much as expected. This is because of the fact that users cannot make a single query which would suffice different Digital Libraries' operability thus arises the issue of interoperability among Digital Libraries which is still an area of concern for developers and users (Maarof & Yahya, 2009). Redundancy of resources is also a big possibility in this case, which also results in wastage of storage space, manpower. Some universities are unable to use their resources to the optimum, using only a feeble portion of the same. Cloud computing here plays a vital role and can tone down the issues with libraries mentioned above.

Problems Faced By Librarians in Managing E-Resources

One important issue faced by usage of libraries is the ability to manage electronic resources. In spite of all the technologically advanced systems to help them, the librarians have a tough task ahead managing resources (Sadeh, 2004). It is their utmost priority to cater to the needs of the organization or institution they are associated with. But the problem is they have to deal with a lot of e-collections, email messages and spreadsheets. They also have to deal with many types of independent systems and data containers which are not integrated with each other. Too often librarians rely on their memory alone to coordinate systems such as the acquisition module of their integrated library system, their alphabetic lists of electronic journals and databases, a Meta search tool, and their local link server. In addition to the initial effort of setting up information in multiple places and the potential lack of consistency between systems, there might also be considerable duplication of effort.

Much of a librarian's ability to carry out necessary tasks is dependent upon personal experience. Moreover, the knowledge and experience gained from dealing with resources is often vested in too few people–sometimes only one–a situation that leaves libraries exposed. Furthermore, providing meaningful metrics, such as detailed cost analyses and statistics on past performance and usage, remains problematic. Without such metrics, managers cannot make fully- informed decisions. With expenditure on e-collections increasing rapidly, a better solution is needed.

Issues Regarding Curriculum Development by Digital Libraries

A curriculum is all the courses of study offered by an educational institute or a course of study. Curriculum development is one of the major areas to be taken care of by educational institutes and educators to provide quality education to students. It involves three main functions: the presentation of material, exploration of material and assessment of learning. Digital Libraries are becoming increasingly important in the field of education, as they provide the specialized staff and students material to explore by distributing resources and also provide links to other sites with prime resources. While traditional libraries support exploration of material, Digital Libraries have enhanced capabilities to support curriculum material exploration. In addition to this, they must also integrate assessment and presentation into a coherent curriculum module (Carver Jr., Hill, & Pooch, 1999). This is a challenging area for Digital Libraries. Also, they are expected to manage complexity and provide a unified interface into increasingly divergent collections of documents to aid easier and faster research and exploration.

The emergence of national Digital Libraries also poses new problems for curriculum developers, professors and students. This is due to the fact that national libraries face several challenges, for example, how to manage geographically separated information resources, how to maintain identity of individual contributors and partners, how to develop effective user interfaces and search engines and how to meet legislative requirements for National Library status.

Table 1. Elements of digital libraries

	Data	Metadata	Processes
Translations of Physical Library Entities	Book Journal Movie	Static Index Classifications Spatial arrangement	Acquiring data Suggesting sources Helping locate sources
New Digital Library Entities	Hypernovel Scientific visualization Computer program	Dynamic index Personalized structure Annotations	Full-text searching Personalizing presentation Retrieving by agents

Taxonomy of Digital Library Issues

Physical libraries provide a good starting point for discussion of digital libraries. Elements of both the physical and digital libraries may be categorized as data, metadata, or processes; these categories are determined in specific instances by the intended use of elements by librarians, patrons, or others. Data, metadata, and processes of the physical library must be translated into the digital domain if they are to be used in the digital library.

Transition of a physical library to a digital library has created quite some concerns. The major concern is translation and preservation of physical data into digital form. Differences between physical library and digital library elements have created many open problems concerning how to adapt the tradition of the physical library into the digital realm (Nürnberg, Furuta, Leggett, Marshall, & Shipman III, 1995).

Table 1 below demonstrates elements in Digital Libraries along two axes.

Each section of the grid is discussed below. Examples of elements that may be thought of as belonging to the section in question are given, followed by an issue particularly relevant to that section. These issues and their positions in the grid are shown in Table 2. As stated earlier, a given element may be thought of as being classified in many different sections on the grid, but elements are placed so that some typical use of that element is highlighted. Also, problems raised in each section may (and often do) apply to other sections as well, but may be thought of as having special significance in their respective sections.

Security Issues in Distributed Digital Libraries

Because of their dynamic nature, providing security for Digital Libraries is quite challenging.

Table 2. Issues raised considering taxonomy of digital libraries

	Data	Metadata	Processes
Translations of Physical Library Entities	What to translate?	How to translate metadata that is dependent on data physically?	How to provide tools for human involvement in these processes?
New Digital Library Entities	How to account for the continual rapid evolution of new data types?	How to insure consistency of separately maintained metadata?	How to distribute computation?

The Digital Libraries are a success if they are able to provide a rich social, legal and economic environment. Hence they are expected to provide a secure environment for development, management, preservation and archiving e-books of proprietary and copyrighted information (Vemulapalli, Halappanavar, & Mukkamala, 2002). The current systems use a variety of techniques for distributed access and search. These techniques such as distributed searching, harvesting and distributed indexing that can be employed in distributed Digital Libraries, spread over multiple autonomous and heterogeneous domains. This makes the libraries more sensitive to security threats and gives rise to the need to develop single domain security systems. Security needs also arise because of the two types of interactions happening, which are interactions between users and Digital Library services and interactions among different Digital Library components.

COPYRIGHT ISSUES

Copyright has been called the "single most vexing barrier to digital library development" (Chepesuik, 1997). The current paper-based concept of copyright breaks down in the digital environment because the control of copies is lost. Copyright is a big issue in Digital Libraries, as thoughts of one author are freely transferred to another without his acknowledgement. A major issue for Digital Libraries is protecting the rights of the author while distributing information. Things are not as simple as they were with the traditional printed work. Digital Libraries are hampered by copyright law, because laws of digital copyrights are still being formed.

The Digital Millennium Copyright Act of 1998 was an act created by the United States with an attempt to deal with the introduction of digital works. This act incorporates two treaties from the year 1996. It criminalizes the attempt to circumvent measures which limit access to copyrighted materials. It also criminalizes the act of attempting to circumvent access control. This act provides an exemption for nonprofit libraries and archives which allows up to three copies to be made, one of which may be digital. This, however, may not be made public or distributed on the Web. Furthermore, it allows libraries and archives to copy a work if its format becomes obsolete. Copyright issue still persists, but if Digital Libraries are exempted from it, the authors might be less inclined to create new works.

ISSUES IN PRESERVATION OF DIGITAL MEDIA

Another important issue is preservation – keeping digital information available in perpetuity. In the preservation of digital materials, the real issue is technical obsolescence. Technical obsolescence in the digital age is like the deterioration of paper in the paper age. Libraries in the pre-digital era had to worry about climate control and the deacidification of books, but the preservation of digital information will mean constantly coming up with new technical solutions.

Storage media like tapes, hard drives and floppy disks have a very short life span considering obsolescence. The data can be refreshed as long as the media are current. But the media used to store digital data become obsolete anywhere from two to five years as they are replaced by a new technology.

Access to content of documents regardless of their format calls for preservation too. While storage medium becomes obsolete and can be shifted from one to the other, what about the format? This issue is bigger than that of obsolete storage media.

To avoid this, conversion technology is used, but that too results in loss of data when migrating from one format to the other.

ISSUES REGARDING EBOOKS

According to Ray Bradbury, "There is more than one way to burn a book. And the world is full of people running about with lit matches."

A book is a carrier of thoughts, emotions, culture, heritage, history and tradition. It is and will always be an integral part of our lives and culture. For most of us, it is difficult to realize how much effort goes into writing a book. It is amazing to discover how effective books are in transferring thoughts and the impact they can have on shaping the society.

Books have seen a transition from printed form to digital form subsequently evolving as e-books. This transition started in 1970s. Speaking generally, a book presented in an electronic form is called an e-book. The emergence of new information handling technologies has significantly influenced the basic nature of conventional paper-based library and information centers. They have created a need for new types of library systems such as polymedia, electronic, digital and the main advantage an e-book has over a printed book is the storage capacity. It is fairly simple to carry several books in electronic form while travelling or moving, as compared to the printed form. But there are people who prefer to read printed books and enjoy the feel of it, which is not present with their electronic counterpart. E-books are the most essential ingredient of a Digital Library. A digital Library is a database of e-books broadly speaking. It is hence very obvious that all the issues and challenges faced by the industries related to e-books are directly related to Digital Libraries as well.

Protecting the Text while Revising an E-Book

Carol Saller, an editor of The Chicago Manual of Style, has noted: When an e-book is sporadically or perhaps even frequently revised, is anyone keeping track? What's the difference between a new printing and a new edition? And does it matter? It may not matter for ephemeral works, but for any work destined for later scrutiny or citation, it is important to be able to identify which version came first.

The ability to modify the published text without notification, tracking, versioning, archiving, or any other means that might provide the original text for readers is destructive to the tradition of the history of the printed word and the tradition of Western scholarship. If we want to know what Galileo wrote, we can still go back to the original text. What if the Catholic Church had had the potential to wipe out completely the record of his writings? What if the government or even a nongovernment entity could destroy, with a simple computer command, the outpourings of the next Thomas Paine? (Hamaker, 2011).

We cannot as a civilization permit our complainers' and dreamers' and thinkers' words to be destroyed by the simple expedient of the ability to "replace, edit or modify the contents" of any e-book. Authors have a right to be wrong. But even the author should not be able to change the text in a previous edition without notification to the reader. Libraries should be the organizations creating mechanisms to protect the very words that are one of their reasons for existence. We need continuity of text, markers of change, versioning, permanent archiving of variant editions if the e-book is to become a significant means of transmitting our culture and heritage.

Pricing of E-Books

The pricing pressure of e-books is significant. Jamie LaRue, Director of the Douglas County Libraries in Colorado told the author (Vinjamuri,

2012), "I saw a decrease in use that was hard to explain because our libraries are busy. Then I looked at our inventory and realized that the problem is that as we shift our dollars to e-books, I am buying fewer items because the prices are so much higher."

The challenge to libraries is not insignificant. Four of the six publishers are not providing e-books to libraries at any price. The other two – Random House and HarperCollins lead the industry with two different models. Random House adjusted e-book pricing in 2012. While the prices on some books were lowered, the most popular titles increased in price, some dramatically. Author Justin Cronin's post-apocalyptic bestseller "The Twelve" whose print edition costs for the Douglas County Libraries $15.51 from Baker & Taylor and whose e-book is priced at $9.99 on Amazon was priced at $84 to Douglas County on October 31st.

E-Books are Licensed, Not Sold

Traditional libraries owned physical books. But the issue with Digital Libraries is that it contains e-books which are e-licensed. They do not belong to the libraries. The libraries acquire a license to lend their resources. The rules for Digital Rights Management apply in such cases, and it may involve a restriction of lending out only one copy at a time for each license. Thus libraries are treated as resellers rather than end users. Hence the law that e-books are sold under a use license just like software, becomes a little complex because the pricing rights of a copyright holder are not absolute.

The solution to this issue is to charge libraries according to cost-per-circulation. This number is easy to calculate. It is equal to the number of lends divided by the cost of the books lent. This method is beneficial both to publishers and libraries as well. The publishers will have easier measurability, flexibility and assured equity. The libraries will have a better access to resources, a lower risk and better financial control.

ENVIRONMENTAL ISSUES

In case of a newly marketed electronic device upon its purchase it is proverbially said "What you just bought is already obsolete". Is it true? With proliferation of smart phones produced by different companies, smart phone upgrades have become tantamount to buying cheap fast food. Most teenagers seem to demand a new laptop every two years. Is e-library concept going to create another pile of electronics junk built from toxic components? According to current state of affairs in the under developed world, what is being done for renewable energy sources is not enough it seems. Was it not more environmentally friendlier when the traditional book titled "Taming of the Shrew" or "Great Expectations" was gifted by a grandfather to his grandson?

Does it suffice to get a nook or kindle and then buy one more gadget the following year, just to satiate the hunger for more and better processors with glittering screen? Who can guarantee that the equipment you have bought would remain compatible with the technology four or five years down the hallway of progress with which current software industry is moving.

HEALTH AND PSYCHOLOGICAL ISSUES

There can be no denying the fact that the advent of Digital Libraries is directly proportional to increased Internet usage hours for the user. A few adverse effects which pose as issues with respect to Digital Libraries are presented below.

Pathological Internet Use May Cause Teen Depression

The usage of Digital Library services implies superfluous online time. According to a new study, using the Internet pathologically, to the point where it resembles addiction puts teenagers at a risk of depression (Rettner, 2010). The researchers say that such extreme use of Internet can be detrimental to adolescents' mental health. Teenagers who are initially free of psychiatric problems may go on to develop depression because of this. Here, an argument may be given that why single out Digital Libraries? They are just one of the many waters irrigating the growing weeds of Internet usage among teenagers. There are several other stronger reasons why teenagers in particular are addicted to Internet. The answer to this argument lies in the fact that Digital Libraries belong to the family of online education paradigms. And it is always a matter of encouragement from parents and teachers when it comes to education. It is always possible to discourage teenagers from other harmful Internet attractions like games, entertainment and social networking, but who can argue about adopting an education method, even if it results in adverse effect on their mental and physical health.

It is not possible to go back to an era where there was no Internet, but a solution to these issues should be taken as a challenge by improving the way the school and society assist young people in making best use of Internet.

Eye Strain

Digital Libraries can undoubtedly be associated with e-books and all the advantages and disadvantages associated with them. With regards to health issues, eye strain is an obvious and well known health concern linked to reading on computer screens. While reading on paper, light reflects off the page and into the eyes in a natural manner. But the computer screen projects light into the eyes and elongated use may cause headaches and possible long term damage to the user's eyesight. E-readers have melded out this effect to some extent, as LED projections used by them dampen eye strain. But the question is what percentage of users has access to e-readers; they still have an overall negative effect.

Greater Student Knowledge Differential

When we talk about usage of Digital Library as an educational resource or a teaching resource in educational institutes or as a knowledge resource in different types of organizations, we cannot neglect the possibility of having to deal with people having different levels of knowledge and IT skills. Earlier, course material was available through educational institutes and all students had access to the same material. The provision and greater access to information via Digital Libraries helps widen the gap between performance of the best and worst student in a class. Students who are lazy and not so computer friendly incessantly lag behind as teachers are inclined towards using latest technology as teaching resource owing to current demand of technological advancement in the society. Consequently, at some point or the other, one or group of users becomes frustrated due to lack of pace in the class. Students who have a poor network access are at a distinct disadvantage when it comes to utilizing online resources. This how to handle these widening knowledge differentials is a matter of concern for all educators and researchers in this field.

Lack in Concentration and Motivation

The concept of Digital Libraries is directly related to online reading ethics. The ambience of a brick and mortar Library is totally different as compared to the environment in which a person sits alone, reading a book online in front of his computer. There can be at least ten different issues bothering him while trying to concentrate on the soft copy of a book on a computer screen. This concern may be understood to some extent if compared with an instance where watching a good movie in a theatre is compared with watching it on the laptop. The major problem in both cases is that with a downloaded file, there is a freedom of choosing a convenient time which suits our busy schedules. Most of the people will vote this as an advantage over being tied down to a time or boundary constraint. But if thought about deeply, the option of freedom actually turns out to be one which is a highly prone to postponement while a person is at the computer; there is always a tendency to surf around for files related to other tasks or Internet for some or the other lucrative reason. Lack of concentration directly results in lack of involvement and consequently a decrease in level of understanding. This is just one psychological factor which is an issue of concern related to online reading.

The question arises whether these technological advancements racing with each other to provide quantity are compromising on the quality.

Judging an Institution on Basis of Technology

Education is developed from books, and a Library is home for books. The importance of developing reading habits can be well understood with the help of the following quote by Ray Bradbury, an America fantasy and fiction writer. Ray says," I spent three days a week for 10 years educating myself in the public library, and it's better than college. People should educate themselves – you can get a complete education for no money. At the end of 10 years, I had read every book in the library and I'd written a thousand stories." Such is the effect of a public library and its resources for someone who understands its importance and benefits.

Digital Libraries are being implemented in most of the major universities and educational institutions around the world. They are evolving and gaining strength in terms of popularity. Not only the privileged few but also the laymen across the world could reap benefits from this relatively cheaper and possibly more convenient form of education. Let us have a look at Digital Library as a facility provided by a degree college. Where does this place a college or an institution, definitely among the advanced technology conscious institutions. The criterion for judging a College in today's time is not the qualified and experienced teachers, but how much technological advanced systems are implemented in it. However, if we ask the similar question- what is the opportunity cost? They say "no pain no gain". So is it going to be only gain or will it be a mix of the two?

The Essence of Teacher-Student Relationship

James Maury "Jim" Henson was the most widely known puppeteer in American television history He writes, in his book 'It's not easy being Green and other things to consider,' "Kids don't remember what you try to teach them. They remember what you are." Children today hardly remember their teachers. The main reason is that technology has taken away the essence of teacher-student relationship. The students and more than them, their parents nowadays are more concerned about what latest technology the educational institute or its teachers use in their classrooms. The qualification and teaching experience of teachers is not exactly a major concern. More emphasis is paid on the teachers' IT skills.

Can we really say that children of modern times remember and respect their teachers as much as they used to in earlier days? The increased dependence on technology has sometimes motivated, but mostly forced the teachers to change their teaching style to that which can be called as 'high tech.' It is always a good idea to adapt and adjust according to growing needs of the modern world, but we need to look carefully at the other side of the coin too. Is it absolutely necessary that adapting to latest technology will guarantee a better educated individual? Is it not possible that a child will lack the advantages of that human interaction which is so important for his psychological and personal development?

ISSUES IN IMPLEMENTATION OF CLOUD COMPUTING FOR DIGITAL LIBRARIES

There is no denying the fact that books are a source of knowledge and information. Also a Library, which is a collection of books, is a reflection of any community. The advancement of technology and science has had a huge impact on the society. It has had its impact in transition and development of Digital libraries as well. The concept of Digital Libraries has been there for quite some time now. But the emergence and evolvement of cloud computing is relatively new. Cloud computing refers to storage of data on the server itself, instead of storing it on the local hardware. This data can then be accessed from any device and from any location, as it is on cloud Internet. It is one of the latest IT technologies in use today. This service is already being used by many industries and organizations to store their data. It is no surprise, that it is now being implemented in Digital Libraries The main reasons for the motivation behind using cloud computing is its ability to enable users to use less hardware, have unlimited storage capacity, use network easily and effectively, share resources by pooling them and use online applications easily and effectively.

The development of cloud computing owes it all to the rapid growth of Internet technologies. But here lies the biggest disadvantage of its implementation. Even though cloud computing is going to benefit the Digital Libraries in some ways; there are difficulties in both phases linked to it, implementation and adaptation.

Increasing Gap between Developed and Developing Nations

Today, the development of a nation is decided on the basis of number of Internet users in that nation. In the context of Digital Libraries and related issues, it is important to discuss and observe the main factor without which it is impossible to imagine the existence of a Digital Library, that is, the Internet. Figure 1 and Figure 2 show the top 20 Internet countries by users and the top 20

Figure 1. Top 20 internet countries by users

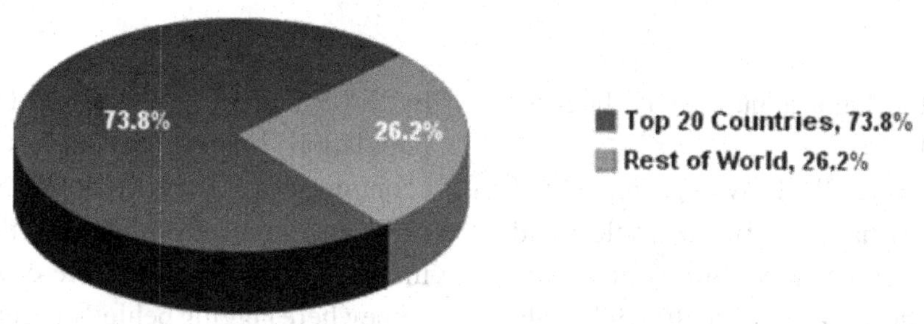

Figure 2. Top 20 countries with highest number of internet users

Top 20 Countries With The Highest Number Of Internet Users

TOP 20 COUNTRIES WITH HIGHEST NUMBER OF INTERNET USERS - JUNE 30, 2012						
#	Country or Region	Population, 2012 Est	Internet Users Year 2000	Internet Users Latest Data	Penetration (% Population)	Users % World
1	China	1,343,239,923	22,500,000	538,000,000	40.1 %	22.4 %
2	United States	313,847,465	95,354,000	245,203,319	78.1 %	10.2 %
3	India	1,205,073,612	5,000,000	137,000,000	11.4 %	5.7 %
4	Japan	127,368,088	47,080,000	101,228,736	79.5 %	4.2 %
5	Brazil	193,946,886	5,000,000	88,494,756	45.6 %	3.7 %
6	Russia	142,517,670	3,100,000	67,982,547	47.7 %	2.8 %
7	Germany	81,305,856	24,000,000	67,483,860	83.0 %	2.8 %
8	Indonesia	248,645,008	2,000,000	55,000,000	22.1 %	2.3 %
9	United Kingdom	63,047,162	15,400,000	52,731,209	83.6 %	2.2 %
10	France	65,630,692	8,500,000	52,228,905	79.6 %	2.2 %
11	Nigeria	170,123,740	200,000	48,366,179	28.4 %	2.0 %
12	Mexico	114,975,406	2,712,400	42,000,000	36.5 %	1.7 %
13	Iran	78,868,711	250,000	42,000,000	53.3 %	1.7 %
14	Korea	48,860,500	19,040,000	40,329,660	82.5 %	1.7 %
15	Turkey	79,749,461	2,000,000	36,455,000	45.7 %	1.5 %
16	Italy	61,261,254	13,200,000	35,800,000	58.4 %	1.5 %
17	Philippines	103,775,002	2,000,000	33,600,000	32.4 %	1.4 %
18	Spain	47,042,984	5,387,800	31,606,233	67.2 %	1.3 %
19	Vietnam	91,519,289	200,000	31,034,900	33.9 %	1.3 %
20	Egypt	83,000,104	450,000	29,809,724	35.6 %	1.2 %
TOP 20 Countries		4,664,486,873	273,374,200	1,776,355,028	38.1 %	73.8 %
Rest of the World		2,353,360,049	87,611,292	629,163,348	26.7 %	26.2 %
Total World Users		7,017,846,922	360,985,492	2,405,518,376	34.3 %	100.0 %

NOTES: (1) Top 20 Internet User Statistics were updated for June 30, 2012. (2) Additional data for individual countries and regions may be found by clicking each country name. (3) The most recent user information comes from data published by Nielsen Online, International Telecommunications Union, Official country reports, and other trustworthy research sources. (4) Data from this site may be cited, giving the due credit and establishing an active link back to www.internetworldstats.com.

countries with the highest number of Internet users respectively.

In 1992, the World Wide Web promoted the use of Internet and it has spread to the whole world to organizations, companies, corporations and individuals in a short span of time. By 1995 only 16 million people used Internet worldwide, that is, less than half percent of the world population. But by 2000 that percentage grew to 5%. It doubled by 2003 and by 2005 reached 15% of world population. Internet growth has a direct socio-economic effect, as all the companies now require skills and knowledge related to the digital world in their job descriptions. Here, people who are somewhere lagging behind in keeping up with the growth in the field of rapid Internet growth are the ones to suffer and lose premium opportunities otherwise befitting them completely.

Digital Divide within a Country

It is always expected that with the advancement spreading more rapidly in urban areas with less preference given to rural areas by the politicians in power, the people residing in rural areas suffer severely with regard to keeping up with the pace of technology. Richer, urban dwellers have more and easier access to Internet than the poorer, rural dwellers. This phenomenon creates a "digital divide" within a country. A larger scenario sees a "global digital divide" where some countries fall further behind other countries in fields of technology, education, democracy, tourism and labor. Figure 3 shows the number of individuals using the Internet per 100 inhabitants.

TECHNICAL ISSUES

Storage

A Digital Library's storage system must be capable of storing a large amount of data in a variety of formats. Accessing this data should also be as fast as possible. Text only documents are easiest to store, but digital video and audio amount to a sizeable storage space and their delivery is time-dependent. Storage is a major challenging area for a digital library set up.

It is very important to choose the correct format of digital data for storage purpose. All formats must be taken into account, also bearing in mind that acquisition and storage can be done in a different format than the distribution. A series of criteria must be studied and correlated with the individual needs of the client. It is also important to keep in mind future requirements and prospects of expansion, so as to avoid the need for migration.

Figure 3. Individuals using internet per 100 inhabitants
Data are from the International Telecommunication Union (ITU,) June 2012.

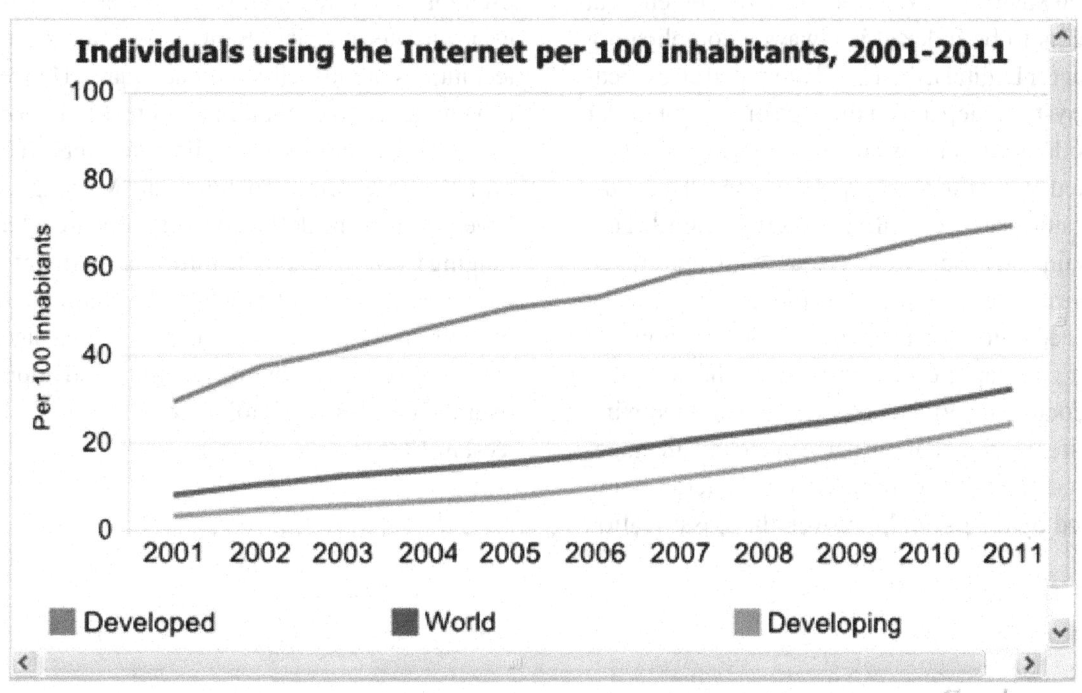

User Interface

The user interface is, perhaps, the most important component of Digital Libraries. It is expected to incorporate a wide variety of techniques to afford rich interaction between the users and the information they seek (Adam, Holowczak, Halem, Lal, & Yesha, 1996). It must display large volumes of data effectively for the user. The users may want to shrink down their search from a huge database to a single document to a specific paragraph. In case of digital multimedia resources, the user might desire to view a certain scene form a particular movie. All these expectations pose a challenge for Digital Libraries and are an interesting topic of research

Indexing and Classification

For better access to the database, it is necessary to have the information in a grouped form. Indexing and classification schemes are used to serve the purpose of searching in a Digital Library (Adam, Holowczak, Halem, Lal, & Yesha, 1996). Since individual perceptions may vary, classifying and indexing objects is filled with pitfalls. With digital data always on the rise, the potential content that remains to be indexed is always a complicating factor for Digital Libraries. Automated classification systems depend on the type of content under consideration. For example classifying novels is quite different form classifying maps. Thus current automated classification efforts are highly domain specific. More issues with automated classification are that even though they can be grouped into two general approaches, none of them can capture the meaning of the words in the document. Video classification and indexing requires system that can parse video into manageable portions. They are based on the queries being posted by the users. Moreover, the classification of musical notation, audio and maps presents additional research challenges.

Information Retrieval

Information retrieval is one of the key areas of Digital Libraries. It is also one of the most fascinating and challenging areas. The efficiency of traditional libraries with regard to ability to find works of interest was directly related to how well they were catalogued. But handling the growing volume of digital works definitely requires more complex information retrieval systems. New tools and technologies have to be designed to allow effective automated semantic classification and searching. The real challenge lies in designing search and retrieval tools that compensate for abbreviated or incomplete cataloging or descriptive information.

In Digital Library domain, there is a variety of information retrieval techniques including metadata searching, full-text document searching and content searching for their data types. An issue with full-text search is that it cannot be applied in finding texts which are a translation of other texts and it has difficulty linking texts published under pseudonyms to real authors. Only an individual user can determine if present information retrieval techniques are effective and adequate. Hence, it is a challenge to find automated methods to create and maintain user profiles and apply these profiles to information retrieval. Many people have put forward definitions of software agents, ranging from an adaptable information filter to an autonomous program which works in conjunction with or on behalf of a human user. These agents can record user actions and reactions and improve over the time (Adam, Holowczak, Halem, Lal, & Yesha, 1996).

EBook Devices

EBooks can be read on a computer device, an e-reader or even some mobile phones. Here again, the increasing options with improving technology has made it difficult to decide which e-books each device is capable of using. Some files are incompatible to use on other devices, restricting the already existing library to fewer e-books. With growing innovations in computer science, there is always a danger of a particular type of file becoming obsolete in near future. Outdated software is another threat to losing out on some of the library resources.

CONCERNS REGARDING VIRTUALIZATION

Virtualization of libraries is no doubt becoming increasingly popular. Everyone nowadays is interested in virtualization of their datacenter. But there are some concerns regarding virtualization which are worth paying attention before planning to virtualize the server.

Single Point of Failure

If the servers are virtualized, care should be taken to see that all virtualized domain controllers are not kept on a single host server. This is a matter of concern, as failure of a single host server may result in the death of all domain controllers controlled by it. Another point of concern is that host server failures are so disruptive, that a proper contingency plan is required to help minimize the impact of an outage.

Whether Virtual Environment Supports All Applications

Some versions of Exchange server are supported only on physical servers. Some common applications are not supported on virtual servers. Thus it should be made sure that all the applications are supported in a virtual environment.

Good Virtualization Candidates

There are some servers which do not make good virtualization candidates. This holds true for servers that run resource-intensive applications or that require special hardware. For example, a dongle is a copy protection device. Some enterprises use a dongle to enforce copy protection. Dongles are almost never supported in a virtual environment.

Most Suitable Virtualization Platform

Owing to mass competition in technology, there are many virtualization products available in the market. All have their own strengths and weaknesses. Therefore, it is a challenge to find out which product will work best for the required situation.

Guest Machines for a Host Server

While virtualizing a datacenter, sometimes the host server is overloaded. This is a matter of concern and it needs some capacity planning ahead of time to determine how many guest machines each host server can realistically accommodate. The reason for this is that every guest machine is different and it should be decided where to place each when beginning the capacity planning process.

Software License

Different software licensing is required for varied virtualization environments. Virtualization of the platforms warrants for different clauses in software licensing.

For example, it is not required to license the Windows operating system on guest machines if we are using Hyper-V. But actual license requirements vary depending on the versions of Windows being used. Hence it is important to understand the license requirements for the operating systems and applications that will be run on the guest machines.

SUMMARY

Digital libraries are here to stay as one of the primary sources of information and knowledge although they might never replace the paper based books. A 'digital library' comprises digital collections, services and infrastructure in different forms of data which certainly is a lifeline for long term scholarly activities. But all that should not be at the cost of privileges such as privacy and stringent regulations on infringements of copy rights. Innovations in technologies should be able to support a healthy physical, social and intellectual environment that is conducive for the morally apt, physically fit and scholastically progressive posterity.

These are some of the concerns which relate to Information Technology's new offspring - cloud computing and e-libraries. With the advent of efficient and easily available infrastructure in the form of cloud computing, e-libraries are becoming widespread. Both aspects of technology have socio-economic advantages over traditional means and methods. But what awaits us in the long run should be a cause of concern for all of us and must be well anticipated.

Concepts of social and technological equilibrium amongst masses should be revisited. Democratization of information and knowledge should be implemented at organizational, governmental and at international level. In doing so considerations must be made to favor anyone who has passion and desire for knowledge while not ignoring a poor individual. Underprivileged ones may be at a disadvantageous position when compared with the elite of a community to attain a timely start in the race of educational competition and in acquiring information. Such manifestos are being recommended on account of ever changing modern technologies, related equipments and resources to get information anytime and anywhere. The explosion of information should be harnessed in such a fashion that differences between desired information and what is accessible could be minimized. Competition between leading hi-tech corporations should be regulated to keep the global environment safe by containing the insanity with which the smart devices retail markets are procuring financial gains for few people while rendering pockets of the masses empty through never ending temptations. Temptations, in the shape of ever glittering touch screens, newer apps and processing power which may never be optimally used by the majority of the users until the next purchasing frenzy!

REFERENCES

Adam, N. R., Holowczak, R., Halem, M., Lal, N., & Yesha, Y. (1996). *Digital library technical committee*. Retrieved from http://cimic3.rutgers.edu/ieee_dltf.html

Carver, C. A., Jr., Hill, J. M. D., & Pooch, U. W. (1999, November). *Emerging curriculum issues in digital libraries*. Paper presented at The 29th ASEE/IEEE Frontiers in Education Conference (pp. 12c2-18 to12c2-23). San Juan, Puerto Rico.

Chepesuik, R. (1997). The future is here: America's libraries go digital. *American Libraries*, *2*(1), 47–49.

Hamaker, C. (2011). *E-Books on fire: Controversies surrounding e-books in libraries*. Retrieved from http://www.infotoday.com/searcher/dec11/Hamaker.shtml

Hutley, S., & Horwood, W. (2002). E-Book readers in Australian public libraries – are they REAL-e worth it? Retrieved from http://www.vala.org.au/vala2002/2002pdf/34HutHor.pdf

Maarof, M., & Yahya, Y. (2009, August 5-7). *Digital libraries interoperability issues*. Paper presented at The International Conference on Electrical Engineering and Informatics. Selangor, Malaysia.

Miniwatts Marketing Group. (2013, March 6). *Internet world stats*. Retrieved from http://www.internetworldstats.com/top20.htm

Nürnberg, P. J., Furuta, R., Leggett, J. J., Marshall, C. C., & Shipman, F. M., III. (1995). *Digital libraries: Issues and architectures*. Retrieved from http://www.csdl.tamu.edu/DL95/papers/nuernberg/nuernberg.html

Pasquali, V., & Aridas, T. (2012, June). *Internet users by country*. Retrieved from http://www.gfmag.com/tools/global-database/ne-data/11942-internet-users.html#axzz2MJiaKu8R

Pingdom. (2010, July 27th). *The top 20 countries on the Internet, and what the future might bring*. Retrieved from http://royal.pingdom.com/2010/07/27/top-20-countries-on-the-internet/

Posey, B. (2010). *10 issues to consider during virtualization planning, Tech Republic downloads*. Retrieved from http://www.techrepublic.com/downloads/10-issues-to-consider-during-virtualization-planning/1468253

Rettner, R. (2010, August 2). Pathological Internet use may cause teen depression. Retrieved from http://www.livescience.com/9556-addicted-technology.html

Sadeh, T. (2004). Developing an electronic resource management system: Verde from Ex Libris. *LIBER Quarterly*, *14*, 322–334.

Saller, C. (2011, September 29). *Typos and worse: When e-books need correcting*. Retrieved from http://chronicle.com/blogs/linguafranca/2011/09/29/typos-and-worse-when-e-books-need-correcting

Vemulapalli, S., Halappanavar, M., & Mukkamala, R. (2002). *Security in distributed digital libraries: Issues and challenges*. Paper presented at The International Conference on Parallel Processing Workshops (ICPPW'02) IEEE. Vancouver, Canada.

Vinjamuri, D. (2012, November). *The wrong war over e-books: Publishers vs. libraries*. Retrieved from http://www.forbes.com/sites/davidvinjamuri/2012/12/11/the-wrong-war-over-eBooks-publishers-vs-libraries

Virkus, S. (2010). *Challenges to building an effective digital library*. Retrieved from http://www.tlu.ee/~sirvir/Information%20and%20Knowledge%20%20Management/Integration%20of%20digital%20libraries%20in%20e-learning/issues_and_challenges_in_creating_digital_libraries.html

Compilation of References

15. *recommended cloud computing management tools.* (2011, March 25). Retrieved from http://www.cloudtweaks.com/2011/03/15-recommended-cloud-computing-management-tools-for-your-business/

3M. *Company.* 3M Cloud Library. Retrieved from https://itunes.apple.com/us/app/3m-cloud-library/id466446054?mt=8

3M. ™ *Cloud Library.* (n.d.). Retrieved from http://solutions.3m.com/wps/portal/3M/en_US/3MLibrarySystems/Home/Products/Cloud+Library/

Abidi, F. & Abidi, H. J. (2012). Cloud libraries: A novel application for cloud computing. *International Journal of Cloud Computing and Services Science (IJ-CLOSER), 1*(3), 79-83.

Adam, N. R., Holowczak, R., Halem, M., Lal, N., & Yesha, Y. (1996). *Digital library technical committee.* Retrieved from http://cimic3.rutgers.edu/ieee_dltf.html

Aggarwal, V. (2008). *Computing in the clouds.* New Delhi, India: Express Compute.

Aggregation, Integration, and Openness: Current Trends in Digital Libraries. (n.d.). Retrieved June 06, 2012, from http://www.kc.tsukuba.ac.jp/dlkc/eproceedings/papers/dlkc04pp105.pdf

Alcalde-Morano, J., Hernández-Ardieta, J. L., Johnston, A., Martinez, D., Zwattendorfer, B., & Stern, M. (2011). *Interface Specification.* Retrieved from https://www.eid-stork.eu/

Alestic. (n.d.). *Ubuntu on Amazon EC2.* Retrieved from http://alestic.com/

Allen, E., & Morris, C. M. (2009). *News from the Library of Congress.* Retrieved from http://www.loc.gov/today/pr/2009/09-140.html and accessed on 15/1/2013 at 2.08

Amazon autoscaling. (n.d.). Retrieved from http://aws.amazon.com/autoscaling/

Amazon CloudFront. (2013). Retrieved from http://aws.amazon.com/cloudfront/

Amazon EC2 AMI tools. (n.d.). Retrieved from http://developer.amazonwebservices.com/connect/entry.jspa?externalID=368&categoryID=251

Amazon EC2 API tools. (n.d.). Retrieved from http://developer.amazonWebservices.com/connect/entry.jspa?externalID=351&categoryID=251

Amazon EC2 libraries for Java, PHP, Perl, C #. (n.d.). Retrieved from http://developer.amazonwebservices.com/connect/kbcategory.jspa?resultOffset=45&categoryID=187

Amazon EC2 service level agreement. (2013). Retrieved from http://aws.amazon.com/ec2-sla/

Amazon EC2 tutorial. (n.d.). Retrieved from http://s3.amazonaws.com/AmazonEC2Tutorial/AmazonEC2Tutorial.html

Amazon elastic block storage (EBS). (n.d.). Retrieved from http://aws.amazon.com/ebs/

Amazon elastic block store. (2013). Retrieved from http://aws.amazon.com/ebs/

Amazon elastic compute cloud. (2013). Retrieved from http://aws.amazon.com/ec2/

Amazon elastic compute cloud. (EC2). (n.d.). Retrieved from http://aws.amazon.com/ec2/

Amazon redshift. (2013). Retrieved from http://aws.amazon.com/redshift/

Amazon relational database service. (2013). Retrieved from http://aws.amazon.com/rds/

Amazon route 53. (2013). Retrieved from http://aws.amazon.com/route53/

Amazon S3 libraries. (n.d.). Retrieved from http://developer.amazonwebservices.com/connect/kbcategory.jspa?resultOffset=0&categoryID=188

Amazon S3 service level agreement. (2013). Retrieved from http://aws.amazon.com/s3-sla/

Amazon simple storage service. (2013). Retrieved from http://aws.amazon.com/s3/

Amazon Web Services. (2013). *What is cloud computing?* Retrieved from http://aws.amazon.com/what-is-aws/

Amrhein, D., de Andrade, A., Armstrong, J., Arasan, E., Bruklis, R., & Cameron, K. … Zappert, F. (2009). *Cloud computing use cases: A white paper produced by the Cloud Computing Use Case Discussion Group.* Retrieved from http://www.cloudbook.net/cloud-computing-use-cases-group

An Overview of Digital Libraries: Issues and Trends. (n.d.). Retrieved July 22, 2012, from http://maltman.hmdc.harvard.edu/papers/DigitalLibraryOverview.pdf

Anderson, C. (2011). *Libraries Operating at Webscale.* Retrieved from http://www.oclc.org/content/dam/oclc/reports/worldshare-management-services/libraries-at-webscale.pdf

Anderson, W. L. (2002). CODATA work in archiving scientific data. In B. Mahon, & E. Siegel (Eds.), *Digital preservation: The record of science* (pp. 63–67). Amsterdam: IOS Press.

Armbrust, M., Fox, A., Griffith, R., Joseph, A., Katz, R., & Konwinski, A. … Zaharia, M. (2009). *Above the clouds: A Berkeley view of cloud.* (Tech. Rep. No. UCB/EECS-2009-28). Berkeley, CA: University of California at Berkeley.

Arora, D., Quraishi, S., & Quraishi, Z. (2011). Application of cloud computing in university libraries. *Pioneer Journal.* Retrieved from http://pioneerjournal.in/conferences/tech-knowledge/12th-national-conference/3654-application-of-cloud-computing-in-university-libraries.html

Athanasopoulos, G., Candela, L., Castelli, D., Innocenti, P., Ioannidis, Y., & Katifori, A. … Ross, S. (2010). *Coordination action on digital library interoperability, best practices and modelling foundations: The Digital Library Reference Model.* Retrieved from http://www.dlorg.eu/uploads/DL%20Reference%20Models/The%20Digital%20Library%20Reference%20Model_v1.0.pdf

Atmos. (n.d.). Retrieved from http://india.emc.com/storage/atmos/atmos.htm#!

Avancini, H., Candela, L., Manzi, A., & Simi, M. (2006). *A powerful and scalable digital library information service.* Retrieved from http://www.ercim.eu/publication/Ercim_News/enw66/ avancini.html

Avancini, H., Candela, L., Manzi, A., & Simi, M. (2006). A powerful and scalable digital library information service. *ERCIM News, 66*, 24–25.

AWS applications. (2013). Retrieved from http://aws.amazon.com/web-mobile-social/

AWS CloudFormation. (2013). Retrieved from http://aws.amazon.com/cloudformation/

AWS identity and access management. (2013). Retrieved from http://aws.amazon.com/iam/

AWS import/export. (2013). Retrieved from http://aws.amazon.com/importexport/

AWS Management Console. (2013). Retrieved from http://aws.amazon.com/console/

AWS public datasets. (n.d.). Retrieved from http://aws.amazon.com/publicdatasets/

AWS security white paper. (2008, September). Retrieved from http://s3.amazonaws.com/aws_blog/AWS_Security_Whitepaper_2008_09.pdf

AWS toolkit for eclipse. (n.d.). Retrieved from http://aws.amazon.com/eclipse/

Ayoub, R. (2011). The 2011 (ISC)2 global information security workforce study. Retrieved from https://www.isc2.org/uploadedFiles/Industry_Resources/FS_WP_ISC%20 Study_020811_MLW_Web.pdf

Badger, L., Bohn, R., Chu, S., Hogan, M., Liu, F., & Kaufmann, V. … Leaf, D. (2011). *US government cloud computing technology roadmap volume II release 1.0 (draft): NIST cloud computing program information technology laboratory*. Retrieved from http://www.nist.gov/itl/cloud/upload/SP_500_293_volumeII.pdf

Bagley, C. (2011). Parting the clouds: Use of dropbox by embedded librarians. In E. M. Corrado, & H. L. Moulaison (Eds.), *Getting started with cloud computing: A LITA guide* (pp. 159–164). New York: Neal-Schuman Publishers.

Baman, P. (2004). Emergence of digital library services in India. In *Proceedings of the 2nd International Convention on Automation of Libraries in Education and Research Institutions* (CALIBER 2004). New Delhi, India.

Bansode, S. Y., & Pujar, S. M. (2012). Cloud computing and libraries. DESIDOC Journal of Library & Information Technology, 32(6). Retrieved January 04, 2013, from http://publications.drdo.gov.in/ojs/index.php/djlit/article/view/2848/1392

Barateiro, J., Antunes, G., Borbinha, J., & Lisboa, P. (2009). Addressing digital preservation: Proposals for new perspectives.[1st *International Workshop on Innovation in Digital Preservation*. Austin, TX: Innovation in Digital Preservation.]. *Proceedings of InDP, 09*, 1.

Barham, P., Dragovic, B., Fraser, K., Hand, S., Harris, T., & Ho, A. … Warfield, A. (2003). Xen and the art of virtualization. In *Proceedings of the 19th ACM Symposium on Operating Systems Principles* (pp. 164-177). Cambridge, UK: University of Cambridge.

Barnatt, C. (2010). *A brief guide to cloud computing*. London: Constable & Robinson.

Behrendt, M., Glasner, B., Kopp, P., Dieckmann, R., Breiter, G., & Pappe, S. … Arsanjani, A. (2011). *Introduction and architecture overview: IBM cloud computing reference architecture 2.0*. Retrieved from http://www.teamswift-solutions.com/CCRA.IBMSubmission.02282011.pdf

Benefits of SHARES participation. (2013). Retrieved from http://www.oclc.org/research/activities/shares/benefits.html

Bergeron, B. (2004). Creating a digital library. *MedGenMed : Medscape General Medicine, 6*(1), 52. PMID:15208563.

Besser, H. (2001). Digital preservation of moving image material?. *The Moving Image, 1*(2).

Besser, H., Trant, J., & Robinson, P. (1993). *Introduction to imaging: Issues in constructing an image database*. Oxford, UK: Oxford University Computing Services.

Blue Ribbon Task Force on Sustainable Digital Preservation and Access. (2010). *Sustainable economics for a digital planet: Ensuring long-term access to digital information.* Retrieved July 3, 2012, from http://brtf.sdsc.edu/biblio/BRTF_Final_Report.pdf

Borbinha, J. (2010). SHAMAN: Sustaining heritage access through multivalent archiving. *ERCIM News, 80.*

Borko, F. (2010). Cloud computing fundamentals. In F. Borko, & A. Escalante (Eds.), *Handbook of cloud computing* (pp. 3–19). New York: Springer Science Business Media, LLC.

Boss, G., Malladi, P., Quan, D., Legregni, L., & Hall, H. (2009). *Cloud computing*. Retrieved from http://www.ibm.com/developerswork/websphere /zones/hipods/library.html

Boss, G., Malladi, P., Quan, S., Legregni, L., & Hall, H. (2007). *Cloud computing. (Tech. Rep.).* Armonk, NY: IBM.

Breeding, M. (2012). *Cloud computing for libraries.* Chicago: ALA TechSource.

Buchanan, G., & Hinze, A. (2005). A generic alerting service for digital libraries. In *Proceedings of the 5th ACM/IEEE-CS Joint Conference on Digital Libraries (JCDL '05)*, pp. 7–11.

Buyya, R., Yeo, C. S., & Venugopal, S. (2008). Market oriented cloud computing vision, hype and reality for delivering IT services as computing utilities. In *Proceedings of 10th IEEE International Conference on High Performance Computing and Communications, Dalian.* (pp. 5-13). Melbourne, Australia: The University of Melbourne.

CALIS-based cloud library service platform. (n.d.). Retrieved from http://www.lw20.com/201202118892529б.html

Callan, J., Smeaton, A., Beaulieu, M., Borlund, P., Brusilovsky, P., & Chalmers, M. ... Toms, E. (2003). Personalization and recommender systems in digital libraries. (Tech. Rep.) Dublin, Ireland: Joint NSF-EU DELOS Working Group.

Carolan, J., & Gaede, S. (2009). *Introduction to cloud computing architecture: White paper.* Retrieved from http://webobjects.cdw.com/webobjects/media/pdf/Sun_CloudComputing.pdf

Carver, C. A., Jr., Hill, J. M. D., & Pooch, U. W. (1999, November). *Emerging curriculum issues in digital libraries.* Paper presented at The 29th ASEE/IEEE Frontiers in Education Conference (pp. 12c2-18 to12c2-23). San Juan, Puerto Rico.

Cenon. (2012). *How universities implement cloud computing.* Retrieved from www.cloud.tweaks.com/2012/02/how-universities-implement-cloud-computing/

CEPH: The future of storage. (2013). Retrieved from http://www.ceph.com

Cervone, H. F. (2010). Managing digital libraries: The view from 3000 feet. *OCLC Systems & Services, 26*(3), 162–165. doi:10.1108/10650751011073607.

Chakraborty, A. K., & Abhik, C. (2013). Cloud computing for knowledge resource centre. In *Proceedings of 2nd International Conference on Academic Libraries* (pp. 68-75). New Delhi, India: Indo American Books Publication.

Chepesuik, R. (1997). The future is here: America's libraries go digital. *American Libraries, 2*(1), 47–49.

Chinnici, R., Moreau, J. J., Ryman, A., & Weerawarana, S. (Eds.). (2007). *Web services description language (WSDL) version 2.0 part 1: Core language.* Retrieved from http://www.w3.org/TR/2007/REC-wsdl20-20070626/

Chronopolis. (2011). Retrieved from http://chronopolis.sdsc.edu/

Cilardo, A., Coppolino, L., Mazzocca, N., & Romano, L. (2006). Elliptic curve cryptography engineering. *Proceedings of the IEEE, 94*(2), 395–406. doi:10.1109/JPROC.2005.862438.

CiteSeerX. (2011). *About CiteSeerX.* Retrieved from http://csxstatic.ist.psu.edu/about

Clement, L., Hately, A., von Riegen, C., & Rogers, T. (Eds.). (2008). *UDDI version 3.0.2: UDDI spec technical committee draft.* Retrieved from http://uddi.org/pubs/uddi_v3.htm

Clercq, J. D. (2002). Single sing-on architectures in infrastructure security. In G. Davida (Ed.), *Proceedings of InfraSec 2002* (pp. 40–58).

Cloud Computing Architecture in Digital Library. (n.d.). Retrieved February 04, 2013, from http://en.wikipedia.org/wiki/cloudcomputing

Cloud computing for business. (n.d.). Retrieved from http://www.business.qld.gov.au/business/running/technology-for-business/cloud-computing-business

Cloud Computing Insights from110 Implementation Projects: IBM Academy of Technology Survey. (2010). Retrieved February 06, 2013, from https://www-304.ibm.com/easyaccess3/fileserve?contentid=215289

Cloud computing issues and impact. (n.d.). Retrieved from http://www.ey.com/Publication/vwLUAssets/Cloud_computing_issues,_impacts_and_insights/$File/Cloud%20computing%20issues%20and%20impacts_14Apr11.pdf

Cloud Computing Security. (2009). *FTC questions cloud computing security.* Retrieved from http://news.cnet.

Cloud computing. (2012). Retrieved from http://en.wikipedia.org/wiki/Cloud_computing#Public_cloud

Cloud computing. (n.d.). Retrieved from http://www.brookings.edu/research/topics/cloud-computing.

Cloud platform. (2013). Retrieved from http://www.citrix.com/products/cloudplatform/try

Cloud studio. (n.d.). Retrieved from http://www.service-cloud.com/node/45

Cloud42. (n.d.). Retrieved from http://cloud42.net/

Colayer. (2009). What is Paas? Retrieved December 29, 2011, from http://ex.colayer.com/_cached/LINK_whatispaas/LINK_whatispaas.html

Collection Development in Digital Libraries. Trends and Problems. (n.d.). Retrieved December 07, 2012, from http://indjst.org/archive/vol.2.issue.11-12/dec09kavitha-29.pdf

Computing, C. (n.d.). Retrieved December 6, 2011, from http://en.wikipedia.org/wiki/Cloud_computing

Corrigan, K. (2012, June 2). Library moves to the cloud. *Gledale News-Press*. Retrieved from http://articles.glendalenewspress.com/2012-06-03/news/tn-gnp-library-moves-to-the-cloud-20120601_1_library-moves-library-systems-library-patrons

Council, C. I. O. (2012). *Creating effective cloud computing contracts for the federal government: Best practices for acquiring IT as a service, in coordination with the Federal Cloud Compliance Committee*. Retrieved from https://cio.gov/wp-content/uploads/downloads/2012/09/cloudbestpractices.pdf

Craig, G. (2009). Fully homomorphic encryption using ideal lattices In M. Mitzenmacher (Ed.). In *Proceedings of STOC '09 the 41st Annual ACM Symposium on Theory of Computing* (pp. 169-174). New York: ACM.

Craig, G. (2010, August 15-19). Toward basing fully homomorphic encryption on worst-case hardness. In T. Rabin (Ed.), *CRYPTO: Proceedings of the 30th Annual Cryptology Conference (2010)*. Santa Barbara, CA (LNCS 6223, pp 116 137).

Dawei Sun, G. C. (2011). *Surveying and analysing security: Privacy and trust issues in cloud computing environments. Advances in Control Engineering and Information Sciences* (pp. 2852–2856). Beijing, China: Elsevier.

Delivering the future of storage. (2013). Retrieved from http://www.inktank.com

Depocas, A., Ippolito, J., Jones, C., & Schaefer, C. A. (2003). *Permanence through change: The variable media approach*. New York: Guggenheim Museum Publications.

Deshpande, R. M., Rahangdale, B., & Bhoskar, R. (2013). Factors responsible for current status of libraries of national institute of technology in India. In *Proceedings of 2nd International Conference on Academic Libraries* (pp. 208-213). New Delhi, India: Indo American Books Publication.

Develop, host, and scale your apps in the cloud. (2013). Retrieved from http://openshift.redhat.com

Dhawan, N. (2011, July 23). Cloud computing can counter illiteracy. *The Times of India*. Retrieved from http://timesofindia.indiatimes.com/tech/careers/education/Cloud-computing-can-counter-illiteracy-Managing-Director-HP-India/articleshow/9335831.cms

Dhawan, S. M. (2013). Library Transformation to the Cloud Environment: Issues and Strategies. In S. M. Dawan, S. Mujumdar, & S. Deshmukh (Eds.), *Library Services through Cloud Computing Moving Libraries to the Web* (pp. 76–81). Delhi, India: Indo American Books.

Dialogic. (2013). *Dialogic making innovation thrive*. Retrieved from http://www.dialogic.com/~/media/products/docs/whitepapers/12023-cloud- computing-wp.pdf

Dictionary.com. (n.d.). Retrieved from http://www.dictionary.reference.com

Diffie, W. (1988). The first ten years of Public Key cryptography.[). New York: IEEE.]. *Proceedings of the IEEE*, *76*, 560–577. doi:10.1109/5.4442.

Digital collection management. (2013). Retrieved from http://www.oclc.org/en-europe/services/digital-collection.html

Digital Library Research. Current Developments and Trends. (n.d.). Retrieved November 07, 2012, from http://eprints.rclis.org/bitstream/10760/4905/1/ASLRcolumn.pdg

Digital Library Technology Trends. (n.d.). Retrieved August 12, 2012, from http://daminfo.wgbh.org/digital_library_trends.pdf

Digital Object Identifier (DOI). An ISBN for the 21st Century. (n.d.). Retrieved June 15, 2011, from http://nopr.niscair.res.in/bitstream/123456789/4123/1/ALIS%20 50%283%29%20101-109.pdf

Digital Technology and Emerging Copy Right Scenario. (n.d.). Retrieved December 08, 2012, from http://nopr.niscair.res.in/bitstream/123456789/4905/1/JIPR%20 8%284%29%20276-301.pdf

D-Lib Magazine. (n.d.). Retrieved November 14, 2012, from http://www.dlib.org/dlib/july01/roes/07roes.html

Doerkson, T. (2008, August 5). *Cloud computing: The user-friendly version of grid computing*. Retrieved from http://jeremygeelan.ulitzer.com/node/593313

Dorey, P. G., & Leite, A. (2011). *Commentary: cloud computing – a security problem or solution?* London: Elsevier. doi:10.1016/j.istr.2011.08.004.

Dura Cloud. (n.d.). Retrieved from http://duracloud.org

EBSCO. (n.d.). Retrieved from www.ebscohost.com/discovery

ECSS. (n.d.). *White paper on software and service architectures, infrastructures and engineering – action paper on the area for the future EU competitiveness volume 2: Background information, version 1.3*. Retrieved from http://www.euecss.eu/contents/documentation/volume%20two_ECSS%20White%20Paper.pdf

EDUCAUSE. (2012). *Top-ten IT issues, 2012*. Retrieved from www.educause.edu/ero/article/topten-it-issues-2012

ElasticFox extension for Mozilla Firefox, developer tools. (n.d.). Retrieved from http://developer.amazonwebservices.com/connect/entry.jspa?externalID=609

Elastra Corp. (n.d.). *An introduction to elastic computing: A new software design, provisioning, and pricing model for online businesses and enterprises*. Retrieved from http://www.marketspaceadvisory.com/cloud/Envisioning-the-Cloud.pdf

Electronic collection management. (2013). Retrieved from http://www.oclc.org/en-europe/services/electronic-collection.html

Elewijt Centre. (2013, February 5). *Open source cloud day*. Retrieved from http://www.opensourcecloudday.be

Engel, F., Klas, C., Brocks, H., Kranstedt, G., Ja¨schke, G., & Hemmje, M. (2009, December). Towards supporting context-oriented information retrieval in a scientific-archive based information life cycle. In Proceedings of Cultural Heritage Online, Empowering Users: An Active Role for User Communities (pp. 135–140). Florence, Italy: Cultural Heritage Online.

Enterprise Features. (n.d.). Retrieved from http://enterprisefeatures.com/2011/03/8-key-advantages-that-cloud-computing-delivers-to-it

Erlandson, R. (2010). Digital culture: The shifting paradigm of systems librarians and systems departments. In E. Iglesias (Ed.), *An overview of the changing role of the systems librarian: Systemic shifts* (pp. 1–12). Cambridge, MA: Woodhead Publishing.

Estefan, J., Laskey, K., McCabe, F., & Thornton, D. (Eds.). (2008). *OASIS reference architecture for service oriented architecture version 1.0: Public review draft 1*. Retrieved from http://docs.oasis-open.org/soa-rm/soa-ra/v1.0/soa-ra-pr-01.pdf

European Commission – IDABC. (2009). *eID Interoperability for PEGS: Update of Country Profiles*. Retrieved from http://ec.europa.eu/idabc/servlets/Doc2ba1.pdf?id=32521

European Commission – MODINIS. (2006). *The Status of Identity Management in European eGovernment initiatives*. Retrieved from http://ec.europa.eu/information_society/activities/ict_psp/documents/identity_management_eu_02_07.pdf

Ex Libris Alma. (n.d.). *The next-generation library services framework*. Retrieved from www.exlibrisgroup.com/category/AlmaOverview

Ex Libris Primo. (n.d.). *Empowering libraries to address user needs*. Retrieved from www.exlibrisgroup.com/category/PrimoOverview

Ex Libris: The bridge to knowledge. (n.d.). Retrieved from http://www.exlibris.co.il/

Farkas, M. (2008). Technology goes local: Collecting local knowledge with social software. *American Libraries, 39*(8), 50.

Farkas, M. G. (2007). *Social software in libraries: Building collaboration, communication, and community online*. Medford, NJ: Information Today.

Fierce, C. I. O. (2009). Securing the cloud: Designing security for a new age. Retrieved from http://i.zdnet.com/whitepapers/eflorida_Securing_Cloud_Designing_Security_New_Age.pdf

Finding Topic Trends in Digital Libraries. (n.d.). Retrieved December 22, 2012, from http://Web.mit.edu/seyda/www/Papers/JCDL09_TopicTrends.pdf

Flickety, K. E. (n.d.). *How to purify air using indoor plants*. Retrieved from http://www.wikihow.com/Purify-the-Air-Using-Plants

Forouzan, B. A. (2007). *Data communications and networking* (4th ed.). New York: McGraw-Hill.

FORTINET. (2011). *Protecting the cloud: Fortinet technologies and services that address your cloud security challenges*. Retrieved from http://www.fortinet.com/sites/default/files/solutionbrief/Protecting%20the%20Cloud.pdf

FOSS4Lib. (n.d.). Retrieved from http://foss4lib.org/

Fox, E. (2012). Digital library source book. Retrieved June 14, 2012, from http://vax.wcsu.edu/library.

Fox, R. (2009). Library in the clouds. *OCLC Systems & Services*, *25*(3), 156–161. doi:10.1108/10650750910982539.

Furht, B., & Escalante, A. (2010). *Handbook of cloud computing* (1st ed.). New York: Springer. doi:10.1007/978-1-4419-6524-0.

Future Improvement of Cloud Computing in Digital Library. (n.d.). Retrieved February 16, 2013, from Cloud Computing in Libraries\Materials\What is Cloud Computing and how will it Affect Libraries Tech Soup for Libraries.html

Garrett, J., & Waters, D. (1996). *Preserving digital information: Report of the task force on archiving of digital information*. Washington, DC: U.S. Commission on Preservation and Access and Research Libraries Group.

Gartner Hype. (2009). *Pricing and positioning cloud computing services*. Ingram Micro Partner Smart Services Division.

Gennaro, R. D. (1996, September 23-26). JSTOR: The Andrew W. Mellon foundation's journal storage project. In A. H. Helal & J. W. Weiss (Eds.), *Proceedings of the 19th International Essen Symposium* (pp. 223-230). Essen, Germany: Universitatsbibliothek Essen.

Gennaro, R. D. (1997, August 31 - September 5). JSTOR: Building an Internet accessible digital archive of retrospective journals. In *Proceedings of the 63rd IFLA General Conference*. IFLA.

Getting started with Amazon EC2. (n.d.). Retrieved from http://paulstamatiou.com/2008/04/05/how-to-getting-started-with-amazon-ec2

Gladney, H. M. (2007). *Preserving digital information*. Berlin: Springer.

GNU operating system. (2013). Retrieved from http://www.gnu.org/licenses/licenses.html

Golden, B. (2009). *The case against cloud computing, part four*. Retrieved from http://www.cio.com/article/480595/The_Case_Against_Cloud_ Computing_Part_Four

Goldner, M. R. (2010). Winds of change: Libraries and cloud computing. *BIBLIOTHEK Forschung und Praxis*, *34*(3), 270–275. doi:10.1515/bfup.2010.042.

Goldwasser, S., & Micali, S. (1982). Probabilistic encryption and how to play mental poker keeping secret all partial information. In *Proceedings of STOC '82 the 14st Annual ACM Symposium on Theory of Computing* (pp. 365-377). New York: ACM.

Google App Engine (GAE). (n.d.). Retrieved from http://code.google.com/appengine/

Google App Engine. (n.d.). Retrieved from http://code.google.com/appengine.

Google. (2012). *Google's approach to IT security: A Google white paper*. Retrieved from https://cloud.google.com/files/Google-CommonSecurity-WhitePaper-v1.4.pdf

Gosavi, N., Shinde, S. S., & Dhakulkar, B. (2012). Use of cloud computing in library and information science field. International Journal of Digital Library Services, 1(3). Retrieved February 04, 2013, from http://www.ijodls.in/uploads/3/6/0/3/3603729/51-60.pdf

Gowda, M. P. (2008). Digital library. In A. K. Sahu (Ed.), *Information management in new millenium: opportunities and challenges for library professionals* (pp. 354–361). New Delhi, India: Ess Ess Publication.

Graham, P. G. (1994). *Intellectual preservation: Electronic preservation of the third kind*. Retrieved June 29, 2012, from http://www.clir.org/pubs/reports/graham/intpres.html

Grant, C. (2012). *Why and how librarians have to shape the new cloud computing platforms*. Retrieved from http://thoughts.care-affiliates.com/2012/06/why-and-how-librarians-have-toshape.html

Gudgin, M., Hadley, M., Mendelsohn, N., Moreau, J. J., Nielsen, H. F., Karmarkar, A., & Lafon, Y. (Eds.). (2007). *SOAP version 1.2. part 1: Messaging framework (2nd ed.).* Retrieved from http://www.w3.org/TR/2007/REC-soap12-part1-20070427/

Gupta, V., & Ansari, M. A. (2006). *Interoperability as a bench mark in digital libraries*. Retrieved from http://ir.inflibnet.ac.in/bitstream/handle/1944/1259/275-280.pdf?sequence=1

Hamaker, C. (2011). *E-Books on fire: Controversies surrounding e-books in libraries*. Retrieved from http://www.infotoday.com/searcher/dec11/Hamaker.shtml

Hamilton, D. (2008, June 4). Cloud computing seen as next wave for technology investors. *Financial Post.*

Han, L., & Wang, L. (2011). Research on digital library platform based on cloud computing. *Advances in Computer Science, Environment, Ecoinformatics, and Education Communications*, *214*, 176–180. doi:10.1007/978-3-642-23321-0_27.

Han, Y. (2010). On the clouds: A new way of computing. *Information Technology & Libraries*, *29*(2), 87–92.

Hayes, B. (2008). Cloud computing. *Communications of the ACM*, *7*(51), 9–11. doi:10.1145/1364782.1364786.

Hazelhurst, S. (2008). Scientific computing using virtual high-performance computing: A case study using the Amazon elastic computing cloud. In *Proceedings of the 2008 Annual Research Conference of the South African Institute of Computer Scientists and Information Technologists on IT Research in Developing Countries: Riding the Wave of Technology* (pp. 94-103). Wilderness, South Africa: University of Witswatersrand.

Heslop, H., Devis, S., & Wilson, A. (2002). *An approach to the preservation of digital record.* Retrieved July 2, 2012, from http://www.naa.gov.au/Images/An-approach-Green-Paper_tcm16-47161.pdf

Hewlett-Packard. (2011). *A white paper: Understanding the HP cloud system reference architecture reference architecture*. Retrieved from www.hp.com/go/cloudsystem

Hickey, A. R. (2010). *20 Coolest cloud platform vendors*. Retrieved from http://www.crn.com/slishows/channel-programs/222400507/20-coolest-cloud-platform-vendors.htm

Hinkle, M. (2010). *Eleven open source cloud computing projects to watch*. Retrieved from http://socializedsoftware.com/2010/01/20/eleven-open-source-cloud-computing-projects-to-watch/

Hosch, W. L. (2009). *Google Inc*. Retrieved from http://search.eb.com/eb/article-9471099

How server virtualization works. (2010, May 17). Retrieved from http://searchservervirtualization.techtarget.com/video/How-server-virtualization-works

Hu, G. (2007). Research on information service model of university library in digital era (D). Tianjin Polytechnic University, 2007(12).

Huang, F. (2008). Research on the development of library information service models in the information culture environment (OJ). Xiangtan University, 2008(7).

Hutley, S., & Horwood, W. (2002). E-Book readers in Australian public libraries – are they REAL-e worth it? Retrieved from http://www.vala.org.au/vala2002/2002pdf/34HutHor.pdf

Hybrid Cloud Computing. (n.d.). Retrieved January 26, 2013, from http://cloudcomputing.sys-con.com

Hybrid cloud Definition. (n.d.). Retrieved from searchcloudcomputing.techtarget.com/definition/hybrid-cloud

IBM Developer Network. (2003). *Web services security*. Retrieved from http://www.ibm.com/developerworks/webservices/library/ws-security.html

IBM. (2002). *IBM developer network: Web services security*. Retrieved from http://www.ibm.com/developerworks/websphere/library/techarticles/0605_chung/0605_chung.html

IBM. (2007). *Understanding SOA security design and implementation*: *IBM Redbook*. Retrieved from http://www.redbooks.ibm.com/abstracts/sg247310.html

Iglesias, E. (2010). The status of the field. In E. Iglesias (Ed.), *An overview of the changing role of the systems librarian: Systemic shifts* (pp. 65–79). Cambridge, MA: Woodhead Publishing. doi:10.1533/9781780630410.

Iglesias, E. (2011). Using Windows home server and Amazon S3 to back up high-resolution digital objects to the cloud. In E. M. Corrado, & H. L. Moulaison (Eds.), *Getting started with cloud computing: A LITA guide* (pp. 143–151). New York: Neal-Schuman Publishers.

Image processing and Cloud computing _ architecture Overview. (n.d.). Retrieved from http://computer-vision-talks.com/2011/04/image-processing-cloud-computing-architecture-overview/

Ingthorsson, O. (2011, November 30). *5 Cloud computing statistics you may find surprising*. Retrieved from http://cloudcomputingtopics.com/2011/11/5-cloud-computing-statistics-you-may-find-surprising/

Innocenti, P., Ross, S., Maceciuvite, E., Wilson, T., Ludwig, J., & Pempe, W. (2009, October). Assessing digital preservation frameworks: The approach of the SHAMAN project. In *Proceedings of MEDES-09 1st International Conference on Management of Emergent Digital EcoSystems* (pp. 412-416). New York: ACM Press.

International Internet Preservation Consortium. (2004). *Mission goal and charter*. Retrieved July 5, 2012, from http://netpreserve.org/about/mission.php

International Internet Preservation Consortium. (2004). *Web curators mailing list*. Retrieved July 5, 2012, from http://netpreserve.org/about/curator.php

International Telecommunication Union. (2012). *Cloud computing in Africa: Situation and perspective*. Retrieved from http://www.itu.int/ITU-D/treg/publications/Cloud_Computing_Afrique-e.pdf

Introducing clouds. (n.d.). Retrieved from http://code.google.com/p/jclouds/

Jacobson, A. (2010, June 26). Cloud computing for library services. Retrieved from http://libraralan.blogspot.com/2010/06/cloud-computing-for-library-services.html

Jacquin, T., De'jean, H., & Chanod, J. P. (2010). Xeproc c: A model-based approach towards document process preservation in research and advanced technology for digital libraries. In M. Lalmas, J. Jose, A. Rauber, F. Sebastiani, & I. Frommholz (Eds.), *Proceedings of the 14th European Conference (ECDL 2010)* (LNCS), (vol. 6273, pp. 538-541). Berlin: Springer Berlin Heidelberg.

James, R. (2010). Records management in the cloud? Records management is the cloud? *Business Information Review, 27*(3), 179–189. doi:10.1177/0266382110377060.

Jeffery, K., & Neidecker-Lutz, B. (2010). The future of cloud computing: Opportunities for European cloud computing beyond 2010. Retrieved from cordis.europa.eu/fp7/ict/ssai/docs/cloud-report-final.pdf

Jianhua Che, Y. D. (2011). Study on the security models and strategies of cloud computing. *International Conference on Power Electronics and Engineering Application* (pp. 586-593). Beijing, China: Elsevier.

Jing, Y., Zhijiang, L., & Suping, Y. (2012). 2012 international workshop on information and electronics engineering (IWIEE): The community library anniance based on cloud computing. *Procedia Engineering, 29*, 2804–2808. doi:10.1016/j.proeng.2012.01.394.

JungleDisk. (n.d.). Retrieved from http://jungledisk.com

Kahle, B. (2001). *The Internet archive*. Retrieved July 29, 2012, from http://archive.org/

Kalpana, T. M., & Gopalakrishnan, S. (2012). Collection development and cloud computing. *International Conference on Collection Development in Digital Environment* (pp. 99-104). Chennai, India: University of Madras.

Kalpana, T. M., & Gopalakrishnan, S. (2012). Increased collection with ecofriendly strategies. *International conference on collection Development in Digital Era* (pp. 421-424). Chennai, India: Univeristy of Madras.

Kalpana, T. M., & Gopalakrishnan, S. (2013). Self sustainability in academic libraries in digital era. In Thanuskodi (Ed.), Challenges in Academic Libraries in Digital Era. Hershey, PA: IGI Global.

Kamoun, F. (2009). Virtualizing the datacenter without compromising server performance. *Ubiquity, 2009*(9), 1-12. doi: 10.1145/1595422.1595424

Kaur, A. (2006). Role of libraries and library professionals in the digital environment. In P. V. Rao (Ed.), *Vistas of information management: Professor H.R. Chopra felicitation volume* (pp. 94–99). Chandigarh, India: Wisdom House Academic.

Khan, S., Khan, S., & Galibeen, S. (2011). Cloud computing an emerging technology: Changing ways of libraries collaboration. *Journal of Library and Information Science, 1*(2), 151–159.

Khater, R. (2010). Cloud computing and the monolithic narrative. Retrieved from http://www.arabmediasociety.com/?article=764

Kitchigami Regional Library System Launches eBooks Service. (2012). Retrieved from http://www.northland-press.com/AREAebookservice11612.html

Knorr, E., & Gruman, G. (2008). *What cloud computing really means*. Retrieved from http://www.infoworld.com/d/cloud-computing/what-cloud-computing-really-means-031

Kodali, N., Farkas, C., & Wijesekera, D. (2004). An authorization model for multimedia digital libraries. *International Journal on Digital Libraries, 4*(3), 139–155. doi:10.1007/s00799-004-0080-1.

Krishna, A. V. N., Vinaya, A. B., & Pandit, S. N. N. (2007). A generalized scheme for data encryption technique using a randomized matrix key. *Journal of Discrete Mathematical Sciences and Cryptography, 10*(1), 73–81. doi:10.1080/09720529.2007.10698109.

Kroski, E. (2009). Library cloud atlas: A guide to cloud computing and storage/stacking the tech. Library Journal. Retrieved February 15, 2011, from http://www.libraryjournal.com/article/CA6695772.html

Kroski, E. (2009, September 10). *Library cloud atlas: A guide to cloud computing and storage stacking the tech.* Retrieved from http://www.libraryjournal.com/article/CA6695772.html

Kruk, S. R., Decker, S., & Zieborak, L. (2005, August 22-26). JeromeDL - adding semantic web technologies to digital libraries. In Proceedings of 16th International Conference, DEXA 2005, Copenhagen, Denmark (pp. 716-725). Berlin: Springer.

Kuali. (n.d.). *Kuali Open Library Environment*. Retrieved from http://kuali.org/ole

Kumar, D. K., M., Y.S.S.R., Ramakrishna, D., & Rohit, A. V. (2012). Application of cloud technology in digital library. *IJCSI International Journal of Computer Science Issues, 9*(3).

Kumar, N. (2013). Cloud computing for academic library: A SWOT analysis. In *Proceedings of 2nd International Conference on Academic Libraries* (pp. 187-198). New Delhi, India: Indo American Books Publication.

Kuribayashi, S. I. (2012). Reducing total power consumption method in cloud computing environment. *International Journal of Computer Networks and Communications, 4*(2), 69–84. doi:10.5121/ijcnc.2012.4205.

Kuyoro, S. O., Ibikunle, F., & Awodele, O. (2011). Cloud computing security issues and challenges.[IJCN]. *International Journal of Computer Networks, 3*(5).

Lakhe, P., Mane, D., & Nakrani, S. (2009). *Guidelines to create and run an Amazon Machine Image (AMI) on Amazon using Linux. (Tech Rep.)*. Pune, India: Tata Research Development and Design Centre.

Lal, M., & Hussain, A. (2010). Digital library: Challenges and opportunities. In R. K. Tiwari (Ed.), *Library Services in Electronic Environment* (pp. 339–343). Gurgaon, India: J.K. Business School.

Lavagnino, M. B. (1997). Networking and the role of the academic systems librarian: An evolutionary perspective. *College & Research Libraries, 58*(3), 217–231.

LeFurgy. B. (2012). *Top 10 digital preservation developments of 2011*. Retrieved from http://blogs.loc.gov/digitalpreservation/2012/01/top-10-digital-preservation-developments-of-2011/ and accessed on 15/1/2013

Leitold, H., & Zwattendorfer, B. (2010). STORK: architecture, implementation and pilots. In *Proceedings of ISSE 2010 Securing Electronic Business Processes: Highlights of the Information Security Solutions Europe 2010 Conference*, (pp. 131-142).

Li, Y., Luan, X., & Li, S. (2009). Libraries Meeting Cloud computing Technology Era.*Academic Library and Information Tribune 2009, 1*(3).

Libraries, D. Technological Advances and Social Impacts. (n.d.). Retrieved June 22, 2011, from [REMOVED HYPERLINK FIELD]http://www.canis.uiuc.edu/news/Computerintro.pdf

Library of Congress. (2002). *Preserving our digital heritage: Plan for the national digital information infrastructure and preservation program.* Retrieved July 3, 2012, from http://www.digitalpreservation.gov/documents/ndiipp_plan.pdf

LibraryThing. (n.d.). Retrieved from http://www.librarything.com/about

Lillard, T. V., Garrison, C. P., Schiller, C. A., & Steele, J. (2010). *Digital forensics for network, Internet and cloud computing: A forensic evidence guide for moving targets and data.* New York: Elsevier.

Liu, J., Zhang, L. J., Hu, B., & He, K. (2012, June). *CCRA: Cloud computing reference architecture. Paper presented at the 9th International Conference on Service Computing (SCC 2012).* Honolulu, HA.

Liu, W., & Cai, H. (2013). Embracing the shift to cloud computing: Knowledge and skills for systems librarians. *OCLC Systems & Services*, *29*(1), 22–29. doi:10.1108/10650751311294528.

Livingstone, R. (2011). *Navigating through the cloud: A plain english guide to surviving the risks, costs and governance pitfalls of cloud computing*. Sydney, Australia: Rob Livingstone.

Luvkush, & Chand, S. (2010). Digital trends in library and role of digital librarian. In R.K.Tiwari (Ed.), Library Services in Electronic Environment (pp. 67-77). Gurgaon, India: J.K. Business School.

Lyman, P., & Hal, R. V. (2003). *How much information?* Retrieved June 17, 2012, from http://www2.sims.berkeley.edu/research/projects/how-much-info-2003/

Lynch, C. A. (2000). From automation to transformation: Forty years of libraries and information technology in higher education. *EDUCAUSE Review*, *35*(1), 60–68.

Maarof, M., & Yahya, Y. (2009, August 5-7). *Digital libraries interoperability issues*. Paper presented at The International Conference on Electrical Engineering and Informatics. Selangor, Malaysia.

MacCarn, D., (1997, January - July). Towards a universal data format for the preservation of media. *SMPTE*, 477-479.

Mallinson, J. C. (1986). Preserving machine-readable archival records for the millenia. *Archivaria*, *22*, 147–152.

Management, D. R. An Integrated Secure Digital Content Distribution Technology. (n.d.). Retrieved December 15, 2012, from http://nopr.niscair.res.in/bitstream/123456789/4878/1/JIPR%209%284%29%20313-331.pdf

Matthews, G., Poulter, A., & Blagg, E. (1997). *Preservation of digital materials, policy and strategy issues for the UK: ISC/NPO studies on the preservation of electronic materials (report 41).* London: BL Research & Innovation.

Mazurek, C., Stroinski, M., Werla, M., & Weglarz, J. (2006). Metadata harvesting in regional digital libraries in PIONIER network, 61-704. Poznan, Poland: Poznan Supercomputing and Networking Centre.

Meiler, P., & Schmeing, M. (2009). *Secure service oriented architectures (SOA) supporting NEC (Tech Rep.).* Brussels, Belgium: North Atlantic Treaty Organization.

Mell, P., & Grance, T. (2009). *The NIST definition of cloud computing*. Retrieved from http://www.nist.gov/itl/cloud/upload/cloud-def-v15.pdf

Mell, P., & Grance, T. (2010). *Effectively and securely using the cloud computing paradigm.* Retrieved from http://www.csrc.nist.gov/groups/SNS/cloud-computing/cloud-computing-v26.ppt

Mell, P., & Grance, T. (2011). The NIST definition of cloud computing: Recommendations of the National Institute of Standards and Technology. Computer Security Division, Information Technology Laboratory, National Institute of Standards and Technology, Retrieved from http://csrc.nist.gov/publications/nistpubs/800-145/SP800-145.pdf

Microsoft Azure. (n.d.). Retrieved from http://www.microsoft.com/azure/

Miller, M. (n.d.). *Cloud computing info graphics*. Retrieved from http://pinterest.com/markmilleritpro/cloud-computing-infographics/

Miller, R. (2011, January 30). Amazon S3 cloud stores 262 billion objects. Retrieved from http://www.datacenterknowledge.com/archives/2011/01/30/amazon-s3-cloud-stores-262-billion-objects/

Miniwatts Marketing Group. (2013, March 6). *Internet world stats*. Retrieved from http://www.internetworldstats.com/top20.htm

Mitchell, E. (2010). Using cloud services for library IT infrastructure. Code4Lib Journal, 9, 3-22. Retrieved January 10, 2013, from http://journal.code4lib.org/articles/2510

Mohlhenrich, J. (1993). *Preservation of electronic formats: Electronic formats for preservation*. Fort Atkinson, WI: Highsmith Press.

Mulvihill, A. (2012). *Ask a librarian*. Retrieved from http://www.highbeam.com/doc/1G1-256071262.html

Nandkishor, G., Sheetal, S., Shinde, S., & Bhagyashree, D. (2012). Use of cloud computing in library and information science field. *International Journal of Digital Library Services*, *2*(3), 51–60.

National Library of Australia. (1997). *Statement of principles: Preservation of and long term access to Australian digital objects*. Canberra, Australia: National Preservation Office.

National Library of Australia. (2003). *Guidelines for the preservation of digital heritage*. Canberra, Australia: United Nations Educational, Scientific, and Cultural Organization.

Netmetix. (n.d.). *Top 10 cloud computing statistics*. Retrieved from http://netmetix.wordpress.com/2011/11/09/top-10-cloud-computing-statistics/

Next generation of archieving. (n.d.). Retrieved from downloads.sys-con-com/download/whitepaper_autonomy_nextgen

NIST. (2013). *Copy data objects out of a cloud*. Retrieved from http://collaborate.nist.gov/twiki-cloud-computing/bin/view/CloudComputing/UseCaseCopyFromCloud

Nürnberg, P. J., Furuta, R., Leggett, J. J., Marshall, C. C., & Shipman, F. M., III. (1995). *Digital libraries: Issues and architectures*. Retrieved from http://www.csdl.tamu.edu/DL95/papers/nuernberg/nuernberg.html

OASIS. (2013). *OASIS privacy management reference model technical committee*. Retrieved from http://www.oasis-open.org/committees/pmrm/charter.php

OCLC. (2013). *Public purpose*. Retrieved from http://www.oclc.org/about/purpose.en.html

OCLC. (2013). *OCLC WorldShare™ management services*. Retrieved from http://www.oclc.org/en-europe/worldshare-management-services.html

OCLC. (2013). *Amlib*. Retrieved from http://www.oclc.org/en-europe/amlib.html

OCLC. (2013). *Cbs*. Retrieved from http://www.oclc.org/en-europe/cbs.html

OCLC. (2013). *Cbs at a glance*. Retrieved March 07, 2013, from http://www.oclc.org/en-europe/cbs/about.html

OCLC. (2013). OLIB. Retrieved from http://www.oclc.org/en-europe/olib.html

OCLC. (2013). Olib at a glance. Retrieved from http://www.oclc.org/en-europe/olib/about.html

OCLC. (n.d.). *WorldCat local: overview*. Retrieved from www.oclc.org/worldcatlocal/overview/default.htm

OCLC. (n.d.). *WorldShare management services: Overview*. Retrieved from www.oclc.org/webscale/overview.htm

ODLIS. Online Dictionary of Library and Information Science. (n.d.). Retrieved November 13, 2012, from http://www.dlib.org

Office of the Privacy Commissioner of Canada. (n.d.). *Fact sheet: Introduction to cloud computing*. Retrieved from http://www.priv.gc.ca/resource/fs-fi/02_05_d_51_cc_e.pdf

Oracle Thinkquest. (2012). *What is CD ROM*. Retrieved June 14, 2012, from http://library.thinkquest.org/26171/whatiscdrom.html

Ort, E. (2005). *Service-oriented architecture and Web services: Concepts, technologies, and tools*. Retrieved from http://www.oracle.com/technetwork/articles/javase/wstools-141839.html

Osei-Poku, W. (2009). *Service oriented architecture*. Retrieved from http://works.bepress.com/raspino/4

Ou, G. (2006). *Introduction to server virtualization.* Retrieved from http://www.techrepublic.com/article/introduction-to-server-virtualization/607494

Padhy, S. C., & Mahapatra, R. K. (2012). Cloud computing: Academic library in Orissa. VSRD Technical & Non-Technical Journal, 3(3). Retrieved January 15, 2013, from http://www.vsrdjournals.com/vsrd/Issue/2012_03_Mar/Web/5_Suresh_Chandra_Padhy_621_Research_Communication_Mar_2012.pdf

Padhy, S. C., & Mahapatra, R. K. (2012). Cloud computing: Academic library in Orissa. *VSRD Technical Non-Technical Journal*, *3*(3), 124–130.

Palanivel, K., & Nagalingam, U. (2011, November). Service-oriented reference model to security for digital library (SORMSDL). In B. R. Babu & P. N. Rao (Eds.). Information Security in the Digital Era: Society for Electronic Transactions and Security, 230-243.

Palanivel, K., Amouda, V., Kuppuswami, S. (2009). A personalized e-learning using web services and semantic web. *International Journal of Computer Engineering and Information Technology Winter ed.*, *21*(5), 27-37.

Palanivel, K., & Kuppuswami, S. (2011). Service-oriented reference architecture for personalized e-learning systems (SORAPES). *International Journal of Computers and Applications*, *24*(5), 35–44. doi:10.5120/2956-3907.

Paliwal, A. (2013, March 15). *Bon appetit with sun: Down to earth.* Retrieved from http://www.downtoearth.org.in/content/bon-appetit-sun

Pasquali, V., & Aridas, T. (2012, June). *Internet users by country.* Retrieved from http://www.gfmag.com/tools/global-database/ne-data/11942-internet-users.html#axzz2MJiaKu8R

Peter, S. (2009). *Securing the cloud: F5 white paper.* Retrieved from http://i.zdnet.com/whitepapers/eflorida_Securing_Cloud_Designing_Security_New_Age.pdf

Peters, C. (2010). *What is cloud computing and how will it affect libraries?* Retrieved from http://www.techsoupforlibraries.org/blog/what-is-cloud-computing-and-how-will-it-affect-libraries

Peters, C. (2013). *What is cloud computing and how will it affect libraries?* Retrieved from http://www.techsoupforlibraries.org/

Pettey, C., & Forsling, C. (2009). Gartner highlights five attributes of cloud computing. Retrieved December 28, 2011, from http://www.gartner.com/it/page.jsp?id=1035013

Pillai, A. S., & Swasthimathi, L. S. (2012). Study on open source cloud computing platforms. *International Journal of Multidisciplinary Management Studies*, *2*(7), 31–39.

Pingdom. (2010, July 27th). *The top 20 countries on the Internet, and what the future might bring.* Retrieved from http://royal.pingdom.com/2010/07/27/top-20-countries-on-the-internet/

Polaris Library Systems. (n.d.). Retrieved from http: // www.gisinfosystems.com/

Pomerantz, J. (2003). Integrating digital reference service into the digital library environment. In R. D. Lankes, S. Nicholson, & A. Goodrum (Eds.), *The Digital Reference Research Agenda* (pp. 23–47). Chicago: Association of College and Research Libraries.

Posey, B. (2010). *10 issues to consider during virtualization planning, Tech Republic downloads.* Retrieved from http://www.techrepublic.com/downloads/10-issues-to-consider-during-virtualization-planning/1468253

Pradeep, B. T., & Bhuvan, U. (n.d.). *CiteSeerx: A cloud perspective.* Retrieved on 1st March 2013 from http://static.usenix.org/event/hotcloud10/tech/full_papers/Teregowda.pdf

Pratha, L., Mattam, M., Ambati, V., & Reddy, R. (2006, November 17). *Multimedia digital library: Performance and scalability issues.* Paper presented at the 2nd International Conference on Universal Digital Library. Hyderabad, India.

Pricing cloud services: Cost structures. (2009, February 23). Retrieved from http://gettogreen.blogspot.in/2009/02/cloud-computing-cost-structure-and.html

Primary Research Group. (2011). *Survey of library use of cloud computing.* New York: Primary Research Group.

Privacy in Cloud. (2009). *Risks to privacy and confidentiality from cloud computing.* Retrieved from http://www.worldprivacyforum.org/pdf/WPF_Cloud_privacy_Report.pdf/

Private cloud (internal cloud or corporate cloud) definition. (n.d.). Retrieved from searchcloudcomputing.techtarget.com/definition/private-cloud

Public Key cryptography. (2000). *Standard Specifications for Public Key Cryptography*. Retrieved from http://www. Stanadard Specifications for Public Key cryptography, IEEE Standard

Public Key. (n.d). Public key algorithm. *Retrieved from*http:// wikipedia.org/wiki/Public-key_cryptography

Ramasamy, R. R., Prabakar, M. A., Devi, M. I., & Suguna, M. (2009). Knapsack based ECC encryption and decryption. *International Journal of Network Security*, *9*(3), 218–226.

Recent Trends in Statewide Academic Library Consortia. (n.d.). Retrieved June 22, 2011, from http://www.thefreelibrary.com/Recent+trends+in+statewide+academic+library+consortia-a019192264

Reddy, T. R. (2012). Digital era: Utilize of cloud computing technology in digital library. International Journal of Digital Library Services, 2, 92-106. Retrieved November 23, 2012, from http://www.ijodls.in/uploads/3/6/0/3/3603729/92-106.pdf

Reddy, T. R. (2012). Digital era: Utilize Of cloud computing technology in digital library. *International Journal of Digital Library Services*, *2*(2), 92–106.

Reed Elsevier. (2013). *About us*. Retrieved from http://www.reedelsevier.com/aboutus/Pages/Home.aspx

Reed, P. R., Jr. (2004). *Reference architecture: The best of best practices*. Retrieved from http://www.ibm.com/developerworks/rational/library/2774.html

Report, E. D. U. C. A. U. S. E. (2010). *Seven things you should know about cloud security*. Retrieved from net.educause.edu/ir/library/pdf/EST1008.pdf.

Resource sharing. (2013). Retrieved from http://www.oclc.org/en-europe/services/resource-sharing.html

Rettner, R. (2010, August 2). Pathological Internet use may cause teen depression. Retrieved from http://www.livescience.com/9556-addicted-technology.html

Rhoton, J. (2009). *Cloud computing explained: Implementation handbook for enterprises*. Retrieved from http://www.amazon.com/Cloud-Computing-Explained-Implementation-ebook/dp/B003LO1H2W

RightScale. (n.d.). Retrieved from http://www.rightscale.com/

Risks and Benefits of Cloud Computing (n.d.). Retrieved from http://blogs.sap.com/innovation/cloud-computing/risks-and-benefits-of-cloud-computing-020025

Rittenhouse, J. W., & Ransome, J. F. (2010). *Cloud computing implementation, management and security*. Boca Raton, FL: CRC Press / Taylor & Francis Group.

Romero, N. L. (2012). Cloud computing in library automation: Benefits and drawbacks. *The Bottom Line: Managing Library Finances*, *25*(3), 110–114.

Roscoria, T. (2011, August 1). *4 university libraries move down the virtualization path*. Retrieved from http://www.centerdigitaled.com/infrastructure/4-University-Libraries-Move-Down-the-Virtualization-Path.html

Rothenberg, J. (1995). Ensuring the longevity of digital documents. *Scientific American*, *272*(1), 42. doi:10.1038/scientificamerican0195-42.

Rupley, S. (2009, November 26). *11 Top open source resources for cloud computing*. Retrieved from http://gigaom.com/2009/11/06/10-top-open-source-resources-for-cloud-computing/

S3Fox. (n.d.). Retrieved from http://www.s3fox.net/

Sachdeva, M., Rana, P., Kapoor, R., & Shahid, M. (2011). Cloud computing: Pay as you go technology. In *Proceedings of the 5th National Conference on Computing for National Development*. (pp. 161-166). New Delhi, India: BVICAM.

Sadeh, T. (2004). Developing an electronic resource management system: Verde from Ex Libris. *LIBER Quarterly*, *14*, 322–334.

Sadeh, T. (2007). Time for a change: New approaches for a new generation of library users. *New Library World*, *108*(7/8), 307–316. doi:10.1108/03074800710763608.

Saini, S. (2010). Digital library in new millennium: Opportunities and challenges for library professionals. In S. P. Singh (Ed.), *ICT impact on knowledge and information management* (pp. 204–209). New Delhi, India: Arihant Prakashan.

Saini, S., & Chand, S. (2011). Digital library: Challenges in the global world. In N. K. Swain, D. C. Ojha, & M. S. Rana (Eds.), *Paradigm shift in technological advancement in librarianship* (pp. 257–266). Jodhpur, India: Scientific.

SalesForce. (n.d.). Retrieved from http://www.salesforce.com/in/

Saller, C. (2011, September 29). *Typos and worse: When e-books need correcting*. Retrieved from http://chronicle.com/blogs/linguafranca/2011/09/29/typos-and-worse-when-e-books-need-correcting

Sanchati, R., & Kulkarni, G. (2011). Cloud computing in digital and university libraries. Global Journal of Computer Science and Technology, 11, 12. Retrieved January 07, 2013, from http://globaljournals.org/GJCST_Volume11/6-Cloud-Computing-in-Digital-and-University.pdf

Sanchati, R., & Kulkarni, G. (2011). Cloud computing in digital and university libraries. *Global J. Comp. Sci. Technol.*, *11*(12), 37–42.

Sangam, S. L., & Leena, V. (2000). Digital library services. In R. Vengan, H. R. Mohan, & K. S. Raghavan (Eds.), Information services in a networked environment in India (pp. 1.107-1.112). Ahmedabad, India: Inflibnet centre.

Scale, E. M. S. (2009). Cloud computing and collaboration. *Library Hi Tech News*, *26*(9), 10–13. doi:10.1108/07419050911010741.

Scale, E. M. S. (2010). Assessing the impact of cloud computing and Web collaboration on the work of distance library services. *Journal of Library Administration*, *50*, 933–950. doi:10.1080/01930826.2010.488995.

Scholarly Digital Library Initiatives. World vs. India. (n.d.). Retrieved June 22, 2011, from http://publications.drdo.gov.in/ojs/index.php/djlit/article/viewFile/219/122

Search cloud computing. (n.d.). Retrieved from http://searchcloudcomputing.techtarget.com/

SerialsSolutions. (n.d.). *The summon service*. Retrieved from www.serialssolutions.com/en/services/summon/

Service level agreement in cloud computing. (n.d.). Retrieved from http://knoesis.wright.edu/library/download/OOPSLA_cloud_wsla_v3.pdf

Shagin, A. (2012). *Benefits of cloud computing*. Retrieved from http://blogs.sap.com/innovation/cloud-computing/risks-and-benefits-of-cloudcomputing-020025

Sharif, A. M. (2010). It's written in the cloud: The hype and promise of cloud computing. *J. Enterprise Inf. Manag.*, *23*(2), 131–134. doi:10.1108/17410391011019732.

Sherikar, A., Jange, S., & Jadhav, S. (2006). *Digital reference services in the Web based information world*. Paper presented at the Convention on Automation of Libraries in Education and Research Institutions (CALIBER 2006). Gulbarga, India.

Shivakumar, B. L., Raju, T., & Revathy, H. (2010). Cloud computing: A dark lining in the dark clouds of crisis management of economic slowdown. *Asia Pacific Business Review*, *6*(3), 99–105.

Shrawankar, M. G., & Dhage, S. (2011). Enhancements in libraries using cloud computing. In *Proceedings of the 2nd National Conference on Information and Communication Technology NCICT(5)*. New York: Foundation of Computer Science.

Sierra. (n.d.). Retrieved from http://sierra.iii.com/

Simple storage service APIs: Sample code and libraries. (n.d.). http://developer.amazonwebservices.com/connect/kbcategory.jspa?categoryID=188

Singh, B., & Sirohi, K. (2013). Cloud computing use case for library. In *Proceedings of 2nd International Conference on Academic Libraries* (pp. 30-39). New Delhi, India: Indo American Books Publication.

Sinha, R., & Sanyal, R. (2011). *Creating aggregative digital repository in distributed environment using service oriented architecture: New dimensions in special libraries services*. Paper presented at the International Conference of Asia Special Libraries (ICoASL 2011). Tokyo, Japan.Thurlow, I., Duke, A., & Davies, J. (2006). *Applying semantic web technology in a digital library*. Paper presented at European Semantic Web Conference (ESWC 2006). Budva, Montenegro.

SISIS-SunRise. (2013). Retrieved from http://www.oclc.org/en-europe/sunrise.html

Slash dot effect. (n.d.). Retrieved from http://en.wikipedia.org/wiki/Slashdot_effect

SlideShare. (n.d.). *Intro to Amazon S3*. Retrieved from http://www.slideshare.net/parn09/intro-to-amazon-s3-presentation

Sood, S. K. (2012). A combined approach to ensure data security in cloud computing. *Journal of Network and Computer Applications*, *35*, 1831–1838. doi:10.1016/j.jnca.2012.07.007.

Source Forge. (2013). *SeerSuite*. Retrieved from http://sourceforge.net/projects/citeseerx/?source=navbar

Stallings, W. (2006). *Cryptography and Network Security* (4th ed.). Upper Saddle River, NJ: Prentice Hall.

Stanford University. (2008). *LOCKSS*. Retrieved July 29, 2012, from http://lockss.stanford.edu/

Stehlé, D., & Steinfeld, R. (2010, December 5-9). Faster fully homomorphic encryption. In M. Abe (Ed.), *ASIACRYPT: Proceedings of the 16th International Conference on the Theory and Application of Cryptology and Information Security (2010)*. Singapore (LCNS 6477, pp 377-394).

Subramanyam, G. V. B. (2012). *Cloud-based reference architecture: Design factors of financial supply chain systems*. Retrieved from http://cloudcomputing.sys-con.com/node/2112881

Sultan, N. (2010). Cloud computing for education: A new dawn? *International Journal of Information Management*, *30*(2), 109–116. doi:10.1016/j.ijinfomgt.2009.09.004.

SUSE Cloud 1.0. (2013). Retrieved from http://www.suse.com/documentation/suse_cloud10/

Symantec. (2011). The secure cloud: Best practices for cloud adoption. Retrieved from https://www4.symantec.com/mktginfo/whitepaper/TheSecureCloudBestPracticesforCloudAdoption_cta52644.pdf

Symmetric key. (n.d). *Symmetric key algorithm*. Retrieved from http://wikipedia.org/wiki/Symmetric-key algorithm/

Teregowda, P., Urgaonkar, B., & Giles, C. L. (2011). Cloud computing: A digital libraries perspective. In *Proceedings of the 2010 IEEE 3rd International Conference on Cloud Computing*, (pp. 115-122). IEEE.

Teregowda, P., Urgaonkar, B., & Lee Giles, C. (2010). Cloud computing: A digital libraries perspective. Paper presented at IEEE Cloud 2010, Computer Science and Engineering. Pennsylvania State University, University Park, PA.

TerraPod. (n.d.). Retrieved from www.terrapodcast.com/

Terrence, W. (n.d.). *Features of cloud computing*. Retrieved from http://en.wikipedia.org/wiki/cloud-computing

The Digital Library at Sapienza- University di Roma and the Effort for Open Access. (n.d.). Retrieved December 22, 2012, from http://eprints.rclis.org/bitstream/10760/8575/1/bids.pdf

Thomas, P. Y. (2011). Cloud computing: A potential paradigm for practicing the scholarship of teaching and learning. *The Electronic Library*, *29*(2), 214–224. doi:10.1108/02640471111125177.

Thoughts from Carl Grant. (2012, June 28). *Why and how librarians have to shape the new cloud computing platforms*. Retrieved from http://thoughts.care-affiliates.com/2012/06/why-and-how-libraries-have-to-shape.html

Tomer, C., & Alman, S. W. (2011). Cloudcomputing for LIS education. In E. M. Corrado, & H. L. Moulasion (Eds.), *Getting started with Cloud computing* (pp. 59–68). New York: Neal Schuman.

Top five cloud computing security issues. (2009, April 29). Retrieved from file:///F:/presentations/cloud%20computing%20security%20issues/Top-five-cloud-computing-security-issues.htm

U.S. Department of Health and Human Services. (n.d.). *The security rule*. Retrieved from http://www.hhs.gov/ocr/privacy/hipaa/administrative/securityrule/

UKOLN. (2002). *CURL exemplars in digital archives (cedars)*. Retrieved July 29, 2012, from http://www.ukoln.ac.uk/metadata/cedars/

Vaquero, L. M., Rodero-Merino, L., Caceres, J., & Lindner, M. (2009). A break in the clouds: Towards a cloud definition. In S. I. G. C. O. M. M. Acm (Ed.), *Computer communication review 2009* (pp. 50–55). New York: ACM Press.

Vaquero, L., Rodero-Merino, L., Caceres, J., & Lindner, M. (2009). A break in the clouds: Towards a cloud definition. *ACM SIGCOMM Computer Communication Review*, *39*(1), 50–55. doi:10.1145/1496091.1496100.

Varadarajan, S. (1997). Virtual local area networks. Retrieved from http://www.cis.ohio-state.edu/

Vaughan, J. (2011). *Web scale discovery services*. Chicago: ALA Techsource Publications.

Vemulapalli, S., Halappanavar, M., & Mukkamala, R. (2002). *Security in distributed digital libraries: Issues and challenges.* Paper presented at The International Conference on Parallel Processing Workshops (ICPPW'02) IEEE. Vancouver, Canada.

Vengan, R. (2000). Digital library: A challenge to library and information professionals. In R. Vengan, H. R. Mohan, & K. S. Raghavan (Eds.), *Information services in a networked environment in India* (pp. 2.89–2.92). Ahmedabad, India: Inflibnet Centre.

Vinjamuri, D. (2012, November). *The wrong war over e-books: Publishers vs. libraries.* Retrieved from http://www.forbes.com/sites/davidvinjamuri/2012/12/11/the-wrong-war-over-eBooks-publishers-vs-libraries

Vinoski, S. (2004). Web services notifications. *IEEE Internet Computing, 892*, 86–90. doi:10.1109/MIC.2004.1273491.

Virkus, S. (2010). *Challenges to building an effective digital library.* Retrieved from http://www.tlu.ee/~sirvir/Information%20and%20Knowledge%20%20Management/Integration%20of%20digital%20libraries%20in%20e-learning/issues_and_challenges_in_creating_digital_libraries.html

Virtualization of the desktops. (n.d.). Retrieved from http://www.intelligroup.com/ppt/WhitepaperDesktop-Virtualization.pdf

VMWare. (2009). *Securing the cloud: A view of cloud computing, security implications and best practices.* Retrieved from http://www.vmware.com/files/pdf/cloud/VMware-Savvis-Cloud-WP-en.pdf

Voas, J., & Zhang, J. (2009). Cloud computing: New wine or just a new bottle. *IT Professional, 11*(2), 15–17. doi:10.1109/MITP.2009.23.

Vogels, W. (2008, October). *A Head in the clouds: The power of infrastructure service.* Paper presented at the First Workshop on Cloud Computing and its Applications (CCA 2008). Chicago.

Wang, J. (2012). From the ground to the cloud: A practice at California State University, East Bay. *CALA Occasional Paper Series, 10*, 1-8.

Wikipedia. (2012). *Digital preservation coaliation.* Retrieved July 3, 2012, from http://en.wikipedia.org/wiki/Digital_Preservation_Coalition

Wikipedia. (2013). *National Institute of Technology.* Retrieved from http://en.wikipedia.org/wiki/National_Institutes_of_Technology

Wikipedia. (2013) *Amazon web services.* Retrieved from http://en.wikipedia.org/wiki/Amazon_Web_Services

Wikipedia. (2013). *OCLC.* Retrieved from http://en.wikipedia.org/wiki/OCLC

Wikipedia. (n.d.). *Cloud computing.* Retrieved from http://en.wikipedia.org/wiki/Cloud_computing

Wikipedia. (n.d.). *Desktop as a service.* Retrieved from http://en.wikipedia.org/wiki/Desktop_as_a_service

Wikipedia. (n.d.). *Information Common.* Retrieved from http://en.wikipedia.org/wiki/Information_Commons

Wilson, T. C. (1998). *The systems librarian: Designing roles, defining skills.* Chicago: American Library Association.

Winds of change: Libraries and cloud computing. (n.d.). Retrieved from http://www.oclc.org/multimedia/2011/files/IFLA-winds-of-change-paper.pdf

Winget, M. (2005, June 7-11). *Digital preservation of new media art through exploration of established symbolic representation systems.* Paper presented at the ACM/IEEE Joint Conference on Digital Libraries' 2005 Doctoral Consortium. Denver, CO.

Xiaona, F., & Lingyun, B. (2010). Application of cloud computing in university library user service model. In *Proceedings of the 3rd International Conference on Advanced Computer Theory and Engineering (ICACTE).* ICACTE.

Yang, M., & Yuan, X. (2009). *Digital Libraries under the Cloud Computing Environment (J)* (p. 9). Library Development.

Yang, S. Q. (2012). Move into the cloud, shall we? *Library Hi Tech News*, (1): 4–7. doi:10.1108/07419051211223417.

Yuvaraj, M., & Singh, A. P. (2012). Cloud computing in conjunction with libraries: Descriptive literature review. *Asia Pacific Journal of Library and Information Science, 2*(2).

Zhang, Y., Wu, J., & Zhuang, Y. (2004). *The personalized services in CADAL digital library*. Retrieved from http://www.ulib.org/conference/2006/23.pdf

Zhao, Y. (2012). *Enterprise and solution architecture forum, 2012*. Retrieved from www. Architechllc.com.

Zheng, Q., Chen, Z., & Bai, X. (2003). *Research on the application of notification service for service-oriented digital library*. Retrieved from http://www.ulib.org/conference/2006/27.pdf

Zheng, X., & Fang, Y. (2010). *An AIS-based cloud security model*. Paper presented at the International Conference on Intelligent Control and Information Processing (ICICIP). Dalian, China.

Zheng, Q., Chen, Z., & Bai, X. (2003). *Research on the application of notification service for service-oriented digital library*. China: Shanghai Jiao Tong University Library.

Zissis, D., & Lekkas, D. (2012). Addressing cloud computing security issues. *Future Generation Computer Systems*, 583–592. doi:10.1016/j.future.2010.12.006.

Zoho. (2013). Retrieved from http://www.zoho.com/company.html

Zwattendorfer, B., & Tauber, A. (2012, December 10-12). Secure cross-cloud single sign-on (SSO) using eIDs. In *Proceedings of The 7th International Conference for Internet Technology and Secured Transactions* (pp. 150-155). London: ICITST.

About the Contributors

Sangeeta N. Dhamdhere is working as a Librarian in Modern College of Arts, Science and Commerce, Ganesh-Khind, Pune, India. She has more than 12 years of experience as a librarian. She has completed a couple of computer-related courses and has expertise in library automation and digital library. She has published more than 21 papers in national and international journals. She has received VLIR fellowship in the year 2008 to attend an International Training Program STIMULATE-8 at Brussels, Belgium. She is a member of a few LIS national and international associations and presently pursuing her Ph.D. and working on a few research projects. She is an Editorial Board Member of a few International Peer Reviewed Journals and Magazines.

* * *

Pawan R. Agrawal, born July 14, 1982, is working as Assistant Librarian at Silvassa Institute of Higher Learning, Government College of Arts, Commerce and Science, Silvassa, Union Territory of Dadra and Nagar Haveli. He has earned his BLISc, and MLISc degrees from The Maharaja Sayajirao University of Baroda and currently pursuing his Ph.D. from the same university. He is the author of a several research and conceptual papers in library and information science. He was awarded two gold medals for achieving highest marks in BLIS. He is an academic counsellor at Indira Gandhi National Open University (IGNOU), New Delhi, and Dr. Babasaheb Ambedkar Open University (BAOU), Ahmedabad. He is also serving International Journal of Digital Library Services as Associate Editor, and International Journal of Information Dissemination and Technology as a member of the editorial board. He can be reached at pawanagrawal4u4u@gmail.com.

Nihal Alam did his Postgraduate work in Documentation and Information Science (ADIS) from Indian Statistical Institute, Bangalore Centre under the DRTC Unit and working as Research Associate in TERI (The Energy and Resource Institute (TERI), New Delhi. His qualifications are based upon a unique combination of education, skills, and work experience. As he successfully completed two projects of 6 months each on building a portal by using open source software on Geographic Information System and another project on a state-of-art-report which gives the consolidated information to the microbiology specialist. Furthermore, he is involved in several digitization projects in the Indira Gandhi National Centre for the Arts (IGNCA), New Delhi, Children Book Trust (CBT), and TERI. He is also responsible as a teammate in different projects sponsored by the ministry to TERI in bringing out innovative information services and product for users, and proficient in designing and developing interactive library portal, promotional materials (print, video, etc.) in coordination with librarian and other experts.

Donald Russell Bailey is an international scholar in digital teaching, learning, and research and is currently Library Director at Providence College, Rhode Island, USA. Dr. Bailey has taught Western languages, literatures and cultures, comparative pedagogy and education (emphasizing East Asian educational opportunities) since 1973. Since 1994 he has served as a faculty administrator in higher education libraries in the US. He is best known for his work in The Commons (Information, Learning, Library, and Faculty Commons). His 2008 book, *Transforming Library Service Through Information Commons: Case Studies for the Digital Age* (with Barbara Tierney) has sold several thousand copies and continues to serve as a resource for libraries in the digital age. He is a frequent speaker internationally (US, Scotland, Czech Republic, Hong Kong, Hungary) and is currently pursuing the role of libraries in creating digital knowledge, especially digital humanities: drbailey@providence.edu, http://works.bepress.com/d_r_bailey/

Ranjana D. Bhoskar born on October 6, 1982, has 6 years of professional experience in Library and Information Science. She had a One month Apprenticeship in Central Reference Library, Kolkata, from January 1, 2007 to January 31, 2007. Her duties were: Processing of English and Marathi books, assigning classification number, cataloguing as per AACR-II. She has taught cataloguing. She has 4 years teaching experience. She has done library housekeeping operations, handling of "LIBSYS" automation software, stacking of books, handled circulation section, handled reference section and back volume section, handled e-resources services through INDEST consortium, document delivery services, record maintain books for binding, handled acquisition section and cataloguing section, handled barcode systems, handled RFID systems, KIOSK system and digital library, stock verification of books at social welfare section, book bank section, general section and reference section. Her present interests include: creating Institutional Repository at VNIT, Digital Library Applications and Services, Customer Care and Virtual Library Initiatives.

Egbert De Smet, after graduating from secondary studies (classical languages), studied 'Political and Social Sciences' with emphasis on Sociology at the University of Antwerp, Belgium. After obtaining his degree, he started to work as a researcher at the University of Antwerp in a project about 'Literature and Society,' followed by a project on Cultural Social Indicators from its initial establishment in 1983, worked as academic co-coordinator for the Interuniversity Special Degree in Information and Library Science, still at the University of Antwerp, and obtained his Ph.D. with a project on automated online Community Information. He worked two years as Training Manager for INASP, Oxford (UK) while continuing to lecture at the University of Antwerp. After the reorganization of the Special Degree to an informal 'postacademic training' programme, he continues to work as a project coordinator for the University of Antwerp, specializing in information aspects and library technology in international development, mainly focusing on the ISIS-technology.

Ravikant M. Deshpande, (25-11-1953), was a graduate in 1973, postgraduate in 1989 and got his doctorate in Library and Information Science in 2004 has more than 30 years of experience in the same field. Dr. Deshpande taught Reference Services and resources B.LIB.SC and Applications of Computers to Information Science MLISC, attended more than 100 -125 Workshops/Seminars/Symposia. Dr. Deshpande directed ISTE sponsored short-term courses. Dr. Deshpande visited the UK twice in the year of 1991 and 1996 as Research Fellow at University of Ealing's, London, and Research Visitor to University of Huddersfield, UK, respectively. He observed the functioning of Library Automation, Digital Library, Online Access to Periodicals, and so forth, as a part of his studies. Dr. Deshpande has worked as University Librarian in KKSU Ramtek for 22 months in 2000-2001. He was first University Librarian and shared the responsibilities of registrar. He pioneered Library Automation in 1993 at VNIT, Nagpur (Earlier VTCE). He was instrumental in making operational the information at VNIT via Library Automation, Digital Library, and RFID. Dr. Deshpande's present interest is in customer care; digitization of local resources, cloud computing, and emerging technology based services in the field of Library and Information Science.

S. Gopalakrishnan is Head-Resource Centre of National Institute of Fashion Technology, Chennai. Holds two Postgraduates and did his Ph.D. in Library and Information Science. Apart from his regular academic qualification, he also holds Green Belt in Six Sigma. He has presented papers in various national and international seminars and published articles in seminar volumes, festschrift, and in peer review journals. He has 18 years of teaching and administrative experience. He is also a member in various doctoral committees for selection of candidates and served as External Examiner for Doctoral studies in various universities. He is one of the co-principle investigators in developing e-content for 120 Fashion Design and Technology subjects under NME-ICT project sponsored by MHRD, Govt. of India. Currently he is guiding five candidates for their doctoral programme. The main area of Research is User Behaviour, Knowledge Management, Networking, and Performance Evaluation. He was deputed to visit various fashion institutes and the Resource Centers in the countries such as The Netherlands, UK, and USA.

Namita Gupta is an educationist in the field of Computer Science. Her current association with International Maritime College Oman as Mathematics and IT Lecturer has multiplied the author's passion for producing and sharing new and interesting ideas related to IT and mathematics. Her postgraduate degree in mathematics led naturally to another logically enriching subject. Hence computer science came along as a passion to indulge into the forever growing and challenging world of technology, driving her to achieve a Masters in Computer Application, and now en route to complete Ph.D. in the field of Data Mining and Artificial Intelligence. She had her first research paper presented and published in the conference proceedings of 'International Conference on Knowledge Management and Resource Sharing' held at Waljat College, Muscat.

Harshila Jain-Bagoria completed Electrical Engineering, MBA (Finance), NET. She has 3 years of corporate experience in the area of banking and 2 years of academic experience. She has attended many international and national conferences/seminars. Presently working as Assistant Professor, Maharaja College of Management, Udaipur.

T. M. Kalpana, Librarian, Shri AMM Murugappa Chettiar Research Centre, Chennai, holds two Postgraduates in Commerce and Library and Information Science. She has attended many National and International Conferences and presented papers. She has won "Best Paper Award" two times in national conferences. Currently she is pursuing her Ph.D. in Library and Information Science. She has around 10 years of teaching and administrative experience. The main area of research is Self-Sustainability of Library and its resources.

Praveen Kapoor is Dy. Librarian at University of Petroleum and Energy Studies. He has about 11 years of experience in librarianship in various organizations and his area of interest is library automation, knowledge management, digital library, and resource sharing. He has received Master of Library and Information Science from IGNOU and M. Com. from Annamalai University. He is a life member of the Indian Library Association and Management Library Network (MANLIBNET). He has presented papers in national conferences and written papers in different journals in the field of Library and Information Science

Ranjan Karmakar did an associateship in Information Science (AIS) with specialization in "Knowledge Management" from NISCAIR (erstwhile INSDOC) and M.Com from Kalyani University with first class. He passed MLIS from Annamalai University and also UGC - NET Qualified two times (June and December 2012). He has knowledge in ICT applications to library and information activities and digital library software like DSpace and GSDL. He has worked in the library at Indian Institute of Technology Ropar, Punjab; India Habitat centre, New Delhi. Currently working in TERI and member of Library Professionals Association (LPA) and Ranganthan Research Circle (RRC), New Delhi.

A. V. N. Krishna received his BE (Mechanical) from Osmania University, ME (Mechanical) from Sivaji University, M.Tech (Computer Science) from B.I.T. Ranchi, and his Ph.D. from the Department of Computer Science and Engineering, Acharya Nagarjuna University, Andhra Pradesh, India. His doctoral work done, he now works as a Principal and Professor of Computer Science and Engineering in Pujya Shri Madhavanji College of Engineering and Technology, JNTUH, Hyderabad. His main research interests include computer networks; network security, simulation and modeling, and so forth. He is guiding five students for their Ph.D. work.

S. Kuppuswami received the M.Sc. degree in Applied Electronics, University of Madras and the Ph.D. degree in computer science from Universite' de Rennes I, France. He is a professor in the Department of Computer Science, Pondicherry University. He worked in ISRO Bangalore as a trainee and developed a unit for the Bhaskara II satellite. He was also a National expert of UNIDO for setting up information technology centre at Neyveli Lignite Corporation, Neyveli. He was awarded an Indo-French Research Fellowship for the year 1983 and CNRS (France) Best Thesis Award for the year 1986 (Prix de These CNRS - 1986). Currently he is writing Computer Science Textbooks in Tamil under funding from Tamilnadu State Council for Higher Education, Chennai, India. His research interests are Object Oriented Systems, Neural Networks, Multimedia and Tamil computers. Presently he is working as the principal of Pondicherry University. He has more than 20 years of experience in the field of teaching and research in various colleges and Pondicherry University.

Ramdas Lihitkar is working as Librarian in Govt. Institute of Science, Nagpur. He has been in LIS Profession Since 2001, MLISc, Gold Medallist from Bhopal University, Bhopal. He is contributory faculty in DLISc, RTM, Nagpur University, Nagpur, He is teaching Research Methodology. He worked as a Librarian Govt. Rajaram College, Kolhapur from 2001 to 2003 and Govt. College of Education Bhandara from 2005 to 2008. He has experience teaching and guiding for UGC NET/SET, P.O. and other competitive examinations in remedial coaching classes of RTM Nagpur University, Nagpur. He has published several papers in seminars, conferences, and journals at the national and international level and has more than 50 papers to his credit. He is a life member of professional association viz. DLA, ILA, and VLA. Joint Secretary of Alumni Association of Department of LISc, RTMNU from 2011. He has presented papers at International Conference at Malaysia and Thailand. He is a recognized research guide for Ph.D. in Library and Information Science in the faculty of Social Science of Rashtrasant Tukadoji Maharaj Nagpur University. He is a subject expert member in R.T.M. Nagpur University and Government nominee of selection/placement Expert Committee. E-mail: rlihitkar1975@gmail.com, (M) 9420865083.

Nilima D. Likhar born on January 25, 1985 has 4 years of professional experience in Library and Information Science. One month Apprenticeship in Central Reference Library, Kolkata, Date: 1st January 2009 to 31st January 2009. Duties: Processing of English and Marathi books, assigning classification number, cataloguing as per AACR-II. She has done Library Housekeeping Operations, Handling of "LIBSYS" Automation Software, Stacking of Books, Handled Circulation Section, Handled Reference Section and Back Volume Section, Handled E-Resources Services through INDEST Consortium, Document Delivery Services, Record Maintain Books for Binding, Handled Acquisition Section, Cataloguing Section, Handled Barcode Systems, Handled RFID Systems, KIOSK System and Digital Library, Stock Verification of Books at Social Welfare Section, Book Bank Section, General Section and Reference Section. She has a present interest in creating Digital Library Applications and Services, Customer Care and Virtual Library Initiatives. She has written two articles in the various National Seminars and Conferences and attended various workshops.

Deepak Mane holds a Master's degree in Computer Science. He had technical proficiency in Public Cloud, Private Cloud, Big Data, and Disaster Recovery. Presently he is working with Cloud Consultant/ Architect with Tata Consultancy Services. For the last 11 years Deepak Mane has provided consulting and architectural services to large corporations and companies in USA, UK, and Europe. He is also working as a mentor for Kresit IIT, Mumbai. He has provided guidance on multiple projects for students. He also conducted a series of workshop and seminars on cloud computing, data mining and big data for more than 50 colleges in India.

Jameson Mbale received his Ph.D. Degree in Computer Science from Harbin Institute of Technology, China, in 2003. He obtained M.Sc. Degree in Computer Science from Shanghai University in 1996 and B.A. in Mathematics and Computer Science at University of Zambia in 1993 in Zambia. He is an Associate Professor in the Department of Computer Science at the University of Namibia. He is the founder and coordinator of Centre of Excellence in Telecommunications and Information Technology. His research interest is in security in cloud computing, wireless networking, telecommunications and e-learning, and he has published papers in these areas.

K. Palanivel received his B.E. in Computer Science and Engineering and M. Tech. in Computer Science and Engineering from Bhrathiar University, Coimbatore and Pondicherry University, Puducherry, in 1994 and 1998 respectively. He cleared the National Level Eligibility test conducted by University Grants Commission, New Delhi, in 1998. Presently he is pursuing his Ph.D. in Computer Science and Engineering at Pondicherry University since 2008. He joined as Technical Assistant in 1995. Presently he is working as Systems Analyst in Computer Centre of Pondicherry University. His field of interest is software engineering, computer networks, and design patterns. He became the member of Indian Society of Technical Education in 2004. He has more than 10 years of experience in the field of computer applications, teaching, and research at Pondicherry University.

Reema Parashar has obtained B. Lib and Inf.sc and M. Lib and Inf. Sc. during 2010 to 2012 from Department of Library and Information Science, Dr. Hari singh Gour University, Sagar, M.P. and M.A. (Geography) during 2006 to 2008 from University of Rajasthan. Currently she is working as Assistant Librarian at Ch. Garshi Ram Public School, Lakshmangarh, Sikar, and Rajasthan. She has 2 years of Administrative and Technical experience. Her areas of interest are digital library, library automation, library consortium, and so forth.

Vijay Parashar has obtained B. Lib and Inf.sc and M. Lib and Inf. Sc. during 2003 to 2004 from Department of Library and Information Science, Rajasthan University, and M. Phil in 2009 from Annamalai University and diploma in computer hardware and networking during 2012 to 2013. Currently he is pursuing his Ph.D. in Library and Information Science and working as I/c Library at Mody Institute of Technology and Science: Deemed University. He has 10 years of Administrative and Technical experience. He published numerous papers in national and international journals. He is a life member of Indian Library Association (ILA), Indian Association of Special Libraries and Information Centres (IASLIC), and Jaipur Association of Library and Information Science (JALIS). His areas of interest are digital library, library automation, electronic resource management, cloud computing, library consortium, and so forth.

Bharati Vasant Patle, born on February 14, 1977, has 5 years of professional experience in Library and Information Science. She has taught Reference Sources. She has 2 years of teaching experience. Bharati Vasant Patle has done library housekeeping operations, handling of "LIBSYS" automation software, stacking of books, handled circulation section, handled reference section and back volume section, handled, e-resources services through INDEST consortium, document delivery services, record maintain books for binding, handled acquisition section, cataloguing section, handled barcode systems, handled RFID systems, KIOSK system and digital library, stock verification of books at social welfare section, book bank section, general section and reference section. Her present interest is creating Institutional Repository at VNIT, digital library applications and services, customer care and virtual library initiatives. She has written four articles in the various national seminars and conferences and attended various workshops.

Suvarna H. Paunikar, born on November 23, 1985, has 5 years of professional experience in Library and Information Science. She has done library housekeeping operations, handling of "LIBSYS" automation software, stacking of books, handled circulation section, handled reference section and back volume section, handled e-resources services through INDEST consortium, document delivery services, record/maintain books for binding, handled acquisition section, cataloguing section, handled barcode systems, handled RFID systems, KIOSK system and digital library, stock verification of books at social welfare section, book bank section, general section and reference section. Her present interest is creating digital library applications and services, customer care and virtual library initiatives. She has written four articles in the various national seminars and conferences and attended various workshops.

Ajay Rawat is Assistant Professor, Department of Computer Science and Engineering, University of Petroleum and Energy Studies. He received his M.S. degree from BITS Pilani, Rajasthan. He has more than 8 years of experience in teaching and industry. His research interest includes mobile agent and cloud computing. He is currently doing his Ph.D. in Mobile Agent. He has published various papers in national and international journals.

Syed Asim Raza Rizvi is an accomplished educator with multicultural awareness, excellent teaching credentials, and a background in teaching with nearly 14 years of "hands-on" high quality teaching experience. The author believes that teaching is an amalgam of art and science which spring from passion for both the fields. Passion, if steered with sanity, is a force that can help in the cultivation of progressive, cultured, prosperous, and congenial communities. Syed is a proponent of progress in information technology as a tool that supports healthy environment for balanced coexistence of people from varied cultures and countries. Syed's academic background in the fields of Computer Science and Economics allows him to view the technology through the spectacles of proportionate structure of scientific developments. This structure could be based on methods that are critical to economizing resources by efficient use of the available technology.

Surbhi Saini is Research Scholar (Library Science) IGNOU University. She is presently associated with IGNOU University in Research and Teaching Assistant (RTA) Scheme for North East Region. She has job experience from ICMR Institute, NIB, Noida, NCIDE, IGNOU and NISCAIR, Delhi. She did graduation B.Sc Biotechnology from M.J.P. Rohilkhand University, university topper in B.Lib and I.Sc from the same university. She did M.Lib and I.Sc from Bundelkhand University. She is qualified UGC-NET Dec 2011. In the publication area, she has 26 papers published in various national, international conference proceedings, and journals. She has also contributed four chapters in four books. She got the Best Paper Award–paper was entitled "Digital Library in New Millennium: Opportunities and Challenges for Library Professionals"–in National Conference on ICT Impact on Knowledge and Information Management at Greater Noida on September 19, 2010 published in University News. She got the CSIR Research Intern Award Library Science in NISCAIR, New Delhi in 2008.

Satish S. Sharma is Ph.D. in HR, M. Phil in OB, MBA in HR and Master's Degree in Applied Industrial Psychology. He has 20 years of academic and research experience in the field of HRM, OB, and IR. He has written many books in the area of HR and OB, and has attended many International and National Conferences/Seminars. More than 50 papers have also been published in Journals. CMD and Professor in Management, Maharaja Group of Colleges, Udaipur.

Rama Sushil is Professor cum Principal of IT in SGRRITS India. She has a doctorate from IIT Roorkee, 2010, and was a research student in Hirosaki University, Japan, 1999. She did her MCA with Honors from MMM Eng. College. Her international academic visits include USA, Italy, Japan, Taiwan, and so forth. Many research papers in International and National Journals are in her credit. She has written a book titled "Artificial Intelligence" and a chapter also on M-Commerce. She is Editor-in-Chief of World Research Journal of Transaction of Algorithms. Fields of interest: mobile computing, mobile agent technology, modeling, simulation, Adv. DS and algorithms. IEEE, CSI member.

Mohan Lal Vishwakarma has obtained M.Lib and Inf. Sc. during 2008 to 2010 from Department of Library and Information Science, Banaras Hindu University, Varanasi and qualified UGC- NET. Currently working as Assistant Librarian at Mody Institute of Technology and Science: Deemed University Lakshmangarh, Sikar, Rajasthan, he has 2.5 years of administrative and technical experience. He is a life member of the Indian Library Association (ILA), Indian Association of Special Libraries and Information Centers (IASLIC), Indian Association of Teachers of Library and Information Science (IATLIS), Society for the Advancement of Library and Information Science (SALIS), Society for Promotion of Libraries in U.P. (SPL). His areas of interest are digital library, library automation, library consortium, and so forth.

Nisha Yadav has obtained B.Lib and Inf.sc and M.Lib and Inf. Sc. during 2006 to 2008 from the Department of Library and Information Science, Bundelkhand University, Jhanshi, U.P and M.Com during 2003 to 2005 from Bundelkhand University, Jhanshi, U.P. Currently she is working as Assistant Librarian at Mody Institute of Technology and Science: Deemed University Lakshmangarh, Sikar, Rajasthan. She has 4 years of administrative and technical experience. Her areas of interest are digital library, library automation, library consortium, and so forth. She is a life member of Society for Promotion of Libraries in U.P. (SPL).

Mayank Yuvaraj, an arts graduate from Delhi University, did his postgraduate work in Library and Information Science from Banaras Hindu University. He secured the BHU Gold medal in 2011 for securing the highest marks. Presently he is a Junior Research Fellow and doing his research on implication of Cloud Computing in Indian Academic Libraries in the department of Library and Information Science, Banaras Hindu University. His research interests include Cloud Computing, Knowledge Management, Social Networking, Information Retrieval, and Webometrics.

Index

N

O

P

Q

R

S

T

U

V

W

Z